WORLD'S GREAT PLAYS

WORLD'S
Great Plays

With an Introduction by

GEORGE JEAN NATHAN

CLEVELAND AND NEW YORK

THE WORLD PUBLISHING COMPANY

Published by THE WORLD PUBLISHING COMPANY

2231 West 110th Street · Cleveland 2 · Ohio

Decorations by Bernard Childs

3HC757

Contents

Introduction

THE WIDELY PROMULGATED NOTION that plays are not meant to be read but to be acted calls for some editing. Plays are meant to be acted well; if they are not thus well acted it is better that they be read than seen. Since it is a matter for regret that the acting visited upon the better plays in this day and age is not often up to the quality of the plays themselves and since proficient acting seems frequently to be reserved for the lesser specimens of drama, the reading of important plays results in an added vital illusion, to say nothing of a considerable aesthetic comfort.

The library arm-chair accordingly sometimes gives birth to a stage beyond and above the theatre's stage. The fancy casts the plays more accurately, and sets the scene more handsomely, and reads into the lines an eloquence and power that cajole the imagination even more greatly than it may be cajoled in a seat in the playhouse. Small wonder, therefore, that the publishing of drama in book form has witnessed such an enormous increase in late years.

The present volume, while it definitely does not claim to present to you the world's greatest plays, at least gives you for your reading pleasure and satisfaction seven that bulk large in the theatre's drama and that are acceptedly representative of the dramatic art in its general flower.

Lysistrata is doubtless the most widely known of any of Aristophanes' plays, and the one that has provoked the most moral indignation, though why, it is difficult for cooler intellects to make out. Observed Schlegel in his celebrated *Lectures on Dramatic Art and Literature*, "It is in such bad repute that we must mention it lightly and rapidly, just as we would tread over hot embers." Yet he concluded, "Notwithstanding the mad indecencies . . . its purpose, when stripped of these, is upon the whole very innocent: the longing for the enjoyment of domestic joys, so often interrupted by the absence of the husbands, is to be the means of putting an end to the calamitous war by which Greece had so long been torn in pieces." Aristophanes' plea for peace is similarly, though in different terms, present in both the *Peace* and the *Acharnæ*. Yet the superb satire and high wit of *Lysistrata* have persisted in remaining no apology for its "mad indecencies" in the minds of the extravagantly pure. So, art's struggle against morality.

Originally produced by its author in 411 B.C. at a critical hour in the Peloponnesian War and playing the leading role himself when the actor hired for it refused to appear in it, fearing the public's indignation, the play has since often been performed on the stages of the western world and, for all occasional puritanical objection, is generally accepted as a sterling example of what was once referred to as the "frivolous" classic Greek drama. The adjective is poorly chosen. In the play's so-called frivolity there is a philosophy, albeit lightly expounded, that is basically far removed from the frivolous and that contains within it a substantial measure of sound human reasoning and inescapable sense.

Faust, Goethe's poetic masterpiece, provides a striking example of a play that profits one more from a reading than from a seeing, at least as it has been seen on the stage thus far. The stage, in whatever land, seems to have been completely baffled by it. It has been cut on occasion into nothingness; it has been distorted out of much of its form and meaning; or it has been so wretchedly played that it has quickly lost its audience's attention and interest. But, nonetheless, its deathless theme has persisted in a variety of forms: in the opera of Gounod, in spectacle as in the Lew Morrison version, in European ballet and pantomime, even, God wot, in the puppet play and the musical show form.

The legends of Faust, upon which Goethe founded his drama, were first gathered in a book, published in Germany in 1587, called *The History of Dr. Faustus, the Notorious Magician and Master of the Black Art, etc.* Marlowe's play, *The Tragical History of Doctor Faustus,* appeared a year or so later. (It was played in Germany very early in the seventeenth century.) The first part of Goethe's great tragedy did not appear until 1808, the second part not until 1831. There have been numerous other stage versions of the theme, among them Calderon's early *El Magico Prodigioso.*

Faust has been termed a literary epitome of Goethe's life, since he devoted himself to it intermittently for a period of three-score years.

Bygmester Solness, or *The Master Builder* as it is known in the English-speaking countries, was written by Ibsen late in his career and, though accepted as one of his masterpieces, has been the subject of wide critical debate since its first production toward the end of the nineteenth century. The debate has not been over its quality, upon which there has been no lack of agreement but over its exact meaning, or at least the meaning its author intended. Such argument, however, has attached equally to other of the great Norwegian's works, notably *The Wild Duck, The Lady From the Sea,* and *Little Eyolf,* since there are always critics who are not happy unless everything, in whatever art form, is as clear to them as ABC. If the exact meaning of even a poem or piece of music is not readily to be grasped, they find themselves ill at ease, and the work of art in question aesthetically dubious.

The symbolic dramatist is always beset by such criticism, and Ibsen has been one of the sorest sufferers. The earlier portions of *The Master Builder* appear to be lucid enough to even his most contentious critics, since the story of Solness' fear of the younger generation and his determination to resist the changes it will inevitably bring calls for no blue-print. Nor does the entrance of Hilda as the representative of that generation. But what follows, predicated on Solness' early promise to her to reward her at the end of a decade with a kingdom, seems to have proved confounding. There are, of course, various ways in which to interpret Ibsen's symbols, perhaps one as valid as another, yet the simplest would appear to be to accept Hilda as the symbol of Solness' youthful aspiration which drives him to attempt something beyond him and visits upon him in the end the tragedy of his own dreams. Other interpretations are, as noted, quite possible. A favorite is the theory that Ibsen designed Hilda as a symbol of youth unable to grasp actualities and thus unwittingly contriving the wreck of Solness. Another, albeit far-fetched one, is that the play as a whole is simply a symbolic treatment of Ibsen's own poetic career. You may take your choice and add even further interpretations if you will. It seems to me, however, that the one which I have specified is in all likelihood the most rational and in the end perhaps the most critically satisfactory.

Cyrano de Bergerac is a sterling example of the swashbuckling drama of the last century. First produced in 1897, it provides in its plume-sweeping romance and wondrous improbabilities not only the theatrical escape from dramatic realism so close to the fancy of a liberal share of theatregoers, but in its poetic raptures and humors a warming holiday from the stage's too frequent prosaicism. In it there comes to life a rich fairy tale for such adults as still dream of impossible loves and adventures and, with all its grotesqueries, it sounds upon its fantastic E-string the melodious note of reassurance to be found at the rainbow's end. Some of its scenes are among the most memorable in the modern theatre and, though its heroic bravado may suggest to the woefully realistic mind nothing so much as the crowing of a rained-on rooster, there is deep in its fabric nevertheless all the handsome bravery of all those creatures amongst us on earth from whom a careless Providence withheld at birth the prettier gifts it bestowed on luckier men.

The Cherry Orchard, first produced in the early years of the present century, is Chekhov's chef d'œuvre, a far greater achievement than his *The Three Sisters, The Sea Gull* or *Uncle Vanya.* It marks the perfection of the form of dramaturgy which he introduced into the theatre and which has since exercised its influence in many directions. Plot in the sense that it is commonly understood is made subservient to character situation and the action, such as it is, proceeds chemically from within, and with the quiet force of quiet waters slowly troubled into turmoil. The theme, in so far as it may be stated at all, may be described as the pitiable hopelessness of hope. There is no more telling scene in all modern drama than that which concludes the play: the sound of the axes indicating that the prized orchard is meeting its doom and that the old order has had its day and the new order is taking over.

The implications of any truly fine play always sweep over and beyond it, and the implications of this of the celebrated Russian sound their wistful note long afterward in the auditors' spirit. For in the brother and sister there is part of their auditors, and in their tragedy there is an echo of the common tragedy that befalls, in one form or another, the hopes of mankind. One loses what one deeply cherishes and what has become part of one's pride and life, for the world in its thoughtless march reckons without sympathy, and leaves the pride of them that can not battle it tattered in its pragmatic winds.

In the way of sheer theatre O'Neill has negotiated little that surpasses *The Emperor Jones.* From beginning to end it holds the spectator—and the reader, I venture, no less—under its spell. Its cumulative dramatic effect is irresistible. Although he has written plays that bulk larger in his career, he has written none that affords greater testimony to his uncommon dramaturgical skill. That skill is sometimes lost sight of by the layman in his rapt immersion in O'Neill's plotting, for the playwright is as expert in mere story telling as in the difficult conversion of it into the dramaturgical form. Yet it remains that in the matter of pure dramaturgy, as his discerning critics know, he has no rival in the American field.

The present play was written in the autumn of 1920, which was one of O'Neill's more productive years. In the same autumn he wrote *Diff'rent;* in the summer he wrote *Anna Christie;* in the winter, *Gold.* The impact of *The Emperor Jones* upon an audience is tremendous. The tom-toms, starting, as Richard Dana Skinner has aptly observed, at the rate of the human pulse beat and rising bit by bit as a fevered pulse would rise, lay hold of the emotions of the audience no less than those of Brutus Jones and sweep it along into the drama's powerful climax. The sound effect is one of the most theatrically impressive that O'Neill has managed: superior to the soft surge of the sea in his admirable one-act play, *The Moon of the Caribbees* or to the dynamo's whirr in *Dynamo.* But, unlike such effects in the hands of numerous other playwrights, it is not extraneous; it is of the warp and woof of the play itself.

In O'Neill's gallery of characters, Jones looms notably large. The dramatist has worked subtly into his psychology and into the psychology of the Negro more generally, more subtly than he succeeded in doing in the instance of *All God's Chillun Got Wings,* which he wrote three years later. What you find here is a crafty study of the black man's dream of release from bondage to the white man and, upon the dream's coming true, his defeat by the very tricks of the white man which through his practice have brought him that release, or what he imagines is release. In the business of the silver bullets which bring death to Jones, O'Neill has further indicated a symbolic imagination rare in the American drama. The whole of the latter part of the play, indeed, with its thunder of fancy, lifts that drama to heights which it had not before achieved.

O'Casey's *The Plough and the Stars,* in conclusion, is one of the finest plays to have come out of Ireland; not only that, it takes its place as one of the classics of the modern world theatre. Into it O'Casey has poured his most moving tragedy and his most relieving comedy, and has managed with the highest dexterity to orchestrate both into a symphony of the Irish spirit. Fluther, like his Joxer in *Juno and the Paycock,* is one of the great comic creations, and as played originally by Arthur Sinclair promptly took its place in the rich file of Abbey comic portraits.

No other modern Irish dramatist has surpassed O'Casey in the deep richness of dramatic writing that is the mark of this play. His tears well up from a profound understanding of its people, as his humor bursts forth from an understanding no less sharp and comprehensive. What he has achieved is a kind of biography of the Celtic psyche. Although in *Juno* that humor is also present, although there are flashes of the poetic feeling in his *The Silver Tassie* and *Within the Gates,* and although the purple of both shine intermittently in his *Purple Dust,* in the estimation of the present writer *The Plough and the Stars* remains his masterpiece.

GEORGE JEAN NATHAN

Lysistrata

BY ARISTOPHANES

CHARACTERS

Lysistrata
Calonice
Myrrhine
Lampito
Stratyllis, etc.
Chorus of Women

Magistrate
Cinesias
Spartan Herald
Envoys
Athenians
Porter, Market-Loungers, etc.
Chorus of Old Men

Lysistrata

SCENE I

Outside LYSISTRATA's *house, near the Acropolis.*
LYSISTRATA *stands alone with the Propylaea at her back.*

LYSISTRATA

If they were trysting for a Bacchanal,
A feast of Pan or Colias or Genetyllis,
The tambourines would block the rowdy streets,
But now there's not a woman to be seen
Except—ah, yes—this neighbour of mine yonder.
(*Enter* CALONICE.)
Good day, Calonice.

CALONICE

Good day, Lysistrata.
But what has vexed you so? Tell me, child.
What are these black looks for? It doesn't suit you
To knit your eyebrows up glumly like that.

LYSISTRATA

Calonice, it's more than I can bear,
I am hot all over with blushes for our sex.
Men say we're slippery rogues—

CALONICE

And aren't they right?

LYSISTRATA

Yet summoned on the most tremendous business
For deliberation, still they snuggle in bed.

CALONICE

My dear, they'll come. It's hard for women, you know,
To get away. There's so much to do.
Husbands to be patted and put in good tempers:
Servants to be poked out: children washed
Or soothed with lullays or fed with mouthfuls of pap.

LYSISTRATA

But I tell you, here's a far more weighty object.

CALONICE

What is it all about, dear Lysistrata,
That you've called the women hither in a troop?
What kind of an object is it?

LYSISTRATA

A tremendous thing!

CALONICE

And long?

LYSISTRATA

Indeed, it may be very lengthy.

CALONICE

Then why aren't they here?

LYSISTRATA

No man's connected with it;
If that was the case, they'd soon come fluttering along.
No, no. It concerns an object I've felt over
And turned this way and that for sleepless nights.

CALONICE

It must be fine to stand such long attention.

LYSISTRATA

So fine it comes to this—Greece saved by Woman!

CALONICE

By Woman? Wretched thing, I'm sorry for it.

LYSISTRATA

Our country's fate is henceforth in our hands:
To destroy the Peloponnesians root and branch—

CALONICE

What could be nobler!

LYSISTRATA

Wipe out the Boeotians—

CALONICE

Not utterly. Have mercy on the eels! *

* The Boeotian eels were highly esteemed delicacies in Athens.

LYSISTRATA

But with regards to Athens, note I'm careful
Not to say any of these nasty things;
Still, thought is free. . . . But if the women join us
From Peloponnesus and Boeotia, then
Hand in hand we'll rescue Greece.

CALONICE

How could we do
Such a big wise deed? We women who dwell
Quietly adorning ourselves in a back-room
With gowns of lucid gold and gawdy toilets
Of stately silk and dainty little slippers. . . .

LYSISTRATA

These are the very armaments of the rescue.
These crocus-gowns, this outlay of the best myrrh,
Slippers, cosmetics dusting beauty, and robes
With rippling creases of light.

CALONICE

Yes, but how?

LYSISTRATA

No man will lift a lance against another—

CALONICE

I'll run to have my tunic dyed crocus.

LYSISTRATA

Or take a shield—

CALONICE

I'll get a stately gown.

LYSISTRATA

Or unscabbard a sword—

CALONICE

Let me buy a pair of slippers.

LYSISTRATA

Now, tell me, are the women right to lag?

CALONICE

They should have turned birds, they should have grown wings and flown.

LYSISTRATA

My friend, you'll see that they are true Athenians:
Always too late. Why, there's not a woman
From the shoreward demes arrived, not one from Salamis.

CALONICE

I know for certain they awoke at dawn,
And got their husbands up if not their boat sails.

LYSISTRATA

And I'd have staked my life the Acharnian dames
Would be here first, yet they haven't come either!

CALONICE

Well anyhow there is Theagenes' wife
We can expect—she consulted Hecate.
But look, here are some at last, and more behind them.
See . . . where are they from?

CALONICE

From Anagyra they come.

LYSISTRATA

Yes, they generally manage to come first.

(*Enter* MYRRHINE.)

MYRRHINE

Are we late, Lysistrata? . . . What is that?
Nothing to say?

LYSISTRATA

I've not much to say for you,
Myrrhine, dawdling on so vast an affair.

MYRRHINE

I couldn't find my girdle in the dark.
But if the affair's so wonderful, tell us, what is it?

LYSISTRATA

No, let us stay a little longer till
The Peloponnesian girls and the girls of Boeotia
Are here to listen.

MYRRHINE

That's the best advice.
Ah, there comes Lampito.

(*Enter* LAMPITO.)

LYSISTRATA

Welcome Lampito!
Dear Spartan girl with a delightful face,

Washed with the rosy spring, how fresh you look
In the easy stride of your sleek slenderness,
Why you could strangle a bull!

LAMPITO

I think I could.
It's frae exercise and kicking high behint.*

LYSISTRATA

What lovely breasts to own!

LAMPITO

Oo . . . your fingers
Assess them, ye tickler, wi' such tender chucks
I feel as if I were an altar-victim.

LYSISTRATA

Who is this youngster?

LAMPITO

A Boeotian lady.

LYSISTRATA

There never was much undergrowth in Boeotia,
Such a smooth place, and this girl takes after it.

CALONICE

Yes, I never saw a skin so primly kept.

LYSISTRATA

This girl?

LAMPITO

A sonsie open-looking jinker!
She's a Corinthian.

LYSISTRATA

Yes, isn't she
Very open, in some ways particularly.

LAMPITO

But who's garred this Council o' Women to meet here?

LYSISTRATA

I have.

LAMPITO

Propound then what you want o' us.

MYRRHINE

What is the amazing news you have to tell?

LYSISTRATA

I'll tell you, but first answer one small question.

MYRRHINE

As you like.

LYSISTRATA

Are you not sad your children's fathers
Go endlessly off soldiering afar
In this plodding war? I am willing to wager
There's not one here whose husband is at home.

CALONICE

Mine's been in Thrace, keeping an eye on Eucrates
For five months past.

* The translator has put the speech of the Spartan characters in Scotch dialect, which is related to English about as was the Spartan dialect to the speech of Athens. The Spartans, in their character, anticipated the shrewd, canny, uncouth Scotch highlander of modern times.

MYRRHINE

And mine left me for Pylos
Seven months ago at least.

LAMPITO

And as for mine
No sooner has he slipped out frae the line
He straps his shield and he's snickt off again.

LYSISTRATA

And not the slightest glitter of a lover!
And since the Milesians betrayed us, I've not seen
The image of a single upright man
To be a marble consolation to us.
Now will you help me, if I find a means
To stamp the war out.

MYRRHINE

By the two Goddesses, Yes!
I will though I've to pawn this very dress
And drink the barter-money the same day.

CALONICE

And I too though I'm split up like a turbot
And half is hackt off as the price of peace.

LAMPITO

And I too! Why, to get a peep at the shy thing
I'd clamber up to the tip-top o' Taygetus.

LYSISTRATA

Then I'll expose my mighty mystery.
O women, if we would compel the men
To bow to Peace, we must refrain—

MYRRHINE

From what?
O tell us!

LYSISTRATA

Will you truly do it then?

MYRRHINE

We will, we will, if we must die for it.

LYSISTRATA

We must refrain from every depth of love. . . .
Why do you turn your backs? Where are you going?
Why do you bite your lips and shake your heads?
Why are your faces blanched? Why do you weep?
Will you or won't you, or what do you mean?

MYRRHINE

No, I won't do it. Let the war proceed.

CALONICE

No, I won't do it. Let the war proceed.

LYSISTRATA

You too, dear turbot, you that said just now
You didn't mind being split right up in the least?

CALONICE

Anything else! O bid me walk in fire
But do not rob us of that darling joy.

What else is like it, dearest Lysistrata?

LYSISTRATA

And you?

MYRRHINE

O please give me the fire instead.

LYSISTRATA

Lewd to the least drop in the tiniest vein,
Our sex is fitly food for Tragic Poets,
Our whole life's but a pile of kisses and babies.
But, hardy Spartan, if you join with me
All may be righted yet. O help me, help me.

LAMPITO

It's a sair, sair thing to ask of us, by the Twa,
A lass to sleep her lane and never fill
Love's lack except wi' makeshifts. . . . But let it be.
Peace maun be thought of first.

LYSISTRATA

My friend, my friend!
The only one amid this herd of weaklings.

CALONICE

But if—which heaven forbid—we should refrain
As you would have us, how is Peace induced?

LYSISTRATA

By the two Goddesses, now can't you see
All we have to do is idly sit indoors
With smooth roses powdered on our cheeks,
Our bodies burning naked through the folds
Of shining Amorgos' silk, and meet the men
With our dear Venus-plats plucked trim and neat.
Their stirring love will rise up furiously,
They'll beg our arms to open. That's our time!
We'll disregard their knocking, beat them off—
And they will soon be rabid for a Peace.
I'm sure of it.

LAMPITO

Just as Menelaus, they say,
Seeing the bosom of his naked Helen
Flang down the sword.

CALONICE

But we'll be tearful fools
If our husbands take us at our word and leave us.

LYSISTRATA

There's only left then, in Pherecrates' phrase,
To flay a skinned dog—flay more our flayed desires.

CALONICE

Bah, proverbs will never warm a celibate.
But what avail will your scheme be if the men
Drag us for all our kicking on to the couch?

LYSISTRATA

Cling to the doorposts.

CALONICE

But if they should force us?

LYSISTRATA

Yield then, but with a sluggish, cold indifference.
There is no joy to them in sullen mating.
Besides we have other ways to madden them;
They cannot stand up long, and they've no delight
Unless we fit their aim with merry succour.

CALONICE

Well if you must have it so, we'll all agree.

LAMPITO

For us I ha' no doubt. We can persuade
Our men to strike a fair an' decent Peace,
But how will ye pitch out the battle-frenzy
O' the Athenian populace?

LYSISTRATA

I promise you
We'll wither up that curse.

LAMPITO

I don't believe it.
Not while they own ane trireme oared an' rigged,
Or a' those stacks an' stacks an' stacks o' siller.

LYSISTRATA

I've thought the whole thing out till there's no flaw.
We shall surprise the Acropolis today:
That is the duty set the older dames.
While we sit here talking, they are to go
And under pretence of sacrificing, seize it.

LAMPITO

Certie, that's fine; all's warking for the best.

LYSISTRATA

Now quickly, Lampito, let us tie ourselves
To this high purpose as tightly as the hemp of words
Can knot together.

LAMPITO

Set out the terms in detail
And we'll a' swear to them.

LYSISTRATA

Of course. . . . Well then
Where is our Scythianess? Why are you staring?
First lay the shield, boss downward, on the floor
And bring the victim's inwards.

CALONICE

But, Lysistrata,
What is this oath that we're to swear?

LYSISTRATA

What oath!
In Aeschylus they take a slaughtered sheep
And swear upon a buckler. Why not we?

CALONICE

O Lysistrata, Peace sworn on a buckler!

LYSISTRATA

What oath would suit us then?

CALONICE

Something burden bearing
Would be our best insignia. . . . A white horse!
Let's swear upon its entrails.

LYSISTRATA

A horse indeed!

CALONICE

Then what will symbolise us?

LYSISTRATA

This, as I tell you—
First set a great dark bowl upon the ground
And disembowel a skin of Thasian wine,
Then swear that we'll not add a drop of water.

LAMPITO

Ah, what aith could clink pleasanter than that!

LYSISTRATA

Bring me a bowl then and a skin of wine.

CALONICE

My dears, see what a splendid bowl it is;
I'd not say No if asked to sip it off.

LYSISTRATA

Put down the bowl. Lay hands, all, on the victim.
Skiey Queen who givest the last word in arguments,
And thee, O Bowl, dear comrade, we beseech:
Accept our oblation and be propitious to us.

CALONICE

What healthy blood, la, how it gushes out!

LAMPITO

An' what a leesome fragrance through the air.

LYSISTRATA

Now, dears, if you will let me, I'll speak first.

CALONICE

Only if you draw the lot, by Aphrodite!

LYSISTRATA

So, grasp the brim, you, Lampito, and all.
You, Calonice, repeat for the rest
Each word I say. Then you must all take oath
And pledge your arms to the same stern conditions—

LYSISTRATA

To husband or lover I'll not open arms

CALONICE

To husband or lover I'll not open arms

LYSISTRATA

Though love and denial may enlarge his charms.

CALONICE

Though love and denial may enlarge his charms.
O, O, my knees are failing me, Lysistrata!

LYSISTRATA

But still at home, ignoring him, I'll stay,

CALONICE

But still at home, ignoring him, I'll stay,

LYSISTRATA

Beautiful, clad in saffron silks all day.

CALONICE

Beautiful, clad in saffron silks all day.

LYSISTRATA

If then he seizes me by dint of force,

CALONICE

If then he seizes me by dint of force,

LYSISTRATA

I'll give him reason for a long remorse.

CALONICE

I'll give him reason for a long remorse.

LYSISTRATA

I'll never lie and stare up at the ceiling,

CALONICE

I'll never lie and stare up at the ceiling,

LYSISTRATA

Nor like a lion on all fours go kneeling.

CALONICE

Nor like a lion on all fours go kneeling.

LYSISTRATA

If I keep faith, then bounteous cups be mine.

CALONICE

If I keep faith, then bounteous cups be mine.

LYSISTRATA

If not, to nauseous water change this wine.

CALONICE

If not, to nauseous water change this wine.

LYSISTRATA

Do you all swear to this?

MYRRHINE

We do, we do.

LYSISTRATA

Then I shall immolate the victim thus.

(*She drinks.*)

CALONICE

Here now, share fair, haven't we made a pact?
Let's all quaff down that friendship in our turn.

LAMPITO

Hark, what caterwauling hubbub's that?

LYSISTRATA

As I told you,
The women have appropriated the citadel.
So, Lampito, dash off to your own land
And raise the rebels there. These will serve as hostages,
While we ourselves take our places in the ranks
And drive the bolts right home.

CALONICE

But won't the men
March straight against us?

LYSISTRATA

And what if they do?
No threat shall creak our hinges wide, no torch
Shall light a fear in us; we will come out
To Peace alone.

CALONICE

That's it, by Aphrodite!
As of old let us seem hard and obdurate.

(LAMPITO *and some go off; the others go up into the Acropolis.*)

SCENE II

Outside the Acropolis.
Chorus of OLD MEN *enter to attack the captured Acropolis.*

MEN

Make room, Draces, move ahead; why your shoulder's chafed, I see,
With lugging uphill these lopped branches of the olive-tree.
How upside-down and wrong-way-round a long life sees things grow.
Ah, Strymodorus, who'd have thought affairs could tangle so?

The women whom at home we fed,
Like witless fools, with fostering bread,
Have impiously come to this—
They've stolen the Acropolis,
With bolts and bars our orders flout
And shut us out.

Come, Philurgus, bustle thither; lay our faggots on the ground,
In neat stacks beleaguering the insurgents all around;
And the vile conspiratresses, plotters of such mischief dire,
Pile and burn them all together in one vast and righteous pyre:
Fling with our own hands Lycon's wife to fry in the thickest fire.
By Demeter, they'll get no brag while I've a vein to beat!
Cleomenes himself was hurtled out in sore defeat.
His stiff-backed Spartan pride was bent.

Out, stripped of all his arms, he went:
A pigmy cloak that would not stretch
To hide his rump (the draggled wretch),
Six sprouting years of beard, the spilth
Of six years' filth.

That was a siege! Our men were ranged in lines of seventeen deep
Before the gates, and never left their posts there, even to sleep.
Shall I not smite the rash presumption then of foes like these,
Detested both of all the gods and of Euripides—
Else, may the Marathon-plain not boast my trophied victories!

Ah, now, there's but a little space
To reach the place!
A deadly climb it is, a tricky road
With all this bumping load:
A pack-ass soon would tire. . . .

How these logs bruise my shoulders! further still
Jog up the hill,
And puff the fire inside,
Or just as we reach the top we'll find it's died.
Ough, phew!
I choke with the smoke.

Lord Heracles, how acrid-hot
Out of the pot
This mad-dog smoke leaps, worrying me
And biting angrily. . . .
'Tis Lemnian fire that smokes,
Or else it would not sting my eyelids thus. . . .
Haste, all of us;
Athene invokes our aid.
Laches, now or never the assault must be made!
Ough, phew!
I choke with the smoke.

Thanked be the gods! The fire peeps up and crackles as it should.
Now why not first slide off our backs these weary loads of wood
And dip a vine-branch in the brazier till it glows, then straight
Hurl it at the battering-ram against the stubborn gate?
If they refuse to draw the bolts in immediate compliance,
We'll set fire to the wood, and smoke will strangle their defiance.
Phew, what a spluttering drench of smoke! Come, now from off my back. . . .
Is there no Samos-general to help me to unpack?
Ah there, that's over! For the last time now it's galled my shoulder.
Flare up thine embers, brazier, and dutifully smoulder,
To kindle a brand, that I the first may strike the citadel.
Aid me, Lady Victory, that a triumph-trophy may tell
How we did anciently this insane audacity quell!

(*Enter Chorus of* WOMEN.)

WOMEN

What's that rising yonder? That ruddy glare, that smoky skurry?
O is it something in a blaze? Quick, quick, my comrades, hurry!

Nicodice, helter-skelter!
Or poor Calyce's in flames
And Cratylla's stifled in the welter.
O these dreadful old men
And their dark laws of hate!

There, I'm all of a tremble lest I turn out to be too late.
I could scarcely get near to the spring though I rose before dawn,
What with tattling of tongues and rattling of pitchers in one jostling din
With slaves pushing in! . . .

Still here at last the water's drawn
And with it eagerly I run
To help those of my friends who stand
In danger of being burned alive.
For I am told a dribbling band
Of greybeards hobble to the field,
Great faggots in each palsied hand,
As if a hot bath to prepare,
And threatening that out they'll drive
These wicked women or soon leave them charring into ashes there.

O Goddess, suffer not, I pray, this harsh deed to be done,
But show us Greece and Athens with their warlike acts repealed!
For this alone, in this thy hold,
Thou Goddess with the helm of gold,
We laid hands on thy sanctuary,
Athene. . . . Then our ally be
And where they cast their fires of slaughter
Direct our water!

STRATYLLIS

(*Caught*)

Let me go!

WOMEN

You villainous old men, what's this you do?
No honest man, no pious man, could do such things as you.

MEN

Ah ha, here's something most original, I have no doubt:
A swarm of women sentinels to man the walls without.

WOMEN

So then we scare you, do we? Do we seem a fearful host?
You only see the smallest fraction mustered at this post.

MEN

Ho, Phaedrias, shall we put a stop to all these chattering tricks?
Suppose that now upon their backs we splintered these our sticks?

WOMEN

Let us lay down the pitchers, so our bodies will be free,
In case these lumping fellows try to cause some injury.

MEN

O hit them hard and hit again and hit until they run away,
And perhaps they'll learn, like Bupalus, not to have too much to say.

WOMEN

Come on, then—do it! I won't budge, but like a dog I'll bite
At every little scrap of meat that dangles in my sight.

MEN

Be quiet, or I'll bash you out of any years to come.

WOMEN

Now you just touch Stratyllis with the top-joint of your thumb.

MEN

What vengeance can you take if with my fists your face I beat?

WOMEN

I'll rip you with my teeth and strew your entrails at your feet.

MEN

Now I appreciate Euripides' strange subtlety:
Woman is the most shameless beast of all the beasts that be.

WOMEN

Rhodippe, come, and let's pick up our water-jars once more.

MEN

Ah cursed drab, what have you brought this water hither for?

WOMEN

What is your fire for then, you smelly corpse? Yourself to burn?

MEN

To build a pyre and make your comrades ready for the urn.

WOMEN

And I've the water to put out your fire immediately.

MEN

What, you put out my fire?

WOMEN

Yes, sirrah, as you soon will see.

MEN

I don't know why I hesitate to roast you with this flame.

WOMEN

If you have any soap you'll go off cleaner than you came.

MEN

Cleaner, you dirty slut?

WOMEN

A nuptial-bath in which to lie!

MEN

Did you hear that insolence?

WOMEN

I'm a free woman, I.

MEN

I'll make you hold your tongue.

WOMEN

Henceforth you'll serve in no more juries.

MEN

Burn off her hair for her.

WOMEN

Now forward, water, quench their furies!

MEN

O dear, O dear!

WOMEN

So . . . was it hot?

MEN

Hot! . . . Enough, O hold.

WOMEN

Watered, perhaps you'll bloom again—why not?

MEN

Brrr, I'm wrinkled up from shivering with cold.

WOMEN

Next time you've fire you'll warm yourself and leave us to our lot.

(MAGISTRATE *enters with attendant* SCYTHIANS.)

MAGISTRATE

Have the luxurious rites of the women glittered
Their libertine show, their drumming tapped out crowds,
The Sabazian Mysteries summoned their mob,
Adonis been wept to death on the terraces,
As I could hear the last day in the Assembly?
For Demostratus—let bad luck befoul him—
Was roaring, "We must sail for Sicily,"

While a woman, throwing herself about in a dance
Lopsided with drink, was shrilling out "Adonis,
Woe for Adonis." Then Demostratus shouted,
"We must levy hoplites at Zacynthus,"
And there the woman, up to the ears in wine,
Was screaming "Weep for Adonis" on the house top,
The scoundrelly politician, that lunatic ox,
Bellowing bad advice through tipsy shrieks:
Such are the follies wantoning in them.

MEN

O, if you knew their full effrontery!
All of the insults they've done, besides sousing us
With water from their pots to our public disgrace
For we stand here wringing our clothes like grown-up infants.

MAGISTRATE

By Poseidon, justly done! For in part with us
The blame must lie for dissolute behaviour
And for the pampered appetites they learn.
Thus grows the seedling lust to blossoming:
We go into a shop and say, "Here, goldsmith,
You remember the necklace that you wrought my wife;
Well, the other night in fervour of a dance
Her clasp broke open. Now I'm off for Salamis;
If you've the leisure, would you go tonight
And stick a bolt pin into her opened clasp."
Another goes to a cobbler, a soldierly fellow,
Always standing up erect, and says to him,
"Cobbler, a sandal strap of my wife's pinches her,
Hurts her little toe in a place where she's sensitive.
Come at noon and see if you can stretch out wider
This thing that troubles her, loosen its tightness."
And so you view the result. Observe my case—
I, a magistrate, come here to draw
Money to buy oar blades, and what happens?
The women slam the door full in my face.
But standing still's no use. Bring me a crowbar,
And I'll chastise this their impertinence.
What do you gape at, wretch, with dazzled eyes?
Peering for a tavern, I suppose.
Come, force the gates with crowbars, prise them apart!
I'll prise away myself too. . . .

(LYSISTRATA *appears.*)

LYSISTRATA

Stop this banging.
I'm coming of my own accord. . . . Why bars?
It is not bars we need but common sense.

MAGISTRATE

Indeed, you slut! Where is the archer now?
Arrest this woman, tie her hands behind.

LYSISTRATA

If he brushes me with a finger, by Artemis,
The public menial, he'll be sorry for it.

MAGISTRATE

Are you afraid? Grab her about the middle.
Two of you then, lay hands on her and end it.

CALONICE

By Pandrosos! if your hand touches her
I'll spread you out and trample on your guts.

MAGISTRATE

My guts! Where is the other archer gone?
Bind that minx there who talks so prettily.

MYRRHINE

By Phosphor, if your hand moves out her way
You'd better have a surgeon somewhere handy.

MAGISTRATE

You too! Where is that archer? Take that woman.
I'll put a stop to these surprise parties.

STRATYLLIS

By the Tauric Artemis, one inch nearer
My fingers, and it's a bald man that'll be yelling.

MAGISTRATE

Tut tut, what's here? Deserted by my archers. . . .
But surely women never can defeat us;
Close up your ranks, my Scythians. Forward at them.

LYSISTRATA

By the Goddesses, you'll find that here await you
Four companies of most pugnacious women
Armed cap-a-pie from the topmost louring curl
To the lowest angry dimple.

MAGISTRATE

On, Scythians, bind them.

LYSISTRATA

On, gallant allies of our high design,
Vendors of grain-eggs-pulse-and-vegetables,
Ye garlic-tavern-keepers of bakeries,
Strike, batter, knock, hit, slap, and scratch our foes,
Be finely imprudent, say what you think of them. . . .
Enough! retire and do not rob the dead.

MAGISTRATE

How basely did my archer-force come off.

LYSISTRATA

Ah, ha, you thought it was a herd of slaves
You had to tackle, and you didn't guess
The thirst for glory ardent in our blood.

MAGISTRATE

By Apollo, I know well the thirst that heats you—
Especially when a wine-skin's close.

MEN

You waste your breath, dear magistrate, I fear, in answering back.
What's the good of argument with such a rampageous pack?
Remember how they washed us down (these very clothes I wore)
With water that looked nasty and that smelt so even more.

WOMEN

What else to do, since you advanced too dangerously nigh.
If you should do the same again, I'll punch you in the eye.
Though I'm a stay-at-home and most a quiet life enjoy,
Polite to all and every (for I'm naturally coy),
Still if you wake a wasps' nest then of wasps you must beware.

MEN

How may this ferocity be tamed? It grows too great to bear.
Let us question them and find if they'll perchance declare
The reason why they strangely dare
To seize on Cranaos' citadel,
His eyrie inaccessible,
This shrine above the precipice,
The Acropolis.
Probe them and find what they mean with this idle talk; listen, but watch they don't try to deceive.
You'd be neglecting your duty most certainly if now this mystery unplumbed you leave.

MAGISTRATE

Women there! Tell what I ask you, directly. . . .
Come, without rambling, I wish you to state
What's your rebellious intention in barring up thus on our noses our own temple-gate.

LYSISTRATA

To take first the treasury out of your management, and so stop the war through the absence of gold.

MAGISTRATE

Is gold then the cause of the war?

LYSISTRATA

Yes, gold caused it and miseries more, too many to be told.
'Twas for money, and money alone, that Pisander with all of the army of mob-agitators
Raised up revolutions. But, as for the future, it won't be worth while to set up to be traitors.
Not an obol they'll get as their loot, not an obol! while we have the treasure-chest in our command.

MAGISTRATE

What then is that you propose?

LYSISTRATA

Just this—merely to take the exchequer henceforth in hand.

MAGISTRATE

The exchequer!

LYSISTRATA

Yes, why not? Of our capabilities you have had various clear evidences.
Firstly remember we have always administered soundly the budget of all home expenses.

MAGISTRATE

But this matter's different.

LYSISTRATA

How is it different?

MAGISTRATE

Why, it deals chiefly with war-time supplies.

LYSISTRATA

But we abolish war straight by our policy.

MAGISTRATE

What will you do if emergencies arise?

LYSISTRATA

Face them our own way.

MAGISTRATE

What *you* will?

LYSISTRATA

Yes *we* will!

MAGISTRATE

Then there's no help for it: we're all destroyed.

LYSISTRATA

No, willy-nilly you must be safeguarded.

MAGISTRATE

What madness is this?

LYSISTRATA

Why, it seems you're annoyed.
It must be done, that's all.

MAGISTRATE

Such awful oppression never,
O never in the past yet I bore.

LYSISTRATA

You must be saved, sirrah—that's all there is to it.

MAGISTRATE

If we don't want to be saved?

LYSISTRATA

All the more.

MAGISTRATE

Why do you women come prying and meddling in matters of state touching war-time and peace?

LYSISTRATA

That I will tell you.

MAGISTRATE

O tell me or quickly I'll—

LYSISTRATA

Hearken awhile and from threatening cease.

MAGISTRATE

I cannot, I cannot; it's growing too insolent.

WOMEN

Come on; you've far more than we have to dread.

MAGISTRATE

Stop from your croaking, old carrion-crow there. . . . Continue.

LYSISTRATA

Be calm then and I'll go ahead.
All the long years when the hopeless war dragged along, we, unassuming, forgotten in quiet,
Endured without question, endured in our loneliness all your incessant child's antics and riot.

Our lips we kept tied, though aching with silence, though well all the while in our silence we knew
How wretchedly everything still was progressing by listening dumbly the daylong to you.
For always at home you continued discussing the war and its politics loudly, and we
Sometimes would ask you, our hearts deep with sorrowing, though we spoke lightly, though happy to see,
"What's to be inscribed on the side of the Treaty-stone? What, dear, was said in the Assembly today?"
"Mind your own business," he'd answer me growlingly, "hold your tongue, woman, or else go away."
And so I would hold it.

WOMEN

I'd not be silent for any man living on earth, no, not I!

MAGISTRATE

Not for a staff?

LYSISTRATA

Well, so I did nothing but sit in the house, feeling dreary, and sigh,
While ever arrived some fresh tale of decisions more foolish by far and presaging disaster.
Then I would say to him, "O my dear husband, why still do they rush on destruction the faster?"
At which he would look at me sideways, exclaiming, "Keep for your web and your shuttle your care,
Or for some hours hence your cheeks will be sore and hot; leave this alone, war is Man's sole affair!"

MAGISTRATE

By Zeus, but a man of fine sense, he.

LYSISTRATA

How sensible?
You dotard, because he at no time had lent
His intractable ears to absorb from our counsel one temperate word of advice, kindly meant?
But when at the last in the streets we heard shouted (everywhere ringing the ominous cry)
"Is there no one to help us, no saviour in Athens?" and, "No, there is no one," come back in reply.
At once a convention of all wives through Hellas here for a serious purpose was held,
To determine how husbands might yet back to wisdom despite their reluctance in time be compelled.
Why then delay any longer? It's settled. For the future you'll take up our old occupation.
Now in turn you're to hold tongue, as we did, and listen while we show the way to recover the nation.

MAGISTRATE

You talk to *us!* Why, you're mad. I'll not stand it.

LYSISTRATA

Cease babbling, you fool; till I end, hold your tongue.

MAGISTRATE

If I should take orders from one who wears veils, may my neck straightaway be deservedly wrung.

LYSISTRATA

O if that keeps pestering you,
I've a veil here for your hair,
I'll fit you out in everything
As is only fair.

CALONICE

Here's a spindle that will do.

MYRRHINE

I'll add a wool-basket too.

LYSISTRATA

Girdled now sit humbly at home,
Munching beans, while you card wool and comb. For war from now on is the Women's affair.

WOMEN

Come then, down pitchers, all,
And on, courageous of heart,
In our comradely venture
Each taking her due part.

I could dance, dance, dance, and be fresher after,
I could dance away numberless suns,
To no weariness let my knees bend.
Earth I could brave with laughter,
Having such wonderful girls here to friend.
O the daring, the gracious, the beautiful ones!
Their courage unswerving and witty
Will rescue our city.

O sprung from the seed of most valiant-wombed grand-mothers, scions of savage and dangerous nettles!
Prepare for the battle, all. Gird up your angers. Our way the wind of sweet victory settles.

LYSISTRATA

O tender Eros and Lady of Cyprus, some flush of beauty I pray you devise
To flash on our bosoms and, O Aphrodite, rosily gleam on our valorous thighs!
Joy will raise up its head through the legions warring and all of the far-serried ranks of mad-love
Bristle the earth to the pillared horizon, pointing in vain to the heavens above.
I think that perhaps then they'll give us our title—
Peace-makers.

MAGISTRATE

What do you mean? Please explain.

LYSISTRATA

First, we'll not see you now flourishing arms about into the Marketing place clang again.

WOMEN

No, by the Paphian.

LYSISTRATA

Still I can conjure them as past where the herbs stand or crockery's sold
Like Corybants jingling (poor sots) fully armoured, they noisily round on their promenade strolled.

MAGISTRATE

And rightly; that's discipline, they—

LYSISTRATA

But what's sillier than to go on an errand of buying a fish
Carrying along an immense Gorgon-buckler instead of the usual platter or dish?

A phylarch I lately saw, mounted on horse-back, dressed for the part with long ringlets and all,
Stow in his helmet the omelet bought steaming from an old woman who kept a food-stall.
Nearby a soldier, a Thracian, was shaking wildly his spear, like Tereus in the play,
To frighten a fig-girl while unseen the ruffian filched from her fruit-trays the ripest away.

MAGISTRATE

How, may I ask, will your rule re-establish order and justice in lands so tormented?

LYSISTRATA

Nothing is easier.

MAGISTRATE

Out with it speedily—what is this plan that you boast you've invented?

LYSISTRATA

If, when yarn we are winding, it chances to tangle, then, as perchance you may know, through the skein
This way and that still the spool we keep passing till it is finally clear all again:
So to untangle the War and its errors, ambassadors out on all sides we will send
This way and that, here, there and round about—soon you will find that the War has an end.

MAGISTRATE

So with these trivial tricks of the household, domestic analogies of threads, skeins and spools,
You think that you'll solve such a bitter complexity, unwind such political problems, you fools!

LYSISTRATA

Well, first as we wash dirty wool so's to cleanse it, so with a pitiless zeal we will scrub
Through the whole city for all greasy fellows; burrs, too, the parasites, off we will rub.
That verminous plague of insensate place-seekers soon between thumb and forefinger we'll crack.
All who inside Athens' walls have their dwelling into one great common basket we'll pack.
Disenfranchised or citizens, allies or aliens, pell-mell the lot of them in we will squeeze.
Till they discover humanity's meaning. . . . As for disjointed and far colonies,
Them you must never from this time imagine as scattered about just like lost hanks of wool.
Each portion we'll take and wind in to this centre, inward to Athens each loyalty pull,
Till from the vast heap where all's piled together at last can be woven a strong Cloak of State.

MAGISTRATE

How terrible is it to stand here and watch them carding and winding at will with our fate,
Witless in war as they are.

LYSISTRATA

What of us then, who ever in vain for our children must weep
Borne but to perish afar and in vain?

MAGISTRATE

Not that, O let that one memory sleep!

LYSISTRATA

Then while we should be companioned still merrily, happy as brides may, the livelong night,
Kissing youth by, we are forced to lie single. . . . But leave for a moment our pitiful plight,
It hurts even more to behold the poor maidens helplessly wrinkling in staler virginity.

MAGISTRATE

Does not a man age?

LYSISTRATA

Not in the same way. Not as a woman grows withered, grows he.
He, when returned from the war, though grey-headed, yet if he wishes can choose out a wife.
But she has no solace save peering for omens, wretched and lonely the rest of her life.

MAGISTRATE

But the old man will often select—

LYSISTRATA

O why not finish and die?
A bier is easy to buy,
A honey cake I'll knead you with joy,
This garland will see you are decked.

CALONICE

I've a wreath for you too.

MYRRHINE

I also will fillet you.

LYSISTRATA

What more is lacking? Step aboard the boat.
See, Charon shouts ahoy.
You're keeping him, he wants to shove afloat.

MAGISTRATE

Outrageous insults! Thus my place to flout!
Now to my fellow magistrates I'll go
And what you've perpetrated on me show.

LYSISTRATA

Why are you blaming us for laying you out?
Assure yourself we'll not forget to make
The third day offering early for your sake.

(MAGISTRATE *retires,* LYSISTRATA *returns within.*)

OLD MEN

All men who call your loins your own, awake at last, arise
And strip to stand in readiness. For as it seems to me
Some more perilous offensive in their heads they now devise.

I'm sure a Tyranny
Like that of Hippias
In this I detect. . . .
They mean to put us under
Themselves I suspect,
And that Laconians assembling
At Cleisthenes' house have played
A trick-of-war and provoked them
Madly to raid
The Treasury, in which term I include
The pay for my food.

For is it not preposterous
They should talk this way to us

On a subject such as battle!
And, women as they are, about bronze bucklers dare to prattle—
Make alliance with the Spartans—people I for one
Like very hungry wolves would always most sincerely shun. . . .
Some dirty game is up their sleeve, I believe.
A Tyranny, no doubt . . . but they won't catch me, that I know.
Henceforth on my guard I'll go,
A sword with myrtle-branches wreathed for ever in my hand,
And under arms in the Public Place I'll take my watchful stand,
Shoulder to shoulder with Aristogeiton. Now my staff I'll draw
And start at once by knocking that shocking
Hag upon the jaw.

WOMEN

Your own mother will not know you when you get back to the town.
But first, my friends and allies, let us lay these garments down,
And all ye fellow-citizens, hark to me while I tell
What will aid Athens well.
Just as is right, for I
Have been a sharer
In all the lavish splendour
Of the proud city.
I bore the holy vessels
At seven, then
I pounded barley
At the age of ten,
And clad in yellow robes,
Soon after this,
I was Little Bear to
Brauronian Artemis;
Then neckletted with figs,
Grown tall and pretty,
I was a Basket-bearer,
And so it's obvious I should
Give you advice that I think good,
The very best I can.
It should not prejudice my voice that I'm not born a man,
If I say something advantageous to the present situation.
For I'm taxed too, and as a toll provide men for the nation.
While, miserable greybeards, you,
It is true,
Contribute nothing of any importance whatever to our needs;
But the treasure raised against the Medes
You've squandered, and do nothing in return, save that you make
Our lives and persons hazardous by some imbecile mistake.
What can you answer? Now be careful, don't arouse my spite,
Or with my slipper I'll take you napping,
faces slapping
Left and right.

MEN

What villainies they contrive!
Come, let vengeance fall,
You that below the waist are still alive,
Off with your tunics at my call—
Naked, all.
For a man must strip to battle like a man.
No quaking, brave steps taking, careless what's ahead, whiteshoed, in the nude, onward bold,
All ye who garrisoned Leipsidrion of old. . . .
Let each one wag
As youthfully as he can,
And if he has the cause at heart
Rise at least a span.

We must take a stand and keep to it,

For if we yield the smallest bit
To their importunity.
Then nowhere from their inroads will be left to us immunity.
But they'll be building ships and soon their navies will attack us,
As Artemisia did, and seek to fight us and to sack us.
And if they mount, the Knights they'll rob
Of a job,
For everyone knows how talented they all are in the saddle,
Having long practised how to straddle;
No matter how they're jogged there up and down, they're never thrown.
Then think of Myron's painting, and each horse-backed Amazon
In combat hand-to-hand with men.
. . . Come, on these women fall,
And in pierced wood-collars let's stick
quick
The necks of one and all.

WOMEN

Don't cross me or I'll loose
The Beast that's kennelled here. . . .
And soon you will be howling for a truce,
Howling out with fear.
But my dear,
Strip also, that women may battle unhindered. . . .
But you, you'll be too sore to eat garlic more, or one black bean,
I really mean, so great's my spleen, to kick you black and blue
With these my dangerous legs.
I'll hatch the lot of you,
If my rage you dash on,
The way the relentless Beetle
Hatched the Eagle's eggs.

Scornfully aside I set
Every silly old-man threat
While Lampito's with me.
Or dear Ismenia, the noble Theban girl. Then let decree
Be hotly piled upon decree; in vain will be your labours,
You futile rogue abominated by your suffering neighbours.
To Hecate's feast I yesterday went—
Off I sent
To our neighbours in Boeotia, asking as a gift to me
For them to pack immediately
That darling dainty thing . . . a good fat eel* I meant of course;
But they refused because some idiotic old decree's in force.
O this strange passion for decrees nothing on earth can check,
Till someone puts a foot out tripping you,
and slipping you
Break your neck.

* *Vide supra*, p. 16.

SCENE III

Inside the Acropolis gates.
LYSISTRATA *enters in dismay.*

WOMEN

Dear Mistress of our martial enterprise,
Why do you come with sorrow in your eyes?

LYSISTRATA

O 'tis our naughty femininity,
So weak in one spot, that hath saddened me.

WOMEN

What's this? Please speak.

LYSISTRATA

Poor women, O so weak!

WOMEN

What can it be? Surely your friends may know.

LYSISTRATA

Yea, I must speak it though it hurt me so.

WOMEN

Speak; can we help? Don't stand there mute in need.

LYSISTRATA

I'll blurt it out then—our women's army's mutinied.

WOMEN

O Zeus!

LYSISTRATA

What use is Zeus to our anatomy?
Here is the gaping calamity I meant:
I cannot shut their ravenous appetites
A moment more now. They are all deserting.
The first I caught was sidling through the postern
Close by the Cave of Pan: the next hoisting herself
With rope and pulley down: a third on the point
Of slipping past: while a fourth malcontent, seated
For instant flight to visit Orsilochus
On bird-back, I dragged off by the hair in time. . . .
They are all snatching excuses to sneak home.
Look, there goes one. . . . Hey, what's the hurry?

1ST WOMAN

I must get home. I've some Milesian wool
Packed wasting away, and moths are pushing through it.

LYSISTRATA

Fine moths indeed, I know. Get back within.

1ST WOMAN

By the Goddesses, I'll return instantly.
I only want to stretch it on my bed.

LYSISTRATA

You shall stretch nothing and go nowhere either.

1ST WOMAN

Must I never use my wool then?

LYSISTRATA

If needs be.

2ND WOMAN

How unfortunate I am! O my poor flax!
It's left at home unstript.

LYSISTRATA

So here's another
That wishes to go home and strip her flax.
Inside again!

2ND WOMAN

No, by the Goddess of Light,
I'll be back as soon as I have flayed it properly.

LYSISTRATA

You'll not flay anything. For if you begin
There'll not be one here but has a patch to be flayed.

3RD WOMAN

O holy Eilithyia, stay this birth
Till I have left the precincts of the place!

LYSISTRATA

What nonsense is this?

3RD WOMAN

I'll drop it any minute.

LYSISTRATA

Yesterday you weren't with child.

3RD WOMAN

But I am today.
O let me find a midwife, Lysistrata.
O quickly!

LYSISTRATA

Now what story is this you tell?
What is this hard lump here?

3RD WOMAN

It's a male child.

LYSISTRATA

By Aphrodite, it isn't. Your belly's hollow,
And it has the feel of metal. . . . Well, I soon can see.
You hussy, it's Athene's sacred helm,
And you said you were with child.

3RD WOMAN

And so I am.

LYSISTRATA

Then why the helm?

3RD WOMAN

So if the throes should take me
Still in these grounds I could use it like a dove
As a laying-nest in which to drop the child.

LYSISTRATA

More pretexts! You can't hide your clear intent,
And anyway why not wait till the tenth day
Meditating a brazen name for your brass brat?

WOMAN

And I can't sleep a wink. My nerve is gone
Since I saw that snake-sentinel of the shrine.

WOMAN

And all those dreadful owls with their weird hooting!

Though I'm wearied out, I can't
close an eye.

LYSISTRATA

You wicked women, cease from
juggling lies.
You want your men. But what of
them as well?
They toss as sleepless in the lonely
night,
I'm sure of it. Hold out awhile,
hold out,
But persevere a teeny-weeny longer.
An oracle has promised Victory
If we don't wrangle. Would you
hear the words?

WOMEN

Yes, yes, what is it?

LYSISTRATA

Silence then, you chatterboxes.
Here—
*Whenas the swallows flocking in
one place from the hoopoes
Deny themselves love's gambols
any more,
All woes shall then have ending
and great Zeus the Thunderer
Shall put above what was below
before.*

WOMEN

Will the men then always be kept
under us?

LYSISTRATA

*But if the swallows squabble among
themselves and fly away
Out of the temple, refusing to agree,
Then The Most Wanton Birds in
all the World
They shall be named for ever.
That's his decree.*

WOMAN

It's obvious what it means.

LYSISTRATA

Now by all the gods
We must let no agony deter from
duty,
Back to your quarters. For we are
base indeed,
My friends, if we betray the oracle.
(*She goes out.*)

SCENE IV

Outside the Acropolis.
Enter Chorus of OLD MEN *and* WOMEN.

OLD MEN

I'd like to remind you of a fable
they used to employ,
When I was a little boy:
How once through fear of the mar-
riage-bed a young man,
Melanion by name, to the wilder-
ness ran,
And there on the hills he
dwelt.
For hares he wove a net
Which with his dog he set—
Most likely he's there yet.
For he never came back home, so
great was the fear he felt.
I loathe the sex as much as he,

And therefore I no less shall be
As chaste as was Melanion.

MAN

Grann'am, do you much mind men?

WOMAN

Onions you won't need, to cry.

MAN

From my foot you shan't escape.

WOMAN

What thick forests I espy.

MEN

So much Myronides' fierce beard
And thundering black back were feared,
That the foe fled when they were shown—
Brave he as Phormion.

WOMEN

Well, I'll relate a rival fable just to show to you
A different point of view:
There was a rough-hewn fellow, Timon, with a face
That glowered as though a thorn-bush in a wild, bleak place.
He too decided on flight,
This very Furies' son,
All the world's ways to shun
And hide from everyone,
Spitting out curses on all knavish men to left and right.
But though he reared this hate for men,
He loved the women even then,
And never thought them enemies.

WOMAN

O your jaw I'd like to break.

MAN

That I fear do you suppose?

WOMAN

Learn what kicks my legs can make.

MAN

Raise them up, and you'll expose—

WOMAN

Nay, you'll see there, I engage,
All is well kept despite my age,
And tended smooth enough to slip
From my adversary's grip.
(LYSISTRATA *appears.*)

LYSISTRATA

Hollo there, hasten hither to me. Skip fast along.

WOMAN

What is this? Why the noise?

LYSISTRATA

A man, a man! I spy a frenzied man!
He carries Love upon him like a staff.
O Lady of Cyprus, and Cythera, and Paphos,
I beseech you, keep our minds and hands to the oath.

WOMAN

Where is he, whoever he is?

LYSISTRATA

By the Temple of Chloe.

WOMAN

Yes, now I see him, but who can he be?

LYSISTRATA

Look at him. Does anyone recognise his face?

MYRRHINE

I do. He is my husband, Cinesias.

LYSISTRATA

You know how to work. Play with him, lead him on,
Seduce him to the cozening-point—kiss him, kiss him,
Then slip your mouth aside just as he's sure of it,
Ungirdle every caress his mouth feels at
Save that the oath upon the bowl has locked.

MYRRHINE

You can rely on me.

LYSISTRATA

I'll stay here to help
In working up his ardor to its height
Of vain magnificence. . . . The rest to their quarters.
(*Enter* CINESIAS.)
Who is this that stands within our lines?

CINESIAS

I.

LYSISTRATA

A man?

CINESIAS

Too much a man!

LYSISTRATA

Then be off at once.

CINESIAS

Who are you that thus eject me?

LYSISTRATA

Guard for the day.

CINESIAS

By all the gods, then call Myrrhine hither.

LYSISTRATA

So, call Myrrhine hither! Who are you?

CINESIAS

I am her husband Cinesias, son of Anthros.

LYSISTRATA

Welcome, dear friend! That glorious name of yours
Is quite familiar in our ranks. Your wife
Continually has it in her mouth.
She cannot touch an apple or an egg
But she must say, "This to Cinesias!"

CINESIAS

O is that true?

LYSISTRATA

By Aphrodite, it is.
If the conversation strikes on men, your wife
Cuts in with, "All are boobies by Cinesias."

CINESIAS

Then call her here.

LYSISTRATA

And what am I to get?

CINESIAS

This, if you want it. . . . See, what I have here.
But not to take away.

LYSISTRATA

Then I'll call her.

CINESIAS

Be quick, be quick. All grace is wiped from life
Since she went away. O sad, sad am I
When there I enter on that loneliness,
And wine is unvintaged of the sun's flavour.
And food is tasteless. But I've put on weight.

MYRRHINE

(*Above*)
I love him O so much! but he won't have it.
Don't call me down to him.

CINESIAS

Sweet little Myrrhine!
What do you mean? Come here.

MYRRHINE

O no I won't.
Why are you calling me? You don't want me.

CINESIAS

Not want you! with this week-old strength of love.

MYRRHINE

Farewell.

CINESIAS

Don't go, please don't go, Myrrhine.
At least you'll hear our child. Call your mother, lad.

CHILD

Mummy . . . mummy . . . mummy!

CINESIAS

There now, don't you feel pity for the child?
He's not been fed or washed now for six days.

MYRRHINE

I certainly pity him with so heartless a father.

CINESIAS

Come down, my sweetest, come for the child's sake.

MYRRHINE

A trying life it is to be a mother!
I suppose I'd better go.
(*She comes down.*)

CINESIAS

How much younger she looks,
How fresher and how prettier! Myrrhine,
Lift up your lovely face, your disdainful face;
And your ankle . . . let your scorn step out its worst;
It only rubs me to more ardor here.

MYRRHINE

(*Playing with the child*)
You're as innocent as he's iniquitous.
Let me kiss you, honey-petling, mother's darling.

CINESIAS

How wrong to follow other women's counsel
And let loose all these throbbing voids in yourself
As well as in me. Don't you go throb-throb?

MYRRHINE

Take away your hands.

CINESIAS

Everything in the house
Is being ruined.

MYRRHINE

I don't care at all.

CINESIAS

The roosters are picking all your web to rags.
Do you mind that?

MYRRHINE

Not I.

CINESIAS

What time we've wasted
We might have drenched with Paphian laughter, flung
On Aphrodite's Mysteries. O come here.

MYRRHINE

Not till a treaty finishes the war.

CINESIAS

If you must have it, then we'll get it done.

MYRRHINE

Do it and I'll come home. Till then I am bound.

CINESIAS

Well, can't your oath perhaps be got around?

MYRRHINE

No . . . no . . . still I'll not say that I don't love you.

CINESIAS

You love me! Then dear girl, let me also love you.

MYRRHINE

You must be joking. The boy's looking on.

CINESIAS

Here, Manes, take the child home! . . . There, he's gone.
There's nothing in the way now. Come to the point.

MYRRHINE

Here in the open! In plain sight?

CINESIAS

In Pan's cave.
A splendid place.

MYRRHINE

Where shall I dress my hair again
Before returning to the citadel?

CINESIAS

You can easily primp yourself in the Clepsydra.

MYRRHINE

But how can I break my oath?

CINESIAS

Leave that to me,
I'll take all risk.

MYRRHINE

Well, I'll make you comfortable.

CINESIAS

Don't worry. I'd as soon lie on the grass.

MYRRHINE

No, by Apollo, in spite of all your faults
I won't have you lying on the nasty earth.

(*From here* MYRRHINE *keeps on going off to fetch things.*)

CINESIAS

Ah, how she loves me.

MYRRHINE

Rest there on the bench,
While I arrange my clothes. O what a nuisance,
I must find some cushions first.

CINESIAS

Why some cushions?
Please don't get them!

MYRRHINE

What? The plain, hard wood?
Never, by Artemis! That would be too vulgar.

CINESIAS

Open your arms!

MYRRHINE

No. Wait a second.

CINESIAS

O . . .
Then hurry back again.

MYRRHINE

Here the cushions are.
Lie down while I– O dear! But what a shame,
You need more pillows.

CINESIAS

I don't want them, dear.

MYRRHINE

But I do.

CINESIAS

Thwarted affection mine,
They treat you just like Heracles at a feast
With cheats of dainties, O disappointing arms!

MYRRHINE

Raise up your head.

CINESIAS

There, that's everything at last.

MYRRHINE

Yes, all.

CINESIAS

Then run to my arms, you golden girl.

MYRRHINE

I'm loosening my girdle now. But you've not forgotten?
You're not deceiving me about the Treaty?

CINESIAS

No, by my life, I'm not.

MYRRHINE

Why, you've no blanket.

CINESIAS

It's not the silly blanket's warmth but yours I want.

MYRRHINE

Never mind. You'll soon have both.
I'll come straight back.

CINESIAS

The woman will choke me with her coverlets.

MYRRHINE

Get up a moment.

CINESIAS

I'm up high enough.

MYRRHINE

Would you like me to perfume you?

CINESIAS

By Apollo, no!

MYRRHINE

By Aphrodite, I'll do it anyway.

CINESIAS

Lord Zeus, may she soon use up all the myrrh.

MYRRHINE

Stretch out your hand. Take it and rub it in.

CINESIAS

Hmm, it's not as fragrant as might be; that is,
Not before it's smeared. It doesn't smell of kisses.

MYRRHINE

How silly I am: I've brought you Rhodian scents.

CINESIAS

It's good enough, leave it, love.

MYRRHINE

You must be jesting.

CINESIAS

Plague rack the man who first compounded scent!

MYRRHINE

Here, take this flask.

CINESIAS

I've a far better one.
Don't tease me, come here, and get nothing more.

MYRRHINE

I'm coming. . . . I'm just drawing off my shoes. . . .
You're sure you will vote for Peace?

CINESIAS

I'll think about it.
(She runs off.)
I'm dead: the woman's worn me all away.
She's gone and left me with an anguished pulse.

MEN

Baulked in your amorous delight
How melancholy is your plight.
With sympathy your case I view;
For I am sure it's hard on you.
What human being could sustain
This unforeseen domestic strain,
And not a single trace
Of willing women in the place!

CINESIAS

O Zeus, what throbbing suffering!

MEN

She did it all, the harlot, she
With her atrocious harlotry.

WOMEN

Nay, rather call her darling-sweet.

MEN

What, sweet? She's a rude, wicked thing.

CINESIAS

A wicked thing, as I repeat.
O Zeus, O Zeus,
Canst Thou not suddenly let loose
Some twirling hurricane to tear
Her flapping up along the air
And drop her, when she's whirled around,
Here to the ground

Neatly impaled upon the stake
That's ready upright for her sake.
(*He goes out.*)
(*Enter* SPARTAN HERALD *and* MAGISTRATE.)

HERALD

Where gabs the Senate an' the Prytanes?
I've fetcht despatches for them.

MAGISTRATE

Are you a man
Or a monstrosity?

HERALD

My scrimp-brained lad,
I'm a herald, as ye see, who hae come frae Sparta
Anent a Peace.

MAGISTRATE

Then why do you hide that lance
That sticks out under your arms?

HERALD

I've brought no lance.

MAGISTRATE

Then why do you turn aside and hold your cloak
So far out from your body? Is your groin swollen
With stress of travelling?

HERALD

By Castor, I'll swear
The man is wud.

MAGISTRATE

Indeed, your cloak is wide,
My rascal fellow.

HERALD

But I tell ye No!
Enow o' fleering!

MAGISTRATE

Well, what is it then?

HERALD

It's my despatch cane.

MAGISTRATE

Of course—a Spartan cane!
But speak right out. I know all this too well.
Are new privations springing up in Sparta?

HERALD

Och, hard as could be: in lofty lusty columns
Our allies stand united. We maun get Pellene.

MAGISTRATE

Whence has this evil come? Is it from Pan?

HERALD

No. Lampito first ran asklent, then the ithers
Sprinted after her example, and blocked, the hizzies,
Their wames unskaithed against our every fleech.

MAGISTRATE

What did you do?

HERALD

We are broken, and bent double,
Limp like men carrying lanthorns in great winds
About the city. They winna let us even
Wi' lightest neif skim their primsie pretties
Till we've concluded Peace-terms wi' a' Hellas.

MAGISTRATE

So the conspiracy is universal;
This proves it. Then return to Sparta. Bid them
Send envoys with full powers to treat of Peace;
And I will urge the Senate here to choose
Plenipotentiary ambassadors,
As argument adducing this connection.

HERALD

I'm off. Your wisdom nane could contravert.

(*They retire.*)

MEN

There is no beast, no rush of fire, like woman so untamed.
She calmly goes her way where even panthers would be shamed.

WOMEN

And yet you are fool enough, it seems, to dare to war with me,
When for your faithful ally you might win me easily.

MEN

Never could the hate I feel for womankind grow less.

WOMEN

Then have your will. But I'll take pity on your nakedness.
For I can see just how ridiculous you look, and so
Will help you with your tunic if close up I now may go.

MEN

Well, that, by Zeus, is no scoundrel-deed, I frankly will admit.
I only took them off myself in a scoundrel raging-fit.

WOMEN

Now you look sensible, and that you're men no one could doubt.
If you were but good friends again, I'd take the insect out
That hurts your eye.

MEN

Is that what's wrong? That nasty bitie thing.
Please squeeze it out, and show me what it is that makes this sting.
It's been paining me a long while now.

WOMEN

Well I'll agree to that,
Although you're most unmannerly. O what a giant gnat.
Here, look! It comes from marshy Tricorysus, I can tell.

MEN

O thank you. It was digging out a veritable well.
Now that it's gone, I can't hold back my tears. See how they fall.

WOMEN

I'll wipe them off, bad as you are, and kiss you after all.

MEN

I won't be kissed.

WOMEN

O yes, you will. Your wishes do not matter.

MEN

O botheration take you all! How you cajole and flatter.
A hell it is to live with you; to live without, a hell:
How truly was that said. But come, these enmities let's quell.

You stop from giving orders and I'll stop from doing wrong.
So let's join ranks and seal our bargain with a choric song.

CHORUS

Athenians, it's not our intention
To sow political dissension
By giving any scandal mention;
But on the contrary to promote good feeling in the state
By word and deed. We've had enough calamities of late.
So let a man or woman but divulge
They need a trifle, say,
Two minas, three or four,
I've purses here that bulge.
There's only one condition made
(Indulge my whim in this I pray)—
When Peace is signed once more,
On no account am I to be repaid.

And I'm making preparation
For a gay select collation
With some youths of reputation.
I've managed to produce some soup and they're slaughtering for me
A sucking-pig: its flesh should taste as tender as could be.
I shall expect you at my house today.
To the baths make an early visit,
And bring your children along;
Don't dawdle on the way.
Ask no one; enter as if the place
Was all your own—yours henceforth is it.
If nothing chances wrong,
The door will then be shut bang in your face.

(*The* SPARTAN AMBASSADORS *approach.*)

CHORUS

Here come the Spartan envoys with long, worried beards.
Hail, Spartans how do you fare?
Did anything new arise?

SPARTANS

No need for a clutter o' words. Do ye see our condition?

CHORUS

The situation swells to greater tension.
Something will explode soon.

SPARTANS

It's awfu' truly.
But come, let us wi' the best speed we may
Scribble a Peace.

CHORUS

I notice that our men
Like wrestlers poised for contest, hold their clothes
Out from their bellies. An athlete's malady!
Since exercise alone can bring relief.

(*The* ATHENIANS *enter.*)

ATHENIANS

Can anyone tell us where Lysistrata is?
There is no need to describe our men's condition,
It shows up plainly enough.

CHORUS

It's the same disease.
Do you feel a jerking throbbing in the morning?

ATHENIANS

By Zeus, yes! In these straits I'm racked all through,
Unless Peace is soon declared, we shall be driven

In the void of women to try
Cleisthenes.

CHORUS

Be wise and cover those things with your tunics.
Who knows what kind of person may perceive you?

ATHENIANS

By Zeus, you're right.

SPARTANS

By the Twa Goddesses,
Indeed ye are. Let's put our tunics on.

ATHENIANS

Hail O my fellow-sufferers, hail Spartans.

SPARTANS

O hinnie darling, what a waefu' thing
If they had seen us wi' our lunging waddies!

ATHENIANS

Tell us then, Spartans, what has brought you here?

SPARTANS

We come to treat o' Peace.

ATHENIANS

Well spoken there!
And we the same. Let us call out Lysistrata
Since she alone can settle the Peace-terms.

SPARTANS

Call out Lysistratus too if ye don't mind.

CHORUS

No indeed. She hears your voices and she comes.

(*Enter* LYSISTRATA.)

Hail, Wonder of all women! Now you must be in turn
Hard, shifting, clear, deceitful, noble, crafty, sweet, and stern.
The foremost men of Hellas, smitten by your fascination,
Have brought their tangled quarrels here for your sole arbitration.

LYSISTRATA

An easy task if their love's raging home-sickness
Doesn't start trying out how well each other
Will serve instead of us. But I'll know at once
If they do. O where's that girl, Reconciliation?
Bring first before me the Spartan delegates,
And see you lift no rude or violent hands—
None of the churlish ways our husbands used.
But lead them courteously, as women should.
And if they grudge fingers, guide them by other methods,
And introduce them with ready tact. The Athenians
Draw by whatever offers you a grip.
Now, Spartans, stay here facing me. Here you,
Athenians. Both hearken to my words.
I am a woman, but I'm not a fool.
And what of natural intelligence I own
Has been filled out with the remembered precepts
My father and the city-elders taught me.

First I reproach you both sides equally
That when at Pylae and Olympia,
At Pytho and the many other shrines
That I could name, you sprinkle from one cup
The altars common to all Hellenes, yet
You wrack Hellenic cities, bloody Hellas
With deaths of her own sons, while yonder clangs
The gathering menace of barbarians.

ATHENIANS

We cannot hold it in much longer now.

LYSISTRATA

Now unto you, O Spartans, do I speak.
Do you forget how your own countryman,
Pericleidas, once came hither suppliant
Before our altars, pale in his purple robes,
Praying for an army when in Messenia
Danger growled, and the Sea-god made earth quaver?
Then with four thousand hoplites Cimon marched
And saved all Sparta. Yet base ingrates now,
You are ravaging the soil of your preservers.

ATHENIANS

By Zeus, they do great wrong, Lysistrata.

SPARTANS

Great wrang, indeed. O! What a luscious wench!

LYSISTRATA

And now I turn to the Athenians.
Have you forgotten too how once the Spartans
In days when you wore slavish tunics, came
And with their spears broke a Thessalian host
And all the partisans of Hippias?
They alone stood by your shoulder on that day.
They freed you, so that for the slave's short skirt
You should wear the trailing cloak of liberty.

SPARTANS

I've never seen a nobler woman anywhere.

ATHENIANS

Nor I one with such prettily jointing hips.

LYSISTRATA

Now, brethren twined with mutual benefactions,
Can you still war, can you suffer such disgrace?
Why not be friends? What is there to prevent you?

SPARTANS

We're agreed, gin that we get this tempting Mole.

LYSISTRATA

Which one?

SPARTANS

That ane we've wanted to get into,
O for sae lang. . . . Pylos, of course.

ATHENIANS

By Poseidon,
Never!

LYSISTRATA

Give it up.

ATHENIANS

Then what will we do?
We need that ticklish place united to us—

LYSISTRATA

Ask for some other lurking-hole in return.

ATHENIANS

Then, ah, we'll choose this snug thing here, Echinus,
Shall we call the nestling spot? And this backside haven,
These desirable twin promontories, The Maliac,
And then of course these Megarean Legs.

SPARTANS

Not that, O surely not that, never that.

LYSISTRATA

Agree! Now what are two legs more or less?

ATHENIANS

I want to strip at once and plough my land.

SPARTANS

And mine I want to fertilize at once.

LYSISTRATA

And so you can, when Peace is once declared.
If you mean it, get your allies' heads together
And come to some decision.

ATHENIANS

What allies?
There's no distinction in our politics:
We've risen as one man to this conclusion;
Every ally is jumping-mad to drive it home.

SPARTANS

And ours the same, for sure.

ATHENIANS

The Carystians first!
I'll bet on that.

LYSISTRATA

I agree with all of you.
Now off, and cleanse yourselves for the Acropolis,
For we invite you all in to a supper
From our commissariat baskets. There at table
You will pledge good behaviour and uprightness;
Then each man's wife is his to hustle home.

ATHENIANS

Come, as quickly as possible.

SPARTANS

As quick as ye like.
Lead on.

ATHENIANS

O Zeus, quick, quick, lead quickly on.

(*They hurry off.*)

CHORUS

Broidered stuffs on high I'm heaping,
Fashionable cloaks and sweeping

Trains, not even gold gawds keeping.
Take them all, I pray you, take them all (I do not care)
And deck your children—your daughter, if the Basket she's to bear.

Come, everyone of you, come in and take
Of this rich hoard a share.
Nought's tied so skilfully
But you its seal can break
And plunder all you spy inside.
I've laid out all that I can spare,
And therefore you will see
Nothing unless than I you're sharper-eyed.
If lacking corn a man should be
While his slaves clamour hungrily
And his excessive progeny,
Then I've a handfull of grain at home which is always to be had,
And to which in fact a more-than-life-size loaf I'd gladly add.

Then let the poor bring with them bag or sack
And take this store of food.
Manes, my man, I'll tell
To help them all to pack
Their wallets full. But O take care.
I had forgotten; don't intrude,
Or terrified you'll yell.
My dog is hungry too, and bites —beware!

SCENE V

In front of a banqueting hall.
Some LOUNGERS *from the market with torches approach. The* PORTER *bars their entrance.*

1ST MARKET-LOUNGER

Open the door.

PORTER

Here move along.

1ST MARKET-LOUNGER

What's this?
You're sitting down. Shall I singe you with my torch?
That's vulgar! O I couldn't do it . . . yet
If it would gratify the audience,
I'll mortify myself.

2ND MARKET-LOUNGER

And I will too.
We'll both be crude and vulgar, yes we will.

PORTER

Be off at once now or you'll be wailing
Dirges for your hair. Get off at once,
And see you don't disturb the Spartan envoys
Just coming out from the splendid feast they've had.

(*The banqueters begin to come out.*)

1ST ATHENIAN

I've never known such a pleasant banquet before,
And what delightful fellows the Spartans are.
When we are warm with wine, how wise we grow.

2ND ATHENIAN

That's only fair, since sober we're such fools.
This is the advice I'd give the Athenians—
See our ambassadors are always drunk.
For when we visit Sparta sober, then
We're on the alert for trickery all the while
So that we miss half of the things they say,
And misinterpret things that were never said,
And then report the muddle back to Athens.
But now we're charmed with each other. They might cap
With the Telamon-catch instead of the Cleitagora,
And we'd applaud and praise them just the same;
We're not too scrupulous in weighing words.

PORTER

Why, here the rascals come again to plague me.
Won't you move on, you sorry loafers there!

MARKET-LOUNGER

Yes, by Zeus, they're already coming out.

SPARTANS

Now hinnie dearest, please tak' up your pipe
That I may try a spring an' sing my best
In honour o' the Athenians an' oursels.

ATHENIANS

Aye, take your pipe. By all the gods, there's nothing
Could glad my heart more than to watch you dance.

SPARTANS

Mnemosyne,
Let thy fire storm these younkers,
O tongue wi' stormy ecstasy
My Muse that knows
Our deeds and theirs, how when at sea
Their navies swooped upon
The Medes at Artemision—
Gods for their courage, did they strike
Wrenching a triumph frae their foes;
While at Thermopylae
Leonidas' army stood: wild-boars they were like,
Wild-boars that wi' fierce threat
Their terrible tusks whet;
The sweat ran streaming down each twisted face,
Faem blossoming i' strange petals o' death
Panted frae mortal breath,
The sweat drenched a' their bodies i' that place,
For the hurly-burly o' Persians glittered more
Than the sands on the shore.

Come, Hunting Girl, an' hear my prayer—
You whose arrows whizz in woodlands, come an' bless
This Peace we swear.
Let us be fenced wi' agelong amity,
O let this bond stick ever firm through thee
In friendly happiness.
Henceforth no guilefu' perjury be seen!
O hither, hither O
Thou wildwood queen.

LYSISTRATA

Earth is delighted now, peace is the voice of earth.
Spartans, sort out your wives: Athenians, yours.
Let each catch hands with his wife and dance his joy
Dance out his thanks, be grateful in music,
And promise reformation with his heels.

ATHENIANS

O Dancers, forward. Lead out the Graces,
Call Artemis out;
Then her brother, the Dancer of Skies,
That gracious Apollo.
Invoke with a shout
Dionysus out of whose eyes
Breaks fire on the maenads that follow;
And Zeus with his flares of quick lightning, and call
Happy Hera, Queen of all,
And all the Daimons summon hither to be
Witnesses of our revelry
And of the noble Peace we have made,
Aphrodite our aid.
Io Paieon, Io, cry—
For victory, leap!
Attained by me, leap!
Euoi Euoi Euai Euai.

SPARTANS

Piper, gie us the music for a new sang.
(*They sing.*)

Leaving again lovely lofty Taygetus
Hither O Spartan Muse, hither to greet us,
And wi' our choric voice to raise
To Amyclean Apollo praise,
And Tyndareus' gallant sons whose days
Along Eurotas' banks merrily pass,
An' Athene o' the House o' Brass.

Now the dance begin;
Dance, making swirl your fringe o' woolly skin,
While we join voices
To hymn dear Sparta that rejoices
I' a beautifu' sang,
An' loves to see
Dancers tangled beautifully,
For the girls i' tumbled ranks
Alang Eurotas' banks
Like wanton fillies thrang,
Frolicking there
An' like Bacchantes shaking the wild air
To comb a giddy laughter through the hair,
Bacchantes that clench thyrsi as they sweep
To the ecstatic leap.

An' Helen, Child o' Leda, come
Thou holy, nimble, graceful Queen,
Lead thou the dance, gather thy joyous tresses up i' bands
An' play like a fawn. To madden them, clap thy hands,
And sing praise to the warrior goddess templed i' our lands,
Her o' the House o' Brass.

Faust

BY JOHANN WOLFGANG VON GOETHE

TRANSLATED FROM THE GERMAN BY BAYARD TAYLOR

Faust

DEDICATION

Again ye come, ye hovering Forms! I find ye,
As early to my clouded sight ye shone!
Shall I attempt, this once, to seize and bind ye?
Still o'er my heart is that illusion thrown?
Ye crowd more near! Then, be the reign assigned ye,
And sway me from your misty, shadowy zone!
My bosom thrills, with youthful passion shaken,
From magic airs that round your march awaken.

Of joyous days ye bring the blissful vision;
The dear, familiar phantoms rise again,
And, like an old and half-extinct tradition,
First Love returns, with Friendship in his train.
Renewed is Pain: with mournful repetition
Life tracks his devious, labyrinthine chain,
And names the Good, whose cheating fortune tore them
From happy hours, and left me to deplore them.

They hear no longer these succeeding measures,
The souls, to whom my earliest songs I sang:
Dispersed the friendly troop, with all its pleasures,
And still, alas! the echoes first that rang!
I bring the unknown multitude my treasures;
Their very plaudits give my heart a pang,
And those beside, whose joy my Song so flattered,
If still they live, wide through the world are scattered.

And grasps me now a long-unwonted yearning
For that serene and solemn Spirit-Land:
My song, to faint Æolian murmurs turning,
Sways like a harp string by the breezes fanned.
I thrill and tremble; tear on tear is burning,
And the stern heart is tenderly unmanned.
What I possess, I see far distant lying,
And what I lost, grows real and undying.

PRELUDE ON THE STAGE

MANAGER, DRAMATIC POET, MERRY-ANDREW.

MANAGER

You two, who oft a helping hand
Have lent, in need and tribulation,
Come, let me know your expectation
Of this, our enterprise, in German land!
I wish the crowd to feel itself well treated,
Especially since it lives and lets me live;
The posts are set, the booth of boards completed,
And each awaits the banquet I shall give.
Already there, with curious eyebrows raised,
They sit sedate, and hope to be amazed.
I know how one the People's taste may flatter,
Yet here a huge embarrassment I feel:
What they're accustomed to, is no great matter,
But then, alas! they've read an awful deal.
How shall we plan, that all be fresh and new,—
Important matters, yet attractive too?
For 'tis my pleasure to behold them surging,
When to our booth the current sets apace,
And with tremendous, oft-repeated urging,
Squeeze onward through the narrow gate of grace:
By daylight even, they push and cram in
To reach the seller's box, a fighting host,
And as for bread, around a baker's door, in famine,
To get a ticket break their necks almost.
This miracle alone can work the Poet

On men so various: now, my friend, pray show it.

POET

Speak not to me of yonder motley masses,
Whom but to see, puts out the fire of Song!
Hide from my view the surging crowd that passes,
And in its whirlpool forces us along!
No, lead me where some heavenly silence glasses
The purer joys that round the Poet throng,—
Where Love and Friendship still divinely fashion
The bonds that bless, the wreaths that crown his passion!

Ah, every utterance from the depths of feeling
The timid lips have stammeringly expressed,—

Now failing, now, perchance, success revealing,—
Gulps the wild Moment in its greedy breast;
Or oft, reluctant years its warrant sealing,
Its perfect stature stands at last confessed!
What dazzles, for the Moment spends its spirit:
What's genuine, shall Posterity inherit.

MERRY-ANDREW

Posterity! Don't name the word to me!
If *I* should choose to preach Posterity,
Where would you get contemporary fun?
That men *will* have it, there's no blinking:
A fine young fellow's presence, to my thinking,
Is something worth, to every one.

Who genially his nature can outpour,
Takes from the People's moods no irritation;
The wider circle he acquires, the more
Securely works his inspiration.
Then pluck up heart, and give us sterling coin!
Let Fancy be with her attendants fitted,—
Sense, Reason, Sentiment, and Passion join,—
But have a care, lest Folly be omitted!

MANAGER

Chiefly, enough of incident prepare!
They come to look, and they prefer to stare.
Reel off a host of threads before their faces,
So that they gape in stupid wonder: then
By sheer diffuseness you have won their graces,
And are, at once, most popular of men.
Only by mass you touch the mass; for any
Will finally, himself, his bit select:
Who offers much, brings something unto many,
And each goes home content with the effect.
If you've a piece, why, just in pieces give it:
A hash, a stew, will bring success, believe it!
'Tis easily displayed, and easy to invent.
What use, a Whole compactly to present?
Your hearers pick and pluck, as soon as they receive it!

POET

You do not feel, how such a trade debases;
How ill it suits the Artist, proud and true!
The botching work each fine pretender traces
Is, I perceive, a principle with you.

MANAGER

Such a reproach not in the least offends;
A man who some result intends
Must use the tools that best are fitting.
Reflect, soft wood is given to you for splitting,
And then, observe for whom you write!
If one comes bored, exhausted quite,

Another, satiate, leaves the banquet's tapers,
And, worst of all, full many a wight
Is fresh from reading of the daily papers.
Idly to us they come, as to a masquerade,
Mere curiosity their spirits warming:
The ladies with themselves, and with their finery, aid,
Without a salary their parts performing.
What dreams are yours in high poetic places?
You're pleased, forsooth, full houses to behold?
Draw near, and view your patrons' faces!
The half are coarse, the half are cold.
One, when the play is out, goes home to cards;
A wild night on a wench's breast another chooses:
Why should you rack, poor, foolish bards,
For ends like these, the gracious Muses?
I tell you, give but more—more, ever more, they ask:
Thus shall you hit the mark of gain and glory.
Seek to confound your auditory!
To satisfy them is a task.—
What ails you now? Is't suffering, or pleasure?

POET

Go, find yourself a more obedient slave!
What! shall the Poet that which Nature gave,
The highest right, supreme Humanity,
Forfeit so wantonly, to swell your treasure?
Whence o'er the heart his empire free?
The elements of Life how conquers he?
Is't not his heart's accord, urged outward far and dim,
To wind the world in unison with him?
When on the spindle, spun to endless distance,
By Nature's listless hand the thread is twirled,
And the discordant tones of all existence
In sullen jangle are together hurled,
Who, then, the changeless orders of creation
Divides, and kindles into rhythmic dance?
Who brings the One to join the general ordination,
Where it may throb in grandest consonance?
Who bids the storm to passion stir the bosom?
In brooding souls the sunset burn above?
Who scatters every fairest April blossom
Along the shining path of Love?
Who braids the noteless leaves to crowns, requiting
Desert with fame, in Action's every field?
Who makes Olympus sure, the Gods uniting?
The might of Man, as in the Bard revealed.

MERRY-ANDREW

So, these fine forces, in conjunction,
Propel the high poetic function,
As in a love-adventure they might play!
You meet by accident; you feel, you stay,

And by degrees your heart is tangled;
Bliss grows apace, and then its course is jangled;
You're ravished quite, then comes a touch of woe,
And there's a neat romance, completed ere you know!
Let us, then, such a drama give!
Grasp the exhaustless life that all men live!
Each shares therein, though few may comprehend:
Where'er you touch, there's interest without end.
In motley pictures little light,
Much error, and of truth a glimmering mite,
Thus the best beverage is supplied,
Whence all the world is cheered and edified.
Then, at your play, behold the fairest flower
Of youth collect, to hear the revelation!
Each tender soul, with sentimental power,
Sucks melancholy food from your creation;
And now in this, now that, the leaven works.
For each beholds what in his bosom lurks.
They still are moved at once to weeping or to laughter,
Still wonder at your flights, enjoy the show they see:
A mind, once formed, is never suited after;
One yet in growth will ever grateful be.

POET

Then give me back that time of pleasures,
While yet in joyous growth I sang,—
When, like a fount, the crowding measures
Uninterrupted gushed and sprang!
Then bright mist veiled the world before me,
In opening buds a marvel woke,
As I the thousand blossoms broke,
Which every valley richly bore me!
I nothing had, and yet enough for youth—
Joy in Illusion, ardent thirst for Truth.
Give, unrestrained, the old emotion,
The bliss that touched the verge of pain,
The strength of Hate, Love's deep devotion,—
O, give me back my youth again!

MERRY-ANDREW

Youth, good my friend, you certainly require
When foes in combat sorely press you;
When lovely maids, in fond desire,
Hang on your bosom and caress you;
When from the hard-won goal the wreath
Beckons afar, the race awaiting;
When, after dancing out your breath,
You pass the night in dissipating:—
But that familiar harp with soul
To play,—with grace and bold expression,
And towards a self-erected goal
To walk with many a sweet digression,—
This, aged Sirs, belongs to you,
And we no less revere you for that reason:
Age childish makes, they say, but 'tis not true;
We're only genuine children still, in Age's season!

MANAGER

The words you've bandied are sufficient;
'Tis deeds that I prefer to see:
In compliments you're both proficient,
But might, the while, more useful be.
What need to talk of Inspiration?
'Tis no companion of Delay.
If Poetry be your vocation,
Let Poetry your will obey!
Full well you know what here is wanting;
The crowd for strongest drink is panting,
And such, forthwith, I'd have you brew.
What's left undone to-day, To-morrow will not do.
Waste not a day in vain digression:
With resolute, courageous trust
Seize every possible impression,
And make it firmly your possession;
You'll then work on, because you must.
Upon our German stage, you know it,
Each tries his hand at what he will;
So, take of traps and scenes your fill,
And all you find, be sure to show it!
Use both the great and lesser heavenly light,—
Squander the stars in any number,
Beasts, birds, trees, rocks, and all such lumber,
Fire, water, darkness, Day and Night!
Thus, in our booth's contracted sphere,
The circle of Creation will appear,
And move, as we deliberately impel,
From Heaven, across the World, to Hell!

PROLOGUE IN HEAVEN

THE LORD. THE HEAVENLY HOST. *Afterwards* MEPHISTOPHELES.
(*The* THREE ARCHANGELS *come forward.*)

RAPHAEL

The sun-orb sings, in emulation,
'Mid brother-spheres, his ancient round:
His path predestined through Creation
He ends with step of thunder-sound.
The angels from his visage splendid
Draw power, whose measure none can say;
The lofty works, uncomprehended,
Are bright as on the earliest day.

GABRIEL

And swift, and swift beyond conceiving,
The splendor of the world goes round,
Day's Eden-brightness still relieving
The awful Night's intense profound:
The ocean-tides in foam are breaking,
Against the rocks' deep bases hurled,
And both, the spheric race partaking,
Eternal, swift, are onward whirled!

MICHAEL

And rival storms abroad are surging
From sea to land, from land to sea.
A chain of deepest action forging

Round all, in wrathful energy.
There flames a desolation, blazing
Before the Thunder's crashing way:
Yet, Lord, Thy messengers are praising
The gentle movement of Thy Day.

THE THREE

Though still by them uncomprehended,
From these the angels draw their power,
And all Thy works, sublime and splendid,
Are bright as in Creation's hour.

MEPHISTOPHELES

Since Thou, O Lord, deign'st to approach again
And ask us how we do, in manner kindest,
And heretofore to meet myself wert fain,
Among Thy menials, now, my face Thou findest.
Pardon, this troop I cannot follow after
With lofty speech, though by them scorned and spurned:
My pathos certainly would move Thy laughter,
If Thou hadst not all merriment unlearned.
Of suns and worlds I've nothing to be quoted;
How men torment themselves, is all I've noted.
The little god o' the world sticks to the same old way,
And is as whimsical as on Creation's day.
Life somewhat better might content him,
But for the gleam of heavenly light which Thou hast lent him:
He calls it Reason—thence his power's increased,
To be far beastlier than any beast.
Saving Thy Gracious Presence, he to me
A long-legged grasshopper appears to be,
That springing flies, and flying springs,
And in the grass the same old ditty sings.
Would he still lay among the grass he grows in!
Each bit of dung he seeks, to stick his nose in.

THE LORD

Hast thou, then, nothing more to mention?
Com'st ever, thus, with ill intention?
Find'st nothing right on earth, eternally?

MEPHISTOPHELES

No, Lord! I find things, there, still bad as they can be.
Man's misery even to pity moves my nature;
I've scarce the heart to plague the wretched creature.

THE LORD

Know'st Faust?

MEPHISTOPHELES

The Doctor Faust?

THE LORD

My servant, he!

MEPHISTOPHELES

Forsooth! He serves you after strange devices:
No earthly meat or drink the fool suffices:

His spirit's ferment far aspireth;
Half conscious of his frenzied, crazed unrest,
The fairest stars from Heaven he requireth,
From Earth the highest raptures and the best,
And all the Near and Far that he desireth
Fails to subdue the tumult of his breast.

THE LORD

Though still confused his service unto Me,
I soon shall lead him to a clearer morning.
Sees not the gardener, even while buds his tree,
Both flower and fruit the future years adorning?

MEPHISTOPHELES

What will you bet? There's still a chance to gain him,
If unto me full leave you give,
Gently upon *my* road to train him!

THE LORD

As long as he on earth shall live,
So long I make no prohibition.
While Man's desires and aspirations stir,
He cannot choose but err.

MEPHISTOPHELES

My thanks! I find the dead no acquisition,
And never cared to have them in my keeping.
I much prefer the cheeks where ruddy blood is leaping,
And when a corpse approaches, close my house:
It goes with me, as with the cat the mouse.

THE LORD

Enough! What thou hast asked is granted.
Turn off this spirit from his fountain-head;
To trap him, let thy snares be planted,
And him, with thee, be downward led;
Then stand abashed, when thou art forced to say:
A good man, through obscurest aspiration,
Has still an instinct of the one true way.

MEPHISTOPHELES

Agreed! But 'tis a short probation.
About my bet I feel no trepidation.
If I fulfil my expectation,
You'll let me triumph with a swelling breast:
Dust shall he eat, and with a zest,
As did a certain snake, my near relation.

THE LORD

Therein thou'rt free, according to thy merits;
The like of thee have never moved My hate.
Of all the bold, denying Spirits,
The waggish knave least trouble doth create.
Man's active nature, flagging, seeks too soon the level;
Unqualified repose he learns to crave;
Whence, willingly, the comrade him I gave,
Who works, excites, and must create, as Devil
But ye, God's sons in love and duty,
Enjoy the rich, the ever-living Beauty!

Creative Power, that works eternal schemes,
Clasp you in bonds of love, relaxing never,
And what in wavering apparition gleams
Fix in its place with thoughts that stand forever!

(*Heaven closes: the* ARCHANGELS *separate.*)

MEPHISTOPHELES

(*Solus*)

I like, at times, to hear The Ancient's word,
And have a care to be most civil:
It's really kind of such a noble Lord
So humanly to gossip with the Devil!

FIRST PART OF THE TRAGEDY

I

NIGHT

A lofty-arched, narrow, Gothic chamber. FAUST, *in a chair at his desk, restless.*

FAUST

I've studied now Philosophy
And Jurisprudence, Medicine,—
And even, alas! Theology,—
From end to end, with labor keen;
And here, poor fool! with all my lore
I stand, no wiser than before:
I'm Magister—yea, Doctor—hight,
And straight or cross-wise, wrong or right,
These ten years long, with many woes,
I've led my scholars by the nose,—
And see, that nothing can be known!
That knowledge cuts me to the bone.
I'm cleverer, true, than those fops of teachers,
Doctors and Magisters, Scribes and Preachers;
Neither scruples nor doubts come now to smite me,
Nor Hell nor Devil can longer affright me.

For this, all pleasure am I foregoing;
I do not pretend to aught worth knowing,
I do not pretend I could be a teacher
To help or convert a fellow creature.
Then, too, I've neither lands nor gold,
Nor the world's least pomp or honor hold—
No dog would endure such a curst existence!
Wherefore, from Magic I seek assistance,
That many a secret perchance I reach
Through spirit-power and spirit-speech,

And thus the bitter task forego
Of saying the things I do not know,—
That I may detect the inmost force
Which binds the world, and guides its course;
Its germs, productive powers explore,
And rummage in empty words no more!

O full and splendid Moon, whom I
Have, from this desk, seen climb the sky
So many a midnight,—would thy glow
For the last time beheld my woe!
Ever thine eye, most mournful friend,
O'er books and papers saw me bend;
But would that I, on mountains grand,
Amid thy blessed light could stand,
With spirits through mountain caverns hover,
Float in thy twilight the meadows over,
And, freed from the fumes of lore that swathe me,
To health in thy dewy fountains bathe me!
Ah, me! this dungeon still I see,
This drear, accursed masonry,
Where even the welcome daylight strains
But duskly through the painted panes.
Hemmed in by many a toppling heap
Of books worm-eaten, gray with dust,
Which to the vaulted ceiling creep,
Against the smoky paper thrust,—
With glasses, boxes, round me stacked,
And instruments together hurled,
Ancestral lumber, stuffed and packed—
Such is my world: and what a world!

And do I ask, wherefore my heart
Falters, oppressed with unknown needs?
Why some inexplicable smart
All movement of my life impedes?
Alas! in living Nature's stead,
Where God His human creature set,
In smoke and mould the fleshless dead
And bones of beasts surround me yet!

Fly! Up, and seek the broad, free land!
And this one Book of Mystery
From Nostradamus' very hand,
Is't not sufficient company?
When I the starry courses know,
And Nature's wise instruction seek,
With light and power my soul shall glow,
As when to spirits spirits speak.
'Tis vain, this empty brooding here,
Though guessed the holy symbols be:
Ye, Spirits, come—ye hover near—
Oh, if you hear me, answer me!
(*He opens the Book, and perceives the sign of the Macrocosm.*)
Ha! what a sudden rapture leaps from this
I view, through all my senses swiftly flowing!
I feel a youthful, holy, vital bliss
In every vein and fibre newly glowing.
Was it a God, who traced this sign,
With calm across my tumult stealing,
My troubled heart to joy unsealing,

With impulse, mystic and divine,
The powers of Nature here, around my path, revealing?
Am I a God?—so clear mine eyes!
In these pure features I behold
Creative Nature to my soul unfold.
What says the sage, now first I recognize:
"The spirit-world no closures fasten;
Thy sense is shut, thy heart is dead:
Disciple, up! untiring, hasten
To bathe thy breast in morning-red!"

(*He contemplates the sign.*)

How each the Whole its substance gives,
Each in the other works and lives!
Like heavenly forces rising and descending,
Their golden urns reciprocally lending,
With wings that winnow blessing
From Heaven through Earth I see them pressing,
Filling the All with harmony unceasing!
How grand a show! but, ah! a show alone.
Thee, boundless Nature, how make thee my own?
Where you, ye beasts? Founts of all Being, shining,
Whereon hang Heaven's and Earth's desire,
Whereto our withered hearts aspire,—
Ye flow, ye feed: and am I vainly pining?

(*He turns the leaves impatiently, and perceives the sign of the Earth-Spirit.*)

How otherwise upon me works this sign!
Thou, Spirit of the Earth, art nearer:
Even now my powers are loftier, clearer;
I glow, as drunk with new-made wine:
New strength and heart to meet the world incite me,
The woe of earth, the bliss of earth, invite me,
And though the shock of storms may smite me,
No crash of shipwreck shall have power to fright me!
Clouds gather over me—
The moon conceals her light—
The lamp's extinguished!—
Mists rise,—red, angry rays are darting
Around my head!—There falls
A horror from the vaulted roof,
And seizes me!
I feel thy presence, Spirit I invoke!
Reveal thyself!
Ha! in my heart what rending stroke!
With new impulsion
My senses heave in this convulsion!
I feel thee draw my heart, absorb, exhaust me:
Thou must! thou must! and though my life it cost me!

(*He seizes the book, and mysteriously pronounces the sign of the Spirit. A ruddy flame flashes: the Spirit appears in the flame.*)

SPIRIT

Who calls me?

FAUST

(*With averted head*)

Terrible to see!

SPIRIT

Me hast thou long with might attracted,
Long from my sphere thy food exacted,
And now—

FAUST

Woe! I endure not thee!

SPIRIT

To view me is thine aspiration,
My voice to hear, my countenance to see;
Thy powerful yearning moveth me,
Here am I!—what mean perturbation
Thee, superhuman, shakes? Thy soul's high calling, where?
Where is the breast, which from itself a world did bear,
And shaped and cherished—which with joy expanded,
To be our peer, with us, the Spirits, banded?
Where art thou, Faust, whose voice has pierced to me,
Who towards me pressed with all thine energy?
He art thou, who, my presence breathing, seeing,
Trembles through all the depths of being,
A writhing worm, a terror-stricken form?

FAUST

Thee, form of flame, shall I then fear?
Yes, I am Faust: I am thy peer!

SPIRIT

In the tides of Life, in Action's storm,
A fluctuant wave,
A shuttle free,
Birth and the Grave,
An eternal sea,
A weaving, flowing
Life, all-glowing,
Thus at Time's humming loom 'tis my hand prepares
The garment of Life which the Deity wears!

FAUST

Thou, who around the wide world wendest,
Thou busy Spirit, how near I feel to thee!

SPIRIT

Thou'rt like the Spirit which thou comprehendest,
Not me!
(*Disappears.*)

FAUST

(*Overwhelmed*)

Not thee!
Whom then?
I, image of the Godhead!
Not even like thee!
(*A knock*)
O Death!—I know it—'tis my Famulus!
My fairest luck finds no fruition:
In all the fullness of my vision
The soulless sneak disturbs me thus!
(*Enter* WAGNER, *in dressing-gown and night-cap, a lamp in his hand.* FAUST *turns impatiently.*)

WAGNER

Pardon, I heard your declamation;
'Twas sure an old Greek tragedy you read?
In such an art I crave some preparation,
Since now it stands one in good stead.
I've often heard it said, a preacher
Might learn, with a comedian for a teacher.

FAUST

Yes, when the priest comedian is by nature,
As haply now and then the case may be.

WAGNER

Ah, when one studies thus, a prisoned creature,
That scarce the world on holidays can see,—
Scarce through a glass, by rare occasion,
How shall one lead it by persuasion?

FAUST

You'll ne'er attain it, save you know the feeling,
Save from the soul it rises clear,
Serene in primal strength, compelling
The hearts and minds of all who hear.
You sit forever gluing, patching;
You cook the scraps from others' fare;
And from your heap of ashes hatching
A starveling flame, ye blow it bare!
Take children's, monkeys' gaze admiring,
If such your taste, and be content;
But ne'er from heart to heart you'll speak inspiring,
Save your own heart is eloquent!

WAGNER

Yet through delivery orators succeed;
I feel that I am far behind, indeed.

FAUST

Seek thou the honest recompense!
Beware, a tinkling fool to be!
With little art, clear wit and sense
Suggest their own delivery;
And if thou'rt moved to speak in earnest,
What need, that after words thou yearnest?
Yes, your discourses, with their glittering show,
Where ye for men twist shredded thought like paper,
Are unrefreshing as the winds that blow
The rustling leaves through chill autumnal vapor!

WAGNER

Ah, God! but Art is long,
And Life, alas! is fleeting.
And oft, with zeal my critic-duties meeting,
In head and breast there's something wrong.
How hard it is to compass the assistance
Whereby one rises to the source!
And, haply, ere one travels half the course
Must the poor devil quit existence.

FAUST

Is parchment, then, the holy fount before thee,
A draught wherefrom thy thirst forever slakes?
No true refreshment can restore thee,
Save what from thine own soul spontaneous breaks.

WAGNER

Pardon! a great delight is granted
When, in the spirit of the ages planted,
We mark how, ere our times, a sage has thought,
And then, how far his work, and grandly, we have brought.

FAUST

O yes, up to the stars at last!
Listen, my friend: the ages that are past
Are now a book with seven seals protected:
What you the Spirit of the Ages call

Is nothing but the spirit of you all,
Wherein the Ages are reflected.
So, oftentimes, you miserably mar it!
At the first glance who sees it runs away.
An offal-barrel and a lumber-garret,
Or, at the best, a Punch-and-Judy play,
With maxims most pragmatical and hitting,
As in the mouths of puppets are befitting!

WAGNER

But then, the world—the human heart and brain!
Of these one covets some slight apprehension.

FAUST

Yes, of the kind which men attain!
Who dares the child's true name in public mention?
The few, who thereof something really learned,
Unwisely frank, with hearts that spurned concealing,
And to the mob laid bare each thought and feeling,
Have evermore been crucified and burned.
I pray you, Friend, 'tis now the dead of night;
Our converse here must be suspended.

WAGNER

I would have shared your watches with delight,
That so our learned talk might be extended.
To-morrow, though, I'll ask, in Easter leisure,
This and the other question, at your pleasure.
Most zealously I seek for erudition:
Much do I know—but to know all is my ambition.

(*Exit.*)

FAUST

(*Solus*)

That brain, alone, not loses hope, whose choice is
To stick in shallow trash forevermore,—
Which digs with eager hand for buried ore,
And, when it finds an angle-worm, rejoices!

Dare such a human voice disturb the flow,
Around me here, of spirit-presence fullest?
And yet, this once my thanks I owe
To thee, of all earth's sons the poorest, dullest!
For thou hast torn me from the desperate state
Which threatened soon to overwhelm my senses:
The apparition was so giant-great,
It dwarfed and withered all my soul's pretences!

I, image of the Godhead, who began—
Deeming Eternal Truth secure in nearness—
To sun myself in heavenly light and clearness,
And laid aside the earthly man;—
I, more than Cherub, whose free force had planned
To flow through Nature's veins in glad pulsation,
To reach beyond, enjoying in creation
The life of Gods, behold my expiation!
A thunder-word hath swept me from my stand.

With thee I dare not venture to compare me.
Though I possessed the power to draw thee near me,
The power to keep thee was denied my hand.
When that ecstatic moment held me,
I felt myself so small, so great;
But thou hast ruthlessly repelled me
Back upon Man's uncertain fate.
What shall I shun? Whose guidance borrow?
Shall I accept that stress and strife?
Ah! every deed of ours, no less than every sorrow,
Impedes the onward march of life.

Some alien substance more and more is cleaving
To all the mind conceives of grand and fair;
When this world's Good is won by our achieving,
The Better, then, is named a cheat and snare.
The fine emotions, whence our lives we mould,
Lie in the earthly tumult dumb and cold.
If hopeful Fancy once, in daring flight,
Her longings to the Infinite expanded,
Yet now a narrow space contents her quite,
Since Time's wild wave so many a fortune stranded.
Care at the bottom of the heart is lurking:
Her secret pangs in silence working,
She, restless, rocks herself, disturbing joy and rest:
In newer masks her face is ever drest,
By turns as house and land, as wife and child, presented,—
As water, fire, as poison, steel:
We dread the blows we never feel,
And what we never lose is yet by us lamented!
I am not like the Gods! That truth is felt too deep:
The worm am I, that in the dust doth creep,—
That, while in dust it lives and seeks its bread,
Is crushed and buried by the wanderer's tread.

Is not this dust, these walls within them hold,
The hundred shelves, which cramp and chain me,
The frippery, the trinkets thousandfold,
That in this mothy den restrain me?
Here shall I find the help I need?
Shall here a thousand volumes teach me only
That men, self-tortured, everywhere must bleed,—
And here and there one happy man sits lonely?
What mean'st thou by that grin, thou hollow skull,
Save that thy brain, like mine, a cloudy mirror,
Sought once the shining day, and then, in twilight dull,
Thirsting for Truth, went wretchedly to Error?
Ye instruments, forsooth, but jeer at me
With wheel and cog, and shapes uncouth of wonder;
I found the portal, you the keys should be;
Your wards are deftly wrought, but drive no bolts asunder!
Mysterious even in open day,
Nature retains her veil, despite our clamors:
That which she doth not willingly display

Cannot be wrenched from her with levers, screws, and hammers.
Ye ancient tools, whose use I never knew,
Here, since my father used ye, still ye moulder:
Thou, ancient scroll, hast worn thy smoky hue
Since at this desk the dim lamp wont to smoulder.
'Twere better far, had I my little idly spent,
Than now to sweat beneath its burden, I confess it!
What from your fathers' heritage is lent,
Earn it anew, to really possess it!
What serves not, is a sore impediment:
The Moment's need creates the thing to serve and bless it!

Yet, wherefore turns my gaze to yonder point so lightly?
Is yonder flash a magnet for mine eyes?
Whence, all around me, glows the air so brightly,
As when in woods at night the mellow moonbeam lies?

I hail thee, wondrous, rarest vial!
I take thee down devoutly, for the trial:
Man's art and wit I venerate in thee.
Thou summary of gentle slumber-juices,
Essence of deadly finest powers and uses,
Unto thy master show thy favor free!
I see thee, and the stings of pain diminish;
I grasp thee, and my struggles slowly finish:
My spirit's flood-tide ebbeth more and more.
Out on the open ocean speeds my dreaming;
The glassy flood before my feet is gleaming,
A new day beckons to a newer shore!

A fiery chariot, borne on buoyant pinions,
Sweeps near me now! I soon shall ready be
To pierce the ether's high, unknown dominions,
To reach new spheres of pure activity!
This godlike rapture, this supreme existence,
Do I, but now a worm, deserve to track?
Yes, resolute to reach some brighter distance,
On Earth's fair sun I turn my back!
Yes, let me dare those gates to fling asunder,
Which every man would fain go slinking by!
'Tis time, through deeds this word of truth to thunder:
That with the height of Gods Man's dignity may vie!
Nor from that gloomy gulf to shrink affrighted,
Where Fancy doth herself to self-born pangs compel,—
To struggle toward that pass benighted,
Around whose narrow mouth flame all the fires of Hell,—
To take this step with cheerful resolution,
Though Nothingness should be the certain, swift conclusion!

And now come down, thou cup of crystal clearest!
Fresh from thine ancient cover thou appearest,
So many years forgotten to my thought!
Thou shon'st at old ancestral banquets cheery,

The solemn guests thou madest merry,
When one thy wassail to the other brought.
The rich and skilful figures o'er thee wrought,
The drinker's duty, rhyme-wise to explain them,
Or in one breath below the mark to drain them,
From many a night of youth my memory caught.
Now to a neighbor shall I pass thee never,
Nor on thy curious art to test my wit endeavor:
Here is a juice whence sleep is swiftly born.
It fills with browner flood thy crystal hollow;
I chose, prepared it: thus I follow,—
With all my soul the final drink I swallow,
A solemn festal cup, a greeting to the morn!
(*He sets the goblet to his mouth.*)
(*Chime of bells and choral song.*)

CHORUS OF ANGELS

Christ is arisen!
Joy to the Mortal One,
Whom the unmerited,
Clinging, inherited
Needs did imprison.

FAUST

What hollow humming, what a sharp, clear stroke,
Drives from my lip the goblet's, at their meeting?
Announce the booming bells already woke
The first glad hour of Easter's festal greeting?
Ye choirs, have ye begun the sweet, consoling chant,
Which, through the night of Death, the angels ministrant
Sang, God's new Covenant repeating?

CHORUS OF WOMEN

With spices and precious
Balm, we arrayed him;
Faithful and gracious,
We tenderly laid him:
Linen to bind him
Cleanlily wound we:
Ah! when we would find him,
Christ no more found we!

CHORUS OF ANGELS

Christ is ascended!
Bliss hath invested him,—
Woes that molested him,
Trials that tested him,
Gloriously ended!

FAUST

Why, here in dust, entice me with your spell,
Ye gentle, powerful sounds of Heaven?
Peal rather there, where tender natures dwell.
Your messages I hear, but faith has not been given;
The dearest child of Faith is Miracle.
I venture not to soar to yonder regions
Whence the glad tidings hither float;
And yet, from childhood up familiar with the note,
To Life it now renews the old allegiance.
Once Heavenly Love sent down a burning kiss
Upon my brow, in Sabbath silence holy;
And, filled with mystic presage, chimed the church-bell slowly,
And prayer dissolved me in a fervent bliss.

A sweet, uncomprehended yearning
Drove forth my feet through woods and meadows free,
And while a thousand tears were burning,
I felt a world arise for me.
These chants, to youth and all its sports appealing,
Proclaimed the Spring's rejoicing holiday;
And Memory holds me now, with childish feeling,
Back from the last, the solemn way.
Sound on, ye hymns of Heaven, so sweet and mild!
My tears gush forth: the Earth takes back her child!

CHORUS OF DISCIPLES

Has He, victoriously,
Burst from the vaulted
Grave, and all-gloriously
Now sits exalted?
Is He, in glow of birth,
Rapture creative near?
Ah! to the woe of earth
Still we are native here.
We, his aspiring
Followers, Him we miss;
Weeping, desiring,
Master, Thy bliss!

CHORUS OF ANGELS

Christ is arisen,
Out of Corruption's womb:
Burst ye the prison,
Break from your gloom!
Praising and pleading him,
Lovingly needing him,
Brotherly feeding him,
Preaching and speeding him,
Blessing, succeeding him,
Thus is the Master near,—
Thus is He here!

II

BEFORE THE CITY-GATE

Pedestrians of all kinds come forth.

SEVERAL APPRENTICES

Why do you go that way?

OTHERS

We're for the Hunters'-lodge, to-day.

THE FIRST

We'll saunter to the Mill, in yonder hollow.

AN APPRENTICE

Go to the River Tavern, I should say.

SECOND APPRENTICE

But then, it's not a pleasant way.

THE OTHERS

And what will *you?*

A THIRD

As goes the crowd, I follow.

A FOURTH

Come up to Burgdorf? There you'll find good cheer,
The finest lasses and the best of beer,

And jolly rows and squabbles, trust me!

A FIFTH

You swaggering fellow, is your hide
A third time itching to be tried?
I won't go there, your jolly rows disgust me!

SERVANT-GIRL

No,—no! I'll turn and go to town again.

ANOTHER

We'll surely find him by those poplars yonder.

THE FIRST

That's no great luck for me, 'tis plain.
You'll have him, when and where you wander:
His partner in the dance you'll be,—
But what is all your fun to me?

THE OTHER

He's surely not alone to-day:
He'll be with Curly-head, I heard him say.

A STUDENT

Deuce! how they step, the buxom wenches!
Come, Brother! we must see them to the benches.
A strong, old beer, a pipe that stings and bites,
A girl in Sunday clothes,—these three are my delights.

CITIZEN'S DAUGHTER

Just see those handsome fellows, there!
It's really shameful, I declare;—
To follow servant-girls, when they
Might have the most genteel society to-day!

SECOND STUDENT

(*To the First*)

Not quite so fast! Two others come behind,—
Those, dressed so prettily and neatly.
My neighbor's one of them, I find,
A girl that takes my heart, completely.
They go their way with looks demure,
But they'll accept us, after all, I'm sure.

THE FIRST

No, Brother! not for me their formal ways.
Quick! lest our game escape us in the press:
The hand that wields the broom on Saturdays
Will best, on Sundays, fondle and caress.

CITIZEN

He suits me not at all, our new-made Burgomaster!
Since he's installed, his arrogance grows faster.
How has he helped the town, I say?
Things worsen,—what improvement names he?
Obedience, more than ever, claims he,
And more than ever we must pay!

BEGGAR

(*Sings*)

Good gentlemen and lovely ladies,
So red of cheek and fine of dress,
Behold, how needful here your aid is,
And see and lighten my distress!

Let me not vainly sing my ditty;
He's only glad who gives away:
A holiday, that shows your pity,
Shall be for me a harvest-day!

ANOTHER CITIZEN

On Sundays, holidays, there's naught I take delight in,
Like gossiping of war, and war's array,
When down in Turkey, far away,
The foreign people are a-fighting.
One at the window sits, with glass and friends,
And sees all sorts of ships go down the river gliding:
And blesses then, as home he wends
At night, our times of peace abiding.

THIRD CITIZEN

Yes, Neighbor! that's my notion, too:
Why, let them break their heads, let loose their passions,
And mix things madly through and through,
So, here, we keep our good old fashions!

OLD WOMAN

(*To the* CITIZEN'S DAUGHTER)

Dear me, how fine! So handsome, and so young!
Who wouldn't lose his heart, that met you?
Don't be so proud! I'll hold my tongue,
And what you'd like I'll undertake to get you.

CITIZEN'S DAUGHTER

Come, Agatha! I shun the witch's sight
Before folks, lest there be misgiving:
'Tis true, she showed me, on Saint Andrew's Night,
My future sweetheart, just as he were living.

THE OTHER

She showed me mine, in crystal clear,
With several wild young blades, a soldier-lover:
I seek him everywhere, I pry and peer,
And yet, somehow, his face I can't discover.

SOLDIERS

Castles, with lofty
Ramparts and towers,
Maidens disdainful
In Beauty's array,
Both shall be ours!
Bold is the venture,
Splendid the pay!
Lads, let the trumpets
For us be suing,—
Calling to pleasure,
Calling to ruin.
Stormy our life is;
Such is its boon!
Maidens and castles
Capitulate soon.
Bold is the venture,
Splendid the pay!
And the soldiers go marching,
Marching away!

FAUST AND WAGNER

FAUST

Released from ice are brook and river
By the quickening glance of the gracious Spring;
The colors of hope to the valley cling,
And weak old Winter himself must shiver,
Withdrawn to the mountains, a crownless king.

Whence, ever retreating, he sends again
Impotent showers of sleet that darkle
In belts across the green o' the plain.
But the sun will permit no white to sparkle;
Everywhere form in development moveth;
He will brighten the world with the tints he loveth,
And, lacking blossoms, blue, yellow, and red,
He takes these gaudy people instead.
Turn thee about, and from this height
Back on the town direct thy sight.
Out of the hollow, gloomy gate,
The motley throngs come forth elate:
Each will the joy of the sunshine hoard,
To honor the Day of the Risen Lord!
They feel, themselves, their resurrection:
From the low, dark rooms, scarce habitable;
From the bonds of Work, from Trade's restriction;
From the pressing weight of roof and gable;
From the narrow, crushing streets and alleys;
From the churches' solemn and reverend night,
All come forth to the cheerful light.
How lively, see! the multitude sallies,
Scattering through gardens and fields remote,
While over the river, that broadly dallies,
Dances so many a festive boat;
And overladen, nigh to sinking,
The last full wherry takes the stream.
Yonder afar, from the hill-paths blinking,
Their clothes are colors that softly gleam.
I hear the noise of the village, even;
Here is the People's proper Heaven;
Here high and low contented see!
Here I am Man,—dare man to be!

WAGNER

To stroll with you, Sir Doctor, flatters;
'Tis honor, profit, unto me.
But I, alone, would shun these shallow matters,
Since all that's coarse provokes my enmity.
This fiddling, shouting, ten-pin rolling
I hate,—these noises of the throng:
They rave, as Satan were their sports controlling,
And call it mirth, and call it song!

PEASANTS, UNDER THE LINDEN-TREE

(*Dance and Song*)

All for the dance the shepherd dressed,
In ribbons, wreath, and gayest vest
Himself with care arraying:
Around the linden lass and lad
Already footed it like mad:
Hurrah! hurrah!
Hurrah—tarara-la!
The fiddle-bow was playing.

He broke the ranks, no whit afraid,
And with his elbow punched a maid,
Who stood, the dance surveying:
The buxom wench, she turned and said:
"Now, you I call a stupid-head!"
Hurrah! hurrah!

Hurrah—tarara-la!
"Be decent while you're staying!"

Then round the circle went their flight,
They danced to left, they danced to right:
Their kirtles all were playing.
They first grew red, and then grew warm,
And rested, panting, arm in arm,—
Hurrah! hurrah!
Hurrah—tarara-la!
And hips and elbows straying.

Now, don't be so familiar here!
How many a one has fooled his dear,
Waylaying and betraying!
And yet, he coaxed her soon aside,
And round the linden sounded wide.
Hurrah! hurrah!
Hurrah-tarara-la!
And the fiddle-bow was playing.

OLD PEASANT

Sir Doctor, it is good of you,
That thus you condescend, to-day,
Among this crowd of merry folk,
A highly-learned man, to stray.
Then also take the finest can,
We fill with fresh wine, for your sake:
I offer it, and humbly wish
That not alone your thirst is slake,—
That, as the drops below its brink,
So many days of life you drink!

FAUST

I take the cup you kindly reach,
With thanks and health to all and each.
(*The People gather in a circle about him.*)

OLD PEASANT

In truth, 'tis well and fitly timed,
That now our day of joy you share,
Who heretofore, in evil days,
Gave us so much of helping care.
Still many a man stands living here,
Saved by your father's skilful hand,
That snatched him from the fever's rage
And stayed the plague in all the land.
Then also you, though but a youth,
Went into every house of pain:
Many the corpses carried forth,
But you in health came out again.
No test or trial you evaded:
A Helping God the helper aided.

ALL

Health to the man, so skilled and tried,
That for our help he long may abide!

FAUST

To Him above bow down, my friends,
Who teaches help, and succor sends!
(*He goes on with* WAGNER.)

WAGNER

With what a feeling, thou great man, must thou
Receive the people's honest veneration!
How lucky he, whose gifts his station
With such advantages endow!
Thou'rt shown to all the younger generation:
Each asks, and presses near to gaze;
The fiddle stops, the dance delays.
Thou goest, they stand in rows to see,
And all the caps are lifted high;

A little more, and they would bend the knee
As if the Holy Host came by.

FAUST

A few more steps ascend, as far as yonder stone!—
Here from our wandering will we rest contented.
Here, lost in thought, I've lingered oft alone,
When foolish fasts and prayers my life tormented.
Here, rich in hope and firm in faith,
With tears, wrung hands and sighs, I've striven,
The end of that far-spreading death
Entreating from the Lord of Heaven!
Now like contempt the crowd's applauses seem:
Couldst thou but read, within mine inmost spirit,
How little now I deem,
That sire or son such praises merit!
My father's was a sombre, brooding brain,
Which through the holy spheres of Nature groped and wandered,
And honestly, in his own fashion, pondered
With labor whimsical, and pain:
Who, in his dusky work-shop bending,
With proved adepts in company,
Made, from his recipes unending,
Opposing substances agree.
There was a Lion red, a wooer daring,
Within the Lily's tepid bath espoused,
And both, tormented then by flame unsparing,
By turns in either bridal chamber housed.
If then appeared, with colors splendid,
The young Queen in her crystal shell,
This was the medicine—the patients' woes soon ended,
And none demanded: who got well?
Thus we, our hellish boluses compounding,
Among these vales and hills surrounding,
Worse than the pestilence, have passed.
Thousands were done to death from poison of my giving;
And I must hear, by all the living,
The shameless murderers praised at last!

WAGNER

Why, therefore, yield to such depression?
A good man does his honest share
In exercising, with the strictest care,
The art bequeathed to his possession!
Dost thou thy father honor, as a youth?
Then may his teaching cheerfully impel thee:
Dost thou, as man, increase the stores of truth?
Then may thine own son afterwards excel thee.

FAUST

O happy he, who still renews
The hope, from Error's deeps to rise forever!
That which one does not know, one needs to use;
And what one knows, one uses never.
But let us not, by such despondence, so
The fortune of this hour embitter!
Mark how, beneath the evening sunlight's glow,

The green-embosomed houses glitter!
The glow retreats, done is the day of toil;
It yonder hastes, new fields of life exploring;
Ah, that no wing can lift me from the soil,
Upon its track to follow, follow soaring!
Then would I see eternal Evening gild
The silent world beneath me glowing,
On fire each mountain-peak, with peace each valley filled,
The silver brook to golden rivers flowing.
The mountain-chain, with all its gorges deep,
Would then no more impede my godlike motion;
And now before mine eyes expands the ocean
With all its bays, in shining sleep!
Yet, finally, the weary god is sinking;
The new-born impulse fires my mind,—
I hasten on, his beams eternal drinking,
The Day before me and the Night behind,
Above me heaven unfurled, the floor of waves beneath me,—
A glorious dream! though now the glories fade.
Alas! the wings that lift the mind no aid
Of wings to lift the body can bequeath me.
Yet in each soul is born the pleasure
Of yearning onward, upward and away,
When o'er our heads, lost in the vaulted azure,
The lark sends down his flickering lay,—
When over crags and piny highlands
The poising eagle slowly soars,
And over plains and lakes and islands
The crane sails by to other shores.

WAGNER

I've had, myself, at times, some odd caprices,
But never yet such impulse felt, as this is.
One soon fatigues, on woods and fields to look,
Now would I beg the bird his wing to spare us:
How otherwise the mental raptures bear us
From page to page, from book to book!
Then winter nights take loveliness untold,
As warmer life in every limb had crowned you;
And when your hands unroll some parchment rare and old,
All Heaven descends, and opens bright around you!

FAUST

One impulse art thou conscious of, at best;
O, never seek to know the other!
Two souls, alas! reside within my breast,
And each withdraws from, and repels, its brother.
One with tenacious organs holds in love
And clinging lust the world in its embraces;
The other strongly sweeps, this dust above,
Into the high ancestral spaces.
If there be airy spirits near,
'Twixt Heaven and Earth on potent errands fleeing,
Let them drop down the golden atmosphere,

And bear me forth to new and varied being!
Yea, if a magic mantle once were mine,
To waft me o'er the world at pleasure,
I would not for the costliest stores of treasure—
Not for a monarch's robe—the gift resign.

WAGNER

Invoke not thus the well-known throng,
Which through the firmament diffused is faring,
And danger thousand-fold, our race to wrong,
In every quarter is preparing.
Swift from the North the spirit-fangs so sharp
Sweep down, and with their barbéd points assail you;
Then from the East they come, to dry and warp
Your lungs, till breath and being fail you:
If from the Desert sendeth them the South,
With fire on fire your throbbing forehead crowning,
The West leads on a host, to cure the drouth
Only when meadow field, and you are drowning.
They gladly hearken, prompt for injury,—
Gladly obey, because they gladly cheat us;
From Heaven they represent themselves to be,
And lisp like angels, when with lies they meet us.
But, let us go! 'Tis gray and dusky all:
The air is cold, the vapors fall.
At night, one learns his house to prize:—
Why stand you thus, with such astonished eyes?
What, in the twilight, can your mind so trouble?

FAUST

Seest thou the black dog coursing there, through corn and stubble?

WAGNER

Long since: yet deemed him not important in the least.

FAUST

Inspect him close: for what tak'st thou the beast?

WAGNER

Why, for a poodle who has lost his master,
And scents about, his track to find.

FAUST

Seest thou the spiral circles, narrowing faster,
Which he, approaching, round us seems to wind?
A streaming trail of fire, if I see rightly,
Follows his path of mystery.

WAGNER

It may be that your eyes deceive you slightly;
Naught but a plain black poodle do I see.

FAUST

It seems to me that with enchanted cunning
He snares our feet, some future chain to bind.

WAGNER

I see him timidly, in doubt, around us running,

Since, in his master's stead, two strangers doth he find.

FAUST

The circle narrows: he is near!

WAGNER

A dog thou seest, and not a phantom, here!
Behold him stop—upon his belly crawl—
His tail set wagging: canine habits, all!

FAUST

Come, follow us! Come here, at least!

WAGNER

'Tis the absurdest, drollest beast.
Stand still, and you will see him wait;
Address him, and he gambols straight;
If something's lost, he'll quickly bring it,—
Your cane, if in the stream you fling it.

FAUST

No doubt you're right: no trace of mind, I own,
Is in the beast: I see but drill, alone.

WAGNER

The dog, when he's well educated,
Is by the wisest tolerated.
Yes he deserves your favor thoroughly,—
The clever scholar of the students, he!

(*They pass in the city-gate.*)

III

THE STUDY

FAUST

(*Entering, with the poodle*)

Behind me, field and meadow sleeping,
I leave in deep, prophetic night,
Within whose dread and holy keeping
The better soul awakes to light.
The wild desires no longer win us,
The deeds of passion cease to chain;
The love of Man revives within us,
The love of God revives again.

Be still, thou poodle; make not such racket and riot!
Why at the threshold wilt snuffing be?
Behind the stove repose thee in quiet!
My softest cushion I give to thee.
As thou, up yonder, with running and leaping
Amused us hast, on the mountain's crest,
So now I take thee into my keeping,
A welcome, but also a silent, guest.

Ah, when, within our narrow chamber
The lamp with friendly lustre glows,
Flames in the breast each faded ember,

And in the heart, itself that knows.
Then Hope again lends sweet assistance,
And Reason then resumes her speech:
One yearns, the rivers of existence,
The very founts of Life, to reach.

Snarl not, poodle! To the sound that rises,
The sacred tones that my soul embrace,
This bestial noise is out of place.
We are used to see, that Man despises
What he never comprehends,
And the Good and the Beautiful vilipends,
Finding them often hard to measure:
Will the dog, like man, snarl *his* displeasure?

But ah! I feel, though will thereto be stronger,
Contentment flows from out my breast no longer.
Why must the stream so soon run dry and fail us,
And burning thirst again assail us?
Therein I've borne so much probation!
And yet, this want may be supplied us;
We call the Supernatural to guide us;
We pine and thirst for Revelation,
Which nowhere worthier is, more nobly sent,
Than here, in our New Testament.
I feel impelled, its meaning to determine,—
With honest purpose, once for all,
The hallowed Original
To change to my beloved German.

(*He opens a volume, and commences.*)

'Tis written: "In the Beginning was the *Word*."
Here am I balked: who, now can help afford?
The *Word*?—impossible so high to rate it;
And otherwise must I translate it,
If by the Spirit I am truly taught.
Then thus: "In the Beginning was the *Thought*."
This first line let me weigh completely,
Lest my impatient pen proceed too fleetly.
Is it the *Thought* which works, creates, indeed?
"In the Beginning was the *Power*," I read.
Yet, as I write, a warning is suggested,
That I the sense may not have fairly tested.
The Spirit aids me: now I see the light!
"In the Beginning was the *Act*," I write.

If I must share my chamber with thee,
Poodle, stop that howling, prithee!
Cease to bark and bellow!
Such a noisy, disturbing fellow
I'll no longer suffer near me.
One of us, dost hear me!
Must leave, I fear me.
No longer guest-right I bestow;
The door is open, art free to go.
But what do I see in the creature?
Is that in the course of nature?

Is't actual fact? or Fancy's shows?
How long and broad my poodle grows!
He rises mightily:
A canine form that cannot be!
What a spectre I've harbored thus!
He resembles a hippopotamus,
With fiery eyes, teeth terrible to see:
O, now am I sure of thee!
For all of thy half-hellish brood
The Key of Solomon is good.

SPIRITS

(*In the corridor*)

Some one, within, is caught!
Stay without, follow him not!
Like the fox in a snare,
Quakes the old hell-lynx there.
Take heed—look about!
Back and forth hover,
Under and over,
And he'll work himself out.
If your aid avail him,
Let it not fail him;
For he, without measure,
Has wrought for our pleasure.

FAUST

First, to encounter the beast,
The Words of the Four be addressed:
Salamander, shine glorious!
Wave, Undine, as bidden!
Sylph, be thou hidden!
Gnome, be laborious!

Who knows not their sense
(These elements),—
Their properties
And power not sees,—
No mastery he inherits
Over the Spirits.

Vanish in flaming ether,
Salamander!
Flow foamingly together,
Undine!
Shine in meteor-sheen,
Sylph!
Bring help to hearth and shelf,
Incubus! Incubus!
Step forward, and finish thus!

Of the Four, no feature
Lurks in the creature.
Quiet he lies, and grins disdain:
Not yet, it seems, have I given him pain.
Now, to undisguise thee,
Hear me exorcise thee!
Art thou, my gay one,
Hell's fugitive stray-one?
The sign witness now,
Before which they bow,
The cohorts of Hell!

With hair all bristling, it begins to swell.

Base Being, hearest thou?
Knowest and fearest thou
The One, unoriginate,
Named inexpressibly,
Through all Heaven impermeate,
Pierced irredressibly!

Behind the stove still banned,
See it, an elephant, expand!
It fills the space entire,
Mist-like melting, ever faster.
'Tis enough: ascend no higher,—
Lay thyself at the feet of the Master!
Thou seest, not vain the threats I bring thee:
With holy fire I'll scorch and sting thee!
Wait not to know
The threefold dazzling glow!
Wait not to know
The strongest art within my hands!

MEPHISTOPHELES

(While the vapor is dissipating, steps forth from behind the stove, in the costume of a Travelling Scholar)
Why such a noise? What are my lord's commands?

FAUST

This was the poodle's real core,
A travelling scholar, then? The *casus* is diverting.

MEPHISTOPHELES

The learned gentleman I bow before:
You've made me roundly sweat, that's certain!

FAUST

What is thy name?

MEPHISTOPHELES

A question small, it seems,
For one whose mind the Word so much despises;
Who, scorning all external gleams,
The depths of being only prizes.

FAUST

With all you gentlemen, the name's a test,
Whereby the nature usually is expressed.
Clearly the latter it implies
In names like Beelzebub, Destroyer, Father of Lies.
Who art thou, then?

MEPHISTOPHELES

Part of that Power, not understood,
Which always wills the Bad, and always works the Good.

FAUST

What hidden sense in this enigma lies?

MEPHISTOPHELES

I am the Spirit that Denies!
And justly so: for all things, from the Void
Called forth, deserve to be destroyed:
'Twere better, then, were naught created.
Thus, all which you as Sin have rated,—
Destruction,—aught with Evil blent,—
That is my proper element.

FAUST

Thou nam'st thyself a part, yet show'st complete to me?

MEPHISTOPHELES

The modest truth I speak to thee.
If Man, that microcosmic fool, can see
Himself a whole so frequently,
Part of the Part am I, once All, in primal Night,—
Part of the Darkness which brought forth the Light,
The haughty Light, which now disputes the space,
And claims of Mother Night her ancient place.
And yet, the struggle fails; since Light, howe'er it weaves,
Still, fettered, unto bodies cleaves:
It flows from bodies, bodies beautifies;
By bodies is its course impeded;
And so, but little time is needed,
I hope, ere, as the bodies die, it dies!

FAUST

I see the plan thou art pursuing:
Thou canst not compass general ruin,
And hast on smaller scale begun.

MEPHISTOPHELES

And truly 'tis not much, when all is done.
That which to Naught is in resistance set,—
The Something of this clumsy world,—has yet,
With all that I have undertaken,
Not been by me disturbed or shaken:
From earthquake, tempest, wave, volcano's brand,
Back into quiet settle sea and land!
And that damned stuff, the bestial, human brood,—
What use, in having that to play with?
How many have I made away with!
And ever circulates a newer, fresher blood.
It makes me furious, such things beholding:
From Water, Earth, and Air unfolding,
A thousand germs break forth and grow,
In dry, and wet, and warm, and chilly;
And had I not the Flame reserved, why, really,
There's nothing special of my own to show!

FAUST

So, to the actively eternal
Creative force, in cold disdain
You now oppose the fist infernal,
Whose wicked clench is all in vain!
Some other labor seek thou rather,
Queer Son of Chaos, to begin!

MEPHISTOPHELES

Well, we'll consider: thou canst gather
My views, when next I venture in.
Might I, perhaps, depart at present?

FAUST

Why thou shouldst ask, I don't perceive.
Though our acquaintance is so recent,
For further visits thou hast leave.
The window's here, the door is yonder;
A chimney, also, you behold.

MEPHISTOPHELES

I must confess that forth I may not wander,
My steps by one slight obstacle controlled,—
The wizard's-foot, that on your threshold made is.

FAUST

The pentagram prohibits thee?
Why, tell me now, thou Son of Hades,
If that prevents, how cam'st thou in to me?
Could such a spirit be so cheated?

MEPHISTOPHELES

Inspect the thing: the drawing's not completed.
The outer angle, you may see,
Is open left—the lines don't fit it.

FAUST

Well,—Chance, this time, has fairly hit it!
And thus, thou'rt prisoner to me?
It seems the business has succeeded.

MEPHISTOPHELES

The poodle naught remarked, as after thee he speeded;
But other aspects now obtain:
The Devil can't get out again.

FAUST

Try, then, the open window-pane!

MEPHISTOPHELES

For Devils and for spectres this is law:
Where they have entered in, there also they withdraw.
The first is free to us; we're governed by the second.

FAUST

In Hell itself, then, laws are reckoned?
That's well! So might a compact be
Made with you gentlemen—and binding,—surely?

MEPHISTOPHELES

All that is promised shall delight thee purely;
No skinflint bargain shalt thou see.
But this is not of swift conclusion;
We'll talk about the matter soon.
And now, I do entreat this boon—
Leave to withdraw from my intrusion.

FAUST

One moment more I ask thee to remain,
Some pleasant news, at least, to tell me.

MEPHISTOPHELES

Release me, now! I soon shall come again;
Then thou, at will, mayst question and compel me.

FAUST

I have not snares around thee cast;
Thyself hast led thyself into the meshes.
Who traps the Devil, hold him fast!
Not soon a second time he'll catch a prey so precious.

MEPHISTOPHELES

An't please thee, also I'm content to stay,
And serve thee in a social station;
But stipulating, that I may
With arts of mine afford thee recreation.

FAUST

Thereto I willingly agree,
If the diversion pleasant be.

MEPHISTOPHELES

My friend, thou'lt win, past all pretences,
More in this hour to soothe thy senses,
Than in the year's monotony.
That which the dainty spirits sing thee,
The lovely pictures they shall bring thee,
Are more than magic's empty show.
Thy scent will be to bliss invited;
Thy palate then with taste delighted,
Thy nerves of touch ecstatic glow!
All unprepared, the charm I spin:
We're here together, so begin!

SPIRITS

Vanish, ye darking
Arches above him!
Loveliest weather,
Born of blue ether,
Break from the sky!
O that the darkling
Clouds had departed!
Starlight is sparkling,

Tranquiller-hearted
Suns are on high.
Heaven's own children
In beauty bewildering,
Waveringly bending,
Pass as they hover;
Longing unending
Follows them over.
They, with their glowing
Garments, out-flowing,
Cover, in going,
Landscape and bower,
Where, in seclusion,
Lovers are plighted,
Lost in illusion.
Bower on bower!
Tendrils unblighted!
Lo! in a shower
Grapes that o'ercluster
Gush into must, or
Flow into rivers
Of foaming and flashing
Wine, that is dashing
Gems, as it boundeth
Down the high places,
And spreading, surroundeth
With crystalline spaces,
In happy embraces,
Blossoming forelands,
Emerald shore-lands!
And the winged races
Drink, and fly onward—
Fly ever sunward
To the enticing
Islands, that flatter,
Dipping and rising
Light on the water!
Hark, the inspiring
Sound of their quiring!
See, the entrancing
Whirl of their dancing!
All in the air are
Freer and fairer.
Some of them scaling
Boldly the highlands,
Others are sailing,
Circling the islands;
Others are flying;
Life-ward all hieing,—
All for the distant
Star of existent
Rapture and Love!

MEPHISTOPHELES

He sleeps! Enough, ye fays! your airy number
Have sung him truly into slumber:
For this performance I your debtor prove.—
Not yet art thou the man, to catch the Fiend and hold him!—
With fairest images of dreams infold him.
Plunge him in seas of sweet untruth!
Yet, for the threshold's magic which controlled him,
The Devil needs a rat's quick tooth.
I use no lengthened invocation:
Here rustles one that soon will work my liberation.

The lord of rats and eke of mice,
Of flies and bed-bugs, frogs and lice,
Summons thee hither to the door-sill,
To gnaw it where, with just a morsel
Of oil, he paints the spot for thee:—
There com'st thou, hopping on to me!
To work, at once! The point which made me craven
Is forward, on the ledge, engraven.
Another bite makes free the door:
So, dream thy dreams, O Faust, until we meet once more!

FAUST

(*Awaking*)

Am I again so foully cheated?
Remains there naught of lofty spirit-sway,
But that a dream the Devil counterfeited,
And that a poodle ran away?

IV

THE STUDY

FAUST. MEPHISTOPHELES.

FAUST

A knock? Come in! Again my quiet broken?

MEPHISTOPHELES

'Tis I!

FAUST

Come in!

MEPHISTOPHELES

Thrice must the words be spoken.

FAUST

Come in, then!

MEPHISTOPHELES

Thus thou pleasest me.
I hope we'll suit each other well;
For now, thy vapors to dispel,
I come, a squire of high degree,
In scarlet coat, with golden trimming,
A cloak in silken lustre swimming,
A tall cock's-feather in my hat,
A long, sharp sword for show or quarrel,—
And I advise thee, brief and flat,
To don the self-same gay apparel,
That, from this den released, and free,
Life be at last revealed to thee!

FAUST

This life of earth, whatever my attire,
Would pain me in its wonted fashion.
Too old am I to play with passion;
Too young, to be without desire.
What from the world have I to gain?
Thou shalt abstain—renounce—refrain!
Such is the everlasting song
That in the ears of all men rings,—
That unrelieved, our whole life long,
Each hour, in passing, hoarsely sings.
In very terror I at morn awake,
Upon the verge of bitter weeping,
To see the day of disappointment break,
To no one hope of mine—not one—its promise keeping:—
That even each joy's presentiment
With wilful cavil would diminish,
With grinning masks of life prevent
My mind its fairest work to finish!
Then, too, when night descends, how anxiously
Upon my couch of sleep I lay me:
There, also, comes no rest to me,
But some wild dream is sent to fray me.
The God that in my breast is owned
Can deeply stir the inner sources;
The God, above my powers enthroned,
He cannot change external forces.
So, by the burden of my days oppressed,
Death is desired, and Life a thing unblest!

MEPHISTOPHELES

And yet is never Death a wholly welcome guest.

FAUST

O fortunate, for whom, when victory glances,
The bloody laurels on the brow he bindeth!
Whom, after rapid, maddening dances,
In clasping maiden-arms he findeth!
O would that I, before that spirit-power,
Ravished and rapt from life, had sunken!

MEPHISTOPHELES

And yet, by some one, in that nightly hour,
A certain liquid was not drunken.

FAUST

Eavesdropping, ha! thy pleasure seems to be.

MEPHISTOPHELES

Omniscient am I not; yet much is known to me.

FAUST

Though some familiar tone, retrieving
My thoughts from torment, led me on,
And sweet, clear echoes came, deceiving
A faith bequeathed from Childhood's dawn,
Yet now I curse whate'er entices
And snares the soul with visions vain;
With dazzling cheats and dear devices
Confines it in this cave of pain!
Cursed be, at once, the high ambition
Wherewith the mind itself deludes!
Cursed be the glare of apparition
That on the finer sense intrudes!
Cursed be the lying dream's impression
Of name, and fame, and laurelled brow!
Cursed, all that flatters as possession,
As wife and child, as knave and plow!
Cursed Mammon be, when he with treasures
To restless action spurs our fate!
Cursed when, for soft, indulgent leisures,
He lays for us the pillows straight!
Cursed be the vine's transcendent nectar,—
The highest favor Love lets fall!
Cursed, also, Hope!—cursed Faith, the spectre!
And cursed be Patience most of all!

CHORUS OF SPIRITS

(Invisible)

Woe! woe!
Thou hast it destroyed,
The beautiful world,
With powerful fist:
In ruin 'tis hurled,
By the blow of a demigod shattered!
The scattered
Fragments into the Void we carry,
Deploring
The beauty perished beyond restoring.
Mightier
For the children of men,
Brightlier

Build it again,
In thine own bosom build it anew!
Bid the new career
Commence,
With clearer sense,
And the new songs of cheer
Be sung thereto!

MEPHISTOPHELES

These are the small dependants
Who give me attendance.
Hear them, to deeds and passion
Counsel in shrewd old-fashion!
Into the world of strife,
Out of this lonely life
That of senses and sap has betrayed thee,
They would persuade thee.
This nursing of the pain forego thee,
That, like a vulture, feeds upon thy breast!
The worst society thou find'st will show thee
Thou art a man among the rest.
But 'tis not meant to thrust
Thee into the mob thou hatest!
I am not one of the greatest,
Yet, wilt thou to me entrust
Thy steps through life, I'll guide thee,—
Will willingly walk beside thee,—
Will serve thee at once and forever
With best endeavor,
And, if thou art satisfied,
Will as servant, slave, with thee abide.

FAUST

And what shall be my counter-service therefor?

MEPHISTOPHELES

The time is long: thou need'st not now insist.

FAUST

No—no! The Devil is an egotist,
And is not apt, without a why or wherefore,
"For God's sake," others to assist.
Speak thy conditions plain and clear!
With such a servant danger comes, I fear.

MEPHISTOPHELES

Here, an unwearied slave, I'll wear thy tether,
And to thine every nod obedient be:
When *There* again we come together,
Then shalt thou do the same for me.

FAUST

The *There* my scruples naught increases.
When thou hast dashed this world to pieces,
The other, then, its place may fill.
Here, on this earth, my pleasures have their sources;
Yon sun beholds my sorrows in his courses;
And when from these my life itself divorces,
Let happen all that can or will!
I'll hear no more: 'tis vain to ponder
If there we cherish love or hate,
Or, in the spheres we dream of yonder,
A High and Low our souls await.

MEPHISTOPHELES

In this sense, even, canst thou venture.
Come, bind thyself by prompt indenture,
And thou mine arts with joy shalt see:
What no man ever saw, I'll give to thee.

FAUST

Canst thou, poor Devil, give me whatsoever?
When was a human soul, in its supreme endeavor,
E'er understood by such as thou?
Yet, hast thou food which never satiates, now,—
The restless, ruddy gold hast thou,
That runs, quicksilver-like, one's fingers through,—
A game whose winnings no man ever knew,—
A maid that, even from my breast,
Beckons my neighbor with her wanton glances,
And Honor's godlike zest,
The meteor that a moment dances,—
Show me the fruits that, ere they're gathered, rot,
And trees that daily with new leafage clothe them!

MEPHISTOPHELES

Such a demand alarms me not:
Such treasures have I, and can show them.
But still the time may reach us, good my friend,
When peace we crave and more luxurious diet.

FAUST

When on an idler's bed I stretch myself in quiet,
There let, at once, my record end!
Canst thou with lying flattery rule me,
Until, self-pleased, myself I see,—
Canst thou with rich enjoyment fool me,
Let that day be the last for me!
The bet I offer.

MEPHISTOPHELES

Done!

FAUST

And heartily!
When thus I hail the Moment flying:
"Ah, still delay—thou art so fair!"
Then bind me in thy bonds undying,
My final ruin then declare!
Then let the death-bell chime the token,
Then art thou from thy service free!
The clock may stop, the hand be broken,
Then Time be finished unto me!

MEPHISTOPHELES

Consider well: my memory good is rated.

FAUST

Thou hast a perfect right thereto.
My powers I have not rashly estimated:
A slave am I, whate'er I do—
If thine, or whose? 'tis needless to debate it.

MEPHISTOPHELES

Then at the Doctors'-banquet I, to-day,
Will as a servant wait behind thee.
But one thing more! Beyond all risk to bind thee,
Give me a line or two, I pray.

FAUST

Demand'st thou, Pedant, too, a document?
Hast never known a man, nor proved his word's intent?
Is't not enough, that what I speak to-day
Shall stand, with all my future days agreeing?

In all its tides sweeps not the world away,
And shall a promise bind my being?
Yet this delusion in our hearts we bear:
Who would himself therefrom deliver?
Blest he, whose bosom Truth makes pure and fair!
No sacrifice shall he repent of ever.
Nathless a parchment, writ and stamped with care,
A spectre is, which all to shun endeavor.
The word, alas! dies even in the pen,
And wax and leather keep the lordship then.
What wilt from me, Base Spirit, say?—
Brass, marble, parchment, paper, clay?
The terms with graver, quill, or chisel, stated?
I freely leave the choice to thee.

MEPHISTOPHELES

Why heat thyself, thus instantly,
With eloquence exaggerated?
Each leaf for such a pact is good;
And to subscribe thy name thou'lt take a drop of blood.

FAUST

If thou therewith art fully satisfied,
So let us by the farce abide.

MEPHISTOPHELES

Blood is a juice of rarest quality.

FAUST

Fear not that I this pact shall seek to sever!
The promise that I make to thee
Is just the sum of my endeavor.
I have myself inflated all too high;
My proper place is thy estate:
The Mighty Spirit deigns me no reply,
And Nature shuts on me her gate.
The thread of Thought at last is broken,
And knowledge brings disgust unspoken.
Let us the sensual deeps explore,
To quench the fervors of glowing passion!
Let every marvel take form and fashion
Through the impervious veil it wore!
Plunge we in Time's tumultuous dance,
In the rush and roll of Circumstance!
Then may delight and distress,
And worry and success,
Alternately follow, as best they can:
Restless activity proves the man!

MEPHISTOPHELES

For you no bound, no term is set.
Whether you everywhere be trying,
Or snatch a rapid bliss in flying,
May it agree with you, what you get!
Only fall to, and show no timid balking.

FAUST

But thou hast heard, 'tis not of joy we're talking.
I take the wildering whirl, enjoyment's keenest pain,
Enamored hate, exhilarant disdain.
My bosom, of its thirst for knowledge sated,
Shall not, henceforth, from any pang be wrested,

And all of life for all mankind created
Shall be within mine inmost being tested:
The highest, lowest forms my soul shall borrow,
Shall heap upon itself their bliss and sorrow,
And thus, my own sole self to all their selves expanded,
I too, at last, shall with them all be stranded!

MEPHISTOPHELES

Believe me, who for many a thousand year
The same tough meat have chewed and tested,
That from the cradle to the bier
No man the ancient leaven has digested!
Trust one of us, this Whole supernal
Is made but for a God's delight!
He dwells in splendor single and eternal,
But *us* he thrusts in darkness, out of sight,
And *you* he dowers with Day and Night.

FAUST

Nay, but I will!

MEPHISTOPHELES

A good reply!
One only fear still needs repeating:
The art is long, the time is fleeting.
Then let thyself be taught, say I!
Go, league thyself with a poet,
Give the rein to his imagination,
Then wear the crown, and show it,
Of the qualities of his creation,—
The courage of the lion's breed,
The wild stag's speed,
The Italian's fiery blood,
The North's firm fortitude!
Let him find for thee the secret tether
That binds the Noble and Mean together,
And teach thy pulses of youth and pleasure
To love by rule, and hate by measure!
I'd like, myself, such a one to see:
Sir Microcosm his name should be.

FAUST

What am I, then, if 'tis denied my part
The crown of all humanity to win me,
Whereto yearns every sense within me?

MEPHISTOPHELES

Why, on the whole, thou'rt—what thou art.
Set wigs of million curls upon thy head, to raise thee,
Wear shoes an ell in height,—the truth betrays thee,
And thou remainest—what thou art.

FAUST

I feel, indeed, that I have made the treasure
Of human thought and knowledge mine, in vain;
And if I now sit down in restful leisure,
No fount of newer strength is in my brain:
I am no hair's-breadth more in height,
Nor nearer to the Infinite.

MEPHISTOPHELES

Good Sir, you see the facts precisely
As they are seen by each and all.

We must arrange them now, more wisely,
Before the joys of life shall pall.
Why, Zounds! Both hands and feet are, truly—
And head and virile forces—thine:
Yet all that I indulge in newly,
Is't thence less wholly mine?
If I've six stallions in my stall,
Are not their forces also lent me?
I speed along, completest man of all,
As though my legs were four-and-twenty.
Take hold, then! let reflection rest,
And plunge into the world with zest!
I say to thee, a speculative wight
Is like a beast on moorlands lean,
That round and round some fiend misleads to evil plight,
While all about lie pastures fresh and green.

FAUST

Then how shall we begin?

MEPHISTOPHELES

We'll try a wider sphere.
What place of martyrdom is here!
Is't life, I ask, is't even prudence,
To bore thyself and bore the students?
Let Neighbor Paunch to that attend!
Why plague thyself with threshing straw forever?
The best thou learnest, in the end
Thou dar'st not tell the youngsters—never!
I hear one's footsteps, hither steering.

FAUST

To see him now I have no heart.

MEPHISTOPHELES

So long the poor boy waits a hearing,
He must not unconsoled depart.
Thy cap and mantle straightway lend me!
I'll play the comedy with art.
(*He disguises himself.*)
My wits, be certain, will befriend me.
But fifteen minutes' time is all I need;
For our fine trip, meanwhile, prepare thyself with speed!
(*Exit* FAUST.)

MEPHISTOPHELES
(*In* FAUST's *long mantle*)

Reason and Knowledge only thou despise,
The highest strength in man that lies!
Let but the Lying Spirit bind thee
With magic works and shows that blind thee,
And I shall have thee fast and sure!—
Fate such a bold, untrammelled spirit gave him,
As forwards, onwards, ever must endure;
Whose over-hasty impulse drave him
Past earthly joys he might secure.
Dragged through the wildest life, will I enslave him,
Through flat and stale indifference;
With struggling, chilling, checking, so deprave him
That, to his hot, insatiate sense,
The dream of drink shall mock, but never lave him:
Refreshment shall his lips in vain implore—
Had he not made himself the Devil's, naught could save him,
Still were he lost forevermore!
(*A* STUDENT *enters.*)

STUDENT

A short time, only, am I here,
And come, devoted and sincere,
To greet and know the man of fame,
Whom men to me with reverence name.

MEPHISTOPHELES

Your courtesy doth flatter me:
You see a man, as others be.
Have you, perchance, elsewhere begun?

STUDENT

Receive me now, I pray, as one
Who comes to you with courage good,
Somewhat of cash, and healthy blood:
My mother was hardly willing to let me;
But knowledge worth having I fain would get me.

MEPHISTOPHELES

Then you have reached the right place now.

STUDENT

I'd like to leave it, I must avow;
I find these walls, these vaulted spaces
Are anything but pleasant places.
'Tis all so cramped and close and mean;
One sees no tree, no glimpse of green,
And when the lecture-halls receive me,
Seeing, hearing, and thinking leave me.

MEPHISTOPHELES

All that depends on habitude.
So from its mother's breasts a child
At first, reluctant, takes its food,
But soon to seek them is beguiled.
Thus, at the breasts of Wisdom clinging,
Thou'lt find each day a greater rapture bringing.

STUDENT

I'll hang thereon with joy, and freely drain them;
But tell me, pray, the proper means to gain them.

MEPHISTOPHELES

Explain, before you further speak,
The special faculty you seek.

STUDENT

I crave the highest erudition;
And fain would make my acquisition
All that there is in Earth and Heaven,
In Nature and in Science too.

MEPHISTOPHELES

Here is the genuine path for you;
Yet strict attention must be given.

STUDENT

Body and soul thereon I'll wreak;
Yet, truly, I've some inclination
On summer holidays to seek
A little freedom and recreation.

MEPHISTOPHELES

Use well your time! It flies so swiftly from us;
But time through order may be won, I promise.
So, Friend (my views to briefly sum),

First, the *collegium logicum.*
There will your mind be drilled
and braced,
As if in Spanish boots 'twere laced,
And thus, to graver paces brought,
'Twill plod along the path of
thought,
Instead of shooting here and there,
A will-o'-the-wisp in murky air.
Days will be spent to bid you know,
What once you did at a single blow,
Like eating and drinking, free and
strong,—
That one, two, three! thereto be-
long.
Truly the fabric of mental fleece
Resembles a weaver's masterpiece,
Where a thousand threads one
treadle throws,
Where fly the shuttles hither and
thither,
Unseen the threads are knit to-
gether,
And an infinite combination grows.
Then, the philosopher steps in
And shows, no otherwise it could
have been:
The first was so, the second so,
Therefore the third and fourth
are so;
Were not the first and second, then
The third and fourth had never
been.
The scholars are everywhere be-
lievers,
But never succeed in being weavers.
He who would study organic ex-
istence,
First drives out the soul with rigid
persistence;
Then the parts in his hand he may
hold and class,
But the spiritual link is lost, alas!
Encheiresin naturæ, this Chemistry
names,
Nor knows how herself she banters
and blames!

STUDENT

I cannot understand you quite.

MEPHISTOPHELES

Your mind will shortly be set aright,
When you have learned, all things
reducing,
To classify them for your using.

STUDENT

I feel as stupid, from all you've said,
As if a mill-wheel whirled in my
head!

MEPHISTOPHELES

And after—first and foremost duty—
Of Metaphysics learn the use and
beauty!
See that you most profoundly gain
What does not suit the human
brain!
A splendid word to serve, you'll find
For what goes in—or won't go in—
your mind.
But first, at least this half a year,
To order rigidly adhere;
Five hours a day, you understand,
And when the clock strikes, be on
hand!
Prepare beforehand for your part
With paragraphs all got by heart,
So you can better watch, and look
That naught is said but what is in
the book:
Yet in thy writing as unwearied be,
As did the Holy Ghost dictate to
thee!

STUDENT

No need to tell me twice to do it!
I think, how useful 'tis to write;
For what one has, in black and
white,
One carries home and then goes
through it.

MEPHISTOPHELES

Yet choose thyself a faculty!

STUDENT

I cannot reconcile myself to Jurisprudence.

MEPHISTOPHELES

Nor can I therefore greatly blame you students:
I know what science this has come to be.
All rights and laws are still transmitted
Like an eternal sickness of the race,—
From generation unto generation fitted,
And shifted round from place to place.
Reason becomes a sham, Beneficence a worry:
Thou art a grandchild, therefore woe to thee!
The right born with us, ours in verity,
This to consider, there's, alas! no hurry.

STUDENT

My own disgust is strengthened by your speech:
O lucky he, whom you shall teach!
I've almost for Theology decided.

MEPHISTOPHELES

I should not wish to see you here misguided:
For, as regards this science, let me hint
'Tis very hard to shun the false direction;
There's so much secret poison lurking in 't,
So like the medicine, it baffles your detection.
Hear, therefore, one alone, for that is best, in sooth,
And simply take your master's words for truth.
On *words* let your attention centre!
Then through the safest gate you'll enter
The temple-halls of Certainty.

STUDENT

Yet in the word must some idea be.

MEPHISTOPHELES

Of course! But only shun too over-sharp a tension,
For just where fails the comprehension,
A word steps promptly in as deputy.
With words 'tis excellent disputing;
Systems to words 'tis easy suiting;
On words 'tis excellent believing;
No word can ever lose a jot from thieving.

STUDENT

Pardon! With many questions I detain you,
Yet must I trouble you again.
Of Medicine I still would fain
Hear one strong word that might explain you.
Three years is but a little space,
And, God! who can the field embrace?
If one some index could be shown,
'Twere easier groping forward, truly.

MEPHISTOPHELES

(*Aside*)

I'm tired enough of this dry tone,—
Must play the Devil again, and fully.

(*Aloud*)
To grasp the spirit of Medicine is easy:
Learn of the great and little world your fill,
To let it go at last, so please ye,
Just as God will!
In vain that through the realms of science you may drift;
Each one learns only—just what learn he can:
Yet he who grasps the Moment's gift,
He is the proper man.
Well-made you are, 'tis not to be denied,
The rest a bold address will win you;
If you but in yourself confide,
At once confide all others in you.
To lead the women, learn the special feeling!
Their everlasting aches and groans,
In thousand tones,
Have all one source, one mode of healing;
And if your acts are half discreet,
You'll always have them at your feet.
A title first must draw and interest them,
And show that yours all other arts exceeds;
Then, as a greeting, you are free to touch and test them,
While, thus to do, for years another pleads.
You press and count the pulse's dances,
And then, with burning sidelong glances,
You clasp the swelling hips, to see
If tightly laced her corsets be.

STUDENT

That's better, now! The How and Where, one sees.

MEPHISTOPHELES

My worthy friend, gray are all theories,
And green alone Life's golden tree.

STUDENT

I swear to you, 'tis like a dream to me.
Might I again presume, with trust unbounded,
To hear your wisdom thoroughly expounded?

MEPHISTOPHELES

Most willingly, to what extent I may.

STUDENT

I cannot really go away:
Allow me that my album first I reach you,—
Grant me this favor, I beseech you!

MEPHISTOPHELES

Assuredly.
(*He writes, and returns the book.*)

STUDENT

(*Reads*)
Eritis sicut Deus, scientes bonum et malum.
(*Closes the book with reverence, and withdraws.*)

MEPHISTOPHELES

Follow the ancient text, and the snake thou wast ordered to trample!
With all thy likeness to God, thou'lt yet be a sorry example!
(FAUST *enters.*)

FAUST

Now, whither shall we go?

MEPHISTOPHELES

As best it pleases thee.
The little world, and then the great, we'll see.
With what delight, what profit winning,
Shalt thou sponge through the term beginning!

FAUST

Yet with the flowing beard I wear,
Both ease and grace will fail me there.
The attempt, indeed, were a futile strife;
I never could learn the ways of life.
I feel so small before others, and thence
Should always find embarrassments.

MEPHISTOPHELES

My friend, thou soon shalt lose all such misgiving:
Be thou but self-possessed, thou hast the art of living!

FAUST

How shall we leave the house, and start?
Where hast thou servant, coach and horses?

MEPHISTOPHELES

We'll spread this cloak with proper art,
Then through the air direct our courses.
But only, on so bold a flight,
Be sure to have thy luggage light.
A little burning air, which I shall soon prepare us,
Above the earth will nimbly bear us,
And, if we're light, we'll travel swift and clear:
I gratulate thee on thy new career!

V

AUERBACH'S CELLAR IN LEIPZIG

CAROUSAL OF JOLLY COMPANIONS.

FROSCH

Is no one laughing? no one drinking?
I'll teach you how to grin, I'm thinking.
To-day you're like wet straw, so tame;
And usually you're all aflame.

BRANDER

Now that's your fault; from you we nothing see,
No beastliness and no stupidity.

FROSCH

(*Pours a glass of wine over* BRANDER'S *head*)
There's both together!

BRANDER

Twice a swine!

FROSCH

You wanted them: I've given you mine.

SIEBEL

Turn out who quarrels—out the door!
With open throat sing chorus, drink and roar!
Up! holla! ho!

ALTMAYER

Woe's me, the fearful bellow!
Bring cotton, quick! He's split my ears, that fellow.

SIEBEL

When the vault echoes to the song,
One first perceives the bass is deep and strong.

FROSCH

Well said! and out with him that takes the least offence!
Ah, tara, lara, da!

ALTMAYER

Ah, tara, lara, da!

FROSCH

The throats are tuned, commence!
(*Sings*)
The dear old holy Roman realm,
How does it hold together?

BRANDER

A nasty song! Fie! a political song—
A most offensive song! Thank God, each morning, therefore,
That you have not the Roman realm to care for!
At least, I hold it so much gain for me,
That I nor Chancellor nor Kaiser be.
Yet also we must have a ruling head, I hope,
And so we'll choose ourselves a Pope.
You know the quality that can
Decide the choice, and elevate the man.

FROSCH

(*Sings*)
Soar up, soar up, Dame Nightingale!
Ten thousand times my sweetheart hail!

SIEBEL

No, greet my sweetheart not! I tell you, I'll resent it.

FROSCH

My sweetheart greet and kiss! I dare you to prevent it!
(*Sings*)
Draw the latch! the darkness makes:
Draw the latch! the lover wakes.
Shut the latch! the morning breaks.

SIEBEL

Yes, sing away, sing on, and praise, and brag of her!
I'll wait my proper time for laughter:
Me by the nose she led, and now she'll lead you after.
Her paramour should be an ugly gnome,
Where four roads cross, in wanton play to meet her:
An old he-goat, from Blocksberg coming home,
Should his good-night in lustful gallop bleat her!
A fellow made of genuine flesh and blood
Is for the wench a deal too good.

Greet her? Not I: unless, when meeting,
To smash her windows be a greeting!

BRANDER

(*Pounding on the table*)

Attention! Hearken now to me!
Confess, Sirs, I know how to live.
Enamored persons here have we,
And I, as suits their quality,
Must something fresh for their advantage give.
Take heed! 'Tis of the latest cut, my strain,
And all strike in at each refrain!

(*He sings.*)

There was a rat in the cellar-nest,
Whom fat and butter made smoother:
He had a paunch beneath his vest
Like that of Doctor Luther.
The cook laid poison cunningly,
And then as sore oppressed was he
As if he had love in his bosom.

CHORUS

(*Shouting*)

As if he had love in his bosom!

BRANDER

He ran around, he ran about,
His thirst in puddles laving;
He gnawed and scratched the house throughout,
But nothing cured his raving.
He whirled and jumped, with torment mad,
And soon enough the poor beast had,
As if he had love in his bosom.

CHORUS

As if he had love in his bosom!

BRANDER

And driven at last, in open day,
He ran into the kitchen,
Fell on the hearth, and squirming lay,
In the last convulsion twitching.
Then laughed the murderess in her glee:
"Ha! ha! he's at his last gasp," said she,
"As if he had love in his bosom!"

CHORUS

As if he had love in his bosom!

SIEBEL

How the dull fools enjoy the matter!
To me it is a proper art
Poison for such poor rats to scatter.

BRANDER

Perhaps you'll warmly take their part?

ALTMAYER

The bald-pate pot-belly I have noted:
Misfortune tames him by degrees;
For in the rat by poison bloated
His own most natural form he sees.

FAUST AND MEPHISTOPHELES.

MEPHISTOPHELES

Before all else, I bring thee hither
Where boon companions meet together,
To let thee see how smooth life runs away.

Here, for the folk, each day's a holiday:
With little wit, and ease to suit them,
They whirl in narrow, circling trails,
Like kittens playing with their tails;
And if no headache persecute them,
So long the host may credit give,
They merrily and careless live.

BRANDER

The fact is easy to unravel,
Their air's so odd, they've just returned from travel:
A single hour they've not been here.

FROSCH

You've verily hit the truth! Leipzig to me is dear:
Paris in miniature, how it refines its people!

SIEBEL

Who are the strangers, should you guess?

FROSCH

Let me alone! I'll set them first to drinking,
And then, as one a child's tooth draws, with cleverness,
I'll worm their secret out, I'm thinking.
They're of a noble house, that's very clear:
Haughty and discontented they appear.

BRANDER

They're mountebanks, upon a revel.

ALTMAYER

Perhaps.

FROSCH

Look out, I'll smoke them now!

MEPHISTOPHELES
(*To* FAUST)

Not if he had them by the neck, I vow,
Would e'er these people scent the Devil!

FAUST

Fair greeting, gentlemen!

SIEBEL

Our thanks: we give the same.
(*Murmurs, inspecting* MEPHISTOPHELES *from the side*)
In one foot is the fellow lame?

MEPHISTOPHELES

Is it permitted that we share your leisure?
In place of cheering drink, which one seeks vainly here,
Your company shall give us pleasure.

ALTMAYER

A most fastidious person you appear.

FROSCH

No doubt 'twas late when you from Rippach started?
And supping there with Hans occasioned your delay?

MEPHISTOPHELES

We passed, without a call, to-day.
At our last interview, before we parted

Much of his cousins did he speak, entreating
That we should give to each his kindly greeting.
(*He bows to* FROSCH.)

ALTMAYER

(*Aside*)

You have it now! he understands.

SIEBEL

A knave sharp-set!

FROSCH

Just wait awhile: I'll have him yet.

MEPHISTOPHELES

If I am right, we heard the sound
Of well-trained voices, singing chorus;
And truly, song must here rebound
Superbly from the arches o'er us.

FROSCH

Are you, perhaps, a virtuoso?

MEPHISTOPHELES

O no! my wish is great, my power is only so-so.

ALTMAYER

Give us a song!

MEPHISTOPHELES

If you desire, a number.

SIEBEL

So that it be a bran-new strain!

MEPHISTOPHELES

We've just traced our way from Spain,
The lovely land of wine, and song, and slumber.

(*Sings*)

There was a king once reigning,
Who had a big black flea—

FROSCH

Hear, hear! A flea! D'ye rightly take the jest?
I call a flea a tidy guest.

MEPHISTOPHELES

(*Sings*)

There was a king once reigning,
Who had a big black flea,
And loved him past explaining,
As his own son were he.
He called his man of stitches;
The tailor came straightway:
Here, measure the lad for breeches,
And measure his coat, I say!

BRANDER

But mind, allow the tailor no caprices:
Enjoin upon him, as his head is dear,
To most exactly measure, sew and shear,
So that the breeches have no creases!

MEPHISTOPHELES

In silk and velvet gleaming
He now was wholly drest—
Had a coat with ribbons streaming,
A cross upon his breast.
He had the first of stations,
A minister's star and name;
And also all his relations
Great lords at court became.

And the lords and ladies of honor
Were plagued, awake and in bed;
The queen she got them upon her,
The maids were bitten and bled.
And they did not dare to brush them,
Or scratch them, day or night:
We crack them and we crush them,
At once, whene'er they bite.

CHORUS
(*Shouting*)
We crack them and we crush them,
At once, whene'er they bite!

FROSCH
Bravo! bravo! that was fine.

SIEBEL
Every flea may it so befall!

BRANDER
Point your fingers and nip them all!

ALTMAYER
Hurrah for Freedom! Hurrah for wine!

MEPHISTOPHELES
I fain would drink with you, my glass to Freedom clinking,
If 'twere a better wine that here I see you drinking.

SIEBEL
Don't let us hear that speech again!

MEPHISTOPHELES
Did I not fear the landlord might complain,
I'd treat these worthy guests, with pleasure,
To some from out our cellar's treasure.

SIEBEL
Just treat, and let the landlord me arraign!

FROSCH
And if the wine be good, our praises shall be ample.
But do not give too very small a sample;
For, if its quality I decide,
With a good mouthful I must be supplied.

ALTMAYER
(*Aside*)
They're from the Rhine! I guessed as much, before.

MEPHISTOPHELES
Bring me a gimlet here!

BRANDER
What shall therewith be done?
You've not the casks already at the door?

ALTMAYER
Yonder, within the landlord's box of tools, there's one!

MEPHISTOPHELES
(*Takes the gimlet. To* FROSCH)
Now, give me of your taste some intimation.

FROSCH
How do you mean? Have you so many kinds?

MEPHISTOPHELES

The choice is free: make up your minds.

ALTMAYER

(*To* FROSCH)

Aha! you lick your chops, from sheer anticipation.

FROSCH

Good! if I have the choice, so let the wine be Rhenish!
Our Fatherland can best the sparkling cup replenish.

MEPHISTOPHELES

(*Boring a hole in the edge of the table, at the place where* FROSCH *sits*)

Get me a little wax, to make the stoppers, quick!

ALTMAYER

Ah! I perceive a juggler's trick.

MEPHISTOPHELES

(*To* BRANDER)

And you?

BRANDER

Champagne shall be my wine,
And let it sparkle fresh and fine!

MEPHISTOPHELES

(*Bores: in the meantime one has made the wax stoppers, and plugged the holes with them.*)

BRANDER

What's foreign one can't always keep quite clear of,
For good things, oft, are not so near;
A German can't endure the French to see or hear of,
Yet drinks their wines with hearty cheer.

SIEBEL

(*As* MEPHISTOPHELES *approaches his seat*)

For me, I grant, sour wine is out of place;
Fill up my glass with sweetest, will you?

MEPHISTOPHELES

(*Boring*)

Tokay shall flow at once, to fill you!

ALTMAYER

No—look me, Sirs, straight in the face!
I see you have your fun at our expense.

MEPHISTOPHELES

O no! with gentlemen of such pretence,
That were to venture far, indeed.
Speak out, and make your choice with speed!
With what a vintage can I serve you?

ALTMAYER

With any—only satisfy our need.
(*After the holes have been bored and plugged.*)

MEPHISTOPHELES

(*With singular gestures*)

Grapes the vine-stem bears,
Horns the he-goat wears!

The grapes are juicy, the vines are wood,
The wooden table gives wine as good!
Into the depths of Nature peer,—
Only believe there's a miracle here!

Now draw the stoppers, and drink your fill!

ALL

(*As they draw out the stoppers, and the wine which has been desired flows into the glass of each*)
O beautiful fountain, that flows at will!

MEPHISTOPHELES

But have a care that you nothing spill!
(*They drink repeatedly.*)

ALL

(*Sing*)
As 'twere five hundred hogs, we feel
So cannibalic jolly!

MEPHISTOPHELES

See, now, the race is happy—it is free!

FAUST

To leave them is my inclination.

MEPHISTOPHELES

Take notice, first! their bestiality
Will make a brilliant demonstration.

SIEBEL

(*Drinks carelessly: the wine spills upon the earth, and turns to flame*)
Help! Fire! Help! Hell-fire is sent!

MEPHISTOPHELES

(*Charming away the flame*)
Be quiet, friendly element!
(*To the revellers*)
A bit of purgatory 'twas for this time, merely.

SIEBEL

What mean you? Wait!—you'll pay for't dearly!
You'll know us, to your detriment.

FROSCH

Don't try that game a second time upon us!

ALTMAYER

I think we'd better send him packing quietly.

SIEBEL

What, Sir! you dare to make so free,
And play your hocus-pocus on us!

MEPHISTOPHELES

Be still, old wine-tub.

SIEBEL

Broomstick, you!
You face it out, impertinent and heady?

BRANDER

Just wait! a shower of blows is ready.

ALTMAYER

(*Draws a stopper out of the table: fire flies in his face*)
I burn! I burn!

SIEBEL

'Tis magic! Strike—
The knave is outlawed! Cut him as you like!
(*They draw their knives, and rush upon* MEPHISTOPHELES.)

MEPHISTOPHELES

(*With solemn gestures*)
False word and form of air,
Change place, and sense ensnare!
Be here—and there!
(*They stand amazed and look at each other.*)

ALTMAYER

Where am I? What a lovely land!

FROSCH

Vines? Can I trust my eyes?

SIEBEL

And purple grapes at hand!

BRANDER

Here, over this green arbor bending,
See what a vine! what grapes depending!
(*He takes* SIEBEL *by the nose: the others do the same reciprocally, and raise their knives.*)

MEPHISTOPHELES

(*As above*)
Loose, Error, from their eyes the band,
And how the Devil jests, be now enlightened!
(*He disappears with* FAUST: *the revellers start and separate.*)

SIEBEL

What happened?

ALTMAYER

How?

FROSCH

Was that your nose I tightened?

BRANDER

(*To* SIEBEL)
And yours that still I have in hand?

ALTMAYER

It was a blow that went through every limb!
Give me a chair! I sink! my senses swim.

FROSCH

But what has happened, tell me now?

SIEBEL

Where is he? If I catch the scoundrel hiding,
He shall not leave alive, I vow.

ALTMAYER

I saw him with these eyes upon a wine-cask riding
Out of the cellar-door, just now.
Still in my feet the fright like lead is weighing.
(*He turns towards the table.*)
Why! If the fount of wine should still be playing?

SIEBEL

'Twas all deceit, and lying, false design!

BRANDER

But with the grapes how was it, pray?

FROSCH

And yet it seemed as I were drinking wine.

ALTMAYER

Shall one believe no miracles, just say!

VI

WITCHES' KITCHEN

Upon a low hearth stands a great caldron, under which a fire is burning. Various figures appear in the vapors which rise from the caldron. An ape sits beside it, skims it, and watches lest it boil over. The he-ape, with the young ones, sits near and warms himself. Ceiling and walls are covered with the most fantastic witch-implements.

FAUST. MEPHISTOPHELES.

FAUST

These crazy signs of witches' craft repel me!
I shall recover, dost thou tell me,
Through this insane, chaotic play?
From an old hag shall I demand assistance?
And will her foul mess take away
Full thirty years from my existence?
Woe's me, canst thou naught better find!
Another baffled hope must be lamented:
Has Nature, then, and has a noble mind
Not any potent balsam yet invented?

MEPHISTOPHELES

Once more, my friend, thou talkest sensibly.
There is, to make thee young, a simpler mode and apter;
But in another book 'tis writ for thee,
And is a most eccentric chapter.

FAUST

Yet will I know it.

MEPHISTOPHELES

Good! the method is revealed
Without or gold or magic or physician.
Betake thyself to yonder field,
There hoe and dig, as thy condition;
Restrain thyself, thy sense and will
Within a narrow sphere to flourish;
With unmixed food thy body nourish;
Live with the ox as ox, and think it not a theft
That thou manur'st the acre which thou reapest;—

That, trust me, is the best mode left,
Whereby for eighty years thy youth thou keepest!

FAUST

I am not used to that; I cannot stoop to try it—
To take the spade in hand, and ply it.
The narrow being suits me not at all.

MEPHISTOPHELES

Then to thine aid the witch must call.

FAUST

Wherefore the hag, and her alone?
Canst thou thyself not brew the potion?

MEPHISTOPHELES

That were a charming sport, I own:
I'd build a thousand bridges meanwhile, I've a notion.
Not Art and Science serve, alone;
Patience must in the work be shown.
Long is the calm brain active in creation;
Time, only, strengthens the fine fermentation.
And all, belonging thereunto,
Is rare and strange, howe'er you take it:
The Devil taught the thing, 'tis true,
And yet the Devil cannot make it.
(*Perceiving the* ANIMALS)
See, what a delicate race they be!
That is the maid! the man is he!
(*To the* ANIMALS)
It seems the mistress has gone away?

THE ANIMALS

Carousing, to-day!
Off and about,
By the chimney out!

MEPHISTOPHELES

What time takes she for dissipating?

THE ANIMALS

While we to warm our paws are waiting.

MEPHISTOPHELES
(*To* FAUST)

How findest thou the tender creatures?

FAUST

Absurder than I ever yet did see.

MEPHISTOPHELES

Why, just such talk as this, for me,
Is that which has the most attractive features!
(*To the* ANIMALS)
But tell me now, ye curséd puppets,
Why do ye stir the porridge so?

THE ANIMALS

We're cooking watery soup for beggars.

MEPHISTOPHELES

Then a great public you can show.

THE HE-APE
(*Comes up and fawns on* MEPHISTOPHELES)

O cast thou the dice!
Make me rich in a trice,
Let me win in good season!
Things are badly controlled,

And had I but gold,
So had I my reason.

MEPHISTOPHELES

How could the ape be sure his luck enhances,
Could he but try the lottery's chances!
(In the meantime the young apes have been playing with a large ball, which they now roll forward.)

THE HE-APE

The world's the ball:
Doth rise and fall,
And roll incessant:
Like glass doth ring,
A hollow thing,—
How soon will't spring,
And drop, quiescent?
Here bright it gleams,
Here brighter seems:
I live at present!
Dear son, I say,
Keep thou away!
Thy doom is spoken!
'Tis made of clay,
And will be broken.

MEPHISTOPHELES

What means the sieve?

THE HE-APE
(Taking it down)

Wert thou the thief,
I'd know him and shame him.
(He runs to the SHE-APE, *and lets her look through it.)*
Look through the sieve!
Know'st thou the thief,
And darest not name him?

MEPHISTOPHELES
(Approaching the fire)

And what's this pot?

HE-APE AND SHE-APE

The fool knows it not!
He knows not the pot,
He knows not the kettle!

MEPHISTOPHELES

Impertinent beast!

THE HE-APE

Take the brush here, at least,
And sit down on the settle!
(He invites MEPHISTOPHELES *to sit down.)*

FAUST

(Who during all this time has been standing before a mirror, now approaching and now retreating from it)
What do I see? What heavenly form revealed
Shows through the glass from Magic's fair dominions!
O lend me, Love, the swiftest of thy pinions,
And bear me to her beauteous field!
Ah, if I leave this spot with fond designing,
If I attempt to venture near,
Dim, as through gathering mist, her charms appear!—
A woman's form, in beauty shining!
Can woman, then, so lovely be?
And must I find her body, there reclining,
Of all the heavens the bright epitome?
Can Earth with such a thing be mated?

MEPHISTOPHELES

Why, surely, if a God first plagues Himself six days,
Then, self-contented, *Bravo!* says,

Must something clever be created.
This time, thine eyes be satiate!
I'll yet detect thy sweetheart and ensnare her,
And blest is he, who has the lucky fate,
Some day, as bridegroom, home to bear her.

(FAUST *gazes continually in the mirror.* MEPHISTOPHELES, *stretching himself out on the settle, and playing with the brush, continues to speak.*)

So sit I, like the King upon his throne:
I hold the sceptre, here,—and lack the crown alone.

THE ANIMALS

(*Who up to this time have been making all kinds of fantastic movements together bring a crown to* MEPHISTOPHELES *with great noise*)

O be thou so good
With sweat and with blood
The crown to belime!

(*They handle the crown awkwardly and break it into two pieces, with which they spring around.*)

'Tis done, let it be!
We speak and we see,
We hear and we rhyme!

FAUST

(*Before the mirror*)

Woe's me! I fear to lose my wits.

MEPHISTOPHELES

(*Pointing to the* ANIMALS)

My own head, now, is really nigh to sinking.

THE ANIMALS

If lucky our hits,
And everything fits,
'Tis thoughts, and we're thinking!

FAUST

(*As above*)

My bosom burns with that sweet vision;
Let us, with speed, away from here!

MEPHISTOPHELES

(*In the same attitude*)

One must, at least, make this admission—
They're poets, genuine and sincere.

(*The caldron, which the* SHE-APE *has up to this time neglected to watch, begins to boil over: there ensues a great flame, which blazes out the chimney. The* WITCH *comes careering down through the flame, with terrible cries.*)

THE WITCH

Ow! ow! ow! ow!
The damnéd beast—the curséd sow!
To leave the kettle, and singe the Frau!
Accurséd fere!

(*Perceiving* FAUST *and* MEPHISTOPHELES)

What is that here?
Who are you here?
What want you thus?
Who sneaks to us?
The fire-pain
Burn bone and brain!

(*She plunges the skimming-ladle into the caldron, and scatters flames towards*

FAUST, MEPHISTOPHELES, *and the* ANIMALS. *The* ANIMALS *whimper.*)

MEPHISTOPHELES

(*Reversing the brush, which he has been holding in his hand, and striking among the jars and glasses*)

In two! in two!
There lies the brew!
There lies the glass!
The joke will pass,
As time, foul ass!
To the singing of thy crew.

(*As the* WITCH *starts back, full of wrath and horror*)

Ha! know'st thou me? Abomination, thou!
Know'st thou, at last, thy Lord and Master?
What hinders me from smiting now
Thee and thy monkey-sprites with fell disaster?
Hast for the scarlet coat no reverence?
Dost recognize no more the tall cock's-feather?
Have I concealed this countenance?—
Must tell my name, old face of leather?

THE WITCH

O pardon, Sir, the rough salute!
Yet I perceive no cloven foot;
And both your ravens, where are *they* now?

MEPHISTOPHELES

This time, I'll let thee 'scape the debt;
For since we two together met,
'Tis verily full many a day now.
Culture, which smooth the whole world licks,
Also unto the Devil sticks.
The days of that old Northern phantom now are over:
Where canst thou horns and tail and claws discover?
And, as regards the foot, which I can't spare, in truth,
'Twould only make the people shun me;
Therefore I've worn, like many a spindly youth,
False calves these many years upon me.

THE WITCH

(*Dancing*)

Reason and sense forsake my brain,
Since I behold Squire Satan here again!

MEPHISTOPHELES

Woman, from such a name refrain!

THE WITCH

Why so? What has it done to thee?

MEPHISTOPHELES

It's long been written in the Book of Fable;
Yet, therefore, no whit better men we see:
The Evil One has left, the evil ones are stable.
Sir Baron call me thou, then is the matter good;
A cavalier am I, like others in my bearing.
Thou hast no doubt about my noble blood:
See, here's the coat-of-arms that I am wearing!

(*He makes an indecent gesture.*)

THE WITCH

(Laughs immoderately)

Ha! ha! That's just your way, I know:
A rogue you are, and you were always so.

MEPHISTOPHELES

(To FAUST*)*

My friend, take proper heed, I pray!
To manage witches, this is just the way.

THE WITCH

Wherein, Sirs, can I be of use?

MEPHISTOPHELES

Give us a goblet of the well-known juice!
But, I must beg you, of the oldest brewage;
The years a double strength produce.

THE WITCH

With all my heart! Now, here's a bottle,
Wherefrom, sometimes, I wet my throttle,
Which, also, not the slightest, stinks;
And willingly a glass I'll fill him.

(Whispering)

Yet, if this man without due preparation drinks,
As well thou know'st, within an hour 'twill kill him.

MEPHISTOPHELES

He is a friend of mine, with whom it will agree,
And he deserves thy kitchen's best potation:
Come, draw thy circle, speak thine adjuration,
And fill thy goblet full and free!

THE WITCH

(With fantastic gestures draws a circle and places mysterious articles therein; meanwhile the glasses begin to ring, the caldron to sound, and make a musical accompaniment. Finally she brings a great book, and stations in the circle the Apes, who are obliged to serve as reading-desk, and to hold the torches. She then beckons FAUST *to approach.)*

FAUST

(To MEPHISTOPHELES*)*

Now, what shall come of this? the creatures antic,
The crazy stuff, the gestures frantic,—
All the repulsive cheats I view,—
Are known to me, and hated, too.

MEPHISTOPHELES

O, nonsense! That's a thing for laughter;
Don't be so terribly severe!
She juggles you as doctor now, that, after,
The beverage may work the proper cheer.

(He persuades FAUST *to step into the circle.)*

THE WITCH

(Begins to declaim, with much emphasis, from the book)

See, thus it's done!
Make ten of one,
And two let be,

Make even three,
And rich thou'lt be.
Cast o'er the four!
From five and six
(The witch's tricks)
Make seven and eight,
'Tis finished straight!
And nine is one,
And ten is none.
This is the witch's once-one's-one!

FAUST

She talks like one who raves in fever.

MEPHISTOPHELES

Thou'lt hear much more before we leave her.
'Tis all the same: the book I can repeat,
Such time I've squandered o'er the history:
A contradiction thus complete
Is always for the wise, no less than fools, a mystery.
The art is old and new, for verily
All ages have been taught the matter,—
By Three and One, and One and Three,
Error instead of Truth to scatter.
They prate and teach, and no one interferes;
All from the fellowship of fools are shrinking.
Man usually believes, if only words he hears,
That also with them goes material for thinking!

THE WITCH
(*Continues*)

The lofty skill
Of Science, still
From all men deeply hidden!
Who takes no thought,
To him 'tis brought,
'Tis given unsought, unbidden!

FAUST

What nonsense she declaims before us!
My head is nigh to split, I fear:
It seems to me as if I hear
A hundred thousand fools in chorus.

MEPHISTOPHELES

O Sibyl excellent, enough of adjuration!
But hither bring us thy potation,
And quickly fill the beaker to the brim!
This drink will bring my friend no injuries:
He is a man of manifold degrees,
And many draughts are known to him.

(*The* WITCH, *with many ceremonies, pours the drink into a cup; as* FAUST *sets it to his lips, a light flame arises.*)

Down with it quickly! Drain it off!
'Twill warm thy heart with new desire:
Art with the Devil hand and glove,
And wilt thou be afraid of fire?

(*The* WITCH *breaks the circle:* FAUST *steps forth.*)

MEPHISTOPHELES

And now, away! Thou dar'st not rest.

THE WITCH

And much good may the liquor do thee!

MEPHISTOPHELES
(*To the* WITCH)

Thy wish be on Walpurgis Night expressed;
What boon I have, shall then be given unto thee.

THE WITCH

Here is a song, which, if you sometimes sing,
You'll find it of peculiar operation.

MEPHISTOPHELES
(*To* FAUST)

Come, walk at once! A rapid occupation
Must start the needful perspiration,
And through thy frame the liquor's potence fling.
The noble indolence I'll teach thee then to treasure,
And soon thou'lt be aware, with keenest thrills of pleasure,
How Cupid stirs and leaps, on light and restless wing.

FAUST

One rapid glance within the mirror give me,
How beautiful that woman-form!

MEPHISTOPHELES

No, no! The paragon of all, believe me,
Thou soon shalt see, alive and warm.
(*Aside*)
Thou'lt find, this drink thy blood compelling,
Each woman beautiful as Helen!

VII

STREET

FAUST. MARGARET (*passing by*).

FAUST

Fair lady, let it not offend you,
That arm and escort I would lend you!

MARGARET

I'm neither lady, neither fair,
And home I can go without your care.
(*She releases herself, and exit.*)

FAUST

By Heaven, the girl is wondrous fair!
Of all I've seen, beyond compare;
So sweetly virtuous and pure,
And yet a little pert, be sure!
The lip so red, the cheek's clear dawn,
I'll not forget while the world rolls on!
How she cast down her timid eyes,
Deep in my heart imprinted lies:
How short and sharp of speech was she,
Why, 'twas a real ecstasy!
(MEPHISTOPHELES *enters.*)

FAUST

Hear, of that girl I'd have possession!

MEPHISTOPHELES

Which, then?

FAUST

The one who just went by.

MEPHISTOPHELES

She, there? She's coming from confession,
Of every sin absolved; for I,
Behind her chair was listening nigh.
So innocent is she, indeed,
That to confess she had no need.
I have no power o'er souls so green.

FAUST

And yet, she's older than fourteen.

MEPHISTOPHELES

How now! You're talking like Jack Rake,
Who every flower for himself would take,
And fancies there are no favors more,
Nor honors, save for him in store;
Yet always doesn't the thing succeed.

FAUST

Most Worthy Pedagogue, take heed!
Let not a word of moral law be spoken!
I claim, I tell thee, all my right;
And if that image of delight
Rest not within mine arms to-night,
At midnight is our compact broken.

MEPHISTOPHELES

But think, the chances of the case!
I need, at least, a fortnight's space,
To find an opportune occasion.

FAUST

Had I but seven hours for all,
I should not on the Devil call,
But win her by my own persuasion.

MEPHISTOPHELES

You almost like a Frenchman prate;
Yet, pray, don't take it as annoyance!
Why, all at once, exhaust the joyance?
Your bliss is by no means so great
As if you'd use, to get control,
All sorts of tender rigmarole,
And knead and shape her to your thought,
As in Italian tales 'tis taught.

FAUST

Without that, I have appetite.

MEPHISTOPHELES

But now, leave jesting out of sight!
I tell you, once for all, that speed
With this fair girl will not succeed;
By storm she cannot captured be;
We must make use of strategy.

FAUST

Get me something the angel keeps!
Lead me thither where she sleeps!
Get me a kerchief from her breast,—
A garter that her knee has pressed!

MEPHISTOPHELES

That you may see how much I'd fain
Further and satisfy your pain,
We will no longer lose a minute;
I'll find her room to-day, and take you in it.

FAUST

And shall I see—possess her?

MEPHISTOPHELES

No!
Unto a neighbor she must go,
And meanwhile thou, alone, mayst glow

With every hope of future pleasure,
Breathing her atmosphere in fullest measure.

FAUST

Can we go thither?

MEPHISTOPHELES

'Tis too early yet.

FAUST

A gift for her I bid thee get!
(*Exit.*)

MEPHISTOPHELES

Presents at once? That's good: he's certain to get at her!
Full many a pleasant place I know,
And treasures, buried long ago:
I must, perforce, look up the matter.
(*Exit.*)

VIII

EVENING

A SMALL, NEATLY KEPT CHAMBER.

MARGARET

(*Plaiting and binding up the braids of her hair*)
I'd something give, could I but say
Who was that gentleman, to-day.
Surely a gallant man was he,
And of a noble family;
And much could I in his face behold,—
And he wouldn't, else, have been so bold!
(*Exit.*)

MEPHISTOPHELES. FAUST.

MEPHISTOPHELES

Come in, but gently: follow me!

FAUST

(*After a moment's silence*)
Leave me alone, I beg of thee!

MEPHISTOPHELES

(*Prying about*)
Not every girl keeps things so neat.

FAUST

(*Looking around*)
O welcome, twilight soft and sweet,
That breathes throughout this hallowed shrine!
Sweet pain of love, bind thou with fetters fleet
The heart that on the dew of hope must pine!
How all around a sense impresses
Of quiet, order, and content!
This poverty what bounty blesses!
What bliss within this narrow den is pent!
(*He throws himself into a leathern arm-chair near the bed.*)
Receive me, thou, that in thine open arms
Departed joy and pain wert wont to gather!
How oft the children, with their ruddy charms,
Hung here, around this throne, where sat the father!

Perchance my love, amid the childish band,
Grateful for gifts the Holy Christmas gave her,
Here meekly kissed the grandsire's withered hand.
I feel, O maid! thy very soul
Of order and content around me whisper,—
Which leads thee with its motherly control,
The cloth upon thy board bids smoothly thee unroll,
The sand beneath thy feet makes whiter, crisper.
O dearest hand, to thee 'tis given
To change this hut into a lower heaven!
And here!

(*He lifts one of the bed-curtains.*)

What sweetest thrill is in my blood!
Here could I spend whole hours, delaying:
Here Nature shaped, as if in sportive playing,
The angel blossom from the bud.
Here lay the child, with Life's warm essence
The tender bosom filled and fair,
And here was wrought, through holier, purer presence,
The form diviner beings wear!

And I? What drew me here with power?
How deeply am I moved, this hour!
What seek I? Why so full my heart, and sore?
Miserable Faust! I know thee now no more.

Is there a magic vapor here?
I came, with lust of instant pleasure,
And lie dissolved in dreams of love's sweet leisure!
Are we the sport of every changeful atmosphere?

And if, this moment, came she in to me,
How would I for the fault atonement render!
How small the giant lout would be,
Prone at her feet, relaxed and tender!

MEPHISTOPHELES

Be quick! I see her there, returning.

FAUST

Go! go! I never will retreat.

MEPHISTOPHELES

Here is a casket, not unmeet,
Which elsewhere I have just been earning.
Here, set it in the press, with haste!
I swear, 'twill turn her head, to spy it:
Some baubles I therein had placed,
That you might win another by it.
True, child is child, and play is play.

FAUST

I know not, should I do it?

MEPHISTOPHELES

Ask you, pray?
Yourself, perhaps, would keep the bubble?
Then I suggest, 'twere fair and just
To spare the lovely day your lust,
And spare to me the further trouble.
You are not miserly, I trust?
I rub my hands, in expectation tender—

(*He places the casket in the press, and locks it again.*)

Now quick, away!
The sweet young maiden to betray,

So that by wish and will you bend her;
And you look as though
To the lecture-hall you were forced to go,—
As if stood before you, gray and loath,
Physics and Metaphysics both!
But away!

(*Exeunt.*)

MARGARET

(*With a lamp*)

It is so close, so sultry, here!

(*She opens the window.*)

And yet 'tis not so warm outside.
I feel, I know not why, such fear!—
Would mother came!—where can she bide?
My body's chill and shuddering,—
I'm but a silly, fearsome thing!

(*She begins to sing, while undressing.*)

There was a King in Thule,
Was faithful till the grave,—
To whom his mistress, dying,
A golden goblet gave.

Naught was to him more precious;
He drained it at every bout:
His eyes with tears ran over,
As oft as he drank thereout.

When came his time of dying,
The towns in his land he told,
Naught else to his heir denying
Except the goblet of gold.

He sat at the royal banquet
With his knights of high degree,
In the lofty hall of his fathers
In the Castle by the Sea.

There stood the old carouser,
And drank the last life-glow;
And hurled the hallowed goblet
Into the tide below.

He saw it plunging and filling,
And sinking deep in the sea:
Then fell his eyelids forever,
And never more drank he!

(*She opens the press in order to arrange her clothes, and perceives the casket of jewels.*)

How comes that lovely casket here to me?
I locked the press, most certainly.
'Tis truly wonderful! What can within it be?
Perhaps 'twas brought by some one as a pawn,
And mother gave a loan thereon?
And here there hangs a key to fit:
I have a mind to open it.
What is that? God in Heaven! Whence came
Such things? Never beheld I aught so fair!
Rich ornaments, such as a noble dame
On highest holidays might wear!
How would the pearl-chain suit my hair?
Ah, who may all this splendor own?

(*She adorns herself with the jewelry, and steps before the mirror.*)

Were but the ear-rings mine, alone!
One has at once another air.
What helps one's beauty, youthful blood?
One may possess them, well and good;
But none the more do others care.
They praise us half in pity, sure:
To gold still tends,
On gold depends
All, all! Alas, we poor!

IX

PROMENADE

FAUST, *walking thoughtfully up and down. To him* MEPHISTOPHELES.

MEPHISTOPHELES

By all love ever rejected! By hell-fire hot and unsparing!
I wish I knew something worse, that I might use it for swearing!

FAUST

What ails thee? What is't gripes thee, elf?
A face like thine beheld I never.

MEPHISTOPHELES

I would myself unto the Devil deliver,
If I were not a Devil myself!

FAUST

Thy head is out of order, sadly:
It much becomes thee to be raving madly.

MEPHISTOPHELES

Just think, the pocket of a priest should get
The trinkets left for Margaret!
The mother saw them, and, instanter,
A secret dread began to haunt her.
Keen scent has she for tainted air;
She snuffs within her book of prayer,
And smells each article, to see
If sacred or profane it be;
So here she guessed, from every gem,
That not much blessing came with them.
"My child," she said, "ill-gotten good
Ensnares the soul, consumes the blood.
Before the Mother of God we'll lay it;
With heavenly manna she'll repay it!"
But Margaret thought, with sour grimace,
"A gift-horse is not out of place,
And, truly! godless cannot be
The one who brought such things to me."
A parson came, by the mother bidden:
He saw, at once, where the game was hidden,
And viewed it with a favor stealthy.
He spake: "That is the proper view,—
Who overcometh, winneth too.
The Holy Church has a stomach healthy:
Hath eaten many a land as forfeit,
And never yet complained of surfeit:
The Church alone, beyond all question,
Has for ill-gotten goods the right digestion."

FAUST

A general practice is the same,
Which Jew and King may also claim.

MEPHISTOPHELES

Then bagged the spangles, chains, and rings,
As if but toadstools were the things,
And thanked no less, and thanked no more
Than if a sack of nuts he bore,—
Promised them fullest heavenly pay,
And deeply edified were they.

FAUST

And Margaret?

MEPHISTOPHELES

Sits unrestful still,
And knows not what she should, or will;
Thinks on the jewels, day and night,
But more on him who gave her such delight.

FAUST

The darling's sorrow gives me pain.
Get thou a set for her again!
The first was not a great display.

MEPHISTOPHELES

O yes, the gentleman finds it all child's-play!

FAUST

Fix and arrange it to my will;
And on her neighbor try thy skill!
Don't be a Devil stiff as paste,
But get fresh jewels to her taste!

MEPHISTOPHELES

Yes, gracious Sir, in all obedience!
(*Exit* FAUST.)
Such an enamored fool in air would blow
Sun, moon, and all the starry legions,
To give his sweetheart a diverting show.
(*Exit.*)

X

THE NEIGHBOR'S HOUSE

MARTHA
(*Solus*)

God forgive my husband, yet he
Hasn't done his duty by me!
Off in the world he went straightway,—
Left me lie in the straw where I lay,
And, truly, I did naught to fret him:
God knows I loved, and can't forget him!
(*She weeps.*)
Perhaps he's even dead! Ah, woe!—
Had I a certificate to show!

MARGARET
(*Comes*)

Dame Martha!

MARTHA

Margaret! what's happened thee?

MARGARET

I scarce can stand, my knees are trembling!
I find a box, the first resembling,
Within my press! Of ebony,—
And things, all splendid to behold,
And richer far than were the old.

MARTHA

You mustn't tell it to your mother!
'Twould go to the priest, as did the other.

MARGARET

Ah, look and see—just look and see!

MARTHA

(Adorning her)

O, what a blessed luck for thee!

MARGARET

But, ah! in the streets I dare not bear them,
Nor in the church be seen to wear them.

MARTHA

Yet thou canst often this way wander,
And secretly the jewels don,
Walk up and down an hour, before the mirror yonder,—
We'll have our private joy thereon.
And then a chance will come, a holiday,
When, piece by piece, can one the things abroad display,
A chain at first, then other ornament:
Thy mother will not see, and stories we'll invent.

MARGARET

Whoever could have brought me things so precious?
That something's wrong, I feel suspicious.

(A knock)

Good Heaven! My mother can that have been?

MARTHA

(Peeping through the blind)

'Tis some strange gentleman.— Come in!

(MEPHISTOPHELES *enters.*)

MEPHISTOPHELES

That I so boldly introduce me,
I beg you, ladies, to excuse me.

(Steps back reverently, on seeing MARGARET.*)*

For Martha Schwerdtlein I'd inquire!

MARTHA

I'm she: what does the gentleman desire?

MEPHISTOPHELES

(Aside to her)

It is enough that you are she:
You've a visitor of high degree.
Pardon the freedom I have ta'en,—
Will after noon return again.

MARTHA

(Aloud)

Of all things in the world! Just hear—
He takes thee for a lady, dear!

MARGARET

I am a creature young and poor:
The gentleman's too kind, I'm sure.
The jewels don't belong to me.

MEPHISTOPHELES

Ah, not alone the jewelry!
The look, the manner, both betray—
Rejoiced am I that I may stay!

MARTHA

What is your business? I would fain—

MEPHISTOPHELES

I would I had a more cheerful strain!
Take not unkindly its repeating:
Your husband's dead, and sends a greeting.

MARTHA

Is dead? Alas, that heart so true!
My husband dead! Let me die, too!

MARGARET

Ah, dearest dame, let not your courage fail!

MEPHISTOPHELES

Hear me relate the mournful tale!

MARGARET

Therefore I'd never love, believe me!
A loss like this to death would grieve me.

MEPHISTOPHELES

Joy follows woe, woe after joy comes flying.

MARTHA

Relate his life's sad close to me!

MEPHISTOPHELES

In Padua buried, he is lying
Beside the good Saint Antony,
Within a grave well consecrated,
For cool, eternal rest created.

MARTHA

He gave you, further, no commission?

MEPHISTOPHELES

Yes, one of weight, with many sighs:
Three hundred masses buy, to save him from perdition!
My hands are empty, otherwise.

MARTHA

What! Not a pocket-piece? no jewelry?
What every journeyman within his wallet spares,
And as a token with him bears,
And rather starves or begs, than loses?

MEPHISTOPHELES

Madam, it is a grief to me;
Yet, on my word, his cash was put to proper uses.
Besides, his penitence was very sore,
And he lamented his ill fortune all the more.

MARGARET

Alack, that men are so unfortunate!
Surely for his soul's sake full many a prayer I'll proffer.

MEPHISTOPHELES

You well deserve a speedy marriage-offer:
You are so kind, compassionate.

MARGARET

O, no! As yet, it would not do.

MEPHISTOPHELES

If not a husband, then a beau for you!
It is the greatest heavenly blessing,
To have a dear thing for one's caressing.

MARGARET

The country's custom is not so.

MEPHISTOPHELES

Custom, or not! It happens, though.

MARTHA

Continue, pray!

MEPHISTOPHELES

I stood beside his bed of dying.
'Twas something better than manure.–

Half-rotten straw: and yet, he died a Christian, sure,
And found that heavier scores to his account were lying.
He cried: "I find my conduct wholly hateful!
To leave my wife, my trade, in manner so ungrateful!
Ah, the remembrance makes me die!
Would of my wrong to her I might be shriven!"

MARTHA
(*Weeping*)

The dear, good man! Long since was he forgiven.

MEPHISTOPHELES

"Yet she, God knows! was more to blame than I."

MARTHA

He lied! What! On the brink of death he slandered?

MEPHISTOPHELES

In the last throes his senses wandered,
If I such things but half can judge.
He said: "I had no time for play, for gaping freedom:
First children, and then work for bread to feed 'em,—
For bread, in the widest sense, to drudge,
And could not even eat my share in peace and quiet!"

MARTHA

Had he all love, all faith forgotten in his riot?
My work and worry, day and night?

MEPHISTOPHELES

Not so: the memory of it touched him quite.
Said he: "When I from Malta went away
My prayers for wife and little ones were zealous,
And such a luck from Heaven befell us,
We made a Turkish merchantman our prey,
That to the Soldan bore a mighty treasure.
Then I received, as was most fit,
Since bravery was paid in fullest measure,
My well-apportioned share of it."

MARTHA

Say, how? Say, where? If buried, did he own it?

MEPHISTOPHELES

Who knows, now, whither the four winds have blown it?
A fair young damsel took him in her care,
As he in Naples wandered round, unfriended;
And she much love, much faith to him did bear,
So that he felt it till his days were ended.

MARTHA

The villain! From his children thieving!
Even all the misery on him cast
Could not prevent his shameful way of living!

MEPHISTOPHELES

But see! He's dead therefrom, at last.
Were I in *your* place, do not doubt me,
I'd mourn him decently a year,
And for another keep, meanwhile, my eyes about me.

MARTHA

Ah, God! another one so dear
As was my first, this world will hardly give me.
There never was a sweeter fool than mine,
Only he loved to roam and leave me,
And foreign wenches and foreign wine,
And the damned throw of dice, indeed.

MEPHISTOPHELES

Well, well! That might have done, however,
If he had only been as clever,
And treated *your* slips with as little heed.
I swear, with this condition, too,
I would, myself, change rings with you.

MARTHA

The gentleman is pleased to jest.

MEPHISTOPHELES
(*Aside*)

I'll cut away, betimes, from here:
She'd take the Devil at his word, I fear.
(*To* MARGARET)
How fares the heart within your breast?

MARGARET

What means the gentleman?

MEPHISTOPHELES
(*Aside*)

Sweet innocent, thou art!
(*Aloud*)
Ladies, farewell!

MARGARET

Farewell!

MARTHA

A moment, ere we part!
I'd like to have a legal witness,
Where, how, and when he died, to certify his fitness.
Irregular ways I've always hated;
I want his death in the weekly paper stated.

MEPHISTOPHELES

Yes, my good dame, a pair of witnesses
Always the truth establishes.
I have a friend of high condition,
Who'll also add his deposition.
I'll bring him here.

MARTHA

Good Sir, pray do!

MEPHISTOPHELES

And this young lady will be present, too?
A gallant youth! has travelled far:
Ladies with him delighted are.

MARGARET

Before him I should blush, ashamed.

MEPHISTOPHELES

Before no king that could be named!

MARTHA

Behind the house, in my garden, then,
This eve we'll expect the gentlemen.

XI

A STREET

FAUST. MEPHISTOPHELES.

FAUST

How is it? under way? and soon complete?

MEPHISTOPHELES

Ah, bravo! Do I find you burning?
Well, Margaret soon will still your yearning:
At Neighbor Martha's you'll this evening meet.
A fitter woman ne'er was made
To ply the pimp and gypsy trade!

FAUST

'Tis well.

MEPHISTOPHELES

Yet something is required from us.

FAUST

One service pays the other thus.

MEPHISTOPHELES

We've but to make a deposition valid
That now her husband's limbs, outstretched and pallid,
At Padua rest, in consecrated soil.

FAUST

Most wise! And first, of course, we'll make the journey thither?

MEPHISTOPHELES

Sancta simplicitas! no need of such a toil:
Depose, with knowledge or without it, either!

FAUST

If you've naught better, then, I'll tear your pretty plan!

MEPHISTOPHELES

Now, there you are! O holy man!
Is it the first time in your life you're driven
To bear false witness in a case?
Of God, the world and all that in it has a place,
Of Man, and all that moves the being of his race,
Have you not terms and definitions given
With brazen forehead, daring breast?
And, if you'll probe the thing profoundly,
Knew you so much—and you'll confess it roundly!—
As here of Schwerdtlein's death and place of rest?

FAUST

Thou art, and thou remain'st, a sophist, liar.

MEPHISTOPHELES

Yes, knew I not more deeply thy desire.

For wilt thou not, no lover fairer,
Poor Margaret flatter, and ensnare her?
And all thy soul's devotion swear her?

FAUST

And from my heart.

MEPHISTOPHELES

'Tis very fine!
Thine endless love, thy faith assuring,
The one almighty force enduring,—
Will that, too, prompt this heart of thine?

FAUST

Hold! hold! It will!—If such my flame,
And for the sense and power intense
I seek, and cannot find, a name;
Then range with all my senses through creation,
Craving the speech of inspiration,
And call this ardor, so supernal,
Endless, eternal and eternal,—
Is that a devilish lying game?

MEPHISTOPHELES

And yet I'm right!

FAUST

Mark this, I beg of thee!
And spare my lungs henceforth: whoever
Intends to have the right, if but his tongue be clever,
Will have it, certainly.
But come: the further talking brings disgust,
For thou art right, especially since I must.

XII

GARDEN

MARGARET *on* FAUST'S *arm.* MARTHA *and* MEPHISTOPHELES *walking up and down.*

MARGARET

I feel, the gentleman allows for me,
Demeans himself, and shames me by it;
A traveller is so used to be
Kindly content with any diet.
I know too well that my poor gossip can
Ne'er entertain such an experienced man.

FAUST

A look from thee, a word, more entertains
Than all the lore of wisest brains.
(*He kisses her hand.*)

MARGARET

Don't incommode yourself! How could you ever kiss it!
It is so ugly, rough to see!

What work I do,—how hard and steady is it!
Mother is much too close with me.
(They pass.)

MARTHA

And you, Sir, travel always, do you not?

MEPHISTOPHELES

Alas, that trade and duty us so harry!
With what a pang one leaves so many a spot,
And dares not even now and then to tarry!

MARTHA

In young, wild years it suits your ways,
This round and round the world in freedom sweeping;
But then come on the evil days,
And so, as bachelor, into his grave a-creeping,
None ever found a thing to praise.

MEPHISTOPHELES

I dread to see how such a fate advances.

MARTHA

Then, worthy Sir, improve betimes your chances!
(They pass.)

MARGARET

Yes, out of sight is out of mind!
Your courtesy an easy grace is;
But you have friends in other places,
And sensibler than I, you'll find.

FAUST

Trust me, dear heart! what men call sensible
Is oft mere vanity and narrowness.

MARGARET

How so?

FAUST

Ah, that simplicity and innocence ne'er know
Themselves, their holy value, and their spell!
That meekness, lowliness, the highest graces
Which Nature portions out so lovingly—

MARGARET

So you but think a moment's space on me,
All times I'll have to think on you, all places!

FAUST

No doubt you're much alone?

MARGARET

Yes, for our household small has grown,
Yet must be cared for, you will own.
We have no maid: I do the knitting, sewing, sweeping,
The cooking, early work and late, in fact;
And mother, in her notions of housekeeping,
Is so exact!
Not that she needs so much to keep expenses down:
We, more than others, might take comfort, rather:
A nice estate was left us by my father,
A house, a little garden near the town.

But now my days have less of noise and hurry;
My brother is a soldier,
My little sister's dead.
True, with the child a troubled life I led,
Yet I would take again, and willing, all the worry,
So very dear was she.

FAUST

An angel, if like thee!

MARGARET

I brought it up, and it was fond of me.
Father had died before it saw the light,
And mother's case seemed hopeless quite,
So weak and miserable she lay;
And she recovered, then, so slowly, day by day.
She could not think, herself, of giving
The poor wee thing it's natural living;
And so I nursed it all alone
With milk and water: 'twas my own.
Lulled in my lap with many a song,
It smilèd, and tumbled, and grew strong.

FAUST

The purest bliss was surely then thy dower.

MARGARET

But surely, also, many a weary hour.
I kept the baby's cradle near
My bed at night: if't even stirred, I'd guess it,
And waking, hear.
And I must nurse it, warm beside me press it,
And oft, to quiet it, my bed forsake,
And dandling back and forth the restless creature take,
Then at the wash-tub stand, at morning's break;
And then the marketing and kitchen-tending,
Day after day, the same thing, never-ending.
One's spirits, Sir, are thus not always good,
But then one learns to relish rest and food.

(*They pass.*)

MARTHA

Yes, the poor women are bad off, 'tis true:
A stubborn bachelor there's no converting.

MEPHISTOPHELES

It but depends upon the like of you,
And I should turn to better ways than flirting.

MARTHA

Speak plainly, Sir, have you no one detected?
Has not your heart been anywhere subjected?

MEPHISTOPHELES

The proverb says: One's own warm hearth
And a good wife, are gold and jewels worth.

MARTHA

I mean, have you not felt desire, though ne'er so slightly?

MEPHISTOPHELES

I've everywhere, in fact, been entertained politely.

MARTHA

I meant to say, were you not touched in earnest, ever?

MEPHISTOPHELES

One should allow one's self to jest with ladies never.

MARTHA

Ah, you don't understand!

MEPHISTOPHELES

I'm sorry I'm so blind:
But I am sure—that you are very kind.

FAUST

(They pass.)
And me, thou angel! did'st thou recognize,
As through the garden-gate I came?

MARGARET

Did you not see it? I cast down my eyes.

FAUST

And thou forgiv'st my freedom, and the blame
To my impertinence befitting,
As the Cathedral thou wert quitting?

MARGARET

I was confused, the like ne'er happened me;
No one could ever speak to my discredit.
Ah, thought I, in my conduct has he read it—
Something immodest or unseemly free?
He seemed to have the sudden feeling
That with this wench 'twere very easy dealing.
I will confess, I knew not what appeal
On your behalf, here, in my bosom grew;
But I was angry with myself, to feel
That I could not be angrier with you.

FAUST

Sweet darling!

MARGARET

Wait a while!
(She plucks a star-flower, and pulls off the leaves, one after the other.)

FAUST

Shall that a nosegay be?

MARGARET

No, it is just in play.

FAUST

How?

MARGARET

Go! you'll laugh at me.
(She pulls off the leaves and murmurs.)

FAUST

What murmurest thou?

MARGARET
(*Half aloud*)
He loves me—loves me not.

FAUST
Thou sweet, angelic soul!

MARGARET
(*Continues*)
Loves me—not—loves me—not—
(*Plucking the last leaf, she cries with frank delight:*)
He loves me!

FAUST
Yes, child! and let this blossom-word
For thee be speech divine! He loves thee!
Ah, know'st thou what it means? He loves thee!
(*He grasps both her hands.*)

MARGARET
I'm all a-tremble!

FAUST
O tremble not! but let this look,
Let this warm clasp of hands declare thee
What is unspeakable!
To yield one wholly, and to feel a rapture
In yielding, that must be eternal!
Eternal!—for the end would be despair.
No, no,—no ending! no ending!

MARTHA
(*Coming forward*)
The night is falling.

MEPHISTOPHELES
Ay! we must away.

MARTHA
I'd ask you, longer here to tarry,
But evil tongues in this town have full play.
It's as if nobody had nothing to fetch and carry,
Nor other labor,
But spying all the doings of one's neighbor:
And one becomes the talk, do whatsoe'er one may.
Where is our couple now?

MEPHISTOPHELES
Flown up the alley yonder,
The wilful summer-birds!

MARTHA
He seems of her still fonder.

MEPHISTOPHELES
And she of him. So runs the world away!

XIII

A GARDEN-ARBOR

MARGARET *comes in, conceals herself behind the door, puts her finger to her lips, and peeps through the crack.*

MARGARET

He comes!

FAUST

(*Entering*)

Ah, rogue! a tease thou art:
I have thee!

(*He kisses her.*)

MARGARET

(*Clasping him, and returning the kiss*)

Dearest man! I love thee from my heart.

(MEPHISTOPHELES *knocks.*)

FAUST

(*Stamping his foot*)

Who's there?

MEPHISTOPHELES

A friend!

FAUST

A beast!

MEPHISTOPHELES

'Tis time to separate.

MARTHA

(*Coming*)

Yes, Sir, 'tis late.

FAUST

May I not, then, upon you wait?

MARGARET

My mother would—farewell!

FAUST

Ah, can I not remain?

Farewell!

MARTHA

Adieu!

MARGARET

And soon to meet again!

(*Exeunt* FAUST *and* MEPHISTOPHELES.)

MARGARET

Dear God! However is it, such
A man can think and know so much?
I stand ashamed and in amaze,
And answer "Yes" to all he says,
A poor, unknowing child! and he—
I can't think what he finds in me!

(*Exit.*)

XIV

FOREST AND CAVERN

FAUST

(*Solus*)

Spirit sublime, thou gav'st me, gav'st me all
For which I prayed. Not unto me in vain
Hast thou thy countenance revealed in fire.
Thou gav'st me Nature as a kingdom grand,
With power to feel and to enjoy it. Thou
Not only cold, amazed acquaintance yield'st,
But grantest, that in her profoundest breast
I gaze, as in the bosom of a friend.
The ranks of living creatures thou dost lead
Before me, teaching me to know my brothers
In air and water and the silent wood.
And when the storm in forest roars and grinds,
The giant firs, in falling, neighbor boughs
And neighbor trunks with crushing weight bear down,
And falling, fill the hills with hollow thunders,—
Then to the cave secure thou leadest me,
Then show'st me mine own self, and in my breast
The deep, mysterious miracles unfold.
And when the perfect moon before my gaze
Comes up with soothing light, around me float
From every precipice and thicket damp
The silvery phantoms of the ages past,
And temper the austere delight of thought.

That nothing can be perfect unto Man
I now am conscious. With this ecstasy,
Which brings me near and nearer to the Gods,
Thou gav'st the comrade, whom I now no more
Can do without, though, cold and scornful, he
Demeans me to myself, and with a breath,
A word, transforms thy gifts to nothingness.
Within my breast he fans a lawless fire,
Unwearied, for that fair and lovely form:
Thus in desire I hasten to enjoyment,
And in enjoyment pine to feel desire.

(MEPHISTOPHELES *enters.*)

MEPHISTOPHELES

Have you not led this life quite long enough?
How can a further test delight you?
'Tis very well, that once one tries the stuff,
But something new must then requite you.

FAUST

Would there were other work for thee!
To plague my day auspicious thou returnest.

MEPHISTOPHELES

Well! I'll engage to let thee be:
Thou darest not tell me so in earnest.
The loss of thee were truly very slight,—
A comrade crazy, rude, repelling:
One has one's hands full all the day and night;
If what one does, or leaves undone, is right,
From such a face as thine there is no telling.

FAUST

There is, again, thy proper tone!—
That thou hast bored me, I must thankful be!

MEPHISTOPHELES

Poor Son of Earth, how couldst thou thus alone
Have led thy life, bereft of me?
I, for a time, at least, have worked thy cure;
Thy fancy's rickets plague thee not at all:
Had I not been, so hadst thou, sure,
Walked thyself off this earthly ball.
Why here to caverns, rocky hollows slinking,
Sit'st thou, as 'twere an owl a-blinking?
Why suck'st, from sodden moss and dripping stone,
Toad-like, thy nourishment alone?
A fine way, this, thy time to fill!
The Doctor's in thy body still.

FAUST

What fresh and vital forces, canst thou guess,
Spring from my commerce with the wilderness?
But, if thou hadst the power of guessing,
Thou wouldst be devil enough to grudge my soul the blessing.

MEPHISTOPHELES

A blessing drawn from supernatural fountains!
In night and dew to lie upon the mountains;
All Heaven and Earth in rapture penetrating;
Thyself to Godhood haughtily inflating;
To grub with yearning force through Earth's dark marrow,
Compress the six days' work within thy bosom narrow,—
To taste, I know not what, in haughty power,
Thine own ecstatic life on all things shower,
Thine earthly self behind thee cast,
And then the lofty instinct, thus—
(*With a gesture:*)
at last,—
I daren't say how—to pluck the final flower!

FAUST

Shame on thee!

MEPHISTOPHELES

Yes, thou findest that unpleasant!
Thou hast the moral right to cry me "shame!" at present.
One dares not that before chaste ears declare,
Which chaste hearts, notwithstanding, cannot spare;

And, once for all, I grudge thee not the pleasure
Of lying to thyself in moderate measure.
But such a course thou wilt not long endure;
Already art thou o'er-excited,
And, if it last, wilt soon be plighted
To madness and to horror, sure.
Enough of that! Thy love sits lonely yonder,
By all things saddened and oppressed;
Her thoughts and yearnings seek thee, tenderer, fonder,—
A mighty love is in her breast.
First came thy passion's flood and poured around her
As when from melted snow a streamlet overflows;
Thou hast therewith so filled and drowned her,
That now *thy* stream all shallow shows.
Methinks, instead of in the forests lording,
The noble Sir should find it good,
The love of this young silly blood
At once to set about rewarding.
Her time is miserably long;
She haunts her window, watching clouds that stray
O'er the old city-wall, and far away.
"Were I a little bird!" so runs her song,
Day long, and half night long.
Now she is lively, mostly sad,
Now, wept beyond her tears;
Then again quiet she appears,—
Always love-mad.

FAUST

Serpent! Serpent!

MEPHISTOPHELES
(*Aside*)

Ha! do I trap thee!

FAUST

Get thee away with thine offences,
Reprobate! Name not that fairest thing,
Nor the desire for her sweet body bring
Again before my half-distracted senses!

MEPHISTOPHELES

What wouldst thou, then? She thinks that thou art flown;
And half and half thou art, I own.

FAUST

Yet am I near, and love keeps watch and ward;
Though I were ne'er so far, it cannot falter:
I envy even the Body of the Lord
The touching of her lips, before the altar.

MEPHISTOPHELES

'Tis very well! *My* envy oft reposes
On your twin-pair, that feed among the roses.

FAUST

Away, thou pimp!

MEPHISTOPHELES

You rail, and it is fun to me.
The God, who fashioned youth and maid,
Perceived the noblest purpose of His trade,
And also made their opportunity.
Go on! It is a woe profound!
'Tis for your sweetheart's room you're bound,
And not for death, indeed.

FAUST

What are, within her arms, the heavenly blisses?
Though I be glowing with her kisses,
Do I not always share her need?
I am the fugitive, all houseless roaming,
The monster without air or rest,
That like a cataract, down rocks and gorges foaming,
Leaps, maddened, into the abyss's breast!
And side-wards she, with young unwakened senses,
Within her cabin on the Alpine field
Her simple, homely life commences,
Her little world therein concealed.
And I, God's hate flung o'er me,
Had not enough, to thrust
The stubborn rocks before me
And strike them into dust!
She and her peace I yet must undermine:
Thou, Hell, hast claimed this sacrifice as thine!
Help, Devil! through the coming pangs to push me;
What must be, let it quickly be!
Let fall on me her fate, and also crush me,—
One ruin whelm both her and me!

MEPHISTOPHELES

Again it seethes, again it glows!
Thou fool, go in and comfort her!
When such a head as thine no outlet knows,
It thinks the end must soon occur.
Hail him, who keeps a steadfast mind!
Thou, else, dost well the devil-nature wear:
Naught so insipid in the world I find
As is a devil in despair.

XV

MARGARET'S ROOM

MARGARET

(*At the spinning-wheel, alone*)

My peace is gone,
My heart is sore:
I never shall find it,
Ah, nevermore!

Save I have him near,
The grave is here;
The world is gall
And bitterness all.

My poor weak head
Is racked and crazed;
My thought is lost,
My senses mazed.

My peace is gone,
My heart is sore:
I never shall find it,
Ah, nevermore!

To see him, him only,
At the pane I sit;
To meet him, him only,
The house I quit.

His lofty gait,
His noble size,
The smile of his mouth,
The power of his eyes,

And the magic flow
Of his talk, the bliss
In the clasp of his hand,
And, ah! his kiss!

My peace is gone,
My heart is sore:
I never shall find it,
Ah, nevermore!

My bosom yearns
For him alone;
Ah, dared I clasp him,
And hold, and own!

And kiss his mouth,
To heart's desire,
And on his kisses
At last expire!

XVI

MARTHA'S GARDEN

MARGARET. FAUST.

MARGARET

Promise me, Henry!—

FAUST

What I can!

MARGARET

How is't with thy religion, pray?
Thou art a dear, good-hearted man,
And yet, I think, dost not incline that way.

FAUST

Leave that, my child! Thou know'st my love is tender;
For love, my blood and life would I surrender,
And as for Faith and Church, I grant to each his own.

MARGARET

That's not enough: we must believe thereon.

FAUST

Must we?

MARGARET

Would that I had some influence!
Then, too, thou honorest not the Holy Sacraments.

FAUST

I honor them.

MARGARET

Desiring no possession
'Tis long since thou hast been to mass or to confession.
Believest thou in God?

FAUST

My darling, who shall dare
"I believe in God!" to say?
Ask priest or sage the answer to declare,
And it will seem a mocking play,
A sarcasm on the asker.

MARGARET

Then thou believest not!

FAUST

Hear me not falsely, sweetest countenance!
Who dare express Him?
And who profess Him,
Saying: I believe in Him!
Who, feeling, seeing,
Deny His being,
Saying: I believe Him not!
The All-enfolding,
The All-upholding,
Folds and upholds he not
Thee, me, Himself?
Arches not there the sky above us?
Lies not beneath us, firm, the earth?
And rise not, on us shining,
Friendly, the everlasting stars?
Look I not, eye to eye, on thee,
And feel'st not, thronging
To head and heart, the force,
Still weaving its eternal secret,
Invisible, visible, round thy life?
Vast as it is, fill with that force thy heart,
And when thou in the feeling wholly blessed art,
Call it, then, what thou wilt,—
Call it Bliss! Heart! Love! God!
I have no name to give it!
Feeling is all in all:
The Name is sound and smoke,
Obscuring Heaven's clear glow.

MARGARET

All that is fine and good, to hear it so:
Much the same way the preacher spoke,
Only with slightly different phrases.

FAUST

The same thing, in all places,
All hearts that beat beneath the heavenly day—
Each in its language—say;
Then why not I, in mine, as well?

MARGARET

To hear it thus, it may seem passable;
And yet, some hitch in't there must be
For thou hast no Christianity.

FAUST

Dear love!

MARGARET

I've long been grieved to see
That thou art in such company.

FAUST

How so?

MARGARET

The man who with thee goes, thy mate,
Within my deepest, inmost soul I hate.
In all my life there's nothing
Has given my heart so keen a pang of loathing,
As his repulsive face has done.

FAUST

Nay, fear him not, my sweetest one!

MARGARET

I feel his presence like something ill.
I've else, for all, a kindly will,
But, much as my heart to see thee yearneth,
The secret horror of him returneth;

And I think the man a knave, as I live!
If I do him wrong, may God forgive!

FAUST

There must be such queer birds, however.

MARGARET

Live with the like of him, may I never!
When once inside the door comes he,
He looks around so sneeringly,
And half in wrath:
One sees that in nothing no interest he hath:
'Tis written on his very forehead
That love, to him, is a thing abhorréd.
I am so happy on thine arm,
So free, so yielding, and so warm,
And in his presence stifled seems my heart.

FAUST

Foreboding angel that thou art!

MARGARET

It overcomes me in such degree,
That wheresoe'er he meets us, even,
I feel as though I'd lost my love for thee.
When he is by, I could not pray to Heaven.
That burns within me like a flame,
And surely, Henry, 'tis with thee the same.

FAUST

There, now, is thine antipathy!

MARGARET

But I must go.

FAUST

Ah, shall there never be
A quiet hour, to see us fondly plighted,
With breast to breast, and soul to soul united?

MARGARET

Ah, if I only slept alone!
I'd draw the bolts to-night, for thy desire;
But mother's sleep so light has grown,
And if we were discovered by her,
'Twould be my death upon the spot!

FAUST

Thou angel, fear it not!
Here is a phial: in her drink
But three drops of it measure,
And deepest sleep will on her senses sink.

MARGARET

What would I not, to give thee pleasure?
It will not harm her, when one tries it?

FAUST

If 'twould, my love, would I advise it?

MARGARET

Ah, dearest man, if but thy face I see,
I know not what compels me to thy will:
So much have I already done for thee,
That scarcely more is left me to fulfil.

(*Exit.*)

(*Enter* MEPHISTOPHELES.)

MEPHISTOPHELES

The monkey! Is she gone?

FAUST

Hast played the spy again?

MEPHISTOPHELES

I've heard, most fully, how she drew thee.
The Doctor has been catechised, 'tis plain;
Great good, I hope, the thing will do thee.
The girls have much desire to ascertain
If one is prim and good, as ancient rules compel:
If there he's led, they think, he'll follow them as well.

FAUST

Thou, monster, wilt nor see nor own
How this pure soul, of faith so lowly,
So loving and ineffable,—
The faith alone
That her salvation is,—with scruples holy
Pines, lest she hold as lost the man she loves so well!

MEPHISTOPHELES

Thou, full of sensual, super-sensual desire,
A girl by the nose is leading thee.

FAUST

Abortion, thou, of filth and fire!

MEPHISTOPHELES

And then, how masterly she reads physiognomy!
When I am present she's impressed, she knows not how;
She in my mask a hidden sense would read:
She feels that surely I'm a genius now,—
Perhaps the very Devil, indeed!
Well, well,—to-night—?

FAUST

What's that to thee?

MEPHISTOPHELES

Yet my delight 'twill also be!

XVII

AT THE FOUNTAIN

MARGARET *and* LISBETH *with pitchers.*

LISBETH

Hast nothing heard of Barbara?

MARGARET

No, not a word. I go so little out.

LISBETH

It's true, Sibylla said, to-day.
She's played the fool at last, there's not a doubt.
Such taking-on of airs!

MARGARET

How so?

LISBETH

It stinks!
She's feeding two, whene'er she eats and drinks.

MARGARET

Ah!

LISBETH

And so, at last, it serves her rightly.
She clung to the fellow so long and tightly!
That was a promenading!
At village and dance parading!
As the first they must everywhere shine,
And he treated her always to pies and wine,
And she made a to-do with her face so fine;
So mean and shameless was her behavior,
She took all the presents the fellow gave her.
'Twas kissing and coddling, on and on!
So now, at the end, the flower is gone.

MARGARET

The poor, poor thing!

LISBETH

Dost pity her, at that?
When one of us at spinning sat,
And mother, nights ne'er let us out the door
She sported with her paramour.
On the door-bench, in the passage dark,
The length of the time they'd never mark.
So now her head no more she'll lift,
But do church-penance in her sinner's shift!

MARGARET

He'll surely take her for his wife.

LISBETH

He'd be a fool! A brisk young blade
Has room, elsewhere, to ply his trade.
Besides, he's gone.

MARGARET

That is not fair!

LISBETH

If him she gets, why let her beware!
The boys shall dash her wreath on the floor,
And we'll scatter chaff before her door!

(*Exit.*)

MARGARET
(*Returning home*)

How scornfully I once reviled,
When some poor maiden was beguiled!
More speech than any tongue suffices
I craved, to censure others' vices.
Black as it seemed, I blackened still,
And blacker yet was in my will;
And blessed myself, and boasted high,—
And now—a living sin am I!
Yet—all that drove my heart thereto,
God! was so good, so dear, so true!

XVIII

DONJON

In a niche of the wall a shrine, with an image of the Mater Dolorosa. Pots of flowers before it.

MARGARET

(*Putting fresh flowers in the pots*)

Incline, O Maiden,
Thou sorrow-laden,
Thy gracious countenance upon my pain!

The sword Thy heart in,
With anguish smarting,
Thou lookest up to where Thy Son is slain!

Thou seest the Father;
Thy sad sighs gather,
And bear aloft Thy sorrow and His pain!

Ah, past guessing,
Beyond expressing,
Thy pangs that wring my flesh and bone!
Why this anxious heart so burneth,
Why it trembleth, why it yearneth,
Knowest Thou, and Thou alone!

Where'er I go, what sorrow,
What woe, what woe and sorrow
Within my bosom aches!
Alone, and ah! unsleeping,
I'm weeping, weeping, weeping,
The heart within me breaks.

The pots before my window,
Alas! my tears did wet,
As in the early morning
For thee these flowers I set.

Within my lonely chamber
The morning sun shone red:
I sat, in utter sorrow,
Already on my bed.

Help! rescue me from death and stain!
O Maiden!
Thou sorrow-laden,
Incline Thy countenance upon my pain!

XIX

NIGHT

Street before MARGARET'S *door.*
VALENTINE (*a soldier,* MARGARET'S *brother*).

VALENTINE

When I have sat at some carouse,
Where each to each his brag allows,
And many a comrade praised to me
His pink of girls right lustily,
With brimming glass that spilled the toast,
And elbows planted as in boast:
I sat in unconcerned repose,
And heard the swagger as it rose.
And stroking then my beard, I'd say,
Smiling, the bumper in my hand:
"Each well enough in her own way,
But is there one in all the land
Like sister Margaret, good as gold,—
One that to her can a candle hold?"
Cling! clang! "Here's to her!" went around
The board: "He speaks the truth!" cried some;
"In her the flower o' the sex is found!"
And all the swaggerers were dumb.
And now!—I could tear my hair with vexation,
And dash out my brains in desperation!
With turned-up nose each scamp may face me,
With sneers and stinging taunts disgrace me,
And, like a bankrupt debtor sitting,
A chance-dropped word may set me sweating!

Yet, though I thresh them all together,
I cannot call them liars, either.

But what comes sneaking, there, to view?
If I mistake not, there are two.
If *he's* one, let me at him drive!
He shall not leave the spot alive.

FAUST. MEPHISTOPHELES.

FAUST

How from the window of the sacristy
Upward th'eternal lamp sends forth a glimmer,
That, lessening side-wards, fainter grows and dimmer,
Till darkness closes from the sky!
The shadows thus within my bosom gather.

MEPHISTOPHELES

I'm like a sentimental tom-cat, rather,
That round the tall fire-ladders sweeps,
And stealthy, then, along the coping creeps:
Quite virtuous, withal, I come,

A little thievish and a little frolicsome.
I feel in every limb the presage
Forerunning the grand Walpurgis-Night:
Day after to-morrow brings its message,
And one keeps watch then with delight.

FAUST

Meanwhile, may not the treasure risen be,
Which there, behind, I glimmering see?

MEPHISTOPHELES

Shalt soon experience the pleasure,
To lift the kettle with its treasure.
I lately gave therein a squint—
Saw splendid lion-dollars in't.

FAUST

Not even a jewel, not a ring,
To deck therewith my darling girl?

MEPHISTOPHELES

I saw, among the rest, a thing
That seemed to be a chain of pearl.

FAUST

That's well, indeed! For painful is it
To bring no gift when her I visit.

MEPHISTOPHELES

Thou shouldst not find it so annoying,
Without return to be enjoying.
Now, while the sky leads forth its starry throng,
Thou'lt hear a masterpiece, no work completer:
I'll sing her, first, a moral song,
The surer, afterwards, to cheat her.

(*Sings to the cither*)

What dost thou here
In daybreak clear,
Kathrina dear,
Before thy lover's door?
Beware! the blade
Lets in a maid,
That out a maid
Departeth nevermore!

The coaxing shun
Of such an one!
When once 'tis done
Good-night to thee, poor thing!
Love's time is brief:
Unto no thief
Be warm and lief,
But with the wedding-ring!

VALENTINE

(*Comes forward*)

Whom wilt thou lure? God's-element!
Rat-catching piper, thou!—perdition!
To the Devil, first, the instrument!
To the Devil, then, the curst musician!

MEPHISTOPHELES

The cither's smashed! For nothing more 'tis fitting.

VALENTINE

There's yet a skull I must be splitting!

MEPHISTOPHELES

(*To* FAUST)

Sir Doctor, don't retreat, I pray!
Stand by: I'll lead, if you'll but tarry:
Out with your spit, without delay!
You've but to lunge, and I will parry.

VALENTINE

Then parry that!

MEPHISTOPHELES

Why not? 'tis light.

VALENTINE

That, too!

MEPHISTOPHELES

Of course.

VALENTINE

I think the Devil must fight!
How is it, then? my hand's already lame.

MEPHISTOPHELES

(*To* FAUST)

Thrust home!

VALENTINE

(*Falls*)

O God!

MEPHISTOPHELES

Now is the lubber tame!
But come, away! 'Tis time for us to fly;
For there arises now a murderous cry.
With the police 'twere easy to compound it,
But here the penal court will sift and sound it.

(*Exit with* FAUST.)

MARTHA

(*At the window*)

Come out! Come out!

MARGARET

(*At the window*)

Quick, bring a light!

MARTHA

(*As above*)

They swear and storm, they yell and fight!

PEOPLE

Here lies one dead already—see!

MARTHA

(*Coming from the house*)

The murderers, whither have they run?

MARGARET

(*Coming out*)

Who lies here?

PEOPLE

'Tis thy mother's son!

MARGARET

Almighty God! what misery!

VALENTINE

I'm dying! That is quickly said,
And quicker yet 'tis done.
Why howl, you women there? Instead,
Come here and listen, every one!

(*All gather around him.*)

My Margaret, see! still young thou art,
But not the least bit shrewd or smart,
Thy business thus to slight:
So this advice I bid thee heed—
Now that thou art a whore indeed,
Why, be one then, outright!

MARGARET

My brother! God! such words to me?

VALENTINE

In this game let our Lord God be!
What's done's already done, alas!
What follows it, must come to pass.
With one begin'st thou secretly,
Then soon will others come to thee,
And when a dozen thee have known,
Thou'rt also free to all the town.

When Shame is born and first appears,
She is in secret brought to light,
And then they draw the veil of night
Over her head and ears;
Her life, in fact, they're loath to spare her.
But let her growth and strength display,
She walks abroad unveiled by day,
Yet is not grown a whit the fairer.
The uglier she is to sight,
The more she seeks the day's broad light.
The time I verily can discern
When all the honest folk will turn
From thee, thou jade! and seek protection
As from a corpse that breeds infection.
Thy guilty heart shall then dismay thee,
When they but look thee in the face:—
Shalt not in a golden chain array thee,
Nor at the altar take thy place!
Shalt not, in lace and ribbons flowing,
Make merry when the dance is going!
But in some corner, woe betide thee!
Among the beggars and cripples hide thee;
And so, though even God forgive,
On earth a damned existence live!

MARTHA

Commend your soul to God for pardon,
That you your heart with slander harden!

VALENTINE

Thou pimp most infamous, be still!
Could I thy withered body kill,
'Twould bring, for all my sinful pleasure,
Forgiveness in the richest measure.

MARGARET

My brother! This is Hell's own pain!

VALENTINE

I tell thee, from thy tears refrain!
When thou from honor didst depart
It stabbed me to the very heart.
Now through the slumber of the grave
I go to God as a soldier brave.

(*Dies.*)

XX

CATHEDRAL

SERVICE, ORGAN *and* ANTHEM.

MARGARET *among much people: the* EVIL SPIRIT *behind* MARGARET.

EVIL SPIRIT

How otherwise was it, Margaret,
When thou, still innocent,
Here to the altar cam'st,
And from the worn and fingered book
Thy prayers didst prattle,
Half sport of childhood,
Half God within thee!
Margaret!
Where tends thy thought?
Within thy bosom
What hidden crime?
Pray'st thou for mercy on thy mother's soul,
That fell asleep to long, long torment, and through thee?
Upon thy threshold whose the blood?
And stirreth not and quickens
Something beneath thy heart,
Thy life disquieting
With most foreboding presence?

MARGARET

Woe! woe!
Would I were free from the thoughts
That cross me, drawing hither and thither,
Despite me!

CHORUS

Dies iræ, dies illa,
Solvet sæclum in favilla!
(*Sound of the organ*)

EVIL SPIRIT

Wrath takes thee!
The trumpet peals!
The graves tremble!
And thy heart
From ashy rest
To fiery torments
Now again requickened,
Throbs to life!

MARGARET

Would I were forth!
I feel as if the organ here
My breath takes from me,
My very heart
Dissolved by the anthem!

CHORUS

Judex ergo cum sedebit,
Quidquid latet, adparebit,
Nil inultum remanebit.

MARGARET

I cannot breathe!
The massy pillars
Imprison me!
The vaulted arches
Crush me!—Air!

EVIL SPIRIT

Hide thyself! Sin and shame

Stay never hidden.
Air? Light?
Woe to thee!

CHORUS

Quid sum miser tunc dicturus,
Quem patronem rogaturus,
Cum vix justus sit securus?

EVIL SPIRIT

They turn their faces,
The glorified, from thee:
The pure, their hands to offer,
Shuddering, refuse thee!
Woe!

CHORUS

Quid sum miser tunc dicturus?

MARGARET

Neighbor! your cordial!
(*She falls in a swoon.*)

XXI

WALPURGIS-NIGHT

The Hartz Mountains.

District of Schierke and Elend.

FAUST. MEPHISTOPHELES.

MEPHISTOPHELES

Dost thou not wish a broomstick-steed's assistance?
The sturdiest he-goat I would gladly see:
The way we take, our goal is yet some distance.

FAUST

So long as in my legs I feel the fresh existence,
This knotted staff suffices me.
What need to shorten so the way?
Along this labyrinth of vales to wander,
Then climb the rocky ramparts yonder,
Wherefrom the fountain flings eternal spray,
Is such delight, my steps would fain delay.
The spring-time stirs within the fragrant birches,
And even the fir-tree feels it now:
Should then our limbs escape its gentle searches?

MEPHISTOPHELES

I notice no such thing, I vow!
'Tis winter still within my body:
Upon my path I wish for frost and snow.
How sadly rises, incomplete and ruddy,
The moon's lone disk, with its belated glow,
And lights so dimly, that, as one advances,
At every step one strikes a rock or tree!
Let us, then, use a Jack-o'-lantern's glances:

I see one yonder, burning merrily.
Ho, there! my friend! I'll levy thine attendance:
Why waste so vainly thy resplendence?
Be kind enough to light us up the steep!

WILL-O'-THE-WISP

My reverence, I hope, will me enable
To curb my temperament unstable;
For zigzag courses we are wont to keep.

MEPHISTOPHELES

Indeed? he'd like mankind to imitate!
Now, in the Devil's name, go straight,
Or I'll blow out his being's flickering spark!

WILL-O'-THE-WISP

You are the master of the house, I mark,
And I shall try to serve you nicely.
But then, reflect: the mountain's magic-mad to-day,
And if a will-o'-the-wisp must guide you on the way,
You mustn't take things too precisely.

FAUST, MEPHISTOPHELES, WILL-O'-THE-WISP
(In alternating song)

We, it seems, have entered newly
In the sphere of dreams enchanted.
Do thy bidding, guide us truly,
That our feet be forwards planted
In the vast, the desert spaces!

See them swiftly changing places,
Trees on trees beside us trooping,
And the crags above us stooping,
And the rocky snouts, outgrowing,—
Hear them snoring, hear them blowing!
O'er the stones, the grasses, flowing
Stream and streamlet seek the hollow.
Hear I noises? songs that follow?
Hear I tender love-petitions?
Voices of those heavenly visions?
Sounds of hope, of love undying!
And the echoes, like traditions
Of old days, come faint and hollow.

Hoo-hoo! Shoo-hoo! Nearer hover
Jay and screech-owl, and the plover,—
Are they all awake and crying?
Is't the salamander pushes,
Bloated-bellied, through the bushes?
And the roots, like serpents twisted,
Through the sand and boulders toiling,
Fright us, weirdest links uncoiling
To entrap us, unresisted:
Living knots and gnarls uncanny
Feel with polypus-antennæ
For the wanderer. Mice are flying,
Thousand-colored, herd-wise hieing
Through the moss and through the heather!
And the fire-flies wink and darkle,
Crowded swarms that soar and sparkle,
And in wildering escort gather!

Tell me, if we still are standing,
Of if further we're ascending?
All is turning, whirling, blending,
Trees and rocks with grinning faces,
Wandering lights that spin in mazes,
Still increasing and expanding!

MEPHISTOPHELES

Grasp my skirt with heart undaunted!
Here a middle-peak is planted,
Whence one seëth, with amaze,
Mammon in the mountain blaze.

FAUST

How strangely glimmers through the hollows
A dreary light, like that of dawn!
Its exhalation tracks and follows
The deepest gorges, faint and wan.
Here steam, there rolling vapor sweepeth;
Here burns the glow through film and haze:
Now like a tender thread it creepeth,
Now like a fountain leaps and plays.
Here winds away, and in a hundred
Divided veins the valley braids:
There, in a corner pressed and sundered,
Itself detaches, spreads and fades.
Here gush the sparkles incandescent
Like scattered showers of golden sand;—
But, see! in all their height, at present,
The rocky ramparts blazing stand.

MEPHISTOPHELES

Has not Sir Mammon grandly lighted
His palace for this festal night?
'Tis lucky thou hast seen the sight;
The boisterous guests approach that were invited.

FAUST

How raves the tempest through the air!
With what fierce blows upon my neck 'tis beating!

MEPHISTOPHELES

Under the old ribs of the rock retreating,
Hold fast, lest thou be hurled down the abysses there!
The night with the mist is black;
Hark! how the forests grind and crack!
Frightened, the owlets are scattered:
Hearken! the pillars are shattered,
The evergreen palaces shaking!
Boughs are groaning and breaking,
The tree-trunks terribly thunder,
The roots are twisting asunder!
In frightfully intricate crashing
Each on the other is dashing,
And over the wreck-strewn gorges
The tempest whistles and surges!
Hear'st thou voices higher ringing?
Far away, or nearer singing?
Yes, the mountain's side along,
Sweeps an infuriate glamouring song!

WITCHES
(In chorus)

The witches ride to the Brocken's top,
The stubble is yellow, and green the crop.
There gathers the crowd for carnival:
Sir Urian sits over all.

And so they go over stone and stock;
The witch she —s, and —s the buck.

A VOICE

Alone, old Baubo's coming now;
She rides upon a farrow-sow.

CHORUS

Then honor to whom the honor is due!
Dame Baubo first, to lead the crew!
A tough old sow and the mother thereon,
Then follow the witches, every one.

A VOICE

Which way com'st thou hither?

VOICE

O'er the Ilsen-stone.
I peeped at the owl in her nest alone:
How she stared and glared!

VOICE

Betake thee to Hell!
Why so fast and so fell?

VOICE

She has scored and has flayed me:
See the wounds she has made me!

WITCHES
(*Chorus*)

The way is wide, the way is long:
See, what a wild and crazy throng!
The broom it scratches, the fork it thrusts,
The child is stifled, the mother bursts.

WIZARDS
(*Semichorus*)

As doth the snail in shell, we crawl:
Before us go the women all.
When towards the Devil's House we tread,
Woman's a thousand steps ahead.

OTHER SEMICHORUS

We do not measure with such care:
Woman in thousand steps is there,
But howsoe'er she hasten may,
Man in one leap has cleared the way.

VOICE
(*From above*)

Come on, come on, from Rocky Lake!

VOICE
(*From below*)

Aloft we'd fain ourselves betake.
We've washed, and are bright as ever you will,
Yet we're eternally sterile still.

BOTH CHORUSES

The wind is hushed, the star shoots by,
The dreary moon forsakes the sky;
The magic notes, like spark on spark,
Drizzle, whistling through the dark.

VOICE
(From below)

Halt, there! Ho, there!

VOICE
(From above)

Who calls from the rocky cleft below there?

VOICE
(Below)

Take me, too! take me, too!
I'm climbing now three hundred years,
And yet the summit cannot see:
Among my equals I would be.

BOTH CHORUSES

Bears the broom and bears the stock,
Bears the fork and bears the buck:
Who cannot raise himself to-night
Is evermore a ruined wight.

HALF-WITCH
(Below)

So long I stumble, ill bestead,
And the others are now so far ahead!
At home I've neither rest nor cheer,
And yet I cannot gain them here.

CHORUS OF WITCHES

To cheer the witch will salve avail;
A rag will answer for a sail;
Each trough a goodly ship supplies;
He ne'er will fly, who now not flies.

BOTH CHORUSES

When round the summit whirls our flight,
Then lower, and on the ground alight;
And far and wide the heather press
With witchhood's swarms of wantonness!
(They settle down.)

MEPHISTOPHELES

They crowd and push, they roar and clatter!
They whirl and whistle, pull and chatter!
They shine, and spirt, and stink, and burn!
The true witch-element we learn.
Keep close! or we are parted, in our turn.
Where art thou?

FAUST
(In the distance)
Here!

MEPHISTOPHELES

What! whirled so far astray?
Then house-right I must use, and clear the way.
Make room! Squire Voland comes! Room, gentle rabble, room!
Here, Doctor, hold to me: in one jump we'll resume
An easier space, and from the crowd be free:
It's too much, even for the like of me.
Yonder, with special light, there's something shining clearer
Within those bushes; I've a mind to see.
Come on! we'll slip a little nearer.

FAUST

Spirit of Contradiction! On! I'll follow straight.

'Tis planned most wisely, if I judge aright:
We climb the Brocken's top in the Walpurgis-Night,
That arbitrarily, here, ourselves we isolate.

MEPHISTOPHELES

But see, what motley flames among the heather!
There is a lively club together:
In smaller circles one is not alone.

FAUST

Better the summit, I must own:
There fire and whirling smoke I see.
They seek the Evil One in wild confusion:
Many enigmas there might find solution.

MEPHISTOPHELES

But there enigmas also knotted be.
Leave to the multitude their riot!
Here will we house ourselves in quiet.
It is an old, transmitted trade,
That in the greater world the little worlds are made.
I see stark-nude young witches congregate,
And old ones, veiled and hidden shrewdly:
On my account be kind, nor treat them rudely!
The trouble's small, the fun is great.
I hear the noise of instruments attuning,—
Vile din! yet one must learn to bear the crooning.
Come, come along! It *must* be, I declare!
I'll go ahead and introduce thee there,
Thine obligation newly earning.
That is no little space: what say'st thou, friend?
Look yonder! thou canst scarcely see the end:
A hundred fires along the ranks are burning.
They dance, they chat, they cook, they drink, they court:
Now where, just tell me, is there better sport?

FAUST

Wilt thou, to introduce us to the revel,
Assume the part of wizard or of devil?

MEPHISTOPHELES

I'm mostly used, 'tis true, to go incognito,
But on a gala-day one may his orders show.
The Garter does not deck my suit,
But honored and at home is here the cloven foot.
Perceiv'st thou yonder snail? It cometh, slow and steady;
So delicately its feelers pry,
That it hath scented me already:
I cannot here disguise me, if I try.
But come! we'll go from this fire to a newer:
I am the go-between, and thou the wooer.

(*To some, who are sitting around dying embers:*)

Old gentlemen, why at the outskirts? Enter!
I'd praise you if I found you snugly in the centre,
With youth and revel round you like a zone:
You each, at home, are quite enough alone.

GENERAL

Say, who would put his trust in nations,
Howe'er for them one may have worked and planned?
For with the people, as with women,
Youth always has the upper hand.

MINISTER

They're now too far from what is just and sage.
I praise the old ones, not unduly:
When we were all-in-all, then, truly,
Then was the real golden age.

PARVENU

We also were not stupid, either,
And what we should not, often did;
But now all things have from their bases slid,
Just as we meant to hold them fast together.

AUTHOR

Who, now, a work of moderate sense will read?
Such works are held as antiquate and mossy;
And as regards the younger folk, indeed,
They never yet have been so pert and saucy.

MEPHISTOPHELES

(*Who all at once appears very old*)

I feel that men are ripe for Judgment-Day,
Now for the last time I've the witches'-hill ascended:
Since to the lees *my* cask is drained away,
The world's, as well, must soon be ended.

HUCKSTER-WITCH

Ye gentlemen, don't pass me thus!
Let not the chance neglected be!
Behold my wares attentively:
The stock is rare and various.
And yet, there's nothing I've collected—
No shop, on earth, like this you'll find!—
Which has not, once, sore hurt inflicted
Upon the world, and on mankind.
No dagger's here, that set not blood to flowing;
No cup, that hath not once, within a healthy frame
Poured speedy death, in poison glowing:
No gems, that have not brought a maid to shame;
No sword, but severed ties for the unwary,
Or from behind struck down the adversary.

MEPHISTOPHELES

Gossip! the times thou badly comprehendest:
What's done has happed—what haps, is done!
'Twere better if for novelties thou sendest:
By such alone can we be won.

FAUST

Let me not lose myself in all this pother!
This is a fair, as never was another!

MEPHISTOPHELES

The whirlpool swirls to get above:
Thou'rt shoved thyself, imagining to shove.

FAUST

But who is that?

MEPHISTOPHELES

Note her especially,
'Tis Lilith.

FAUST

Who?

MEPHISTOPHELES

Adam's first wife is she.
Beware the lure within her lovely tresses,
The splendid sole adornment of her hair!
When she succeeds therewith a youth to snare,
Not soon again she frees him from her jesses.

FAUST

Those two, the old one with the young one sitting,
They've danced already more than fitting.

MEPHISTOPHELES

No rest to-night for young or old!
They start another dance: come now, let us take hold!

FAUST

(*Dancing with the young witch*)

A lovely dream once came to me;
I then beheld an apple-tree,
And there two fairest apples shone:
They lured me so, I climbed thereon.

THE FAIR ONE

Apples have been desired by you,
Since first in Paradise they grew;
And I am moved with joy, to know
That such within my garden grow.

MEPHISTOPHELES

(*Dancing with the old one*)

A dissolute dream once came to me:
Therein I saw a cloven tree,
Which had a — — —;
Yet, — as 'twas, I fancied it.

THE OLD ONE

I offer here my best salute
Unto the knight with cloven foot!
Let him a — — prepare,
If him — — — does not scare.

PROKTOPHANTASMIST

Accurséd folk! How dare you venture thus?
Had you not, long since, demonstration
That ghosts can't stand on ordinary foundation?
And now you even dance, like one of us!

THE FAIR ONE

(*Dancing*)

Why does he come, then, to our ball?

FAUST

(*Dancing*)

O, everywhere on him you fall!
When others dance, he weighs the matter:
If he can't every step bechatter,
Then 'tis the same as were the step not made;

But if you forwards go, his ire is most displayed.
If you would whirl in regular gyration
As he does in his dull old mill,
He'd show, at any rate, good-will,—
Especially if you heard and heeded his hortation.

PROKTOPHANTASMIST

You still are here? Nay, 'tis a thing unheard!
Vanish, at once! We've said the enlightening word.
The pack of devils by no rules is daunted:
We are so wise, and yet is Tegel haunted.
To clear the folly out, how have I swept and stirred!
'Twill ne'er be clean: why, 'tis a thing unheard!

THE FAIR ONE

Then cease to bore us at our ball!

PROKTOPHANTASMIST

I tell you, spirits, to your face,
I give to spirit-despotism no place;
My spirit cannot practise it at all.

(*The dance continues.*)

Naught will succeed, I see, amid such revels;
Yet something from a tour I always save,
And hope, before my last step to the grave,
To overcome the poets and the devils.

MEPHISTOPHELES

He now will seat him in the nearest puddle;
The solace this, whereof he's most assured:
And when upon his rump the leeches hang and fuddle,
He'll be of spirits and of Spirit cured.

(*To* FAUST, *who has left the dance:*)

Wherefore forsakest thou the lovely maiden,
That in the dance so sweetly sang?

FAUST

Ah! in the midst of it there sprang
A red mouse from her mouth—sufficient reason!

MEPHISTOPHELES

That's nothing! One must not so squeamish be;
So the mouse was not gray, enough for thee.
Who'd think of that in love's selected season?

FAUST

Then saw I—

MEPHISTOPHELES

What?

FAUST

Mephisto, seest thou there,
Alone and far, a girl most pale and fair?
She falters on, her way scarce knowing,
As if with fettered feet that stay her going.
I must confess, it seems to me
As if my kindly Margaret were she.

MEPHISTOPHELES

Let the thing be! All thence have evil drawn:

It is a magic shape, a lifeless eidolon.
Such to encounter is not good:
Their blank, set stare benumbs the human blood,
And one is almost turned to stone.
Medusa's tale to thee is known.

FAUST

Forsooth, the eyes they are of one whom, dying,
No hand with loving pressure closed;
That is the breast whereon I once was lying,—
The body sweet, beside which I reposed!

MEPHISTOPHELES

'Tis magic all, thou fool, seduced so easily!
Unto each man his love she seems to be.

FAUST

The woe, the rapture, so ensnare me,
That from her gaze I cannot tear me!
And, strange! around her fairest throat
A single scarlet band is gleaming,
No broader than a knife-blade seeming!

MEPHISTOPHELES

Quite right! The mark I also note.
Her head beneath her arm she'll sometimes carry;
'Twas Perseus lopped it, her old adversary.
Thou crav'st the same illusion still!
Come, let us mount this little hill;
The Prater shows no livelier stir,
And, if they've not bewitched my sense,
I verily see a theatre.
What's going on?

SERVIBILIS

'Twill shortly recommence:
A new performance—'tis the last of seven.
To give that number is the custom here:
'Twas by a Dilettante written,
And Dilettanti in the parts appear.
That now I vanish, pardon, I entreat you!
As Dilettante I the curtain raise.

MEPHISTOPHELES

When I upon the Blocksberg meet you,
I find it good: for that's your proper place.

XXII

WALPURGIS-NIGHT'S DREAM

OBERON AND TITANIA'S GOLDEN WEDDING.

INTERMEZZO

MANAGER

Sons of Mieding, rest to-day!
Needless your machinery:
Misty vale and mountain gray,
That is all the scenery.

HERALD

That the wedding golden be,
Must fifty years be rounded:
But *the Golden* give to me,
When the strife's compounded.

OBERON

Spirits, if you're here, be seen—
Show yourselves, delighted!
Fairy king and fairy queen,
They are newly plighted.

PUCK

Cometh Puck, and, light of limb,
Whisks and whirls in measure:
Come a hundred after him,
To share with him the pleasure.

ARIEL

Ariel's song is heavenly-pure,
His tones are sweet and rare ones:
Though ugly faces he allure,
Yet he allures the fair ones.

OBERON

Spouses, who would fain agree,
Learn how we were mated!
If your pairs would loving be,
First be separated!

TITANIA

If her whims the wife control,
And the man berate her,
Take him to the Northern Pole,
And her to the Equator!

ORCHESTRA. TUTTI.
(*Fortissimo*)

Snout of fly, mosquito-bill,
And kin of all conditions,
Frog in grass, and cricket-trill,—
These are the musicians!

SOLO

See the bagpipe on our track!
'Tis the soap-blown bubble:
Hear the *schnecke-schnicke-schnack*
Through his nostrils double!

SPIRIT, JUST GROWING INTO FORM

Spider's foot and paunch of toad,
And little wings—we know 'em!
A little creature 'twill not be,
But yet, a little poem.

A LITTLE COUPLE

Little step and lofty leap
Through honey-dew and fragrance:
You'll never mount the airy steep
With all your tripping vagrance.

INQUISITIVE TRAVELLER

Is't but masquerading play?
See I with precision?
Oberon, the beauteous fay,
Meets, to-night, my vision!

ORTHODOX

Not a claw, no tail I see!
And yet, beyond a cavil,
Like "the Gods of Greece," must he
Also be a devil.

NORTHERN ARTIST

I only seize, with sketchy air,
Some outlines of the tourney;
Yet I betimes myself prepare
For my Italian journey.

PURIST

My bad luck brings me here, alas!
How roars the orgy louder!
And of the witches in the mass,
But only two wear powder.

YOUNG WITCH

Powder becomes, like petticoat,
A gray and wrinkled noddy;
So I sit naked on my goat,
And show a strapping body.

MATRON

We've too much tact and policy
To rate with gibes a scolder;
Yet, young and tender though you be,
I hope to see you moulder.

LEADER OF THE BAND

Fly-snout and mosquito-bill,
Don't swarm so round the Naked!
Frog in grass and cricket-trill,
Observe the time, and make it!

WEATHERCOCK
(*Towards one side*)

Society to one's desire!
Brides only, and the sweetest!
And bachelors of youth and fire.
And prospects the completest!

WEATHERCOCK
(*Towards the other side*)

And if the Earth don't open now
To swallow up each ranter,
Why, then will I myself, I vow,
Jump into hell instanter!

XENIES

Us as little insects see!
With sharpest nippers flitting,
That our Papa Satan we
May honor as is fitting.

HENNINGS

How, in crowds together massed,
They are jesting, shameless!
They will even say, at last,
That their hearts are blameless.

MUSAGETES

Among this witches' revelry
His way one gladly loses;
And, truly, it would easier be
Than to command the Muses.

CI-DEVANT GENIUS OF THE AGE

The proper folks one's talents laud:
Come on, and none shall pass us!
The Blocksberg has a summit broad,
Like Germany's Parnassus.

INQUISITIVE TRAVELLER

Say, who's the stiff and pompous man?
He walks with haughty paces:
He snuffles all he snuffle can:
"He scents the Jesuits' traces."

CRANE

Both clear and muddy streams, for me
Are good to fish and sport in:
And thus the pious man you see
With even devils consorting.

WORLDLING

Yes, for the pious, I suspect,
All instruments are fitting;
And on the Blocksberg they erect
Full many a place of meeting.

DANCER

A newer chorus now succeeds!
I hear the distant drumming.
"Don't be disturbed! 'tis, in the reeds,
The bittern's changeless booming."

DANCING-MASTER

How each his legs in nimble trip
Lifts up, and makes a clearance!
The crooked jump, the heavy skip,
Nor care for the appearance.

GOOD FELLOW

The rabble by such hate are held,
To maim and slay delights them:
As Orpheus' lyre the brutes compelled,
The bagpipe here unites them.

DOGMATIST

I'll not be led by any lure
Of doubts or critic-cavils:
The Devil must be something, sure,—
Or how should there be devils?

IDEALIST

This once, the fancy wrought in me
Is really too despotic:
Forsooth, if I am all I see,
I must be idiotic!

REALIST

This racking fuss on every hand,
It gives me great vexation;
And, for the first time, here I stand
On insecure foundation.

SUPERNATURALIST

With much delight I see the play,
And grant to these their merits,
Since from the devils I also may
Infer the better spirits.

SCEPTIC

The flame they follow, on and on,
And think they're near the treasure:
But *Devil* rhymes with *Doubt* alone,
So I am here with pleasure.

LEADER OF THE BAND

Frog in green, and cricket-trill,
Such dilettants!—perdition!
Fly-snout and mosquito-bill,—
Each one's a fine musician!

THE ADROIT

Sans souci, we call the clan
Of merry creatures so, then;
Go a-foot no more we can,
And on our heads we go, then.

THE AWKWARD

Once many a bit we sponged, but now,
God help us! that is done with:
Our shoes are all danced out, we trow,
We've but naked soles to run with.

WILL-O'-THE WISPS

From the marshes we appear,
Where we originated;
Yet in the ranks, at once, we're here
As glittering gallants rated.

SHOOTING-STAR

Darting hither from the sky,
In star and fire light shooting,
Cross-wise now in grass I lie:
Who'll help me to my footing?

THE HEAVY FELLOWS

Room! and round about us, room!
Trodden are the grasses:
Spirits also, spirits come,
And they are bulky masses.

PUCK

Enter not so stall-fed quite,
Like elephant-calves about one!
And the heaviest weight to-night
Be Puck, himself, the stout one!

ARIEL

If loving Nature at your back,
Or Mind, the wings uncloses,
Follow up my airy track
To the mount of roses!

ORCHESTRA
(*Pianissimo*)

Cloud and trailing mist o'erhead
Are now illuminated:
Air in leaves, and wind in reed,
And all is dissipated.

XXIII

DREARY DAY

A Field.

FAUST. MEPHISTOPHELES.

FAUST

In misery! In despair! Long wretchedly astray on the face of the earth, and now imprisoned! That gracious, ill-starred creature shut in a dungeon as a criminal, and given up to fearful torments! To this has it come! to this!—Treacherous, contemptible spirit, and thou hast concealed it from me!—Stand, then,—stand! Roll the devilish eyes wrathfully in thy head! Stand and defy me with thine intolerable presence! Imprisoned! In irretrievable misery! Delivered up to evil spirits, and to condemning, unfeeling Man! And thou hast lulled me, meanwhile, with the most insipid dissipations, hast concealed from me her increasing wretchedness, and suffered her to go helplessly to ruin!

MEPHISTOPHELES

She is not the first.

FAUST

Dog! Abominable monster! Transform him, thou Infinite Spirit! transform the reptile again into his dog-shape, in which it pleased him often at night to scamper on before me, to roll himself at the feet of the unsuspecting wanderer, and hang upon his shoulders when he fell! Transform him again into his favorite likeness, that he may crawl upon his belly in the dust before me,—that I may trample him, the outlawed, under foot! Not the first! O woe! woe which no human soul can grasp, that more than one being should sink into the depths of this misery,—that the first, in its writhing death-agony under the eyes of the Eternal Forgiver, did not expiate the guilt of all others! The misery of this single one pierces to the very marrow of my life; and thou art calmly grinning at the fate of thousands!

MEPHISTOPHELES

Now we are already again at the end of our wits, where the understanding of you men runs wild. Why didst thou enter into fellowship with us, if thou canst not carry it out? Wilt fly, and art not secure against dizziness? Did we thrust ourselves upon thee, or thou thyself upon us?

FAUST

Gnash not thus thy devouring teeth at me! It fills me with horrible disgust. Mighty, glorious Spirit, who hast vouchsafed to me Thine apparition, who knowest my heart and my soul, why fetter me to the felon-comrade, who feeds on mischief and gluts himself with ruin?

MEPHISTOPHELES

Hast thou done?

FAUST

Rescue her, or woe to thee! The fearfullest curse be upon thee for thousands of ages!

MEPHISTOPHELES

I cannot loosen the bonds of the Avenger, nor undo his bolts. Rescue her? Who was it that plunged her into ruin? I, or thou?

(FAUST *looks around wildly.*)
Wilt thou grasp the thunder? Well that it has not been given to you, miserable mortals! To crush to pieces the innocent respondent—that is the tyrant-fashion of relieving one's self in embarrassments.

FAUST

Take me thither! She shall be free!

MEPHISTOPHELES

And the danger to which thou wilt expose thyself? Know that the guilt of blood, from thy hand, still lies upon the town! Avenging spirits hover over the spot where the victim fell, and lie in wait for the returning murderer.

FAUST

That, too, from thee? Murder and death of a world upon thee, monster! Take me thither, I say, and liberate her!

MEPHISTOPHELES

I will convey thee there; and hear, what I can do! Have I all the power in Heaven and on Earth? I will becloud the jailer's senses: get possession of the key, and lead her forth with human hand! I will keep watch: the magic steeds are ready, I will carry you off. So much is in my power.

FAUST

Up and away!

XXIV

NIGHT

Open Field.

FAUST *and* MEPHISTOPHELES *speeding onward on black horses.*

FAUST

What weave they there round the raven-stone?

MEPHISTOPHELES

I know not what they are brewing and doing.

FAUST

Soaring up, sweeping down, bowing and bending!

MEPHISTOPHELES

A witches'-guild.

FAUST

They scatter, devote and doom!

MEPHISTOPHELES

On! on!

XXV

DUNGEON

FAUST

(With a bunch of keys and a lamp, before an iron door)

A shudder, long unfelt, comes o'er me;
Mankind's collected woe o'erwhelms me, here.
She dwells within the dark, damp walls before me,
And all her crime was a delusion dear!
What! I delay to free her?
I dread, once again to see her?
On! my shrinking but lingers Death more near.

(He grasps the lock: the sound of singing is heard inside.)

My mother, the harlot,
Who put me to death;
My father, the varlet,
Who eaten me hath!
Little sister, so good,
Laid my bones in the wood,
In the damp moss and clay:
Then was I a beautiful bird o' the wood;
Fly away! Fly away!

FAUST

(*Unlocking*)

She does not dream her lover listens near;
That he the rattling chain, the rustling straw, can hear.

(*He enters.*)

MARGARET

(*Hiding herself on the pallet*)

Woe! woe! They come. O death of bitterness!

FAUST

(*Whispering*)

Hush! hush! The hour is come that frees thee.

MARGARET

(*Throwing herself before him*)

Art thou a man, then pity my distress!

FAUST

Thy cries will wake the guards, and they will seize thee!

(*He takes hold of the fetters to unlock them.*)

MARGARET

(*On her knees*)

Who, headsman! unto thee such power
Over me could give?
Thou'rt come for me at midnight hour:
Have mercy on me, let me live!
Is't not soon enough when morning chime has run?

(*She rises.*)

And I am yet so young, so young!
And now Death comes, and ruin!
I, too, was fair, and that was my undoing.
My love was near, but now he's far;
Torn lies the wreath, scattered the blossoms are.
Seize me not thus so violently!
Spare me! What have I done to thee?
Let me not vainly entreat thee!
I never chanced, in all my days, to meet thee!

FAUST

Shall I outlive this misery?

MARGARET

Now am I wholly in thy might.
But let me suckle, first, my baby!
I blissed it all this livelong night;
They took 't away, to vex me, maybe,
And now they say I killed the child outright.
And never shall I be glad again.
They sing songs about me! 'tis bad of the folk to do it!
There's an old story has the same refrain;
Who bade them so construe it?

FAUST

(*Falling upon his knees*)

Here lieth one who loves thee ever,
The thraldom of thy woe to sever.

MARGARET

(*Flinging herself beside him*)

O let us kneel, and call the Saints to hide us!
Under the steps beside us,
The threshold under,
Hell heaves in thunder!
The Evil One
With terrible wrath
Seeketh a path
His prey to discover!

FAUST

(*Aloud*)

Margaret! Margaret!

MARGARET

(*Attentively listening*)

That was the voice of my lover!

(*She springs to her feet: the fetters fall off.*)

Where is he? I heard him call me.
I am free! No one shall enthrall me.
To his neck will I fly,
On his bosom lie!
On the threshold he stood, and *Margaret!* calling,
Midst of Hell's howling and noises appalling,
Midst of the wrathful, infernal derision,
I knew the sweet sound of the voice of the vision!

FAUST

'Tis I!

MARGARET

'Tis thou! O, say it once again!

(*Clasping him*)

'Tis he! 'tis he! Where now is all my pain?
The anguish of the dungeon, and the chain?
'Tis thou! Thou comest to save me,
And I am saved!—
Again the street I see
Where first I looked on thee;
And the garden, brightly blooming,
Where I and Martha wait thy coming.

FAUST

(*Struggling to leave*)

Come! Come with me!

MARGARET

Delay, now!
So fain I stay, when thou delayest!

(*Caressing him*)

FAUST

Away, now!
If longer here thou stayest,
We shall be made to dearly rue it.

MARGARET

Kiss me!—canst no longer do it?
My friend, so short a time thou'rt missing,
And hast unlearned thy kissing?
Why is my heart so anxious, on thy breast?
Where once a heaven thy glances did create me,
A heaven thy loving words expressed,
And thou didst kiss, as thou wouldst suffocate me—
Kiss me!
Or I'll kiss thee!

(*She embraces him.*)

Ah, woe! thy lips are chill,
And still.
How changed in fashion
Thy passion!
Who has done me this ill?

(*She turns away from him.*)

FAUST

Come, follow me! My darling, be more bold:
I'll clasp thee, soon, with warmth a thousand-fold;
But follow now! 'Tis all I beg of thee.

MARGARET

(*Turning to him*)

And is it thou? Thou, surely, certainly?

FAUST

'Tis I! Come on!

MARGARET

Thou wilt unloose my chain,
And in thy lap wilt take me once again.

How comes it that thou dost not shrink from me?—
Say, dost thou know, my friend, whom thou mak'st free?

FAUST

Come! come! The night already vanisheth.

MARGARET

My mother have I put to death;
I've drowned the baby born to thee.
Was it not given to thee and me?
Thee, too!—'Tis thou! It scarcely true doth seem—
Give me thy hand! 'Tis not a dream!
Thy dear, dear hand!—But, ah, 'tis wet!
Why, wipe it off! Methinks that yet
There's blood thereon.
Ah, God! what hast thou done?
Nay, sheathe thy sword at last!
Do not affray me!

FAUST

O, let the past be past!
Thy words will slay me!

MARGARET

No, no! Thou must outlive us.
Now I'll tell thee the graves to give us:
Thou must begin to-morrow
The work of sorrow!
The best place give to my mother,
Then close at her side my brother,
And me a little away,
But not too very far, I pray!
And here, on my right breast, my baby lay!
Nobody else will lie beside me!—
Ah, within thine arms to hide me,
That was a sweet and a gracious bliss,
But no more, no more can I attain it!
I would force myself on thee and constrain it,
And it seems thou repellest my kiss:
And yet 'tis thou, so good, so kind to see!

FAUST

If thou feel'st it is I, then come with me!

MARGARET

Out yonder?

FAUST

To freedom.

MARGARET

If the grave is there,
Death lying in wait, then come!
From here to eternal rest:
No further step—no, no!
Thou goest away! O Henry, if I could go!

FAUST

Thou canst! Just will it! Open stands the door.

MARGARET

I dare not go: there's no hope any more.
Why should I fly? They'll still my steps waylay!
It is so wretched, forced to beg my living,
And a bad conscience sharper misery giving!
It is so wretched, to be strange, forsaken,
And I'd still be followed and taken!

FAUST

I'll stay with thee.

MARGARET

Be quick! Be quick!
Save thy perishing child!
Away! Follow the ridge
Up by the brook,
Over the bridge,
Into the wood,
To the left, where the plank is placed
In the pool!
Seize it in haste!
'Tis trying to rise,
'Tis struggling still!
Save it! Save it!

FAUST

Recall thy wandering will!
One step, and thou art free at last!

MARGARET

If the mountain we had only passed!
There sits my mother upon a stone,—
I feel an icy shiver!
There sits my mother upon a stone,
And her head is wagging ever.
She beckons, she nods not, her heavy head falls o'er;
She slept so long that she wakes no more.
She slept, while we were caressing:
Ah, those were the days of blessing!

FAUST

Here words and prayers are nothing worth;
I'll venture, then, to bear thee forth.

MARGARET

No—let me go! I'll suffer no force!
Grasp me not so murderously!
I've done, else, all things for the love of thee.

FAUST

The day dawns: Dearest! Dearest!

MARGARET

Day? Yes, the day comes,—the last day breaks for me!
My wedding-day it was to be!
Tell no one thou has been with Margaret!
Woe for my garland! The chances
Are over—'tis all in vain!
We shall meet once again,
But not at the dances!
The crowd is thronging, no word is spoken:
The square below
And the streets overflow:
The death-bell tolls, the wand is broken.
I am seized, and bound, and delivered—
Shoved to the block—they give the sign!
Now over each neck has quivered
The blade that is quivering over mine.
Dumb lies the world like the grave!

FAUST

O had I ne'er been born!

MEPHISTOPHELES
(*Appears outside*)

Off! or you're lost ere morn.
Useless talking, delaying and praying!
My horses are neighing:
The morning twilight is near.

MARGARET

What rises up from the threshold here?
He! he! suffer him not!
What does he want in this holy spot?
He seeks me!

FAUST

Thou shalt live.

MARGARET

Judgment of God! myself to thee I give.

MEPHISTOPHELES

(*To* FAUST)

Come! or I'll leave her in the lurch, and thee!

MARGARET

Thine am I, Father! rescue me!
Ye angels, holy cohorts, guard me,
Camp around, and from evil ward me!
Henry! I shudder to think of thee.

MEPHISTOPHELES

She is judged!

VOICE

(*From above*)
She is saved!

MEPHISTOPHELES

(*To* FAUST)
Hither to me!
(*He disappears with* FAUST.)

VOICE

(*From within, dying away*)
Henry! Henry!

The Master Builder

BY HENRIK IBSEN

TRANSLATED FROM
THE NORWEGIAN BY
EDMUND GOSSE AND
WILLIAM ARCHER

CHARACTERS

HALVARD SOLNESS, *the Master Builder.*
ALINE SOLNESS, *his wife.*
DOCTOR HERDAL, *physician.*
KNUT BROVIK, *formerly an architect, now in* SOLNESS'S *employment.*
RAGNAR BROVIK, *his son, draughtsman.*
KAIA FOSLI, *his niece, book-keeper.*
MISS HILDA WANGEL.
SOME LADIES.
A CROWD IN THE STREET.
The action passes in and about the house of SOLNESS.

The Master Builder

ACT ONE

A plainly-furnished work-room in the house of HALVARD SOLNESS. *Folding doors on the left lead out to the hall. On the right is the door leading to the inner rooms of the house. At the back is an open door into the draughtsmen's office. In front, on the left, a desk with books, papers, and writing materials. Further back than the folding door, a stove. In the right-hand corner, a sofa, a table, and one or two chairs. On the table a water-bottle and glass. A smaller table, with a rocking-chair and arm-chair, in front on the right. Lighted lamps with shades on the table in the draughtsmen's office, on the table in the corner, and on the desk.*

In the draughtsmen's office sit KNUT BROVIK *and his son* RAGNAR, *occupied with plans and calculations. At the desk in the outer office stands* KAIA FOSLI, *writing in the ledger.* KNUT BROVIK *is a spare old man with white hair and beard. He wears a rather threadbare but well-brushed black coat, spectacles, and a somewhat discolored white neckcloth.* RAGNAR BROVIK *is a well-dressed, light-haired man of about thirty, who stoops a little.* KAIA FOSLI *is a slightly-built girl, a little over twenty, carefully dressed, and delicate-looking. She has a green shade over her eyes.—All three go on working for some time in silence.*

KNUT BROVIK (*rises suddenly, as if in distress, from the table; breathes heavily and laboriously as he comes forward into the doorway*). No, I can't bear it much longer!

KAIA (*going up to him*). You're feeling very ill this evening, aren't you, Uncle?

BROVIK. Oh, I seem to get worse every day.

RAGNAR (*has risen and advances*). You ought to go home, father. Try to get a little sleep——

BROVIK (*impatiently*). Go to bed, I suppose? Would you have me stifled outright?

KAIA. Then take a little walk.

RAGNAR. Yes, do. I will come with you.

BROVIK (*with warmth*). I'll not go till he comes! I'm determined to have it out this evening with—(*in a tone of suppressed bitterness*)—with him—with the chief.

KAIA (*anxiously*). Oh no, uncle,—do wait awhile before doing *that!*

RAGNAR. Yes, better wait, father!

BROVIK (*draws his breath laboriously*). Ha—ha—! *I* haven't much time for waiting.

KAIA (*listening*). Hush! I hear him on the stairs. (*All three go back to their work. A short silence.*)

(HALVARD SOLNESS *comes in through the hall door. He is a man of mature age, healthy and vigorous, with close-cut curly hair, dark mustache and dark thick eyebrows. He wears a grayish-green buttoned jacket with an upstanding collar and broad lapels. On his head he wears a soft gray felt hat, and he has one or two light portfolios under his arm.*)

SOLNESS (*near the door, points towards the draughtsmen's office, and asks in a whisper*): Are they gone?

KAIA (*softly, shaking her head*). No. (*She takes the shade off her eyes.* SOLNESS *crosses the room, throws his hat on a chair, places the portfolios on the table by the sofa, and approaches the desk again.* KAIA *goes on writing without intermission, but seems nervous and uneasy.*)

SOLNESS (*aloud*). What is that you're entering, Miss Fosli?

KAIA (*starts*). Oh, it's only something that——

SOLNESS. Let me look at it, Miss Fosli. (*Bends over her, pretends to be looking into the ledger, and whispers*): Kaia?

KAIA (*softly, still writing*). Well?

SOLNESS. Why do you always take that shade off when I come?

KAIA (*as before*). I look so ugly with it on.

SOLNESS (*smiling*). Then you don't like to look ugly, Kaia?

KAIA (*half glancing up at him*). Not for all the world. Not in *your* eyes.

SOLNESS (*strokes her hair gently*). Poor, poor little Kaia——

KAIA (*bending her head*). Hush, they can hear you!

(SOLNESS *strolls across the room to the right, turns and pauses at the door of the draughtsmen's office.*)

SOLNESS. Has any one been here for me?

RAGNAR (*rising*). Yes, the young couple who want a villa built out at Lövstrand.

SOLNESS (*growling*). Oh, those two! They must wait. I'm not quite clear about the plans yet.

RAGNAR (*Advancing, with some hesitation*). They were very anxious to have the drawings at once.

SOLNESS (*as before*). Yes, of course—so they all are.

BROVIK (*looks up*). They say they're longing so to get into a house of their own.

SOLNESS. Yes, yes—we know all that! And so they're content to take whatever's offered them. They get a—a roof over their heads—an address—but nothing to call a home. No thank you! In that case, let them apply to somebody else. Tell them *that*, the next time they call.

BROVIK (*pushes his glasses up on to his forehead and looks in astonishment at him*). To somebody else? Are you prepared to give up the commission?

SOLNESS (*impatiently*). Yes, yes, yes, devil take it! If that's to be the way of it. —Rather that, than build away at random. (*Vehemently*) Besides, I know very little about these people as yet.

BROVIK. The people are safe enough. Ragnar knows them. He's a friend of the family. Perfectly safe people.

SOLNESS. Oh, safe—safe enough! That's not at all what I mean. Good lord—don't *you* understand me either? (*Angrily*) I won't have anything to do with these strangers. They may apply to whom they please, so far as I'm concerned.

BROVIK (*rising*). Do you really mean it?

SOLNESS (*sulkily*). Yes I do.—For once in a way. (*He comes forward.*) (BROVIK *exchanges a glance with* RAGNAR, *who makes a warning gesture. Then* BROVIK *comes into the front room.*)

BROVIK. May I have a few words with you?

SOLNESS. Certainly.

BROVIK (*to* KAIA). Just go in there for a moment, Kaia.

KAIA (*uneasily*). Oh, but Uncle——

BROVIK. Do as I say, child. And shut the door after you.
(KAIA *goes reluctantly into the draughtsmen's office, glances anxiously and entreatingly at* SOLNESS, *and shuts the door.*)

BROVIK (*lowering his voice a little*). I don't want the poor children to know how ill I am.

SOLNESS. Yes, you've been looking very poorly of late.

BROVIK. It will soon be all over with me. My strength is ebbing from day to day.

SOLNESS. Won't you sit down?

BROVIK. Thanks—may I?

SOLNESS (*placing the arm-chair more conveniently*). Here—take this chair.—And now?

BROVIK (*has seated himself with difficulty*). Well, you see, it's about Ragnar. That's what weighs most upon me. What is to become of him?

SOLNESS. Of course your son will stay with me as long as ever he likes.

BROVIK. But that's just what he doesn't like. He feels that he can't stay any longer.

SOLNESS. Why, I should say he was very well off here. But if he wants a rise, I shouldn't object to——

BROVIK. No, no! It's not *that.* (*Impatiently*) But sooner or later he, too, must have a chance of doing something on his own account.

SOLNESS (*without looking at him*). Do you think that Ragnar has quite talent enough to stand alone?

BROVIK. No, that's just the heartbreaking part of it—I've begun to have my doubts about the boy. For you've never said so much as—as one encouraging word about him. And yet I can't help thinking there must be something in him—he can't possibly be without talent.

SOLNESS. Well, but he has learnt nothing—nothing thoroughly, I mean. Except, of course, to draw.

BROVIK (*looks at him with covert hatred, and says hoarsely*): You had learned little enough of the business when you were in my employment. But that didn't prevent you from setting to work—(*breathing with difficulty*)—and pushing your way up, and taking the wind out of my sails—mine, and other people's.

SOLNESS. Yes, you see—circumstances favored me.

BROVIK. You're right there. Everything favored you. But then how can you have the heart to let me go to my grave—without having seen what Ragnar is fit for? And of course I'm anxious to see them married, too—before I go.

SOLNESS (*sharply*). Is it she who wishes it?

BROVIK. Not Kaia so much as Ragnar—he talks about it every day. (*Appealingly*) You must—you *must* help him to get some independent work now! I *must* see something that the lad has done. Do you hear?

SOLNESS (*peevishly*). You can't expect me to drag commissions down from the moon for him!

BROVIK. He has the chance of a capital commission at this very moment. A big bit of work.

SOLNESS (*uneasily, startled*). Has he?

BROVIK. If *you* would give your consent.

SOLNESS. What sort of work do you mean?

BROVIK (*with some hesitation*). He can have the building of that villa out at Lövstrand.

SOLNESS. That! Why, I'm going to build that myself!

BROVIK. Oh, you don't much care about doing it.

SOLNESS (*flaring up*). Don't care! I! Who dares to say that?

BROVIK. You said so yourself just now.

SOLNESS. Oh, never mind what I *say.*—Would they give Ragnar the building of that villa?

BROVIK. Yes. You see, he knows the family. And then—just for the fun of the thing—he's made drawings and estimates and so forth——

SOLNESS. Are they pleased with the drawings? The people who've got to live in the house?

BROVIK. Yes. If you would only look through them and approve of them——

SOLNESS. Then they would let Ragnar build their home for them?

BROVIK. They were immensely pleased with his idea. They thought it exceedingly original, they said.

SOLNESS. Oho! Original! Not the old-fashioned stuff that *I'm* in the habit of turning out.

BROVIK. It seemed to them *different.*

SOLNESS (*with suppressed irritation*). So it was to see Ragnar that they came here—whilst I was out!

BROVIK. They came to call upon you—and at the same time to ask whether you would mind retiring——

SOLNESS (*angrily*). Retire? I?

BROVIK. In case you thought that Ragnar's drawings——

SOLNESS. I? Retire in favor of your son?

BROVIK. Retire from the agreement, they meant.

SOLNESS. Oh, it comes to the same thing. (*Laughs angrily.*) So that's it, is it? Halvard Solness is to see about retiring now! To make room for younger men! For the very youngest, perhaps! He's got to make room! Room! Room!

BROVIK. Why, good heavens! there's surely room for more than one single man——

SOLNESS. Oh, there's not so very much room to spare either. But be that as it may—I will never retire! I will never give way to anybody! Never of my own free will. Never in this world will I do *that!*

BROVIK (*rises with difficulty*). Then I am to pass out of life without any certainty? Without a gleam of happiness? Without any faith or trust in Ragnar? Without having seen a single piece of work of his doing? Is that to be the way of it?

SOLNESS (*turns half aside, and mutters*). H'm—don't ask more just now.

BROVIK. But answer me this one thing. Am I to pass out of life in such utter poverty?

SOLNESS (*seems to struggle with

himself; finally he says in a low but firm voice): You must pass out of life as best you can.

BROVIK. Then be it so. (*He goes up the room.*)

SOLNESS (*following him, half in desperation*). Don't you understand that I *cannot* help it? I am what I am, and I can't change my nature!

BROVIK. No, no; you evidently can't. (*Reels and supports himself against the sofa-table.*) May I have a glass of water?

SOLNESS. By all means. (*Fills a glass and hands it to him.*)

BROVIK. Thanks. (*Drinks and puts the glass down again.*)
(SOLNESS *goes up and opens the door of the draughtsmen's office.*)

SOLNESS. Ragnar—you must come and take your father home.
(RAGNAR *rises quickly. He and* KAIA *come into the work-room.*)

RAGNAR. What's the matter, father?

BROVIK. Give me your arm. Now let us go.

RAGNAR. All right. You'd better put your things on, too, Kaia.

SOLNESS.—Miss Fosli must stay—just a moment. There's a letter I want written.

BROVIK (*looks at* SOLNESS). Good-night. Sleep well—if you can.

SOLNESS. Good-night.

(BROVIK *and* RAGNAR *go out through the hall-door.* KAIA *goes to the desk.* SOLNESS *stands with bent head, to the right, by the arm-chair.*)

KAIA (*dubiously*). Is there any letter——?

SOLNESS (*curtly*). No, of course not. (*Looks sternly at her.*) Kaia!

KAIA (*anxiously, in a low voice*). Yes?

SOLNESS (*points imperatively to a spot on the floor*). Come here! At once!

KAIA (*hesitatingly*). Yes.

SOLNESS (*as before*). Nearer!

KAIA (*obeying*). What do you want with me?

SOLNESS (*looks at her for a while*). Is it you I have to thank for all this?

KAIA. No, no, don't think that!

SOLNESS. But confess now—you want to get married!

KAIA (*softly*). Ragnar and I have been engaged for four or five years, and so——

SOLNESS. And so you think it's time there were an end of it. Isn't that so?

KAIA. Ragnar and Uncle say I *must*. So I suppose I'll have to give in.

SOLNESS (*more gently*). Kaia, don't you really care a little bit for Ragnar, too?

KAIA. I cared very much for Ragnar once—before I came here to you.

SOLNESS. But you don't now? Not in the least?

KAIA (*passionately, clasping her hands and holding them out towards him*). Oh, you know very well that there's only *one* person I care for now! One, and one only, in all the world. I shall never care for any one else again!

SOLNESS. Yes, you say that. And yet you go away from me—leave me alone here with everything on my hands.

KAIA. But couldn't I stay with you, even if Ragnar——?

SOLNESS (*repudiating the idea*). No, no, that's quite impossible. If Ragnar leaves me and starts work on his own account, then of course he'll need you himself.

KAIA (*wringing her hands*). Oh, I feel as if I *couldn't* be separated from you! It's quite, quite impossible!

SOLNESS. Then be sure you get those foolish notions out of Ragnar's mind. Marry him as much as you please—(*alters his tone*) I mean—don't let him throw up his good situation with me. For then I can keep *you* too, my dear Kaia.

KAIA. Oh yes, how lovely that would be, if it could only be managed.

SOLNESS (*clasps her head with his two hands and whispers*): For I *can't* get on without you, you see. I must have you with me every single day.

KAIA (*in nervous exaltation*). My God! My God!

SOLNESS (*kisses her hair*). Kaia—Kaia!

KAIA (*sinks down before him*). Oh, how good you are to me! How unspeakably good you are!

SOLNESS (*vehemently*). Get up! For goodness' sake get up! I think I hear some one!
(*He helps her to rise. She staggers over to the desk.* MRS. SOLNESS *enters by the door on the right. She looks thin and wasted with grief, but shows traces of bygone beauty. Blonde ringlets. Dressed with good taste, wholly in black. Speaks somewhat slowly and in a plaintive voice.*)

MRS. SOLNESS (*in the doorway*). Halvard!

SOLNESS (*turns*). Oh, are you there, dear——?

MRS. SOLNESS (*with a glance at* KAIA). I'm afraid I'm disturbing you.

SOLNESS. Not in the least. Miss Fosli has only a short letter to write.

MRS. SOLNESS. Yes, so I see.

SOLNESS. What do you want with me, Aline?

MRS. SOLNESS. I merely wanted to tell you that Dr. Herdal is in the drawing-room. Won't you come and see him, Halvard?

SOLNESS (*looks suspiciously at her*). H'm—is the doctor so very anxious to talk to me?

MRS. SOLNESS. Well, not exactly anxious. He really came to see me; but he would like to say how-do-you-do to you at the same time.

SOLNESS (*laughs to himself*). Yes, I dare say. Well, you must ask him to wait a little.

MRS. SOLNESS. Then you'll come in later on?

SOLNESS. Perhaps I will. Later on, later on, dear. Presently.

MRS. SOLNESS (*glancing again at* KAIA). Well now, don't forget, Halvard. (*Withdraws and closes the door behind her.*)

KAIA (*softly*). Oh dear, oh dear—I'm sure Mrs. Solness thinks ill of me in some way!

SOLNESS. Oh, not in the least. Not more than usual at any rate. But you'd better go now, all the same, Kaia.

KAIA. Yes, yes, now I must go.

SOLNESS (*severely*). And mind you get that matter settled for me. Do you hear?

KAIA. Oh, if it only depended on *me*——

SOLNESS. I *will* have it settled, I say! And to-morrow too—not a day later!

KAIA (*terrified*). If there's nothing else for it, I'm quite willing to break off the engagement.

SOLNESS (*angrily*). Break it off! Are you mad? Would you think of breaking it off?

KAIA (*distracted*). Yes, if necessary. For I *must*—I *must* stay here with you! I can't leave you! That's utterly—utterly impossible!

SOLNESS (*with a sudden outburst*). But deuce take it—how about Ragnar then! It's Ragnar that I——

KAIA (*looks at him with terrified eyes*). It is chiefly on Ragnar's account, that—that you——?

SOLNESS (*collecting himself*). No, no, of course not! You don't understand me either. (*Gently and softly*) Of course it's *you* I want to keep—you above everything, Kaia. But for that very reason you must prevent Ragnar too from throwing up his situation. There, there,—now go home.

KAIA. Yes, yes—good-night, then.

SOLNESS. Good-night. (*As she is going*) Oh! stop a moment! Are Ragnar's drawings in there?

KAIA. I didn't see him take them with him.

SOLNESS. Then just go in and find them for me. I might perhaps glance over them.

KAIA (*happy*). Oh yes, please do!

SOLNESS. For your sake, Kaia dear. Now, let me have them at once, please.
(KAIA *hurries into the draughtsmen's office, searches anxiously in the table-drawer, finds a portfolio and brings it with her.*)

KAIA. Here are all the drawings.

SOLNESS. Good. Put them down there on the table.

KAIA (*putting down the portfolio*). Good-night, then. (*Beseechingly*) And think kindly of me.

SOLNESS. Oh, that I always do. Good-night, my dear little Kaia. (*Glances to the right.*) Go, go now!
(MRS. SOLNESS *and* DR. HERDAL *enter by the door on the right. He is a stoutish, elderly man, with a round, good-humored face, clean shaven, with thin, light hair, and gold spectacles.*)

MRS. SOLNESS (*still in the doorway*). Halvard, I cannot keep the doctor any longer.

SOLNESS. Well then, come in here.

MRS. SOLNESS (*to* KAIA, *who is turning down the desk lamp*). Have you finished the letter already, Miss Fosli?

KAIA (*in confusion*). The letter—?

SOLNESS. Yes, it was quite a short one.

MRS. SOLNESS. It must have been very short.

SOLNESS. You may go now, Miss Fosli. And please come in good time to-morrow morning.

KAIA. I will be sure to. Good-night, Mrs. Solness. (*She goes out by the hall-door.*)

MRS. SOLNESS. She must be quite an acquisition to you, Halvard, this Miss Fosli.

SOLNESS. Yes, indeed. She's useful in all sorts of ways.

MRS. SOLNESS. So it seems.

DR. HERDAL. Is she good at book-keeping, too?

SOLNESS. Well—of course she's had a good deal of practice during these two years. And then she's so nice and obliging in every possible way.

MRS. SOLNESS. Yes, that must be very delightful.

SOLNESS. It *is*. Especially when one doesn't get too much of that sort of thing.

MRS. SOLNESS (*in a tone of general remonstrance*). Can *you* say that, Halvard?

SOLNESS. Oh, no, no, my dear Aline; I beg your pardon.

MRS. SOLNESS. There's no occasion. Well, then, doctor, you'll come back later on and have a cup of tea with us?

DR. HERDAL. I've only a professional visit to pay, and then I'll come back.

MRS. SOLNESS. Thank you. (*She goes out by the door on the right.*)

SOLNESS. Are you in a hurry, doctor?

DR. HERDAL. No, not at all.

SOLNESS. May I have a little chat with you?

DR. HERDAL. With the greatest of pleasure.

SOLNESS. Then let us sit down. (*He motions the doctor to take the rocking-chair and sits down himself in the arm-chair.*)

SOLNESS (*looks searchingly at him*). Tell me, did you notice anything odd about Aline?

DR. HERDAL. Do you mean just now when she was here?

SOLNESS. Yes, in her manner to me. Did you notice anything?

DR. HERDAL (*smiling*). Well, I admit—one couldn't well avoid noticing that your wife—h'm——

SOLNESS. Well?

DR. HERDAL.—That your wife isn't particularly fond of this Miss Fosli.

SOLNESS. Is that all? I've noticed that myself.

DR. HERDAL. And I must say it doesn't surprise me.

SOLNESS. What doesn't?

DR. HERDAL. That she shouldn't exactly approve of you seeing so much of another woman, all day and every day.

SOLNESS. No, no, I suppose you're right there—and Aline too. But it's impossible to make any change.

DR. HERDAL. Could you not engage a clerk?

SOLNESS. The first man that came to hand? No thanks—that would never do for me.

DR. HERDAL. But now, if your wife——? Suppose, with her delicate health, all this tries her too much?

SOLNESS. Well then there's no help for it—I could almost say. I *must* keep Kaia Fosli. No one else could fill her place.

DR. HERDAL. No one else?

SOLNESS (*curtly*). No, no one.

DR. HERDAL (*drawing his chair closer*). Now listen to me, my dear Mr. Solness. May I ask you a question, quite between ourselves?

SOLNESS. By all means.

DR. HERDAL. Women, you see—in certain matters, they have a deucedly keen intuition——

SOLNESS. They have indeed. There's not the least doubt of that. But——?

DR. HERDAL. Well, tell me now—if your wife can't endure this Kaia Fosli——?

SOLNESS. Well, what then?

DR. HERDAL.—hasn't she got just—just the least little bit of reason for this involuntary dislike?

SOLNESS (*looks at him and rises*). Oho!

DR. HERDAL. Now don't be offended—but *hasn't* she?

SOLNESS (*with curt decision*). No.

DR. HERDAL. No reason of any sort?

SOLNESS. No other reason than her own suspicious nature.

DR. HERDAL. I know you've known a good many women in your time.

SOLNESS. Yes, I have.

DR. HERDAL. And have been a good deal taken with some of them, too?

SOLNESS. Oh yes, I don't deny it.

DR. HERDAL. But as regards Miss Fosli, then—there's nothing of that sort in the case?

SOLNESS. No; nothing at all—on *my* side.

DR. HERDAL. But on her side?

SOLNESS. I don't think you have any right to ask that question, doctor.

DR. HERDAL. Well, you know, we were discussing your wife's intuition.

SOLNESS. So we were. And for that matter—(*lowers his voice*)—Aline's intuition, as you call it—in a certain sense, it's not been so far out.

DR. HERDAL. Ah! there we have it!

SOLNESS (*sits down*). Doctor Herdal—I'm going to tell you a strange story—if you care to listen to it.

DR. HERDAL. I like listening to strange stories.

SOLNESS. Very well then. I daresay you recollect that I took Knut Brovik and his son into my service—after the old man's business had gone to the dogs.

DR. HERDAL. Yes, so I've understood.

SOLNESS. You see, they really are clever fellows, these two. Each of them has talent in his way. But then the son took it into his head to get engaged; and the next thing, of course, was that he wanted to get married—and begin to build on his own account. That's the way with all these young people.

DR. HERDAL (*laughing*). Yes, they've a bad habit of wanting to marry.

SOLNESS. Just so. But of course that

didn't suit *my* plans; for I needed Ragnar myself—and the old man, too. He's exceedingly good at calculating bearing-strains and cubic contents—and all that sort of devilry, you know.

DR. HERDAL. Oh yes, no doubt that's very important.

SOLNESS. Yes, it is. But Ragnar was absolutely bent on setting to work for himself. He wouldn't hear of anything else.

DR. HERDAL. But he has stayed with you all the same.

SOLNESS. Yes, I'll tell you how that came about. One day this girl, Kaia Fosli, came to see them on some errand or other. She had never been here before. And when I saw how utterly infatuated they were with each other, the thought occurred to me: If only I could get her into the office here, then perhaps Ragnar too would stay where she is.

DR. HERDAL. That was not at all a bad idea.

SOLNESS. Yes, but at the time I didn't breathe a word of what was in my mind. I merely stood and looked at her, and kept wishing intently that I could have her here. Then I talked to her a little, in a friendly way—about one thing and another. And then she went away.

DR. HERDAL. Well?

SOLNESS. Well then, next day, pretty late in the evening, when old Brovik and Ragnar had gone home, she came here again, and behaved as if I had made an arrangement with her.

DR. HERDAL. An arrangement? What about?

SOLNESS. About the very thing my mind had been fixed on. But I hadn't said one single word about it.

DR. HERDAL. That was most extraordinary.

SOLNESS. Yes, wasn't it? And now she wanted to know what she was to do here, whether she could begin the very next morning, and so forth.

DR. HERDAL. Don't you think she did it in order to be with her sweetheart?

SOLNESS. That was what occurred to me at first. But no, that wasn't it. She seemed to drift quite away from *him*—when once she had come here to me.

DR. HERDAL. She drifted over to you, then?

SOLNESS. Yes, entirely. If I happen to look at her when her back is turned, I can tell that she feels it. She quivers and trembles the moment I come near her. What do you think of that?

DR. HERDAL. H'm—that's not very hard to explain.

SOLNESS. Well, but what about the other thing? That she believed I had said to her what I had only wished and willed—silently—inwardly—to myself? What do you say to that? Can you explain that, Dr. Herdal?

DR. HERDAL. No, I won't undertake to do that.

SOLNESS. I felt sure you wouldn't; and so I've never cared to talk about it till now. But it's a cursed nuisance to me in the long run, you understand. Here have I got to go on day after day pretending—. And it's a shame to treat her so, too, poor girl. (*Vehemently*) But I *can't* do anything else. For if *she* runs away from me—then Ragnar will be off too.

DR. HERDAL. And you haven't told your wife the rights of the story?

SOLNESS. No.

DR. HERDAL. Then why on earth don't you?

SOLNESS (*looks fixedly at him and says in a low voice*): Because I seem to find a sort of—of salutary self-torture in allowing Aline to do me an injustice.

DR. HERDAL (*shakes his head*). I don't in the least understand what you mean.

SOLNESS. Well, you see, it's like paying off a little bit of a huge, immeasurable debt——

DR. HERDAL. To your wife?

SOLNESS. Yes; and that always helps to relieve one's mind a little. One can breathe more freely for a while, you see.

DR. HERDAL. No, goodness knows, I don't see at all——

SOLNESS (*breaking off, rises again*). Well, well, well—then we won't talk any more about it. (*He saunters across the room, returns, and stops beside the table. Looks at the doctor with a sly smile*) I suppose you think you've drawn me out nicely now, doctor?

DR. HERDAL (*with some irritation*). Drawn you out? Again I haven't the faintest notion what you mean, Mr. Solness.

SOLNESS. Oh come, out with it; for I've seen it quite clearly, you know.

DR. HERDAL. *What* have you seen?

SOLNESS (*in a low voice, slowly*). That you've been quietly keeping an eye upon me.

DR. HERDAL. That *I* have! And why in all the world should I do *that*?

SOLNESS. Because you think that I—— (*Passionately*) Well, devil take it—you think the same of me as Aline does.

DR. HERDAL. And what does *she* think about you?

SOLNESS (*having recovered his self-control*). She has begun to think that I'm—that I'm—ill.

DR. HERDAL. Ill! *You!* She has never

hinted such a thing to me. Why, what can she think is the matter with you?

SOLNESS (*leans over the back of the chair and whispers*): Aline has made up her mind that I am mad. *That's* what she thinks.

DR. HERDAL (*rising*). Why, my dear, good fellow—!

SOLNESS. Yes, on my soul she does! I tell you it's so! And she has got you to think the same. Oh, I can assure you, doctor, I see it in your face as clearly as possible. You don't take me in so easily, I can tell you.

DR. HERDAL (*looks at him in amazement*). Never, Mr. Solness—never has such a thought entered my mind.

SOLNESS (*with an incredulous smile*). Really? Has it not?

DR. HERDAL. No, never! Nor your wife's mind either, I'm convinced. I could almost swear to that.

SOLNESS. Well, I wouldn't advise you to. For, in a certain sense, you see, perhaps—perhaps she's not so far wrong in thinking something of the kind.

DR. HERDAL. Come now, I really must say—

SOLNESS (*interrupting with a sweep of his hand*). Well, well, my dear doctor—don't let us discuss this any further. We had better agree to differ. (*Changes to a tone of quiet merriment.*) But look here now, doctor—hm—

DR. HERDAL. Well?

SOLNESS. Since you don't believe that I am—ill—and crazy—and mad, and so forth—

DR. HERDAL. What then?

SOLNESS. Then I daresay you fancy that I'm an extremely happy man?

DR. HERDAL. Is *that* mere fancy?

SOLNESS (*laughs*). No, no—of course not! Heaven forbid! Only think—to be Solness the master builder! Halvard Solness! What could be more delightful?

DR. HERDAL. Yes, I must say it seems to me you've had the luck on your side to an astounding degree.

SOLNESS (*suppresses a gloomy smile*). So I have. I can't complain on *that* score.

DR. HERDAL. First of all that grim old robber's castle was burnt down for you. And that was certainly a great piece of luck.

SOLNESS (*seriously*). It was the home of Aline's family. Remember that.

DR. HERDAL. Yes, it must have been a great grief to *her*.

SOLNESS. She hasn't got over it to this day—not in all these twelve or thirteen years.

DR. HERDAL. Ah, but what followed

must have been the worst blow for her.

SOLNESS. The one thing with the other.

DR. HERDAL. But you—yourself—*you* rose upon the ruins. You began as a poor boy from a country village—and now you're at the head of your profession. Ah, yes, Mr. Solness, you've undoubtedly had the luck on your side.

SOLNESS (*looks doubtfully across at him*). Yes, but that's just what makes me so horribly afraid.

DR. HERDAL. Afraid? Because you have the luck on your side!

SOLNESS. It terrifies me—terrifies me every hour of the day. For sooner or later the luck must turn, you see.

DR. HERDAL. Oh, nonsense! What should make the luck turn?

SOLNESS (*with firm assurance*). The younger generation.

DR. HERDAL. Pooh! The younger generation! You're not laid on the shelf yet, I should hope. Oh no—your position here is probably firmer now than it has ever been.

SOLNESS. The luck *will* turn. I know it—I feel the day approaching. Some one or other will take it into his head to say: Give *me* a chance! And then all the rest will come clamoring after him, and shake their fists at me and shout: Make room—make room—make room! Yes, just you see, doctor—presently the younger generation will come knocking at my door——

DR. HERDAL (*laughing*). Well, and what if they do?

SOLNESS. What if they do? Then there's an end of Halvard Solness. (*There is a knock at the door on the left.*)

SOLNESS (*starts*). What's that? Didn't you hear something?

DR. HERDAL. Some one is knocking at the door.

SOLNESS (*loudly*). Come in.
(HILDA WANGEL *enters through the hall door. She is of middle height, supple, and delicately built. Somewhat sunburnt. Dressed in a tourist costume, with skirt caught up for walking, a sailor's collar open at the throat, and a small sailor hat on her head. Knapsack on back, plaid shawl in strap, and alpenstock.*)

HILDA (*goes straight up to* SOLNESS, *her eyes sparkling with happiness*). Good-evening!

SOLNESS (*looks doubtfully at her*). Good-evening——

HILDA (*laughs*). I almost believe you don't recognize me!

SOLNESS. No—I must admit that—just for the moment——

DR. HERDAL (*approaching*). But *I* recognize you, my dear young lady——

HILDA (*pleased*). Oh, is it you that—

DR. HERDAL. Of course it is. (*To* SOLNESS) We met at one of the mountain stations this summer. (*To* HILDA) What became of the other ladies?

HILDA. Oh, they went westward.

DR. HERDAL. They didn't much like all the fun we used to have in the evenings.

HILDA. No, I believe they didn't.

DR. HERDAL (*holds up his finger at her*). And I'm afraid it can't be denied that you flirted a little with us.

HILDA. Well, that was better fun than to sit there knitting stockings with all those old women.

DR. HERDAL (*laughs*). There I entirely agree with you!

SOLNESS. Have you come to town this evening?

HILDA. Yes, I've just arrived.

DR. HERDAL. Quite alone, Miss Wangel?

HILDA. Oh yes!

SOLNESS. Wangel? Is your name Wangel?

HILDA (*looks in amused surprise at him*). Yes, of course it is.

SOLNESS. Then you must be the daughter of the district doctor up at Lysanger?

HILDA (*as before*). Yes, who else's daughter should I be?

SOLNESS. Oh, then I suppose we met up there, that summer when I was building a tower on the old church.

HILDA (*more seriously*). Yes, of course it was then we met.

SOLNESS. Well, that's a long time ago.

HILDA (*looks hard at him*). It's just the ten years.

SOLNESS. You must have been a mere child then, I should think.

HILDA (*carelessly*). Well, I was twelve or thirteen.

DR. HERDAL. Is this the first time you've ever been up to town, Miss Wangel?

HILDA. Yes, it is indeed.

SOLNESS. And don't you know any one here?

HILDA. Nobody but you. And of course, your wife.

SOLNESS. So you know *her* too?

HILDA. Only a little. We spent a few days together at the sanatorium.

SOLNESS. Ah, up there?

HILDA. She said I might come and

pay her a visit if ever I came up to town. (*Smiles*) Not that that was necessary.

SOLNESS. Odd that she should never have mentioned it.
(HILDA *puts her stick down by the stove, takes off the knapsack and lays it and the plaid on the sofa.* DR. HERDAL *offers to help her.* SOLNESS *stands and gazes at her.*)

HILDA (*going towards him*). Well, now I must ask you to let me spend the night here.

SOLNESS. I'm sure we can manage that.

HILDA. For I've no other clothes than those I stand in, except a change of linen in my knapsack. And that has to go to the wash, for it's very dirty.

SOLNESS. Oh yes, we'll see to that. Now I'll just let my wife know——

DR. HERDAL. Meanwhile, I'll visit my patient.

SOLNESS. Yes, do; and come again later on.

DR. HERDAL (*playfully, with a glance at* HILDA). Oh that I will, you may be very certain! (*Laughs*) So your prediction has come true, Mr. Solness!

SOLNESS. How so?

DR. HERDAL. The younger generation *did* come knocking at your door.

SOLNESS (*cheerfully*). Yes, but in a very different way from what I meant.

DR. HERDAL. Very different, yes. That's undeniable.
(*He goes out by the hall-door.* SOLNESS *opens the door on the right and speaks into the side room.*)

SOLNESS. Aline! Will you come in here, please. Here's a friend of yours—Miss Wangel.

MRS. SOLNESS (*appears in the doorway*). Who do you say it is? (*Sees* HILDA) Oh, is it you, Miss Wangel? (*Goes up to her and offers her hand.*) So you've come to town after all.

SOLNESS. Miss Wangel has this moment arrived; and she would like to stay the night here.

MRS. SOLNESS. Here with us? Oh yes, with pleasure.

SOLNESS. So as to get her things a little in order, you see.

MRS. SOLNESS. I will do the best I can for you. It's no more than my duty. I suppose your trunk is coming on later?

HILDA. I *have* no trunk.

MRS. SOLNESS. Well, it will be all right, I daresay. In the meantime, you must excuse my leaving you here with my husband until I can get a room made a little comfortable for you.

SOLNESS. Can't we give her one of

the nurseries? *They* are all ready as it is.

MRS. SOLNESS. Oh yes. There we have room and to spare. (*To* HILDA) Sit down now and rest a little.

(*She goes out to the right.* HILDA, *with her hands behind her back, strolls about the room and looks at various objects.* SOLNESS *stands in front, beside the table, also with his hands behind his back, and follows her with his eyes.*)

HILDA (*stops and looks at him*). Have you several nurseries?

SOLNESS. There are three nurseries in the house.

HILDA. That's a lot. Then I suppose you have a great many children?

SOLNESS. No. We have no child. But now *you* can be the child here, for the time being.

HILDA. For to-night, yes. I sha'n't cry. I mean to sleep as sound as a stone.

SOLNESS. Yes, you must be very tired, I should think.

HILDA. Oh no! But all the same— It's so delicious to lie and dream.

SOLNESS. Do you dream much of nights?

HILDA. Oh yes! Almost always.

SOLNESS. What do you dream about most?

HILDA. I sha'n't tell you to-night. Another time, perhaps.

(*She again strolls about the room, stops at the desk and turns over the books and papers a little.*)

SOLNESS (*approaching*). Are you searching for anything?

HILDA. No, I'm merely looking at all these things. (*Turns*) Perhaps I mustn't?

SOLNESS. Oh, by all means.

HILDA. Is it you that writes in this great ledger?

SOLNESS. No, it's my book-keeper.

HILDA. Is it a woman?

SOLNESS (*smiles*). Yes.

HILDA. One you employ here, in your office?

SOLNESS. Yes.

HILDA. Is she married?

SOLNESS. No, she's single.

HILDA. Ah!

SOLNESS. But I believe she's soon going to be married.

HILDA. That's a good thing for *her*.

SOLNESS. But not such a good thing for *me*. For then I shall have nobody to help me.

HILDA. Can't you get hold of some one else who'll do just as well?

SOLNESS. Perhaps *you* would stop here and—and write in the ledger?

HILDA (*measures him with a glance*). Yes, I daresay! No, thanks —nothing of that sort for *me*—(*She again strolls across the room, and sits down in the rocking-chair.* SOLNESS *too goes to the table.* HILDA *continues*):—for there must surely be other things than *that* to be done here. (*Looks smilingly at him.*) Don't you think so too?

SOLNESS. Of course. First and foremost, I suppose you want to make a round of the shops, and get yourself up in the height of fashion.

HILDA (*amused*). No, I think I shall let *that* alone.

SOLNESS. Indeed!

HILDA. For you must know I've run through all my money.

SOLNESS (*laughs*). Neither trunk nor money, then!

HILDA. Neither one nor the other. But never mind—it doesn't matter now.

SOLNESS. Come now, I like you for *that.*

HILDA. Only for *that?*

SOLNESS. For that among other things. (*Sits in the arm-chair.*) Is your father alive still?

HILDA. Yes, father's alive.

SOLNESS. Perhaps you're thinking of studying here?

HILDA. No, that hadn't occurred to me.

SOLNESS. But I suppose you'll be stopping for some time.

HILDA. That must depend upon circumstances.
(*She sits awhile rocking herself and looking at him, half seriously, half with a suppressed smile. Then she takes off her hat and puts it on the table in front of her.*)

HILDA. Mr. Solness!

SOLNESS. Well?

HILDA. Have you a very bad memory?

SOLNESS. A bad memory? No, not that I'm aware of.

HILDA. Then haven't you anything to say to me about what happened up there?

SOLNESS (*in momentary surprise*). Up at Lysanger? (*Indifferently*) Why, it was nothing much to talk about, it seems to me.

HILDA (*looks reproachfully at him*). How can you sit there and say such things?

SOLNESS. Well, then, *you* talk to *me* about it.

HILDA. When the tower was finished, we had grand doings in the town.

SOLNESS. Yes, I sha'n't easily forget that day.

HILDA (*smiles*). Won't you? That's good of you!

SOLNESS. Good?

HILDA. There was music in the churchyard—and many, many hundreds of people. We school girls were dressed in white; and we all carried flags.

SOLNESS. Ah yes, those flags—I can tell you I remember them!

HILDA. Then you climbed up over the scaffolding, straight to the very top; and you had a great wreath with you; and you hung that wreath right away up on the weathercock.

SOLNESS (*curtly interrupting*). I always did that in those days. It's an old custom.

HILDA. It was so wonderfully thrilling to stand below and look up at you. Fancy, if he should fall over! He—the master builder himself!

SOLNESS (*as if to lead her away from the subject*). Yes, yes, yes, that might very well have happened, too. For one of those white-frocked little devils,—she went on in such a way, and screamed up at me so——

HILDA (*sparkling with pleasure*). "Hurrah for Mr. Solness!" Yes!

SOLNESS. —and waved and flourished with her flag so that I—so that it almost made me giddy to look at it.

HILDA (*in a lower voice, seriously*). That little devil—that was *I*.

SOLNESS (*fixes his eyes steadily upon her*). I'm sure of that now. It *must* have been you.

HILDA (*lively again*). Oh, it was so gloriously thrilling! I couldn't have believed there was a builder in the whole world that could have built such a tremendously high tower. And then, that you yourself should stand at the very top of it, as large as life! And that you shouldn't be the least bit dizzy! It was that above everything that made one—made one dizzy to think of.

SOLNESS. How could you be so certain that I wasn't——?

HILDA (*scouting the idea*). No indeed! Oh no! I knew that instinctively. For if you had been you could never have stood up there and sung.

SOLNESS (*looks at her in astonishment*). Sung? Did I sing?

HILDA. Yes, I should think you did.

SOLNESS (*shakes his head*). I've never sung a note in my life.

HILDA. Yes, you sang then. It sounded like harps in the air.

SOLNESS (*thoughtfully*). This is very strange—all this.

HILDA (*is silent awhile, looks at him and says in a low voice*): But then,—it was after that—that the *real* thing happened.

SOLNESS. The real thing?

HILDA (*sparkling with vivacity*).

Yes, I surely don't need to remind you of *that*?

SOLNESS. Oh yes, do remind me a little of *that,* too.

HILDA. Don't you remember that a great dinner was given in your honor at the Club?

SOLNESS. Yes, to be sure. It must have been the same afternoon, for I left the place next morning.

HILDA. And from the Club you were invited to come round to our house to supper.

SOLNESS. Quite right, Miss Wangel. It's wonderful how all these trifles have impressed themselves on your mind.

HILDA. Trifles! I like that! Perhaps it was a trifle, too, that I was *alone* in the room when you came in?

SOLNESS. *Were* you alone?

HILDA (*without answering him*). You didn't call me a little devil *then.*

SOLNESS. No, I probably didn't.

HILDA. You said I was lovely in my white dress, and that I looked like a little princess.

SOLNESS. I've no doubt you did, Miss Wangel.—And besides—I was feeling so buoyant and free that day——

HILDA. And then you said that when I grew up I should be *your* princess.

SOLNESS (*laughing a little*). Dear, dear—did I say *that* too?

HILDA. Yes, you did. And when I asked how long I should have to wait, you said that you would come again in ten years—like a troll—and carry me off—to Spain or some such place. And you promised you would buy me a kingdom there.

SOLNESS (*as before*). Yes, after a good dinner one doesn't haggle about the halfpence. But did I really *say* all that?

HILDA (*laughs to herself*). Yes. And you told me, too, what the kingdom was to be called.

SOLNESS. Well, what was it?

HILDA. It was to be called the kingdom of Orangia,* you said.

SOLNESS. Well, that was an appetizing name.

HILDA. No, I didn't like it a bit; for it seemed as though you wanted to make game of me.

SOLNESS. I'm sure *that* can't have been my intention.

HILDA. No, I should hope not—considering what you did next——

SOLNESS. What in the world did I do next?

HILDA. Well, that's the finishing touch, if you've forgotten *that* too.

* In the original "Appelsinia," "appelsin" meaning "orange."

I should have thought one couldn't help remembering such a thing as that.

SOLNESS. Yes, yes, just give me a hint, and then perhaps–Well?

HILDA (*looks fixedly at him*). You came and kissed me, Mr. Solness.

SOLNESS (*open-mouthed, rising from his chair*). *I* did!

HILDA. Yes, indeed you did. You took me in both your arms, and bent my head back, and kissed me –many times.

SOLNESS. Now, really, my dear Miss Wangel—!

HILDA (*rises*). You surely don't mean to deny it?

SOLNESS. Yes, I do. I deny it altogether!

HILDA (*looks scornfully at him*). Oh, indeed!
(*She turns and goes slowly close up to the stove, where she remains standing motionless, her face averted from him, her hands behind her back. Short pause.*)

SOLNESS (*goes cautiously up behind her*). Miss Wangel!—

HILDA (*is silent and does not move*).

SOLNESS. Don't stand there like a statue. You must have dreamt all this. (*Lays his hand on her arm.*) Now just listen—

HILDA (*makes an impatient movement with her arm*).

SOLNESS (*as a thought flashes upon him*). Or—! Wait a moment! There is something under all this, you may depend!

HILDA (*does not move*).

SOLNESS (*in a low voice, but with emphasis*). I must have *thought* all that. I must have *wished* it–have *willed* it–have *longed* to do it. And then—. May not that be the explanation?

HILDA (*is still silent*).

SOLNESS (*impatiently*). Oh very well, deuce take it all–then I *did* do it, I suppose!

HILDA (*turns her head a little, but without looking at him*). Then you admit it now?

SOLNESS. Yes–whatever you like.

HILDA. You came and put your arms round me?

SOLNESS. Oh, yes.

HILDA. And bent my head back?

SOLNESS. Very far back.

HILDA. And kissed me?

SOLNESS. Yes, I did.

HILDA. Many times?

SOLNESS. As many as ever you like.

HILDA (*turns quickly towards him*

and has once more the sparkling expression of gladness in her eyes). Well, you see, I got it out of you at last!

SOLNESS *(with a slight smile)*. Yes—just think of my forgetting such a thing as that.

HILDA *(again a little sulky, retreats from him)*. Oh, you've kissed so many people in your time, I suppose.

SOLNESS. No, you mustn't think *that* of me.
(HILDA *seats herself in the arm-chair.* SOLNESS *stands and leans against the rocking-chair.*)

SOLNESS *(looks observantly at her)*. Miss Wangel?

HILDA. Yes?

SOLNESS. How *was* it now? What came of all this—between us two?

HILDA. Why, nothing more came of it. You know that quite well. For then the other guests came in, and then—bah!

SOLNESS. Quite so! The others came in. To think of my forgetting *that* too!

HILDA. Oh, you haven't really forgotten anything: you're only a little ashamed of it all. I'm sure one doesn't forget things of that kind.

SOLNESS. No, one would suppose not.

HILDA *(lively again, looks at him)*. Perhaps you've even forgotten what day it was?

SOLNESS. What day?

HILDA. Yes, on what day did you hang the wreath on the tower? Well? Tell me at once!

SOLNESS. H'm—I confess I've forgotten the particular day. I only know it was ten years ago. Some time in the autumn.

HILDA *(nods her head slowly several times)*. It was ten years ago—on the 19th of September.

SOLNESS. Yes, it must have been about that time. Fancy your remembering that too! *(Stops)* But wait a moment—! Yes—it's the 19th of September today.

HILDA. Yes, it is; and the ten years are gone. And you didn't come—as you had promised me.

SOLNESS. Promised you? Threatened, I suppose you mean?

HILDA. I don't think there was any sort of threat in *that*.

SOLNESS. Well then, a little bit of a hoax.

HILDA. Was that all you wanted to do? To hoax me?

SOLNESS. Well, or to have a little joke with you! Upon my soul I don't recollect. But it must have been something of that kind; for you were a mere child then.

HILDA. Oh, perhaps I wasn't quite

such a child either. Not such a mere chit as you imagine.

SOLNESS (*looks searchingly at her*). Did you really and seriously expect me to come again?

HILDA (*conceals a half-teasing smile*). Yes, indeed! I did expect *that* of you.

SOLNESS. That I should come back to your home, and take you away with me?

HILDA. Just like a troll—yes.

SOLNESS. And make a princess of you?

HILDA. That's what you promised.

SOLNESS. And give you a kingdom as well?

HILDA (*looks up at the ceiling*). Why not? Of course it needn't have been an actual, every-day sort of a kingdom.

SOLNESS. But something else just as good?

HILDA. Yes, at least as good. (*Looks at him a moment.*) I thought if you could build the highest church-towers in the world, you could surely manage to raise a kingdom of one sort or another as well.

SOLNESS (*shakes his head*). I can't quite make you out, Miss Wangel.

HILDA. Can't you? To me it seems all so simple.

SOLNESS. No, I can't make up my mind whether you mean all you say, or are simply having a joke with me.

HILDA (*smiles*). Hoaxing you, perhaps? I, too?

SOLNESS. Yes, exactly. Hoaxing—both of us. (*Looks at her.*) Is it long since you found out that I was married?

HILDA. I've known it all along. Why do you ask me *that?*

SOLNESS (*lightly*). Oh, well, it just occurred to me. (*Looks earnestly at her, and says in a low voice*): What have you come for?

HILDA. I want my kingdom. The time is up.

SOLNESS (*laughs involuntarily*). What a girl you are!

HILDA (*gayly*). Out with my kingdom, Mr. Solness! (*Raps with her fingers.*) The kingdom on the table!

SOLNESS (*pushing the rocking-chair nearer and sitting down*). Now, seriously speaking—what have you come for? What do you really want to do here?

HILDA. Oh, first of all, I want to go round and look at all the things that you've built.

SOLNESS. That will give you plenty of exercise.

HILDA. Yes, I know you've built a tremendous lot.

SOLNESS. I have indeed—especially of late years.

HILDA. Many church-towers among the rest? Immensely high ones?

SOLNESS. No. I build no more church-towers now. Nor churches either.

HILDA. What *do* you build then?

SOLNESS. Homes for human beings.

HILDA (*reflectively*). Couldn't you build a little—a little bit of a church-tower over these homes as well?

SOLNESS (*starting*). What do you mean by *that?*

HILDA. I mean—something that points—points up into the free air. With the vane at a dizzy height.

SOLNESS (*pondering a little*). Strange that you should say *that* —for that's just what I'm most anxious to do.

HILDA (*impatiently*). Then why don't you do it?

SOLNESS (*shakes his head*). No, the people won't have it.

HILDA. Fancy their not wanting it!

SOLNESS (*more lightly*). But now I'm building a new home for myself—just opposite here.

HILDA. For yourself?

SOLNESS. Yes. It's almost finished. And on that there's a tower.

HILDA. A high tower?

SOLNESS. Yes.

HILDA. Very high?

SOLNESS. No doubt people will say that it's too high—too high for a dwelling-house.

HILDA. I'll go out and look at that tower the first thing tomorrow morning.

SOLNESS (*sits with his hand under his cheek and gazes at her*). Tell me, Miss Wangel—what is your name? Your Christian name, I mean?

HILDA. Why, Hilda, of course.

SOLNESS (*as before*). Hilda? Ah?

HILDA. Don't you remember *that?* You called me Hilda yourself—that day when you misbehaved.

SOLNESS. Did I really?

HILDA. But then you said *"little* Hilda"; and I didn't like that.

SOLNESS. Oh, you didn't like that, Miss Hilda?

HILDA. No, not at such a time as that. But—"Princess Hilda"—that will sound very well, I think.

SOLNESS. Very well indeed. Princess Hilda of—of—what was to be the name of the kingdom?

HILDA. Pooh! I won't have anything to do with *that* stupid kingdom.

I've set my heart upon quite a different one!

SOLNESS (*has leaned back in the chair, still gazing at her*). Isn't it strange——? The more I think of it now, the more it seems to me as though I had gone about all these years torturing myself with—h'm——

HILDA. With what?

SOLNESS. With the effort to recover something—some experience, which I seemed to have forgotten. But I never had the least inkling of what it would be.

HILDA. You should have tied a knot in your pocket-handkerchief, Mr. Solness.

SOLNESS. In that case, I should simply have had to go racking my brains to discover what the knot could mean.

HILDA. Oh yes, I suppose there are trolls of *that* kind in the world, too.

SOLNESS (*rises slowly*). What a good thing it is that *you* have come to me now.

HILDA (*looks deeply into his eyes*). *Is* it a good thing?

SOLNESS. For I've been so lonely here. I've been gazing so helplessly at it all. (*In a lower voice*) I must tell you—I've begun to be so afraid —so terribly afraid of the younger generation.

HILDA (*with a little snort of contempt*). Pooh—is the younger generation a thing to be afraid of?

SOLNESS. It is indeed. And that's why I've locked and barred myself in. (*Mysteriously*) I tell you the younger generation will one day come and thunder at my door! They'll break in upon me!

HILDA. Then I should say you ought to go out and open the door to the younger generation.

SOLNESS. Open the door?

HILDA. Yes. Let them come in to you on friendly terms, as it were.

SOLNESS. No, no, no! The younger generation—it means retribution, you see. It comes, as if under a new banner, heralding the turn of fortune.

HILDA (*rises, looks at him, and says with a quivering twitch of her lips*). Can *I* be of any use to you, Mr. Solness?

SOLNESS. Yes, you can indeed! For you, too, come—under a new banner, it seems to me. Youth marshalled against youth——!
(DR. HERDAL *comes in by the hall-door.*)

DR. HERDAL. What—you and Miss Wangel here still?

SOLNESS. Yes. We've had no end of things to talk about.

HILDA. Both old and new.

DR. HERDAL. Have you really?

HILDA. Oh, it has been the greatest fun. For Mr. Solness—he has such a miraculous memory. All the least little details he remembers instantly. (MRS. SOLNESS *enters by the door on the right.*)

MRS. SOLNESS. Well, Miss Wangel, your room is quite ready for you now.

HILDA. Oh, how kind you are to me!

SOLNESS (*to* MRS. SOLNESS). The nursery?

MRS. SOLNESS. Yes, the middle one. But first let us go in to supper.

SOLNESS (*nods to* HILDA). Hilda shall sleep in the nursery.

MRS. SOLNESS (*looks at him*). Hilda?

SOLNESS. Yes, Miss Wangel's name is Hilda. I knew her when she was a child.

MRS. SOLNESS. Did you really, Halvard? Well, shall we go? Supper is on the table.

(*She takes* DR. HERDAL'S *arm and goes out with him to the right.* HILDA *has meanwhile been collecting her travelling things.*)

HILDA (*softly and rapidly to* SOLNESS). Is it true, what you said? *Can* I be of use to you?

SOLNESS (*takes the things from her*). *You* are the very one I have most needed.

HILDA (*looks at him with happy, wondering eyes and clasps her hands*). Oh heavens, how lovely—!

SOLNESS (*eagerly*). What—?

HILDA. Then I *have* my kingdom!

SOLNESS (*involuntarily*). Hilda—!

HILDA (*again with the quivering twitch of her lips*). *Almost*–I was going to say.
(*She goes out to the right.* SOLNESS *follows her.*)

ACT TWO

A prettily furnished small drawing-room in the house of SOLNESS. *In the back, a glass-door leading out to the veranda and garden. The right-hand corner is cut off transversely by a large bay-window, in which are flower-stands. The left-hand corner is similarly cut off by a transverse wall, in which is a small door papered like the wall. On each side, an ordinary door. In front, on the right, a console table with a large mirror over it. Well-filled stands of plants and flowers. In front, on the left, a sofa with a table and chairs. Further back, a bookcase. Well forward in the room, before the bay-window, a small table and some chairs. It is early in the day.*

SOLNESS *sits by the little table with* RAGNAR BROVIK'S *portfolio open in front of him. He is turning the drawings over and closely examining some of them.* MRS. SOLNESS *walks about noiselessly with a small watering-pot, attending to her flowers. She is dressed in black as before. Her hat, cloak and parasol lie on a chair near the mirror. Unobserved by her,* SOLNESS *now and again follows her with his eyes. Neither of them speaks.*

KAIA FOSLI *enters quietly by the door on the left.*

SOLNESS (*turns his head and says in an off-hand tone of indifference*). Well, is that you?

KAIA. I merely wished to let you know I've come.

SOLNESS. Yes, yes, that's all right. Hasn't Ragnar come too?

KAIA. No, not yet. He had to wait a little while to see the doctor. But he's coming presently to hear——

SOLNESS. How is the old man to-day?

KAIA. Not well. He begs you to excuse him, for he must keep his bed to-day.

SOLNESS. Quite so; by all means let him rest. But now, get to your work.

KAIA. Yes. (*Pauses at the door.*) Do you wish to speak to Ragnar when he comes?

SOLNESS. No—I don't know that I've anything special to say to him.
(KAIA *goes out again to the left.* SOLNESS *remains seated, turning over the drawings.*)

MRS. SOLNESS (*over beside the plants*). I wonder if *he* isn't going to die now, as well?

SOLNESS (*looks up at her*). As well as who?

MRS. SOLNESS (*without answering*). Yes, yes—depend upon it, Halvard, old Brovik's going to die too. You'll see that he will.

SOLNESS. My dear Aline, oughtn't you to go out for a little walk?

MRS. SOLNESS. Yes, I suppose I ought to. (*She continues to attend to the flowers.*)

SOLNESS (*bending over the drawings*). Is she still asleep?

MRS. SOLNESS (*looking at him*). Is it Miss Wangel you're sitting there thinking about?

SOLNESS (*indifferently*). I just happened to recollect her.

MRS. SOLNESS. Miss Wangel was up long ago.

SOLNESS. Oh, was she?

MRS. SOLNESS. When I went in to see her, she was busy putting her things in order.
(*She goes in front of the mirror and slowly begins to put on her hat.*)

SOLNESS (*after a short pause*). So we've found a use for one of our nurseries after all, Aline.

MRS. SOLNESS. Yes, we have.

SOLNESS. That seems to me better than to have them all standing empty.

MRS. SOLNESS That emptiness is dreadful; you're right there.

SOLNESS (*closes the portfolio, rises and approaches her*). You'll find that we shall get on far better after this, Aline. Things will be more comfortable. Life will be easier—especially for *you.*

MRS. SOLNESS (*looks at him*). After this?

SOLNESS. Yes, believe me, Aline——

MRS. SOLNESS. Do you mean—because *she* has come here?

SOLNESS (*checking himself*). I mean, of course—when once we've moved into the new house.

MRS. SOLNESS (*takes her cloak*). Ah, do you think so, Halvard? Will it be better then?

SOLNESS. I can't think otherwise. And surely you think so too?

MRS. SOLNESS. I think nothing at all about the new house.

SOLNESS (*cast down*). It's hard for me to hear you say that; for you know it's mainly for your sake that I've built it.
(*He offers to help her on with her cloak.*)

MRS. SOLNESS (*evades him*). The fact is, you do far too much for my sake.

SOLNESS (*with a certain vehemence*). No, no, you really mustn't say that, Aline. I can't bear to hear you say such things.

MRS. SOLNESS. Very well, then I won't say it, Halvard.

SOLNESS. But I stick to what *I* said. You'll see that things'll be easier for you in the new place.

MRS. SOLNESS. Oh heavens—easier for me—!

SOLNESS (*eagerly*). Yes, indeed they will! You may be quite sure of that! For you see—there'll be so very, very much there that'll remind you of your own home——

MRS. SOLNESS. The home that used to be father's and mother's—and that was burnt to the ground——

SOLNESS (*in a low voice*). Yes, yes, my poor Aline. That was a terrible blow for you.

MRS. SOLNESS (*breaking out in lamentation*). You may build as much as ever you like, Halvard—you can never build up again a real home for *me!*

SOLNESS (*crosses the room*). Well, in Heaven's name, let us talk no more about it then.

MRS. SOLNESS. We're not in the habit of talking about it. For you always put the thought away from you——

SOLNESS (*stops suddenly and looks at her*). Do I? And why should I do *that*? Put the thought away from me?

MRS. SOLNESS. Oh yes, Halvard, I understand very well. You're so anxious to spare me—and to find excuses for me too—as much as ever you can.

SOLNESS (*with astonishment in his eyes*). *You!* Is it *you*—yourself, that you're talking about, Aline?

MRS. SOLNESS. Yes, who else should it be but myself?

SOLNESS (*involuntarily, to himself*). *That* too!

MRS. SOLNESS. As for the old house, I wouldn't mind so much about that. When once misfortune was in the air—why——

SOLNESS. Ah, you're right there. Misfortune will have its way—as the saying goes.

MRS. SOLNESS. But it's what came of the fire—the dreadful thing that followed—! *That* is the thing! That, that, that!

SOLNESS (*vehemently*). Don't think about *that*, Aline.

MRS. SOLNESS. Ah, that's exactly what I can't help thinking about. And now, at last, I must speak about it, too; for I don't seem able to bear it any longer. And then never to be able to forgive myself——

SOLNESS (*vehemently*). Yourself?

MRS. SOLNESS. Yes, for I had duties on both sides—both towards you and towards the little ones. I ought to have hardened myself—not to have let the horror take such hold upon me, nor the grief for the burning of my home. (*Wrings her hands.*) Oh, Halvard, if I'd only had the strength!

SOLNESS (*softly, much moved, comes closer*). Aline—you must promise me never to think these thoughts any more. Promise me that, dear!

MRS. SOLNESS. Oh, promise, promise! One can promise anything.

SOLNESS (*clenches his hands and crosses the room*). Oh, but this is hopeless, hopeless! Never a ray of sunlight! Not so much as a gleam of brightness to light up our home!

MRS. SOLNESS. This *is* no home, Halvard.

SOLNESS. Oh no, you may well say that. (*Gloomily*) And God knows whether you're not right in saying that it will be no better for us in the new house, either.

MRS. SOLNESS. It will never be any better. Just as empty—just as desolate—there as here.

SOLNESS (*vehemently*). Why in all the world have we built it then? Can you tell me that?

MRS. SOLNESS. No; you must answer that question for yourself.

SOLNESS (*glances suspiciously at

her). What do you mean by *that,* Aline?

MRS. SOLNESS. What do I mean?

SOLNESS. Yes, in the devil's name! You said it so strangely—as if you had some hidden meaning in it.

MRS. SOLNESS. No, indeed, I assure you——

SOLNESS (*comes closer*). Oh, come now—I know what I know. I've both my eyes and my ears about me, Aline—you may depend upon that!

MRS. SOLNESS. Why, what are you talking about? What is it?

SOLNESS (*places himself in front of her*). Do you mean to say you don't find a kind of lurking, hidden meaning in the most innocent word I happen to say?

MRS. SOLNESS. *I*, do you say? I do that?

SOLNESS (*laughs*). Ho-ho-ho! It's natural enough, Aline! When you've a sick man on your hands——

MRS. SOLNESS (*anxiously*). *Sick?* Are you ill, Halvard?

SOLNESS (*violently*). A half-mad man, then! A crazy man! Call me what you will.

MRS. SOLNESS (*feels gropingly for a chair and sits down*). Halvard—for God's sake——

SOLNESS. But you're wrong, both you and the doctor. That's not what's the matter with me.

(*He walks up and down the room.* MRS. SOLNESS *follows him anxiously with her eyes. Finally he goes up to her.*)

SOLNESS (*calmly*). In reality there's nothing whatever wrong with me.

MRS. SOLNESS. No, there isn't, is there? But then what is it that troubles you so?

SOLNESS. Why this, that I often feel ready to sink under this terrible burden of debt——

MRS. SOLNESS. Debt, do you say? But you owe no one anything, Halvard!

SOLNESS (*softly, with emotion*). I owe a boundless debt to you—to you—to you, Aline.

MRS. SOLNESS (*rises slowly*). What is behind all this? You may just as well tell me at once.

SOLNESS. But there *is* nothing behind it. I've never done you any wrong—not wittingly and wilfully, at any rate. And yet—and yet it seems as though a crushing debt rested upon me and weighed me down.

MRS. SOLNESS. A debt to me?

SOLNESS. Chiefly to you.

MRS. SOLNESS. Then you are—ill after all, Halvard.

SOLNESS (*gloomily*). I suppose I must be—or not far from it. (*Looks towards the door to the right, which is opened at this moment.*) Ah, now it grows lighter.

(HILDA WANGEL *comes in. She has made some alterations in her dress, and let down her skirt.*)

HILDA. Good-morning, Mr. Solness!

SOLNESS (*nods*). Slept well?

HILDA. Quite deliciously! As if in a cradle. Oh—I lay and stretched myself like—like a princess!

SOLNESS (*smiles a little*). You were thoroughly comfortable then?

HILDA. I should think so.

SOLNESS. And no doubt you dreamed, too.

HILDA. Yes, I did. But *that* was horrid.

SOLNESS. Indeed?

HILDA. Yes, for I dreamed I was falling over a frightfully high, sheer precipice. Do you never have that kind of dream?

SOLNESS. Oh yes—now and then——

HILDA. It's tremendously thrilling—when you fall and fall——

SOLNESS. It seems to make one's blood run cold.

HILDA. Do you draw your legs up under you while you're falling?

SOLNESS. Yes, as high as ever I can.

HILDA. So do I.

MRS. SOLNESS (*takes her parasol*). I must go into town now, Halvard. (*To* HILDA) And I'll try to get one or two things that may be of use to you.

HILDA (*making a motion to throw her arms round her neck*). Oh, you dear, sweet Mrs. Solness! You're really much too kind to me! Frightfully kind——

MRS. SOLNESS (*deprecatingly, freeing herself*). Oh, far from it. It's only my duty, so I'm very glad to do it.

HILDA (*offended, pouts*). But really, I think I'm quite fit to be seen in the streets—now that I've put my dress to rights. Or do you think I'm not?

MRS. SOLNESS. To tell you the truth, I think people would stare at you a little.

HILDA (*contemptuously*). Pooh! Is that all? That only amuses me.

SOLNESS (*with suppressed ill-humor*). Yes, but people might take it into their heads that *you* were mad too, you see.

HILDA. Mad? Are there so many mad people here in town, then?

SOLNESS (*points to his own forehead*). Here you see *one* at all events.

HILDA. You—Mr. Solness!

MRS. SOLNESS. Oh, don't talk like that, my dear Halvard!

SOLNESS. Haven't you noticed *that* yet?

HILDA. No, I certainly haven't. (*Reflects and laughs a little.*) And yet —perhaps in one single thing.

SOLNESS. Ah, do you hear *that*, Aline?

MRS. SOLNESS. What is that one single thing, Miss Wangel?

HILDA. No, I won't say.

SOLNESS. Oh yes, do!

HILDA. No thanks—I'm not so mad as all that.

MRS. SOLNESS. When you and Miss Wangel are alone, I daresay she'll tell you, Halvard.

SOLNESS. Ah—you think she will?

MRS. SOLNESS. Oh yes, certainly. For you've known her so well in the past. Ever since she was a child —you tell me.
(*She goes out by the door on the left.*)

HILDA (*after a little while*). Does you wife dislike me very much?

SOLNESS. Did you think you noticed anything of the kind?

HILDA. Didn't you notice it yourself?

SOLNESS (*evasively*). Aline has become exceedingly shy with strangers of late years.

HILDA. Has she really?

SOLNESS. But if only you could get to know her thoroughly—Ah, she's so nice—and so kind—and so good at heart.

HILDA (*impatiently*). But if she's all that—what made her say that about her duty?

SOLNESS. Her duty?

HILDA. She said that she would go out and buy something for me, because it was her *duty*. Oh I can't bear that ugly, horrid word!

SOLNESS. Why not?

HILDA. It sounds so cold, and sharp, and stinging. Duty—duty—duty. Don't *you* think so, too? Doesn't it seem to sting you?

SOLNESS. H'm—haven't thought much about it.

HILDA. Yes, it does. And if she's so nice—as you say she is—why should she talk in that way?

SOLNESS. But, good Lord, what would you have had her say, then?

HILDA. She might have said she would do it because she had taken a tremendous fancy to me. She might have said something like that—something really warm and cordial, you understand.

SOLNESS (*looks at her*). Is that how you'd like to have it?

HILDA. Yes, precisely.
(*She wanders about the room, stops at the bookcase and looks at the books.*)

HILDA. What a lot of books you have!

SOLNESS. Yes, I've got together a good many.

HILDA. Do you read them all, too?

SOLNESS. I used to try to. Do you read much?

HILDA. No, never! I've given it up. For it all seems so irrelevant.

SOLNESS. That's just my feeling.
(HILDA *wanders about a little, stops at the small table, opens the portfolio and turns over the contents.*)

HILDA. Are all these drawings yours?

SOLNESS. No, they're drawn by a young man whom I employ to help me.

HILDA. Some one you've taught?

SOLNESS. Oh yes, no doubt he's learnt something from me, too.

HILDA (*sits down*). Then I suppose he's very clever. (*Looks at a drawing.*) Isn't he?

SOLNESS. Oh, he's not bad. For *my* purpose——

HILDA. Oh yes—I'm sure he's frightfully clever.

SOLNESS. Do you think you can see that in the drawings?

HILDA. Pooh—these scrawlings! But if he's been learning from *you*——

SOLNESS. Oh, as far as that goes—there are plenty of people here that have learnt from *me*, and have come to little enough for all that.

HILDA (*looks at him and shakes her head*). No, I can't for the life of me understand how you can be so stupid.

SOLNESS. Stupid? Do you think I'm so very stupid?

HILDA. Yes, I do indeed. If you're content to go about here teaching all these people——

SOLNESS (*with a slight start*). Well, and why not?

HILDA (*rises, half-serious, half-laughing*). No indeed, Mr. Solness! What can be the good of that? No one but yourself should be allowed to build. You should stand quite alone—do it all yourself. Now you know it.

SOLNESS (*involuntarily*). Hilda——!

HILDA. Well!

SOLNESS. How in the world did that come into your head?

HILDA. Do you think I'm so very far wrong then?

SOLNESS. No, that's not what I mean. But now I'll tell you something.

HILDA. Well?

SOLNESS. I keep on—incessantly—in silence and alone—brooding on that very thought.

HILDA. Yes, that seems to me perfectly natural.

SOLNESS (*looks somewhat searchingly at her*). Perhaps you've already noticed it?

HILDA. No, indeed I haven't.

SOLNESS. But just now—when you said you thought I was—off my balance? In one thing you said——

HILDA. Oh, I was thinking of something quite different.

SOLNESS. What was it?

HILDA. I'm not going to tell you.

SOLNESS (*crosses the room*). Well, well—as you please. (*Stops at the bow-window.*) Come here and I'll show you something.

HILDA (*approaching*). What is it?

SOLNESS. Do you see—over there in the garden——?

HILDA. Yes?

SOLNESS (*points*). Right above the great quarry——?

HILDA. That new house, you mean?

SOLNESS. The one that's being built, yes. Almost finished.

HILDA. It seems to have a very high tower.

SOLNESS. The scaffolding is still up.

HILDA. Is that your new house?

SOLNESS. Yes.

HILDA. The house you're soon going to move into?

SOLNESS. Yes.

HILDA (*looks at him*). Are there nurseries in *that* house, too?

SOLNESS. Three, as there are here.

HILDA. And no child.

SOLNESS. And there never will be one.

HILDA (*with a half-smile*). Well, isn't it just as I said——

SOLNESS. That——?

HILDA. That you *are* a little—a little mad after all.

SOLNESS. Was that what you were thinking of?

HILDA. Yes, of all the empty nurseries I slept in.

SOLNESS (*lowers his voice*). We *have* had children—Aline and I.

HILDA (*looks eagerly at him*). Have you——?

SOLNESS. Two little boys. They were of the same age.

HILDA. Twins, then.

SOLNESS. Yes, twins. It's eleven or twelve years ago now.

HILDA (*cautiously*). And so both of them—? You have lost both the twins, then?

SOLNESS (*with quiet emotion*). We only kept them about three weeks. Or scarcely so much. (*Bursts forth*) Oh, Hilda, I can't tell you what a good thing it is for me that you have come! For now at last I have some one I can talk to!

HILDA. Can't you talk to—to *her*, too?

SOLNESS. Not about this. Not as I want to talk and must talk. (*Gloomily*) And not about so many other things, too.

HILDA (*in a subdued voice*). Was that all you meant when you said you needed me?

SOLNESS. That was mainly what I meant—at all events, yesterday. For to-day I'm not so sure. (*Breaking off*) Come here and let us sit down, Hilda. Sit there on the sofa—so that you can look into the garden. (HILDA *seats herself in the corner of the sofa.* SOLNESS *brings a chair closer.*) Would you like to hear about it?

HILDA. Yes, I shall love to sit and listen to you.

SOLNESS (*sits down*). Then I'll tell you all about it.

HILDA. Now I can see both the garden and you, Mr. Solness. So now, tell away! Go on!

SOLNESS (*points towards the bow-window*). Out there on the rising ground—where you see the new house—

HILDA. Yes?

SOLNESS. Aline and I lived there in the first years of our married life. There was an old house up there that had belonged to her mother; and we inherited it, and the whole of the great garden with it.

HILDA. Was there a tower on *that* house, too?

SOLNESS. No, nothing of the kind. From the outside it looked like a great, dark, ugly wooden box; but, all the same, it was snug and comfortable enough inside.

HILDA. Then did you pull down the ramshackle old place?

SOLNESS. No, it was burnt down.

HILDA. The whole of it?

SOLNESS. Yes.

HILDA. Was that a great misfortune for you?

SOLNESS. That depends on how you look at it. As a builder, the fire was the making of me—

HILDA. Well, but—?

SOLNESS. It was just after the birth of the two little boys.

HILDA. The poor little twins, yes.

SOLNESS. They came healthy and

bonny into the world. And they were growing too—you could see the difference from day to day.

HILDA. Little children do grow quickly at first.

SOLNESS. It was the prettiest sight in the world to see Aline lying with the two of them in her arms. But then came the night of the fire——

HILDA (*excitedly*). What happened? Do tell me! Was any one burnt?

SOLNESS. No, not that. Every one got safe and sound out of the house——

HILDA. Well, and what then?

SOLNESS. The fright had shaken Aline terribly. The alarm—the escape—the break-neck hurry—and then the ice-cold night air—for they had to be carried out just as they lay—both she and the little ones——

HILDA. Was it too much for them?

SOLNESS. Oh no, *they* stood it well enough. But Aline fell into a fever, and it affected her milk. She would insist on nursing them herself; because it was her duty, she said. And both our little boys, they—(*clenching his hands*)—they—oh!

HILDA. They didn't get over *that*?

SOLNESS. No, *that* they didn't get over. That was how we lost them.

HILDA. It must have been terribly hard for you.

SOLNESS. Hard enough for me; but ten times harder for Aline. (*Clenching his hands in suppressed fury*) Oh, that such things should be allowed to happen here on earth! (*Shortly and firmly*) From the day I lost them, I had no heart for building churches.

HILDA. Didn't you like building the church tower in our town?

SOLNESS. I didn't like it. I know how free and happy I felt when that tower was finished.

HILDA. *I* know that, too.

SOLNESS. And now I shall never—never build anything of that sort again! Neither churches nor church towers.

HILDA (*nods slowly*). Nothing but houses for people to live in.

SOLNESS. Homes for human beings, Hilda.

HILDA. But homes with high towers and pinnacles upon them.

SOLNESS. If possible. (*Adopts a lighter tone*) Well, you see, as I said, that fire was the making of me—as a builder, I mean.

HILDA. Why don't you call yourself an architect, like the others?

SOLNESS. I haven't been systematically enough taught for that. Most of what I know, I've found out for myself.

HILDA. But you succeeded all the same.

SOLNESS. Yes, thanks to the fire. I laid out almost the whole of the garden in villa-lots; and *there* I was able to build entirely after my own heart. So I came to the front with a rush.

HILDA (*looks keenly at him*). You must surely be a very happy man —situated as you are.

SOLNESS (*gloomily*). Happy? Do *you* say that, too—like all the rest of them?

HILDA. Yes, I should say you must be. If you could only get the two little children out of your head——

SOLNESS (*slowly*). The two little children—they're not so easy to forget, Hilda.

HILDA (*somewhat uncertainly*). Do you still feel their loss so much—after all these years?

SOLNESS (*looks fixedly at her, without replying*). A happy man, you said——

HILDA. Well now, *are* you not happy—in other respects?

SOLNESS (*continues to look at her*). When I told you all this about the fire—h'm——

HILDA. Well?

SOLNESS. Was there not one special thought that you—that you seized upon?

HILDA (*reflects in vain*). No. What thought should that be?

SOLNESS (*with subdued emphasis*). It was simply and solely by that fire that I was enabled to build homes for human beings. Cosy, comfortable, bright homes, where father and mother and the whole troop of children can live in safety and gladness, feeling what a happy thing it is to be alive in the world —and most of all to belong to each other—in great things and in small.

HILDA (*ardently*). Well, and isn't it a great happiness for you to be able to build such beautiful homes?

SOLNESS. The price, Hilda! The terrible price I had to pay for it!

HILDA. But can you *never* get over that?

SOLNESS. No. That I might build homes for others, I had to forego—to forego for all time—the home that might have been my own. I mean a home for a troop of children—and for father and mother, too.

HILDA (*cautiously*). But need you have done that? For all time, you say?

SOLNESS (*nods slowly*). *That* was the price of this happiness that people talk about. (*Breathes heavily*) This happiness—h'm—this happiness was not to be bought any cheaper, Hilda.

HILDA (*as before*). But may it not come right even yet?

SOLNESS. Never in this world—never. That is another consequence of the fire—and of Aline's illness afterwards.

HILDA (*looks at him with an indefinable expression*). And yet you build all these nurseries?

SOLNESS (*seriously*). Have you never noticed, Hilda, how the impossible—how it seems to beckon and cry aloud to one?

HILDA. (*reflecting*). The impossible? (*With animation*) Yes, indeed! Is that how *you* feel too?

SOLNESS. Yes, I do.

HILDA. Then there must be—a little of the troll in you too?

SOLNESS. Why of the troll?

HILDA. What would *you* call it, then?

SOLNESS (*rises*). Well, well, perhaps you're right. (*Vehemently*) But how can I help turning into a troll, when this is how it always goes with me in everything—in everything!

HILDA. How do you mean?

SOLNESS (*speaking low, with inward emotion*). Mark what I say to you, Hilda. All that I have succeeded in doing, building, creating—all the beauty, security, cheerful comfort—ay, and magnificence too—(*clenches his hands*)—oh, isn't it terrible even to think of——!

HILDA. *What* is so terrible?

SOLNESS. That all this I have to make up for, to pay for—not in money, but in human happiness. And not with my own happiness only, but with other people's too. Yes, yes, do you see that, Hilda? That is the price which my position as an artist has cost me—and others. And every single day I have to look on while the price is paid for me anew. Over again, and over again—and over again forever.

HILDA (*rises and looks steadily at him*). Now I can see you're thinking of—of *her*.

SOLNESS. Yes, mainly of Aline. For Aline—she, too, had her vocation in life, just as much as I had mine. (*His voice quivers.*) But her vocation has had to be stunted, and crushed, and shattered—in order that mine might force its way to—to a sort of great victory. For you must know that Aline—she, too, had a turn for building.

HILDA. She? For building?

SOLNESS (*shakes his head*). Not houses, and towers, and spires—not such things as I work away at——

HILDA. Well, but *what*, then?

SOLNESS (*softly, with emotion*). For building up the souls of little children, Hilda. For building up children's souls in perfect balance, and in noble and beautiful forms. For enabling them to soar up into erect and full-grown human souls. That was Aline's talent. And there it all lies now—unused and unusable forever—of no earthly service to any one—just like the ruins left by a fire.

HILDA. Yes, but even if this were so—

SOLNESS. It *is* so! It *is* so! I know it.

HILDA. Well, but in any case it's not *your* fault.

SOLNESS (*fixes his eyes on her, and nods slowly*). Ah, *that* is the great, the terrible question. *That* is the doubt that's gnawing me—night and day.

HILDA. That?

SOLNESS. Yes. Suppose the fault *was* mine—in a certain sense.

HILDA. Your fault! The fire!

SOLNESS. All of it; the whole thing. And yet, perhaps—I mayn't have had anything to do with it.

HILDA (*looks at him with a troubled expression*). Oh, Mr. Solness, if you can talk like that, I'm afraid you must be—ill, after all.

SOLNESS. H'm—I don't think I shall ever be of quite sound mind on that point.
(RAGNAR BROVIK *cautiously opens the little door in the left-hand corner.* HILDA *comes forward.*)

RAGNAR (*when he sees* HILDA). Oh —I beg pardon, Mr. Solness— (*He makes a movement to withdraw.*)

SOLNESS. No, no, don't go. Let's get it over.

RAGNAR. Oh, yes—if only we could.

SOLNESS. I hear your father is no better?

RAGNAR. Father is fast growing weaker—and therefore I beg and implore you to write a few kind words for me on one of the plans! Something for father to read before he—

SOLNESS (*vehemently*). I won't hear anything more about those drawings of yours!

RAGNAR. Have you looked at them?

SOLNESS. Yes, I have.

RAGNAR. And they're good for nothing? And *I* am good for nothing, too?

SOLNESS (*evasively*). Stay here with me, Ragnar. You shall have everything your own way. And then you can marry Kaia, and live at your ease—and—and happily too, who knows? Only don't think of building on your own account.

RAGNAR. Well, well, then I must go home and tell father what you say —I promised I would. *Is* this what I am to tell father—before he dies?

SOLNESS (*with a groan*). Oh tell him—tell him what you will for me. Best to say nothing at all to him! (*With a sudden outburst*) I *cannot* do anything else, Ragnar!

RAGNAR. May I have the drawings to take with me?

SOLNESS. Yes, take them—take them by all means! They're lying there on the table.

RAGNAR (*goes to the table*). Thanks.

HILDA (*puts her hand on the portfolio*). No, no; leave them here.

SOLNESS. Why?

HILDA. Because I want to look at them too.

SOLNESS. But you *have* been— (*To* RAGNAR) Well, leave them here, then.

RAGNAR. Very well.

SOLNESS. And go home at once to your father.

RAGNAR. Yes, I suppose I must.

SOLNESS (*as if in desperation*). Ragnar—you *must* not ask me to do what's beyond my power! Do you hear, Ragnar? You *must* not!

RAGNAR. No, no. I beg your pardon—
(*He bows, and goes out by the corner door.* HILDA *goes over and sits down on a chair near the mirror.*)

HILDA (*looks angrily at* SOLNESS). That was a very ugly thing to do.

SOLNESS. Do *you* think so, too?

HILDA. Yes, it was horribly ugly—and hard and bad and cruel as well.

SOLNESS. Oh, you don't understand my position.

HILDA. All the same—. No, you oughtn't to be like that.

SOLNESS. You said yourself, only just now, that no one but *I* ought to be allowed to build.

HILDA. *I* may say such things—but *you* mayn't.

SOLNESS. I most of all, surely, who have paid so dear for my position.

HILDA. Oh, yes—with what you call domestic comfort—and that sort of thing.

SOLNESS. And with my peace of soul into the bargain.

HILDA (*rising*). Peace of soul! (*With feeling*) Yes, yes, you're right in that! Poor Mr. Solness—you fancy that—

SOLNESS (*with a quiet, chuckling laugh*). Just sit down again, Hilda, and I'll tell you something funny.

HILDA (*sits down; with intent interest*). Well?

SOLNESS. It sounds such a ludicrous little thing; for, you see, the whole story turns upon nothing but a crack in a chimney.

HILDA. No more than that?

SOLNESS. No, not to begin with.
(*He moves a chair nearer to* HILDA *and sits down.*)

HILDA (*impatiently, taps on her knee*). Well, now for the crack in the chimney!

SOLNESS. I had noticed the split in the flue long, long before the fire. Every time I went up into the attic,

I looked to see if it was still there.

HILDA. And it was?

SOLNESS. Yes; for no one else knew about it.

HILDA. And you said nothing?

SOLNESS. Nothing.

HILDA. And didn't think of repairing the flue either.

SOLNESS. Oh yes, I thought about it—but never got any further. Every time I intended to set to work, it seemed just as if a hand held me back. Not to-day, I thought—to-morrow; and nothing ever came of it.

HILDA. But why did you keep putting it off like that?

SOLNESS. Because I was revolving something in my mind. (*Slowly, and in a low voice*) Through that little black crack in the chimney I might, perhaps, force my way upwards—as a builder.

HILDA (*looking straight in front of her*). That must have been thrilling.

SOLNESS. Almost irresistible—quite irresistible. For at that time it appeared to me a perfectly simple and straightforward matter. I would have had it happen in the winter time—a little before midday. I was to be out driving Aline in the sleigh. The servants at home would have made a huge fire in the stove.

HILDA. For, of course, it was to be bitterly cold that day?

SOLNESS. Rather biting, yes—and they would want Aline to find it thoroughly snug and warm when she came home.

HILDA. I suppose she's very chilly by nature?

SOLNESS. She *is*. And as we drove home, we were to see the smoke.

HILDA. Only the smoke?

SOLNESS. The smoke first. But when we came up to the garden gate, the whole of the old timber-box was to be a rolling mass of flames.—That's how I wanted it to be, you see.

HILDA. Oh, why, *why* couldn't it have happened so!

SOLNESS. You may well say that, Hilda.

HILDA. Well, but now listen, Mr. Solness. Are you perfectly certain that the fire was caused by that little crack in the chimney?

SOLNESS. No, on the contrary—I'm perfectly certain that the crack in the chimney had nothing whatever to do with the fire.

HILDA. What!

SOLNESS. It has been clearly ascertained that the fire broke out in a clothes-cupboard—in a totally different part of the house.

HILDA. Then what's all this nonsense you're talking about the crack in the chimney?

SOLNESS. May I go on talking to you a little, Hilda?

HILDA. Yes, if you'll only talk sensibly,——

SOLNESS. I'll try to. (*He moves his chair nearer.*)

HILDA. Out with it, then, Mr. Solness.

SOLNESS (*confidentially*). Don't you agree with me, Hilda, that there exist special, chosen people who have been endowed with the power and faculty of *desiring* a thing, *craving* for a thing, willing a thing—so persistently and so—so inexorably—that at last it *has* to happen? Don't you believe that?

HILDA (*with an indefinable expression in her eyes*). If that is so, we shall see one of these days—whether *I* am one of the chosen.

SOLNESS. It's not one's self alone that can do such great things. Oh, no—the helpers and the servers—they must do their part too, if it's to be of any good. But they never come of themselves. One has to call upon them very persistently—inwardly, you understand.

HILDA. What are these helpers and servers?

SOLNESS. Oh, we can talk about that some other time. For the present, let us keep to this business of the fire.

HILDA. Don't you think the fire would have happened all the same—even if you hadn't wished for it?

SOLNESS. If the house had been old Knut Brovik's, it would never have burnt down so conveniently for *him.* I'm sure of that; for he doesn't know how to call for the helpers—no, nor for the servers, either. (*Rises in agitation.*) So you see, Hilda—it's my fault, after all, that the lives of the two little boys had to be sacrificed. And do you think it isn't my fault, too, that Aline has never been the woman she should and might have been—and that she most longed to be?

HILDA. Yes, but if it's all the work of those helpers and servers——?

SOLNESS. *Who* called for the helpers and servers? It was *I!* And they came and obeyed my will. (*In increasing excitement*) *That's* what good people call having the luck on your side; but I must tell you what this sort of luck feels like! It feels like a great raw place here on my breast. And the helpers and servers keep on flaying pieces of skin off other people in order to close my sore. But still the sore is not healed—never, never! Oh, if you knew how it can sometimes gnaw and burn.

HILDA (*looks attentively at him*). You *are* ill, Mr. Solness. Very ill, I almost think.

SOLNESS. Say *mad*; for that's what you mean.

HILDA. No, I don't think there's much amiss with your intellect.

SOLNESS. With *what,* then? Out with it!

HILDA. I wonder whether you weren't sent into the world with a sickly conscience.

SOLNESS. Say *mad;* for that's what devilry is that?

HILDA. I mean that your conscience is feeble—too delicately built, as it were—hasn't strength to take a grip of things—to lift and bear what's heavy.

SOLNESS (*growls*). H'm! May I ask, then, what sort of a conscience one ought to have?

HILDA. I should like *your* conscience to be thoroughly robust.

SOLNESS. Indeed? Robust, eh? Is your own conscience robust?

HILDA. Yes, I think it is. I've never noticed that it wasn't.

SOLNESS. It hasn't been put very severely to the test, I should think.

HILDA (*with a quivering of the lips*). Oh, it wasn't such a simple matter to leave father—I'm so awfully fond of him.

SOLNESS. Dear me! for a month or two——

HILDA. I don't think I shall ever go home again.

SOLNESS. Never? Then why did you leave him?

HILDA (*half-seriously, half-banteringly*). Have you forgotten again that the ten years are up?

SOLNESS. Oh, nonsense. Was anything wrong at home? Eh?

HILDA (*quite seriously*). It *was* this something within me that drove and spurred me here—and allured and attracted me, too.

SOLNESS (*eagerly*). There we have it! There we have it, Hilda! There's a troll in you too, as in me. For it's the troll in one, you see—it's *that* that calls to the powers outside us. And then you *must* give in—whether you will or no.

HILDA. I almost think you're right, Mr. Solness.

SOLNESS (*walks about the room*). Oh, there are devils innumerable abroad in the world, Hilda, that one never *sees!*

HILDA. Devils, too?

SOLNESS (*stops*). Good devils and bad devils; light-haired devils and black-haired devils. If only you could always tell whether it's the light or the dark ones that have got hold of you! (*Paces about.*) Ho, ho! Then it would be simple enough!

HILDA (*follows him with her eyes*). Or if one had a really vigorous, radiantly healthy conscience—so that one *dared* to do what one *would.*

SOLNESS (*stops beside the console table*). I believe, now, that most people are just as puny creatures as I am in this respect.

HILDA. I shouldn't wonder.

SOLNESS (*leaning against the table*). In the sagas— Have you read any of the old sagas?

HILDA. Oh yes! When I used to read books, I——

SOLNESS. In the sagas you read about vikings, who sailed to foreign lands, and plundered and burned and killed men——

HILDA. And carried off women——

SOLNESS ——and kept them in captivity——

HILDA. ——took them home in their ships——

SOLNESS. ——and behaved to them like—like the very worst of trolls.

HILDA (*looks straight before her with a half-veiled look*). I think *that* must have been thrilling.

SOLNESS (*with a short, deep laugh*). To carry off women, eh?

HILDA. To *be* carried off.

SOLNESS (*looks at her a moment*). Oh, indeed.

HILDA (*as if breaking the thread of conversation*). But what made you speak of these vikings, Mr. Solness?

SOLNESS. Because *those* fellows must have had robust consciences, if you like! When they got home again they could eat and drink, and be as happy as children. And the women, too! They often wouldn't leave them on any account. Can you understand that, Hilda?

HILDA. Those women I can understand exceedingly well.

SOLNESS. Oho! Perhaps you could do the same yourself?

HILDA. Why not?

SOLNESS. Live—of your own free will—with a ruffian like that?

HILDA. If it was a ruffian I had come to love——

SOLNESS. *Could* you come to love a man like that?

HILDA. Good heavens, you know very well one can't choose whom one's going to love.

SOLNESS (*looks meditatively at her*). Oh no, I suppose it's the troll within one that's responsible for that.

HILDA (*half laughing*). And all those blessed devils, that *you* know so well—both the light-haired and the dark-haired ones.

SOLNESS (*quietly and warmly*). Then I hope with all my heart that the devils will choose carefully for you, Hilda.

HILDA. For me they *have* chosen already—once and for all.

SOLNESS (*looks earnestly at her*). Hilda, you are like a wild bird of the woods.

HILDA. Far from it. I don't hide myself away under the bushes.

SOLNESS. No, no. There's rather something of the bird of prey in you.

HILDA. That's nearer it—perhaps. (*Very vehemently*) And why not a bird of prey? Why shouldn't *I* go a-hunting—I, as well as the rest? Carry off the prey I want—if I can only get my claws into it, and have my own way with it.

SOLNESS. Hilda,—do you know what you are?

HILDA. Yes, I suppose I'm a strange sort of bird.

SOLNESS. No. You are like a dawning day. When I look at you, I seem to be looking towards the sunrise.

HILDA. Tell me, Mr. Solness—are you certain that you've never called me to you?—Inwardly, you know?

SOLNESS (*softly and slowly*). I almost think I must have.

HILDA. What did you want with me?

SOLNESS. You are the younger generation, Hilda.

HILDA (*smiles*). That younger generation that you're so afraid of.

SOLNESS (*nods slowly*). And which, in my heart, I yearn towards so deeply.

(HILDA *rises, goes to the little table, and fetches* RAGNAR BROVIK'S *portfolio.*)

HILDA (*holds out the portfolio to him*). We were talking of these drawings——

SOLNESS (*shortly, waving them away*). Put those things away! I've seen enough of them.

HILDA. Yes, but you have to write your approval on them.

SOLNESS. Write my approval on them? Never!

HILDA. But the poor old man is lying at death's door! Can't you give him and his son this pleasure before they're parted? And perhaps he might get the commission to carry them out, too.

SOLNESS. Yes, that's just what he would get. He's made sure of that—has my fine gentleman!

HILDA. Then good heavens—if that's so—can't you tell the least little bit of a lie for once?

SOLNESS. A lie? (*Raging*) Hilda—take those devil's drawings out of my sight!

HILDA (*draws the portfolio a little nearer to herself*). Well, well, well—don't bite me.—You talk of trolls—but I think you go on like a troll yourself. (*Looks round*) Where do you keep your pen and ink?

SOLNESS. There's nothing of the sort in here.

HILDA (*goes towards the door*). But in the office where that young lady is——

SOLNESS. Stay where you are, Hilda! —I ought to tell a lie, you say. Oh yes, for the sake of his old father I might well do that—for in my time I've crushed him, trodden him under foot——

HILDA. Him, too?

SOLNESS. I needed room for myself. But this Ragnar—he must on no account be allowed to come to the front.

HILDA. Poor fellow, there's surely no fear of that. If he has nothing in him——

SOLNESS (*comes closer, looks at her, and whispers*): If Ragnar Brovik comes to the front he will strike *me* to the earth. Crush me—as I crushed his father.

HILDA. Crush you? Has he the ability for that?

SOLNESS. Yes, you may depend upon it *he* has the ability! He is the younger generation that stands ready to knock at my door—to make an end of Halvard Solness.

HILDA (*looks at him with quiet reproach*). And yet you would bar him out. Fie, Mr. Solness!

SOLNESS. The fight I have been fighting has cost heart's blood enough.—And I'm afraid, too, that the helpers and servers won't obey me any longer.

HILDA. Then you must go ahead without them. There's nothing else for it.

SOLNESS. It's hopeless, Hilda. The luck is bound to turn. A little sooner or a little later. Retribution is inexorable.

HILDA (*in distress putting her hands over her ears*). Don't talk like that! Do you want to kill me? To take from me what is more than my life?

SOLNESS. And what is that?

HILDA. The longing to see you great. To see you, with a wreath in your hand, high, high up upon a church-tower. (*Calm again*) Come, out with your pencil now. You must have a pencil about you!

SOLNESS (*takes out his pocket-book*). I have one here.

HILDA (*puts the portfolio on the sofa-table*). Very well. Now let us two sit down here, Mr. Solness. (SOLNESS *seats himself at the table.*)

HILDA (*behind him leaning over the back of the chair*). And now we'll write on the drawings. We must write very, very nicely and cordially—for this horrid Ruar—or whatever his name is.

SOLNESS (*writes a few words, turns his head and looks at her*). Tell me one thing, Hilda.

HILDA. Yes?

SOLNESS. If you've been waiting for me all these ten years——

HILDA. What then?

SOLNESS. Why have you never written to me? Then I could have answered you.

HILDA (*hastily*). No, no, no! That was just what I didn't want.

SOLNESS. Why not?

HILDA. I was afraid the whole thing might fall to pieces.—But we were going to write on the drawings, Mr. Solness.

SOLNESS. So we were.

HILDA (*bends forward and looks over his shoulder while he writes*). Mind now! kindly and cordially! Oh how I hate—how I hate this Ruald——

SOLNESS (*writing*). Have you never really cared for anyone, Hilda?

HILDA (*harshly*). What do you say?

SOLNESS. Have you never cared for any one?

HILDA. For any one else, I suppose you mean?

SOLNESS (*looks up at her*). For any one else, yes. Have you never? In all these ten years? Never?

HILDA. Oh yes, now and then. When I was perfectly furious with you for not coming.

SOLNESS. Then you did take an interest in other people, too?

HILDA. A little bit—for a week or so. Good heavens, Mr. Solness, you surely know how such things come about.

SOLNESS. Hilda—what is it you've come for?

HILDA. Don't waste time in talking. The poor old man might go and die in the mean time.

SOLNESS. Answer me, Hilda. What do you want of me?

HILDA. I want my kingdom.

SOLNESS. H'm——
(*He gives a rapid glance towards the door on the left, and then goes on writing on the drawings. At the same moment* MRS. SOLNESS *enters; she has some packages in her hand.*)

MRS. SOLNESS. Here are a few things I've got for you, Miss Wangel. The large parcels will be sent later on.

HILDA. Oh, how very, very kind of you!

MRS. SOLNESS. Only my simple duty. Nothing more than that.

SOLNESS (*reading over what he has written*). Aline!

MRS. SOLNESS. Yes?

SOLNESS. Did you notice whether the—the book-keeper was out there?

MRS. SOLNESS. Yes, of course, *she* was there.

SOLNESS (*puts the drawings in the portfolio*). H'm——

MRS. SOLNESS. She was standing at the desk, as she always is—when *I* go through the room.

SOLNESS (*rises*). Then I'll give this to her, and tell her that——

HILDA (*takes the portfolio from him*). Oh, no, let me have the pleasure of doing that! (*Goes to the door, but turns*) What's her name?

SOLNESS. Her name is Miss Fosli.

HILDA. Pooh, that sounds so cold. Her Christian name, I mean?

SOLNESS. Kaia—I believe.

HILDA (*opens the door and calls out*). Kaia, come in here! Make haste! Mr. Solness wants to speak to you.
(KAIA FOSLI *appears at the door.*)

KAIA (*looking at him in alarm*). Here I am.

HILDA (*handing her the portfolio*). See here, Kaia? You can take these home; Mr. Solness has written on them now.

KAIA. Oh, at last!

SOLNESS. Give them to the old man as soon as you can.

KAIA. I will go straight home with them.

SOLNESS. Yes, do. Now Ragnar will have a chance of building for himself.

KAIA. Oh, may he come and thank you for all——

SOLNESS (*harshly*). I won't have any thanks. Tell him *that* from me.

KAIA. Yes, I will——

SOLNESS. And tell him at the same time that henceforward I don't require his services—nor yours either.

KAIA (*softly and quiveringly*). Not mine either?

SOLNESS. You will have other things to think of now, and to attend to; and that's a very good thing for you. Well, go home with the drawings now, Miss Fosli. Quickly! Do you hear?

KAIA (*as before*). Yes, Mr. Solness. (*She goes out.*)

MRS. SOLNESS. Heavens! what deceitful eyes she has.

SOLNESS. She? That poor little creature?

MRS. SOLNESS. Oh—I can see what I can see, Halvard.——Are you really dismissing them?

SOLNESS. Yes.

MRS. SOLNESS. Her as well?

SOLNESS. Wasn't that what you wished?

MRS. SOLNESS. But how can you get on without *her*——? Oh well, no doubt you have some one else in reserve, Halvard.

HILDA (*playfully*). Well, *I* for one am not the person to stand at that desk.

SOLNESS. Never mind, never mind—it'll be all right, Aline. Now all you have to do is to think about moving into our new home—as quickly as you can. This evening we'll hang up the wreath—(*turns to* HILDA)—right on the very pinnacle of the tower. What do you say to that, Miss Hilda?

HILDA (*looks at him with sparkling eyes*). It'll be splendid to see you so high up once more.

SOLNESS. Me!

MRS. SOLNESS. For Heaven's sake, Miss Wangel, don't imagine such a thing! My husband!—when he always gets so dizzy!

HILDA. *He* get dizzy! No, I know quite well he doesn't.

MRS. SOLNESS. Oh, yes, indeed he does.

HILDA. But I've seen him with my own eyes right up at the top of a high church-tower.

MRS. SOLNESS. Yes, I hear people talk of that; but it's utterly impossible——

SOLNESS (*vehemently*). Impossible—impossible, yes! But there I stood all the same!

MRS. SOLNESS. Oh, how can you say so, Halvard? Why, you can't even bear to go out on the second-story balcony here. You've always been like that.

SOLNESS. You may perhaps see something different this evening.

MRS. SOLNESS (*in alarm*). No, no, no! Please God, I shall never see that! I'll write at once to the doctor—and I'm sure he won't let you do it.

SOLNESS. Why, Aline——!

MRS. SOLNESS. Oh, you know you're ill, Halvard. This *proves* it! Oh God—Oh God!
(*She goes hastily out to the right.*)

HILDA (*looks intently at him*). Is it so, or is it not?

SOLNESS. That I turn dizzy?

HILDA. That *my* master builder *dares* not—*cannot*—climb as high as he builds?

SOLNESS. Is that the way you look at it?

HILDA. Yes.

SOLNESS. I believe there's scarcely a corner in me safe from you.

HILDA (*looks towards the bow-window*). Up there, then. Right up there——

SOLNESS (*approaches her*). You might have the topmost chamber in the tower, Hilda—there you might live like a princess.

HILDA (*indefinably, between earnest and jest*). Yes, that's what you promised me.

SOLNESS. *Did* I really?

HILDA. Fie, Mr. Solness! You said, I should be a princess, and that you would give me a kingdom. And then you went and——Well!

SOLNESS (*cautiously*). Are you quite certain that this is not a dream—

a fancy, that has fixed itself in your mind?

HILDA (*sharply*). Do you mean that you didn't do it?

SOLNESS. I scarcely know myself. (*More softly*) But now I know *so much* for certain, that I——

HILDA. That you——? Say it at once!

SOLNESS. ——that I *ought* to have done it.

HILDA (*in a bold outburst*). Don't tell me *you* can ever be dizzy!

SOLNESS. This evening, then, we'll hang up the wreath—Princess Hilda.

HILDA (*with a bitter curve of the lips*). Over your new home, yes.

SOLNESS. Over the new house, which will never be a *home* for *me*.
(*He goes out through the garden door.*)

HILDA (*looks straight in front of her with a far-away expression, and whispers to herself. The only words audible are*): ——frightfully thrilling——

ACT THREE

A large, broad veranda attached to SOLNESS's *dwelling-house. Part of the house, with outer door leading to the veranda, is seen to the left. A railing along the veranda to the right. At the back, from the end of the veranda, a flight of steps leads down to the garden below. Tall old trees in the garden spread their branches over the veranda and towards the house. Far to the right, in among the trees, a glimpse is caught of the lower part of the new villa, with scaffolding round so much as is seen of the tower. In the background the garden is bounded by an old wooden fence. Outside the fence, a street with low, tumble-down cottages.*

Evening sky with sun-lit clouds.

On the veranda a garden bench stands along the wall of the house, and in front of the bench a long table. On the other side of the table, an arm-chair and some stools. All the furniture is of wicker-work.

MRS. SOLNESS, *wrapped in a large white crape shawl, sits resting in the arm-chair and gazes over to the right. Shortly after,* HILDA WANGEL *comes up the flight of steps from the garden. She is dressed as in the last act and wears her hat. She has in her bodice a little nosegay of small common flowers.*

MRS. SOLNESS (*turning her head a little*). Have you been round the garden, Miss Wangel?

HILDA. Yes, I've been taking a look at it.

MRS. SOLNESS. And found some flowers too, I see.

HILDA. Yes, indeed. There are such heaps of them in among the bushes.

MRS. SOLNESS. Are there really? Still? You see I scarcely ever go there.

HILDA (*closer*). What! Don't you take a run down into the garden every day, then?

MRS. SOLNESS (*with a faint smile*). I don't "run" anywhere, nowadays.

HILDA. Well, but don't you go down now and then, to look at all the lovely things there?

MRS. SOLNESS. It has all become so strange to me. I'm almost afraid to see it again.

HILDA. Your own garden!

MRS. SOLNESS. I don't feel that it is *mine* any longer.

HILDA. What do you mean——?

MRS. SOLNESS. No, no, it *is* not—not as it was in my mother's and father's time. They have taken away so much—so much of the garden, Miss Wangel. Fancy—they've parcelled it out—and built houses for strangers—people that I don't know. And *they* can sit and look in upon me from their windows.

HILDA (*with a bright expression*). Mrs. Solness?

MRS. SOLNESS. Yes?

HILDA. May I stay here with you a little?

MRS. SOLNESS. Yes, by all means, if you care to.

(HILDA *moves a stool close to the arm-chair and sits down.*)

HILDA. Ah—one can sit here and sun oneself like a cat.

MRS. SOLNESS (*lays her hand softly on* HILDA'S *neck*). It's nice of you to be willing to sit with *me*. I thought you wanted to go in to my husband.

HILDA. What should I want with him?

MRS. SOLNESS. To help him, I thought.

HILDA. No, thanks. And besides, he's not in. He's over there with his workmen. But he looked so fierce that I didn't dare to talk to him.

MRS. SOLNESS. He's so kind and gentle in reality.

HILDA. *He!*

MRS. SOLNESS. You don't really know him yet, Miss Wangel.

HILDA (*looks affectionately at her*). Are you pleased at the thought of moving over to the new house?

MRS. SOLNESS. I *ought* to be pleased; for it's what Halvard wants——

HILDA. Oh, not just on that account, surely.

MRS. SOLNESS. Yes, yes, Miss Wangel; for it's simply my duty to submit myself to *him*. But very often it's dreadfully difficult to force one's mind to obedience.

HILDA. Yes, *that* must be difficult indeed.

MRS. SOLNESS. I can tell you it is—when one has so many faults as I have——

HILDA. When one has gone through so much as *you* have——

MRS. SOLNESS. How do you know about that?

HILDA. Your husband told me.

MRS. SOLNESS. To me he very seldom mentions these things.—Yes, I can tell you I've gone through more than enough trouble in my life, Miss Wangel.

HILDA (*looks sympathetically at her and nods slowly*). Poor Mrs. Solness. First of all there was the fire——

MRS. SOLNESS (*with a sigh*). Yes, everything that was *mine* was burnt.

HILDA. And then came what was worse.

MRS. SOLNESS (*looking inquiringly at her*). Worse?

HILDA. The worst of all.

MRS. SOLNESS. What do you mean?

HILDA (*softly*). You lost the two little boys.

MRS. SOLNESS. Oh yes, the boys. But you see, *that* was a thing apart. That was a dispensation of Providence; and in such things one can only bow in submission—yes, and be thankful, too.

HILDA. Then are you so?

MRS. SOLNESS. Not always, I'm sorry to say. I know well enough that it's my duty—but all the same I *cannot*.

HILDA. No, no, I think that's only natural.

MRS. SOLNESS. And often and often I have to remind myself that it was a righteous punishment for me—

HILDA. Why?

MRS. SOLNESS. Because I hadn't fortitude enough in misfortune.

HILDA. But I don't see that——

MRS. SOLNESS. Oh, no, no, Miss Wangel—don't talk to me any more about the two little boys. We ought to feel nothing but joy in thinking of *them;* for they are so happy—so happy now. No, it's the *small* losses in life that cut one to the heart—the loss of all that other people look upon as almost nothing.

HILDA (*lays her arms on* MRS. SOLNESS' *knees and looks at her affectionately*). Dear Mrs. Solness—tell me what things you mean!

MRS. SOLNESS. As I say, only little things. All the old portraits were burnt on the walls. And all the old silk dresses were burnt, that had belonged to the family for generations and generations. And all mother's and grandmother's lace—that was burnt too. And only think—the jewels too! (*Sadly*) And then all the dolls.

HILDA. The dolls?

MRS. SOLNESS (*choking with tears*). I had nine lovely dolls.

HILDA. And *they* were burnt too?

MRS. SOLNESS. All of them. Oh, it was hard—so hard for me.

HILDA. Had you put by all these dolls, then? Ever since you were little?

MRS. SOLNESS. I hadn't put them by. The dolls and I had gone on living together.

HILDA. After you were grown up?

MRS. SOLNESS. Yes, long after that.

HILDA. After you were married too?

MRS. SOLNESS. Oh yes, indeed. So long as he didn't see it.—But they were all burnt up, poor things. No one thought of saving them. Oh, it's so miserable to think of. You mustn't laugh at me, Miss Wangel.

HILDA. I'm not laughing in the least.

MRS. SOLNESS. For you see, in a certain sense there was life in them, too. I carried them under my heart—like little unborn children.

(DR. HERDAL, *with his hat in his hand, comes out through the door and observes* MRS. SOLNESS *and* HILDA.)

DR. HERDAL. Well, Mrs. Solness, so you're sitting out here catching cold?

MRS. SOLNESS. I find it so pleasant and warm here to-day.

DR. HERDAL. Yes, yes. But is there anything going on here? I got a note from you.

MRS. SOLNESS (*rises*). Yes, there's something I must talk to you about.

DR. HERDAL. Very well; then perhaps we'd better go in. (*To* HILDA) Still in your mountaineering dress, Miss Wangel?

HILDA (*gayly, rising*). Yes—in full uniform! But to-day I'm not going climbing and breaking my neck. We two will stop quietly below and look on, doctor.

DR. HERDAL. What are we to look on at?

MRS. SOLNESS (*softly, in alarm, to* HILDA). Hush, hush—for God's sake! He's coming! Try to get that idea out of his head. And let us be friends, Miss Wangel. Don't you think we can?

HILDA (*throws her arms impetuously round* MRS. SOLNESS' *neck*). O, if we only could!

MRS. SOLNESS (*gently disengages herself*). There, there, there! There he comes, doctor. Let me have a word with you.

DR. HERDAL. Is it about *him?*

MRS. SOLNESS. Yes, to be sure it's about him. Do come in.
(*She and the doctor enter the house. Next moment* SOLNESS *comes up from the garden by the flight of steps. A serious look comes over* HILDA'S *face.*)

SOLNESS (*glances at the house-door, which is closed cautiously from within*). Have you noticed, Hilda, that as soon as I come, she goes?

HILDA. I've noticed that as soon as you come, you make her go.

SOLNESS. Perhaps so. But I cannot help it. (*Looks observantly at her.*) Are you cold, Hilda? I think you look so.

HILDA. I've just come up out of a tomb.

SOLNESS. What do you mean by *that?*

HILDA. That I've got chilled through and through, Mr. Solness.

SOLNESS (*slowly*). I believe I understand—

HILDA. What brings you up here just now?

SOLNESS. I caught sight of you from over there.

HILDA. But then you must have seen her too?

SOLNESS. I knew she would go at once if I came.

HILDA. Is it very painful for you that she should avoid you in this way?

SOLNESS. In one sense, it's a relief as well.

HILDA. Not to have her before your eyes?

SOLNESS. Yes.

HILDA. Not to be always seeing how heavily the loss of the little boys weighs upon her?

SOLNESS. Yes. Chiefly that.
(HILDA *drifts across the veranda with her hands behind her back, stops at the railing and looks out over the garden.*)

SOLNESS (*after a short pause*). Did you have a long talk with her?
(HILDA *stands motionless and does not answer.*)

SOLNESS. Had you a long talk, I asked?
(HILDA *is silent as before.*)

SOLNESS. What was she talking about, Hilda?
(HILDA *continues silent.*)

SOLNESS. Poor Aline! I suppose it was about the little boys.

HILDA (*a nervous shudder runs through her; then she nods hurriedly once or twice*).

SOLNESS. She will never get over it

—never in this world. (*Approaches her.*) Now you're standing there again like a statue; just as you stood last night.

HILDA (*turns and looks at him with great serious eyes*). I am going away.

SOLNESS (*sharply*). Going away!

HILDA. Yes.

SOLNESS. But I won't allow you to.

HILDA. What am I to do *here* now?

SOLNESS. Simply to *be* here, Hilda!

HILDA (*measures him with a look*). Oh, thank you. You know it wouldn't end there.

SOLNESS (*without consideration*). So much the better.

HILDA (*vehemently*). I *can't* do any harm to one I *know!* I can't take away anything that belongs to her.

SOLNESS. Who wants you to do that?

HILDA (*continuing*). A stranger, yes! for that's quite a different thing. A person I've never set eyes on. But one that I've come into close contact with——! No! Oh no! Ugh!

SOLNESS. Yes, but I never proposed you should.

HILDA. Oh, Mr. Solness, you know quite well what the end of it would be. And that's why I'm going away.

SOLNESS. And what's to become of me when you're gone? What shall I have to live for *then*?—After that?

HILDA (*with the indefinable look in her eyes*). It's surely not so hard for *you*. You have your duties to her. Live for those duties.

SOLNESS. Too late. These powers—these—these——

HILDA. ——devils——

SOLNESS. Yes, these devils. And the troll within me as well—they have drawn all the life-blood out of her. (*Laughs in desperation*) They did it for my *happiness*. Yes, yes! (*Sadly*) And now she's dead—for my sake. And I am chained alive to a dead woman. (*In wild anguish*) *I—I* who *cannot* live without joy in life!

(HILDA *walks round the table and seats herself on the bench with her elbows on the table, and her head supported by her hands.*)

HILDA (*sits and looks at him awhile*). What will you build next?

SOLNESS (*shakes his head*). I don't believe I shall build much more.

HILDA. Not those cozy, happy homes for mother and father, and for the troop of children?

SOLNESS. I wonder whether there will be any use for such homes in the times that are coming.

HILDA. Poor Mr. Solness! And you have gone all these ten years—and staked your whole life—on that alone.

SOLNESS. Yes, you may well say so, Hilda.

HILDA (*with an outburst*). Oh, it all seems to me so foolish—so foolish!

SOLNESS. All what?

HILDA. Not to be able to grasp at your own happiness—at your own life! Merely because some one you know happens to stand in the way!

SOLNESS. One whom you have no right to set aside.

HILDA. I wonder whether one really *hasn't* the right? And yet, and yet——. Oh! if one could only sleep the whole thing away!
(*She lays her arms flat down on the table, rests the left side of her head on her hand and shuts her eyes.*)

SOLNESS (*turns the arm-chair and sits down at the table*). Had *you* a cosy, happy home—up with your father, Hilda?

HILDA (*without stirring, answers as if half asleep*). I had only a cage.

SOLNESS. And you're determined not to return to it?

HILDA (*as before*). The wild bird never wants to go into the cage.

SOLNESS. Rather range through the free air—

HILDA (*still as before*). The bird of prey loves to range—

SOLNESS (*lets his eyes rest on her*). If only one had the viking-spirit in life——

HILDA (*in her usual voice; opens her eyes but does not move*). And the other thing? Say what *that* was!

SOLNESS. A robust conscience.
(HILDA *sits upon the bench with animation. Her eyes have once more the sparkling expression of gladness.*)

HILDA (*nods to him*). *I* know what you're going to build next!

SOLNESS. Then you know more than I do, Hilda.

HILDA. Yes, builders are such stupid people.

SOLNESS. What is it to be then?

HILDA (*nods again*). The castle.

SOLNESS. What castle?

HILDA. *My* castle, of course.

SOLNESS. Do you want a castle now?

HILDA. Don't you owe me a kingdom, I'd like to know?

SOLNESS. You say I do.

HILDA. Well—you admit you owe me this kingdom. And you can't have a kingdom without a royal castle, I should think!

SOLNESS (*more and more ani-*

mated). Yes, they usually go together.

HILDA. Good! Then build it for me this moment!

SOLNESS (*laughing*). Must you have that on the instant, too?

HILDA. Yes, to be sure! For the ten years are up now, and I'm not going to wait any longer. So—out with the castle, Mr. Solness!

SOLNESS. It's no light matter to owe you anything, Hilda.

HILDA. You should have thought of that before. It's too late now. So—(*tapping the table*)—the castle on the table! It's *my* castle. I will have it *at once!*

SOLNESS (*more seriously, leans over towards her, with his arms on the table*). What sort of castle have you imagined, Hilda?
(*Her expression becomes more and more veiled. She seems gazing inwards at herself.*)

HILDA (*slowly*). My castle shall stand on a height—on a very great height—with a clear outlook on all sides, so that I can see far—far around.

SOLNESS. And no doubt it's to have a high tower?

HILDA. A tremendously high tower. And at the very top of the tower there shall be a balcony. And I will stand out upon it——

SOLNESS (*involuntarily clutches at his forehead*). How can you like to stand at such a dizzy height——?

HILDA. Yes, I will! Right up there will I stand and look down on the other people—on those that are building churches, and homes for mother and father and the troop of children. And *you* may come up and look on at it, too.

SOLNESS (*in a low tone*). Is the builder to be allowed to come up beside the princess?

HILDA. If the builder *will.*

SOLNESS (*more softly*). Then I think the builder will come.

HILDA (*nods*). The builder—he'll come.

SOLNESS. But he'll never be able to build any more. Poor builder!

HILDA (*animated*). Oh yes, he will! We two will set to work together. And then we'll build the loveliest—the very loveliest—thing in all the world.

SOLNESS (*intently*). Hilda, tell me what that is!

HILDA (*looks smilingly at him, shakes her head a little, pouts, and speaks as if to a child*). Builders—they are such very—very stupid people.

SOLNESS. Yes, no doubt they're stupid. But now tell me what it is—the loveliest thing in the world—that we two are to build together?

HILDA (*is silent a little while, then says with an indefinable expression in her eyes*). Castles in the air.

SOLNESS. Castles in the air?

HILDA (*nods*). Castles in the air, yes! Do you know what sort of thing a castle in the air is?

SOLNESS. It's the loveliest thing in the world, you say.

HILDA (*rises with vehemence, and makes a gesture of repulsion with her hands*). Yes, to be sure it is! Castles in the air—they're so easy to take refuge in. And so easy to build, too—(*looks scornfully at him*)—especially for the builders who have a—a dizzy conscience.

SOLNESS (*rises*). After this day we two will build together, Hilda.

HILDA (*with a half-dubious smile*). A *real* castle in the air?

SOLNESS. Yes. One with a firm foundation under it.

(RAGNAR BROVIK *comes out from the house. He is carrying a large green wreath with flowers and silken ribbons.*)

HILDA (*with an outburst of pleasure*). The wreath! Oh, that'll be glorious!

SOLNESS (*in surprise*). Have *you* brought the wreath, Ragnar?

RAGNAR. I promised the foreman I would.

SOLNESS (*relieved*). Ah, then I suppose your father's better?

RAGNAR. No.

SOLNESS. Wasn't he cheered by what I wrote?

RAGNAR. It came too late.

SOLNESS. Too late!

RAGNAR. When she came with it he was unconscious. He had had a stroke.

SOLNESS. Why, then, you must go home to him. You must attend to your father!

RAGNAR. He doesn't need me any more.

SOLNESS. But surely you ought to be with him.

RAGNAR. *She* is sitting by his bed.

SOLNESS (*rather uncertainly*). Kaia?

RAGNAR (*looking darkly at him*). Yes—Kaia.

SOLNESS. Go home, Ragnar—both to him and to her. Give *me* the wreath.

RAGNAR (*suppresses a mocking smile*). You don't mean that you yourself——

SOLNESS. I will take it down to them myself. (*Takes the wreath from him.*) And now, you go home; we don't require you to-day.

RAGNAR. I know you don't require me any more; but to-day I shall stop.

SOLNESS. Well, stop then, since you're bent upon it.

HILDA (*at the railing*). Mr. Solness, I will stand here and look on at you.

SOLNESS. At me!

HILDA. It will be fearfully thrilling.

SOLNESS (*in a low tone*). We'll talk about that another time, Hilda. (*He goes down the flight of steps with the wreath, and away through the garden.*)

HILDA (*looks after him, then turns to* RAGNAR). You might at least have thanked him, I think.

RAGNAR. Thanked him? Ought I to have thanked *him*?

HILDA. Yes, of course you ought!

RAGNAR. I think it's rather you I ought to thank.

HILDA. How can you say such a thing?

RAGNAR (*without answering her*). But I advise you to take care, Miss Wangel! For you don't know *him* rightly yet.

HILDA (*ardently*). Oh, I know him better than any one!

RAGNAR (*laughs in exasperation*). Thank him, when he's held me down year after year! When he made father disbelieve in me—made me disbelieve in myself. And all merely that he might——!

HILDA (*as if divining something*). That he might——? Tell me at once!

RAGNAR. That he might keep her with him.

HILDA (*with a start towards him*). The girl at the desk!

RAGNAR. Yes.

HILDA (*threateningly, clenching her hands*). That is not true! You're telling falsehoods about him!

RAGNAR. I wouldn't believe it either until to-day—when she said so herself.

HILDA (*as if beside herself*). *What* did she say? I *will* know! At once! at once!

RAGNAR. She said that he had taken possession of her mind—her whole mind—centred all her thoughts upon himself alone. She says that she can never leave him—that she will remain here, where *he* is——

HILDA (*with flashing eyes*). She won't be allowed to!

RAGNAR (*as if feeling his way*). Who won't allow her?

HILDA (*rapidly*). *He* won't either?

RAGNAR. Oh no—I understand the whole thing now. After this she would merely be—in the way.

HILDA. You understand nothing—since you can talk like that! No, *I* will tell you why he kept hold of her.

RAGNAR. Well then, why?

HILDA. In order to keep hold of *you.*

RAGNAR. Has he told you so?

HILDA. No, but it is so. It *must* be so! (*Wildly*) I will—I *will* have it so!

RAGNAR. And at the very moment when you came—he let her go.

HILDA. It was *you—you* that he let go! What do you suppose he cares about strange women like her?

RAGNAR (*reflects*). Is it possible that all this time he's been afraid of me?

HILDA. *He* afraid! I wouldn't be so conceited if I were you.

RAGNAR. Oh, he must have seen long ago that I had something in me, too. Besides—cowardly—that's just what he is, you see.

HILDA. He! Oh yes, I'm likely to believe *that.*

RAGNAR. In a certain sense he *is* cowardly—he, the great master builder. He's not afraid of robbing others of their life's happiness—as he has done both for my father and for me. But when it comes to climbing a paltry bit of scaffolding—he'll do anything rather than *that.*

HILDA. Oh, you should just have seen him high, high up—at the dizzy height where I once saw him.

RAGNAR. Did you see that?

HILDA. Yes, indeed I did. How free and great he looked as he stood and fastened the wreath to the church vane!

RAGNAR. I know that he ventured that, *once* in his life—one solitary time. It's a tradition among us younger men. But no power on earth would induce him to do it again.

HILDA. To-day he will do it again!

RAGNAR (*scornfully*). Yes, I daresay!

HILDA. We shall see it.

RAGNAR. That neither you nor I will see.

HILDA (*with uncontrolled vehemence*). I *will* see it! I *will* and *must* see it!

RAGNAR. But he won't do it. He simply daren't do it. For you see he can't get over this infirmity—master builder though he be.

(MRS. SOLNESS *comes from the house on to the veranda.*)

MRS. SOLNESS (*looks around*). Isn't he here? Where has he gone to?

RAGNAR. Mr. Solness is down with the men.

HILDA. He took the wreath with him.

MRS. SOLNESS (*terrified*). Took the wreath with him! Oh God! Oh God! Brovik—you must go down to him! Get him to come back here!

RAGNAR. Shall I say you want to speak to him, Mrs. Solness?

MRS. SOLNESS. Oh yes, do! No, no—don't say that *I* want anything! You can say that somebody is here, and that he must come at once.

RAGNAR. Good. I will do so, Mrs. Solness.
(*He goes down the flight of steps and away through the garden.*)

MRS. SOLNESS. Oh, Miss Wangel, you can't think how anxious I feel about him.

HILDA. Is there anything in this to be so terribly frightened about?

MRS. SOLNESS. Oh yes; surely you can understand. Just think, if he were really to do it! If he should take it into his head to climb up the scaffolding!

HILDA (*eagerly*). Do you think he will?

MRS. SOLNESS. Oh, one can never tell what he might take into his head. I'm afraid there's nothing he mightn't think of doing.

HILDA. Aha! Perhaps you think that he's—well——?

MRS. SOLNESS. Oh, I don't know what to think about him now. The doctor has been telling me all sorts of things; and putting it all together with several things I've heard him say——
(DR. HERDAL *looks out through the door.*)

DR. HERDAL. Isn't he coming soon?

MRS. SOLNESS. Yes, I think so. I've sent for him at any rate.

DR. HERDAL (*coming closer*). I'm afraid you'll have to go in, my dear lady——

MRS. SOLNESS. Oh no! Oh no! I shall stay out here and wait for Halvard.

DR. HERDAL. But some ladies have just come to call on you——

MRS. SOLNESS. Good heavens, that too! And just at this moment!

DR. HERDAL. They say they positively must see the ceremony.

MRS. SOLNESS. Well, well, I suppose I must go to them after all. It's my duty.

HILDA. Can't you ask the ladies to go away?

MRS. SOLNESS. No; that would never do. Now that they're here, it's my duty to see them. But do you stay out here in the mean time, and receive him when he comes.

DR. HERDAL. And try to occupy his attention as long as possible——

MRS. SOLNESS. Yes, do, dear Miss Wangel. Keep as firm hold of him as ever you can.

HILDA. Wouldn't it be best for you to do that?

MRS. SOLNESS. Yes; God knows that is *my* duty. But when one has duties in so many directions——

DR. HERDAL (*looks towards the garden*). There he's coming!

MRS. SOLNESS. And I have to go in!

DR. HERDAL (*to* HILDA). Don't say anything about *my* being here.

HILDA. Oh no! I dare say I shall find something else to talk to Mr. Solness about.

MRS. SOLNESS. And be sure you keep firm hold of him. I believe *you* can do it best.
(MRS. SOLNESS *and* DR. HERDAL *go into the house.* HILDA *remains standing on the veranda.* SOLNESS *comes from the garden up the flight of steps.*)

SOLNESS. Somebody wants me, I hear.

HILDA. Yes; it's I, Mr. Solness.

SOLNESS. Oh, is it you, Hilda? I was afraid it might be Aline or the Doctor.

HILDA. You're very easily frightened, it seems!

SOLNESS. Do you think so?

HILDA. Yes; people say that you're afraid to climb about—on the scaffoldings, you know.

SOLNESS. Well, that's quite a special thing.

HILDA. Then it's true that you're afraid to do it.

SOLNESS. Yes. I am.

HILDA. Afraid of falling down and killing yourself?

SOLNESS. No, not of that.

HILDA. Of what then?

SOLNESS. I'm afraid of retribution, Hilda.

HILDA. Of retribution? (*Shakes her head*) I don't understand that.

SOLNESS. Sit down, and I'll tell you something.

HILDA. Yes, do—at once!
(*She sits on a stool by the railing, and looks expectantly at him.*)

SOLNESS (*throws his hat on the table*). You know that I began by building churches.

HILDA (*nods*). I know that well.

SOLNESS. For, you see, I came as a boy from a pious home in the country; and so it seemed to me that this church building was the noblest task I could set myself.

HILDA. Yes, yes.

SOLNESS. And I venture to say that I built those poor little churches with such honest and warm and heart-felt devotion that—that——

HILDA. That——? Well?

SOLNESS. Well, that I think he ought to have been pleased with me.

HILDA. *He?* What *he?*

SOLNESS. He who was to have the churches, of course! He to whose honor and glory they were dedicated.

HILDA. Oh, indeed! But are you certain, then, that—that he wasn't—pleased with you?

SOLNESS (*scornfully*). *He* pleased with *me!* How can you talk so, Hilda? He who gave the troll in me leave to lord it just as it pleased. He who bade them be at hand to serve me, both day and night—all these—all these——

HILDA. Devils——

SOLNESS. Yes, of both kinds. Oh no, he made me feel clearly enough that he wasn't pleased with me. (*Mysteriously*) You see, that was really the reason why he made the old house burn down.

HILDA. Was that why?

SOLNESS. Yes, don't you understand? He wanted to give me the chance of becoming an accomplished master in my own sphere—so that I might build all the more glorious churches for him. At first I didn't understand what he was driving at; but all of a sudden it flashed upon me.

HILDA. When was that?

SOLNESS. It was when I was building the church-tower up at Lysanger.

HILDA. I thought so.

SOLNESS. For you see, Hilda—up there, amid those new surroundings, I used to go about musing and pondering within myself. Then I saw plainly why he had taken my little children from me. It was that I should have nothing else to attach myself to. No such thing as love and happiness, you understand. I was to be only a master builder—nothing else. And all my life long I was to go on building for him. (*Laughs*) But I can tell you nothing came of that.

HILDA. What did you do, then?

SOLNESS. First of all, I searched and tried my own heart——

HILDA. And then?

SOLNESS. Then I did the *impossible*—I no less than *he*.

HILDA. The impossible?

SOLNESS. I had never before been able to climb up to a great, free height. But that day, I did it.

HILDA (*leaping up*). Yes, yes, you did!

SOLNESS. And when I stood there, high over everything, and was hanging the wreath over the vane, I said to him: Hear me now, thou Mighty One! From this day forward I will be a free builder—I too, in my sphere—just as thou in thine. I will never build any more churches for thee—only homes for human beings.

HILDA (*with great sparkling eyes*). *That* was the song that I heard through the air!

SOLNESS. But afterwards his turn came.

HILDA. What do you mean?

SOLNESS (*looks disconsolately at her*). Building homes for human beings is not worth sixpence, Hilda.

HILDA. Do you say *that* now?

SOLNESS. Yes, for now I *see* it. Men have no use for these homes of theirs—to be happy in. And I shouldn't have had any use for such a home, if I'd had one. (*With a quiet, bitter laugh*) See, that is the upshot of the whole affair, however far back I look. Nothing really built; nor anything sacrificed for the chance of building. Nothing, nothing! the whole is nothing!

HILDA. Then you will never build anything more?

SOLNESS (*with animation*). On the contrary, I'm just going to begin.

HILDA. What, then? What will you build? Tell me at once!

SOLNESS. I believe there's only one possible dwelling-place for human happiness—and that's what I'm going to build now.

HILDA (*looks firmly at him*). Mr. Solness—you mean our castles in the air.

SOLNESS. The castles in the air—yes.

HILDA. I'm afraid you would turn dizzy before we got half-way up.

SOLNESS. Not if I can mount hand in hand with you, Hilda.

HILDA (*with an expression of suppressed resentment*). Only with me? Won't there be others of the party?

SOLNESS. Who else should there be?

HILDA. Oh—that girl—that Kaia at the desk. Poor thing—don't you want to take her with you too?

SOLNESS. Oho! Was it about her that Aline was talking to you?

HILDA. Is it so—yes or no?

SOLNESS (*vehemently*). I won't answer such a question! You must believe in me, utterly and entirely!

HILDA. All these ten years I've believed in you so fully—so fully.

SOLNESS. You must go on believing in me!

HILDA. Then let me see you stand free and high up!

SOLNESS (*sadly*). Oh, Hilda—it's not every day that I can do that.

HILDA (*passionately*). I will have you do it! I will have it! (*Imploringly*) Just once more, Mr. Solness! Do the *impossible* once again!

SOLNESS (*stands and looks deep into her eyes*). *If* I try it, Hilda, I will stand up there and talk to him as I did that time before.

HILDA (*in rising excitement*). What will you say to him?

SOLNESS. I will say to him: Hear me, Mighty Lord—thou may'st judge me as seems best to thee. But hereafter I will build nothing but the loveliest thing in the world——

HILDA (*carried away*). Yes—yes—yes!

SOLNESS. —build it together with a princess, whom I love——

HILDA. Yes, tell him that! Tell him that!

SOLNESS. Yes. And then I will say to him: Now I shall go down and throw my arms round her and kiss her——

HILDA. —many times! Say that!

SOLNESS. —many, many times, I will say.

HILDA. And then——?

SOLNESS. Then I will wave my hat—and come down to the earth—and do as I said to him.

HILDA (*with outstretched arms*). Now I see you again as I did when there was song in the air!

SOLNESS (*looks at her with his head bowed*). How have you become what you are, Hilda?

HILDA. How have you made me what I am?

SOLNESS (*shortly and firmly*). The princess shall have her castle.

HILDA (*jubilant, clapping her hands*). Oh, Mr. Solness——! My lovely, lovely castle. Our castle in the air!

SOLNESS. On a firm foundation.

(*In the street a crowd of people have assembled, vaguely seen through the trees. Music of wind-instruments is heard far away behind the new house.* MRS. SOLNESS, *with a fur collar round her neck,* DOCTOR HERDAL, *with her white shawl on his arm, and some ladies, come out on the veranda.* RAGNAR BROVIK *comes at the same time up from the garden.*)

MRS. SOLNESS (*to* RAGNAR). Are we to have music, too?

RAGNAR. Yes. It's the band of the Masons' Union. (*To* SOLNESS) The foreman asked me to tell you that he's ready now to go up with the wreath.

SOLNESS (*takes his hat*). All right. I'll go down to him myself.

MRS. SOLNESS (*anxiously*). What have you to do down there, Halvard?

SOLNESS (*curtly*). I must be down below with the men.

MRS. SOLNESS. Yes, down below—only down below.

SOLNESS. That's where I always stand—on everyday occasions.

(*He goes down the flight of steps and away through the garden.*)

MRS. SOLNESS (*calls after him over

the railing). But do beg the man to be careful when he goes up! Promise me that, Halvard!

DR. HERDAL (*to* MRS. SOLNESS). Don't you see that I was right? He's given up all thought of that folly.

MRS. SOLNESS. Oh, what a relief! Twice workmen have fallen, and each time they were killed on the spot. (*Turns to* HILDA) Thank you, Miss Wangel, for having kept such a firm hold upon him. I should never have had my own way with him.

DR. HERDAL (*playfully*). Yes, yes, Miss Wangel, you know how to keep firm hold on a man, when you give your mind to it.

(MRS. SOLNESS *and* DR. HERDAL *go up to the ladies, who are standing nearer to the steps and looking over the garden.* HILDA *remains standing beside the railing in the foreground.* RAGNAR *goes up to her.*)

RAGNAR (*with suppressed laughter, half whispering*). Miss Wangel, do you see all those young fellows down in the street?

HILDA. Yes.

RAGNAR. They're my fellow-students come to look at the master.

HILDA. What do they want to look at *him* for?

RAGNAR. They want to see how he daren't climb to the top of his own house.

HILDA. Oh, *that's* what those boys want, is it?

RAGNAR (*spitefully and scornfully*). He's kept us down so long, that man. Now we're going to see him keep quietly down below himself.

HILDA. You won't see that—not this time.

RAGNAR (*smiles*). Indeed! Then where shall we see him?

HILDA. High—high up by the vane! That's where you'll see him!

RAGNAR (*laughs*). Him! Oh yes, I daresay!

HILDA. His *will* is to reach the top —so at the top you shall see him.

RAGNAR. His *will*, yes; that I can easily believe. But he simply *can't* do it. His head would swim round, long, long before he got halfway. He'd have to crawl down again on his hands and knees.

DR. HERDAL (*points across*). Look! there goes the foreman up the ladders.

MRS. SOLNESS. And of course he's got the wreath to carry too. Oh, I do hope he'll be careful!

RAGNAR (*stares incredulously and shouts*). Why, but it's——

HILDA (*breaking out in jubilation*). It's the master builder himself.

MRS. SOLNESS (*screams with terror*). Yes, it's Halvard! O my great God——! Halvard! Halvard!

DR. HERDAL. Hush! Don't shout to him!

MRS. SOLNESS (*half beside herself*). I must go to him! I must bring him down again.

DR. HERDAL (*holds her*). Don't move, any of you! Not a sound!

HILDA (*immovable, follows* SOLNESS *with her eyes*). He climbs and climbs. Higher and higher! Higher and higher! Look! Just look!

RAGNAR (*breathless*). He *must* turn now. He can't possibly help it.

HILDA. He climbs and climbs. He'll soon be at the top now.

MRS. SOLNESS. Oh, I shall die of terror. I can't bear to see it!

DR. HERDAL. Then don't look up at him.

HILDA. There, he's standing on the topmost planks! Right at the top!

DR. HERDAL. Nobody must move! Do you hear?

HILDA (*exulting, with quiet intensity*). At last! At last! Now I see him great and free again!

RAGNAR (*almost voiceless*). But this is im—

HILDA. So I have seen him all through these ten years. How secure he stands! Frightfully thrilling all the same. Look at him! Now he's hanging the wreath round the vane!

RAGNAR. I feel as if I were looking at something utterly impossible.

HILDA. Yes, it *is* the *impossible* that he's doing now! (*With the indefinable expression in her eyes*) Can you see any one else up there with him?

RAGNAR. There is no one else.

HILDA. Yes, there is one he is striving with.

RAGNAR. You are mistaken.

HILDA. Then do you hear no song in the air, either?

RAGNAR. It must be the wind in the tree-tops.

HILDA. *I* hear a song—a mighty song! (*Shouts in wild jubilation and glee*) Look, look! Now he's waving his hat! He's waving it to us down here! Oh, wave, wave back to him! For now it's finished! (*Tears the white shawl from the doctor, waves it, and shouts up to* SOLNESS) Hurrah for Master Builder Solness!

DR. HERDAL. Stop! Stop! For God's sake—!

(*The ladies on the veranda wave their pocket-handkerchiefs, and the shouts of "Hurrah" are taken up in the street below. Then they are suddenly silenced, and the crowd bursts out into a shriek of horror. A human body, with planks and fragments of wood, is vaguely perceived crashing down behind the trees.*)

MRS. SOLNESS AND THE LADIES (*at the same time*). He's falling! He's falling!

(MRS. SOLNESS *totters, falls backwards, swooning, and is caught, amid cries and confusion, by the ladies. The crowd in the street breaks down the fence and storms into the garden. At the same time* DR. HERDAL, *too, rushes down thither. A short pause.)*

HILDA (*stares fixedly upwards, and says as if petrified*): *My* Master Builder.

RAGNAR (*supports himself, trembling, against the railing*). He must be dashed to pieces—killed on the spot.

ONE OF THE LADIES (*whilst Mrs. Solness is carried into the house*). Run down for the doctor——

RAGNAR. I can't stir a foot——

ANOTHER LADY. Then call to some one!

RAGNAR (*tries to call out*). How is it? Is he alive?

A VOICE (*below, in the garden*). Mr. Solness is dead!

OTHER VOICES (*nearer*). The head is all crushed.—He fell right into the quarry.

HILDA (*turns to* RAGNAR, *and says quietly*): I can't see him up there now.

RAGNAR. This is terrible. So, after all, he could not do it.

HILDA (*as if in quiet spell-bound triumph*). But he mounted right to the top. And I heard harps in the air. (*Waves her shawl in the air, and shrieks with wild intensity*) *My—my* Master Builder!

Cyrano de Bergerac

BY EDMOND ROSTAND

AN ACTING VERSION

TRANSLATED FROM
THE FRENCH BY
HAROLD WHITEHALL

CHARACTERS

CYRANO DE BERGERAC
CHRISTIAN DE NEUVILLETTE
COUNT DE GUICHE
RAGUENEAU
LE BRET
DE VALVERT
LIGNIÈRE
MONTFLEURY
BELLEROSE
JODELET
CUIGY
BRISSAILLE
CARBON DE CASTEL-JALOUX
THE GASCONY CADETS
FIRST FOP
SECOND FOP
THIRD FOP
AN ANNOYING BORE
TWO MUSKETEERS
PAGES
A SPANISH OFFICER
A LIGHT-HORSEMAN

THE DOORKEEPER
THE CITIZEN
HIS SON
A PICKPOCKET
A SPECTATOR
A MEMBER OF THE WATCH
THE CAPUCHIN
TWO MUSICIANS (PAGES)
POETS
PASTRY COOKS

ROXANE
MOTHER MARGUERITE
SISTER MARTHE
LISE
A REFRESHMENT GIRL
THE DUENNA
SISTER CLAIRE
AN ACTRESS
THE SOUBRETTE
THE FLOWER-GIRL

The Crowd, Citizens of Paris, Tradesmen, Fops, Musketeers, Pickpockets, Pastry Cooks, Poets, Gascony Cadets, Actors, Violinists, Pages, Children, Spanish Soldiers, Spectators, *Précieuses,* Actresses, Citizens' Wives, Nuns, etc.

TIME: *The first four acts in 1640; the fifth in 1655.*

Cyrano de Bergerac

ACT ONE

A THEATRICAL PERFORMANCE AT THE HÔTEL DE BOURGOGNE

SCENE I

The Hall of the Hôtel de Bourgogne, Paris, in 1640. A sort of "real" tennis court adapted and decorated for use as a theater. It was, in actual fact, the first theater in the French capital. The auditorium is oblong, but we see it as a triangle; one of its sides runs from downstage right to upstage left and forms an angle with the stage, which is seen obliquely. The wings on both sides of this stage are cluttered with benches. Its curtain is two tapestries which can be drawn apart. Above the Harlequin draperies (covering the top and sides of the stage front) are the Royal Arms of Louis XIII. Wide steps lead down from the stage platform to the auditorium. On each side of these steps, places for the violinists of the orchestra. The footlights are candles.

Two tiers of galleries in the auditorium, one above the other; the lower is divided into boxes. No seats in the pit, our stage proper. At the back of the pit, that is to say downstage right, a few tiered benches; under a staircase leading to the upper seats and visible only in its lowest portion is a sort of refreshment stand furnished with small candelabra, vases of flowers, glasses, plates of cakes, bottles, etc.

The entrance to this theater is center backstage under the boxes. It is a large door, half-way open to admit the audience. On the door-panels, in several corners and above the refreshment stand, are red posters reading LA CLORISE.

At the rise of the curtain, the auditorium is in half darkness and empty. Chandeliers have been lowered to the center of the pit in readiness for lighting.

The audience arriving gradually: CAVALIERS, CITIZENS, LACKEYS, PAGES, *a* PICKPOCKET, *the* DOORKEEPER, *etc. Then the* FOPS *(Fr. les Marquis),* CUIGY, BRISSAILLE, *the* REFRESHMENT GIRL, VIOLINISTS *of the orchestra, etc.*

(An uproar of voices behind the door. A CAVALIER *enters suddenly.)*

DOORKEEPER (*following him*). Hey! Your fifteen cents!

CAVALIER. I come in free.

DOORKEEPER. Why?

CAVALIER. I belong to the King's Light Horse.

DOORKEEPER (*to another* CAVALIER *just entering*). And you?

SECOND CAVALIER. I don't have to pay.

DOORKEEPER. But——

SECOND CAVALIER. I'm a Musketeer.

FIRST CAVALIER (*to* SECOND). The play doesn't start till two o'clock. The pit is empty. Let's fence a while.
(*They fence with foils they have brought.*)

LACKEY (*entering*). Pst— Flanquin!

ANOTHER (*already in*). You, Champagne?

FIRST LACKEY (*revealing articles drawn from his doublet*). Cards. Dice. (*Sits on the ground.*) Let's go.

SECOND (*also sitting*). All right, my lad.

FIRST LACKEY (*unpocketing a candle-end which he lights and sticks on the floor*). I've stolen a little of my master's luster.

MEMBER OF THE WATCH (*to a* FLOWER-GIRL *walking in*). It's a treat to come in before they light up. (*Puts his arm around her.*)

CAVALIER (*hit by a foil*). *Touché!*

CARD-PLAYER. Clubs!

MEMBER OF THE WATCH (*pursuing girl*). A kiss!

FLOWER-GIRL (*evading him*). They'll see us.

MEMBER OF THE WATCH (*dragging her into a dark corner*). Not a chance!

A MAN (*joining others on the ground who have brought refreshments*). When you come in early, it's nice to have a snack.

A CITIZEN (*leading in his son*). Let's stand here, son.

CARD-PLAYER. Aces— Three of a kind!

A MAN (*sitting down on the ground with the others already seated and taking a bottle from under his cloak*). Your genuine toper will gulp down bourgogne (*Drinks*) in the Hôtel de Bourgogne.

CITIZEN (*to his son*). You'd think we were in the stews. (*Points at the drinker with his cane*) Boozers! (*One of the fencers, recoiling, jostles him*) Brawlers! (*Stumbles among the card-players*) Gamblers!

MEMBER OF THE WATCH (*behind him, pestering the girl*). Kiss?

CITIZEN (*hurriedly drawing his son*

away). Good Heavens! To think that in a place like this they actually played Rotrou!

HIS SON. Even Corneille.

A BAND OF PAGES (*entering hand in hand, singing and dancing*). Tra la la la la la la la lu!

DOORKEEPER (*severely, to the* PAGES). No nonsense, lads.

FIRST PAGE (*with wounded dignity*). Sir, the very idea! (*To the* SECOND PAGE *as soon as the* DOORKEEPER *has turned his back*) Got some string?

SECOND PAGE. *And* a fishhook.

FIRST PAGE. We could fish for wigs (*Pointing*) up there.

A PICKPOCKET (*calling together around him several tough-looking men*). Now, young crooks, here's the lay. Seeing as it's your first try at lifting purses, you—

SECOND PAGE (*calling others already in the upper gallery*). Hey! Got your blow-guns?

THIRD PAGE (*from above*). I'll say. Peas, too. (*Peppers them with peas.*)

CITIZEN'S SON (*to* CITIZEN). What's the play?

CITIZEN. "Clorise."

SON. Who wrote it?

CITIZEN. Monsieur Balthazar Baro. A masterpiece that—

(*Walks towards the back arm in arm with his son.*)

PICKPOCKET (*to his confederates*). You cut the lace knee-ruffles just like this—

A SPECTATOR (*to another, pointing towards an upper corner*). Look, I was up there, the first night of "The Cid."

PICKPOCKET (*motioning as if picking pockets*). Snitch the watches—

CITIZEN (*coming forward again with his son*). You'll see some famous actors—

PICKPOCKET (*his hands suggesting furtive little jerks*). Then the handkerchiefs—

CITIZEN. Montfleury—

SOMEONE (*shouting from the upper gallery*). Light up!

CITIZEN. Bellerose, l'Épy, la Beaupré, Jodelet—

A PAGE (*in the pit*). Here's the refreshment girl.

REFRESHMENT GIRL (*behind the refreshment stand*). Oranges, milk, raspberry press, citronade.
(*Confusion at the door.*)

TENOR VOICE. Room, you louts!

A LACKEY (*surprised*). Fops? In the pit?

ANOTHER LACKEY. Oh, for the moment.
(*Enter a group of young noblemen.*)

FOP (*seeing the hall is half empty*). What! Have we come in like haberdashers? No fuss disturbing people? No stepping on their toes? Too bad. (*Finding himself among other noblemen already in*) Cuigy! Brissaille!
(*General embracing.*)

CUIGY. Faithful comrades! Yes, we came before they lit the candles.

FOP. Oh, don't mention it! It puts me in such a temper——

ANOTHER FOP. Take heart, Marquis. Here comes the lamplighter.

ENTIRE AUDIENCE (*hailing the entrance of the lamplighter*). Hurrah! (*They crowd around the chandeliers as he lights them.* LIGNIÈRE *enters the pit arm in arm with* CHRISTIAN DE NEUVILLETTE. LIGNIÈRE, *somewhat untidy, has the look of an aristocratic drunkard.* CHRISTIAN, *dressed in an elegant but somewhat old-fashioned style, appears preoccupied; his attention is fixed on the boxes.*)

SCENE II

The same; CHRISTIAN, LIGNIÈRE; *then* RAGUENEAU, *and* LE BRET.

CUIGY. Lignière!

BRISSAILLE (*laughing*). What! Not drunk yet?

LIGNIÈRE (*in a low voice to* CHRISTIAN). Shall I present you? (*Sign of assent from* CHRISTIAN) Baron de Neuvillette.
(*An exchange of bows.*)

THE AUDIENCE (*cheering the rise of the first lighted chandelier*). Hurrah!

CUIGY (*to* BRISSAILLE, *while looking at* CHRISTIAN). Handsome fellow . . . very!

FIRST FOP (*overhearing*). Pfui!

LIGNIÈRE (*presenting them to* CHRISTIAN). Messieurs de Cuigy, de Brissaille.

CHRISTIAN (*bowing*). Delighted.

FIRST FOP (*to* SECOND). Handsome enough, but scarcely dressed in style.

LIGNIÈRE (*to* CUIGY). He is just in from Touraine.

CHRISTIAN. Yes, I've not been over twenty days in town. I enter the Guards tomorrow, as Gascony Cadet.

FIRST FOP (*looking over the people entering the boxes*). There's Judge Aubrey's wife.

REFRESHMENT GIRL. Oranges, milk —

THE VIOLINISTS (*tuning up*). La! . . . La!

CUIGY (*to* CHRISTIAN, *motioning to-*

wards the auditorium which is rapidly filling). Quite a crowd.

CHRISTIAN. Quite.

FIRST FOP. All the smart set.
(*The fops identify the various elegantly turned-out ladies entering the boxes. Exchange of bows and smiles.*)

SECOND FOP. Mesdames de Guéménée . . .

CUIGY. De Bois-Dauphin . . .

FIRST FOP. Whom we've all loved—in our time.

BRISSAILLE. De Chavigny —

SECOND FOP. Who is playing with all our hearts.

LIGNIÈRE. Look there! Monsieur de Corneille is back from Rouen.

CITIZEN'S SON (*to his father*). Is the Academy here?

CITIZEN. Several members. (*Pointing*) Boudu, Boissat, Cureau de la Chambre, Porchères, Colomby, Bourzeys, Bourdon, Arbaud—immortal, deathless names! Wonderful!

FIRST FOP. Attention! Our *précieuses* are going to their seats. Barthénoïde, Urimédonte, Cassandace, Félixérie . . .

SECOND FOP. Exquisite names! Divine! Do you know them all, Marquis?

FIRST FOP. All their names, Marquis.

LIGNIÈRE (*drawing* CHRISTIAN *aside*). Look, my friend, I came to do you a favor. But since the lady isn't here, I shall go back to my cups.

CHRISTIAN (*imploringly*). You must stay! You lampoon the Court and Town. You know everyone. Only you can tell me her name. The one I'm dying with love for.

FIRST VIOLINIST (*striking his stand with his bow*). Ready, gentlemen! (*He raises his bow.*)

REFRESHMENT GIRL. Macaroons, lemonade . . .
(*The violinists start playing.*)

CHRISTIAN. I'm afraid she's too experienced, too subtly cultured, for a plain and timid soldier such as I am. I have no claim to wit; no courage to address her. I'm bewildered by this fancy modern language— That's the place, back there. That empty box. That's where she always sits.

LIGNIÈRE (*starting to leave*). Well, I'll be off.

CHRISTIAN (*stopping him*). You've got to stay.

LIGNIÈRE. I can't. D'Assoucy is waiting at the tavern. I'd shrivel with thirst here.

REFRESHMENT GIRL (*passing in front of him with her tray*). Orangeade?

LIGNIÈRE. Pfui!

REFRESHMENT GIRL. Milk?

LIGNIÈRE. Pfui again!

REFRESHMENT GIRL. Muscatel?

LIGNIÈRE. Wait a minute. (*To* CHRISTIAN) At that, I might stay a little longer. Let us test this Muscatel. (*Sits down by the refreshment stand. The girl pours out some Muscatel.*)

THE AUDIENCE (*applauding the entrance of a plump, lively little fellow*). Ragueneau! Hurrah!

LIGNIÈRE (*to* CHRISTIAN). Ragueneau, the famous pastry-cook.

RAGUENEAU (*in a pastry-cook's Sunday best, making a bee-line for* LIGNIÈRE). Have you seen Monsieur Cyrano?

LIGNIÈRE (*introducing* RAGUENEAU *to* CHRISTIAN). The pastry-cook of players and of poets.

RAGUENEAU (*plainly confused*). You honor me too much.

LIGNIÈRE. Quiet, Maecenas!

RAGUENEAU. These gentlemen give me custom—

LIGNIÈRE. On credit. A most talented poet himself—

RAGUENEAU. So they say! So they say!

LIGNIÈRE. Mad about poetry.

RAGUENEAU. It is true that for an odelet—

LIGNIÈRE. You pay a tart—

RAGUENEAU (*deprecatingly*). Oh, a tartlet.

LIGNIÈRE. Pure modesty! And what do you pay for a villanelle?

RAGUENEAU. Rolls—

LIGNIÈRE (*severely*). Vanilla rolls! He loves the theater, too. Don't you?

RAGUENEAU. Idolize it!

LIGNIÈRE. And pay for your seat in cakes, isn't that so? Confidentially, what did your seat cost today?

RAGUENEAU. Four custards. Fifteen cream puffs. (*Looking everywhere at once*) Monsieur Cyrano isn't here. What a surprise!

LIGNIÈRE. Why?

RAGUENEAU. Montfleury is going to act.

LIGNIÈRE. Why, yes! That walking wine-cask plays Phédon's rôle tonight. What's that to Cyrano?

RAGUENEAU. Don't you know? He has forbidden Montfleury to take the stage again for an entire month. He detests him.

LIGNIÈRE (*who has reached his fourth glass*). Well?

RAGUENEAU. Montfleury is going to act!

CUIGY (*who has drawn near with

his companions). Cyrano can't stop him.

RAGUENEAU. I have come to see.

FIRST FOP. Who is this Cyrano?

CUIGY. Quite a hand with a rapier.

SECOND FOP. A gentleman?

CUIGY. He'll do. He is a Cadet in the Guards. (*Indicating a gentleman walking here and there as if in search of someone*) His friend, Le Bret, could tell you. (*Calling*) Le Bret! (LE BRET *comes up.*) Looking for Bergerac?

LE BRET. I'm uneasy——

CUIGY. I appeal to you. Isn't he quite extraordinary?

LE BRET (*affectionately*). The most exquisite spirit under the moon!

RAGUENEAU. Rhymester!

CUIGY. Swordster!

BRISSAILLE. Physicist!

LE BRET. Lutanist!

LIGNIÈRE. And what a strange looking fellow to boot!

RAGUENEAU. He's scarcely the kind of man our sober Philippe de Champaigne would choose to paint. But the late Jacques Callot now—he might have put Cyrano among his masques as the maddest fire-eater of them all. Imagine him: triple-plumed felt hat, doublet puffed out with half a dozen skirts, cloak lifted by his sword like the insolent tail-feathers of a fighting-cock. He's prouder than any bravo that Gascony, the Mother Goose of bravos, ever weaned. And, to cap all, from his Punchinello ruff he sports . . . a nose. Gentlemen, what a nose! A nose to end all noses! Anyone else nosed like that and you'd say, "Impossible! A pure exaggeration!" Then you would smile and think, "He'll take it off." But Cyrano, he never takes it off.

LE BRET (*nodding his head*). He never takes it off—and you don't mention it, or else——

RAGUENEAU (*proudly*). His sword is one blade of the shears of Fate.

FIRST FOP (*shrugging his shoulders*). I'll wager he won't come.

RAGUENEAU. I'll bet a chicken à la Ragueneau he will!

FIRST FOP (*laughing*). Done! (*Admiring murmurs.* ROXANE *has just appeared in her box. She seats herself in front, her duenna at the back.* CHRISTIAN, *paying the* REFRESHMENT GIRL, *fails to see her.*)

SECOND FOP (*with inchoate cries of admiration*). Gentlemen! She is too, too ravishing!

FIRST FOP. A peach that smiles with strawberry lips.

SECOND FOP. But cold—cold. If you came close you'd catch cold—in the heart.

CHRISTIAN (*looks up, sees* ROXANE, *and grips* LIGNIÈRE'S *arm*). That's her!

LIGNIÈRE (*looking*). So she's the one.

CHRISTIAN. Quick! Tell me. I'm afraid.

LIGNIÈRE (*sipping his Muscatel*). Magdeleine Robin, called Roxane. A genuine *précieuse.*

CHRISTIAN. So I feared.

LIGNIÈRE. Heart-free. Orphan. Cousin of the Cyrano they've just mentioned—
(*At this moment, a very fashionable nobleman, wearing the ribbon of the Order of the Holy Ghost across his chest, enters the box and stands talking for a while with* ROXANE.)

CHRISTIAN (*starting*). Who is that man?

LIGNIÈRE (*blinking, a little drunk*). Well! Well! The Count de Guiche. Loves her, but married to the niece of Armand de Richelieu. Wants to marry off Roxane to a certain sorry lord, Monsieur de Valvert, a viscount—and accommodating. She doesn't consent, but well— De Guiche has ways and means! He could make things unpleasant for an unprotected girl. Matter of fact, I've revealed his sly maneuvering in a song which— Ho! He ought to bear me malice! The ending was really biting. Listen!—
(*He rises staggering, lifts his glass, is about to sing.*)

CHRISTIAN. No! Good-bye!

LIGNIÈRE. You're going?

CHRISTIAN. To Monsieur de Valvert's.

LIGNIÈRE. Careful. *He'll* kill *you.* (*Indicating* ROXANE *by the direction of his glance*) Wait. Some one's looking.

CHRISTIAN. So she is!
(*He muses on* ROXANE. *The group of pickpockets, seeing his head in the air and mouth open, close in on him.*)

LIGNIÈRE. I am the one to go. I am thirsty. My friends are waiting—in the taverns. (*Goes out, unsteady on his feet.*)

LE BRET (*who has completed a turn round the auditorium, in a relieved tone to Ragueneau*). No Cyrano yet.

RAGUENEAU (*incredulously*). All the same——

LE BRET. I can only hope he didn't see the play-bill.

THE AUDIENCE. Curtain! Curtain!

SCENE III

The same, without LIGNIÈRE; DE GUICHE, VALVERT, *then* MONTFLEURY. DE GUICHE, *who has left* ROXANE'S *box, crosses the pit, surrounded by obsequious noblemen, among them the* VISCOUNT DE VALVERT.

A FOP. How they fawn on this De Guiche!

ANOTHER. Just another Gascon.

THE FIRST. A cold and subtle Gascon. That kind go far. We'd better pay respects.
(*They approach De Guiche.*)

SECOND FOP. Magnificent ribbons! What color, Count de Guiche? *Kiss-me-darling,* or *Hind's Breast?*

DE GUICHE. This is *Sick Spaniard.*

FIRST FOP. Singularly fitting! For soon, thanks to your valor, things will go ill for Spaniards there in Flanders.

DE GUICHE. I am going on the stage. Will you join me? (*Followed by all the fops and noblemen he proceeds toward the stage. He turns and calls*) Come on, Valvert!

CHRISTIAN (*listening and looking on, starts at the name*). The Viscount, eh? Well! Into that face of his I'll throw my—— (*Putting his hand in his pocket, he finds the hand of a pickpocket. Turns quickly*) What's this?

THE PICKPOCKET. Ow!

CHRISTIAN (*without letting him go*). I was looking for a glove.

PICKPOCKET (*with a piteous smile*). And you found a hand. (*Changing tone and whispering hastily*) If you'll let me go, I'll tell you a secret.

CHRISTIAN (*still keeping hold*). Well?

PICKPOCKET. Lignière. He just left you——

CHRISTIAN (*still keeping hold*). Yes?

PICKPOCKET. He's near his last gasp. A song he made displeased a certain great personage. A hundred men—I'm one of them—will ambush him tonight.

CHRISTIAN. A hundred! Who hired them?

PICKPOCKET. A secret.

CHRISTIAN (*shrugging*). Oh!

PICKPOCKET (*with great dignity*). Professional secret.

CHRISTIAN. Where will they be posted?

PICKPOCKET. Right on his way home near the Porte de Nesle. Better warn him.

CHRISTIAN (*letting his wrist go*). Where can I find him?

PICKPOCKET. Scour the taverns,—the Golden Wine-Press, the Fir-Cone, the Sundered Belt, the Torches Twain, the Three Funnels—leave a note of warning everywhere.

CHRISTIAN. I'll go. Ruffians! One against a hundred! (*Looking lovingly at* ROXANE) To have to leave her! (*Looking angrily at Valvert*) And him! But I've got to save Lignière. (*He runs out.*)
(DE GUICHE, *the* VISCOUNT, *the* FOPS, *all the nobles have vanished behind the curtain, to take their seats on the benches on the stage. The pit is completely full. Not an empty seat in the galleries and boxes.*)

THE AUDIENCE. Curtain!

A CITIZEN (*whose wig, hooked by a page in the upper gallery, flies away on the end of a string*). My wig!

JOYOUS SHOUTS. He is bald! Good for the pages! Ha! ha! ha!

CITIZEN (*furious, shaking his fists*). Little demon!

LAUGHTER AND SHOUTS (*beginning very loudly, then gradually diminishing*). Ha! ha! ha! ha! ha! ha!
(*Dead silence.*)

LE BRET (*surprised*). Why this sudden silence? (*A spectator whispers to him.*) Really?

SPECTATOR. On the best possible authority.

MURMURS (*through the audience*). Goodness—— Is he here?—— No!—— Yes!—— In the box with the grille.—— The Cardinal!—— The Cardinal!—— The Cardinal!

A PAGE. The devil! No more fun for us!
(*Three taps on the stage announce the rise of the curtain. Everyone silent with expectation.*)

VOICE OF A FOP (*behind the curtain, breaking the silence*). Snuff that candle!

ANOTHER FOP (*poking his head through the opening in the curtain*). A chair!
(*A chair is passed from hand to hand over the heads of the audience. A fop, taking it, disappears, after throwing several kisses at the boxes.*)

A SPECTATOR. Silence!
(*The three knocks are repeated. The curtain opens. The fops sit along the sides, in impudent poses. The back-drop represents the bluish setting suited to a pastoral. Four little crystal chandeliers light the stage. The violinists play softly.*)

LE BRET (*under his breath, to* RAGUENEAU). Is Montfleury coming on stage?

RAGUENEAU (*also under his breath*). Yes, he has to begin.

LE BRET. And Cyrano isn't here?

RAGUENEAU. I've lost my wager.

LE BRET. So much the better.
(*Sound of bagpipes.* MONTFLEURY *appears on the stage. Enormously fat, dressed in shepherd's costume, his hat trimmed with roses over one ear, he is blowing a beribboned bagpipe.*)

THE PIT (*applauding*). Bravo! Montfleury! Montfleury!

MONTFLEURY (*after bowing, commences his role of Phédon*).

"Happy the man, who in some solitude,
Far from the Court, in exile self-imbued,
Can list the breath of Zephyr in the wood—"

VOICE (*from the middle of the pit*). Rascal, didn't I exile you for a month?
(*Astonishment. Everyone turns round. Murmurs.*)

DIFFERENT VOICES. Hey!— What?— What is it?
(*People in the boxes stand to look.*)

CUIGY. There he is.

LE BRET (*terrified*). Cyrano!

THE VOICE. You king of clowns, get off that stage at once!

THE WHOLE AUDIENCE (*indignant*). Oh!

MONTFLEURY. But sir!—

THE VOICE. Oh! You'll be stubborn, will you?

DIFFERENT VOICES (*from the pit and boxes*). Hush! Enough! Act, Montfleury! Nothing to fear!

MONTFLEURY (*in a trembling voice*).

"Can list the breath of Zephyr in the wood—"

THE VOICE (*more menacing*). Must I plant the wood on your shoulders, you monarch of rascals?
(*An arm furnished with a cane leaps out above the heads of the audience.*)

MONTFLEURY (*in a voice growing gradually fainter*).

"Happy the man who in—"
(*The cane waves in the air.*)

THE VOICE. Out you go!

THE PIT. Oh!

MONTFLEURY (*choking*).

"Happy the man who in some sol—"
(CYRANO *emerges from the pit and stands on a chair, arms folded, hat cocked on one side, mustache bristling. His nose is terrifying.*)

CYRANO. Oh! I shall become really vexed!
(*Sensation at the sight of him.*)

SCENE IV

The same; CYRANO, *then* BELLEROSE, JODELET.

MONTFLEURY (*to the* FOPS). Come to my aid, gentlemen.

A FOP (*indifferently*). On with the play, then.

CYRANO. Paunch! If you persist, I shall have to slap your face.

THE FOP. That's enough from you!

CYRANO. The young gentlemen will be seen, not heard. Otherwise, my cane might spoil their ribbons.

ALL THE FOPS (*standing*). This is too much. Montfleury —

CYRANO. Either he goes off, or I will slash his ears off, and (*Gesturing*) rip him up!

A VOICE. Say!

CYRANO. He'd better go!

ANOTHER VOICE. Now wait a moment—

CYRANO. Not gone yet? (*Making the motion of rolling up his sleeves*) I'm going to slice that fat sausage on the stage as if it were a sideboard.

MONTFLEURY (*collecting all his dignity*). Sir, when you insult me, you insult the Muse!

CYRANO (*with great politeness*). If this Muse, who never knew you, ever knew you as you stand there, fat and lumpish as a pot, she'd kick you with her buskin.

THE PIT. Montfleury! Montfleury! Give us Baro's play!

CYRANO (*to those shouting around him*). Have pity on my scabbard. If you persist, it must yield up its mortal soul.
(*The circle around him widens immediately.*)

THE CROWD (*drawing back*). Careful now!

CYRANO (*to* MONTFLEURY). Off the stage with you!

THE CROWD (*approaching, grumbling*). Oh! Oh!

CYRANO (*turning around suddenly*). Any objections?
(*Another general withdrawal.*)

A VOICE (*at the back, singing*).

Monsieur de Cyrano,
Your tyrannous caprice,
Turns Cyrano to Tyrano:—
They shall act "La Clorise."

THE WHOLE AUDIENCE (*singing*). La Clorise, La Clorise!

CYRANO. If I hear that song again, I will knock you all down, every man Jack of you!

CITIZEN. Do you think you are a Samson?

CYRANO. Lend me your jawbone, sir?

A LADY (*in one of the boxes*). This is unheard of!

A NOBLEMAN. Scandalous!

A CITIZEN. Vexatious!

A PAGE. And they call this entertainment!

THE PIT (*hissing*). Montfleury! Cyrano!

CYRANO. Silence, everybody.

THE PIT (*in a frenzy*). Hee-haw! Baa! Woof-woof! Cock-a-doodle-doo!

CYRANO. Silence!—

A PAGE. Mee-ow!

CYRANO. Silence! I must insist on silence! Good! Now here's a general challenge to the pit. Come on, young heroes, shall I write down your names? Each in his proper turn? I'll give you numbered tickets. Who'll be first? You, sir? No! You? No! I promise I'll dispatch you with due honors. Just lift your finger if you want to die. (*Silence*) Perhaps it's modesty. You don't like looking at a *naked* blade? What, not a single name? Not a finger lifted? Very well, to proceed! (*Turning toward the stage where* MONTFLEURY *is waiting in an agony of apprehension*) I want to see the theater healed of this monstrous canker. If all else fails—(*he puts his hand on his sword*) the lancet.

MONTFLEURY. I think—
(CYRANO *gets down from the chair, seats himself in the middle of the circle his words have cleared, and makes himself thoroughly at home.*)

CYRANO. Full moon, I shall clap three times. At the third—eclipse!

THE PIT (*amused*). Hurrah!

CYRANO (*clapping his hands*). One!

MONTFLEURY. I—

VOICE (*from the boxes*). Stay!

THE PIT. He will stay!—He won't stay!

MONTFLEURY. Gentlemen, I think—

CYRANO. Two!

MONTFLEURY. I am sure it would be better—

CYRANO. Three!
(MONTFLEURY *disappears, as if through a trap-door. Burst of laughter, whistles, and hoots.*)

THE CROWD. Coward! Come back!

CYRANO (*delighted, tips back in his chair and crosses his legs*). Let him come back if he dares!

A CITIZEN. Ah! There's the actors' spokesman.
(BELLEROSE *comes forward and bows.*)

THE BOXES. There's Bellerose. (*Applauding*) Bellerose!

BELLEROSE (*with great elegance*). Most noble gentlemen—

THE PIT. No! No! Jodelet! Give us Jodelet!

JODELET (*advancing, speaking through his nose*). Big bunch of calves!

THE PIT. Hurrah! Bravo! Excellent! Bravo! Jodelet!

JODELET. No bravo, if you please! The fat tragedian, whose paunch you all adore, has felt—

THE PIT. He's a coward!

JODELET. –has felt obliged to leave!

THE PIT. Send him back on!

SOME. No!

OTHERS. Yes!

A YOUNG MAN (*to* CYRANO). But, after all, sir, why should you hate Montfleury?

CYRANO (*graciously, still seated*). Young gosling, for two reasons, either alone sufficient. First: he is a wretched actor, howling and grunting like a water-carrier the verses that should soar away on wings. Second: that's my secret.

OLD CITIZEN (*behind him*). But you rob us of "Clorise" for no good reason. I'm stubborn enough to want to know that secret.

CYRANO (*respectfully, turning his chair to face the citizen*). Old mule, this Baro's verses count for less than zero. No harm in interrupting *them.*

THE PRÉCIEUSES (*in the boxes*). What, our own Baro! How could he say it? Heavens above!

CYRANO (*gallantly, facing his chair towards the boxes*). You lovely beings, gleaming like bepetalled flowers, you cup-bearers of dreams whose smiles make even death enchanting, you should inspire our verse, not stoop to criticise it.

BELLEROSE. But the ticket-money must be given back.

CYRANO (*facing his chair towards the stage*). That's the first rational remark I've heard. I'm not the man to rend the robe of Thespis. (*Rising and throwing a bag on the stage*) Here! Catch this purse on the fly and hold your tongue.

AUDIENCE (*dazzled*). Oh! Oh!

JODELET (*hastily grabbing the purse and testing its weight*). For this price, sir, I freely give you leave to come every day and cancel "La Clorise"—

AUDIENCE. Hoo! Hoo!

JODELET. –even if we're all hissed down for it.

BELLEROSE. Clear the house!

JODELET. Yes! clear the house! (*The audience begins to go out.* CYRANO *looks on with a satisfied air. But people linger to hear the ensuing scene, and the general exit ceases. The women in the boxes, already standing with their cloaks on, stop to listen; finally sit down again.*)

LE BRET (*to* CYRANO). Of all the madness!

A BORE (*who has come up to* CYRANO). This is scandalous. The great Montfleury! But the Duke de Candale is his patron; he'll protect him! Who is your patron?

CYRANO. No one.

BORE. No one?

CYRANO. No one.

BORE. No great lord to shield you with his name?

CYRANO (*irritated*). No one! I've told you twice. Must I repeat again? No! No protector! (*His hand on his sword*) A protectress, yes!

BORE. You're leaving town, of course?

CYRANO. It all depends.

BORE. The Duke de Candale has a long arm.

CYRANO. Not as long as mine (*Pointing to his sword*) with this extension.

BORE. But you don't pretend to think—

CYRANO. I do pretend.

BORE. But—

CYRANO. Now about face!

BORE. But—

CYRANO. About face! Or tell me why you contemplate my nose.

BORE (*bewildered*). I—

CYRANO (*advancing*). Why is it strange?

BORE (*recoiling*). Your honor is mistaken—

CYRANO. Is it pliant, swaying like a trunk?

BORE (*again recoiling*). I didn't say—

CYRANO. Hooked like the beak of an owl?

BORE. I—

CYRANO. With a wart on the top?

BORE. But—

CYRANO. Or a fly sauntering over it? What's so unusual?

BORE. Oh!

CYRANO. Is it so freakish?

BORE. But I know enough to keep my eyes away!

CYRANO. And why, please, should you keep your eyes away?

BORE. I heard——

CYRANO. Disgusting, eh?

BORE. Sir!

CYRANO. The color seems unwholesome——?

BORE. Sir!

CYRANO. The shape obscene?

BORE. Oh! Not at all!

CYRANO. Why so disparaging? Perhaps you find my nose a trifle large?

BORE (*stammering*). I find it small, quite small—in fact, minute!

CYRANO. Oh! That's your line of ridicule? So! My nose is small?

BORE. Merciful Heaven!

CYRANO. My nose is huge! Enormous! Why, you pip-nosed, snub-nosed flat-head, know that I glory in this appendage of mine! A large nose is the sign manifest of such a man as I am—courteous, witty, liberal in opinions, fired with courage. Such a man, poor fool, you could never hope to be, for the inglorious face my hand is going to find above your collar, is just as bare——
(*He slaps his face.*)

BORE. Ow!

CYRANO. —of pride, imagination, lyricism, romantic fancy, sparkle, and rich life,—as bare, in short, of nose as that (*He turns him around by the shoulders, suiting the action to the word*) my boot will find beneath your backbone.

BORE (*running off*). Help! Help! The Watch!

CYRANO. Let this be warning to all curious fellows making pleasantries about the middle of my face. If the jester is of noble birth, my treatment will be different,—steel instead of boot-leather, in front and higher up.

DE GUICHE (*who has descended from the stage with the* FOPS). The man grows tiresome.

THE VISCOUNT DE VALVERT (*shrugging*). And boastful.

DE GUICHE. Will no one answer him?

VISCOUNT. No one? Wait. I'll launch a shaft to scare him. (*He swaggers up to* CYRANO, *who is watching him, and stands in front of him with a conceited air.*) You—you have—— your—— ah—— nose is very large!

CYRANO (*gravely*). Very.

VISCOUNT (*smiling*). Ha! Ha!

CYRANO (*unperturbed*). Is that all?

VISCOUNT. Sir——

CYRANO. That's a mite brief, young man. You might make, Lord, how many remarks, merely by changing tone. For instance, listen:— Aggressive: "Sir, if I had that nose, they should amputate at once." Friendly interest: "It must get in your cups; you ought to have a pitcher made for drinking." Descriptive: "It's a rock! A peak! A cape! A cape, I said? A whole peninsula." Inquisitive: "What do you use that oblong casket for, inkstand or scissors-case?" Gracious: "Are you so fond of birds, that in paternal fashion you tender for their little feet that perch?" Quarrelsome: "When you smoke your pipe, sir, does the smoke ever leave your nostrils without some neighbor crying, 'Chimney fire'?" Warning: "With that weight pulling at your head, take care you don't fall forward on the ground!" Tender: "Have a little parasol made, lest the sun fade its hue." Pedantic: "Only the beast that Aristophanes calls Hippocampelephantocamelos could carry such flesh and bone beneath its brows." Lordly: "What, my friend, you say that hook is in style? Surely convenient to hang one's hat on!" Emphatic: "No wind except the mistral, O magisterial nose, could give you cold all over." Dramatic: "When it bleeds, there's your Red Sea!" Admiring: "What a sign for a perfumer!" Lyrical: "Oh, art thou Triton breathing in that conch?" Naïve: "What are the visiting hours at this monument?" Respectful: "My deep respects, sir! You have, so to speak, a gable all your own, fronting the street." Rustic: "Yon's a nose what is a nose. It's a great turnip or dwarf melon else." Military: "Defense against cavalry." Practical: "Is it up in a raffle? Surely, sir, it's bound to take first prize." Finally, in weeping parody of De Viau's *Pyramus:*

> "There's the nose that spoiled the face endowed to him by Nature.
> Its master's symmetries are lost. It makes him blush, the traitor!"

That, my friend, or something very like it, is what you might have said if you had the merest spice of letters and of wit. But of wit, most ridiculous of creatures, you never had an atom, and of letters, only the four that spell out *fool!* What's more, even if you had the necessary invention to offer such mad jests before these galleries filled with nobles, you couldn't have uttered the quarter of the half of the beginning of the first. To myself I offer them with verve; but no one else may offer them to me.

DE GUICHE (*trying to drag away the petrified* VISCOUNT). Viscount, come away!

VISCOUNT (*stifled with anger*). Such arrogant airs he gives himself, this country lout! He—he— doesn't even wear gloves! He goes about ribbonless, bowless, braidless——

CYRANO. My elegance I keep for my character. Not foppish in my dress, I am the less vain, the more perfectly accoutred. I don't go from home leaving insult uncleansed, my honor soiled with wearing, my scruples black as mourning, my conscience yellow from the slumber still unwiped from its eyes. When I go abroad, everything shines fresh and cleanly, plumed as I am with sincere independence. Not my figure but my soul I stiffen up with stays; and thus, wearing the ribbands of fulfilled achievement, curling the mustachios of my wit, I go my way through the crowd, letting truth ring out like clanking spurs.

VISCOUNT. But, sir—

CYRANO. I have no gloves? Too bad! I had one left of a very old pair. It was much in my way; I threw it in someone's face.

VISCOUNT. Knavish rascal! Ridiculous, ill-mannered boor!

CYRANO (*taking off his hat and bowing as if the* VISCOUNT *were introducing himself*). Charmed! And I am Cyrano-Savinien-Hercule de Bergerac.
(*Laughter.*)

VISCOUNT (*exasperated*). Buffoon!

CYRANO (*with a sudden cry as if seized with cramp*). Oh!

VISCOUNT (*who was going away, turning around*). What else did he say?

CYRANO (*grimacing, as if in agony*). She gets stiff when not used. This comes of idleness!

VISCOUNT. What's the matter?

CYRANO. My sword's asleep. It tingles.

VISCOUNT (*drawing his*). So be it!

CYRANO. I shall give you the most charming little thrust.

VISCOUNT (*scornfully*). Poet!

CYRANO. Precisely, sir, a poet! Such a poet that while we fence I am going to make a ballade, improvized.

VISCOUNT. A ballade?

CYRANO. You don't know what that is, I suppose.

VISCOUNT. Sir—

CYRANO (*as if reciting a lesson*). The ballade, then, is composed of three stanzas of eight lines each—

VISCOUNT (*stamping*). Oh!

CYRANO (*continuing*). —with an envoy of four.

VISCOUNT. You—

CYRANO. At one and the same time, I shall compose a ballade, and fight you. At the last line, I shall kill you.

VISCOUNT. No!

CYRANO. No? (*Declaiming*) "BALLADE OF THE DUEL WHICH MONSIEUR DE BERGERAC FOUGHT WITH A NINCOMPOOP IN THE HÔTEL DE BOURGOGNE."

VISCOUNT. What might that be?

CYRANO. That is the title.

AUDIENCE (*frenzied with excitement*). Room! This is fun! Make way! No noise!
(*Tableau. Circle of curious spectators in the pit, the fops and officers mixed in with citizens and common people. Pages climb on people's shoulders to get a better view. In the boxes, all the ladies are standing. On the right,* DE GUICHE *and his attendant nobles. Left,* LE BRET, RAGUENEAU, CUIGY, *etc.*)

CYRANO (*closing his eyes for a moment*). Wait! I am choosing my rhymes. There, I've found them! (*As he recites, he suits the action to the words.*)

With grace I toss my plumed *chapeau:*
With languid grace, my mantle shed.
I draw my well-tried rapier—so!—
And circle you with catlike tread.
Was Céladon the better-bred?
Could Scaramouche such style essay?
Young Myrmidon, your Fate's foresaid:
The envoy's end, and then *touché!*

(*Their swords meet.*)

If you'd kept silent, *comme il faut,*
No need to riddle you; instead,
Now I must beat my brains to know
Where I shall spit you,—heart, or head,
Or on that badge unmerited!
Wait! Now I have it, clear as day!
Your paunch shall put my point to bed!
The envoy's end, and then *touché!*

I need another rhyme in *—o!*
You disengage? Your color's fled?
Then you're a goose that daren't say "Boh,"
And that's my rhyme. Your thrust is sped;
I block it with my parry, spread
Your guard with this new counter, play
My blade till your blade drops like lead!
The envoy's end, and then *touché!*

(*He announces solemnly.*)

Envoy.

Prince! To the living God, who bled
Upon the cross, 'tis best you pray!
I lunge! I feint! You're good as dead!

(*The* VISCOUNT *staggers;* CYRANO *bows.*)

The envoy's end! And . . . so! . . . *touché!*
(*Cheers. Applause in the boxes. Showers of flowers and handkerchiefs. Officers mob* CYRANO *with congratulations.* RAGUENEAU *dances with joy.* LE BRET *is both happy and disconsolate. The* VISCOUNT'S *friends, supporting him in their arms, lead him away.*)

THE CROWD (*in a long shout*). Hurrah!

A LIGHT-HORSEMAN. Superb!

A WOMAN. So pretty!

RAGUENEAU. Wonderful!

A FOP. Novel!

LE BRET. Mad!

VARIOUS MEMBERS OF THE CROWD (*surrounding* CYRANO). Compliments!— Congratulate you!— Bravo!

A WOMAN'S VOICE. He is a hero!

A MUSKETEER (*swiftly approaching* CYRANO *with outstretched hand*). Sir, allow me! Exceedingly well done! I'm speaking as something of a judge. Naturally, I first expressed my approval by stamping. (*He withdraws.*)

CYRANO (*to* CUIGY). What is that gentleman's name?

CUIGY. He's D'Artagnan.

LE BRET (*to* CYRANO, *taking his arm*). Now, let us have a talk.

CYRANO. Let this crowd thin out. (*To* BELLEROSE) May I stay?

BELLEROSE (*with marked respect*). Most certainly.
(*Shouting outside.*)

JODELET (*after looking out*). Montfleury. They're hooting him.

BELLEROSE (*solemnly*). *Sic transit.* (*Changing tone,—to the* DOORKEEPER *and* CANDLE-SNUFFER) Sweep out! Close the doors! But don't put out the lights. We'll be back after dinner to rehearse a new farce for tomorrow.
(*Exeunt* JODELET *and* BELLEROSE *after impressive bows to* CYRANO.)

THE DOORKEEPER (*to* CYRANO). Aren't you dining?

CYRANO. I? No.
(*The* DOORKEEPER *retires.*)

LE BRET (*to* CYRANO). Not dining? Why not?

CYRANO (*proudly*). Because (*changing his tone when the* DOORKEEPER *has gone*)—I have no money.

LE BRET (*making the motion of throwing a bag*). Oh! The bag of crowns?

CYRANO. Paternal allowance, your life was but a day!

LE BRET. How will you live the rest of the month?

CYRANO. I have nothing left.

LE BRET. Silly to throw away that bag!

CYRANO. But what a splendid gesture.

REFRESHMENT GIRL (*coughing behind her little counter*). Hm! (CYRANO *and* LE BRET *turn; she comes up somewhat frightened.*) Sir, to know you're hungry,—that breaks my heart. (*Indicating the refreshment stand*) I have everything needed there. (*Impulsively*) Take what you wish.

CYRANO (*taking off his hat*). Dear child, though Gascon pride forbids that I accept the smallest trifle from your fingers, I could not hurt your feelings by refusing. Therefore, I'll accept—(*he goes to the stand to select something*)—some little something: a single grape! (*She wishes to give him the bunch; he takes one grape.*) Just one! This glass of (*stopping her as she starts to pour out wine*)—water! And half a macaroon! (*He puts back the other half.*)

LE BRET. Stupid!

REFRESHMENT GIRL. Oh! Something more!

CYRANO. Why, yes! Your hand to kiss. (*He kisses the hand she extends as though it were that of a princess.*)

REFRESHMENT GIRL. I thank you, sir. (*She curtsies.*) Good night! (*Exit.*)

SCENE V

CYRANO, LE BRET, *then the* DOORKEEPER.

CYRANO (*to* LE BRET). Now I'll listen. (*He places the macaroon before him.*) The main course. (*The glass of water*) Beverage. (*The grape*) Dessert. (*He sits down.*) I'll sit down to my feast. Pardon, my friend, I was terribly hungry. (*Eating*) What were you saying?

LE BRET. I was saying these fops with their bellicose airs will ruin your reason if you listen only to them. Talk to sensible people; you'll soon find out the effect of your escapade.

CYRANO (*finishing his macaroon*). Terrific.

LE BRET. The Cardinal—

CYRANO (*beaming*). The Cardinal—was he there?

LE BRET. Yes. He must have found it—

CYRANO. Quite unusual.

LE BRET. Nevertheless—

CYRANO. Oh, he's a playwright himself. It wouldn't bother him to see a rival's play disturbed.

LE BRET. The trouble with you is you're getting too many enemies on your hands.

CYRANO (*starting on the grape*). How many, approximately, have I made today?

LE BRET. Forty-eight, not counting women.

CYRANO. Particularize!

LE BRET. Montfleury, the old citizen, De Guiche, the Viscount, Baro, the playwright, the entire Academy——

CYRANO. That's enough. You'll kill me with joy.

LE BRET. But this kind of life—where will it lead you? What's behind it?

CYRANO. I was wandering in a maze. Too many courses, too many complicated resolutions. So I took——

LE BRET. Well?

CYRANO. —the simplest possible. I decided—in all things and at all times—to deserve admiration.

LE BRET (*shrugging*). So that's that! But your hatred for Montfleury—what's your motive, your real motive?

CYRANO (*rising*). That fat Silenus, so paunched that his own navel is beyond him, thinks he's God's gift to women. As he murders his lines, his toad's eyes turn to sheep's eyes. I've hated him since that evening when he first looked at *her*. It was like watching a slug sliding down a flower.

LE BRET (*astonished*). Good God! Is it possible——

CYRANO (*with a bitter smile*). That I should be in love? (*Changing his tone and speaking gravely*) I am in love.

LE BRET. Who? You never told me.

CYRANO. My love? Why, just consider. This nose of mine, a quarter-hour ahead no matter where I go, would nightmare dreams of love with Nature's ugliest duckling. Whom do I love then? Why, naturally, the loveliest of all.

LE BRET. The loveliest of all?

CYRANO. The loveliest in the world. The wittiest! The subtlest! (*Dejectedly*) The fairest!

LE BRET. Good God! Who can she be?

CYRANO. A deadly peril, but without intention; exquisite beauty, without self-admiration; a musk rose, Nature's snare, with love enambushed. Whoever knows her smile, he knows perfection. Graceful she is in all things; divinity is in her merest gesture. And thou, O Venus, could never mount thy shell, nor thou, Diana, walk thy flowered woods, as she mounts in her chair or walks through Paris!

LE BRET. The devil! I know all now. It's very plain.

CYRANO. Plain? It's crystal clear.

LE BRET. Your cousin, Magdeleine Robin.

CYRANO. Precisely. It's Roxane.

LE BRET. Well, that's only as it should be. You love her? Tell her so. In her eyes, today has covered you with glory.

CYRANO (*indicating his nose*). My dear fellow, tell me what hope of glory, what hope of any kind, this protuberance of mine could ever leave me. I'm not a fool,—don't cherish such illusions! And yet, sometimes, in the violet hour of twilight, I can be touched—even I! —with secret longings. In some still garden where the very hour is fragrant, my poor sinner of a nose senses the breath of April, and my eyes drift down a silver shaft of moonlight to trail some woman on her lover's arm. I can dream then how it would be to walk slowly in the moonlight with someone on my arm. Elated, I forget myself. But suddenly, why, there's the shadow of my profile on the wall, and then—

LE BRET (*touched*). My poor friend.

CYRANO. Friend, I'm not without my dismal hours, knowing myself so ugly, so alone.

LE BRET (*hastily, seizing his hand*). What! Tears? From you?

CYRANO. Not that! No, never that! That would be much too ugly, if tears should glide along this nose of mine. The divine grace of tears, while I'm their master, shall never touch such monstrous ugliness. Nothing on earth is more sublime than tears, and no least one, through any fault of mine, shall find the ridicule of being laughed at.

LE BRET. Love's just a game of chance. No need for sadness!

CYRANO (*shaking his head*). I love Cleopatra. Have I the look of Caesar? I idolize Berenice. Would you take me for Titus?

LE BRET. Where's your courage? Your spirit? Why, that little girl, just now when she offered you refreshment—you saw her eyes.

CYRANO (*impressed*). That's true.

LE BRET. You see! And when Roxane herself went pale as she watched you duelling—

CYRANO. Roxane went pale?

LE BRET. —it shows her heart and mind were struck with admiration. Why don't you speak to her?

CYRANO. I can't! It's the one thing on earth that I'm afraid of. She'd laugh in my nose.

THE DOORKEEPER (*ushering someone in*). Someone for you, sir.

CYRANO (*recognizing the duenna*). Oh God! Her duenna!

SCENE VI

CYRANO, LE BRET, *and the* DUENNA.

DUENNA (*with an elaborate curtsey*). Someone wants to know where she can meet her valiant cousin—secretly.

CYRANO (*disturbed*). Meet me?

DUENNA (*curtsies*). Meet you! There are things to be told.

CYRANO. What things?

DUENNA (*curtsies again*). Some things!

CYRANO (*staggering*). My God!

DUENNA. Someone's going early—very early—tomorrow morning to hear mass at Saint-Roch.

CYRANO (*hanging on* LE BRET *for support*). Oh, my God!

DUENNA. On the way back, where could one . . . step in . . . to have a little talk?

CYRANO (*completely distracted*). Where? O-o-oh! My God!

DUENNA. Quickly, please!

CYRANO. I'm cudgeling my brains —

DUENNA. Well, where?

CYRANO. At—at—Ragueneau's, the pastry-cook's.

DUENNA. Which is where?

CYRANO. In—in Rue— Oh, God! Rue St. Honoré!

DUENNA (*commencing to leave*). Someone will be there. Don't forget. Be there at seven o'clock.

CYRANO. Seven without fail! (*Exit the* DUENNA.)

SCENE VII

CYRANO, LE BRET, *afterwards the actors, actresses,* CUIGY, BRISSAILLE, LIGNIÈRE, *the* DOORKEEPER, *the violinists.*

CYRANO (*clutching* LE BRET'*s arm*). To me! From her! A rendezvous!

LE BRET. I shouldn't think you'd be sad now.

CYRANO. Whatever happens, she at least knows I'm alive.

LE BRET. You'll calm down now?

CYRANO (*beside himself*). Now? Now I shall fulminate frenetically! I want an entire army corps to put to flight! My heart's ten-fold; my arms are twenty-fold! No more killing dwarfs for me! (*Shouting his *head off*) Bring on your giants! (*During his speech, whispering shadows of the actors have been moving about the back of the stage. They begin rehearsing. The violinists are in their seats under the stage.*)

VOICE (*from the stage*). Shhh! Shut up down there! We're in rehearsal.

CYRANO (*laughing*). We're going. (*He goes upstage. Through the large door at the back enter* CUIGY, BRISSAILLE, *and several officers, supporting* LIGNIÈRE, *who is completely drunk.*)

CUIGY. Cyrano!

CYRANO. What's that?

CUIGY. A boiled owl we're bringing in to you.

CYRANO (*recognizing him*). Lignière! What's wrong with him?

CUIGY. He's looking for you.

BRISSAILLE. He can't go home.

LIGNIÈRE (*in a thick voice, showing him a crumpled note*). This note . . . warning . . . a hundred men waiting . . . because of song. Great danger . . . Porte de Nesle. Must get through 'em to get back home. Allow me—hic!—sleep at your . . . house?

CYRANO. A hundred men, you say! You'll sleep at home for all that.

LIGNIÈRE (*frightened*). I daren't——

CYRANO (*commandingly, pointing to the lighted lantern which the* DOORKEEPER *is swinging as he listens*). Take that lantern. (LIGNIÈRE *hurriedly takes it.*) And get going! I'll protect you till I get you home, if I have to tuck you in myself. (*To the officers*) You'd better follow us as witnesses.

CUIGY. But a hundred men——

CYRANO. They're none too many men for me tonight.
(*The actors and actresses approach in costume down from the stage.*)

LE BRET. But why you should protect——

CYRANO. Old grumbler again!

LE BRET. —protect that vulgar sot!

CYRANO (*clapping* LIGNIÈRE *on the shoulder*). Why? Because this sot, this tun of Muscatel, this liquor hogshead, once did a noble deed! One day, when leaving mass, he saw his sweetheart dipping her fingers in the holy water; and he who always runs away from water rushed to the basin, bent his mustache down and drank it, every drop.

AN ACTRESS (*in soubrette costume*). That was real nice, that was!

CYRANO. Wasn't it, my dear?

THE ACTRESS (*to the others*). But why a hundred against one poor poet?

CYRANO. Let's go! (*To the officers*) When you see me rush against them, don't give me aid, no matter what the danger.

ANOTHER ACTRESS (*jumping from the stage*). I'm going to see it.

CYRANO. Come on!

ANOTHER ACTRESS (*jumping down, to an old actor*). Cassandra, are you coming?

CYRANO. Come on, and welcome. Isabelle, Leander, the Doctor—all of you. Come, join your Italian farce as sub-plot to this Spanish tragedy, and cloak its groans with your fantastic din as jingles mask the beat of tambourines.

ALL THE ACTORS (*gleefully*). Hurrah!—Where's my cloak?—Where's my hood?

JODELET. Let us go.

CYRANO (*to the violinists*). Give us a tune, there!
(*The violinists join the forming procession, handing out candles taken from the footlights. It becomes a torch-light procession.*)

CYRANO. Splendid! Officers! Actresses in costume. And twenty steps ahead (*goes to the place he designates at the head of the procession*)—myself, alone, marching under the plumes that Glory herself has given me, proud as Scipio, with three times his nose! You understand? Strictly forbidden to help me. Everyone ready? One, two, three! Doorkeeper, the door!
(*The* DOORKEEPER *opens both sides of the double door. Through it, we glimpse a corner of picturesque old Paris under the moon.*)

CYRANO. Ah! Paris mists away before my eyes. The bluish moonlight floods the sloping roofs,—exquisite setting for the coming action. The Seine below us, under its scarf of haze, is tremulant as a mystic magic-mirror. You shall see . . . what you shall see! But nothing mean or pitiful, I'm sure!

ALL. To the Porte de Nesle!

CYRANO (*at the threshold*). To the Porte de Nesle! (*To the soubrette*) My dear, you asked me why a hundred men have set themselves against this single poet? (*Placidly, drawing his sword*) Because, as everyone knows, the man's my friend.
(*Exit* CYRANO. *Under the flicker of candles, to a tune on the violins, the procession—headed by* LIGNIÈRE, *staggering, followed by the actresses on the arms of the officers, then the actors, frolicking—goes marching off into the night.*)

CURTAIN

ACT TWO

THE POET'S COOKSHOP

The shop of RAGUENEAU, *baker and pastry-cook. It is a very large establishment situated at the corner of the Rue St. Honoré and the Rue de l'Arbre-Sec. A wide vista of these streets, gray in the first light of dawn, looms through the glass of a door, backstage. Downstage, left, a counter overhung by a wrought-iron canopy from which are suspended geese, ducks, and white peacocks. Around the counter, tall bouquets of garden flowers, chiefly sun-flowers, set in high china vases. Further back, left, an enormous fireplace. In front of it, on huge andirons, each supporting a saucepan, roasts drip into grease-pans. Downstage, right, a door. Further back, right, a stairway leading to a little eavesloft, its interior visible through open shutters. This eating-nook, lit by a little Flemish chandelier, is furnished with a table, already laid. A wooden gallery, leading from the top of the stairway, seems to give access to other, similar nooks. In the center of the shop, an iron ring, raised or lowered by means of a rope, is festooned with large chunks of meat and makes a kind of chandelier of game.*

It is the early morning rush period. Ovens glow brightly in the shadow of the stairway. Copper vessels shine; spits turn. Here and there, hams are hanging. Various kinds of food pyramid up on dishes in conventional patterns. Harried scullions, fat cooks, and little cooks' assistants bustle confusedly, their caps decorated with chicken feathers and guinea-fowl wings. Some bring in quincunxes of muffins and whole towns of tiny cakes on sheet-iron trays and wicker stands.

Some of the tables are heaped with cakes and other kinds of eatables. Others, with chairs set around them, await customers. A smaller table in a corner is half hidden under a litter of papers. As the curtain rises, RAGUENEAU *is seated at it, writing.*

SCENE I

RAGUENEAU, *pastry-cooks, then* LISE. RAGUENEAU, *at the small table, writing with an inspired air, and counting on his fingers.*

FIRST PASTRY-COOK (*with sweetmeats arranged in patterns*). Nougat fruits!

SECOND PASTRY-COOK (*with a dish*). Custard!

THIRD PASTRY-COOK (*with a roast decorated with feathers*). Peacock!

FOURTH PASTRY-COOK (*with a plate of cakes*). Rissoles!

FIFTH PASTRY-COOK (*with an earthenware dish*). Sauced filet of beef!

RAGUENEAU (*stops writing; raises his head*). The dawn already silvers on our coppers. Time, Ragueneau, to stifle in your god of song. Lute-time will come again; this is your stove-time. (*He rises. To a cook*) Lengthen this sauce for me; it's far too thick.

COOK. How much?

RAGUENEAU. About three feet. (*Proceeds.*)

COOK. Hey! What's that?

FIRST PASTRY-COOK. Tart!

SECOND PASTRY-COOK. *Torte!*

RAGUENEAU (*in front of the fireplace*). Leave me, O Muse, that your charming eyes be not reddened by this faggot-fire. (*To a pastry-cook who displays bread*) You have not cleft these loaves in the right places; caesuras go *between* the hemistiches. (*To another, displaying an unfinished pasty*) You must roof in this palace-wall of crust. (*To a young apprentice, seated on the floor, spitting poultry*) Son, upon that same interminable spit, alternate humble chicken and haughty turkey, as old Malherbe varied long lines with short ones; and turn your roasts before the fire in strophes.

ANOTHER APPRENTICE (*approaching with a tray covered with a napkin*). Master, thinking of you, I had this baked. I hope you'll like it. (*He uncovers the tray, and displays a huge pastry lyre.*)

RAGUENEAU (*dazzled*). A lyre!

APPRENTICE. Of muffin paste.

RAGUENEAU (*touched*). With candied fruit!

APPRENTICE. Look at the strings. I have made them out of sugar.

RAGUENEAU (*giving him money*). Go, drink my health in this! (*Enter* LISE.) Hush! My wife! Off with you! Hide that money! (*To* LISE, *showing her the lyre apprehensively*) Fine, isn't it?

LISE. Ridiculous!
(*She places a pile of paper bags on the counter.*)

RAGUENEAU. Bags? Good! So thoughtful! (*Examining them*) What! Books I revere! The verses of my friends! Torn! Ripped apart! To make up bags for cracknels! Why, it's Orpheus and the Bacchantes in revival!

LISE (*dryly*). I've the right to use as I see fit the only payment your limp-lined scribblers ever left us.

RAGUENEAU. Ant! You're insulting poetry's grasshoppers.

LISE. Till they began to eat us out of house and home, you never used to call me aunt—let alone backauntie!

RAGUENEAU. And you did this to poetry?

LISE. Nothing but!

RAGUENEAU. What would you do if it were prose?

SCENE II

The same. Two CHILDREN *have just entered the shop.*

RAGUENEAU. Well, children, what do you want?

FIRST CHILD. Three patties, please.

RAGUENEAU (*serving them*). There! Crisp, brown, and piping hot.

SECOND CHILD. Could you wrap them up, please?

RAGUENEAU (*aside*). Alas, one of my precious bags! (*To the* CHILDREN) You're sure you want them wrapped? (*They nod. He takes a bag, and as he starts to wrap the patties, reads aloud*)

"When Ulysses had left Penelope—"

No! Not that! (*He puts it aside and takes another. As he is putting in the patties he sees the writing and reads*) "The fair Apollo —" Nor that! (*Puts it aside.*)

LISE (*impatiently*). Well, what are you waiting for?

RAGUENEAU (*hastily*). Ah! Here we are! (*Resignedly, he takes the third.*) That sonnet to Phyllis— All the same, it's rather hard.

LISE (*shrugging*). It's as well you've made up your mind. Simpleton! (*She climbs on a chair, and begins to arrange dishes on a sideboard.*)

RAGUENEAU (*as soon as her back is turned, calling the* CHILDREN *back from the door*). Quick, children! Give me back that sonnet, and I'll give you six patties for the three. (*The* CHILDREN *give the bag back, quickly take the cakes, and go out.* RAGUENEAU *smoothes out the paper and begins to read, declaiming*) "Phyllis." What! A fleck of butter on that charming name? "Phyllis!" (CYRANO *enters hurriedly.*)

SCENE III

RAGUENEAU, LISE, CYRANO; *then the* MUSKETEER.

CYRANO. What time is it?

RAGUENEAU (*bowing ceremoniously*). Six.

CYRANO (*emotionally*). In one short hour! (*He walks to and fro across the shop.*)

RAGUENEAU (*following him*). Magnificent! I saw it all.

CYRANO. You saw what?

RAGUENEAU. Your duel.

CYRANO. Which?

RAGUENEAU. At the Hôtel de Bourgogne.

CYRANO (*disdainfully*). Oh, that!

RAGUENEAU (*admiringly*). Yes! The duel in verse.

LISE. He talks of nothing else.

CYRANO. No harm in that.

RAGUENEAU (*lunging with a spit*). "The envoy's end, and then *touché!*" Magnificent! "The envoy's end! And . . . so! . . . *touché!*" (*He grows more and more enthusiastic.*) "The envoy's end . . ."

CYRANO. What time is it?

RAGUENEAU (*stopping to look at the clock*). Five after six. "And then *touché!*" (*Straightening up*) Oh, to make a ballade like that!

LISE (*to* CYRANO, *who has absent-mindedly shaken hands with her as he passes her counter*). What have you done to your hand?

CYRANO. Nothing. Just a scratch.

RAGUENEAU. You have been in trouble!

CYRANO. No trouble at all.

LISE (*shaking her finger at him*). I think you're lying.

CYRANO. What! Did my nose quiver? It would take a monstrous lie for that. (*Changing tone*) I'm expecting someone. If all goes well, will you leave us alone?

RAGUENEAU. That's not so easy; my poets are coming.

LISE (*ironically*). For breakfast, on the house!

CYRANO. Get them out of here when I give the signal. What time is it now?

RAGUENEAU. Ten after six.

CYRANO (*seating himself nervously at* RAGUENEAU'*s table and helping himself to paper*). I need a pen.

RAGUENEAU (*offering the one behind his ear*). The quill of a swan. (*Enter a* MUSKETEER, *splendidly mustached and stentorian voiced.*)

MUSKETEER. Hail!
(LISE *goes to him hastily.*)

CYRANO (*turning*). Who's that?

RAGUENEAU. Friend of my wife's. A terrible warrior—so he says!

CYRANO (*motioning* RAGUENEAU *away; to himself*). Come on—write it—seal it—give it her and hurry off. (*Throwing down the pen*) Coward that I am! And yet I'd gladly die if I could speak to her —speak but a single word—(*To* RAGUENEAU) The time?

RAGUENEAU. Quarter after six.

CYRANO (*beating his breast*).—just one lone word of all I have in here! But writing, now—(*Takes up the pen again*) Let's write this *billet-doux*, then, phrased and rephrased in my mind a hundred times, already perfect. Why, all I need to do is let my soul lie by this paper and copy what I see there.

(*He writes. Slender, hesitant shadows move behind the glass window in the door.*)

SCENE IV

RAGUENEAU, LISE, *the* MUSKETEER, CYRANO, *still writing; the poets, dressed in black, their hose falling, splashed with mud.*

LISE (*entering, to* RAGUENEAU). Your mud-larks are here.

FIRST POET (*entering, to* RAGUENEAU). My colleague!

SECOND POET (*shaking* RAGUENEAU'S *hand*). My dear colleague!

THIRD POET. Eagle of pastry-cooks! Your eyrie smells divine.

FOURTH POET. O Phoebus of the spit!

FIFTH POET. Apollo of the dripping pan!

RAGUENEAU (*as they surround, embrace him, and shake his hand*). How easy it is to feel at home with them.

FIRST POET. We were delayed by the crowd at the Porte de Nesle.

SECOND POET. Eight bloody sword-ripped brigands garnished the pavement there.

CYRANO (*raising his head*). Eight? Hm! Seven, I thought. (*Continues writing.*)

RAGUENEAU (*to* CYRANO). You wouldn't happen to know the hero of this slaughter?

CYRANO (*absent-mindedly*). Me? No.

LISE (*to the* MUSKETEER). Do you?

MUSKETEER (*twirling his mustache*). Perhaps I do.

CYRANO (*writing, murmuring a word from time to time*). I adore you!

FIRST POET. They say a single man put the whole troop to flight.

SECOND POET. Amazing sight! The ground strewn with pikes and clubs.

CYRANO (*writing*). As for your eyes—

THIRD POET. Hats scattered on the ground as far as Goldsmiths' quay.

FIRST POET. The deuce! He must have gone berserk—

CYRANO (*writing*). And for your lips—

FIRST POET. —the man who did all this. Some fierce, remorseless giant!

CYRANO (*writing*). I swoon with fear when my eyes rest upon you!

SECOND POET (*snatching a cake*). What's your new poem, Ragueneau?

CYRANO (*writing*). Your devoted admirer—— (*Just as he is about to sign his name, he stops writing, rises, and puts the letter in his doublet.*) No need to sign; I'll give it her myself.

RAGUENEAU (*to the* SECOND POET). I've versified a recipe.

THIRD POET (*stationing himself near a tray of cream puffs*). Let's hear this recipe.

FOURTH POET (*looking at a muffin he has taken*). This muffin's cap is unsymmetrical. (*He takes off the top at a single bite.*)

FIRST POET. This ginger bread ogles a famished poet with almond eyes 'neath brows angelical. (*Takes a piece of ginger bread.*)

SECOND POET. We are listening.

THIRD POET (*gently squeezing a cream puff between his fingers*). This cream puff is driveling cream. It's laughing at me!

SECOND POET (*biting the big pastry lyre*). For the first time in my life, the Lyre sustains me.

RAGUENEAU (*ready to recite, coughs, settles his cap, and strikes pose*). A recipe in verse:—

SECOND POET (*nudging the* FIRST). Stuffing for breakfast?

FIRST POET (*to the* SECOND). Gorging for dinner?

RAGUENEAU. "HOW TO MAKE ALMOND CREAM TARTS"

Whip whites of eggs to lightest texture;
Then next your
Egg-white strain as fine as silk,
Add juice of lemons, one or two,
And quite a few
Spoonfuls of sweetened almond milk!

Now in every tartlet-mold
Your thumb must fold
Such dough as lightens pastry tops.
You line the sides with jellied fruit,
Sugar to suit,
And pour your whip in careful drops

Into the waiting shells! See well
That every shell
Suffers the stove's alchemic arts,
Whence issuing, the merry crew,
Light brown in hue,
Will be delicious cream of almond tarts!

THE POETS (*with their mouths full*). Exquisite! Delicious!

A POET (*choking*). Mmmm—mm! (*They go backstage, eating.*)

CYRANO (*has been watching them; goes up to* RAGUENEAU). Are you ulled to sleep by your own voice? Can't you see how they're stuff-ng?

RAGUENEAU (*with a smile*). I'm not asleep. I don't look, for fear I'd hurt their feelings. When I recite, I get a double pleasure: as I satisfy my little pleasant weakness, I see those things eaten—by those who haven't eaten.

CYRANO (*slapping him on the shoulder*). Oh, I like that! (RAGUENEAU *rejoins his friends.* CYRANO, *a little brusquely*) You, Lise! (LISE, *in amorous conversation with the* MUSKETEER, *starts guiltily and comes towards him*) Is this captain beleaguering you?

LISE (*offended*). Oh! With a single haughty glance I can conquer anyone who dares attack my virtue!

CYRANO. Huh! For a conqueror's eyes, they are pretty badly battered.

LISE (*stifling with rage*). I won't be ridiculed!

CYRANO (*with decision*). *He* shan't be ridicuckolded. I'm fond of him.

LISE. Ah-h-h!

CYRANO (*raising his voice for the benefit of the* MUSKETEER). A word to the wise!
(*He bows to the* MUSKETEER; *looks up at the clock; takes up a place of observation by the door.*)

LISE (*to the* MUSKETEER, *who has merely returned* CYRANO's *bow*). I'm surprised! Why didn't you throw that insult back—in his nose?

MUSKETEER. In his nose—*his* nose? Not me! (*He moves away hastily.* LISE *follows.*)

CYRANO (*from the door at the back, giving* RAGUENEAU *the signal to take the poets out*). Pst!

RAGUENEAU (*showing them the door on the right*). We'll be better off in here. . . .

CYRANO (*impatiently*). Pst! Pst!

RAGUENEAU (*trying to herd them out*). . . . for reading verses.

FIRST POET (*mournfully, his mouth full*). What about the cakes?

SECOND POET. They go with us! (*They make a hurried onslaught on the dishes; then follow* RAGUENEAU *in procession.*)

SCENE V

CYRANO, ROXANE, *the* DUENNA.

CYRANO (*aside*). I'll not show my letter till I know I have a chance. (ROXANE, *masked, followed by the* DUENNA, *appears behind the window. He quickly opens the door.*)

CYRANO. Come in! (*Stepping up to the* DUENNA) Two words with you, Duenna.

DUENNA. Make it four.

CYRANO. Do—you—like—goodies?

DUENNA. Adore them. I could eat them till I'm sick.

CYRANO (*hastily taking paper bags from the counter*). Good! Here are two sonnets by Benserade—

DUENNA. Pfui!

CYRANO. —which I will fill with cream tarts.

DUENNA (*changing expression*). Oh!

CYRANO. Do you like the cake called "puff"?

DUENNA. Delicious! Filled with cream!

CYRANO. I will thrust six into the heart of a poem by Saint-Amant. Into these verses by Chapelain I will put a piece of sponge cake. Hmmm! Somewhat lighter! Oh! and you like fresh cakes?

DUENNA. To distraction!

CYRANO (*filling her arms with the bags*). Then eat these in the street—

DUENNA. But—

CYRANO (*pushing her out*). —and don't come back till they are eaten up.
(*He closes the door, comes to* ROXANE, *removes his hat, and stands at a respectful distance.*)

SCENE VI

CYRANO, ROXANE, *the* DUENNA *for a moment.*

CYRANO. Blest be this above all other moments, when, ceasing to forget I humbly breathe, you come here to say to me—? To tell me—?

ROXANE (*unmasking*). First let me thank you because that foppish fool your sword checked yesterday is one that a great lord, in love with me—

CYRANO. De Guiche?

ROXANE (*dropping her eyes*). —has tried to force upon me, as a husband.

CYRANO. Husband in name only? (*Bowing*) Then I have fought—and this is much the better—not for my ugly nose, but for your lovely eyes.

ROXANE. Next . . . I wished—but for this confession I'll think of you once more as the . . . almost brother I used to play in the park with near the lake.

CYRANO. When you came every summer to Bergerac.

ROXANE. And the reeds gave you wood to make your swords.

CYRANO. And the corn, yellow ringlets for your dolls.

ROXANE. That was our play-time——

CYRANO. —when fruit was bittersweet.

ROXANE. The time when you did everything I wanted.

CYRANO. Short-frocked Roxane, called Magdeleine——

ROXANE. And was I pretty?

CYRANO. You were not ugly.

ROXANE. Sometimes you came running with your hand all bleeding from your climbing. Then, playing mother, I would say, trying to make my childish voice severe: (*Taking his hand*) "What is the meaning of this scratch?" (*Surprised*) Oh, that's too bad! It really is! (CYRANO *tries to withdraw his hand.*) No, show it to me! What? The same child, still? Where did you do it?

CYRANO. Still playing, near the Porte de Nesle.

ROXANE (*sitting down at a table, and dipping her handkerchief in a glass of water*). Put it here.

CYRANO (*also sitting down*). Still prettily, still playfully maternal!

ROXANE. Tell me, while I wipe away a little of this blood, how many were against you?

CYRANO. Oh, some hundred.

ROXANE. Tell me about it.

CYRANO. No! Let it pass! But tell me what you were afraid to tell just now.

ROXANE (*holding his hand*). Now I am not afraid. The perfume of the past has given me courage. Yes, now I think I'll tell you. There's someone that I care for.

CYRANO. Oh!

ROXANE. So far, he doesn't know it.

CYRANO. Oh!

ROXANE. Not yet.

CYRANO. Oh!

ROXANE. But though he doesn't know it, soon he will do.

CYRANO. Oh!

ROXANE. The poor boy has loved me from afar, not dared to tell me——

CYRANO. Oh!

ROXANE. Give me your hand again. You see, it's feverish! I've seen avowal trembling on his lips.

CYRANO. Oh!

ROXANE (*finishes a little bandage made with her handkerchief*). And just imagine, cousin! As it happens, he's in your regiment.

CYRANO. Oh!

ROXANE (*smiling*). A Cadet in your Company!

CYRANO. Oh!

ROXANE. His face bears the stamp of wit and genius; proud, noble, young, intrepid, handsome——

CYRANO (*losing color, rising*). Handsome?

ROXANE. Handsome! Why, what's the matter?

CYRANO. Nothing. It's—(*smilingly indicating his hand*)—it's just a childish hurt.

ROXANE. In short, I love him. Yet I've never even seen him save at the play.

CYRANO. You two have never spoken to each other?

ROXANE. Only our eyes!

CYRANO. How can you know, then?

ROXANE. Under the lindens, in the Place Royale, there's talk. Gossips have hinted——

CYRANO. Cadet, you say?

ROXANE. In the Guards.

CYRANO. And what's his name?

ROXANE. The Baron Christian de Neuvillette.

CYRANO. He's no Cadet!

ROXANE. Yes, since this morning, under Captain de Castel-Jaloux.

CYRANO. How suddenly you throw your heart away! My dear——

DUENNA (*appearing at the door*). The cakes are gone, Monsieur de Bergerac.

CYRANO. Well, read the verses

printed on the bags. (*The* DUENNA *disappears.*) My dear! But what if he should be an ignoramus,—unlearned, uncultivated, lacking wit? *You* know no other love but pretty speeches.

ROXANE. No, he has hair like one of d'Urfé's heroes.

CYRANO. His speech may lack the brightness of his hair.

ROXANE. No! Every word is pointed, I'm quite sure.

CYRANO. His mustache must be super-fine! If he were stupid——

ROXANE (*stamping her foot*). Then I should die at once!

CYRANO (*after a pause*). And you brought me here to tell me that? I scarcely see the sense——

ROXANE. Why yesterday my heart was put to death. They told me all your Company are Gascons. All Gascons, every one of you——

CYRANO. I see. They said we challenge all those quackish youths whom influence gets admitted to our ranks, posing as Gascons but, in fact, not Gascons. That's what they told you, isn't it?

ROXANE (*nods*). I'm concerned!

CYRANO (*between his teeth*). As well you may be!

ROXANE. But yesterday, how invincible you seemed, punishing that rascal, coping with those brutes! I thought, supposing he, whom they all fear——

CYRANO. Enough! I will protect your little baron.

ROXANE. For me? I've always been so very fond of you!

CYRANO. Yes.

ROXANE. And always be his friend?

CYRANO. I will.

ROXANE. And he will never have to fight a duel?

CYRANO. Never! I promise.

ROXANE. You're so very kind, my dear!—— I must go. (*She hastily puts back her mask; throws a veil over her forehead; absent-mindedly*) To think you never got to tell about your last night's exploit! Really, it must be quite unique—— Tell him to write to me. (*She kisses her hand to him.*) So fond of you, my dear!

CYRANO. Yes!

ROXANE. A hundred men against you? Well, good-bye. We're great friends, aren't we?

CYRANO. Naturally! Of course!

ROXANE. Tell him to write to me. A hundred men! You must describe it—later on. Now I must go. A hundred men! What courage!

CYRANO (*bowing*). Believe me, I've done far, far better—since! (*Exit* ROXANE. CYRANO *stands motionless, his eyes lowered. The door at the right opens.* RAGUENEAU *puts his head in.*)

SCENE VII

CYRANO, RAGUENEAU, *the poets,* CARBON DE CASTEL-JALOUX, *the* CADETS, *the crowd, etc.; then* DE GUICHE, CUIGY, *and* BRISSAILLE.

RAGUENEAU. Can we come in?

CYRANO (*immobile*). Yes.
(RAGUENEAU *beckons, and his friends come in again. At the same time,* CARBON DE CASTEL-JALOUX, *in the costume of a Captain of the Guards, appears at the door backstage. Seeing* CYRANO, *he gestures extravagantly to someone outside.*)

CARBON. Here he is!

CYRANO (*raising his head*). Captain!

CARBON (*exultantly*). Our hero! We know everything. Thirty of my Cadets are here—

CYRANO. But— Captain!

CARBON (*trying to get him outside*). They want to greet you.

CYRANO. No.

CARBON. They're across the street, drinking at the Crossed Hilt.

CYRANO. No!

CARBON (*shouting out of the door in a thunderous voice*). The hero refuses. He's out of sorts.

A VOICE (*outside*). The devil he is! (*Uproar outside; noise of clanking swords and approaching boots.*)

CARBON (*rubbing his hands*). Here they come across the street.

THE CADETS (*entering the cookshop*). 'Sblood! 'Struth! 'Sbones! Dog's body! 'Snavel!

RAGUENEAU (*recoiling in alarm*). Gentlemen! Are you all from Gascony?

CADETS. All!

A CADET (*to* CYRANO). Bravo!

CYRANO. Baron!

ANOTHER CADET (*shaking his hands*). Vivat!

CYRANO. Baron!

THIRD CADET. Come to my arms!

CYRANO. Baron!

SEVERAL CADETS. Come to our arms!

CYRANO (*not knowing what to answer*). Baron!— Baron!— Please!

RAGUENEAU. Gentlemen! Are you all barons?

THE CADETS. All!

RAGUENEAU. Are they?

FIRST CADET. You could make a tower of our coronets.

LE BRET (*entering, running to* CYRANO). They're looking everywhere for you—a delirious crowd, led by those who followed you last night.

CYRANO (*in alarm*). You didn't tell them where to find me?

LE BRET (*rubbing his hands*). I certainly did!

A CITIZEN (*entering, followed by others*). The whole world of fashion is here!
(*Outside, the street is crowded with people. Sedan chairs are stopping.*)

LE BRET (*aside to* CYRANO, *smiling*). What about—Roxane?

CYRANO (*hurriedly*). Be quiet, will you!

THE CROWD (*shouting*). Cyrano!!
(*A crowd rushes into the cookshop. Confusion. Cheering.*)

RAGUENEAU (*standing on a table*). My shop is invaded; they are smashing everything! It's wonderful!

PEOPLE (*around* CYRANO). My friend!—My friend!

CYRANO. Yesterday, so many friends were lacking.

LE BRET. Success at last!

FOP (*running up with outstretched hands*). My dear! If you only knew——

CYRANO. Dear? Dear? Where did *we* get drunk together?

ANOTHER FOP. Sir, I'd like to introduce you to some ladies in my carriage.

CYRANO (*coldly*). And who will introduce you first to me?

LE BRET (*surprised*). What's wrong with you?

CYRANO. Be quiet!

A MAN OF LETTERS (*with a pocket-inkstand*). Now if you'll just give me the details——

CYRANO. No!

LE BRET (*nudging him with his elbow*). That's Théophraste Renaudot, inventor of the "Gazette"!

CYRANO. Pfui!

LE BRET. His sheet contains a world of matters. They say it has a future!

A POET (*advancing*). Sir—

CYRANO. Another?

THE POET. I'll make a pentacrostic on your name.

SOMEONE ELSE (*advancing*). Sir!—

CYRANO (*loudly*). Enough's enough! (*The crowd moves off. The people withdraw.* DE GUICHE *appears, escorted by the officers who followed* CYRANO *in the first act, including* CUIGY *and* BRISSAILLE. CUIGY *hastens up.*)

CUIGY (*to* CYRANO). Monsieur de Guiche! (*Murmurs; everybody withdraws.*) Representing the Marshal de Gassion!

DE GUICHE (*bowing to* CYRANO). Who wishes to express his admiration for your current exploit, now newly brought to light!

THE CROWD. Hurrah!

CYRANO (*bowing*). The Marshal is a judge of bravery.

DE GUICHE. He would never have believed it, if these gentlemen hadn't sworn that they had seen it.

CUIGY. With our own eyes!

LE BRET (*in a low voice, to* CYRANO, *who seems abstracted*). Now, really!

CYRANO. Hush!

LE BRET. You seem to be suffering.

CYRANO (*starting, and hastily straightening up*). What! Before these people? (*His mustache bristles; he throws out his chest.*) Suffering? You shall see!

DE GUICHE (*in whose ear* CUIGY *has been whispering*). Your career already abounds in glorious deeds. You're one of these crazy Gascons, aren't you?

CYRANO. A Cadet!

A CADET (*in a terrific voice*). He's one of us!

DE GUICHE (*contemplates the Gascons ranged behind* CYRANO). So! All these haughty gentlemen behind you must be the famous, the renowned—

CARBON. Cyrano!

CYRANO. Captain?

CARBON. Since my Company is here complete and all accounted for, you'd better introduce them to the Count.

CYRANO (*stepping two paces towards De Guiche and indicating the Cadets*).

These are Cadets of Gascony
In Captain Carbon's corps;
They fight and lie outrageously,

These are Cadets of Gascony!
And boast their forebears' ancestry
Who never thieves forebore.
These are Cadets of Gascony
In Captain Carbon's corps.

Hawk-eyed, wolf-fanged, and lank of knee,
Catwhiskered, through the crowd they pour,
Careless of curse and deaf to plea,
Hawk-eyed, wolf-fanged, and lank of knee,
Wearing their plumes beguilingly
On hats agape with holes galore.
Hawk-eyed, wolf-fanged, and lank of knee,
Catwhiskered, through the crowd they pour.

Here's Crack-your-Phiz and Snickersnee—
Such nicknames they adore—
Who'd not love Fame to such degree,
Not Crack-your-Phiz and Snickersnee,
Nor trade so much in duel'ry,
Loved they not Woman more.
Here's Crack-your-Phiz and Snickersnee;
Such nicknames they adore.

These are Cadets of Gascony,
All husbands they abhor;
But welcome wives! With bonhomie,
These same Cadets of Gascony
Will teach you Love's geometry
While cuckoos sing and new horns roar.
These are Cadets of Gascony,
All husbands they ab-whore!

DE GUICHE (*nonchalantly sitting in an armchair brought by* RAGUENEAU). Poets are luxuries we all must have today! Could I be your patron?

CYRANO. Not you, sir, nor anyone.

DE GUICHE. Your spirit yesterday was vastly diverting to my uncle Richelieu. I could further you with him.

LE BRET (*dazzled*). God!

DE GUICHE. I imagine that somewhere around you must have—some—some little thing—some five acts in rhyme?

LE BRET (*whispering*). They'll produce your "Agrippina."

DE GUICHE. Take it to him.

CYRANO (*tempted, somewhat pleased*). Well, really—

DE GUICHE. He's a connoisseur in such things. In your case, I'm quite sure, he'd only need to amend a verse or two.

CYRANO (*glowering*). Impossible! To think he could change a single comma would freeze my blood.

DE GUICHE. On the other hand, when he likes a verse, he'll pay—pay rather well!

CYRANO. But not so well as I do. When I've made verses that I really like, I make the proper payment: I chant them to myself.

DE GUICHE. You're a proud soul.

CYRANO. You've noticed that—already?

A CADET (*entering, his sword strung with battered plumed hats*). Look, Cyrano. Here's strange game we bagged on the quay this morning. Runaways' hats!

CARBON. Spoils of the chase!
(*General laughter.*)

CUIGY. Faith! Whoever set the rascals on will cut up rough today.

BRISSAILLE. Who could it be, I wonder?

DE GUICHE. It was I! (*The laughter stops short.*) I told them to chastise a wretched, drunken rhymester. It's not the kind of thing to soil one's hands with.
(*Strained silence.*)

THE CADET (*in an undertone to* CYRANO, *pointing to the hats*). What's to be done with them? Make a game stew? They're rather high.
(CYRANO *takes the sword strung with hats and salutes with it in such a manner that they slide off with a rush at* DE GUICHE'*s feet.*)

CYRANO. Perhaps you would return these to your friends?

DE GUICHE (*rising, speaking curtly*). Quick! My chair and porters! (*To* CYRANO) As for you, sir—

A VOICE (*outside*). The porters of His Grace the Count de Guiche.

DE GUICHE (*recovering self-control, with a smile*). Have you read "Don Quixote"?

CYRANO. Frequently. Hats off to the hare-brained fellow!

DE GUICHE. Then you would do well to remember—

A PORTER (*appearing at the back*). Here's the chair.

DE GUICHE. —the chapter on the windmills.

CYRANO (*bowing*). Chapter thirteen.

DE GUICHE. For when you attack them, it often happens—

CYRANO. —that my opponents turn with every breeze?

DE GUICHE. —that a windmill's spinning, sail-covered arms, will hurl you in the mud.

CYRANO. Or next door to the stars!
(*Exit* DE GUICHE. *He is seen getting into his chair. His companions withdraw, whispering significantly.* LE BRET *ushers them to the door. The crowd leaves.*)

SCENE VIII

CYRANO, LE BRET; *the* CADETS *sit down at the tables, right and left, and are served with refreshments throughout the scene.*

CYRANO (*bowing ironically to those who leave unceremoniously*). Gentlemen! Gentlemen! Gentlemen!

LE BRET (*returning, throwing up his hands in despair*). This is a pretty pickle!

CYRANO. Enter the old grumbler!

LE BRET. You must admit you can murder opportunity too often. You exaggerate the thing!

CYRANO. Exaggerate? Well, yes—

LE BRET (*triumphantly*). There now!

CYRANO. But for the sake of principle, not to say example, sometimes there's virtue in exaggeration.

LE BRET. Relax that musketeer's soul of yours a little! Think of the sure fortune, the undoubted fame—

CYRANO. What should I do? Seek out a powerful patron as protector, and like the obscure ivy round a tree, obtain support by licking at the bark, climb up by trickery, not by forthright strength? That's not for me! To be like all the rest and dedicate my verse to men of wealth, the financiers,—become a vile and spiritless buffoon in the poor hope some politician's smile might prove not too unfriendly? No, not for me! I'll not lunch every mortal day on insult, nor wear my stomach's casing thin with crawling, nor lacerate these two good knees with kneeling, nor flex my dorsal vertebrae with bowing! I'll pat no cabbage-eating goat with one hand while watering rows of cabbage with the other, nor ever suffer damns to gain faint praise, nor lather perfumed flattery on a beard. I'll never graduate from lap to lap to be the darling of some little circle, nor navigate with madrigals for oars and elderly maidens' sighs to fill my mainsail, or pay my publisher to bring my poems out, or chairman idiots in a grog-shop council—such things are not for me! Some make a single sonnet serve a lifetime. That's not for me! And some are terrorized by vagrant journals, would strive abjectly for a favoring mention in papers like the *Mercury of France*. Most calculate, must always be afraid, grow pale, present petitions —would rather pay a call than write a poem. But not for me! No, never that for me! None of these things for me! Instead . . . to sing, to dream, to laugh while passing by, to be alone and free! To have the observing eye, recording hand, and vibrant voice! To wear your hat as you please and when you please! To duel for *yes* or *no* . . . or poetize them. These are my life! To neglect fame for a journey to the moon; never to write but what comes out of the heart—content with flowers, and fruits, even with leaves, if you pluck them in your own garden plot! Then, when at length you have made a little way, you'll never need to render unto Caesar the things that are not Caesar's but your own; and though, in the end, you may never reach the stature of a great spreading oak or towering linden, you'll at least not be parasitic ivy; you'll climb—not high perhaps—but climb alone.

LE BRET. So be it! Quite alone! But quite alone—not one against the world! Where the devil did you get that mania for making enemies, always, everywhere?

CYRANO. From seeing you make friends! From seeing you smiling at your crowds of friends, your mouth tight-pursed! As for me, I like to give few greetings as I walk. My most joyful words are: One enemy the more!

LE BRET. Sheer lunacy!

CYRANO. Lunacy or not, that's my one vice; displeasure is my one pleasure—the great, final pleasure of being hated! My friend, you've no idea how much better you strut it out under the musketry of hostile eyes; and the least unpleasant stains upon your doublet are those of envious gall and cowards' spite. For you, the easy friendship that surrounds you is like a floating, loose Italian collar: your neck is too pliant for its good—not haughty because there's no restraint, support, or stricture, and your head gives way, pays court to everyone. But hatred irons my ruff into stiff creases that hold my head uplifted and in place. Each enemy is another added pleat, an inconvenience but a ray of splendor. For like a Spanish ruff in every way, hate's collar is the aureole of glory.

LE BRET (*after a short pause, putting his arm through* CYRANO'S). Be proud and bitter to the world, my friend; but, privately, just say, "She doesn't love me."

CYRANO (*quickly*). Quiet!
(CHRISTIAN *has entered and mingled with the* CADETS; *they ignore him; finally, he sits down alone at a little table, where* LISE *waits on him.*)

SCENE IX

CYRANO, LE BRET, *the* CADETS, CHRISTIAN DE NEUVILLETTE.

A CADET (*seated, glass in hand, at a table backstage*). Hey! Cyrano! (CYRANO *turns around.*) The story!

CYRANO. Later!
(*He walks backstage arm in arm with* LE BRET. *They talk quietly.*)

THE CADET (*rising and coming forward*). The story of the fight! It will be the best possible lesson (*stopping in front of* CHRISTIAN'S *table*) for this scared beginner.

CHRISTIAN (*looking up*). Beginner?

ANOTHER CADET. Yes, puny northerner!

CHRISTIAN. Puny?

FIRST CADET (*mockingly*). Monsieur de Neuvillette, one thing you should know: there is one subject never mentioned in this corps, any more than rope in a hanged man's house!

CHRISTIAN. What is it?

ANOTHER CADET (*in a terrifying voice*). Look at me! (*He mysteriously puts his finger to his nose three times.*) Understand?

CHRISTIAN. Oh! It's his——

ANOTHER. Hush! Never utter that word (*indicating* CYRANO, *talking backstage with* LE BRET) or you will have to deal with him.

ANOTHER (*who, while* CHRISTIAN'S *back is turned, has quietly seated himself on the table behind him*). Quite recently, he massacred two snufflers, just for talking through their noses. He didn't like it.

ANOTHER (*hollowly, appearing under the table*). You can't even allude to that fatal cartilage without deceasing long before your time.

ANOTHER (*his hand on* CHRISTIAN'S *shoulder*). A word is enough. What did I say—a word? A single gesture! Reach for your handkerchief and you clutch your shroud!
(*Silence. All around* CHRISTIAN *watch him gravely, their arms folded. He rises and goes to* CARBON DE CASTEL-JALOUX, *who affects to be absorbed in a conversation with an officer.*)

CHRISTIAN. Captain!

CARBON (*turns and looks him up and down*). Sir?

CHRISTIAN. What's to be done, when southerners are boastful?

CARBON. Prove that a northerner can be courageous! (*He turns his back upon him.*)

CHRISTIAN. Thank you!

FIRST CADET (*to* CYRANO). Now for your story.

ALL. The story!

CYRANO (*coming towards them*). My story? Here it is!
(*All draw up stools and chairs, grouping themselves around him, craning their necks.* CHRISTIAN *sits astride a chair.*)

CYRANO. As I marched out alone to meet them, the moon gleamed like a watch; but some careful horologian must have drawn a cloud of cotton over its silver case, for the night changed swift and strangely to the blackest night in the world. Since the quays were unillumined, you couldn't see your——

CHRISTIAN. Nose!
(*Dead silence. Everyone slowly rises in amazement. They watch* CYRANO *with alarm. He stops, stupefied.*)

CYRANO. Who is this person?

A CADET (*in an undertone*). He joined the corps this morning.

CYRANO (*stepping towards* CHRISTIAN). This morning?

CARBON (*also in an undertone*). He calls himself the Baron de Neuvil—

CYRANO (*stops hastily*). So! That's it? (*He pales, then reddens, and starts to rush at* CHRISTIAN *again.*) Well! (*Regaining self-control, hollowly*) Very well!— I was saying —(*Sudden burst of rage*) 'Struth! (*Continuing in his natural voice*) —that nothing could be seen. (*General amazement; they all sit down again, still watching him.*) And so I marched on thinking that a friendless rogue like myself might displease some eminent person, some prince who would trim my—

CHRISTIAN. Nose!
(*Everyone stands again;* CHRISTIAN *rocks back and forth in his chair.*)

CYRANO (*his voice stifled with rage*). Claws; and his claws would be out for me. In short, I'd be placing my—

CHRISTIAN. Nose!

CYRANO. Fingers—'twixt the hammer and the anvil, for this person might have power, to strike me in the—

CHRISTIAN. Nose!

CYRANO (*wiping sweat from his forehead*). —in the back! But I said: "On! Do what you must. On, Cyrano, come what may!" So I went my way in the darkness, until some one gave me a—

CHRISTIAN. Nose-tap!

CYRANO. I parried it—so! There I was—

CHRISTIAN. Nose to nose!

CYRANO (*rushing at him*). Hell and damnation! (*All jump up to watch; controlling himself with difficulty, he continues*)—face to face with a hundred ruffians, smelling so—

CHRISTIAN. You had to hold your nose?

CYRANO (*pale, with a determined smile*). —of onions and sour wine! Forward I rushed, head down!—

CHRISTIAN. And nose to the wind!

CYRANO. I charged! Two I ripped up standing! Another I skewered at a thrust. Then one of them lunges: Snap! I parry, and answer—

CHRISTIAN. Sniff!

CYRANO (*bursting forth*). Damnation! Out! The whole pack of you!

(*All the* CADETS *hurry toward the door.*)

FIRST CADET. The tiger has awakened!

CYRANO. All of you! Leave me alone with this man!

SECOND CADET. Heavens! He'll make mince-meat of him.

RAGUENEAU. Mince-meat?

ANOTHER CADET. Just right for one of your pies.

RAGUENEAU. I feel pale. I'm limp as a napkin.

CARBON. Let's get out of here!

ANOTHER. Not a crumb of him left.

ANOTHER. What's going to happen here would scare anyone to death.

ANOTHER. Terrible! Terrible!
(*They are all gone—some by the back, some by the sides; a few have disappeared up the staircase.* CYRANO *and* CHRISTIAN *stand face to face and stare at each other a moment.*)

SCENE X

CYRANO, CHRISTIAN.

CYRANO. Come to my arms!

CHRISTIAN. Sir——

CYRANO. Brave fellow!

CHRISTIAN. Yes, but——

CYRANO. Extremely brave. I like you.

CHRISTIAN. But why all this?

CYRANO. Your hand! I'm her brother.

CHRISTIAN. Whose?

CYRANO. Hers!

CHRISTIAN. What?

CYRANO. Roxane's.

CHRISTIAN. Heavens! You, her brother?

CYRANO. Almost! Her cousin-brother.

CHRISTIAN. And she's told you——

CYRANO. Everything.

CHRISTIAN. Does she love me?

CYRANO. Possibly.

CHRISTIAN (*shaking both his hands*). How happy I am, Sir, to get to know you!

CYRANO. That's what is called taking a sudden liking.

CHRISTIAN. I'm sorry!

CYRANO (*looking at him with his hand on his shoulder*). It's true! The man is really handsome.

CHRISTIAN. If you only knew how I admire you.

CYRANO. But those noses you threw in my face—

CHRISTIAN. I take them back!

CYRANO. Roxane expects a letter tonight.

CHRISTIAN. Impossible!

CYRANO. What?

CHRISTIAN. To write would kill my chance with her!

CYRANO. How is that?

CHRISTIAN. I am such a numbskull I could kill myself for shame.

CYRANO. You couldn't be, or else you'd never know it. That was no numbskull who bandied words with me.

CHRISTIAN. Oh, you can find words in the heat of conflict. I have a certain easy soldier's wit, but before women it's best I should be silent. Oh, their eyes may shine with kindness as I pass them—

CYRANO. And don't their hearts show kindness when you stop?

CHRISTIAN. No! I am one of those—I know it, and tremble to think of it,—who can never talk of love.

CYRANO. If they'd only been more careful with the model, I might have talked of it quite passably myself.

CHRISTIAN. Oh, to be able to express such things gracefully!

CYRANO. To be some passing musketeer—but handsome!

CHRISTIAN. Roxane is fastidious in such matters—a *précieuse!* I'm sure to disappoint her.

CYRANO (*looking intently at* CHRISTIAN). If I had such an interpreter to speak my soul!

CHRISTIAN (*in despair*). If I had eloquence!

CYRANO (*brusquely*). I'll give it you! Give me your conquering presence in exchange; together we could make a hero of romance!

CHRISTIAN. What?

CYRANO. Could you repeat the things I'll teach you every day?

CHRISTIAN. What are you proposing?

CYRANO. Roxane must never know the truth. Dare you feel the soul I can inspire pass from my leather jerkin into your silken doublet?

CHRISTIAN. But Cyrano!—

CYRANO. Christian, are you willing?

CHRISTIAN. You startle me!

CYRANO. Since you think that, alone, you'll make her heart turn cold, will you let your lips collaborate with my phrases, and caress her heart into flame?

CHRISTIAN. Your eyes are shining.

CYRANO. Well?

CHRISTIAN. Would it please you so very much?

CYRANO (*intoxicated by the prospect*). That? (*Regaining self-control and speaking dispassionately as an artist*) That would . . . fascinate me strangely. A situation worthy of a poet! You as my complement, and I as yours; you in the sun, and I deep in shadow; I as the spirit, you the incarnation.

CHRISTIAN. But the letter should be sent to her at once! I could never hope to write it.

CYRANO (*taking from his doublet the letter he has written*). Here is your letter.

CHRISTIAN. What?

CYRANO. Nothing lacking, except the signature.

CHRISTIAN. Mine? No!

CYRANO. You can send it. Wait! It's quite all right.

CHRISTIAN. You had it written, already?

CYRANO. We poets are never caught without a letter in our pockets—epistles to Chloris, imaginative rondels for sweethearts blown from dreams into the bubble of a name. Take it and use it. Make truths of its pretences. It was more eloquent the less I was sincere. These are complaints and avowals launched at random; take them and make these errant swallows come to roost. Take it and have done with it!

CHRISTIAN. But shouldn't the words be changed? Written haphazard, will it fit Roxane?

CYRANO. Fit her like a glove.

CHRISTIAN. But——

CYRANO. Self-love is self-belief; it has no limitations. Roxane will think that this was made especially for her.

CHRISTIAN. My dearest friend! (*He throws himself into* CYRANO'S *arms. They remain embraced.*)

SCENE XI

CYRANO, CHRISTIAN, *the* GASCONS, *the* MUSKETEER, LISE.

A CADET (*opening the door*). Not a sound—dead silence—I daren't look — (*Puts in his head*) Why!

ALL THE CADETS (*entering and seeing* CYRANO *and* CHRISTIAN *embracing each other*). Oh!—

A CADET. Unbelievable!
(*General consternation.*)

THE MUSKETEER (*jeering*). Well! Well!

CARBON. Our demon is gentle as a disciple, is he? Whoever shall smite him on the one nostril, doth he turn the other also?

MUSKETEER. We can talk about his nose, eh? (*With an air of triumph, calling* LISE *to see*) Hey! Lise! Here's something you should see! (*Sniffing the air affectedly*) Oh! Oh! Shocking! What an odor! (*Going to* CYRANO) Sir, you must have sniffed it. What does it smell of here?

CYRANO (*slapping his face*). A slapdragon!
(*General joy. The Cadets have found their own* CYRANO *again. They turn somersaults in relief.*)

CURTAIN

ACT THREE

ROXANE'S KISS

A small square in the 17th century fashionable quarter of Paris, the old Marais. Old-style houses. Perspectives of narrow streets. At the right, ROXANE'S *house and garden-wall, topped by abundant foliage. Above the door of her house, a balcony and upstairs window. The walls are ivied; the balcony is wreathed in jasmine, festooning from and to the ground. In front of the threshold of the door, a bench. By means of this bench and stones jutting irregularly from the wall, the balcony can easily be climbed.*

At the left, another old house of brick and stone in the same architectural style. The knocker in the door is swathed in linen as though it were a sore thumb.

At the rise of the curtain, ROXANE'S *balcony window is open. The* DUENNA *is seated on the bench. Before her stands* RAGUENEAU *wearing a sort of livery. He is concluding a recital of his woes, drying tearful eyes.*

SCENE I

RAGUENEAU, *the* DUENNA; *then* ROXANE, CYRANO, *and two* PAGES *with lutes.*

RAGUENEAU. And off she went with a musketeer! Alone, ruined, I was hanging myself. I had already left this world, when Monsieur de Bergerac rushed in; cut me down; recommended me to his cousin as a steward. Thus ended my suspense.

DUENNA. But how do you explain your ruination?

RAGUENEAU. Lise loved warriors; I, poets. Mars ate all the stock of cakes that Apollo had left. After that, the end wasn't long in coming.

DUENNA (*rising and calling towards the open window*). Roxane, they are waiting for us. Are you ready?

ROXANE'S VOICE (*from the window*). I am putting on my cloak.

DUENNA (*to* RAGUENEAU, *pointing to the door leftstage*). We're stepping across to Clomire's house. A little meeting in her temple of letters. Someone is going to discourse on the Tender Passion.

RAGUENEAU. The Tender Passion?

DUENNA (*simpering*). To be sure. (*Calling towards the window*) Roxane, hurry down! We'll be too late for the Tender Passion!

ROXANE'S VOICE. I am coming.
(*A tune played on lutes offstage. It becomes louder as the players approach.*)

CYRANO'S VOICE (*offstage, singing*). La! la! la! la!

DUENNA (*in pleased surprise*). A serenade, for us?
(*Enter* CYRANO, *followed by two* PAGES *with lutes.*)

CYRANO. I tell you that is a demi-semi-quaver, you demi-semi-idiot.

FIRST PAGE (*ironically*). What, sir, you know about demi-semi-quavers?

CYRANO. Like all Gassendi's pupils, I know my music.

THE PAGE (*playing and singing*). La la!

CYRANO (*snatching his lute and taking up the musical phrase*). I can continue it. La! la! la! la!

ROXANE (*appearing on the balcony*). Is it you?

CYRANO (*singing his words to the tune*).

"I who come to greet your fairness, pay respects unto your radiance;
I who come to praise your lilies, am enamoured of your roses!"

ROXANE. I am coming down. (*She leaves the balcony.*)

DUENNA (*indicating the* PAGES). Who are these two masters of the lute?

CYRANO. A wager I won from D'Assoucy. We were disputing a point of grammar—this way and that way, yes and no—when suddenly he points to these his constant shadows, these crabs whose claws are skilled in scraping strings, and says: "I'll bet you a whole day's music." He lost. So, until Apollo starts his course again, I have to have these lutanists at my heels, harmonious witnesses of all I do. At first, it was delightful; now, it palls. (*To the* PAGES) Hey! Go and play Montfleury a pavane. (*They proceed upstage. To the* DUENNA) I'm here, as every night, to ask Roxane—— (*To the* PAGES) Play a long time . . . and keep it well off key! (*To the* DUENNA)—whether her heart's delight is still quite faultless.

ROXANE (*coming out of the house*). How handsome. How witty. How I love him!

CYRANO (*smiling*). Christian? Witty?

ROXANE. Even more than you are!

CYRANO. Maybe so.

ROXANE. No one alive can turn so delicately those pretty nothings which are everything. Sometimes his muse is gone; he seems distrait. Then suddenly he says enchanting things.

CYRANO (*incredulous*). Impossible!

ROXANE. Now that's too much. That's you men all over: just because he's handsome you think he can't be clever.

CYRANO. He speaks from the heart, speaks expertly?

ROXANE. He doesn't speak at all; he lyricizes.

CYRANO. And sometimes writes you?

ROXANE. He out-writes writing. Listen to this! (*Declaiming*)

"The more you steal my heart, the more remains."

Well? Good?

CYRANO. Pooh!

ROXANE. And this:

"Since I have need of heart that I may feel,
Then keep this heart of mine, but lend me yours."

CYRANO. Sometimes too much; sometimes not enough. Just how much heart does he want?

ROXANE. You're jealous!

CYRANO (*starting*). What?

ROXANE. One author's jealousy of another. And this——

"Unto your heart, my heart sounds one clear call;
And if my kisses could be written down,
You'd read them with your lips, could they be read at all."

Isn't that the ultimate in delicate affection?

CYRANO (*smiling with satisfaction, in spite of himself*). Ha! Ha! Now those lines—those lines are—well!—(*with affected disdain as he remembers his rôle*)—on the insipid side.

ROXANE. And this——

CYRANO (*delighted*). You know his letters by heart, then?

ROXANE. All of them!

CYRANO. There's no denying it; the man's a flatterer.

ROXANE. Flatterer? He's a veritable master.

CYRANO (*modestly*). Oh!—a master.

ROXANE (*peremptory*). A master!

CYRANO. If you insist, then—a master!

DUENNA (*hurrying downstage*). Monsieur de Guiche! (*To* CYRANO, *pushing him towards the door of the house*) Into the house! He'd better not find you here. It might open his eyes——

ROXANE. Yes, to my cherished secret. He's in love with me—and powerful. He mustn't suspect. He'd knock my affair on the head—and with an axe.

CYRANO (*disappearing through the door*). All right! All right!

SCENE II

ROXANE, DE GUICHE; *the* DUENNA *backstage.*

ROXANE (*making a curtsey to* DE GUICHE). I'm going out.

DE GUICHE. I've come to say goodbye.

ROXANE (*coldly*). Going away?

DE GUICHE. Going to war.

ROXANE (*without any feeling*). Oh!

DE GUICHE. Going tonight.

ROXANE. Oh!

DE GUICHE. I have my orders. Arras is under siege.

ROXANE. Oh! Under siege?

DE GUICHE. Yes. I see my departure seems to leave you cold.

ROXANE. Really?

DE GUICHE. Don't you see I'm heart-broken? When and where shall we ever meet again? . . . By the way, I've been made commander of a regiment.

ROXANE (*indifferently*). Very nice.

DE GUICHE. Yes, commander. Commander of the Regiment of Guards—

ROXANE (*startled*). Of Guards! Oh!

DE GUICHE. —in which your cousin serves, he of the boastful speeches. I imagine I might pay off old scores with him out there.

ROXANE (*choking with emotion*). And the Guards are off to the front?

DE GUICHE (*laughing*). Naturally! That's my regiment.

ROXANE (*aside, slipping down on to the bench*). Christian!

DE GUICHE. Is something wrong?

ROXANE (*much moved*). It's this parting. It makes me sad. To know that a loved one must go off to war!

DE GUICHE (*in pleased surprise*). So after all you can find a word of kindness? For the first time, when I'm leaving you?

ROXANE (*with a change of tone and manner*). You want your revenge against my cousin?—

DE GUICHE (*smiling*). I see. You're for him.

ROXANE. No! Against him.

DE GUICHE. But you meet him sometimes.

ROXANE. Very rarely.

DE GUICHE. He goes around everywhere with one of the Cadets—a certain Neu . . . villen . . . viller . . .

ROXANE. Tall?

DE GUICHE. Fair!

ROXANE. Red-haired.

DE GUICHE. Handsome—

ROXANE. Pfui!

DE GUICHE. —but stupid.

ROXANE. He looks it! (*Changing tone again*) This settling of old scores with Cyrano—you're going to put him under fire, aren't you? A poor revenge. He'll like that. I could suggest something really crushing.

DE GUICHE. What is it?

ROXANE. Let the regiment leave. Keep him and all his dear Cadets back here in Paris, champing at the bit, until the war is over. That's the only way to hurt a man like him: to deprive him of danger is the best of all punishments.

DE GUICHE. A veritable woman after all! Only a woman could invent a trick like that!

ROXANE. He'll eat his heart out—and his friends chew their nails—not to be in the thick of it. Your revenge will count for something.

DE GUICHE (*coming close*). You must really care for me a little! (ROXANE *smiles.*) Roxane, am I wrong in reading a proof of love in the fact that you second my rancor?

ROXANE. You may be right.

DE GUICHE (*showing sealed letters*). Here are the marching orders. One goes to every company except—(*taking one out*)—this one. It's for the Gascony Cadets. (*He puts it in his pocket.*) I'll see personally it is not delivered. (*Laughing*) Ha! Ha! Ha! Cyrano spoils for a fight, does he? And you, you're not above playing a trick or two?

ROXANE. Under certain circumstances.

DE GUICHE (*now very close to her*). I ought to leave tonight, but . . . you drive my senses to distraction. How can I leave, knowing that I have moved you? Listen! I know! There's that convent in the Rue d'Orléans, founded by the syndic of Capuchins, Father Athanasius. A layman can't enter, but I could manage it. They'll hide me up their sleeves; they're liberal-minded. These Capuchins are of Richelieu's household; dreading the uncle, they'll obey his nephew! That's it! People will think I've gone, and I'll come back here masked. My capricious darling, grant me one more day!

ROXANE. But if it's discovered! Your reputation——

DE GUICHE. Bah!

ROXANE. What of the seige at Arras?

DE GUICHE. So much the worse! Is it a bargain?

ROXANE. No!

DE GUICHE. It must be!

ROXANE (*tenderly*). Don't you see I *must* refuse——

DE GUICHE. Oh!

ROXANE. Don't you see you'll have to go—(*aside*) But Christian stays! (*aloud*)—because I want you to be of heroic stature—Antoine!

DE GUICHE. Divinely uttered name! Then you really love the man who——

ROXANE. I love the man for whom I've been afraid.

DE GUICHE (*transported with joy*). Darling! I must go! (*Kisses her hand.*) Happy, now?

ROXANE. Happy? Yes, my dear! (*Exit* DE GUICHE.)

DUENNA (*making a mocking curtsey behind his back*). Yes, my dear!

ROXANE. Whatever you do, don't say a word of this! Cyrano will be furious if he knows I've robbed him of his silly old war. (*Calls towards the house*) Cousin!

SCENE III

ROXANE, *the* DUENNA, CYRANO.

ROXANE. We'll go to Clomire's now. (*Indicating the door, left*) Alcandre's going to speak, and so is Lysimon.

DUENNA (*putting her little finger in her ear*). A little birdie tells me we have missed them.

CYRANO (*to* ROXANE). You wouldn't miss those performing monkeys, would you?
(*They reach Clomire's door.*)

DUENNA (*delighted*). Look, the knocker is swathed in linen. (*To the knocker*) Tough little fellow! They've gagged you so you shan't disturb the speeches. (*She lifts it with infinite care and knocks gently.*)

ROXANE (*as the door opens*). Let's go in. (*From the threshold, to* CYRANO) If Christian comes, as no doubt he will, tell him to wait for me.

CYRANO (*hastily, as she goes in*). By the way! (*She turns around.*) Following the usual trend, what's the interrogation for today? What will you ask him?

ROXANE. About—

CYRANO (*quickly*). About—?

ROXANE. But you must keep mum.

CYRANO. Mum as a wall.

ROXANE. About—precisely nothing! I'm going to say to him, "Out with it! Be quite unbridled! Improvise! Talk of love! Be your splendid best!"

CYRANO (*smiling*). Good.

ROXANE. Hush.

CYRANO. Hush.

ROXANE. Not a word. (*She goes in and closes the door.*)

CYRANO (*bowing to her, after the door is shut*). Our deepest thanks! (*The door reopens;* ROXANE *puts out her head.*)

ROXANE. He might prepare beforehand—

CYRANO. No! The devil he might!

BOTH TOGETHER. Hush!
(*The door closes.*)

CYRANO (*calling*). Christian!

SCENE IV

CYRANO, CHRISTIAN.

CYRANO. I know all we need. Get your memory in trim. Here's a chance to cover yourself with glory. No time to lose. Don't look so sad. Quick! Let's get back to your rooms. I'm going to teach you—

CHRISTIAN. No.

CYRANO. What?

CHRISTIAN. No! I shall wait for Roxane here.

CYRANO. What's got into you? Come on, you've got to learn it quickly—

CHRISTIAN. I tell you no! I'm tired of borrowed letters and borrowed speeches, of playing a part and knowing that I'm afraid. It was all right at first, but now I feel she loves me. I'm not afraid any more; I'm going to speak for myself!

CYRANO. Careful! Look out!

CHRISTIAN. Who told you I don't know how to speak? I'm not as dull as all that. Just wait! But, my friend, your lessons have not been wasted. I shall know how to speak alone to her. And by the living God, I'll know very well how to take her in my arms! (*He sees* ROXANE *reappearing from Clomire's house.*) Here she is now! Cyrano, don't leave me!

CYRANO (*bowing ceremoniously*). Sir, you shall speak for yourself! (*Disappears behind the garden wall.*)

SCENE V

CHRISTIAN, ROXANE; *the* DUENNA, *for a moment.* ROXANE *appears at* CLOMIRE'S *door with the others, from whom she is taking leave. Curtsies and bows.*

ROXANE. Barthénoïde! Alcandre! Grémione!

DUENNA (*pitifully*). Oh! To have missed the discourse on the Tender Passion! (*Goes into* ROXANE'S.)

ROXANE (*bowing again*). Urimédonte! Farewell! (*All bow to* ROXANE, *bow again to each other, separate, and leave by different streets.* ROXANE *sees* CHRISTIAN.) You're here! (*She goes up to him.*)

Evening is falling. They have gone now; and no one else is passing. The air is mild. Let's sit down here and talk. Well, I am listening.

CHRISTIAN (*who has seated himself near her on the bench, after a pause*). I love you.

ROXANE (*closing her eyes*). Yes, speak of love.

CHRISTIAN. I love you!

ROXANE. Yes, that's the theme; what of the variations?

CHRISTIAN. I love—

ROXANE. The variations!

CHRISTIAN. I love you—very much!

ROXANE. Doubtlessly. What else?

CHRISTIAN. What else? I should be happy if you—loved me, too. Roxane, tell me that you love me!

ROXANE (*pouting*). You offer me gruel when I hoped for sweets. Tell me how you love me.

CHRISTIAN. Why, very much indeed.

ROXANE. Oh! Dislabyrinth your feelings!

CHRISTIAN. I want to kiss your throat.

ROXANE. Christian!

CHRISTIAN. I love you.

ROXANE (*starting to rise*). What, again?

CHRISTIAN (*hastily, stopping her*). No! I don't love you—

ROXANE (*sitting down again*). That's just as well!

CHRISTIAN —I adore you!

ROXANE (*rising, beginning to leave him*). Oh!

CHRISTIAN. I know; I'm growing foolish—

ROXANE (*dryly*). I don't like it. No more than if you suddenly turned ugly.

CHRISTIAN. But—

ROXANE. Run after your vanished eloquence!

CHRISTIAN. I—

ROXANE. I know; you love me. Good-bye. (*Goes towards her house.*)

CHRISTIAN. Please! Not so soon! I'll tell you how—

ROXANE (*pushing the door open to go in*). —how you adore me. Yes, I know already. Best go away!

CHRISTIAN. But please! Really, I— (*She shuts the door in his face.*)

CYRANO (*who has looked on, unperceived, for a moment*). A grand success!

SCENE VI

CHRISTIAN, CYRANO; *the* PAGES, *for a moment.*

CHRISTIAN. Won't you help me?

CYRANO. I'm afraid not.

CHRISTIAN. If I can't get back her good graces, I shall die this very instant.

CYRANO. But how the devil can I teach you this very instant?

CHRISTIAN (*seizing his arm*). See that?
(*The balcony window lights up.*)

CYRANO (*moved*). Her window! Hers!

CHRISTIAN. I'll die, I tell you.

CYRANO. Lower your voice.

CHRISTIAN (*whispering*). I'll die!

CYRANO (*thinking aloud*). Yet the night is dark—

CHRISTIAN. Yes?

CYRANO. All's not lost yet, though you don't deserve much else. Stand there, young fool, in front of the balcony. I'll go underneath and prompt you in a whisper.

CHRISTIAN. But—

CYRANO. Shhh!

THE PAGES (*reappearing backstage, to* CYRANO). Hey!

CYRANO. Quiet! (*Puts his finger on his lips.*)

FIRST PAGE (*in an undertone*) We've just administered the serenade to Montfleury—

CYRANO (*low, quickly*). Go and watch for me—you at this corner, you at that. If any inconvenient passer-by should come, play me a tune.

SECOND PAGE. What tune do you want, O follower of Gassendi?

CYRANO. Merry, if it's a woman; mournful, for a man.
(*The* PAGES *vanish, one at each corner.*)

CYRANO. Call her out!

CHRISTIAN. Roxane!

CYRANO (*gathering pebbles, and throwing them at the window*). Wait! Let's try these pebbles.

ROXANE (*slightly opening her window*). Who called me?

CHRISTIAN. I did.

ROXANE. Which "I"?

CHRISTIAN. Christian!

ROXANE (*scornfully*). Oh, you!

CHRISTIAN. I want to speak to you.

CYRANO (*under the balcony*). Good! Good! Keep your voice down.

ROXANE. No, your words are far too halting. Go away!

CHRISTIAN. Can't you forgive?

ROXANE. No! You no longer love me.

CHRISTIAN (*as* CYRANO *prompts him*). Merciful Heavens! Accuse me of loving you no longer, when I love you more than ever!

ROXANE (*arrested in the act of closing the window*). Oh! That's a little better.

CHRISTIAN (*prompted*). Love waxes in me—rocked in my restless heart—my troubled heart—which the—cruel brat has taken for his—cradle.

ROXANE (*stepping out on the balcony*). That *is* better! But since this love is cruel, you were foolish not to choke it in the cradle.

CHRISTIAN (*prompted*). That I attempted also—but in vain; this—new-born child—is a little—Hercules—

ROXANE. Still better!

CHRISTIAN (*prompted*). A child new-born—who strangles as if of naught—the two writhing serpents—Pride and—Doubt.

ROXANE (*advancing, resting her elbows on the balcony*). Very good indeed! But why do you speak with so much hesitation? Have your inventive faculties succumbed to gout?

CYRANO (*pulling* CHRISTIAN *under the balcony and taking his place*). Shhh! This is getting difficult.

ROXANE. Why are you hesitant tonight, I wonder?

CYRANO (*speaking low, like* CHRISTIAN). Because it is tonight, and all my words must search in the shadowed darkness for your ear.

ROXANE. Yet mine find no such hindrance.

CYRANO. They find their way at once? Why, so they ought, since *my* heart is here to welcome them. My heart is wide, profound; your ear is tiny. Besides, your words, descending, rush down quickly, while mine, Roxane, climb at a slower gait.

ROXANE. They climb much better in these last few moments.

CYRANO. They grow accustomed to gymnastic feats.

ROXANE. Indeed I'm far too high from where I'm speaking—

CYRANO. So high, you'd kill me, if from that great height, you dropped one hard word down upon my heart.

ROXANE. I'm coming down myself.

CYRANO (*hastily*). No!

ROXANE. Climb on that seat then, quickly.

CYRANO (*alarmed, slipping back into the darkness*). No, I daren't.

ROXANE. Why not?

CYRANO (*with rising emotion*). Let us take full advantage of this moment, when we can speak, but speaking, cannot see.

ROXANE. Not see each other?

CYRANO. Blessed, heavenly moment! Each can divine the other, nothing more. You sense the blackness of my long, trailing cloak; I glimpse the glimmering whiteness of your gown; I'm but a shadow—you, a gleam of radiance. Can you guess what all this must mean to me? If sometimes I was eloquent——

ROXANE. Oh, you were!

CYRANO. —yet, nonetheless, till this celestial minute, my words could never spring straight from the heart.

ROXANE. How could that be?

CYRANO. Because, till now, I could not speak, save through—(*Pauses.*)

ROXANE (*softly*). Through what?

CYRANO. —the veil of dizziness that mantles all who see you. Tonight, it seems, I speak for the first time.

ROXANE. It's true your voice sounds different.

CYRANO (*feverishly drawing nearer*). Yes, quite different. I'm myself at last. In this protecting darkness, I think I'd dare—(*Stops in confusion.*) Where am I? I cannot tell! Forgive this rush of feeling, so new to me——

ROXANE. So new?

CYRANO (*distracted, trying to regain composure*). New to me, yes! So new to be sincere! Fear of your laughter has always stopped me.

ROXANE. My laughter? Why?

CYRANO. Because of my—impulsiveness. My heart has hid in wit for fear of shame. Often I wished to pluck a star for you; in fear of scorn, I tendered just a flower.

ROXANE. Your flowers had virtues.

CYRANO. This evening, let's forget them.

ROXANE. You never spoke like this before——

CYRANO. My dear, far from the quivers, the torches, and the arrows, let us find other words less dulled by repetition. Leave Lignon's tasteless waters, drunk in drops from the puny goblet of a golden thimble, and see our souls slake their eternal thirst from the great flood of Love's eternal river.

ROXANE. But that wit of yours.

CYRANO. Oh, I made full use of it

at first—to hold you. But now, to speak like some small poetaster is treason to this night, this hour, this garden. Let the bright stars, in one revealing glance, rid us of artifice. By wit's fell alchemy, true sentiment might puff away in vapor, the heart be emptied by its own empty pastimes, and fine refinement be—finality.

ROXANE. Then all your cleverness?—

CYRANO. In love, I hate it. Love's greatest crime is to prolong the fencing beyond the sure, inevitable moment,—moment some men can never hope to know,— when our hearts feel a great love ennobled beyond the dismal grasp of pretty words.

ROXANE. If this should be that moment, what words have you left for me?

CYRANO. Why, this, this, this! Every word that comes, no matter how! Words that I throw in clusters, unarranged! I love— I burn for you— I love you— I am mad! There, that's too much! I can't go on! Your name is like a bell within my heart, and all the time I'm quivering, my Roxane, and all the time the bell shakes with my heart, and all the time it's pealing out your name. All of you that I love, all I remember, comes rushing back to me. You did not know, last year, the twelfth of May, when you left this house in the morning, I was there! Your hair was dressed in a subtly different fashion,—your hair so long to me a blinding radiance. And just as when you look too long in the sun, you see vermilion circles everywhere, when I turned away from your hair's too dazzling flame, my eyes were flecked with shimmering golden blots.

ROXANE (*agitated*). Why! This is love itself!

CYRANO. Beyond all doubt! What else could it be, so terrible and demanding? It vibrates with love's melancholy madness—and yet, there is no selfishness. Though I should love and you should never know, I'd gladly sacrifice all recompense, if sometimes I could hear from far away your gay, untroubled laughter. You understand? Each glance of yours inspires me with new virtues, with new courage. You must know that, and somehow sense my soul climbing the shadows! But then, this night's too perfect as it is. To think that I can speak, that you are listening, outruns the hope of my most sanguine dreams. Since nothing else remains to ask, I'll die. Ah! but these words of mine have set you trembling, over my head among the moon-flecked branches, for you *are* trembling like a leaf-fringed flower. Whether you will or no, I feel your trembling, the adorable quiver of your outstretched hand running along these fragrant jasmine-branches.
(*He passionately kisses the tip of a hanging bough.*)

ROXANE. Yes! I am tremulous and weeping. I love you! I am yours! Your words have cast a spell on me!

CYRANO. Then Death come when it will! It is I, I, who cast this spell on you. I ask but one thing more of Life—

CHRISTIAN (*under the balcony*). A kiss!

ROXANE (*recoiling*). What?

CYRANO. Oh!

ROXANE. You asked for what?

CYRANO. Yes—I—(*In a low voice to* CHRISTIAN) You're much too hasty!

CHRISTIAN. Since she's profoundly stirred, I'll profit by it.

CYRANO (*to* ROXANE). Yes, I—I asked, it's true. But, heavens above, I was far too audacious!

ROXANE (*somewhat disappointed*). You don't insist?

CYRANO. Yes! I insist—insist without insistence. Your modesty is hurt, I know. You must not grant this kiss!

CHRISTIAN (*to* CYRANO, *pulling his cloak*). Why not?

CYRANO. Be quiet, Christian!

ROXANE. What are you whispering?

CYRANO. Scolding myself for having gone too far! Saying: Be quiet, Christian! (*Lutes begin to play.*) Wait! Someone's coming!
(ROXANE *closes her window.* CYRANO *listens to the lutes, one of which plays a merry, the other a mournful air.*)

CYRANO. Sad tune! Gay tune! What's the idea? Man or woman? Oh, I understand. A monk! Some wandering monk!
(*Enter a Capuchin, lantern in hand; he goes from house to house peering at the doors.*)

SCENE VII

CYRANO, CHRISTIAN, *the* CAPUCHIN.

CYRANO (*to the* CAPUCHIN). Who is this new Diogenes with a lantern searching for honest men in *darkness?*

CAPUCHIN. I'm looking for the house of—

CHRISTIAN. He's ruining everything!

CAPUCHIN. —of Madame Magdeleine Robin.

CHRISTIAN. What does he want?

CYRANO (*indicating one of the streets upstage*). That way. Straight ahead. Always straight ahead.

CAPUCHIN. Thank you. I'll say my rosary for you, right to the biggest bead. (*Exit backstage.*)

CYRANO. Good luck! My prayers be on your cowl! (*Returns to* CHRISTIAN.)

SCENE VIII

CYRANO, CHRISTIAN.

CHRISTIAN. Get me that kiss!

CYRANO. No!

CHRISTIAN. Sooner or later—

CYRANO. Yes, that's true. There'll come that moment of intoxication when your lips must meet because her mouth is red, your mustache fair. (*To himself*) I'd rather it were because of other things.

(*Sounds of the window opening.* CHRISTIAN *hides under the balcony.*)

SCENE IX

CYRANO, CHRISTIAN, ROXANE.

ROXANE (*stepping out on the balcony*). Are you still there? We were speaking of a–of a—

CYRANO. Kiss. The word is sweet; why are your lips afraid? If the word burns you, what will the real thing be? No need for fear. A moment past, insensibly, your jesting came to an end; you passed without a qualm from smile to sigh, and from your sighs to tears. Take one step more in the same fearless fashion–from tear to kiss is but an added tremor.

ROXANE. Be still!

CYRANO. A kiss! When all is said, what is a kiss? A vow brought close, a promise more precise! A troth confirmed, a little rosy dot we write above the letter "i" in *loving!* A secret told the lips instead of the ear, infinite instant murmurous of bees, fragrant communion odorous of flowers! The breathing in, a little, of the heart, to taste, with lips, a little of the soul!

ROXANE. Will you be still?

CYRANO. Kisses have been ennobled, my Roxane. The Queen of France, even the Queen herself, allowed the happiest of lords to take one!

ROXANE. Indeed!

CYRANO (*carried away*). Like Buckingham's, my sufferings have been mute; like him, I have adored the Queen you are. Like him, I'm sad and true—

ROXANE. And like him, handsome.

CYRANO (*aside, sobered*). That's true; I was forgetting I am handsome.

ROXANE. Well, climb, and gather up this peerless flower.

CYRANO (*pushing* CHRISTIAN *towards the balcony*). Climb!

ROXANE. This tasting of the soul.

CYRANO. Climb up!

ROXANE. This murmuring of bees.

CYRANO. Climb up, I say!

CHRISTIAN (*hesitating*). It seems to me it isn't quite right now.

ROXANE. This infinite instant.

CYRANO. Will you climb up, you idiot? (*Gives him a push.*)
(CHRISTIAN *springs forward, scales the balcony by means of the bench and jasmines, and leaps over the balustrade.*)

CHRISTIAN. My Roxane! (*Embraces her and bends over her lips.*)

CYRANO. God! what is this torture in my heart? Oh feast of love, at which I'm Lazarus! A vagrant crumb comes falling through the darkness, brushes my lips, and slides into my soul! For on the lips which have enticed Roxane, she kisses words that only I have spoken! (*The lutes are heard.*) Sad tune, gay tune—the monk again! (*In a loud voice, pretending to run from a distance*) Hello!

ROXANE. Who's there?

CYRANO. I. I was just passing. Is Christian there?

CHRISTIAN (*astonished*). Cyrano?

ROXANE. Good evening, cousin!

CYRANO. Good evening, cousin!

ROXANE. I'm coming down.
(*She disappears into the house. Reenter the* CAPUCHIN *backstage.*)

CHRISTIAN (*seeing him*). Him? Again? (*He follows* ROXANE *inside.*)

SCENE X

CYRANO, CHRISTIAN, ROXANE, *the* CAPUCHIN, RAGUENEAU.

CAPUCHIN. It's this one. I'm certain of it. Magdeleine Robin.

CYRANO. You said Ro*lin*.

CAPUCHIN. No! —*bin!* B, i, n,—*bin!*

ROXANE (*appearing at the door followed by* RAGUENEAU *with a lantern, and by* CHRISTIAN). What is it?

CAPUCHIN. A letter.

CHRISTIAN. What?

CAPUCHIN (*to* ROXANE). It can only be about some sacred matter.

It was a right worthy nobleman who——

ROXANE (*to* CHRISTIAN). It's from De Guiche.

CHRISTIAN. He'd never dare!

ROXANE. Well, he won't keep on troubling me for ever. (*Unsealing the letter*) Besides, I love you, and if he—(*Reading by the light of* RAGUENEAU'S *lantern; aside*) "Mademoiselle: The drums are beating. My soldiers are putting on their tunics. They leave immediately. I'm supposed to have left already, yet I'm still here—at the convent. I've disobeyed you. I'm coming to see you, and send this advance word by a simple sheep of a monk who could never guess what it all means. Your smile was altogether too much for me; I *must* see it again. Please arrange matters so that you're alone, and deign to receive this audacious being, already pardoned as he hopes, who signs himself your—etc." (*To the* CAPUCHIN) Father, here's what the letter says. Listen! (*All draw near; she reads aloud*) "Mademoiselle: However hard it may seem, the wishes of the Cardinal must be obeyed. That is why I have chosen a very holy, discreet, and intelligent Capuchin to convey these lines into your charming hands. We desire him to pronounce at once and in your own dwelling (*she turns the page*) the nuptial benediction over you and Christian, who will secretly become your husband. I have sent him to you, knowing that you dislike him. Yet you must resign yourself to the inevitable. You can be sure that Heaven will bless your zeal, and can be assured, Mademoiselle, of the respect of him who has always been your very humble and very—etc."

CAPUCHIN (*beaming*). That worthy nobleman! I said so, you remember. I wasn't afraid; I knew it must be sacred business.

ROXANE (*in an undertone to* CHRISTIAN). Don't I read letters rather well?

CHRISTIAN. Hm!

ROXANE (*aloud, in mock despair*). Oh! This is terrible!

CAPUCHIN (*turning his lantern on* CYRANO). So you're the one?

CHRISTIAN. No! I'm the one!

CAPUCHIN (*turning the light on him, as if suspicious of his handsome appearance*). But—Sir!——

ROXANE (*hurriedly*). Postscript: "Give one hundred and twenty pistoles for the convent."

CAPUCHIN. That worthy, worthy lord! (*To* ROXANE) Resign yourself, my daughter.

ROXANE (*with the expression of a martyr*). I am resigned. (*While* RAGUENEAU *is opening the door for the* CAPUCHIN, *she speaks softly to* CYRANO.) De Guiche will come. Keep him here. Don't let him come in until——

CYRANO. I understand. (*To the* CAPUCHIN) How lengthy is this ceremony?

CAPUCHIN. A quarter of an hour.

CYRANO (*shepherding them towards the house*). Go in! I'm staying here.

ROXANE (*to* CHRISTIAN). Come along. (*They enter.*)

CYRANO (*aside*). How the devil can I hold De Guiche for fifteen minutes? (*He jumps on the bench and climbs on the wall towards the balcony.*) There! Up here! I think my plan might work. (*The lutes begin to play a mournful tune.*) So? A man! (*The tune becomes tragic.*) This time a man for certain. (*He has reached the balcony; he pulls his hat over his eyes, takes off his sword, wraps his cloak about him, and leans over the balustrade.*) No, it's not too high. (*He bestrides the balustrade, grasps with both hands a branch of one of the trees over the garden wall, and prepares to let himself drop.*) A little atmospheric disturbance is forecast. (*Enter* DE GUICHE, *masked, groping in the dark.*)

SCENE XI

CYRANO, DE GUICHE.

DE GUICHE. What can that cursed Capuchin be doing?

CYRANO. The devil! If he should recognize my voice— (*Letting go with one hand, he pretends to turn an invisible key.*) Click, clack! (*Solemnly*) Cyrano, assume the dialect of Bergerac!

DE GUICHE (*looking up at the house*). Yes, that's the one. I don't see well, not with this mask on. (*He starts towards the house;* CYRANO *jumps from the balcony by the aid of the branch, which bends and lets him down lightly between* DE GUICHE *and the door; he pretends to fall very heavily, as if from a height, and lies prone on the ground, motionless, as if stunned.* DE GUICHE, *startled, recoils.*)

DE GUICHE. Hey! What's this? (*By the time he looks up, the branch has already sprung back; he sees nothing but open sky.*) Where did this fellow come from?

CYRANO (*sitting up; in a broad dialect*). From the moon!

DE GUICHE. From the *what*?

CYRANO (*abruptly*). What time is it?

DE GUICHE. Is he out of his mind?

CYRANO. What time is it? What country—day—and season?

DE GUICHE. But—

CYRANO. My head is dazed!

DE GUICHE. My dear sir!—

CYRANO. I fell like a bomb—from the moon.

DE GUICHE (*impatiently*). Oh, come now!—

CYRANO (*rising; in a terrifying voice*). Fell from the moon, I tell you!

DE GUICHE (*recoiling*). All right! If you say so, you fell from the moon. (*Aside*) Probably mad!

CYRANO (*coming up to him*). Not metaphorically, either!

DE GUICHE. But—

CYRANO. But meteorically! Was it a hundred years or just a minute since? I can't tell how long I was falling—falling from that saffron planet yonder.

DE GUICHE (*shrugging*). Maybe so! Let me by!

CYRANO (*interposing*). Where am I? Be quite frank with me. No glozing over. Where—where in the universe—has my meteor fall just landed me?

DE GUICHE. The devil!

CYRANO. I couldn't pick my destination. I fell as I fell. Has my back-end's weight dragged me to earth or onto a moon?

DE GUICHE. Why, sir, I assure you!—

CYRANO (*with a cry of terror that makes* DE GUICHE *recoil further*). Merciful heavens! The people have black faces here!

DE GUICHE (*feeling his face*). What?

CYRANO (*with assumed terror*). The Moors of Algeria! You're a native!

DE GUICHE (*somewhat reassured*). Oh! This mask.

CYRANO (*somewhat reassured*). Then it's Venice or Genoa!

DE GUICHE (*trying to get by him*). There's a lady expecting me—

CYRANO (*completely reassured*). Paris! That's where I am!

DE GUICHE (*smiling in spite of himself*). The fellow's amusing.

CYRANO. You're smiling!

DE GUICHE. Smiling, but you'd better let me by.

CYRANO (*beaming broadly*). So here I am in Paris? (*Brushing himself, bowing, perfectly at ease*) Excuse my appearance. That last cloud-burst spattered me with ether. Quite a trip I've had. My eyes are filled with stardust, and there's still planet hair in my spurs. (*Picking something off his sleeve*) Why, here's a stray wisp from a comet's mane on my doublet. (*He makes a show of blowing it away.*)

DE GUICHE (*beside himself with anger*). Sir!—
(*Just as* DE GUICHE *is about to pass,* CYRANO *stretches out his leg and stops him.*)

CYRANO. If there isn't a tooth from the Great Bear in the calf of my leg! And as I skirted the Trident to avoid one of the prongs, blessed if I didn't land sitting on Libra, right on its scales! That indicator up there must still register my weight! (*Quickly preventing* DE GUICHE *from passing, he takes him by the button of his doublet.*) If you took my nose between your fingers, it would spurt out milk!

DE GUICHE. What? Milk?

CYRANO. From the Milky Way.

DE GUICHE. Hell and—!

CYRANO. Heaven sent me here. (*Folding his arms*) Would you believe what I saw as I fell? Sirius wraps his head every night in a turban. The Little Bear is too little yet to bite. (*Laughing*) As I went through the Lyre I broke a string. (*Proudly*) But I'm planning a book about it, and the golden stars that I brought in my scorched cloak at such great risk and peril will be useful when it's printed, as asterisks!

DE GUICHE. Enough of this! I wish —

CYRANO. Naturally, you would wish —

DE GUICHE. Sir!

CYRANO. –you'd wish to know from my own lips how the moon is made; whether any one lives within its retort-like roundness?

DE GUICHE (*shouting*). No, I don't! I wish—

CYRANO. To know how I got there? Well, the method is my own invention.

DE GUICHE (*discouraged*). Mad!

CYRANO. I didn't use the idiotic flying machine of Regiomontanus or the wooden pigeon of Archytas—

DE GUICHE. Mad!!–but a scholar, nonetheless!

CYRANO. –or anything ever tried before.
(DE GUICHE *succeeds in getting by him and walks towards* ROXANE'S *door.* CYRANO *follows, ready to hold him forcibly.*)

CYRANO. I've found six ways to ravish the virgin skies.

DE GUICHE (*interested, turning*). Six?

CYRANO (*volubly*). My body, tapernude, I could deck with vials filled with the dews gathered from morning skies. Then, when the dews were drawn up to the sun, my form would follow and soar up with them.

DE GUICHE (*surprised; taking a step towards* CYRANO). That's certainly one method.

CYRANO (*drawing back to lead him on*). With burning glasses in a twenty-sided frame, I'd store up air sufficient for my flight by rarefaction in a cedar-chest.

DE GUICHE (*taking another step*). Two!

CYRANO (*drawing further back*).

I'm a pyrotechnician-machinist! I might fashion a steel-triggered cricket, which I'd hurl by successive explosions to the blue fields where stars are pastured.

DE GUICHE (*unsuspiciously following him*). Three!

CYRANO. Since smoke has the property of rising, why not rise on a globe of smoke?

DE GUICHE (*still following; increasingly astonished*). Four!

CYRANO. The Moon, when her crescent is thinnest, sucks out your marrow, O beeves! I'd anoint my body with marrow.

DE GUICHE (*astounded*). Five! (CYRANO, *while talking, has gradually led* DE GUICHE *towards a seat at the other side of the square.*)

CYRANO. Lastly, mounting on an iron disc, I'd fling a lodestone magnet in the air, and as the well-thrown magnet went its way, the iron disc would soar in hot pursuit. Repeat the throw, and, faith, you'd soar indefinitely!

DE GUICHE. Six! Six excellent methods, sir! Which method did you choose?

CYRANO. A seventh.

DE GUICHE. Really? What was that?

CYRANO. You'll never guess.

DE GUICHE (*aside*). He interests me strangely!

CYRANO (*making the sound of waves, and with mysterious gestures*). Hoo-sh! Hoo-sh!

DE GUICHE. Well?

CYRANO. Can't you guess?

DE GUICHE. No!

CYRANO. The sea! The sea, of course! (*Portentously*) At the hour when the tide is surging to the moon, after my sea-bath, lying on the sands, my head first lifting—for you see, my friend, the head holds water in its fringe of hair—upwards I drifted, upwards like an angel, ascending, rising, soaring—no sense of strain!—until I felt a shock! Then——

DE GUICHE (*carried away by curiosity, sits on the seat*). And then? What then?

CYRANO (*returning to his natural speech*). Then is now! The quarter of an hour is over. Now they are married, I'll let you go!

DE GUICHE (*springing to his feet*). What's this? Am I drunk? That voice! (*The doors of the house open. Lackeys carry out lighted candelabra.* CYRANO *takes off his hat.*) That nose! Cyrano?

CYRANO (*bowing*). Precisely! Cyrano! They've just exchanged rings.

DE GUICHE. They've what? Who? (*He turns round. Tableau. Behind the lackeys,* ROXANE *and* CHRISTIAN *holding hands. The* CAPUCHIN *follows them, smiling.* RAGUENEAU *carries a torch. The flurried* DUENNA *brings up the rear in a peignoir.*)

DE GUICHE. Great God in Heaven!

SCENE XII

The same; ROXANE, CHRISTIAN, *the* CAPUCHIN, RAGUENEAU, *the lackeys, the* DUENNA.

DE GUICHE (*to* ROXANE). You! (*Astounded at recognizing* CHRISTIAN) Him? (*Bowing to* ROXANE *with admiration*) You are more than clever! (*To* CYRANO) My compliments, inventor of machines! Your tale would have stopped a saint from entering Paradise. I hope that you noted all the details; they deserve enshrining in a book.

CYRANO (*bowing*). That, sir, is advice I pledge myself to follow.

CAPUCHIN (*indicating the lovers to* DE GUICHE *and shaking his great white beard with satisfaction*). My son, this is a handsome couple you united.

DE GUICHE (*frostily*). Indeed! (*To* ROXANE) Madame, it's time you said good-bye to your husband.

ROXANE. What?

DE GUICHE (*to* CHRISTIAN). Your regiment is on the march. Join it at once!

ROXANE. To go to war?

DE GUICHE. Naturally!

ROXANE. But, Sir, the Cadets are not to go!

DE GUICHE. They'll go, all right! (*Taking out the paper which he had put into his doublet*) Here are their orders. (*To* CHRISTIAN) Deliver that, Baron.

ROXANE (*throwing herself into* CHRISTIAN'S *arms*). Christian!

DE GUICHE (*sneeringly, to* CYRANO). The wedding night is still a long way off.

CYRANO (*aside*). To think he thinks that hurts me terribly!

CHRISTIAN (*to* ROXANE). Oh, your lips again!

CYRANO. Come! Enough's enough.

CHRISTIAN (*continuing to kiss* ROXANE). It's hard to leave her; you couldn't possibly know——

CYRANO (*trying to pull him away*). I know.
(*Drums beat a march in the distance.*)

DE GUICHE (*going upstage*). The regiment is leaving.
(*For the remainder of the scene,* CYRANO *tries to pull* CHRISTIAN *away;* ROXANE *to hold him back.*)

ROXANE (*to* CYRANO). I trust him to your care. Promise me that nothing shall put his life in danger.

CYRANO. I'll try my best, but still I cannot promise—

ROXANE. Promise that he'll be very careful.

CYRANO. I'll do all possible, but—

ROXANE. That during this terrible siege, he'll never take cold.

CYRANO. I'll do my best, but—

ROXANE. And that he'll be faithful—

CYRANO. Yes, yes, certainly! But—

ROXANE. And that he'll write me often!

CYRANO. That I can really promise you!

CURTAIN

ACT FOUR

THE CADETS OF GASCONY

The post occupied at the Siege of Arras in 1640 by the company of CADETS *commanded by* CARBON DE CASTEL-JALOUX. *A talus, or face-slope of an earthwork, crosses the entire backstage area. Beyond it, and extending to the horizon, a broad vista of a plain. The whole countryside is dotted with breastworks and trenches; in the far distance, the walls and roofs of Arras are silhouetted against the sky. There are tents, scattered arms, drums, etc.; sentries posted at even intervals; campfires. Day is just dawning—a Chinese yellow dawn.*

The GASCONY CADETS *are fast asleep, wrapped in their cloaks.* CARBON DE CASTEL-JALOUX *and* LE BRET, *both very pale and very thin, keep watch.* CHRISTIAN, *frontstage, is asleep in his cape among his comrades; his face is visible in the firelight.*

SCENE I

CHRISTIAN, CARBON DE CASTEL-JALOUX, LE BRET, *the* CADETS; *then* CYRANO.

LE BRET. This is dreadful.

CARBON. Not a thing left.

LE BRET. God!

CARBON (*his finger on his lips*). Curse in whispers; you'll wake them up. (*To the* CADETS) Hush! Sleep on. (*To* LE BRET) Those who sleep, have no need of food.

LE BRET. Insomnia is a double hunger. We're suffering from a veritable famine!
(*Shots in the distance.*)

CARBON. Oh, the deuce take their firing. They'll wake my lads. (*To the* CADETS, *who have raised their heads*) Go back to sleep.
(*The heads go down again. More shooting, closer.*)

A CADET (*stirring*). Lord! Again?

CARBON. It's all right. Just Cyrano coming back.
(*Heads fall back again.*)

SENTRY (*offstage*). Who goes there?

CYRANO'S VOICE. Bergerac.

ANOTHER SENTRY (*on the talus slope*). The devil! Who goes there?

CYRANO (*appearing on the rampart*). Bergerac, you idiot. (*He approaches.* LE BRET *goes to meet him.*)

LE BRET. Thank God you're back.

CYRANO (*motioning for quiet*). Hush!

LE BRET. Wounded?

CYRANO. You know well enough they make a habit of missing me every morning.

LE BRET. Still, it's far-fetched to risk your life every morning just to carry a letter.

CYRANO (*stopping in front of* CHRISTIAN). I promised he'd write often. (*Looking down at him*) Asleep, pale, dying of hunger—still handsome in spite of everything! If she only knew, poor girl, how he's starving to death.

LE BRET. Go and get some sleep.

CYRANO. Don't grouse, Le Bret. Here's one comfort for you: to get through the Spanish ranks, I've found a place where they're drunk every night.

LE BRET. Some night you ought to bring us back some food.

CYRANO. I have to travel light to get through. But something is going to happen tonight, I feel it in my bones. If I'm a judge, we French must dine or die.

LE BRET. What do you mean?

CYRANO. I'm not quite sure. You'll soon see——

CARBON. It's a crime what a hungry business this besieging is.

LE BRET. Well, this siege of Arras is a complicated matter. We besiege the town; then, caught like rats in a trap, we're besieged in turn by the Cardinal Prince of Spain.

CYRANO. To finish it off, someone ought to come out and besiege him!

LE BRET. I'm past laughing.

CYRANO. Oh! Oh!

LE BRET. It makes me boil to think that every day you risk a life like yours just to carry— (CYRANO *moves off towards one of the tents.*) Where are you off to?

CYRANO. I'm going to write another! (*He lifts the tent-flap and disappears inside.*)

SCENE II

The same; without CYRANO.

Dawn has brightened from yellow to rose. Arras, on the horizon, is steeped in morning gold. Offstage, far left, the sudden report of a cannon, followed by the beating of drums. Another roll of drums close at hand. The near and far drums answer each other, become merged in a single continuous roll, come very close to the camp, and die away gradually, offstage right. It is the reveille. Noises of the camp awakening. In the distance, voices of officers uttering commands.

CARBON (*sighing*). The reveille—oh me! (*The* CADETS *stir in their cloaks; stretch themselves.*) Succulent slumbers, why must you end? I know only too well what their first words will be!

A CADET (*sitting up*). I'm famished.

ANOTHER. Dying.

ALL (*groaning*). Oh!

CARBON. Get up!

THIRD CADET. I can't take a step.

FOURTH CADET. I can't move a muscle.

THE FIRST (*observing his reflection in his breastplate*). My tongue is yellow; today's air doesn't eat so well.

ANOTHER. My baron's coronet for a speck of Cheshire cheese.

ANOTHER. If they won't put enough in my bread-basket to work up a pint of gastric juice, I'll sulk in my tent all day—like Achilles.

ANOTHER. Oh, for a little bread.

CARBON (*in an undertone, going to* CYRANO'S *tent*). Cyrano!

OTHERS. We're going to die.

CARBON (*still in an undertone, at the door of the tent*). Cyrano, I need your help! You always have a merry quip for them. Come and cheer them up.

SECOND CADET (*dashing at the* FIRST, *who seems to be chewing something*). What are you nibbling?

THE FIRST. Gun-tow, fried with axle-grease in a helmet. This Arras district is a little short of game.

ANOTHER (*entering*). I've just been hunting.

ANOTHER (*entering*). I've been fishing in the Scarpe.

ALL (*rising and rushing towards them*). What! What have you got —pheasant, carp? Come on, show us.

THE FISHERMAN. A minnow.

THE HUNTER. A sparrow.

ALL (*exasperated*). Enough of this! Let's mutiny!

CARBON. Cyrano, you've got to help! (*It is now broad daylight.*)

SCENE III

The same; and CYRANO.

CYRANO (*calmly issuing from his tent, book in hand, a pen behind his ear*). What's wrong here? (*Silence. To the* FIRST CADET) What are you dragging around for?

THE CADET. I've something in my heels that hampers me.

CYRANO. What's that?

THE CADET. My stomach.

CYRANO. The same goes for me.

THE CADET. Doesn't it worry you?

CYRANO. The contrary! It adds inches to my stature.

SECOND CADET. My teeth are sure sharp-set.

CYRANO. The better to bite with—in good time.

A THIRD. My stomach is limp as a rag.

CYRANO. We'll use it for spare drum-skins.

ANOTHER. My ears buzz——

CYRANO. That's not true. Famished stomach: deaf ears. You don't believe me? There, deaf ears! A hungry man won't ever listen to reason.

ANOTHER. Oh, for a few leaves—and a little oil.

CYRANO (*taking off his helmet and quickly thrusting it in his hands*). Why, here's a whole sallet!

ANOTHER. I could devour anything, no matter how tough and dry.

CYRANO (*throwing him his book*). Try the *Iliad.*

ANOTHER. I'll bet the Cardinal has his four meals a day.

CYRANO. A cardinal sin you should avoid! You want him to talk turkey?

THE SAME. I'd not grouse if he sent some wine.

CYRANO. By a portly friar?

THE SAME. Chartreuse or Benedictine—

CYRANO. A cordial emissary!

ANOTHER. I could eat nails.

CYRANO. Where's the iron in your soul?

FIRST CADET (*shrugging*). Go on. Always witty! Always punning! Always words to the point!

CYRANO. Yes! the point—the pointed word. That above all! I should like to die under sunset skies some evening making a last *bon mot* for a noble cause, to sink to the turf, far from the bed of sickness, struck by a worthy sword and adversary; to die with a point at my heart and a pointed word on my lips.

ALL. We're hungry!

CYRANO (*folding his arms*). Is there nothing on earth but food? Come here, old Bertrandou! I know you've been a shepherd. Take from your double leather case one of your shepherd pipes. Blow it! Play for this pack of gormandizers and gluttons the old airs of our homeland, with their ancient, haunting rhythms. Each note a little sister, or the sound of familiar voices,—the cadence slow as the lazy smoke from our native village roofs, and the tune pitched to the lilt of our childhood's Gascon patois. (*The old man sits down and takes out a flute.*) Let the warlike pipe, which mourns today, remember for a moment—as your fingers flutter a sarabande, birdlike upon its stops—that its shrill martial ebony was once a rustic reed. Surprise it with old songs again, the songs of its peaceful youth. (*The old man begins to play Languedocian tunes.*) You weary Gascons, listen! It changes in his fingers. The shrill fife of the roaring camp is the flute of our quiet woods; the stirring call to battle turns to a goatherd's song, to the spirit of moor and forest and our little red-capped shepherds, to the tender green of evening on the reaches of Dordogne. Listen, you weary Gascons! This is your Gascony.
(*All heads are bent; all eyes dreamy. Tears are furtively wiped away on the backs of sleeves and corners of cloaks.*)

CARBON (*in an undertone, to* CYRANO). You're making them weep.

CYRANO. Nostalgia's a nobler pain than hunger. Mental, not physical. Let their sufferings leave their stomachs for a while; it's their hearts that are aching now.

CARBON. You'll weaken them by plucking at their heartstrings.

CYRANO (*signalling a drummer to approach*). Nonsense! They have heroism in their blood. It doesn't take much rousing. All that's needed is— (*At his signal, the drum rolls.*)

ALL (*leaping up and rushing to their arms*). Hey!—What!—What's all this?

CYRANO (*smiling*). —just the beat of a drum! Then, farewell dreams, regrets, homesickness, love. What the flute stirred, vanished with the drum.

A CADET (*looking backstage*). Well, well! If it isn't Monsieur de Guiche.

ALL THE CADETS (*in a low murmur*). Boo!

CYRANO (*smiling*). Such flattering murmurs!

A CADET. He bores us.

ANOTHER. Trying to make an impression with that broad point-lace collar over his armor!

ANOTHER. As if anyone wore linen on armor!

THE FIRST. It's a good thing when you've a carb-uncle on your neck.

THE SECOND. He's proper nephew to that uncle.

ANOTHER. Always the perfect courtier.

CARBON. A Gascon, nonetheless.

THE FIRST. A false Gascon. I don't trust him. Real Gascons ought to be crazy; nothing's more dangerous than a Gascon who can keep his head.

LE BRET. He looks pale.

ANOTHER. He's hungry as any other poor devil. But his breast-plate has studs of silver gilt. *His* stomach-cramps can glitter in the sun.

CYRANO (*hurriedly*). Don't show your sufferings, either! Get out your cards, your pipes, your dice— (*All start playing with cards and dice, on drums, stools, and cloaks spread on the ground. They light long tobacco pipes.*) For my part, I'll be reading Descartes.
(*He walks to and fro, reading a little volume he has taken from his pocket. Tableau. Everyone looks contented and absorbed. Enter* DE GUICHE. *He approaches* CARBON.)

SCENE IV

The same; DE GUICHE.

DE GUICHE (*to* CARBON). Oh!—Good morning! (*They look at each other with open satisfaction; aside*) Green as a corpse!

CARBON (*aside*). His face all eyes!

DE GUICHE (*surveying the* CADETS). So these are the wrong-headed rascals? Gentlemen, I hear from all sides that you scoff at me! That the Cadets, those scions of the hillsides, squireens of Béarn, *pâté de fois gras* barons, have no words too bad for their colonel! That this point-lace collar on my breastplate shocks them profoundly! That nothing restrains their indignation to see a Gascon who is not a beggar! (*Silence. The* CADETS *continue smoking and playing.*) A punishment is indicated! Perhaps your captain——

CARBON. I hold a free commission. No punishment is contemplated.

DE GUICHE. So!

CARBON. I maintain my own Company. They are mine alone—otherwise answerable only to general orders.

DE GUICHE (*struck by an idea*). Ah? Indeed? So that's it? Enough! (*To the* CADETS) I shall treat your blustering with contempt. My conduct under fire needs no boasting advertisement. Take yesterday's action at Bapaume,— my repulse of the Count of Bucquoi. Pouring in my men like an avalanche, I charged three times——

CYRANO (*without looking up from his book*). And lost your white scarf?

DE GUICHE (*surprised and pleased*). Oh, you knew about that? Yes, as I wheeled my horse and rallied my men, a sudden rush of fugitives swept me to the enemy lines. There was danger I'd be shot or taken prisoner. Then, I had an idea. I dropped my white scarf, my only badge of rank. The trick worked. In the general confusion, the Spaniards didn't notice who I was. I got back safely to our lines, rallied my men, pressed home the charge, and won the skirmish. Well? What do you think of it?

(*The* CADETS *have not appeared to listen; at this point, however, their cards and dice-boxes remain in the air; their pipe-puffing stops. Pause.*)

CYRANO. I'd say—that Henry IV, no matter what the odds, would never have lowered his stature by the loss of his white plume.
(*Silent joy. The cards and dice fall. Pipes puff again.*)

DE GUICHE. Yet the stratagem succeeded!
(*The same pause and action as before.*)

CYRANO. Possibly! Possibly! But who'd decline the honor of being a target? (*Cards and dice fall; pipes puff as before.*) There's a difference in our notions of courage. If I'd been present when you dropped your scarf, I'd have picked it up and worn it myself.

DE GUICHE. More of your Gascon bluster!

CYRANO. Bluster? Lend it to me! I'll be first in tonight's attack, wearing it on my shoulder.

DE GUICHE. A typical Gascon offer! You know very well where the scarf is. Back there by the river where the enemy lines are under a hail of grapeshot. No one could get it and survive.

CYRANO (*takes a white scarf from his pocket and hands it to* DE GUICHE). Yet here it is!
(*Silence. The* CADETS *smother laughter by means of cards and dice boxes.* DE GUICHE *turns round*

and looks at them; they recover gravity and continue gambling. One of them unconcernedly whistles the Languedocian air played earlier by the piper.)

DE GUICHE (*taking the scarf*). Many thanks! Now I have it back, I can give the signal I was hesitant to give.
(*He goes to the breastwork, scrambles up, and waves the scarf several times.*)

ALL. What's that for?

THE SENTRY (*on the breastwork*). That man down there! He's running to the enemy, making his escape—

DE GUICHE. Very useful, too! He's a counterfeit Spanish spy. I plant the information he carries to the enemy. They make their dispositions according to my wishes.

CYRANO. The man's a cheat!

DE GUICHE (*returning, coolly knotting his scarf*). A convenient cheat! What were we saying? Oh yes! I was about to tell you something. In the last supreme effort to bring in supplies, the Marshal made a secret sortie to Dourlens. The King's Sutlers are there. He'll join them by way of the fields. But to force his way back, he has taken troops in strength. The Spaniards would have an easy time of it, if they'd attack us now with half our army gone.

CARBON. Lucky they don't know it! Too bad if they attack.

DE GUICHE. They do know it. They're going to attack.

CARBON. What!

DE GUICHE. That spy came to tell me. "Where do you want it?" he said. "I can make them attack at any point you choose. Tell me where you want them to think you're weakest, and that's where their main smash will come." "Good," I said. "Leave camp at once, but keep your eyes on our lines. Where you see my signal, have them attack."

CARBON (*to the* CADETS). Gentlemen, to arms!
(*All leap to their feet. Noise of buckling on of belts and swords.*)

DE GUICHE. They'll be on you in an hour.

FIRST CADET. What! An hour?
(*They all sit down again, and continue their gambling.*)

DE GUICHE (*to* CARBON). The Marshal's forces are on their way back now. You've got to gain us time.

CARBON. And to gain time?

DE GUICHE. You will oblige us by getting killed!

CYRANO. So this is your revenge!

DE GUICHE. I won't claim that if I had liked you, I'd have chosen you and your men for this duty! But your bravery is incomparable. Serving my spite, I also serve my King.

CYRANO. Permit me to express my gratitude.

DE GUICHE. You love to fight, one against a hundred. You'll not complain of lack of opportunity.
(*He walks backstage with* CARBON.)

CYRANO (*to the* CADETS). Gentlemen, we shall add to the Gascon coat-of-arms, which bears six chevrons of azure and of or, the missing chevron—red for blood!
(*Backstage* DE GUICHE *talks in an undertone with* CARBON. *Orders. Preparations for defence.* CYRANO *goes up to* CHRISTIAN, *who stands motionless, arms folded.*)

CYRANO (*laying his hand on his shoulder*). Christian?

CHRISTIAN (*shaking his head*). Roxane!

CYRANO. Poor lad.

CHRISTIAN. I wish my heart's last farewell could be written down in a final, moving letter.

CYRANO. I guessed you'd need it for today. (*He takes a note from his doublet.*) I've written it already.

CHRISTIAN. Let me see!

CYRANO. You really want to?

CHRISTIAN (*taking the note*). Why, yes. (*He opens it, reads, suddenly stops.*) Oh!

CYRANO. What's wrong?

CHRISTIAN. This little spot?

CYRANO (*hastily taking the letter and looking it over with every sign of innocence*). Spot?

CHRISTIAN. It's a tear!

CYRANO. Yes. A poet gets caught at his own game; that's its charm! You understand—this note was very moving. Tears came into my eyes as I wrote it.

CHRISTIAN. Tears?

CYRANO. Yes. To die is nothing. But—never to see her again, that's horrible! For I couldn't—— (CHRISTIAN *looks at him searchingly.*) we couldn't—(*Hastily*) you couldn't——

CHRISTIAN (*snatching the note*). Give me that note!
(*A noise in the distance.*)

A SENTRY'S VOICE. What the hell! Who goes there?
(*Shooting. Voices. Bells.*)

CARBON. What is it?

A SENTRY (*on the breastwork*). A carriage.
(*They all rush to see.*)

VARIOUS VOICES. What! In the camp? It's coming in. It's coming from the enemy. The devil! Fire! No, the coachman is shouting. Shouting what? Listen: Service of the King!
(*The bells come closer.*)

DE GUICHE. What? Service of the King?

(*Everybody comes down and falls in ordered ranks.* DE GUICHE *disappears over the breastwork.*)

CARBON. Hats off, all of you!

DE GUICHE (*offstage*). From the King! Get that crowd out of the way! Make room to draw up!
(*A carriage enters at a trot. It is covered with mud and dust. The curtains are drawn. Two lackeys behind. It comes to a sudden stop.*)

CARBON (*shouting*). Beat a salute!
(*The drums roll. All the* CADETS *remove their helmets.*)

DE GUICHE. Lower the steps!
(*Two* CADETS *rush to the carriage. The door opens.*)

ROXANE (*jumping out of the coach*). Good morning!
(*At the sound of her voice, all the* CADETS, *who were bowing low, jerk up their heads. Complete astonishment.*)

SCENE V

The same; ROXANE.

DE GUICHE. Service of the King! You?

ROXANE. Of Love, the only King!

CYRANO. God in Heaven!

CHRISTIAN (*rushing towards her*). You! Why are you here? Why did you come?

ROXANE. The siege was much too long.

CHRISTIAN. But why did you——

ROXANE. I'll tell you privately.
(*Since she first spoke,* CYRANO *has stood immobile, not daring to look up at her.*)

CYRANO. My God! Dare I look at her?

DE GUICHE. You can't stay here!

ROXANE. Indeed I can! Will someone bring me a drum? (*When it is brought, she sits down on it.*) There, thank you! (*She laughs.*) A patrol fired on my coach! (*Proudly*) It looks as if it were made out of a pumpkin, doesn't it, as in Cinderella? And the lackeys transmogrified from rats? (*Blowing a kiss to* CHRISTIAN) Good morning! (*Surveying them all*) You don't look very gay. Do you know it's rather far to Arras? (*Noticing* CYRANO) Cousin, I'm enchanted!

CYRANO (*approaching*). Oh, indeed! How did you——

ROXANE. How did I find the army? Gracious me! Very easy: I drove wherever the country was laid waste. I had to see such horrors to believe them. Gentlemen, if this is *your* King's service, mine is better.

CYRANO. Plain madness. Where the devil could you get through?

ROXANE. Where? Through the Spaniards.

FIRST CADET. Trust a woman to find the weakest point!

DE GUICHE. How did you manage to get across their lines?

LE BRET. It must have been difficult.

ROXANE. Not very. I drove through as fast as possible. If some hidalgo showed his arrogant face, I let my sweetest smile beam through the door. And since these gentlemen—you French won't mind this—are the most gallant mortals in the world, I had no trouble at all in passing through.

CARBON. Yes, that smile of yours is a certain passport. But they must often have asked you where you were going?

ROXANE. Quite often. I answered, "I'm going to see my lover." Immediately, the fiercest Spaniard closed the carriage door with a gesture a King would envy, motioned away the pointed muskets, and—superb in grace and stateliness, his legs stiff under the fluted lace—swept the air with his plumed hat, and bowed, and said: "Pass on, my señorita!"

CHRISTIAN. But Roxane——

ROXANE. I said, "My lover," yes—forgive me! You see, if I'd said, "My husband," they would never have let me pass.

CHRISTIAN. Roxane——

ROXANE. What's wrong?

DE GUICHE. You'll have to get away from here!

ROXANE. I?

CYRANO. Immediately.

LE BRET. As soon as possible!

CHRISTIAN. Yes.

ROXANE. But why?

CHRISTIAN (*embarrassed*). Because——

CYRANO (*embarrassed*). In three-quarters of an hour——

DE GUICHE (*embarrassed*). Or—an hour——

CARBON (*embarrassed*). It would be better——

LE BRET (*embarrassed*). You might——

ROXANE. I'm staying! You are going to fight.

ALL. Oh! No! Not at all!

ROXANE. He is my husband! (*She throws herself into* CHRISTIAN'S *arms.*) Let me be killed with you.

CHRISTIAN. What eyes you have.

ROXANE. I could tell you why.

DE GUICHE (*despairingly*). This is a really dangerous post.

ROXANE (*turning*). What! Dangerous?

CYRANO. That's why he gave it us.

ROXANE (*to* DE GUICHE). So! You wish to make me a widow?

DE GUICHE. Oh! I assure you——

ROXANE. Now I'm angry. I won't leave. Besides, this is intriguing.

CYRANO. What? Is the *précieuse* a heroine?

ROXANE. Monsieur de Bergerac! After all, I'm your cousin.

A CADET. We'll defend you well.

ROXANE (*increasingly excited*). I think you will, my friends!

ANOTHER (*carried away*). The whole camp smells of orris root.

ROXANE. Luckily I've put on a hat which will look very well in battle! (*Looking at* DE GUICHE) But perhaps it is time for the Count to leave. They might begin to attack.

DE GUICHE (*angry*). That's the last straw! (*Significantly*) I shall go to inspect my guns. When I come back— Well! You have still time to change your mind!

ROXANE. Never!
(*Exit* DE GUICHE.)

SCENE VI

The same; without DE GUICHE.

CHRISTIAN (*imploring*). Roxane, you must!

ROXANE. Never.

FIRST CADET (*to the others*). She'll stay.
(*The* CADETS *hurry around, getting in each other's way, in an effort to make themselves tidy.*)

ALL. A comb!—Soap!—My jacket's torn: a needle!—A ribbon!—Your mirror!—My ruffles!—Your curling iron!—A razor!

ROXANE (*to* CYRANO, *who is still urging her to go*). Nothing will stir me from this place.
(CARBON, *like the others, has tightened his belt, dusted his clothes, brushed his hat, straightened his plume, and pulled down his cuffs. He approaches* ROXANE.)

CARBON (*ceremoniously*). In that case, it is fitting I should present some of these gentlemen who will have the honor of dying before your eyes.
(ROXANE *bows; then stands expectantly, her arm through* CHRISTIAN'S.)

CARBON (*in formal introduction*). Baron de Peyrescous de Colignac!

THE CADET (*bowing*). Madame——

CARBON (*continuing*). Baron de

Casterac de Cahuzac.—Vidame de Malgouyre Estressac Lésbas d'Escarabiot — Chevalier d'Antignac-Juzet.—Baron Hillot de Blagnac-Saléchan de Castel Crabioules——

ROXANE. How many names does each one have?

BARON HILLOT. Swarms! Galaxies!

CARBON (*to* ROXANE). Open your hand. The one with the handkerchief.

ROXANE (*opens her hand; the handkerchief falls*). Why?
(*The whole company rushes forward to retrieve it.*)

CARBON (*quickly snatching it*). My company needed a flag. Faith! Now it has the finest in the camp!

ROXANE (*smiling*). It's somewhat tiny.

CARBON (*fastening the handkerchief to the staff of his captain's lance*). But lace!

A CADET (*to the others*). After looking in that face, give me a single nutshell in my stomach, and I'd die without a qualm.

CARBON (*overhearing, indignant*). Shame! To speak of eating when an exquisite woman——

ROXANE. But the air of the camp is sharp. I'm famished myself. Patties, jellied game, dry wine,—that's my bill of fare. Will you bring it out?

A CADET. Nothing more?

ANOTHER. Good Lord, where could we get it?

ROXANE (*quietly*). From my carriage.

ALL. What?

ROXANE. It needs boning, carving, serving! Look at my coachman a little closer, gentlemen. You'll see he's indispensable. You can have the sauces hot if you so wish.

THE CADETS (*rushing towards the carriage*). Ragueneau! (*Cheers*) Ragueneau! Hurrah!

ROXANE (*watching them compassionately*). Poor lads.

CYRANO (*kissing her hand*). The good fairy.

RAGUENEAU (*standing on the seat like a barker at a fair*). Gentlemen!
(*Wild enthusiasm.*)

THE CADETS. Hurrah! Bravo!

RAGUENEAU. The Spaniards, when *she* passed, didn't investigate the repast!
(*Applause.*)

CYRANO (*in an undertone, to* CHRISTIAN). Ahem! Christian!

RAGUENEAU. Charmed by the fair, they failed to see—(*he displays a dish which he has pulled out from under a seat.*)—the fowl!
(*It is passed from hand to hand amidst applause.*)

CYRANO (*to* CHRISTIAN). Just a word.

RAGUENEAU. And Venus held their eyes, while Diana brought you— (*Brandishing a joint*)—venison! (*Great enthusiasm. The joint is seized by twenty outstretched hands.*)

CYRANO (*to* CHRISTIAN). I *must* speak to you!

ROXANE (*to the* CADETS, *returning with their arms filled with eatables*). Put it down here! (*Assisted by the two imperturbable lackeys from the carriage, she spreads a tablecloth on the grass. To* CHRISTIAN, *just as* CYRANO *is drawing him aside*) Make yourself useful! (CHRISTIAN *assists her.* CYRANO *shows signs of impatience.*)

RAGUENEAU. Truffled peacock.

FIRST CADET (*beaming, as he cuts himself a thick slice of ham*). Thunder! We shan't run our last mile without a final guzzle. (*Hastily checking himself at the sight of* ROXANE) Sorry. Er—final feed.

RAGUENEAU (*throwing cushions from the carriage*). The cushions are overstuffed—with ortolans! (*Uproar. They rip the cushions open. Laughter. Delight.*)

THIRD CADET. Well, dirk my doublet!

RAGUENEAU (*throwing out bottles of red and white wine*). Flasks of ruby! Bottled topaz!

ROXANE (*throwing a folded tablecloth at* CYRANO). Lay out this tablecloth. Lively, now!

RAGUENEAU (*waving one of the carriage lanterns*). Each of the lanterns is a little larder!

CYRANO (*in an undertone to* CHRISTIAN, *as they unfold the tablecloth*). I must speak to you before you speak to her.

RAGUENEAU (*increasingly rhetorical*). The handle of my whip is pure Bologna!

ROXANE (*pouring and serving wine*). They'll kill us all off, will they? Then, *morbleu,* here's a last laugh in the face of the rest of the army. This is for Gascons only. If De Guiche should come—no invitation, mind! (*Going from one to another*) There, take your time! Not so fast! Drink a little! What? Tears?

FIRST CADET. It tastes so good——

ROXANE. Hush! Red or white? Some bread for Monsieur de Carbon! A knife! Your plate! A little crust? Some more? Let me give you some! Champagne? A wing?

CYRANO (*following and helping her, aside*). I adore her. (*His arms are loaded with dishes.*)

ROXANE (*to* CHRISTIAN). What will you have?

CHRISTIAN. Nothing.

ROXANE. Must! This biscuit, in some muscatel—two fingers?

CHRISTIAN (*attempting to detain her*). Why did you come? Really.

ROXANE. Wait! I must think entirely of these poor fellows now. In good time!

LE BRET (*backstage, passing bread on his lance-point to the sentry on the talus*). Here's De Guiche!

CYRANO. Quick! Hide the bottles, dishes, plates, and baskets! Remember, nothing special has happened! (*To* RAGUENEAU) Up on your seat! Everything hidden? (*Everything vanishes in a flash under tents, clothing, cloaks, and hats. Enter* DE GUICHE, *hurriedly. He stops suddenly, sniffs the air. Silence.*)

SCENE VII

The same; DE GUICHE.

DE GUICHE (*sniffing*). What smells so good?

A CADET (*humming unconcernedly*). La! La! La!

DE GUICHE (*looking at him sharply*). What's wrong with you? You're red in the face.

THE CADET. Me? Nothing. Just my blood. It sniffs battle, reddens with joy.

ANOTHER. Pum—pum—pum!

DE GUICHE (*turning*). What is that?

THE CADET (*slightly drunk*). Nothing. Nothing at all. Just a little song. The merest wisp of—

DE GUICHE. You're in high spirits, lad.

THE CADET. That's what danger does to me.

DE GUICHE (*calling* CARBON *to give him orders*). Captain! I—(*Stops when he sees his face.*) The devil! You don't look sad yourself!

CARBON (*reddening; evasively hiding a bottle behind his back*). Really?

DE GUICHE. There is one cannon to spare. I've had it placed (*pointing to the side*) there, in that corner. Your men can use it, if necessary.

A CADET (*staggering*). Such attention!

ANOTHER (*smiling graciously*). Such solicitude!

DE GUICHE. Mad as March hares! (*Dryly*) You're not accustomed to artillery. Look out for the recoil; it goes back suddenly.

THE FIRST CADET. Oh! Shoot!

DE GUICHE (*furious, going towards him*). Well!

THE CADET. A Gascon's cannon never goes back on him.

DE GUICHE (*taking his arm; shaking him*). You're drunk, that's what! On what?

THE CADET (*arrogantly*). The smell of gun-powder.

DE GUICHE (*shrugs, pushes him away, and goes quietly to* ROXANE). There isn't much time, madame! Have you made your decision?

ROXANE. I shall stay.

DE GUICHE. Not escape while you can?

ROXANE. No.

DE GUICHE (*after hesitating briefly*). Then give me a musket.

CARBON. What?

DE GUICHE. I'm staying too.

CYRANO. At last, Sir, you show real courage.

FIRST CADET. In spite of his lace, perhaps he *is* a Gascon.

ROXANE. But why?

DE GUICHE. I'll leave no woman in danger.

SECOND CADET (*to the* FIRST). Don't you think we might give him something to eat?
(*The food magically reappears.*)

DE GUICHE (*his eyes brightening*). Food!

A THIRD CADET (*rubbing his stomach significantly*). Under every jacket.

DE GUICHE (*controlling himself, haughtily*). Do you think I would eat your leavings?

CYRANO (*bowing*). You show improvement.

DE GUICHE (*proudly, with the slightest trace of Gascon accent*). I shall fight on an empty stomach.

FIRST CADET. Ah! the genuine Gascon accent.

DE GUICHE (*laughing*). That to me?

THE CADET. He is one of us!
(*All begin dancing spontaneously.* CARBON *drops out of sight for a moment, and then reappears on the breastwork.*)

CARBON. The pikemen are set. They mean business! (*He indicates a line of pikes above the breastwork.*)

DE GUICHE (*to* ROXANE, *bowing*). Will you honor me with your arm for the review?
(*She takes it; they proceed up the talus. Everyone uncovers and follows.*)

CHRISTIAN (*going to* CYRANO, *hurriedly*). Quick now!
(*When* ROXANE *appears at the breastwork, the pikes, lowered for a salute, disappear. Cheers. She bows.*)

PIKEMEN (*offstage*). Hurrah!

CHRISTIAN. What's it all about?

CYRANO. Roxane. If by any chance she—

CHRISTIAN. Yes!

CYRANO. –should speak about your letters—

CHRISTIAN. My letters! Yes?

CYRANO. Don't be so foolish as to show surprise.

CHRISTIAN. Why?

CYRANO. Need I tell you? Good God, it's quite simple. I thought of it today when she appeared. You have–well—

CHRISTIAN. Hurry up.

CYRANO. You have–have written far more often than you realize!

CHRISTIAN. What?

CYRANO. Damnation! Can't you see it? I interpreted your passion. Sometimes I wrote without telling you about it.

CHRISTIAN. Oh?

CYRANO. It is quite simple.

CHRISTIAN. But how did you manage it? We're surrounded!

CYRANO. Oh, before daylight I could get across—

CHRISTIAN (*folding his arms*). I see! That simple! Did I write twice a week? Three times? Four?

CYRANO. More than that.

CHRISTIAN. Every day?

CYRANO. Every day! Twice a day.

CHRISTIAN (*violently*). You liked that, didn't you? Liked it so much that you'd go and risk your life—

CYRANO (*seeing* ROXANE *return*). Hush! Not while she's here! (*He hurries off to his tent.*)

SCENE VIII

ROXANE, CHRISTIAN; *backstage, constant going and coming of* CADETS; CARBON *and* DE GUICHE *issue orders.*

ROXANE (*running up to* CHRISTIAN). Christian! At last!

CHRISTIAN (*taking her hands*). And now, tell me. Tell me why you came to join me through all these awful roads, through all these lines of soldiers and desperate ruffians.

ROXANE. It was your letters.

CHRISTIAN. Do you know what you're saying?

ROXANE. It's all your doing that I had to run such risks. Your letters moved me beyond all words. Think how many you've written me this last month, and each one more eloquent than the last.

CHRISTIAN. So! For a few little love-letters you have——

ROXANE. Hush! Can't you understand? God knows, I've loved you ever since that evening when your second voice came climbing to my window and made me know your soul. And this last month, your letters have brought me back the voice I heard that evening, the tender voice that enveloped me like an aura. It's all your fault that I simply had to come here! If Ulysses had written her as you did, Penelope wouldn't have stayed at home embroidering. She'd have joined you with the heedless haste of Helen; she'd have sent her embroidery flying——

CHRISTIAN. But——

ROXANE. I read them; I was conquered; I came here—came, utterly your own! Each of your pages was like a petal falling from your soul, and every flaming word so strong, sincere——

CHRISTIAN. Strong, sincere? You felt that there, Roxane?

ROXANE. God knows how I felt it!

CHRISTIAN. So you came?

ROXANE. So I came. Oh, Christian, my master, you'd raise me up if I threw myself at your feet, but the soul that I throw at your feet you can never raise. It is there forever. I came to ask your pardon—this is the time to ask it with Death so close—your pardon for the unforgivable insult of loving you for your great good looks alone.

CHRISTIAN (*in alarm*). Roxane!

ROXANE. Later, my dear, when my love became less shallow,—a fluttering bird trying its untried wings,—your beauty held me but your soul seduced me, and I loved you for both together.

CHRISTIAN. Roxane! And now?

ROXANE. Now? You yourself are the victor over yourself: it is only your soul I love now——

CHRISTIAN. Oh, Roxane——!

ROXANE. You should rejoice. To be loved for a transient garment, would put an ardent and noble heart to torture. But your dear mind eclipses your dear face, obliterates the beauty that first won me; and now that I see, what I saw once I see no more.

CHRISTIAN. Oh!——

ROXANE. You don't like your triumph?

CHRISTIAN (*mournfully*). Roxane! Roxane!

ROXANE. I understand! You can't believe such love——

CHRISTIAN. I don't want such love. I want to be loved for——

ROXANE. —for what you were always loved for till now? You must let yourself be loved in a better fashion.

CHRISTIAN. It was better as it was before.

ROXANE. Won't you understand? It is now that I love you better that I love you at all, loving the only you that is really you. Though your brilliance dazzled me less—

CHRISTIAN (*anticipating the trend*). Hush!

ROXANE. —my love couldn't alter. Though all of your handsomeness suddenly vanished—

CHRISTIAN. Don't say it!

ROXANE. But I do say it!

CHRISTIAN (*brokenly*). You mean—that if I were ugly?—

ROXANE. I swear it would make no difference.

CHRISTIAN. God!

ROXANE. Is your happiness so great then?

CHRISTIAN (*in a stifled voice*). Great? God!

ROXANE. What's wrong?

CHRISTIAN (*gently pushing her away*). Nothing! Excuse me a moment. I have to tell someone something.

ROXANE. But—Christian!

CHRISTIAN (*indicating the* CADETS *backstage*). My love is robbing them of you. Smile on them just a little before they die. You'd better go.

ROXANE (*deeply moved*). Dear, thoughtful Christian.
(*She goes towards the group of* CADETS; *they collect with respectful eagerness around her.*)

SCENE IX

CHRISTIAN, CYRANO; *backstage,* ROXANE *talking with* CARBON *and the group of* CADETS.

CHRISTIAN (*shouting towards* CYRANO'S *tent*). Cyrano?
(CYRANO *comes out, armed for battle.*)

CYRANO. What is it? Why, man, you're white!

CHRISTIAN. All over! She doesn't love me any more.

CYRANO. What?

CHRISTIAN. It's you! She loves you!

CYRANO. Impossible!

CHRISTIAN. She only loves my soul.

CYRANO. No!

CHRISTIAN. Yes! You see it's you she really loves. And you love her!

CYRANO. I?

CHRISTIAN. I know you do.

CYRANO (*slowly*). It happens to be true.

CHRISTIAN. You love her to distraction.

CYRANO. More than that.

CHRISTIAN. Tell her so!

CYRANO. No.

CHRISTIAN. Why not?

CYRANO. Just look at this face of mine.

CHRISTIAN. She would love me if I were ugly.

CYRANO. She told you that?

CHRISTIAN (*pointing to the place where it happened*). There!

CYRANO. I am very glad she said it. But come, come! Don't believe such nonsense. Heavens, I'm very glad she could think a thing like that. But don't take her at her word; don't spoil that handsome face. She'd never forgive me.

CHRISTIAN. That is what I want to see.

CYRANO. No, no.

CHRISTIAN. Tell her everything! Let her make a choice between us.

CYRANO. Don't torment me!

CHRISTIAN. Should I kill your happiness because my looks are passable? That's not right.

CYRANO. And should I bury yours because the accident of birth lets me express the things you doubtless feel?

CHRISTIAN. You must tell her everything!

CYRANO. He persists in tempting me! Bad, too bad!

CHRISTIAN. I am tired of carrying a rival here inside me

CYRANO. Christian!

CHRISTIAN. We had no witness at our secret marriage. It can be set aside, if we survive.

CYRANO. Still obstinate?

CHRISTIAN. Yes, I'll be loved for myself, or not at all! I am going to see what's happening. Wait! I shall walk down to the other end of the post; then I'll return. Meanwhile, tell her; let her make her choice.

CYRANO. It will be you.

CHRISTIAN. I hope so. (*He calls*) Roxane!

CYRANO. No! No! Christian, you mustn't!

ROXANE (*hurrying down*). What is it?

CHRISTIAN. Cyrano wants to tell you—something very important. (*She goes quickly to* CYRANO *Exit* CHRISTIAN.)

SCENE X

ROXANE, CYRANO; *then* LE BRET, CARBON, *the* CADETS, RAGUENEAU, DE GUICHE, *etc.*

ROXANE. Important?

CYRANO (*at his wit's end*). He is gone. (*To* ROXANE) Nothing at all. Heavens! You of all people know how he makes something out of nothing.

ROXANE (*quickly*). Perhaps he didn't believe what I said just now? I thought he didn't believe it.

CYRANO (*taking her hand*). You were telling him the truth?

ROXANE. Yes, yes, I should love him even—(*She stops momentarily.*)

CYRANO (*smiling sadly*). The words won't come out, you see, when I'm here!

ROXANE. But——

CYRANO. I don't much mind. Even if he were ugly? Is that it?

ROXANE. Even if he were ugly! (*Shots offstage*) Listen! They are firing!

CYRANO (*ardently*). Even repulsive?

ROXANE. Repulsive!

CYRANO. Disfigured?

ROXANE. Disfigured!

CYRANO. Grotesque?

ROXANE. Nothing could make him grotesque to me.

CYRANO. You would love him still?

ROXANE. Even more—if possible!

CYRANO (*losing control; aside*). My God, perhaps it's true! Perhaps I've happiness within my grasp. (*To* ROXANE) Roxane—listen! There's something——
(*Enter* LE BRET *hurriedly.*)

LE BRET (*in an undertone*). Cyrano!

CYRANO (*turning*). Well?

LE BRET. Ssssh! (*He whispers to* CYRANO.)

CYRANO (*with a cry, dropping* ROXANE'S *hand*). Oh, no! No!

ROXANE. What's the matter?

CYRANO (*to himself, completely overcome*). All over. That's the end.
(*Renewed firing offstage.*)

ROXANE. What is the matter? This shooting? (*She starts backstage to see for herself.*)

CYRANO. All over! I can never tell her now!

ROXANE (*trying to rush forward*). What's happening?

CYRANO (*hastily, stopping her*). It's nothing.
(*Enter a group of* CADETS *carrying something which they try to conceal from* ROXANE.)

ROXANE (*sharply*). These men—

CYRANO (*drawing her away*). Don't bother about them.

ROXANE. What were you going to say to me just now?

CYRANO. What was I going to say? Why, nothing. Nothing, I can assure you. (*Solemnly*) I assure you that Christian's spirit and his soul were—(*In alarm, trying to correct himself*)—are the greatest—

ROXANE. Were? (*With a scream*) Oh!
(*She rushes forward into the group of* CADETS, *and thrusts them aside.*)

CYRANO. And that's the end!

ROXANE (*sees* CHRISTIAN *lying in his cloak*). Christian!

LE BRET (*to* CYRANO). The enemy's first shot!
(ROXANE *throws herself on* CHRISTIAN's *body. More shooting. Clashing of swords. Noises of conflict. Beating of drums. Followed by the* CADETS, CARBON, *sword in hand, goes to the far side of the talus.*)

CARBON. The attack! To arms!

ROXANE. Christian!

CARBON (*behind the breastwork*). Lively now!

ROXANE. Christian!

CARBON. Form ranks!

ROXANE. Christian!

CARBON. Measure fuses!
(RAGUENEAU *runs up with some water in a helmet.*)

CHRISTIAN (*in a dying voice*). Roxane!
(*The distracted* ROXANE *dips in the water a piece of linen torn from her bosom to bandage his wound.*)

CYRANO (*hurriedly whispering in* CHRISTIAN's *ear*). I have told her everything. You are the only one she loves. (CHRISTIAN *closes his eyes.*)

ROXANE. What, dearest?

CARBON. Ramrods out!

ROXANE (*to* CYRANO). He's not dead—

CARBON. Charges ready!

ROXANE. —but his cheek is growing cold!

CARBON. Aim!

ROXANE. What? A letter in his tunic? For me!

CYRANO (*aside*). My letter!

CARBON. Fire!
(*Reports of massed musketry. Shouting. Noise of battle.*)

CYRANO (*trying to free his hand, which* ROXANE *holds, kneeling*). But Roxane, they need me. They are fighting.

ROXANE (*detaining him*). He's dead, and you were the only one who knew him. (*She weeps gently.*) Wasn't he an exquisite soul, a marvellous being?

CYRANO (*standing, head uncovered*). Yes, Roxane.

ROXANE. An adorable poet of unheard of powers?

CYRANO. Yes, Roxane.

ROXANE. A sublime mind?

CYRANO. Yes, Roxane.

ROXANE. A strange, deep soul, magnificent and charming?

CYRANO (*firmly*). Yes, Roxane.

ROXANE (*throwing herself on* CHRISTIAN's *body*). He's dead!

CYRANO (*aside, drawing his sword*). Nothing is left me but to die! For without knowing, she's mourning me in him.
(*Trumpets in the distance. Enter* DE GUICHE *on the talus, head bare, a wound in his forehead.*)

DE GUICHE (*in a thundering voice*). The trumpets! That's the signal! The French are entering camp with our supplies. Hold fast just a little longer!

ROXANE. Blood. Tears! On *his* letter!

A VOICE (*offstage, shouting*). Surrender!

THE CADETS. Never!

RAGUENEAU (*from the top of his carriage, watching the battle*). The fight's getting hotter!

CYRANO (*to* DE GUICHE, *indicating* ROXANE). Get her away. I'm going to lead a charge.

ROXANE (*kissing the letter, her voice failing*). His blood! His tears!

RAGUENEAU (*jumping down and hurrying to her*). She's fainting!

DE GUICHE (*from the talus, in a furious voice*). Stand fast!

VOICE (*offstage*). Surrender!

CADETS' VOICES. Never!

CYRANO (*to* DE GUICHE). Sir, you have more than proved your courage. (*Pointing to* ROXANE) Escape with her! Save your own life and hers!

DE GUICHE (*runs to* ROXANE, *lifts her in his arms*). Very well! The fight is good as won, if you'll gain us time!

CYRANO. Good! (*To* ROXANE, *as* DE GUICHE *and* RAGUENEAU *carry her*

away, insensible) Roxane! Farewell!
(*Confusion. Shouts. Wounded* CADETS *reappear and fall upon the stage.* CYRANO, *hurrying into the fight, is stopped at the breastwork by* CARBON, *covered with blood.*)

CARBON. We're breaking! I've two halberd wounds myself——

CYRANO (*shouting to the Gascons*). Courage, lads! Stand fast! (*To* CARBON) Never fear. I have two deaths to avenge: my happiness and Christian's. (*They come down,* CYRANO *helping* CARBON. CYRANO *brandishes the lance bearing* ROXANE'S *handkerchief.*) Float, little lace; show them her monogram! (*He plants the lance in the ground, and shouts to the* CADETS.) On them, lads! Crush them! (*To the piper*) Give us a tune there!
(*The piper plays. Some of the wounded get to their feet. Other* CADETS, *rolling down the talus, group themselves around* CYRANO *and the little flag. The coach, covered and filled with men, bristling with arquebuses, becomes a redoubt. Enter a* CADET, *retreating down the talus, still fighting.*)

CADET. They are coming up the slope! (*He falls dead.*)

CYRANO. Give them a rousing welcome!
(*A great array of the enemy suddenly appears above the breastwork. Over their heads, banners of the Imperial forces.*)

CYRANO. Fire!
(*A massed volley.*)

SHOUT (*from the enemy's ranks*). Fire!
(*A murderous volley in reply. Cadets fall on every side.*)

A SPANISH OFFICER (*taking off his hat*). Who are these men, so eager to be killed?

CYRANO (*in the midst of the hail of bullets, reciting*).

"These are Cadets of Gascony
In Captain Carbon's Corps!
They lie and fight outrageously
——"

(*He charges, followed by a few survivors.*)

"These are Cadets of Gascony——"

(*The rest is lost in the din of battle.*)

CURTAIN

ACT FIVE

CYRANO'S GAZETTE

The park of the Convent of the Sisters of the Cross in Paris, fifteen years later (1655). Magnificent shade-trees. Left stage, the chapter-house with several doors opening on a great terraced flight of steps. Center stage, a huge isolated tree within a small oval enclosure. Front right, a semicircular stone seat among boxwood hedges. The entire back-stage is crossed by an avenue of chestnut trees leading, backstage right, to the door of a chapel half hidden among the branches. Through the double screen of trees bounding the avenue, one can catch glimpses of lawns, other avenues, small copses, remote corners of the park, the open sky. The small side door of the chapel opens on a colonnade, festooned with reddening vines, which is eventually lost to sight behind the box-wood bushes, front right.

It is autumn. Over the grass, still fresh and green, all the leaves have turned, though here and there boxwood and yew form dark islands of somber green. Under each tree there is a circle of yellow leaves. Fallen leaves strew the entire stage, crackle under foot in the avenues, half cover the steps and seats.

Between the stone seat, front right, and the tree, center stage, is a big embroidery frame set up on legs. In front of it, a small chair and baskets filled with skeins and balls of colored wool. On the frame, a piece of embroidery has been started. At the rise of the curtain, Sisters of the convent are coming and going in the park. A few are seated on the stone seat around an older nun. Leaves are falling everywhere.

SCENE I

MOTHER MARGUERITE, SISTER MARTHE, SISTER CLAIRE, *other sisters.*

SISTER MARTHE (*to* MOTHER MARGUERITE). Sister Claire glanced in the mirror twice this morning to see how her headdress suits her.

MOTHER MARGUERITE (*to* SISTER CLAIRE). That's very bad.

SISTER CLAIRE. Sister Marthe stole a plum out of a tart this morning. I saw her do it.

MOTHER MARGUERITE (*to* SISTER MARTHE). Very naughty, Sister Marthe.

SISTER CLAIRE. It was only a tiny glance.

SISTER MARTHE. It was only a tiny plum.

MOTHER MARGUERITE. This evening I shall tell Monsieur Cyrano.

SISTER CLAIRE (*alarmed*). No! He'll laugh at me.

SISTER MARTHE. He will say that nuns are very vain.

SISTER CLAIRE. Very greedy.

MOTHER MARGUERITE (*smiling*). And very good.

SISTER CLAIRE. Mother Marguerite, hasn't he come here every Saturday these last ten years?

MOTHER MARGUERITE. Longer! Ever since his cousin first brought her veil of crepe as token of worldly mourning among our linen caps. She settled among us fourteen years ago, her coif a great black bird among our white ones.

SISTER MARTHE. Since she took refuge in this cloister, only Monsieur Cyrano has comforted the grief that can't be comforted.

VARIOUS SISTERS. He is so droll. So merry when he comes. He's a tease. He's nice. We're really fond of him. He likes the angelica paste we make for him.

SISTER MARTHE. All the same, he's not a very good Catholic!

SISTER CLAIRE. We are going to convert him.

THE SISTERS. Yes! Yes! So we are.

MOTHER MARGUERITE. I forbid you to do anything of the kind. Don't worry him; he might not come so often if you did.

SISTER MARTHE. But— Dear God! —

MOTHER MARGUERITE. God knows him very well. Be sure of that.

SISTER MARTHE. But every Saturday, he comes and says to me—and looks so proud of it—"Sister, I ate meat yesterday!"

MOTHER MARGUERITE. Oh! He tells you that? Well, the last time he came, he hadn't eaten anything for two days.

SISTER MARTHE. Mother in Heaven!

MOTHER MARGUERITE. He's poor.

SISTER MARTHE. Who told you so?

MOTHER MARGUERITE. Monsieur Le Bret.

SISTER MARTHE. Doesn't any one try to help him?

MOTHER MARGUERITE. That would offend him.
(*Enter* ROXANE, *in widow's coif and long black veil, on one of the avenues backstage; beside her* DE GUICHE, *magnificently turned out, but growing older. They pace slowly.* MOTHER MARGUERITE *rises.*)

MOTHER MARGUERITE. Come, we must go inside. Madame Magdeleine is walking with a visitor.

SISTER MARTHE (*in an undertone, to* SISTER CLAIRE). Is it the Duke de Grammont?

SISTER CLAIRE (*looking*). I think it is.

SISTER MARTHE. He hasn't been to see her for months.

SISTERS. He is very busy. The Court. The Camp.

SISTER CLAIRE. The cares of the world.
(*Exit* SISTERS. DE GUICHE *and* ROXANE *approach in silence, and stop near the embroidery frame. A pause.*)

SCENE II

ROXANE, *the Duke de Grammont, formerly* COUNT DE GUICHE; *then* LE BRET *and* RAGUENEAU.

DE GUICHE. Will you stay here forever in mourning, your blonde beauty wasted?

ROXANE. Forever.

DE GUICHE. Always faithful to his memory?

ROXANE. Always!

DE GUICHE (*after a pause*). Am I forgiven?

ROXANE (*nodding*). Since I've been here, yes!
(*Another pause.*)

DE GUICHE. He must have been a real person——

ROXANE. You had to know him.

DE GUICHE. Yes! Perhaps I never knew him well enough. I suppose his last letter is still close to your heart?

ROXANE. Hanging from this velvet like a scapulary.

DE GUICHE. Dead. Yet you still love him.

ROXANE. Only half dead, it sometime seems, as though our hearts were still together and his love, still alive, hovering around me.

DE GUICHE (*after another pause*). Does Cyrano ever visit you?

ROXANE. Very often. My faithful cousin is a speaking gazette for me. He's regular as clockwork! His chair is set out for him under this tree,—at least when it's fine; I embroider as I wait for him. Then, on the last stroke of the hour, not even turning my head, I hear his cane on the steps. He sits down, rallies me about my interminable embroidery, tells me the week's events, and—(LE BRET *appears on the steps.*) Ah! There's Le Bret. (LE BRET *approaches.*) How's our friend?

LE BRET. Bad!

DE GUICHE. Oh!

ROXANE (*to* DE GUICHE). An exaggeration!

LE BRET. Everything as I predicted: neglect, poverty, crowds of new enemies made by his epistles. He attacks everything—sham nobles, sham devotion, sham braggarts, plagiarists, everyone, everywhere.

ROXANE. But his sword still inspires profound respect. They'll never get the best of him.

DE GUICHE (*shaking his head*). Who knows?

LE BRET. It's not attacks I fear. It's loneliness and hunger, stealthy December stealing to his room. Those are assassins that will murder him. A new notch in his belt every day. His poor nose yellow as old ivory. Nothing to wear but an old serge suit.

DE GUICHE. There's one who didn't succeed. Just the same, I wouldn't pity him too much.

LE BRET (*with a bitter smile*). My lord!

DE GUICHE. No! Don't pity him too much. He has lived without concessions to the world, free in his thoughts and free in act.

LE BRET (*still bitterly smiling*). But, your Grace!

DE GUICHE (*haughtily*). Yes, I know! I've had everything, you think; he has had nothing? And yet—I'd very gladly shake his hand. (*Bowing to* ROXANE) Good-bye.

ROXANE. I'll see you out.

(DE GUICHE *bows to* LE BRET *and goes with* ROXANE *towards the steps.*)

DE GUICHE (*stopping, as she starts to ascend*). Somehow, I almost envy him. You see: too much success in life will bring, though God knows you've done nothing really wrong, a thousand little self-disgusts whose total is not remorse perhaps but a vague feeling, an obscure sense of . . . almost embarrassment. And a duke's robes may drag within their lining (even as they sweep the rising stairs to eminence) the rustle of withered illusions and dry regrets; just as in climbing slowly towards those doors, your gown of mourning drags the fallen leaves.

ROXANE (*ironically*). A dreamer? You?

DE GUICHE. Perhaps. (*Abruptly, just as he is leaving*) Monsieur Le Bret! (*To* ROXANE) A word with him, if you don't mind. (*In an undertone to* LE BRET) It's true that no one would openly attack your friend, but many hate him. Only yesterday, at a card game in the Queen's Apartment, somebody said to me, "This Cyrano might die by accident."

LE BRET. So!

DE GUICHE. He should go out very seldom and be careful.

LE BRET (*throwing up his arms*). Careful! Careful! He's coming here! I've got to head him off! But how can I—?

ROXANE (*at the head of the steps, to an approaching* SISTER). What is it?

SISTER. Ragueneau, Madame. He wants to see you.

ROXANE. Have him come in. (*To* DE GUICHE *and* LE BRET) Some pitiful story of his latest plight. Starting as author, he has become by turns a singer—

LE BRET. Bath-keeper.

ROXANE. Actor.

LE BRET. Beadle.

ROXANE. Wig-maker.

LE BRET. And virtuoso of the lute.

ROXANE. What will he be today, I wonder?

RAGUENEAU (*entering precipitately*). Madame! (*Seeing* LE BRET) Monsieur!

ROXANE (*smiling*). Tell all your latest troubles to Le Bret. I'll soon be back.

RAGUENEAU. Oh! Madame!—
(*She pays no further attention. Exit* ROXANE *with* DE GUICHE. RAGUENEAU *hurries up to* LE BRET.)

SCENE III

LE BRET, RAGUENEAU.

RAGUENEAU. Perhaps it's for the best since you are here. She oughtn't to know. I was going to see your friend. About twenty paces from his house—and he came out. I hurried up. As he started to turn the corner I started running. Then—there was the window—he was under it—and—accident?—perhaps!—a lackey lets fall a heavy log of wood.

LE BRET. The scoundrels! Cyrano!

RAGUENEAU. I rush up! I look at him!

LE BRET. Horrible!

RAGUENEAU. Our friend, our poet, prostrate on the ground, with a great wound in his head!

LE BRET. Dead?

RAGUENEAU. No. But—dear God! I carried him to his room. His room! You ought to see the place.

LE BRET. Is he suffering?

RAGUENEAU. He's unconscious.

LE BRET. What about a doctor?

RAGUENEAU. One came out of charity.

LE BRET. Poor Cyrano! Break it gently to Roxane. What does the doctor say?

RAGUENEAU. I hardly know—fever, something about the brain. You should see him—his head all bandaged. Let's go at once! There is no one with him to look after him. If he gets up, he'll die.

LE BRET (*pointing offstage right*). This way. Quick! A short cut! Through the chapel!

(ROXANE, *entering, sees them hurrying down the colonnade.*)

ROXANE. Monsieur Le Bret! (LE BRET *and* RAGUENEAU *hurry off without replying.*) Why doesn't Le Bret come back when I call him? More trouble for good old Ragueneau I suppose. (*She descends the steps.*)

SCENE IV

ROXANE *alone; then two* SISTERS *for a moment.*

ROXANE. The last day of September—beautiful. Even my grief, uncomfortable in spring, can find a smile these gentler autumn days. (*She sits down by her embroidery frame. Two* SISTERS *bring a large armchair from the house and set it under the trees.*) My dear old friend's old chair?

SISTER. It's the best the convent has.

ROXANE. Thank you, Sister. (*The* SISTERS *leave.*) He'll soon be here. (*She sits before the embroidery frame. The clock strikes.*) There! It's striking now. Quick, my skeins! Why, it has finished striking. I'm quite surprised. Could he be late now the first time? That Sister at the wicket—where's my thimble? Ah! I've got it!—she must be urging him to penitence. (*Pauses*) She must be urging him at length. He can't be much longer. Apart from that, nothing could prevent—scissors?—here in my bag!—could prevent him from coming. What, a dying leaf? (*She brushes away a leaf which has fallen on the embroidery.*)
(*Enter a* SISTER *at the head of the steps.*)

A SISTER. Monsieur de Bergerac.

SCENE V

ROXANE, CYRANO; *then, for a short while,* SISTER MARTHE.

ROXANE (*without turning around*). What was I saying?
(*She works at her embroidery. Enter* CYRANO, *very pale, his hat pulled down over his eyes. The* SISTER *who announced him withdraws. He descends the steps slowly, leaning on his cane, visibly struggling to keep erect.*)

ROXANE. Oh! these faded shades. How can I make them match? (*To*

CYRANO, *affecting to scold him*) For the first time in fourteen years, you're late!
(CYRANO *reaches the armchair and sits down.*)

CYRANO (*in a merry voice belying his appearance*). Yes, provoking! I am vexed. I was delayed, confound it!

ROXANE. By what?

CYRANO. A quite inopportune visit.

ROXANE (*absent-minded, working*). Some disagreeable person?

CYRANO. Very disagreeable. He won't be denied.

ROXANE. Did you send him away?

CYRANO. Yes. I said: "You'll excuse me. This is Saturday. On Saturdays I visit a certain house. Nothing can prevent me. Come back in an hour."

ROXANE (*lightly*). Well! He'll have to wait to see you; I shan't let you leave before evening.

CYRANO. Perhaps I'll have to leave a little sooner.
(*He closes his eyes and is silent for a moment.* SISTER MARTHE *crosses the park from the chapel to the steps.* ROXANE, *seeing her, beckons.*)

ROXANE (*to* CYRANO). Aren't you going to tease Sister Marthe?

CYRANO (*quickly, opening his eyes*). Why certainly! (*In a comical, blustering voice*) Sister Marthe, come here! (*The* SISTER *approaches.*) Ha! Ha! Ha! Your lovely eyes are wasted on the ground.

SISTER MARTHE (*looking up with a smile*). Really? (*Noticing his face, alarmed*) Oh!

CYRANO (*in a whisper, indicating* ROXANE). Hush! It is nothing—(*Boastfully, aloud*) I ate meat yesterday.

SISTER MARTHE. I knew it. (*Aside*) So that's why he's so pale. Hungry! (*Quickly, in an undertone*) If you'll come up to the refectory, I will make you a big bowl of soup. Won't you come?

CYRANO. Yes indeed!

SISTER MARTHE. For once, you're quite reasonable today.

ROXANE (*hearing them whisper*). Is she trying to convert you?

SISTER MARTHE. Heaven forbid!

CYRANO. It's true. You're always talkative on pious matters; today you haven't preached to me at all. Surprising! (*With affected fury*) Thunderation! I must surprise you too. Wait!—(*Apparently searching for, and finding, a new method of teasing*) Yes! Something completely new. I'll let you pray for me in church tonight.

ROXANE (*smiling*). Oh! Oh!

CYRANO (*laughing*). Sister Marthe is amazed beyond all words.

SISTER MARTHE (*quietly*). I didn't need your permission. (*She leaves.*)

CYRANO (*turning to* ROXANE, *bent over her frame*). Embroidery, alas, I'll never see you finished!

ROXANE. That's the joke I was expecting.
(*A slight gust of wind causes a flurry of falling leaves.*)

CYRANO. Ah! The leaves.

ROXANE (*lifting her head to look across at the avenues*). Venetian yellow. Watch them fall.

CYRANO. How well they fall. In this one short journey from the branch to earth, they show a final beauty. Despite their fear of rotting on the ground, they wish their fall to assume the grace of flight.

ROXANE. Melancholy?

CYRANO (*recollecting himself*). Not at all, Roxane.

ROXANE. Let the leaves fall as they will. Give me the news. Where's my today's gazette?

CYRANO. Why, here it is.

ROXANE. Good.

CYRANO (*paling rapidly, struggling against the pain*). Saturday, the nineteenth: Roxane's gazette of news. After eight full helpings of fine Cette preserves, His Majesty was stricken with a fever; twice-bled, he had his malady arrested, and now his august pulse is back to normal. At the Queen's grand ball, given on Sunday evening, they burned seven hundred and sixty-three wax candles; meanwhile, our troops have beaten John of Austria, four sorcerers have been hanged, and Madame d'Athis has had to give her ailing dog a clyster—

ROXANE. Monsieur de Bergerac, let's leave that out.

CYRANO (*his face contorted*). On Monday, nothing—Lygdamire changed lovers.

ROXANE. Oh.

CYRANO. On Tuesday the Court assembled at Fontainebleau. On Wednesday, La Montglat said "No" to De Fiesque. On Thursday, Mancini was queen of France—or almost. On Friday, La Montglat said "Yes" to De Fiesque. On Saturday, the twenty-sixth—
(*His eyes close. His head drops forward. Silence.*)

ROXANE (*surprised, turns around, looks at him, and rises in alarm*). Has he fainted? (*She runs to him, calling*) Cyrano!

CYRANO (*opens his eyes again; in an uncertain voice*). What is it? What has happened? (*Seeing* ROXANE *bending over him, he hastily readjusts his hat, and draws back in his chair in alarm.*) No! No! I assure you, it's nothing. I'll be all right.

ROXANE. Still—

CYRANO. It's the wound I had at Arras. Sometimes, you know—

ROXANE. My poor friend!

CYRANO. It's nothing. It will go away. (*He smiles with an effort.*) It's gone.

ROXANE (*straightening up, relieved*). Each of us has a wound. I have mine too. The old wound, always fresh—it's still here! (*She puts her hand on her breast.*) Here under this fading letter stained with blood and tears.
(*Twilight begins to fall.*)

CYRANO. His letter. Didn't you say that some day, perhaps, you would let me read it?

ROXANE. You want to read his letter?

CYRANO. Yes, today, now!

ROXANE (*giving him the little bag which hangs around her neck*). Here!

CYRANO (*taking it*). May I open it?

ROXANE. Open it and read it.
(*She returns to her embroidery frame, folds it up, and begins to collect her skeins and balls of wool.*)

CYRANO (*reading*). "Roxane, farewell! Knowing I must die, and as it seems tonight, I send this greeting."

ROXANE (*stopping, surprised*). What, aloud?

CYRANO (*continuing*). "My heart is heavy with love that I never told, and now can never tell. My infatuate eyes——"

ROXANE. How strangely well you read it.
(*Darkness is falling imperceptibly.*)

CYRANO (*continuing*). "—those eyes which found a tremulous joy in this, shall never again embrace your familiar gestures. You can never know how your best trait of all, the way you smooth your forehead, made my cry, 'My best, my own beloved'——"

ROXANE. You are reading——

CYRANO (*continuing*). "—makes me cry——"

ROXANE. That voice——

CYRANO (*continuing*). "Now, in the recollection, 'Love, farewell!' "

ROXANE. That voice I heard long years ago.
(*She approaches very quietly without his noticing, goes behind the armchair, bends over him noiselessly, and looks at the letter. Darkness deepens.*)

CYRANO. "My heart has never left you for a moment; and, still in the other world, I shall be the one who has loved beyond all hope of loving, the one who loved——"

ROXANE (*placing her hand on his shoulder*). How can you read it now? It's dark. (*Startled, he turns round, sees her very close, makes a gesture of alarm, bends his head. A long silence. Then, slowly, clasping her hands*) And so for fourteen years, you've played this part. The old friend coming to amuse me!

CYRANO. Roxane!

ROXANE. It was you!

CYRANO. No, no, Roxane, no!

ROXANE. I ought to have known it by the way you spoke my name.

CYRANO. You're wrong.

ROXANE. It was you.

CYRANO. I assure you——

ROXANE. I see through all your generous trickery. The letters,—they were yours——

CYRANO. No!

ROXANE. The dear mad words were yours.

CYRANO. No.

ROXANE. The voice in the night was yours.

CYRANO. I swear it wasn't.

ROXANE. The soul was yours.

CYRANO. I didn't love you.

ROXANE. You loved me.

CYRANO. It was the other. He was the one who loved you.

ROXANE. *You* loved me!

CYRANO. No! No!

ROXANE. You say it in a faltering voice already.

CYRANO. No! No! I never loved you —dearest love!

ROXANE. Ah! How many things, long dead, are now reborn. Why were you silent all these fourteen years, when on this letter that he never wrote these tears were yours?

CYRANO (*giving her the letter*). The blood was his.

ROXANE. Then why did you let this silence so sublime be broken now?

CYRANO. Why, Roxane?
(LE BRET *and* RAGUENEAU *rush in.*)

SCENE VI

The same; LE BRET, *and* RAGUENEAU.

LE BRET. Sheer madness! I was sure of it. Here he is!

CYRANO (*smiling and straightening up*). Why, naturally. Where else?

LE BRET. He has finished himself, madame, by getting up.

ROXANE. God alive! Then that faintness just now—?

CYRANO. Quite so. I didn't finish my gazette. On Saturday, the twenty-sixth, an hour before his dinner, Monsieur de Bergerac was done to death.
(*He takes off his hat, revealing his bandaged head.*)

ROXANE. What does he mean? Cyrano! Your head all bandaged up? What have they done to you?

CYRANO. "Struck by a worthy sword and adversary; to die with a point at my heart and a pointed word at my lips!" And I said that. How Fate has laughed at me! Here I am murdered, trapped in an ambush, killed by a lackey, with a mere block of wood! Nothing more perfect. A failure in life, and a failure in death.

RAGUENEAU. My dear friend!

CYRANO. Ragueneau! No tears. (*Stretching out his hand to him*) What are you now, my brother?

RAGUENEAU (*through his tears*). I am candle—candle-snuffer, for the plays of Molière.

CYRANO. Molière?

RAGUENEAU. I shall leave him after tomorrow; I'm quite indignant. Yesterday, when they played "Scapin," I saw he had taken an entire scene from you.

LE BRET. An entire scene!

RAGUENEAU. Yes! The famous "What the devil was he doing——?"

LE BRET (*indignantly*). And Molière stole that from you?

CYRANO. Hush! He did right. (*To* RAGUENEAU) Was it effective?

RAGUENEAU (*sobbing*). The people laughed—laughed and laughed!

CYRANO. That's been my life—to prompt and be forgotten. (*To* ROXANE) The night Christian spoke beneath your window—you remember? My whole life's in that moment. While I stayed below within the shadows, others have climbed to take the kiss of glory. It's not unfair. From the grave's brink, I think I must approve: Molière has genius; Christian had beauty. (*Bells sound from the chapel. Sisters pass along the avenue backstage on their way to service.*) For whom the bell is tolling,—they should pray.

ROXANE (*rising and calling*). Sister! Sister!

CYRANO (*holding her back*). No! Don't go for anyone. Too late. When you returned, I should be no longer here. (*The Sisters have entered the chapel; the organ is heard.*) Ah! Harmony was missing; there it is.

ROXANE. I love you; you must live!

CYRANO. No. In the tale of Beauty and the Beast, when the princess says, "I love you," then the prince feels all his ugliness transformed to fairness, transmuted in the sunshine of her words. You see, I'm still the same, still untransformed.

ROXANE. I've been your life's misfortune——

CYRANO. Never that. Quite the reverse. I've never known women's sweetness. My mother—she could scarcely think me handsome. I had no sister. Later, I was afraid to meet a sweetheart's eye. Yet, thanks to you, I've known a woman's friendship—a woman's gown has brushed against my life.

LE BRET (*pointing to the moonlight in the branches*). Your other friend has come to you.

CYRANO (*smiling at the moon*). I see her.

ROXANE. I've loved one man alone. Why must I lose him twice?

CYRANO. Le Bret, I'll climb to the opaline moon tonight and not need my machines——

ROXANE. What are you saying?

CYRANO. They'll send me there to find my Paradise. They must. The souls I love are exiled there. I shall find Socrates and Galileo——

LE BRET (*rebelling*). No! This end's too senseless, too unjust! A poet like him! A heart so great, so lofty! To die! To die like this!

CYRANO. Old grumbler to the last!

LE BRET (*in tears*). Dear friend!

CYRANO (*rising, wild-eyed*). "These are Cadets of Gascony"—the elemental mass!—yes, there's the problem!

LE BRET (*almost proudly*). A scientist, even in delirium!

CYRANO. Copernicus—he said——

ROXANE (*weeping*). Oh!

CYRANO.

> "But what the devil was he doing there,
> How did he come to be in this affair?"

(*Pauses*)

> Philosopher and physicist,
> Musician, poet, duellist,
> Planetary aerialist,
> Skilled at the parry and attack,
> A lover too—unhappy man!
> Here lies Hercule-Savinien
> De Cyrano de Bergerac,
> Who failed in all a mortal can!

Forgive me. I must go now. I can't stay. Moonlight is here to take me home again. (*He falls back in his chair.* ROXANE's *tears bring him to reality. He looks at her and touches her veil with caressing fingers.*) Don't grieve the less for your fine, charming Christian, but when the last great chill has gripped my bones, could you give double meaning to your veil, and, mourning him, mourn me a little also? Could you, Roxane?

ROXANE. I promise—faithfully!

CYRANO (*seized by a great shivering, suddenly rises*). Not here! No! not in this armchair! (*They wish to help him.*) Never! No! Don't support me. (*He leans against the tree.*) Nothing but this tree. (*Pause*) He's on his way now. Already I'm shod in marble—and gloved with lead. But since he's on his way, I shall await him standing——(*he draws his sword.*)—and standing sword in hand!

LE BRET. Cyrano!

ROXANE (*faltering*). Cyrano! (*All draw back in terror.*)

CYRANO. I see him peering now! He dares to look at my nose, that squat-nosed Horror! (*Raising his sword*) What do you say? It's useless? Well, I know it! But the best fight is not for the hope of winning. Far better to fight when you know the fight is hopeless. Who are all these? A thousand of you? So! I know you now—my ancient adversaries. Falsehood! (*Striking the empty air with his sword*) And Cowardice! And Prejudice! Compromise too? (*Striking hard*) I'll make a compact, will I? Why, never! Never! Ah! And here comes Folly! I know you'll better me tonight. No matter! I'll fight, and fight, and fight. (*He sweeps his sword in great circles, then stops, panting.*) Yes! You have robbed me of all now, the laurel and the rose. Take them. Despite your malice, there are things you cannot take. When I enter the mansion of God tonight, my bow shall brush its azure sills with something erect, unspotted, that I carry in spite of you all—(*Starts forward with raised sword*)—and that is—(*The sword drops from his hand; he staggers and falls into the arms of* ROXANE *and* RAGUENEAU.)

ROXANE (*bending over him and kissing his forehead*). And that is?

CYRANO (*reopens his eyes, recognizes her, and smiles*). My undishonored plume!

CURTAIN

The Cherry Orchard

BY ANTON CHEKHOV

CHARACTERS

LYUBOF ANDREYEVNA RANEVSKY, *a landowner*
ANYA, *her daughter, aged seventeen*
BARBARA, *her adopted daughter, aged twenty-seven*
LEONID ANDREYEVITCH GAYEF, *her brother*
YERMOLAI ALEXEYEVITCH LOPAKHIN, *a merchant*
PETER SERGEYEVITCH TROPHIMOF, *a student*
BORIS BORISOVITCH SIMEONOF-PISHTCHIK, *a landowner*
CHARLOTTE IVANOVNA, *a governess*
SIMEON PANTELEYEVITCH EPHIKHODOF, *a clerk*
DUNYASHA (AVDOTYA FYODOROVNA), *a maid*
FIRS,* *a man-servant, aged eighty-seven*
YASHA, *a young man-servant*
A TRAMP
A STATION MASTER
GUESTS
A POST OFFICE CLERK
SERVANTS

The action takes place on MADAME RANEVSKY'S *estate.*

* Pronounced like a Scotsman saying "fierce."

The Cherry Orchard

ACT ONE

A room which is still called the nursery. One door leads to ANYA'S *room. Dawn, the sun will soon rise. It is already May, the cherry-trees are in blossom, but it is cold in the garden and there is a morning frost. The windows are closed.*

Enter DUNYASHA *with a candle, and* LOPAKHIN *with a book in his hand.*

LOPAKHIN. So the train has come in, thank heaven. What is the time?

DUNYASHA. Nearly two. (*Putting the candle out*) It is light already.

LOPAKHIN. How late is the train? A couple of hours at least. (*Yawning and stretching*) What do you think of me? A fine fool I have made of myself. I came on purpose to meet them at the station and then I went and fell asleep, fell asleep as I sat in my chair. What a nuisance it is! You might have woke me up anyway.

DUNYASHA. I thought that you had gone. (*She listens*) That sounds like them driving up.

LOPAKHIN (*listening*). No; they have got to get the luggage out and all that. (*A pause*) Madame Ranevsky has been five years abroad. I wonder what she has become like. What a splendid creature she is! So easy and simple in her ways. I remember when I was a youngster of fifteen my old father (he used to keep a shop here in the village then) struck me in the face with his fist and set my nose bleeding. We had come for some reason or other, I forget what, into the courtyard, and he had been drinking. Madame Ranevsky, I remember it like yesterday, still a young girl, and oh, so slender, brought me to the wash-hand stand here, in this very room, in the nursery. "Don't cry, little peasant," she said, "it'll mend by your wedding."* (*A pause*) "Little peasant!" . . . My father, it is true, was a peasant, and here am I in a white waistcoat and brown boots; a silk purse out of a sow's ear, as you might say; just turned rich, with heaps of money, but when you come to look at it, still a peasant of the peasants. (*Turning over the pages of the book*) Here's this book that I was reading and didn't

* *It'll mend by your wedding:* a proverbial phrase.

understand a word of; I just sat reading and fell asleep.

DUNYASHA. The dogs never slept all night, they knew that their master and mistress were coming.

LOPAKHIN. What's the matter with you, Dunyasha? You're all . . .

DUNYASHA. My hands are trembling, I feel quite faint.

LOPAKHIN. You are too refined, Dunyasha, that's what it is. You dress yourself like a young lady, and look at your hair. You ought not to do it; you ought to remember your place.
(*Enter* EPHIKHODOF *with a nosegay. He is dressed in a short jacket and brightly polished boots which squeak noisily. As he comes in he drops the nosegay.*)

EPHIKHODOF (*picking it up*). The gardener has sent this; he says it is to go in the dining-room. (*Handing it to* DUNYASHA.)

LOPAKHIN. And bring me some kvass.

DUNYASHA. Yes, sir. (*Exit.*)

EPHIKHODOF. There's a frost this morning, three degrees, and the cherry-trees all in blossom. I can't say I think much of our climate; (*sighing*) that is impossible. Our climate is not adapted to contribute; and I should like to add, with your permission, that only two days ago I bought myself a new pair of boots, and I venture to assure you they do squeak beyond all bearing. What am I to grease them with?

LOPAKHIN. Get out; I'm tired of you.

EPHIKHODOF. Every day some misfortune happens to me; but do I grumble? No; I am used to it; I can afford to smile. (*Enter* DUNYASHA, *and hands a glass of kvass to* LOPAKHIN.) I must be going. (*He knocks against a chair, which falls to the ground.*) There you are! (*In a voice of triumph*) You see, if I may venture on the expression, the sort of incidents *inter alia*. It really is astonishing!
(*Exit* EPHIKHODOF.)

DUNYASHA. To tell you the truth, Yermolai Alexeyitch, Ephikhodof has made me a proposal.

LOPAKHIN. Humph!

DUNYASHA. I hardly know what to do. He is such a well-behaved young man, only so often when he talks one doesn't know what he means. It is all so nice and full of good feeling, but you can't make out what it means. I fancy I am rather fond of him. He adores me passionately. He is a most unfortunate man; every day something seems to happen to him. They call him "Twenty-two misfortunes," that's his nickname.

LOPAKHIN (*listening*). There, surely that is them coming!

DUNYASHA. They're coming! Oh, what is the matter with me? I am all turning cold.

LOPAKHIN. Yes, there they are, and no mistake. Let's go and meet them. Will she know me again, I wonder? It is five years since we met.

DUNYASHA. I am going to faint! . . . I am going to faint!
(*Two carriages are heard driving up to the house.* LOPAKHIN *and* DUNYASHA *exeunt quickly. The stage remains empty. A hubbub begins in the neighbouring rooms.* FIRS *walks hastily across the stage, leaning on a walking stick. He has been to meet them at the station. He is wearing an old-fashioned livery and a tall hat; he mumbles something to himself but not a word is audible. The noise behind the scenes grows louder and louder. A voice says: "Let's go this way." Enter* MADAME RANEVSKY, ANYA, CHARLOTTE, *leading a little dog on a chain, all dressed in travelling dresses;* BARBARA *in greatcoat with a kerchief over her head,* GAYEF, SIMEONOF-PISHTCHIK, LOPAKHIN, DUNYASHA, *carrying parcel and umbrella, servants with luggage, all cross the stage.*)

ANYA. Come through this way. Do you remember what room this is, mamma?

MADAME RANEVSKY (*joyfully, through her tears*). The nursery.

BARBARA. How cold it is. My hands are simply frozen. (*To* MADAME RANEVSKY) Your two rooms, the white room and the violet room, are just the same as they were, mamma.

MADAME RANEVSKY. My nursery, my dear, beautiful nursery! This is where I used to sleep when I was a little girl. (*Crying*) I am like a little girl still. (*Kissing* GAYEF *and* BARBARA *and then* GAYEF *again*) Barbara has not altered a bit, she is just like a nun, and I knew Dunyasha at once. (*Kissing* DUNYASHA.)

GAYEF. Your train was two hours late. What do you think of that? There's punctuality for you!

CHARLOTTE (*to* SIMEONOF-PISHTCHIK). My little dog eats nuts.

PISHTCHIK (*astonished*). You don't say so! well I never!
(*All go out but* ANYA *and* DUNYASHA.)

DUNYASHA. At last you've come! (*She takes off* ANYA'*s overcoat and hat.*)

ANYA. I have not slept for four nights on the journey. I am frozen to death.

DUNYASHA. It was Lent when you went away. There was snow on the ground, it was freezing; but now! Oh, my dear! (*Laughing and kissing her*) How I have waited for you, my joy, my light! Oh, I must tell you something at once, I cannot wait another minute.

ANYA (*without interest*). What, again?

DUNYASHA. Ephikhodof, the clerk, proposed to me in Easter week.

ANYA. Same old story. . . . (*Putting her hair straight*) All my hairpins have dropped out. (*She is very tired, staggering with fatigue.*)

DUNYASHA. I hardly know what to think of it. He loves me! oh, how he loves me!

ANYA (*looking into her bedroom, affectionately*). My room, my windows, just as if I had never gone away! I am at home again! When I wake up in the morning I shall run out into the garden. . . . Oh, if only I could get to sleep! I have not slept the whole journey from Paris, I was so nervous and anxious.

DUNYASHA. Monsieur Trophimof arrived the day before yesterday.

ANYA (*joyfully*). Peter?

DUNYASHA. He is sleeping outside in the bathhouse; he is living there. He was afraid he might be in the way. (*Looking at her watch*) I'd like to go and wake him, only Mamzelle Barbara told me not to. "Mind you don't wake him," she said.
(*Enter* BARBARA *with bunch of keys hanging from her girdle.*)

BARBARA. Dunyasha, go and get some coffee, quick. Mamma wants some coffee.

DUNYASHA. In a minute! (*Exit.*)

BARBARA. Well, thank heaven, you have come. Here you are at home again. (*Caressing her*) My little darling is back! My pretty one is back!

ANYA. What I've had to go through!

BARBARA. I can believe you.

ANYA. I left here in Holy Week. How cold it was! Charlotte would talk the whole way and keep doing conjuring tricks. What on earth made you tie Charlotte round my neck.

BARBARA. Well, you couldn't travel alone, my pet. At seventeen!

ANYA. When we got to Paris, it was so cold! There was snow on the ground. I can't talk French a bit. Mamma was on the fifth floor of a big house. When I arrived there were a lot of Frenchmen with her, and ladies, and an old Catholic priest with a book, and it was very uncomfortable and full of tobacco smoke. I suddenly felt so sorry for mamma, oh, so sorry! I took her head in my arms and squeezed it and could not let it go, and then mamma kept kissing me and crying.

BARBARA (*crying*). Don't go on, don't go on!

ANYA. She'd sold her villa near Mentone already. She'd nothing left, absolutely nothing; and I hadn't a farthing either. We only just managed to get home. And mamma won't understand! We get out at a station to have some dinner, and she asks for all the most expensive things and gives the waiters a florin each for a tip; and Charlotte does the same. And Yasha wanted his portion too. It was too awful! Yasha is mamma's new man-servant. We have brought him back with us.

BARBARA. I've seen the rascal.

ANYA. Come, tell me all about everything! Has the interest on the mortgage been paid?

BARBARA. How could it be?

ANYA. Oh dear! Oh dear!

BARBARA. The property will be sold in August.

ANYA. Oh dear! Oh dear!

LOPAKHIN (*looking in at the door and mooing like a cow*). Moo-o (*He goes away again.*)

BARBARA (*laughing through her tears, and shaking her fist at the door*). Oh, I should like to give him one!

ANYA (*embracing* BARBARA *softly*). Barbara, has he proposed to you? (BARBARA *shakes her head.*) And yet I am sure he loves you. Why don't you come to an understanding? What are you waiting for?

BARBARA. I don't think anything will come of it. He has so much to do; he can't be bothered with me; he hardly takes any notice. Confound the man, I can't bear to see him! Everyone talks about our marriage; everyone congratulates me, but, as a matter of fact, there is nothing in it; it's all a dream. (*Changing her tone*) You've got on a brooch like a bee.

ANYA (*sadly*). Mamma bought it for me. (*Going into her room, talking gaily, like a child*) When I was in Paris, I went up in a balloon!

BARBARA. How glad I am you are back, my little pet! my pretty one! (DUNYASHA *has already returned with a coffee-pot and begins to prepare the coffee; standing by the door*) I trudge about all day looking after things, and I think and think. What are we to do? If only we could marry you to some rich man it would be a load off my mind. I would go into a retreat, and then to Kiev, to Moscow; I would tramp about from one holy place to another, always tramping and tramping. What bliss!

ANYA. The birds are singing in the garden. What time is it now?

BARBARA. It must be past two. It is time to go to bed, my darling. (*Following* ANYA *into her room*) What bliss!
(*Enter* YASHA *with a shawl and a travelling bag.*)

YASHA (*crossing the stage, delicately*). May I pass this way, mademoiselle?

DUNYASHA. One would hardly know you, Yasha. How you've changed abroad!

YASHA. Ahem! and who may you be?

DUNYASHA. When you left here I was a little thing like that. (*Indicating with her hand*) My name is Dunyasha, Theodore Kozoyedof's daughter. Don't you remember me?

YASHA. Ahem! You little cucumber! (*He looks round cautiously, then embraces her. She screams and drops a saucer. Exit* YASHA, *hastily.*)

BARBARA (*in the doorway, crossly*). What's all this?

DUNYASHA (*crying*). I've broken a saucer.

BARBARA. Well, it brings luck.
(*Enter* ANYA *from her room.*)

ANYA. We must tell mamma that Peter's here.

BARBARA. I've told them not to wake him.

ANYA (*thoughtfully*). It's just six years since papa died. And only a month afterwards poor little Grisha was drowned in the river; my pretty little brother, only seven years old! It was too much for mamma; she ran away, ran away without looking back. (*Shuddering*) How well I can understand her, if only she knew! (*A pause*) Peter Trophimof was Grisha's tutor; he might remind her.
(*Enters* FIRS *in long coat and white waistcoat.*)

FIRS (*going over to the coffee-pot, anxiously*). My mistress is going to take coffee here. (*Putting on white gloves*) Is the coffee ready? (*Sternly, to* DUNYASHA) Here, girl, where's the cream?

DUNYASHA. Oh, dear! oh, dear! (*Exit hastily.*)

FIRS (*Bustling about the coffee-pot*). Ah, you . . . job-lot!* (*Mumbling to himself*) She's come back from Paris. The master went to Paris once in a post-chaise. (*Laughing.*)

BARBARA. What is it, Firs?

FIRS. I beg your pardon? (*Joyfully*) My mistress has come home; at last I've seen her. Now I'm ready to die. (*He cries with joy.*)
(*Enter* MADAME RANEVSKY, LOPAKHIN, GAYEF *and* PISHTCHIK *in Russian breeches and coat of fine cloth.* GAYEF *as he enters makes gestures as if playing billiards.*)

MADAME RANEVSKY. What was the expression? Let me see. "I'll put the red in the corner pocket; double into the middle——"

GAYEF. I'll chip the red in the right-hand top. Once upon a time, Lyuba, when we were children, we used to sleep here side by side in two little cots, and now I'm fifty-one, and can't bring myself to believe it.

LOPAKHIN. Yes; time flies.

GAYEF. Who's that?

LOPAKHIN. Time flies, I say.

GAYEF. There's a smell of patchouli!

ANYA. I am going to bed. Good-night, mamma. (*Kissing her mother.*)

MADAME RANEVSKY. My beloved little girl! (*Kissing her hands*) Are you glad you're home again? I can't come to my right senses.

* In the original, *nedotëpa,* a word invented by Chekhov, and now established as classical. Derived from *ne,* not, and *dotyapat,* to finish chopping. The implication is: You're a bungling piece of work, chopped out with a hatchet, and not finished at that. "Botchment" or "underbungle" would have been more literal. "You are one of those who never get there," was the Stage Society rendering. Batyushkof looks on it as the key to the whole play (the word occurs several times); they are all *nedotëpas,* Madame Ranevsky, Gayef, Lopakhin, Trophimof, Ephikhodof, Yasha, even the tramp who lurches across in Act II. That is the tragedy of it, and of Russian life.

ANYA. Good-night, uncle.

GAYEF (*kissing her face and hands*). God bless you, little Anya. How like your mother you are! (*To* MADAME RANEVSKY) You were just such another girl at her age, Lyuba.
(ANYA *shakes hands with* LOPAKHIN *and* SIMEONOF-PISHTCHIK, *and exit, shutting her bedroom door behind her.*)

MADAME RANEVSKY. She's very, very tired.

PISHTCHIK. It must have been a long journey.

BARBARA (*to* LOPAKHIN *and* PISHTCHIK). Well, gentlemen, it's past two; time you were off.

MADAME RANEVSKY (*laughing*). You haven't changed a bit, Barbara! (*Drawing her to herself and kissing her*) I'll just finish my coffee, then we'll all go. (FIRS *puts a footstool under her feet.*) Thank you, friend. I'm used to my coffee. I drink it day and night. Thank you, you dear old man. (*Kissing* FIRS.)

BARBARA. I'll go and see if they've got all the luggage. (*She goes out.*)

MADAME RANEVSKY. Can it be me that's sitting here? (*Laughing*) I want to jump and wave my arms about. (*Pausing and covering her face*) Surely I must be dreaming! God knows I love my country. I love it tenderly. I couldn't see out of the window from the train, I was crying so. (*Crying*) However, I must drink my coffee. Thank you, Firs; thank you, you dear old man. I'm so glad to find you still alive.

FIRS. The day before yesterday.

GAYEF. He's hard of hearing.

LOPAKHIN. I've got to be off for Kharkov by the five o'clock train. Such a nuisance! I wanted to stay and look at you and talk to you. You're as splendid as you always were.

PISHTCHIK (*sighing heavily*). Handsomer than ever and dressed like a Parisian . . . perish my waggon and all its wheels!

LOPAKHIN. Your brother, Leonid Andreyitch, says I'm a snob, a money-grubber. He can say what he likes. I don't care a hang. Only I want you to believe in me as you used to; I want your wonderful, touching eyes to look at me as they used to. Merciful God in heaven! My father was your father's serf, and your grandfather's serf before him; but you, you did so much for me in the old days that I've forgotten everything, and I love you like a sister—more than a sister.

MADAME RANEVSKY. I can't sit still! I can't do it! (*Jumping up and walking about in great agitation*) This happiness is more than I can bear. Laugh at me! I am a fool! (*Kissing a cupboard*) My darling old cupboard! (*Caressing a table*) My dear little table!

GAYEF. Nurse is dead since you went away.

MADAME RANEVSKY (*sitting down and drinking coffee*). Yes, Heaven rest her soul. They wrote and told me.

GAYEF. And Anastasi is dead. Squint-eyed Peter has left us and works in the town at the Police Inspector's now. (*Takes out a box of sugar candy from his pocket, and begins to eat it.*)

PISHTCHIK. My daughter Dashenka sent her compliments.

LOPAKHIN. I long to say something charming and delightful to you. (*Looking at his watch*) I'm just off; there's no time to talk. Well, yes, I'll put it in two or three words. You know that your cherry orchard is going to be sold to pay the mortgage: the sale is fixed for the twenty-second of August; but don't you be uneasy, my dear lady; sleep peacefully; there's a way out of it. This is my plan. Listen to me carefully. Your property is only fifteen miles from the town; the railway runs close beside it; and if only you will cut up the cherry orchard and the land along the river into building lots and let it off on lease for villas, you will get at least two thousand five hundred pounds a year out of it.

GAYEF. Come, come! What rubbish you're talking!

MADAME RANEVSKY. I don't quite understand what you mean, Yermolai Alexeyitch.

LOPAKHIN. You will get a pound a year at least for every acre from the tenants, and if you advertise the thing at once, I am ready to bet whatever you like, by the autumn you won't have a clod of that earth left on your hands. It'll all be snapped up. In two words, I congratulate you; you are saved. It's a first-class site, with a good deep river. Only of course you will have to put it in order and clear the ground; you will have to pull down all the old buildings—this house, for instance, which is no longer fit for anything; you'll have to cut down the cherry orchard. . . .

MADAME RANEVSKY. Cut down the cherry orchard! Excuse me, but you don't know what you're talking about. If there is one thing that's interesting, remarkable in fact, in the whole province, it's our cherry orchard.

LOPAKHIN. There's nothing remarkable about the orchard except that it's a very big one. It only bears once every two years, and then you don't know what to do with the fruit. Nobody wants to buy it.

GAYEF. Our cherry orchard is mentioned in Andreyevsky's Encyclopaedia.

LOPAKHIN (*looking at his watch*). If we don't make up our minds or think of any way, on the twenty-second of August the cherry orchard and the whole property will be sold by auction. Come, make up your mind! There's no other way out of it, I swear—absolutely none.

FIRS. In the old days, forty or fifty

years ago, they used to dry the cherries and soak 'em and pickle 'em, and make jam of 'em; and the dried cherries . . .

GAYEF. Shut up, Firs.

FIRS. The dried cherries used to be sent in waggons to Moscow and Kharkov. A heap of money! The dried cherries were soft and juicy and sweet and sweet-smelling then. They knew some way in those days.

MADAME RANEVSKY. And why don't they do it now?

FIRS. They've forgotten. Nobody remembers how to do it.

PISHTCHIK (*to* MADAME RANEVSKY). What about Paris? How did you get on? Did you eat frogs?

MADAME RANEVSKY. Crocodiles.

PISHTCHIK. You don't say so! Well I never!

LOPAKHIN. Until a little while ago there was nothing but gentry and peasants in the villages; but now villa residents have made their appearance. All the towns, even the little ones, are surrounded by villas now. In another twenty years the villa resident will have multiplied like anything. At present he only sits and drinks tea on his verandah, but it is quite likely that he will soon take to cultivating his three acres of land, and then your old cherry orchard will become fruitful, rich and happy. . . .

GAYEF (*angry*). What gibberish! (*Enter* BARBARA *and* YASHA.)

BARBARA (*taking out a key and noisily unlocking an old-fashioned cupboard*). There are two telegrams for you, mamma. Here they are.

MADAME RANEVSKY (*tearing them up without reading them*). They're from Paris. I've done with Paris.

GAYEF. Do you know how old this cupboard is, Lyuba? A week ago I pulled out the bottom drawer and saw a date burnt in it. That cupboard was made exactly a hundred years ago. What do you think of that, eh? We might celebrate its jubilee. It's only an inanimate thing, but for all that it's a historic cupboard.

PISHTCHIK (*astonished*). A hundred years? Well, I never!

GAYEF (*touching the cupboard*). Yes, it's a wonderful thing. . . . Beloved and venerable cupboard; honour and glory to your existence, which for more than a hundred years has been directed to the noble ideals of justice and virtue. Your silent summons to profitable labour has never weakened in all these hundred years. (*Crying*) You have upheld the courage of succeeding generations of our human kind; you have upheld faith in a better future and cherished in us ideals of goodness and social consciousness. (*A pause.*)

LOPAKHIN. Yes. . . .

MADAME RANEVSKY. You haven't changed, Leonid.

GAYEF (*embarrassed*). Off the white in the corner, chip the red in the middle pocket!

LOPAKHIN (*looking at his watch*). Well I must be off.

YASHA (*handing a box to* MADAME RANEVSKY). Perhaps you'll take your pills now.

PISHTCHIK. You oughtn't to take medicine, dear lady. It does you neither good nor harm. Give them here, my friend. (*He empties all the pills into the palm of his hand, blows on them, puts them in his mouth and swallows them down with a draught of kvass.*) There!

MADAME RANEVSKY (*alarmed*). Have you gone off your head?

PISHTCHIK. I've taken all the pills.

LOPAKHIN. Greedy fellow! (*Everyone laughs.*)

FIRS (*mumbling*). They were here in Easter week and finished off a gallon of pickled gherkins.

MADAME RANEVSKY. What's he talking about?

BARBARA. He's been mumbling like that these three years. We've got used to it.

YASHA. Advancing age.
(CHARLOTTE *crosses in a white frock, very thin, tightly laced, with a lorgnette at her waist.*)

LOPAKHIN. Excuse me, Charlotte Ivanovna, I've not paid my respects to you yet. (*He prepares to kiss her hand.*)

CHARLOTTE (*drawing her hand away*). If one allows you to kiss one's hand, you will want to kiss one's elbow next, and then one's shoulder.

LOPAKHIN. I'm having no luck today. (*All laugh.*) Charlotte Ivanovna, do us a conjuring trick.

MADAME RANEVSKY. Charlotte, do do us a conjuring trick.

CHARLOTTE. No, thank you. I'm going to bed.
(*Exit.*)

LOPAKHIN. We shall meet again in three weeks. (*Kissing* MADAME RANEVSKY'S *hand*) Meanwhile, good-bye. I must be off. (*To* GAYEF) So-long. (*Kissing* PISHTCHIK) Ta-ta. (*Shaking hands with* BARBARA, *then with* FIRS *and* YASHA) I hate having to go. (*To* MADAME RANEVSKY) If you make up your mind about the villas, let me know, and I'll raise you five thousand pounds at once. Think it over seriously.

BARBARA (*angrily*). For heaven's sake do go!

LOPAKHIN. I'm going, I'm going. (*Exit.*)

GAYEF. Snob! . . . However, *pardon!* Barbara's going to marry him; he's Barbara's young man.

BARBARA. You talk too much, uncle.

MADAME RANEVSKY. Why, Barbara, I shall be very glad. He's a nice man.

PISHTCHIK. Not a doubt about it. . . . A most worthy individual. My Dashenka, she says . . . oh, she says . . . lots of things. (*Snoring and waking up again at once*) By the by, dear lady, can you lend me twenty-five pounds? I've got to pay the interest on my mortgage to-morrow.

BARBARA (*alarmed*). We can't! We can't!

MADAME RANEVSKY. It really is a fact that I haven't any money.

PISHTCHIK. I'll find it somewhere. (*Laughing*) I never lose hope. Last time I thought: "Now I really am done for, I'm a ruined man," when behold, they ran a railway over my land and paid me compensation. And so it'll be again; something will happen, if not to-day, then to-morrow. Dashenka may win the twenty-thousand-pound prize; she's got a ticket in the lottery.

MADAME RANEVSKY. The coffee's finished. Let's go to bed.

FIRS (*brushing* GAYEF'S *clothes, admonishingly*). You've put on the wrong trousers again. Whatever am I to do with you?

BARBARA (*softly*). Anya is asleep. (*She opens the window quietly.*) The sun's up already; it isn't cold now. Look, mamma, how lovely the trees are. Heavens! what a sweet air! The starlings are singing!

GAYEF (*opening the other window*). The orchard is all white. You've not forgotten it, Lyuba? This long avenue going straight on, straight on, like a ribbon between the trees? It shines like silver on moonlight nights. Do you remember? You've not forgotten?

MADAME RANEVSKY (*looking out into the garden*). Oh, my childhood, my pure and happy childhood! I used to sleep in this nursery. I used to look out from here into the garden. Happiness awoke with me every morning! and the orchard was just the same then as it is now; nothing is altered. (*Laughing with joy*) It is all white, all white! Oh, my cherry orchard! After the dark and stormy autumn and the frosts of winter you are young again and full of happiness; the angels of heaven have not abandoned you. Oh! if only I could free my neck and shoulders from the stone that weighs them down! If only I could forget my past!

GAYEF. Yes; and this orchard will be sold to pay our debts, however impossible it may seem. . . .

MADAME RANEVSKY. Look! There's mamma walking in the orchard . . . in a white frock! (*Laughing with joy*) There she is!

GAYEF. Where?

BARBARA. Heaven help you!

MADAME RANEVSKY. There's no one there, really. It only looked like it; there on the right where the path turns down to the summer-house; there's a white tree that leans over and looks like a woman. (*Enter* TROPHIMOF *in a shabby student uniform and spectacles.*) What a wonderful orchard, with its white masses of blossom and the blue sky above!

TROPHIMOF. Lyubof Andreyevna! (*She looks round at him.*) I only want to say, "How do you do," and go away at once. (*Kissing her hand eagerly*) I was told to wait till the morning, but I hadn't the patience. (MADAME RANEVSKY *looks at him in astonishment.*)

BARBARA (*crying*). This is Peter Trophimof.

TROPHIMOF. Peter Trophimof; I was Grisha's tutor, you know. Have I really altered so much?
(MADAME RANEVSKY *embraces him and cries softly.*)

GAYEF. Come, come, that's enough, Lyuba!

BARBARA (*crying*). I told you to wait till to-morrow, you know, Peter.

MADAME RANEVSKY. My little Grisha! My little boy! Grisha . . . my son. . . .

BARBARA. It can't be helped, mamma. It was the will of God.

TROPHIMOF (*gently, crying*). There, there!

MADAME RANEVSKY (*crying*). He was drowned. My little boy was drowned. Why? What was the use of that, my dear? (*In a softer voice*) Anya's asleep in there, and I am speaking so loud, and making a noise. . . . But tell me, Peter, why have you grown so ugly? Why have you grown so old?

TROPHIMOF. An old woman in the train called me a "mouldy gentleman."

MADAME RANEVSKY. You were quite a boy then, a dear little student, and now your hair's going and you wear spectacles. Are you really still a student? (*Going towards the door.*)

TROPHIMOF. Yes, I expect I shall be a perpetual student.

MADAME RANEVSKY (*kissing her brother and then* BARBARA). Well, go to bed. You've grown old too, Leonid.

PISHTCHIK (*following her*). Yes, yes; time for bed. Oh, oh, my gout! I'll stay the night here. Don't forget, Lyubof Andreyevna, my angel, to-morrow morning . . . twenty-five.

GAYEF. He's still on the same string.

PISHTCHIK. Twenty-five . . . to pay the interest on my mortgage.

MADAME RANEVSKY. I haven't any money, my friend.

PISHTCHIK. I'll pay you back, dear lady. It's a trifling sum.

MADAME RANEVSKY. Well, well, Leonid will give it to you. Let him have it, Leonid.

GAYEF (*ironically*). I'll give it him right enough! Hold your pocket wide!

MADAME RANEVSKY. It can't be helped. . . . He needs it. He'll pay it back.
(*Exeunt* MADAME RANEVSKY, TROPHIMOF, PISHTCHIK *and* FIRS. GAYEF, BARBARA *and* YASHA *remain.*)

GAYEF. My sister hasn't lost her old habit of scattering the money. (*To* YASHA) Go away, my lad! You smell of chicken.

YASHA (*laughing*). You're just the same as you always were, Leonid Andreyevitch!

GAYEF. Who's that? (*To* BARBARA) What does he say?

BARBARA (*to* YASHA). Your mother's come up from the village. She's been waiting for you since yesterday in the servants' hall. She wants to see you.

YASHA. What a nuisance she is!

BARBARA. You wicked, unnatural son!

YASHA. Well, what do I want with her? She might just as well have waited till to-morrow.
(*Exit.*)

BARBARA. Mamma is just like she used to be; she hasn't changed a bit. If she had her way, she'd give away everything she has.

GAYEF. Yes. (*A pause*) If people recommend very many cures for an illness, that means that the illness is incurable. I think and think, I batter my brains; I know of many remedies, very many, and that means really that there is none. How nice it would be to get a fortune left one by somebody! How nice it would be if Anya could marry a very rich man! How nice it would be to go to Yaroslav and try my luck with my aunt the Countess. My aunt is very, very rich, you know.

BARBARA (*crying softly*). If only God would help us!

GAYEF. Don't howl! My aunt is very rich, but she does not like us. In the first place, my sister married a solicitor, not a nobleman. (ANYA *appears in the doorway.*) She married a man who was not a nobleman, and it's no good pretending that she has led a virtuous life. She's a dear, kind, charming creature, and I love her very much, but whatever mitigating circumstances one may find for her, there's no getting round it that she's a sinful woman. You can see it in her every gesture.

BARBARA (*whispering*). Anya is standing in the door!

GAYEF. Who's that? (*A pause*) It's very odd, something's got into my

right eye. I can't see properly out of it. Last Thursday when I was down at the District Court . . .
(ANYA *comes down.*)

BARBARA. Why aren't you asleep, Anya?

ANYA. I can't sleep. It's no good trying.

GAYEF. My little pet! (*Kissing* ANYA'S *hands and face*) My little girl! (*Crying*) You're not my niece; you're my angel; you're my everything. Trust me, trust me. . . .

ANYA. I do trust you, uncle. Everyone loves you, everyone respects you; but dear, dear uncle, you ought to hold your tongue, only to hold your tongue. What were you saying just now about mamma? about your own sister? What was the good of saying that?

GAYEF. Yes, yes. (*Covering his face with her hand*) You're quite right; it was awful of me! Lord, Lord! save me from myself! And a little while ago I made a speech over a cupboard. What a stupid thing to do! As soon as I had done it, I knew it was stupid.

BARBARA. Yes, really, uncle. You ought to hold your tongue. Say nothing; that's all that's wanted.

ANYA. If only you would hold your tongue, you'd be so much happier!

GAYEF. I will! I will! (*Kissing* ANYA'S *and* BARBARA'S *hands*) I'll hold my tongue. But there's one thing I must say; it's business. Last Thursday, when I was down at the District Court, a lot of us were there together, we began to talk about this and that, one thing and another, and it seems I could arrange a loan on note of hand to pay the interest into the bank.

BARBARA. If only Heaven would help us!

GAYEF. I'll go in on Tuesday and talk it over again. (*To* BARBARA) Don't howl! (*To* ANYA) Your mamma shall have a talk with Lopakhin. Of course he won't refuse her. And as soon as you are rested you must go to see your grandmother, the Countess, at Yaroslav. We'll operate from three points, and the trick is done. We'll pay the interest, I'm certain of it. (*Taking sugar candy*) I swear on my honour, or whatever you will, the property shall not be sold. (*Excitedly*) I swear by my hope of eternal happiness! There's my hand on it. Call me a base, dishonourable man if I let it go to auction. I swear by my whole being!

ANYA (*calm again and happy*). What a dear you are, uncle, and how clever! (*Embraces him.*) Now I'm easy again. I'm easy again! I'm happy!
(*Enter* FIRS.)

FIRS (*reproachfully*). Leonid Andreyevitch, have you no fear of God? When are you going to bed?

GAYEF. I'm just off—just off. You get along, Firs. I'll undress myself all right. Come, children, bye-bye! Details to-morrow, but now let's go to bed. (*Kissing* ANYA *and* BARBARA) I'm a good Liberal, a man of the eighties. People abuse the eighties, but I think that I may say I've suffered something for my convictions in my time. It's not for nothing that the peasants love me. We ought to know the peasants; we ought to know with what . . .

ANYA. You're at it again, uncle!

BARBARA. Why don't you hold your tongue, uncle?

FIRS (*angrily*). Leonid Andreyevitch!

GAYEF. I'm coming; I'm coming. Now go to bed. Off two cushions in the middle pocket! I start another life! . . .
(*Exit, with* FIRS *hobbling after him.*)

ANYA. Now my mind is at rest. I don't want to go to Yaroslav; I don't like grandmamma; but my mind is at rest, thanks to Uncle Leonid. (*She sits down.*)

BARBARA. Time for bed. I'm off. Whilst you were away there's been a scandal. You know that nobody lives in the old servants' quarters except the old people, Ephim, Pauline, Evstigney and old Karp. Well, they took to having in all sorts of queer fish to sleep there with them. I didn't say a word. But at last I heard they had spread a report that I had given orders that they were to have nothing but peas to eat; out of stinginess, you understand? It was all Evstigney's doing. "Very well," I said to myself, "you wait a bit." So I sent for Evstigney. (*Yawning*) He comes. "Now then, Evstigney," I said, "you old imbecile, how do you dare . . ." (*Looking at* ANYA) Anya, Anya! (*A pause*) She's asleep. (*Taking* ANYA'S *arm*) Let's go to bed. Come along. (*Leading her away*) Sleep on, my little one! Come along; come along! (*They go towards* ANYA'S *room. In the distance beyond the orchard a shepherd plays his pipe.* TROPHIMOF *crosses the stage and, seeing* BARBARA *and* ANYA, *stops.*) 'Sh! She's asleep, she's asleep! Come along, my love.

ANYA (*drowsily*). I'm so tired! Listen to the bells! Uncle, dear uncle! Mamma! Uncle!

BARBARA. Come along, my love! Come along.
(*Exeunt* BARBARA *and* ANYA *to the bedroom.*)

TROPHIMOF (*with emotion*). My sunshine! My spring!

CURTAIN

ACT TWO

In the open fields; an old crooked half-ruined shrine. Near it a well; big stones, apparently old tombstones; an old bench. Road to the estate beyond. On one side rise dark poplar-trees. Beyond them begins the cherry orchard. In the distance a row of telegraph poles, and, far away on the horizon, the dim outlines of a big town, visible only in fine, clear weather. It is near sunset.

CHARLOTTE, YASHA *and* DUNYASHA *sit on the bench.* EPHIKHODOF *stands by them and plays on a guitar; they meditate.* CHARLOTTE *wears an old peaked cap. She has taken a gun from off her shoulders and is mending the buckle of the strap.*

CHARLOTTE (*thoughtfully*). I have no proper passport. I don't know how old I am; I always feel I am still young. When I was a little girl my father and mother used to go about from one country fair to another, giving performances, and very good ones too. I used to do the *salto mortale* and all sorts of tricks. When papa and mamma died an old German lady adopted me and educated me. Good! When I grew up I became a governess. But where I come from and who I am, I haven't a notion. Who my parents were—very likely they weren't married—I don't know. (*Taking a cucumber from her pocket and beginning to eat it*) I don't know anything about it. (*A pause*) I long to talk so, and I have no one to talk to, I have no friends or relations.

EPHIKHODOF (*playing on the guitar and singing*).

"What is the noisy world to me?
Oh, what are friends and foes?"

How sweet it is to play upon a mandolin!

DUNYASHA. That's a guitar, not a mandolin. (*She looks at herself in a hand-glass and powders her face.*)

EPHIKHODOF. For the madman who loves, it is a mandolin. (*Singing*)

"Oh, that my heart were cheered
By the warmth of requited love."

(YASHA *joins in.*)

CHARLOTTE. How badly these people do sing! Foo! Like jackals howling!

DUNYASHA (*to* YASHA). What happiness it must be to live abroad!

YASHA. Of course it is; I quite agree with you. (*He yawns and lights a cigar.*)

EPHIKHODOF. It stands to reason. Everything abroad has attained a certain culnimation.*

YASHA. That's right.

EPHIKHODOF. I am a man of cultivation; I have studied various remarkable books, but I cannot

* This represents a similar blunder of Ephikhodof's in the original.

fathom the direction of my preferences; do I want to live or do I want to shoot myself, so to speak? But in order to be ready for all contingencies, I always carry a revolver in my pocket. Here it is. (*Showing revolver.*)

CHARLOTTE. That's done. I'm off. (*Slinging the rifle over her shoulder*) You're a clever fellow, Ephikhodof, and very alarming. Women must fall madly in love with you. Brrr! (*Going*) These clever people are all so stupid; I have no one to talk to. I am always alone, always alone; I have no friends or relations, and who I am, or why I exist, is a mystery. (*Exit slowly.*)

EPHIKHODOF. Strictly speaking, without touching upon other matters, I must protest *inter alia* that destiny treats me with the utmost rigour, as a tempest might treat a small ship. If I labour under a misapprehension, how is it that when I woke up this morning, behold, so to speak, I perceived sitting on my chest a spider of præternatural dimensions, like that? (*Indicating with both hands*) And if I go to take a draught of kvass, I am sure to find something of the most indelicate character, in the nature of a cockroach. (*A pause*) Have you read Buckle?* (*A pause; to* DUN-

* Buckle's "History of Civilization" is better known in Russia than here. To have read it is a sort of cachet of popular erudition, equivalent, say, to knowing your Herbert Spencer in England. Ephikhodof is a new type, evolved since the Liberation and the Reforms of Alexander II. He is just the opposite of Lopakhin. Ephikhodof is stupid and has intellectual aspirations. Lopakhin is clever and has no intellectual aspirations.

YASHA. I should like to trouble you, Avdotya Fyodorovna, for a momentary interview.

DUNYASHA. Talk away.

EPHIKHODOF. I should prefer to conduct a *tête-à-tête*. (*Sighing.*)

DUNYASHA (*confused*). Very well, only first please fetch me my cloak. It's by the cupboard. It's rather damp here.

EPHIKHODOF. Very well, mademoiselle. I will go and fetch it, mademoiselle. Now I know what to do with my revolver. (*Takes his guitar and exit, playing.*)

YASHA. Twenty-two misfortunes! Between you and me, he's a stupid fellow. (*Yawning.*)

DUNYASHA. Heaven help him, he'll shoot himself! (*A pause*) I have grown so nervous, I am always in a twitter. I was quite a little girl when they took me into the household, and now I have got quite disused to common life, and my hands are as white as white, like a lady's. I have grown so refined, so delicate and genteel, I am afraid of everything. I'm always frightened. And if you deceive me, Yasha, I don't know what will happen to my nerves.

YASHA (*kissing her*). You little cucumber! Of course every girl ought to behave herself properly; there's nothing I dislike as much as when girls aren't proper in their behaviour.

DUNYASHA. I've fallen dreadfully in love with you. You're so educated; you can talk about anything! (*A pause.*)

YASHA (*yawning*). Yes. . . . The way I look at it is this; if a girl falls in love with anybody, then I call her immoral. (*A pause*) How pleasant it is to smoke one's cigar in the open air. (*Listening*) There's someone coming. It's the missis and the rest of 'em. . . . (DUNYASHA *embraces him hastily.*) Go towards the house as if you'd just been for a bathe. Go by this path or else they'll meet you and think that I've been walking out with you. I can't stand that sort of thing.

DUNYASHA (*coughing softly*). Your cigar has given me a headache. (*Exit.* YASHA *remains sitting by the shrine. Enter* MADAME RANEVSKY, GAYEF *and* LOPAKHIN.)

LOPAKHIN. You must make up your minds once and for all. Time waits for no man. The question is perfectly simple. Are you going to let off the land for villas or not? Answer in one word; yes or no? Only one word!

MADAME RANEVSKY. Who's smoking horrible cigars here? (*She sits down.*)

GAYEF. How handy it is now they've built the railway. (*Sitting*) We've been into town for lunch and back again. . . . Red in the middle! I must just go up to the house and have a game.

MADAME RANEVSKY. There's no hurry.

LOPAKHIN. Only one word—yes or no! (*Entreatingly*) Come, answer the question!

GAYEF (*yawning*). Who's that?

MADAME RANEVSKY (*looking into her purse*). I had a lot of money yesterday but there's hardly any left now. Poor Barbara tries to save money by feeding us all on milk soup; the old people in the kitchen get nothing but peas, and yet I go squandering aimlessly. . . . (*Dropping her purse and scattering gold coins; vexed.*) There, I've dropped it all!

YASHA. Allow me, I'll pick it up. (*Collecting the coins.*)

MADAME RANEVSKY. Yes, please do, Yasha! Whatever made me go into town for lunch? I hate your horrid restaurant with the organ and the tablecloths all smelling of soap. Why do you drink so much, Leonid? Why do you eat so much? Why do you talk so much? You talked too much at the restaurant again, and most unsuitably, about the seventies, and the decadents. And to whom? Fancy talking about decadents to the waiters!

LOPAKHIN. Quite true.

GAYEF (*with a gesture*). I'm incorrigible, that's plain. (*Irritably to* YASHA) What do you keep dodging about in front of me for?

YASHA (*laughing*). I can't hear your voice without laughing.

GAYEF (*to* MADAME RANEVSKY). Either he or I . . .

MADAME RANEVSKY. Go away, Yasha; run along.

YASHA (*handing* MADAME RANEVSKY *her purse*). I'll go at once. (*Restraining his laughter with difficulty*) This very minute. (*Exit.*)

LOPAKHIN. Deriganof, the millionaire, wants to buy your property. They say he'll come to the auction himself.

MADAME RANEVSKY. How did you hear?

LOPAKHIN. I was told so in town.

GAYEF. Our aunt at Yaroslav has promised to send something; but I don't know when, or how much.

LOPAKHIN. How much will she send? Ten thousand pounds? Twenty thousand pounds?

MADAME RANEVSKY. Oh, come . . . A thousand or fifteen hundred at the most.

LOPAKHIN. Excuse me, but in all my life I never met anybody so frivolous as you two, so crazy and unbusiness-like! I tell you in plain Russian your property is going to be sold, and you don't seem to understand what I say.

MADAME RANEVSKY. Well, what are we to do? Tell us what you want us to do.

LOPAKHIN. Don't I tell you every day? Every day I say the same thing over and over again. You must lease off the cherry orchard and the rest of the estate for villas; you must do it at once, this very moment; the auction will be on you in two twos! Try and understand. Once you make up your mind there are to be villas, you can get all the money you want, and you're saved.

MADAME RANEVSKY. Villas and villa residents, oh, please . . . it's so vulgar!

GAYEF. I quite agree with you.

LOPAKHIN. I shall either cry, or scream, or faint. I can't stand it! You'll be the death of me. (*To* GAYEF) You're an old woman!

GAYEF. Who's that?

LOPAKHIN. You're an old woman! (*Going.*)

MADAME RANEVSKY (*frightened*). No, don't go. Stay here, there's a dear! Perhaps we shall think of some way.

LOPAKHIN. What's the good of thinking!

MADAME RANEVSKY. Please don't go; I want you. At any rate it's gayer when you're here. (*A pause*) I keep expecting something to happen, as if the house were going to tumble down about our ears.

GAYEF (*in deep abstraction*). Off the cushion on the corner; double into the middle pocket. . . .

MADAME RANEVSKY. We have been very, very sinful!

LOPAKHIN. You! What sins have you committed?

GAYEF (*eating candy*). They say I've devoured all my substance in sugar candy. (*Laughing.*)

MADAME RANEVSKY. Oh, the sins that I have committed . . . I've always squandered money at random like a mad-woman; I married a man who made nothing but debts. My husband drank himself to death on champagne; he was a fearful drinker. Then for my sins I fell in love and went off with another man; and immediately—that was my first punishment—a blow full on the head . . . here, in this very river . . . my little boy was drowned; and I went abroad, right, right away, never to come back any more, never to see this river again. . . . I shut my eyes and ran, like a mad thing, and *he* came after me, pitiless and cruel. I bought a villa at Mentone, because he fell ill there, and for three years I knew no rest day or night; the sick man tormented and wore down my soul. Then, last year, when my villa was sold to pay my debts, I went off to Paris, and he came and robbed me of everything, left me and took up with another woman, and I tried to poison myself. . . . It was all so stupid, so humiliating. . . . Then suddenly I longed to be back in Russia, in my own country, with my little girl. . . . (*Wiping away her tears*) Lord, Lord, be merciful to me; forgive my sins! Do not punish me any more! (*Taking a telegram from her pocket*) I got this to-day from Paris. . . . He asks to be forgiven, begs me to go back. . . . (*Tearing up the telegram*) Isn't that music I hear? (*Listening.*)

GAYEF. That's our famous Jewish band. You remember? Four fiddles, a flute and a double bass.

MADAME RANEVSKY. Does it still exist? We must make them come up some time; we'll have a dance.

LOPAKHIN (*listening*). I don't hear anything. (*Singing softly*)

"The Germans for a fee will turn
A Russ into a Frenchman."

(*Laughing*) I saw a very funny piece at the theatre last night; awfully funny!

MADAME RANEVSKY. It probably wasn't a bit funny. You people oughtn't to go and see plays; you ought to try to see yourselves; to see what a dull life you lead, and how much too much you talk.

LOPAKHIN. Quite right. To tell the honest truth, our life's an imbecile affair. (*A pause*) My papa was a peasant, an idiot; he understood nothing; he taught me nothing; all he did was to beat me when he was drunk, with a walking-stick. As a matter of fact I'm just as big a blockhead and idiot as he was. I never did any lessons; my handwriting's abominable; I write so badly I'm ashamed before people; like a pig.

MADAME RANEVSKY. You ought to get married.

LOPAKHIN. Yes, that's true.

MADAME RANEVSKY. Why not marry Barbara? She's a nice girl.

LOPAKHIN. Yes.

MADAME RANEVSKY. She's a nice straightforward creature; works all day; and what's most important, she loves you. You've been fond of her for a long time.

LOPAKHIN. Well, why not? I'm quite willing. She's a very nice girl. (*A pause.*)

GAYEF. I've been offered a place in a bank. Six hundred pounds a year. Do you hear?

MADAME RANEVSKY. You in a bank! Stay where you are.
(*Enter* FIRS *carrying an overcoat.*)

FIRS (*to* GAYEF). Put this on, please, master; it's getting damp.

GAYEF (*putting on the coat*). What a plague you are, Firs!

FIRS. What's the use. . . . You went off and never told me. (*Examining his clothes.*)

MADAME RANEVSKY. How old you've got, Firs!

FIRS. I beg your pardon?

LOPAKHIN. She says how old you've got!

FIRS. I've been alive a long time. When they found me a wife, your father wasn't even born yet. (*Laughing*) And when the Liberation came I was already chief valet. But I wouldn't have any Liberation then; I stayed with the master. (*A pause*) I remember how happy everybody was, but why they were happy they didn't know themselves.

LOPAKHIN. It was fine before then. Anyway they used to flog 'em.

FIRS (*mishearing him*). I should think so! The peasants minded the masters, and the masters minded the peasants, but now it's all higgledy-piggledy; you can't make head or tail of it.

GAYEF. Shut up, Firs. I must go into town again to-morrow. I've been promised an introduction to a general who'll lend money on a bill.

LOPAKHIN. You'll do no good. You won't even pay the interest; set your mind at ease about that.

MADAME RANEVSKY (*to* LOPAKHIN). He's only talking nonsense. There's no such general at all.
(*Enter* TROPHIMOF, ANYA *and* BARBARA.)

GAYEFF. Here come the others.

ANYA. Here's mamma.

MADAME RANEVSKY (*tenderly*). Come along, come along, . . . my little ones. . . . (*Embracing* ANYA *and* BARBARA) If only you knew how much I love you both! Sit beside me . . . there, like that. (*Everyone sits.*)

LOPAKHIN. The Perpetual Student's always among the girls.

TROPHIMOF. It's no affair of yours.

LOPAKHIN. He's nearly fifty and still a student.

TROPHIMOF. Stop your idiotic jokes!

LOPAKHIN. What are you losing your temper for, silly?

TROPHIMOF. Why can't you leave me alone?

LOPAKHIN (*laughing*). I should like to know what your opinion is of me?

TROPHIMOF. My opinion of you, Yermolai Alexeyitch, is this. You're a rich man; you'll soon be a millionaire. Just as a beast of prey which devours everything that comes in its way is necessary for the conversion of matter, so you are necessary too.
(*All laugh.*)

BARBARA. Tell us something about the planets, Peter, instead.

MADAME RANEVSKY. No. Let's go on with the conversation we were having yesterday.

TROPHIMOF. What about?

GAYEF. About the proud man.

TROPHIMOF. We had a long talk yesterday, but we didn't come to any conclusion. There is something mystical in the proud man in the sense in which you use the words. You may be right from your point of view, but, if we look at it simple-mindedly, what room is there for pride? Is there any sense in it, when man is so poorly constructed from the physiological point of view, when the vast majority of us are so gross and stupid and profoundly unhappy? We must give up admiring ourselves. The only thing to do is to work.

GAYEF. We shall die all the same.

TROPHIMOF. Who knows? And what does it mean, to die? Perhaps man has a hundred senses, and when he dies only the five senses that we know perish with him, and the other ninety-five remain alive.

MADAME RANEVSKY. How clever you are, Peter.

LOPAKHIN (*ironically*). Oh, extraordinary!

TROPHIMOF. Mankind marches forward, perfecting its strength. Everything that is unattainable for us now will one day be near and clear; but we must work; we must help with all our force those who seek the truth. At present only a few men work in Russia. The vast majority of the educated people that I know seek after nothing, do nothing, and are as yet incapable of work. They call themselves the "Intelligentsia," they say "thou" and "thee" to the servants, they treat the peasants like animals, learn nothing, read nothing serious, do absolutely nothing, only talk about science, and understand little or nothing about art. They are all serious; they all have solemn faces; they only discuss important subjects; they philosophise; but meanwhile the vast majority of us, ninety-nine per cent, live like savages; at the least thing they curse and punch people's heads; they eat like beasts and sleep in dirt and bad air; there are bugs everywhere, evil smells, damp and moral degradation. . . . It's plain that all our clever conversations are only meant to distract our own attention and other people's. Show me where those creches are, that they're always talking so much about; or those reading-rooms. They are only things people write about in novels; they don't really exist at all. Nothing exists but dirt, vulgarity and Asiatic ways. I am afraid of solemn faces; I dislike them; I am afraid of solemn conversations. Let us rather hold our tongues.

LOPAKHIN. Do you know, I get up at five every morning, I work from morning till night; I am always handling my own money or other people's, and I see the sort of men there are about me. One only has to begin to do anything to see how few honest and decent people there are. Sometimes, as I lie awake in bed, I think: "O Lord, you have given us mighty forests, boundless fields and immeasurable horizons, and we, living in their midst, ought really to be giants."

MADAME RANEVSKY. Oh dear, you want giants! They are all very well in fairy stories; but in real life they are rather alarming. (EPHIKHODOF *passes at the back of the scene, playing on his guitar, pensively*) There goes Ephikhodof.

ANYA (*pensively*). There goes Ephikhodof.

GAYEF. The sun has set.

TROPHIMOF. Yes.

GAYEF (*as if declaiming, but not loud*). O Nature, wonderful Nature, you glow with eternal light; beautiful and indifferent, you whom we call our mother, uniting in yourself both life and death, you animate and you destroy. . . .

BARBARA (*entreatingly*). Uncle!

ANYA. You're at it again, uncle!

TROPHIMOF. You'd far better double the red into the middle pocket.

GAYEF. I'll hold my tongue! I'll hold my tongue! (*They all sit pensively. Silence reigns, broken only by the mumbling of old* FIRS. *Suddenly a distant sound is heard as if from the sky, the sound of a string breaking, dying away, melancholy.*)

MADAME RANEVSKY. What's that?

LOPAKHIN. I don't know. It's a lifting-tub given way somewhere away in the mines. It must be a long way off.

GAYEF. Perhaps it's some sort of bird . . . a heron, or something.

TROPHIMOF. Or an owl. . . .

MADAME RANEVSKY (*shuddering*). There's something uncanny about it!

FIRS. The same thing happened before the great misfortune: the owl screeched and the samovar kept humming.

GAYEF. What great misfortune?

FIRS. The Liberation. (*A pause.*)*

MADAME RANEVSKY. Come, everyone, let's go in; it's getting late. (*To* ANYA) You've tears in your

* The sound of a tub falling in a mind is a very old remembrance, an impression of boyhood got in the steppes; Chekhov made use of it once before.

eyes. What is it, little one? (*Embracing her.*)

ANYA. Nothing, mamma. I'm all right.

TROPHIMOF. There's someone coming.

(*A* TRAMP *appears in a torn white peaked cap and overcoat. He is slightly drunk.*)

TRAMP. Excuse me, but can I go through this way straight to the station?

GAYEF. Certainly. Follow this path.

TRAMP. I am uncommonly obliged to you, sir. (*Coughing*) We're having lovely weather. (*Declaiming*) "Brother, my suffering brother" . . . "Come forth to the Volga. Who moans?" . . . (*To* BARBARA) Mademoiselle, please spare a six-pence for a hungry fellow-countryman.

(BARBARA, *frightened, screams.*)

LOPAKHIN (*angrily*). There's a decency for every indecency to observe!

MADAME RANEVSKY. Take this; here you are. (*Fumbling in her purse*) I haven't any silver. . . . Never mind, take this sovereign.

TRAMP. I am uncommonly obliged to you, madam. (*Exit. Laughter.*)

BARBARA (*frightened*). I'm going! I'm going! Oh, mamma, there's nothing for the servants to eat at home, and you've gone and given this man a sovereign.

MADAME RANEVSKY. What's to be done with your stupid old mother? I'll give you up everything I have when I get back. Yermolai Alexeyitch, lend me some more money.

LOPAKHIN. Very good.

MADAME RANEVSKY. Come along, everyone; it's time to go in. We've settled all about your marriage between us, Barbara. I wish you joy.

BARBARA (*through her tears*). You musn't joke about such things, mamma.

LOPAKHIN. Amelia, get thee to a nunnery, go!

GAYEF. My hands are all trembling; it's ages since I had a game of billiards.

LOPAKHIN. Amelia, nymphlet, in thine orisons remember me.

MADAME RANEVSKY. Come along. It's nearly supper-time.

BARBARA. How he frightened me! My heart is simply throbbing.

LOPAKHIN. Allow me to remind you, the cherry orchard is to be sold on the twenty-second of August. Bear that in mind; bear that in mind!

(*All go out except* TROPHIMOF *and* ANYA.)

ANYA (*laughing*). Many thanks to the Tramp for frightening Barbara; at last we are alone.

TROPHIMOF. Barbara's afraid we shall go and fall in love with each other. Day after day she never leaves us alone. With her narrow mind she cannot understand that we are above love. To avoid everything petty, everything illusory, everything that prevents one from being free and happy, that is the whole meaning and purpose of our life. Forward! We march on irresistibly towards that bright star which burns far, far before us! Forward! Don't tarry, comrades!

ANYA (*clasping her hands*). What beautiful things you say! (*A pause*) Isn't it enchanting here to-day!

TROPHIMOF. Yes it's wonderful weather.

ANYA. What have you done to me, Peter? Why is it that I no longer love the cherry orchard as I did? I used to love it so tenderly; I thought there was no better place on earth than our garden.

TROPHIMOF. All Russia is our garden. The earth is great and beautiful; it is full of wonderful places. (*A pause*) Think, Anya, your grandfather, your great-grandfather and all your ancestors were serf-owners, owners of living souls. Do not human spirits look out at you from every tree in the orchard, from every leaf and every stem? Do you not hear human voices? . . . Oh! it is terrible. Your orchard frightens me. When I walk through it in the evening or at night, the rugged bark on the trees glows with a dim light, and the cherry-trees seem to see all that happened a hundred and two hundred years ago in painful and oppressive dreams. Well, well, we have fallen at least two hundred years behind the times. We have achieved nothing at all as yet; we have not made up our minds how we stand with the past; we only philosophise, complain of boredom, or drink vodka. It is so plain that, before we can live in the present, we must first redeem the past, and have done with it; and it is only by suffering that we can redeem it, only by strenuous, unremitting toil. Understand that, Anya.

ANYA. The house we live in has long since ceased to be our house; and I shall go away, I give you my word.

TROPHIMOF. If you have the household keys, throw them in the well and go away. Be free, be free as the wind.

ANYA (*enthusiastically*). How beautifully you put it!

TROPHIMOF. Believe what I say, Anya; believe what I say. I'm not thirty yet; I am still young, still a student; but what I have been through! I am hungry as the winter; I am sick, anxious, poor as a beggar. Fate has tossed me hither and thither; I have been everywhere, everywhere. But wherever I have been, every minute, day and night, my soul has been full of mysterious anticipations. I feel the approach of happiness, Anya; I see it coming. . . .

ANYA (*pensively*). The moon is rising.

(EPHIKHODOF *is heard still playing the same sad tune on his guitar. The moon rises. Somewhere beyond the poplar trees,* BARBARA *is heard calling for* ANYA: *"Anya, where are you?"*)

TROPHIMOF. Yes, the moon is rising. (*A pause*) There it is, there is happiness; it is coming towards us, nearer and nearer; I can hear the sound of its footsteps. . . . And if we do not see it, if we do not know it, what does it matter? Others will see it.

BARBARA (*without*). Anya? Where are you?

TROPHIMOF. There's Barbara again! (*Angrily*) It really is too bad!

ANYA. Never mind. Let us go down to the river. It's lovely there.

TROPHIMOF. Come on! (ANYA *and* TROPHIMOF *go out.*)

BARBARA (*without*). Anya! Anya!

CURTAIN

ACT THREE

A sitting-room separated by an arch from a big drawing-room behind. Chandelier lighted. The Jewish band mentioned in Act II is heard playing on the landing. Evening. In the drawing-room they are dancing the grand rond. SIMEONOF-PISHTCHIK *is heard crying: "Promenade à une paire!"*
The dancers come down into the sitting-room. The first pair consists of PISHTCHIK *and* CHARLOTTE; *the second of* TROPHIMOF *and* MADAME RANEVSKY; *the third of* ANYA *and the* POST OFFICE OFFICIAL; *the fourth of* BARBARA *and the* STATIONMASTER, *etc., etc.* BARBARA *is crying softly and wipes away the tears as she dances. In the last pair comes* DUNYASHA. *They cross the sitting-room.*

PISHTCHIK. Grand rond, balancez . . . Les cavaliers à genou et remerciez vos dames.
(FIRS *in evening dress carries seltzer water across on a tray.* PISHTCHIK *and* TROPHIMOF *come down into the sitting-room.*)

PISHTCHIK. I am a full-blooded man; I've had two strokes already; it's hard work dancing, but, as the saying goes: "If you run with the pack, bark or no, but anyway wag your tail." I'm as strong as a horse. My old father, who was fond of his joke, rest his soul, used to say, talking of our pedigree, that the ancient stock of the Simeonof-Pishtchiks was descended from that very horse that Caligula made a senator. . . . (*Sitting*) But the worst of it is, I've got no money. A hungry dog believes in nothing but meat. (*Snoring and waking up again at once*) I'm just the same . . . it's nothing but money, money, with me.

TROPHIMOF. Yes, it's quite true, there is something horselike about your build.

PISHTCHIK. Well, well . . . a horse

is a jolly creature . . . you can sell a horse.
(*A sound of billiards being played in the next room.* BARBARA *appears in the drawing-room beyond the arch.*)

TROPHIMOF (*teasing her*). Madame Lopakhin! Madame Lopakhin!

BARBARA (*angrily*). Mouldy gentleman!

TROPHIMOF. Yes, I'm a mouldy gentleman, and I'm proud of it.

BARBARA (*bitterly*). We've hired the band, but where's the money to pay for it? (*She goes out.*)

TROPHIMOF (*to* PISHTCHIK). If the energy which you have spent in the course of your whole life in looking for money to pay the interest on your loans had been diverted to some other purpose, you would have had enough of it, I dare say, to turn the world upside down.

PISHTCHIK. Nietzsche the philosopher, a very remarkable man, very famous, a man of gigantic intellect, says in his works that it's quite right to forge banknotes.

TROPHIMOF. What, have you read Nietzsche?

PISHTCHIK. Well . . . Dashenka told me. . . . But I'm in such a hole, I'd forge 'em for two-pence. I've got to pay thirty-one pounds the day after to-morrow. . . . I've got thirteen pounds already. (*Feeling his pockets; alarmed*) My money's gone! I've lost my money! (*Crying*) Where's my money got to? (*Joyfully*) Here it is, inside the lining. . . . It's thrown me all in a perspiration.
(*Enter* MADAME RANEVSKY *and* CHARLOTTE.)

MADAME RANEVSKY (*humming a lezginka**). Why is Leonid so long? What can he be doing in the town? (*To* DUNYASHA) Dunyasha, ask the musicians if they'll have some tea.

TROPHIMOF. The sale did not come off, in all probability.

MADAME RANEVSKY. It was a stupid day for the musicians to come; it was a stupid day to have this dance. . . . Well, well, it doesn't matter. . . . (*She sits down and sings softly to herself.*)

CHARLOTTE (*giving* PISHTCHIK *a pack of cards*). Here is a pack of cards. Think of any card you like.

PISHTCHIK. I've thought of one.

CHARLOTTE. Now shuffle the pack. That's all right. Give them here, oh, most worthy Mr. Pishtchik. Ein, zwei, drei! Now look and you'll find it in your side pocket.

PISHTCHIK (*taking a card from his side pocket*). The Eight of Spades! You're perfectly right. (*Astonished*) Well, I never!

CHARLOTTE (*holding the pack on the palm of her hand, to* TROPHIMOF). Say quickly, what's the top card?

* A lively Caucasian dance in two-four time, popularised by Glinka, and by Rubenstein in his opera, *Demon.*

TROPHIMOF. Well, say the Queen of Spades.

CHARLOTTE. Right! (*To* PISHTCHIK) Now then, what's the top card?

PISHTCHIK. Ace of Hearts.

CHARLOTTE. Right! (*She claps her hands; the pack of cards disappears.*) What a beautiful day we've been having.
(*A mysterious female* VOICE *answers her as if from under the floor: "Yes, indeed, a charming day, mademoiselle."*)

CHARLOTTE. You are my beautiful ideal.

THE VOICE. *"I think you also ferry peautiful, mademoiselle."*

STATIONMASTER (*applauding*). Bravo, Miss Ventriloquist!

PISHTCHIK (*astonished*). Well, I never! Bewitching Charlotte Ivanovna, I'm head over ears in love with you.

CHARLOTTE. In love! (*Shrugging her shoulders*) Are you capable of love? Guter Mensch, aber schlechter Musikant!

TROPHIMOF (*slapping* PISTHCHIK *on the shoulder*). You old horse!

CHARLOTTE. Now attention, please; one more trick. (*Taking a shawl from a chair*) Now here's a shawl, and a very pretty shawl; I'm going to sell this very pretty shawl. (*Shaking it*) Who'll buy? who'll buy?

PISHTCHIK (*astonished*). Well I never!

CHARLOTTE. Ein, zwei, drei! (*She lifts the shawl quickly; behind it stands* ANYA, *who drops a curtsy, runs to her mother, kisses her, then runs up into the drawing-room amid general applause.*)

MADAME RANEVSKY (*applauding*). Bravo! bravo!

CHARLOTTE. Once more. Ein, zwei, drei! (*She lifts up the shawl; behind it stands* BARBARA, *bowing.*)

PISHTCHIK (*astonished*). Well I never!

CHARLOTTE. That's all. (*She throws the shawl over* PISHTCHIK, *makes a curtsy and runs up into the drawing-room.*)

PISHTCHIK (*hurrying after her*). You little rascal . . . there's a girl for you, there's a girl. . . . (*He goes out.*)

MADAME RANEVSKY. And still no sign of Leonid. What he's doing in the town so long, I can't understand. It must be all over by now; the property's sold; or the auction never came off; why does he keep me in suspense so long?

BARBARA (*trying to soothe her*). Uncle has bought it, I am sure of that.

TROPHIMOF (*mockingly*). Of course he has!

BARBARA. Grannie sent him a power of attorney to buy it in her name and transfer the mortgage. She's done it for Anya's sake. I'm perfectly sure that Heaven will help us and uncle will buy it.

MADAME RANEVSKY. Your Yaroslav grannie sent fifteen hundred pounds to buy the property in her name—she doesn't trust us—but it wouldn't be enough even to pay the interest. (*Covering her face with her hands*) My fate is being decided to-day, my fate. . . .

TROPHIMOF (*teasing* BARBARA). Madame Lopakhin!

BARBARA (*angrily*). Perpetual Student! He's been sent down twice from the University.

MADAME RANEVSKY. Why do you get angry, Barbara? He calls you Madame Lopakhin for fun. Why not? You can marry Lopakhin if you like; he's a nice, interesting man; you needn't if you don't; nobody wants to force you, my pet.

BARBARA. I take it very seriously, mamma, I must confess. He's a nice man and I like him.

MADAME RANEVSKY. Then marry him. There's no good putting it off that I can see.

BARBARA. But, mamma, I can't propose to him myself. For two whole years everybody's been talking about him to me, everyone; but he either says nothing or makes a joke of it. I quite understand. He's making money; he's always busy; he can't be bothered with me. If I only had some money, even a little, even ten pounds, I would give everything up and go right away. I would go into a nunnery.

TROPHIMOF (*mocking*). What bliss!

BARBARA (*to* TROPHIMOF). A student ought to be intelligent. (*In a gentler voice, crying*) How ugly you've grown, Peter; how old you've grown! (*She stops crying; to* MADAME RANEVSKY) But I can't live without work, mamma. I must have something to do every minute of the day.
(*Enter* YASHA.)

YASHA (*trying not to laugh*). Ephikhodof has broken a billiard cue. (*Exit.*)

BARBARA. What's Ephikhodof doing here? Who gave him leave to play billiards? I don't understand these people. (*Exit.*)

MADAME RANEVSKY. Don't tease her, Peter. Don't you see that she's unhappy enough already?

TROPHIMOF. I wish she wouldn't be so fussy, always meddling in other people's affairs. The whole summer she's given me and Anya no peace; she is afraid we'll work up a romance between us. What business is it of hers? I'm sure I never gave her any grounds; I'm not likely to be so commonplace. We are above love!

MADAME RANEVSKY. Then I suppose I must be beneath love. (*Deeply agitated*) Why doesn't Leonid come? Oh, if only I knew whether the property's sold or not!

It seems such an impossible disaster, that I don't know what to think. . . . I'm bewildered . . . I shall burst out screaming, I shall do something idiotic. Save me, Peter; say something to me, say something. . . .

TROPHIMOF. Whether the property is sold to-day or whether it's not sold, surely it's all one? It's all over with it long ago; there's no turning back; the path is overgrown. Be calm, dear Lyubof Andreyevna. You mustn't deceive yourself any longer; for once you must look the truth straight in the face.

MADAME RANEVSKY. What truth? You can see what's truth, and what's untruth, but I seem to have lost the power of vision; I see nothing. You settle every important question so boldly; but tell me, Peter, isn't that because you're young, because you have never solved any question of your own as yet by suffering. You look boldly ahead; isn't it only that you don't see or divine anything terrible in the future; because life is still hidden from your young eyes? You are bolder, honester, deeper than we are, but reflect, show me just a finger's breadth of consideration, take pity on me. Don't you see? I was born here, my father and mother lived here, and my grandfather; I love this house; without the cherry orchard my life has no meaning for me, and if it *must* be sold, then for heaven's sake sell me too! (*Embracing* TROPHIMOF *and kissing him on the forehead*) My little boy was drowned here. (*Crying*) Be gentle with me, dear, kind Peter.

TROPHIMOF. You know I sympathise with all my heart.

MADAME RANEVSKY. Yes, yes, but you ought to say it somehow differently. (*Taking out her handkerchief and dropping a telegram*) I am so wretched to-day, you can't imagine! All this noise jars on me, my heart jumps at every sound: I tremble all over; but I can't shut myself up; I am afraid of the silence when I'm alone. Don't be hard on me, Peter; I love you like a son. I would gladly let Anya marry you, I swear it; but you must work, Peter; you must get your degree. You do nothing; Fate tosses you about from place to place; and that's not right. It's true what I say, isn't it? And you must do something to your beard to make it grow better. (*Laughing*) I can't help laughing at you.

TROPHIMOF (*picking up the telegram*). I don't wish to be an Adonis.

MADAME RANEVSKY. It's a telegram from Paris. I get them every day. One came yesterday another to-day. That savage is ill again; he's in a bad way. . . . He asks me to forgive him, he begs me to come; and I really ought to go to Paris and be with him. You look at me sternly; but what am I to do, Peter? What am I to do? He's ill, he's lonely, he's unhappy. Who is to look after him? Who is to keep him from doing stupid things? Who is to give him his medicine when it's time? After all, why should I be ashamed to say it? I love him, that's plain. I love him, I love him. . . . My love is like a stone tied round my neck; it's dragging me down to the bottom; but I love my stone. I can't live without it. (*Squeezing* TROPHIMOF'S *hand*) Don't think ill of me, Peter; don't say anything! Don't say anything!

TROPHIMOF (*crying*). Forgive my bluntness, for heaven's sake; but the man has simply robbed you.

MADAME RANEVSKY. No, no, no! (*Stopping her ears*) You mustn't say that!

TROPHIMOF. He's a rascal; everybody sees it but yourself; he's a petty rascal, a ne'er-do-weel. . . .

MADAME RANEVSKY (*angry but restrained*). You're twenty-six or twenty-seven, and you're still a Lower School boy!

TROPHIMOF. Who cares?

MADAME RANEVSKY. You ought to be a man by now; at your age you ought to understand people who love. You ought to love someone yourself, you ought to be in love! (*Angrily*) Yes, yes! It's not purity with you; it's simply you're smug, a figure of fun, a freak. . . .

TROPHIMOF (*horrified*). What does she say?

MADAME RANEVSKY. "I am above love!" You're not above love; you're simply what Firs calls a "job-lot." At your age you ought to be ashamed not to have a mistress!

TROPHIMOF (*aghast*). This is awful! What does she say? (*Going quickly up into the drawing-room, clasping his head with his hands*) This is something awful! I can't stand it; I'm off . . . (*Goes out, but returns at once.*) All is over between us! (*Goes out to landing.*)

MADAME RANEVSKY (*calling after him*). Stop, Peter! Don't be ridiculous; I was only joking! Peter! (TROPHIMOF *is heard on the landing going quickly down the stairs, and suddenly falling down them with a crash.* ANYA *and* BARBARA *scream. A moment later the sound of laughter.*)

MADAME RANEVSKY. What has happened?
(ANYA *runs in.*)

ANYA (*laughing*). Peter's tumbled downstairs. (*She runs out again.*)

MADAME RANEVSKY. What a ridiculous fellow he is!
(*The* STATIONMASTER *stands in the middle of the drawing-room beyond the arch and recites Alexey Tolstoy's poem, "The Sinner." Everybody stops to listen, but after a few lines the sound of a waltz is heard from the landing and he breaks off. All dance.* TROPHIMOF, ANYA, BARBARA *and* MADAME RANEVSKY *enter from the landing.*)

MADAME RANEVSKY. Come, Peter, come, you pure spirit. . . . I beg your pardon. Let's have a dance. (*She dances with* TROPHIMOF. ANYA *and* RARBARA *dance.*)
(*Enter* FIRS, *and stands his walking-stick by the side door. Enter*

YASHA *by the drawing-room; he stands looking at the dancers.*)

YASHA. Well, grandfather?

FIRS. I'm not feeling well. In the old days it was generals and barons and admirals that danced at our dances, but now we send for the Postmaster and the Stationmaster, and even they make a favour of coming. I'm sort of weak all over. The old master, their grandfather, used to give us all sealing wax, when we had anything the matter. I've taken sealing wax every day for twenty years and more. Perhaps that's why I'm still alive.*

YASHA. I'm sick of you, grandfather. (*Yawning*) I wish you'd die and have done with it.

FIRS. Ah! you . . . job-lot! (*He mumbles to himself.*)
(TROPHIMOF *and* MADAME RANEVSKY *dance beyond the arch and down into the sitting-room.*)

MADAME RANEVSKY. *Merci.* I'll sit down. (*Sitting*) I'm tired.
(*Enter* ANYA.)

ANYA (*agitated*). There was somebody in the kitchen just now saying that the cherry orchard was sold to-day.

MADAME RANEVSKY. Sold? Who to?

ANYA. He didn't say who to. He's gone. (*She dances with* TROPHIMOF. *Both dance up into the drawing-room.*)

YASHA. It was some old fellow chattering; a stranger.

FIRS. And still Leonid Andreyitch doesn't come. He's wearing his light overcoat *demi-saison;* he'll catch cold as like as not. Ah, young wood, green wood!

MADAME RANEVSKY. This is killing me. Yasha, go and find out who it was sold to.

YASHA. Why, he's gone long ago, the old man. (*Laughs.*)

MADAME RANEVSKY (*vexed*). What are you laughing at? What are you glad about?

YASHA. He's a ridiculous fellow is Ephikhodof. Nothing in him. Twenty-two misfortunes!

MADAME RANEVSKY. Firs, if the property is sold, where will you go to?

FIRS. Wherever you tell me, there I'll go.

MADAME RANEVSKY. Why do you look like that? Are you ill? You ought to be in bed.

FIRS (*ironically*). Oh yes, I'll go to bed, and who'll hand the things round, who'll give orders? I've the whole house on my hands.

* If any reader of this book wants to try Firs' treatment, he must soak the sealing wax well in water, and then drink the water.

YASHA. Lyubof Andreyevna! Let me ask a favour of you; be so kind; if you go to Paris again, take me with you, I beseech you. It's absolutely impossible for me to stay here. (*Looking about; sotto voce*) What's the use of talking? You can see for yourself this is a barbarous country; the people have no morals; and the boredom! The food in the kitchen is something shocking, and on the top of it old Firs going about mumbling irrelevant nonsense. Take me back with you; be so kind!
(*Enter* PISHTCHIK.)

PISHTCHIK. May I have the pleasure . . . a bit of a waltz, charming lady? (MADAME RANEVSKY *takes his arm*) All the same, enchanting lady, you must let me have eighteen pounds. (*Dancing*) Let me have . . . eighteen pounds.
(*They go out dancing through the arch.*)

YASHA (*singing to himself*).

"Oh, wilt thou understand
The turmoil of my soul?"
(*Beyond the arch appears a figure in grey tall hat and check trousers, jumping and waving its arms. Cries of "Bravo, Charlotte Ivanovna."*)

DUNYASHA (*stopping to powder her face*). Mamselle Anya tells me I'm to dance; there are so many gentlemen and so few ladies. But dancing makes me giddy and makes my heart beat, Firs Nikolayevitch; and just now the gentlemen from the post office said something so nice to me, oh, so nice! It quite took my breath away. (*The music stops.*)

FIRS. What did he say to you?

DUNYASHA. He said, "You are like a flower."

YASHA (*yawning*). Cad! (*Exit.*)

DUNYASHA. Like a flower! I am so ladylike and refined, I dote on compliments.

FIRS. You'll come to a bad end.
(*Enter* EPHIKHODOF.)

EPHIKHODOF. You are not pleased to see me, Avdotya Fyodorovna, no more than if I were some sort of insect. (*Sighing*) Ah! Life! Life!

DUNYASHA. What do you want?

EPHIKHODOF. Undoubtedly perhaps you are right. (*Sighing*) But of course, if one regards it, so to speak, from the point of view, if I may allow myself the expression, and with apologies for my frankness, you have finally reduced me to a state of mind. I quite appreciate my destiny; every day some misfortune happens to me, and I have long since grown accustomed to it, and face my fortune with a smile. You have passed your word to me, and although I . . .

DUNYASHA. Let us talk of this another time, if you please; but now leave me in peace. I am busy meditating. (*Playing with her fan.*)

EPHIKHODOF. Every day some mis-

fortune befalls me, and yet, if I may venture to say so, I meet them with smiles and even laughter.
(*Enter* BARBARA *from the drawing-room.*)

BARBARA (*to* EPHIKHODOF). Haven't you gone yet, Simeon? You seem to pay no attention to what you're told. (*To* DUNYASHA) You get out of here, Dunyasha. (*To* EPHIKHODOF) First you play billiards and break a cue, and then you march about the drawing-room as if you were a guest!

EPHIKHODOF. Allow me to inform you that it's not your place to call me to account.

BARBARA. I'm not calling you to account; I'm merely talking to you. All you can do is to walk about from one place to another, without ever doing a stroke of work; and why on earth we keep a clerk at all heaven only knows.

EPHIKHODOF (*offended*). Whether I work, or whether I walk, or whether I eat, or whether I play billiards is a question to be decided only by my elders and people who understand.

BARBARA (*furious*). How dare you talk to me like that! How dare you! I don't understand things, don't I? You clear out of here this minute! Do you hear me? This minute!

EPHIKHODOF (*flinching*). I must beg you to express yourself in genteeler language.

BARBARA (*beside herself*). You clear out this instant second! Out you go! (*Following him as he retreats towards the door*) Twenty-two misfortunes! Make yourself scarce! Get out of my sight!
(*Exit* EPHIKHODOF.)

EPHIKHODOF (*without*). I shall lodge a complaint against you.

BARBARA. What! You're coming back, are you? (*Seizing the walking-stick left at the door by* FIRS) Come on! Come on! Come on! I'll teach you! Are you coming? Are you coming? Then take that. (*She slashes with the stick.*)
(*Enter* LOPAKHIN.)

LOPAKHIN. Many thanks; much obliged.

BARBARA (*still angry, but ironical*). Sorry!

LOPAKHIN. Don't mention it. I'm very grateful for your warm reception.

BARBARA. It's not worth thanking me for. (*She walks away, then looks round and asks in a gentle voice*) I didn't hurt you?

LOPAKHIN. Oh no, nothing to matter. I shall have a bump like a goose's egg, that's all.
(*Voices from the drawing-room:* "Lopakhin has arrived! Yermolai Alexeyitch!")

PISHTCHIK. Let my eyes see him, let my ears hear him! (*He and* LOPAKHIN *kiss.*) You smell of brandy, old man. We're having a high time, too.
(*Enter* MADAME RANEVSKY.)

MADAME RANEVSKY. Is it you, Yermolai Alexeyitch? Why have you been so long? Where is Leonid?

LOPAKHIN. Leonid Andreyitch came back with me. He's just coming.

MADAME RANEVSKY (*agitated*). What happened? Did the sale come off? Tell me, tell me!

LOPAKHIN (*embarrassed, afraid of showing his pleasure*). The sale was all over by four o'clock. We missed the train and had to wait till half-past eight. (*Sighing heavily*) Ouf! I'm rather giddy. . . . (*Enter* GAYEF. *In one hand he carries parcels; with the other he wipes away his tears.*)

MADAME RANEVSKY. What happened, Lenya? Come, Lenya! (*Impatiently, crying*) Be quick, be quick, for heaven's sake!

GAYEF (*answering her only with an up and down gesture of the hand; to* FIRS, *crying*). Here, take these. . . . Here are some anchovies and Black Sea herrings. I've had nothing to eat all day. Lord, what I've been through! (*Through the open door of the billiard-room comes the click of the billiard balls and* YASHA'S *voice: "Seven, eighteen!"* GAYEF'S *expression changes; he stops crying.*) I'm frightfully tired. Come and help me change, Firs. (*He goes up through the drawing-room,* FIRS *following.*)

PISHTCHIK. What about the sale? Come on, tell us all about it.

MADAME RANEVSKY. Was the cherry orchard sold?

LOPAKHIN. Yes.

MADAME RANEVSKY. Who bought it?

LOPAKHIN. I did. (*A pause.* MADAME RANEVSKY *is overwhelmed at the news. She would fall to the ground but for the chair and table by her.* BARBARA *takes the keys from her belt, throws them on the floor in the middle of the sitting-room, and goes out.*) I bought it. Wait a bit; don't hurry me; my head's in a whirl; I can't speak. . . . (*Laughing*) When we got to the sale, Deriganof was there already. Leonid Andreyitch had only fifteen hundred pounds, and Deriganof bid three thousand more than the mortgage right away. When I saw how things stood, I went for him and bid four thousand. He said four thousand five hundred. I said five thousand five hundred. He went up by five hundreds, you see, and I went up by thousands. . . . Well, it was soon over. I bid nine thousand more than the mortgage, and got it; and now the cherry orchard is mine! Mine! (*Laughing*) Heaven's alive! Just think of it! The cherry orchard is mine! Tell me that I'm drunk; tell me that I'm off my head; tell me that it's all a dream! . . . (*Stamping his feet*) Don't laugh at me! If only my father and my grandfather could rise from their graves and see the whole affair, how their Yermolai, their flogged and ignorant Yermolai, who used to run about barefooted in the winter, how this same Yermolai had bought a property that hasn't its equal for beauty anywhere in the whole world! I have bought the property where my father and grandfather were slaves, where they weren't even allowed into the kitchen. I'm asleep, it's only a vision, it isn't real. . . . 'Tis the fruit of imagination, wrapped in the mists of ignorance. (*Picking up the keys and smiling affectionately*) She's thrown down her keys; she wants to show that she's no longer mistress here. . . . (*Jingling them together*) Well, well, what's the odds? (*The musicians are heard tuning up.*) Hey, musicians, play! I want to hear you. Come everyone and see Yermolai Lopakhin lay his axe to the cherry orchard, come and see the trees fall down! We'll fill the place with villas; our grandsons and great-grandsons shall see a new life here. . . . Strike up, music! (*The band plays.* MADAME RANEVSKY *sinks into a chair and weeps bitterly. Reproachfully*) Oh, why, why didn't you listen to me? You can't put the clock back now, poor dear. (*Crying*) Oh, that all this were past and over! Oh, that our unhappy topsyturvy life were changed!

PISHTCHIK (*taking him by the arm, sotto voce*). She's crying. Let's go into the drawing-room and leave her alone to . . . Come on. (*Taking him by the arm, and going up towards the drawing-room.*)

LOPAKHIN. What's up? Play your best, musicians! Let everything be as I want. (*Ironically*) Here comes the new squire, the owner of the cherry orchard! (*Knocking up by accident against a table and nearly throwing down the candelabra*) Never mind, I can pay for everything!

(*Exit with* PISHTCHIK. *Nobody remains in the drawing-room or sitting-room except* MADAME RANEVSKY, *who sits huddled together, weeping bitterly. The band plays softly. Enter* ANYA *and* TROPHIMOF *quickly.* ANYA *goes to her mother and kneels before her.* TROPHIMOF *stands in the entry to the drawing-room.*)

ANYA. Mamma! Are you crying, mamma? My dear, good, sweet mamma! Darling, I love you! I bless you! The cherry orchard is sold; it's gone; it's quite true, it's quite true. But don't cry, mamma, you've still got life before you, you've still got your pure and lovely soul. Come with me, darling; come away from here. We'll plant a new garden, still lovelier than this. You will see it and understand, and happiness, deep, tranquil happiness will sink down on your soul, like the sun at eventide, and you'll smile, mamma. Come, darling, come with me!

CURTAIN

ACT FOUR

Same scene as Act I. There are no window-curtains, no pictures. The little furniture left is stacked in a corner, as if for sale. A feeling of emptiness. By the door to the hall and at the back of the scene are piled portmanteaux, bundles, etc. The door is open and the voices of BARBARA and ANYA are audible.

LOPAKHIN *stands waiting.* YASHA *holds a tray with small tumblers full of champagne.* EPHIKHODOF *is tying up a box in the hall. A distant murmur of voices behind the scene; the* PEASANTS *have come to say good-bye.*

GAYEF (*without*). Thank you, my lads, thank you.

YASHA. The common people have come to say good-bye. I'll tell you what I think, Yermolai Alexeyitch; they're good fellows but rather stupid.

(*The murmur of voices dies away. Enter* MADAME RANEVSKY *and* GAYEF *from the hall. She is not crying, but she is pale, her face twitches, she cannot speak.*)

GAYEF. You gave them your purse, Lyuba. That was wrong, very wrong!

MADAME RANEVSKY. I couldn't help it, I couldn't help it! (*Both go out.*)

LOPAKHIN (*calling after them through the doorway*). Please come here! Won't you come here? Just a glass to say good-bye. I forgot to bring any from the town, and could only raise one bottle at the station. Come along. (*A pause*) What, won't you have any? (*Returning from the door*) If I'd known, I wouldn't have bought it. I shan't have any either. (YASHA *sets the tray down carefully on a chair.*) Drink it yourself, Yasha.

YASHA. Here's to our departure! Good luck to them that stay! (*Drinking*) This isn't real champagne, you take my word for it.

LOPAHKIN. Sixteen shillings a bottle. (*A pause*) It's devilish cold in here.

YASHA. The fires weren't lighted today; we're all going away. (*He laughs.*)

LOPAKHIN. What are you laughing for?

YASHA. Just pleasure.

LOPAKHIN. Here we are in October, but it's as calm and sunny as summer. Good building weather. (*Looking at his watch and speaking off*) Don't forget that there's only forty-seven minutes before the train goes. You must start for the station in twenty minutes. Make haste.

(*Enter* TROPHIMOF *in an overcoat, from out of doors.*)

TROPHIMOF. I think it's time we

were off. The carriages are round. What the deuce has become of my goloshes? I've lost 'em. (*Calling off*) Anya, my goloshes have disappeared. I can't find them anywhere!

LOPAKHIN. I've got to go to Kharkov. I'll start in the same train with you. I'm going to spend the winter in Kharkov. I've been loafing about all this time with you people, eating my head off for want of work. I can't live without work, I don't know what to do with my hands; they dangle about as if they didn't belong to me.

TROPHIMOF. Well, we're going now, and you'll be able to get back to your beneficent labours.

LOPAKHIN. Have a glass.

TROPHIMOF. Not for me.

LOPAKHIN. Well, so you're off to Moscow?

TROPHIMOF. Yes, I'll see them into the town, and go on to Moscow tomorrow.

LOPAKHIN. Well, well. . . . I suppose the professors haven't started their lectures yet; they're waiting till you arrive.

TROPHIMOF. It is no affair of yours.

LOPAKHIN. How many years have you been up at the University?

TROPHIMOF. Try and think of some new joke; this one's getting a bit flat. (*Looking for his goloshes*) Look here, I dare say we shan't meet again, so let me give you a bit of advice as a keepsake: Don't flap your hands about! Get out of the habit of flapping. Building villas, prophesying that villa residents will turn into small freeholders, all that sort of thing is flapping too. Well, when all's said and done, I like you. You have thin, delicate, artist fingers; you have a delicate artist soul.

LOPHAKIN (*embracing him*). Goodbye, old chap. Thank you for everything. Take some money off me for the journey if you want it.

TROPHIMOF. What for? I don't want it.

LOPAKHIN. But you haven't got any.

TROPHIMOF. Yes, I have. Many thanks. I got some for a translation. Here it is, in my pocket. (*Anxiously*) I can't find my goloshes anywhere!

BARBARA (*from the next room*). Here, take your garbage away! (*She throws a pair of goloshes on the stage.*)

TROPHIMOF. What are you so cross about, Barbara? Humph! . . . But those aren't *my* goloshes!

LOPAKHIN. In the spring I sowed three thousand acres of poppy and I have cleared four thousand pounds net profit. When my poppies were in flower, what a picture they made! So you see, I cleared four thousand pounds; and I wanted to lend you a bit because I've got it to spare. What's the good of being stuck up? I'm a peasant. . . . As man to man. . . .

TROPHIMOF. Your father was a peasant; mine was a chemist; it doesn't prove anything. (LOPAKHIN *takes out his pocket-book with paper money.*) Shut up, shut up. . . . If you offered me twenty thousand pounds I would not take it. I am a free man; nothing that you value so highly, all of you, rich and poor, has the smallest power over me; it's like thistledown floating on the wind. I can do without you; I can go past you; I'm strong and proud. Mankind marches forward to the highest truth, to the highest happiness possible on earth, and I march in the foremost ranks.

LOPAKHIN. Will you get there?

TROPHIMOF. Yes. (*A pause*) I will get there myself or I will show others the way.
(*The sound of axes hewing is heard in the distance.*)

LOPAKHIN. Well, good-bye, old chap; it is time to start. Here we stand swaggering to each other, and life goes by all the time without heeding us. When I work for hours without getting tired, I get easy in my mind and I seem to know why I exist. But God alone knows what most of the people in Russia were born for. . . . Well, who cares? It doesn't affect the circulation of work. They say Leonid Andreyitch has got a place; he's going to be in a bank and get six hundred pounds a year. . . . He won't sit it out, he's too lazy.

ANYA (*in the doorway*). Mamma says, will you stop cutting down the orchard till she has gone.

TROPHIMOF. Really, haven't you got tact enough for that? (*Goes out by the hall.*)

LOPAKHIN. Of course, I'll stop them at once. What fools they are! (*Goes out after* TROPHIMOF.)

ANYA. Has Firs been sent to the hospital?

YASHA. I told 'em this morning. They're sure to have sent him.

ANYA (*to* EPHIKHODOF, *who crosses*). Simeon Panteleyitch, please find out if Firs has been sent to the hospital.

YASHA (*offended*). I told George this morning. What's the good of asking a dozen times?

EPHIKHODOF. Our centenarian friend, in my conclusive opinion, is hardly worth tinkering; it's time he was dispatched to his forefathers. I can only say I envy him. (*Putting down a portmanteau on a bandbox and crushing it flat*) There you are! I knew how it would be! (*Exit.*)

YASHA (*jeering*). Twenty-two misfortunes!

BARBARA (*without*). Has Firs been sent to the hospital?

ANYA. Yes.

BARBARA. Why didn't they take the note to the doctor?

ANYA. We must send it after them. (*Exit.*)

BARBARA (*from the next room*). Where's Yasha? Tell him his

mother is here. She wants to say good-bye to him.

YASHA (*with a gesture of impatience*). It's enough to try the patience of a saint!
(DUNYASHA *has been busying herself with the luggage. Seeing* YASHA *alone, she approaches him.*)

DUNYASHA. You might just look once at me, Yasha. You are going away, you are leaving me. (*Crying and throwing her arms round his neck.*)

YASHA. What's the good of crying? (*Drinking champagne*) In six days I shall be back in Paris. To-morrow we take the express, off we go, and that's the last of us! I can hardly believe it's true. Vive la France! This place don't suit me. I can't bear it . . . it can't be helped. I have had enough barbarism; I'm fed up. (*Drinking champagne*) What's the good of crying? You be a good girl, and you'll have no call to cry.

DUNYASHA (*powdering her face and looking into a glass*). Write me a letter from Paris. I've been so fond of you, Yasha, ever so fond! I am a delicate creature, Yasha.

YASHA. Here's somebody coming. (*He busies himself with the luggage, singing under his breath.*)
(*Enter* MADAME RANEVSKY, GAYEF, ANYA *and* CHARLOTTE.)

GAYEF. We'll have to be off; it's nearly time. (*Looking at* YASHA) Who is it smells of red herring?

MADAME RANEVSKY. We must take our seats in ten minutes. (*Looking round the room*) Good-bye, dear old house, good-bye, grandpapa! When winter is past and spring comes again, you will be here no more; they will have pulled you down. Oh, think of all these walls have seen! (*Kissing* ANYA *passionately*) My treasure, you look radiant, your eyes flash like two diamonds. Are you happy? very happy?

ANYA. Very, very happy. We're beginning a new life, mamma.

GAYEF (*gaily*). She's quite right, everything's all right now. Till the cherry orchard was sold we were all agitated and miserable; but once the thing was settled finally and irrevocably, we all calmed down and got jolly again. I'm a bank clerk now; I'm a financier . . . red in the middle! And you, Lyuba, whatever you may say, you're looking ever so much better, not a doubt about it.

MADAME RANEVSKY. Yes, my nerves are better; it's quite true. (*She is helped on with her hat and coat.*) I sleep well now. Take my things out, Yasha. We must be off. (*To* ANYA) We shall soon meet again, darling. . . . I'm off to Paris; I shall live on the money your grandmother sent from Yaroslav to buy the property. God bless your grandmother! I'm afraid it won't last long.

ANYA. You'll come back very, very soon, won't you, mamma? I'm going to work and pass the examination at the Gymnase and get a place and help you. We'll read all sorts of books together, won't we, mamma? (*Kissing her mother's hands*) We'll read in the long autumn evenings, we'll read heaps of books, and a new, wonderful world will open up before us. (*Meditating*) . . . Come back, mamma!

MADAME RANEVSKY. I'll come back, my angel. (*Embracing her.*)
(*Enter* LOPAKHIN. CHARLOTTE *sings softly.*)

GAYEF. Happy Charlotte, she's singing.

CHARLOTTE (*taking a bundle of rugs, like a swaddled baby*). Hush-a-bye, baby, on the tree top . . . (*The baby answers, "Wah-wah."*) Hush, my little one, hush, my pretty one! ("*Wah-wah.*") You'll break your mother's heart. (*She throws the bundle down on the floor again.*) Don't forget to find me a new place, please. I can't do without it.

LOPAKHIN. We'll find you a place, Charlotte Ivanovna, don't be afraid.

GAYEF. Everybody's deserting us. Barbara's going. Nobody seems to want us.

CHARLOTTE. There's nowhere for me to live in the town. I'm obliged to go. (*Hums a tune.*) What's the odds?
(*Enter* PISHTCHIK.)

LOPAKHIN. Nature's masterpiece!

PISHTCHIK (*panting*). Oy, oy, let me get my breath again! . . . I'm done up! . . . My noble friends! . . . Give me some water.

GAYEF. Wants some money, I suppose. No, thank you; I'll keep out of harm's way. (*Exit.*)

PISHTCHIK. It's ages since I have been here, fairest lady. (*To* LOPAKHIN) You here? Glad to see you, you man of gigantic intellect. Take this; it's for you. (*Giving* LOPAKHIN *money*) Forty pounds! I still owe you eighty-four.

LOPAKHIN (*amazed, shrugging his shoulders*). It's like a thing in a dream! Where did you get it from?

PISHTCHIK. Wait a bit. . . . I'm hot. . . . A most remarkable thing! Some Englishmen came and found some sort of white clay on my land. (*To* MADAME RANEVSKY.) And here's forty pounds for you, lovely, wonderful lady. (*Giving her money*) The rest another time. (*Drinking water*) Only just now a young man in the train was saying that some . . . some great philosopher advises us all to jump off roofs . . . Jump, he says, and there's an end of it. (*With an astonished air*) Just think of that! More water!

LOPAKHIN. Who were the Englishmen?

PISHTCHIK. I leased them the plot with the clay on it for twenty-four years. But I haven't any time now . . . I must be getting on. I must go to Znoikof's, to Kardamonof's. . . . I owe everybody money. (*Drinking*) Good-bye to everyone; I'll look in on Thursday.

MADAME RANEVSKY. We're just moving into town, and to-morrow I go abroad.

PISHTCHIK. What! (*Alarmed*) What are you going into town for? Why, what's happened to the furniture? . . . Trunks? . . . Oh, it's all right. (*Crying*) It's all right. People of powerful intellect . . . those Englishmen. It's all right. Be happy . . . God be with you . . . it's all right. Everything in this world has to come to an end. (*Kissing* MADAME RANEVSKY'S *hand*) If ever the news reaches you that *I* have come to an end, give a thought to the old . . . horse, and say, "Once there lived a certain Simeonof-Pishtchik, Heaven rest his soul." . . . Remarkable weather we're having. . . . Yes. . . . (*Goes out deeply moved. Returns at once and says from the doorway.*) Dashenka sent her compliments. (*Exit.*)

MADAME RANEVSKY. Now we can go. I have only two things on my mind. One is poor old Firs. (*Looking at her watch*) We can still stay five minutes.

ANYA. Firs has been sent to the hospital already, mamma. Yasha sent him off this morning.

MADAME RANEVSKY. My second anxiety is Barbara. She's used to getting up early and working, and now that she has no work to do she's like a fish out of water. She has grown thin and pale and taken to crying, poor dear. . . . (*A pause*) You know very well, Yermolai Alexeyitch, I always hoped . . . to see her married to you, and as far as I can see, you're looking out for a wife. (*She whispers to* ANYA, *who nods to* CHARLOTTE, *and both go out.*) She loves you; you like her; and I can't make out why you seem to fight shy of each other. I don't understand it.

LOPAKHIN. I don't understand it either, to tell you the truth. It all seems so odd. If there's still time, I'll do it this moment. Let's get it over and have done with it; without you there, I feel as if I should never propose to her.

MADAME RANEVSKY. A capital idea! After all, it doesn't take more than a minute. I'll call her at once.

LOPAKHIN. And here's the champagne all ready. (*Looking at the glasses*) Empty; someone's drunk it. (YASHA *coughs*) That's what they call lapping it up and no mistake!

MADAME RANEVSKY (*Animated*). Capital! We'll all go away. . . . *Allez,* Yasha. I'll call her. (*At the door*) Barbara, leave all that and come here. Come along! (MADAME RANEVSKY *and* YASHA *go out.*)

LOPAKHIN (*looking at his watch*). Yes.

(*A pause. A stifled laugh behind the door; whispering; at last enter* BARBARA.)

BARBARA (*examining the luggage*). Very odd; I can't find it anywhere . . .

LOPAKHIN. What are you looking for?

BARBARA. I packed it myself, and can't remember. (*A pause.*)

LOPAKHIN. Where are you going to-day, Barbara Mikhailovna?

BARBARA. Me? I'm going to the Ragulins'. I'm engaged to go and keep house for them, to be housekeeper or whatever it is.

LOPAKHIN. Oh, at Yashnevo? That's about fifty miles from here. (*A pause*) Well, so life in this house is over now.

BARBARA (*looking at the luggage*). Wherever can it be? Perhaps I put it in the trunk. . . . Yes, life here is over now; there won't be any more . . .

LOPAKHIN. And I'm off to Kharkov at once . . . by the same train. A lot of business to do. I'm leaving Ephikhodof to look after this place. I've taken him on.

BARBARA. Have you?

LOPAKHIN. At this time last year snow was falling already, if you remember; but now it's fine and sunny. Still, it's cold for all that. Three degrees of frost.

BARBARA. Were there? I didn't look. (*A pause*) Besides, the thermometer's broken. (*A pause.*)

A VOICE (*at the outer door*). Yermolai Alexeyitch!

LOPAKHIN (*as if he had only been waiting to be called*). I'm just coming! (*Exit quickly.*)
(BARBARA *sits on the floor, puts her head on a bundle and sobs softly. The door opens and* MADAME RANEVSKY *comes in cautiously.*)

MADAME RANEVSKY. Well? (*A pause*) We must be off.

BARBARA (*no longer crying, wiping her eyes*). Yes, it's time, mamma. I shall get to the Ragulins' all right to-day, so long as I don't miss the train.

MADAME RANEVSKY (*calling off*). Put on your things, Anya.
(*Enter* ANYA, *then* GAYEF *and* CHARLOTTE. GAYEF *wears a warm overcoat with a hood. The servants and drivers come in.* EPHIKHODOF *busies himself about the luggage.*)

MADAME RANEVSKY. Now we can start on our journey.

ANYA (*delighted*). We can start on our journey!

GAYEF. My friends, my dear, beloved friends! Now that I am leaving this house for ever, can I keep silence? Can I refrain from expressing those emotions which fill my whole being at such a moment?

ANYA (*pleadingly*). Uncle!

BARBARA. Uncle, what's the good?

GAYEF (*sadly*). Double the red in the middle pocket. I'll hold my tongue.
(*Enter* TROPHIMOF, *then* LOPAKHIN.)

TROPHIMOF. Come along, it's time to start.

LOPAKHIN. Ephikhodof, my coat.

MADAME RANEVSKY. I must sit here another minute. It's just as if I had never noticed before what the walls and ceilings of the house were like. I look at them hungrily, with such tender love. . . .

GAYEF. I remember, when I was six years old, how I sat in this window on Trinity Sunday, and watched father starting out for church.

MADAME RANEVSKY. Has everything been cleared out?

LOPAKHIN. Apparently everything. (*To* EPHIKHODOF, *putting on his overcoat*) See that everything's in order, Ephikhodof.

EPHIKHODOF (*in a hoarse voice*). You trust me, Yermolai Alexeyitch.

LOPAKHIN. What's up with your voice?

EPHIKHODOF. I was just having a drink of water. I swallowed something.

YASHA (*contemptuously*). Cad!

MADAME RANEVSKY. We're going, and not a soul will be left here.

LOPAKHIN. Until the spring.
(BARBARA *pulls an umbrella out of a bundle of rugs, as if she were brandishing it to strike.* LOPAKHIN *pretends to be frightened.*)

BARBARA. Don't be so silly! I never thought of such a thing.

TROPHIMOF. Come, we'd better go and get in. It's time to start. The train will be in immediately.

BARBARA. There are your goloshes, Peter, by that portmanteau. (*Crying*) What dirty old things they are!

TROPHIMOF (*putting on his goloshes*). Come along.

GAYEF (*much moved, afraid of crying*). The train . . . the station . . . double the red in the middle; doublette to put the white in the corner.

MADAME RANEVSKY. Come on!

LOPAKHIN. Is everyone here? No one left in there? (*Locking the door*) There are things stacked in there; I must lock them up. Come on!

ANYA. Good-bye, house; good-bye, old life!

TROPHIMOF. Welcome, new life!
(*Exit with* ANYA. BARBARA *looks round the room, and exit slowly. Exeunt* YASHA *and* CHARLOTTE *with her dog.*)

LOPAKHIN. Till the spring, then. Go on, everybody. So long! (*Exit.*)
(MADAME RANEVSKY *and* GAYEF *remain alone. They seem to have been waiting for this, throw their arms round each other's necks and sob restrainedly and gently, afraid of being overheard.*)

GAYEF (*in despair*). My sister! my sister!

MADAME RANEVSKY. Oh, my dear, sweet, lovely orchard! My life, my youth, my happiness, farewell! Farewell!

ANYA (*calling gaily without*). Mamma!

TROPHIMOF (*gay and excited*). Aoo!

MADAME RANEVSKY. One last look at the walls and the windows. . . . Our dear mother used to walk up and down this room.

GAYEF. My sister! my sister!

ANYA (*without*). Mamma!

TROPHIMOF (*without*). Aoo!

MADAME RANEVSKY. We're coming. (*They go out.*)

(*The stage is empty. One hears all the doors being locked, and the carriages driving away. All is quiet. Amid the silence the thud of the axes on the trees echoes sad and lonely. The sound of footsteps.* FIRS *appears in the doorway R. He is dressed, as always, in his long coat and white waistcoat; he wears slippers. He is ill.*)

FIRS (*going to the door L. and trying the handle*). Locked. They've gone. (*Sitting on the sofa*) They've forgotten me. Never mind! I'll sit here. Leonid Andreyitch is sure to have put on his cloth coat instead of his fur. (*He sighs anxiously*) He hadn't me to see. Young wood, green wood! (*He mumbles something incomprehensible*) Life has gone by as if I'd never lived. (*Lying down*) I'll lie down. There's no strength left in you; there's nothing, nothing. Ah, you . . . job-lot!

(*He lies motionless. A distant sound is heard, as if from the sky, the sound of a string breaking, dying away, melancholy. Silence ensues, broken only by the stroke of the axe on the trees far away in the cherry orchard.*)

The Emperor Jones

BY EUGENE O'NEILL

CHARACTERS

BRUTUS JONES, *Emperor*
HENRY SMITHERS, *A Cockney Trader*
AN OLD NATIVE WOMAN
LEM, *A Native Chief*
SOLDIERS, *Adherents of Lem*
The Little Formless Fears; Jeff; The Negro Convicts; The Prison Guard; The Planters; The Auctioneer; The Slaves; The Congo Witch-Doctor; The Crocodile God.

The action of the play takes place on an island in the West Indies as yet not self-determined by White Marines. The form of native government is, for the time being, an Empire.

SCENES

Scene I: In the palace of the EMPEROR JONES. Afternoon.
Scene II: The edge of the Great Forest. Dusk.
Scene III: In the Forest. Night.
Scene IV: In the Forest. Night.
Scene V: In the Forest. Night.
Scene VI: In the Forest. Night.
Scene VII: In the Forest. Night.
Scene VIII: Same as Scene Two—the edge of the Great Forest. Dawn.

The Emperor Jones

SCENE ONE

The audience chamber in the palace of the Emperor—a spacious, high-ceilinged room with bare, white-washed walls. The floor is of white tiles. In the rear, to the left of center, a wide archway giving out on a portico with white pillars. The palace is evidently situated on high ground for beyond the portico nothing can be seen but a vista of distant hills, their summits crowded with thick groves of palm trees. In the right wall, center, a smaller arched doorway leading to the living quarters of the palace. The room is bare of furniture with the exception of one huge chair made of uncut wood which stands at center, its back to rear. This is very apparently the Emperor's throne. It is painted a dazzling, eye-smiting scarlet. There is a brilliant orange cushion on the seat and another smaller one is placed on the floor to serve as a footstool. Strips of matting, dyed scarlet, lead from the foot of the throne to the two entrances.

It is late afternoon but the sunlight still blazes yellowly beyond the portico and there is an oppressive burden of exhausting heat in the air.

As the curtain rises, a native negro woman sneaks in cautiously from the entrance on the right. She is very old, dressed in cheap calico, bare-footed, a red bandana handkerchief covering all but a few stray wisps of white hair. A bundle bound in colored cloth is carried over her shoulder on the end of a stick. She hesitates beside the doorway, peering back as if in extreme dread of being discovered. Then she begins to glide noiselessly, a step at a time, toward the doorway in the rear. At this moment, SMITHERS *appears beneath the portico.*

SMITHERS *is a tall, stoop-shouldered man about forty. His bald head, perched on a long neck with an enormous Adam's apple, looks like an egg. The tropics have tanned his naturally pasty face with its small, sharp features to a sickly yellow, and native rum has painted his pointed nose to a startling red. His little, washy-blue eyes are red-rimmed and dart about him like a ferret's. His expression is one of unscrupulous meanness, cowardly and dangerous. He is dressed in a worn riding suit of dirty white drill, puttees, spurs, and wears a white cork helmet. A cartridge belt with an automatic revolver is around his waist. He carries a riding whip in his hand. He sees the woman and stops to watch her suspiciously. Then, making up his mind, he steps quickly on tiptoe into the room. The woman, looking back over her shoulder continually, does not see him until it is too late. When she does* SMITHERS *springs forward and grabs her firmly by the shoulder. She struggles to get away, fiercely but silently.*

SMITHERS (*tightening his grasp—roughly*). Easy! None o' that, me birdie. You can't wiggle out, now I got me 'ooks on yer.

WOMAN (*seeing the uselessness of struggling, gives way to frantic terror, and sinks to the ground, embracing his knees supplicatingly*). No tell him! No tell him, Mister!

SMITHERS (*with great curiosity*). Tell 'im? (*Then scornfully*) Oh, you mean 'is bloomin' Majesty. What's the gaime, any'ow? What are you sneakin' away for? Been stealin' a bit, I s'pose. (*He taps her bundle with his riding whip significantly.*)

WOMAN (*shaking her head vehemently*). No, me no steal.

SMITHERS. Bloody liar! But tell me what's up. There's somethin' funny goin' on. I smelled it in the air first thing I got up this mornin'. You blacks are up to some devilment. This palace of 'is is like a bleedin' tomb. Where's all the 'ands? (*The woman keeps sullenly silent.* SMITHERS *raises his whip threateningly.*) Ow, yer won't, won't yer? I'll show yer what's what.

WOMAN (*coweringly*). I tell, Mister. You no hit. They go—all go. (*She makes a sweeping gesture toward the hills in the distance.*)

SMITHERS. Run away—to the 'ills?

WOMAN. Yes, Mister. Him Emperor—Great Father. (*She touches her forehead to the floor with a quick mechanical jerk.*) Him sleep after eat. Then they go—all go. Me old woman. Me left only. Now me go too.

SMITHERS (*his astonishment giving way to an immense, mean satisfaction*). Ow! So that's the ticket! Well, I know bloody well wot's in the air—when they runs orf to the 'ills. The tom-tom'll be thumping out there bloomin' soon. (*With extreme vindictiveness*) And I'm bloody glad of it, for one! Serve 'im right! Puttin' on airs, the stinkin' nigger! 'Is Majesty! Gawd blimey! I only 'opes I'm there when they takes 'im out to shoot 'im. (*Suddenly*) 'E's still 'ere all right, ain't 'e?

WOMAN. Him sleep.

SMITHERS. 'E's bound to find out soon as 'e wakes up. 'E's cunnin' enough to know when 'is time's come. (*He goes to the doorway on right and whistles shrilly with his fingers in his mouth. The old woman springs to her feet and runs out of the doorway, rear.* SMITHERS *goes after her, reaching for his revolver.*) Stop or I'll shoot! (*Then stopping—indifferently*) Pop orf then, if yer like, yer black cow. (*He stands in the doorway, looking after her.*)

(JONES *enters from the right. He is a tall, powerfully-built, full-blooded negro of middle age. His features are typically negroid, yet there is something decidedly distinctive about his face—an underlying strength of will, a hardy, self-reliant confidence in himself that inspires respect. His eyes are alive with a keen, cunning intelligence. In manner he is shrewd, suspicious, evasive. He wears a light blue uniform coat, sprayed with brass buttons, heavy gold chevrons on his shoulders, gold braid on the collar, cuffs, etc. His pants are bright red with a light blue stripe down the side. Patent leather laced boots with brass spurs, and a belt with a long-barreled, pearl-handled revolver in a holster complete his make up. Yet there is something not altogether ridiculous about his grandeur. He has a way of carrying it off.*)

JONES (*not seeing anyone—greatly irritated and blinking sleepily—shouts*). Who dare whistle dat way in my palace? Who dare wake up de Emperor? I'll git de hide frayled off some o' you niggers sho'!

SMITHERS (*showing himself—in a manner half-afraid and half-defiant*). It was me whistled to yer. (*As* JONES *frowns angrily*) I got news for yer.

JONES (*putting on his suavest manner, which fails to cover up his contempt for the white man*). Oh, it's you, Mister Smithers. (*He sits down on his throne with easy dignity.*) What news you got to tell me?

SMITHERS (*coming close to enjoy his discomfiture*). Don't yer notice nothin' funny today?

JONES (*coldly*). Funny? No. I ain't perceived nothin' of de kind!

SMITHERS. Then yer ain't so foxy as I thought yer was. Where's all your court? (*sarcastically*) the Generals and the Cabinet Ministers and all?

JONES (*imperturbably*). Where dey mostly runs to minute I closes my eyes—drinkin' rum and talkin' big down in de town. (*Sarcastically*) How come you don't know dat? Ain't you sousin' with 'em most every day?

SMITHERS (*stung but pretending indifference—with a wink*). That's part of the day's work. I got ter—ain't I—in my business?

JONES (*contemptuously*). Yo' business!

SMITHERS (*imprudently enraged*). Gawd blimey, you was glad enough for me ter take yer in on it when you landed here first. You didn' 'ave no 'igh and mighty airs in them days!

JONES (*his hand going to his revolver like a flash—menacingly*). Talk polite, white man! Talk polite, you heah me! I'm boss heah now, is you fergettin'? (*The Cockney seems about to challenge this last statement with the facts but something in the other's eyes holds and cows him.*)

SMITHERS (*in a cowardly whine*). No 'arm meant, old top.

JONES (*condescendingly*). I accepts yo' apology. (*Lets his hand fall from his revolver.*) No use'n you rakin' up ole times. What I was den is one thing. What I is now's another. You didn't let me in on yo' crooked work out o' no kind feelin's dat time. I done de dirty work fo' you—and most o' de brain work, too, fo' dat matter—and I was wu'th money to you, dat's de reason.

SMITHERS. Well, blimey, I give yer a start, didn't I?—when no one else would. I wasn't afraid to 'ire you like the rest was—'count of the story about your breakin' jail back in the States.

JONES. No, you didn't have no s'cuse to look down on me fo' dat. You been in jail you'self more'n once.

SMITHERS (*furiously*). It's a lie! (*Then trying to pass it off by an attempt at scorn*) Garn! Who told yer that fairy tale?

JONES. Dey's some tings I ain't got to be tole. I kin see 'em in folk's eyes. (*Then after a pause—meditatively*) Yes, you sho' give me a start. And it didn't take long from dat time to git dese fool, woods' niggers right where I wanted dem. (*With pride*) From stowaway to Emperor in two years! Dat's goin' some!

SMITHERS (*with curiosity*). And I bet you got yer pile o' money 'id safe some place.

JONES (*with satisfaction*). I sho' has! And it's in a foreign bank where no pusson don't ever git it out but me no matter what come. You didn't s'pose I was holdin' down dis Emperor job for de glory in it, did you? Sho'! De fuss and glory part of it, dat's only to turn de heads o' de low-flung, bush niggers dat's here. Dey wants de big circus show for deir money. I gives it to 'em an' I gits de money. (*With a grin*) De long green, dat's me every time! (*Then rebukingly*) But you ain't got no kick agin me, Smithers. I'se paid you back all you done for me many times. Ain't I pertected you and winked at all de crooked tradin' you been doin' right out in de broad day? Sho' I has—and me makin' laws to stop it at de same time! (*He chuckles.*)

SMITHERS (*grinning*). But, meanin' no 'arm, you been grabbin' right and left yourself, ain't yer? Look at the taxes you've put on 'em! Blimey! You've squeezed 'em dry!

JONES (*chuckling*). No, dey ain't *all* dry yet. I'se still heah, ain't I?

SMITHERS (*smiling at his secret thought*). They're dry right now, you'll find out. (*Changing the subject abruptly*) And as for me breakin' laws, you've broke 'em all yerself just as fast as yer made 'em.

JONES. Ain't I de Emperor? De laws don't go for him. (*Judicially*) You heah what I tells you, Smithers. Dere's little stealin' like you does, and dere's big stealin' like I does. For de little stealin' dey gits you in jail soon or late. For de big stealin' dey makes you Emperor and puts you in de Hall o' Fame when you croaks. (*Reminiscently*) If dey's one thing I learns in ten years on de Pullman ca's listenin' to de white quality talk, it's dat same fact. And when I gits a chance to use it I winds up Emperor in two years.

SMITHERS (*unable to repress the genuine admiration of the small *fry for the large*). Yes, yer turned the bleedin' trick, all right. Blimey, I never seen a bloke 'as 'ad the bloomin' luck you 'as.

JONES (*severely*). Luck? What you mean—luck?

SMITHERS. I suppose you'll say as that swank about the silver bullet ain't luck—and that was what first got the fool blacks on yer side the time of the revolution, wasn't it?

JONES (*with a laugh*). Oh, dat silver bullet! Sho' was luck. But I makes dat luck, you heah? I loads de dice! Yessuh! When dat murderin' nigger ole Lem hired to kill me takes aim ten feet away and his gun misses fire and I shoots him dead, what you heah me say?

SMITHERS. You said yer'd got a charm so's no lead bullet'd kill yer. You was so strong only a silver bullet could kill yer, you told 'em. Blimey, wasn't that swank for yer—and plain, fat-'eaded luck?

JONES (*proudly*). I got brains and I uses 'em quick. Dat ain't luck.

SMITHERS. Yer know they wasn't 'ardly liable to get no silver bullets. And it was luck 'e didn't 'it you that time.

JONES (*laughing*). And dere all dem fool bush niggers was kneelin' down and bumpin' deir heads on de ground like I was a miracle out o' de Bible. Oh, Lawd, from dat time on I has dem all eatin' out of my hand. I cracks de whip and dey jumps through.

SMITHERS (*with a sniff*). Yankee bluff done it.

JONES. Ain't a man's talkin' big what makes him big—long as he makes folks believe it? Sho', I talks large when I ain't got nothin' to back it up, but I ain't talkin' wild just de same. I knows I kin fool 'em—I *knows* it—and dat's backin' enough fo' my game. And ain't I got to learn deir lingo and teach some of dem English befo' I kin talk to 'em? Ain't' dat wuk? You ain't never learned ary word er it, Smithers, in de ten years you been heah, dough you knows it's money in yo' pocket tradin' wid 'em if you does. But you'se too shiftless to take de trouble.

SMITHERS (*flushing*). Never mind about me. What's this I've 'eard about yer really 'avin' a silver bullet moulded for yourself?

JONES. It's playin' out my bluff. I has de silver bullet moulded and I tells 'em when de time comes I kills myself wid it. I tells 'em dat's 'cause I'm de on'y man in de world big enuff to git me. No use'n deir tryin'. And dey falls down and bumps deir heads. (*He laughs.*) I does dat so's I kin take a walk in peace widout no jealous nigger gunnin' at me from behind de trees.

SMITHERS (*astonished*). Then you 'ad it made—'onest?

JONES. Sho' did. Heah she be. (*He takes out his revolver, breaks it, and takes the silver bullet out of one chamber.*) Five lead an' dis silver baby at de last. Don't she shine pretty? (*He holds it in his hand, looking at it admiringly, as if strangely fascinated.*)

SMITHERS. Let me see. (*Reaches out his hand for it.*)

JONES (*harshly*). Keep yo' hands whar dey b'long, white man. (*He replaces it in the chamber and puts the revolver back on his hip.*)

SMITHERS (*snarling*). Gawd Blimey! Think I'm a bleedin' thief, you would.

JONES. No, 'tain't dat. I knows you'se scared to steal from me. On'y I ain't 'llowin' nary body to touch dis baby. She's my rabbit's foot.

SMITHERS (*sneering*). A bloomin' charm, wot? (*Venomously*) Well, you'll need all the bloody charms you 'as before long, s' 'elp me!

JONES (*judicially*). Oh, I'se good for six months yit 'fore dey gits sick o' my game. Den, when I sees trouble comin', I makes my get-away.

SMITHERS. Ho! You got it all planned, ain't yer?

JONES. I ain't no fool. I knows dis Emperor's time is sho't. Dat why I make hay when de sun shine. Was you thinkin' I'se aimin' to hold down dis job for life? No, suh! What good is gittin' money if you stays back in dis raggedy country? I wants action when I spends. And when I sees dese niggers gittin' up deir nerve to tu'n me out, and I'se got all de money in sight, I resigns on de spot and beats it quick.

SMITHERS. Where to?

JONES. None o' yo' business.

SMITHERS. Not back to the bloody States, I'll lay my oath.

JONES (*suspiciously*). Why don't I? (*Then with an easy laugh*) You mean 'count of dat story 'bout me breakin' from jail back dere? Dat's all talk.

SMITHERS (*skeptically*). Ho, yes!

JONES (*sharply*). You ain't 'sinuatin' I'se a liar, is you?

SMITHERS (*hastily*). No, Gawd strike me! I was only thinkin' o' the bloody lies you told the blacks 'ere about killin' white men in the States.

JONES (*angered*). How come dey're lies?

SMITHERS. You'd 'ave been in jail if you 'ad, wouldn't yer then? (*With venom*) And from what I've 'eard, it ain't 'ealthy for a black to kill a white man in the States. They burns 'em in oil, don't they?

JONES (*with cool deadliness*). You mean lynchin' 'd scare me? Well, I tells you, Smithers, maybe I does kill one white man back dere. Maybe I does. And maybe I kills another right heah 'fore long if he don't look out.

SMITHERS (*trying to force a laugh*). I was on'y spoofin' yer. Can't yer take a joke? And you was just sayin' you'd never been in jail.

JONES (*in the same tone—slightly boastful*). Maybe I goes to jail dere for gettin' in an argument wid razors ovah a crap game. Maybe I gits twenty years when dat colored man die. Maybe I gits in 'nother argument wid de prison guard was overseer ovah us when we're wukin' de road. Maybe he hits me wid a whip and I splits his head wid a shovel and runs away and files de chain off my leg and gits away safe. Maybe I does all dat an' maybe I don't. It's a story I tells you so's you knows I'se de kind of man dat if you evah repeats one word of it, I ends yo' stealin' on dis yearth mighty damn quick!

SMITHERS (*terrified*). Think I'd peach on yer? Not me! Ain't I always been yer friend?

JONES (*suddenly relaxing*). Sho' you has—and you better be.

SMITHERS (*recovering his composure—and with it his malice*). And just to show yer I'm yer friend, I'll tell yer that bit o' news I was goin' to.

JONES. Go ahead! Shoot de piece. Must be bad news from de happy way you look.

SMITHERS (*warningly*). Maybe it's gettin' time for you to resign—with that bloomin' silver bullet, wot? (*He finishes with a mocking grin.*)

JONES (*puzzled*). What's dat you say? Talk plain.

SMITHERS. Ain't noticed any of the guards or servants about the place today, I 'aven't.

JONES (*carelessly*). Dey're all out in de garden sleepin' under de trees. When I sleeps, dey sneaks a sleep, too, and I pretends I never suspicions it. All I got to do is to ring de bell and dey come flyin', makin' a bluff dey was wukin' all de time.

SMITHERS (*in the same mocking tone*). Ring the bell now an' you'll bloody well see what I means.

JONES (*startled to alertness, but preserving the same careless tone*). Sho' I rings. (*He reaches below the throne and pulls out a big, common dinner bell which is painted the same vivid scarlet as the throne. He rings this vigorously—then stops to listen. Then he goes to both doors, rings again, and looks out.*)

SMITHERS (*watching him with malicious satisfaction, after a pause—mockingly*). The bloody ship is sinkin' an' the bleedin' rats 'as slung their 'ooks.

JONES (*in a sudden fit of anger flings the bell clattering into a corner*). Low-flung, woods' niggers! (*Then catching* SMITHERS' *eye on him, he controls himself and suddenly bursts into a low chuckling laugh.*) Reckon I overplays my hand dis once! A man can't take de pot on a bob-tailed flush all de time. Was I sayin' I'd sit in six months mo'? Well, I'se changed my mind den. I cashes in and resigns de job of Emperor right dis minute.

SMITHERS (*with real admiration*). Blimey, but you're a cool bird, and no mistake.

JONES. No use'n fussin'. When I knows de game's up I kisses it good-by widout no long waits.

Dey've all run off to de hills, ain't dey?

SMITHERS. Yes—every bleedin' man jack of 'em.

JONES. Den de revolution is at de post. And de Emperor better git his feet smokin' up de trail. (*He starts for the door in rear.*)

SMITHERS. Goin' out to look for your 'orse? Yer won't find any. They steals the 'orses first thing. Mine was gone when I went for 'im this mornin'. That's wot first give me a suspicion of wot was up.

JONES (*alarmed for a second, scratches his head, then philosophically*). Well, den I hoofs it. Feet, do yo' duty! (*He pulls out a gold watch and looks at it.*) Three-thuty. Sundown's at six-thuty or dereabouts. (*Puts his watch back—with cool confidence*) I got plenty o' time to make it easy.

SMITHERS. Don't be so bloomin' sure of it. They'll be after you 'ot and 'eavy. Ole Lem is at the bottom o' this business an' 'e 'ates you like 'ell. 'E'd rather do for you than eat 'is dinner, 'e would!

JONES (*scornfully*). Dat fool no-count nigger! Does you think I'se scared o' him? I stands him on his thick head more'n once befo' dis, and I does it again if he comes in my way— (*Fiercely*) And dis time I leave him a dead nigger fo' sho'!

SMITHERS. You'll 'ave to cut through the big forest—an' these blacks 'ere can sniff and follow a trail in the dark like 'ounds. You'd 'ave to 'ustle to get through that forest in twelve hours even if you knew all the bloomin' trails like a native.

JONES (*with indignant scorn*). Look-a-heah, white man! Does you think I'se a natural bo'n fool? Give me credit fo' havin' some sense, fo' Lawd's sake! Don't you s'pose I'se looked ahead and made sho' of all de chances? I'se gone out in dat big forest, pretendin' to hunt, so many times dat I knows it high an' low like a book. I could go through on dem trails wid my eyes shut. (*With great contempt*) Think dese ign'rent bush niggers dat ain't got brains enuff to know deir own names even can catch Brutus Jones? Huh, I s'pects not! Not on yo' life! Why, man, de white men went after me wid bloodhounds where I come from an' I jes' laughs at 'em. It's a shame to fool dese black trash around heah, dey're so easy. You watch me, man. I'll make dem look sick, I will. I'll be 'cross de plain to de edge of de forest by time dark comes. Once in de woods in de night, dey got a swell chance o' findin' dis baby! Dawn tomorrow I'll be out at de oder side and on de coast whar dat French gunboat is stayin'. She picks me up, takes me to Martinique when she go dar, and dere I is safe wid a mighty big bankroll in my jeans. It's easy as rollin' off a log.

SMITHERS (*maliciously*). But s'posin' somethin' 'appens wrong an they do nab yer?

JONES (*decisively*). Dey don't—dat's de answer.

SMITHERS. But, just for argyment's sake—what'd you do?

JONES (*frowning*). I'se got five lead bullets in dis gun good enuff fo' common bush niggers—and after dat I got de silver bullet left to cheat 'em out o' gittin' me.

SMITHERS (*jeeringly*). Ho, I was fergettin' that silver bullet. You'll bump yourself orf in style, won't yer? Blimey!

JONES (*gloomily*). You kin bet yo' whole roll on one thing, white man. Dis baby plays out his string to de end and when he quits, he quits wid a bang de way he ought. Silver bullet ain't none too good for him when he go, dat's a fac'! (*Then shaking off his nervousness —with a confident laugh*) Sho'! What is I talkin' about? Ain't come to dat yit and I never will—not wid trash niggers like dese yere. (*Boastfully*) Silver bullet bring me luck anyway. I kin outguess, outrun, outfight, an' outplay de whole lot o' dem all ovah de board any time o' de day er night! You watch me! (*From the distant hills comes the faint, steady thump of a tom-tom, low and vibrating. It starts at a rate exactly corresponding to normal pulse beat—72 to the minute—and continues at a gradually accelerating rate from this point uninterruptedly to the very end of the play.*)
(JONES *starts at the sound. A strange look of apprehension creeps into his face for a moment as he listens. Then he asks, with an attempt to regain his most casual manner*) What's dat drum beatin' fo'?

SMITHERS (*with a mean grin*). For you. That means the bleedin' ceremony 'as started. I've 'eard it before and I knows.

JONES. Cer'mony? What cer'mony?

SMITHERS. The blacks is 'oldin' a bloody meetin', 'avin' a war dance, gettin' their courage worked up b'fore they starts after you.

JONES. Let dem! Dey'll sho' need it!

SMITHERS. And they're there 'oldin' their 'eathen religious service—makin' no end of devil spells and charms to 'elp 'em against your silver bullet. (*He guffaws loudly.*) Blimey, but they're balmy as 'ell!

JONES (*a tiny bit awed and shaken in spite of himself*). Huh! Takes more'n dat to scare dis chicken!

SMITHERS (*scenting the other's feeling—maliciously*). Ternight when it's pitch black in the forest, they'll 'ave their pet devils and ghosts 'oundin' after you. You'll find yer bloody 'air 'll be standin' on end before termorrow mornin'. (*Seriously*) It's a bleedin' queer place, that stinkin' forest, even in daylight. Yer don't know what might 'appen in there, it's that rotten still. Always sends the cold shivers down my back minute I gets in it.

JONES (*with a contemptuous sniff*). I ain't no chicken-liver like you is. Trees an' me, we'se friends, and dar's a full moon comin' bring me light. And let dem po' niggers make all de fool spells dey'se a min' to. Does yo' s'pect I'se silly enuff to b'lieve in ghosts an' ha'nts an' all dat ole woman's talk?

G'long, white man! You ain't talkin' to me. (*With a chuckle*) Doesn't you know dey's got to do wid a man was member in good standin' o' de Baptist Church? Sho' I was dat when I was porter on de Pullmans, befo' I gits into my little trouble. Let dem try deir heathen tricks. De Baptist Church done pertect me and land dem all in hell. (*Then with more confident satisfaction*) And I'se got little silver bullet o' my own, don't forgit!

SMITHERS. Ho! You 'aven't give much 'eed to your Baptist Church since you been down 'ere. I've 'eard myself you 'ad turned yer coat an' was takin' up with their blarsted witch-doctors, or whatever the 'ell yer calls the swine.

JONES (*vehemently*). I pretends to! Sho' I pretends! Dat's part o' my game from de fust. If I finds out dem niggers believes dat black is white, den I yells it out louder 'n deir loudest. It don't git me nothin' to do missionary work for de Baptist Church. I'se after de coin, an' I lays my Jesus on de shelf for de time bein'. (*Stops abruptly to look at his watch—alertly*) But I ain't got de time to waste on no more fool talk wid you. I'se gwine away from heah dis secon'. (*He reaches in under the throne and pulls out an expensive Panama hat with a bright multi-colored band and sets it jauntily on his head.*) So long, white man! (*With a grin*) See you in jail sometime, maybe!

SMITHERS. Not me, you won't. Well, I wouldn't be in yer bloody boots for no bloomin' money, but 'ere's wishin' yer luck just the same.

JONES (*contemptuously*). You're de frightenedest man evah I see! I tells you I'se safe's 'f I was in New York City. It takes dem niggers from now to dark to git up de nerve to start somethin'. By dat time, I'se got a head start dey never kotch up wid.

SMITHERS (*maliciously*). Give my regards to any ghosts yer meets up with.

JONES (*grinning*). If dat ghost got money, I'll tell him never ha'nt you less'n he wants to lose it.

SMITHERS (*flattered*). Garn! (*Then curiously*) Ain't yer takin' no luggage with yer?

JONES. I travels light when I wants to move fast. And I got tinned grub buried on de edge o' de forest. (*Boastfully*) Now say dat I don't look ahead an' use my brains! (*With a wide, liberal gesture*) I will all dat's left in de palace to you—and you better grab all you kin sneak away wid befo' dey gits here.

SMITHERS (*gratefully*). Righto—and thanks ter yer. (*As* JONES *walks toward the door in rear—cautioningly*) Say! Look 'ere, you ain't goin' out that way, are yer?

JONES. Does you think I'd slink out de back door like a common nigger? I'se Emperor yit, ain't I? And de Emperor Jones leaves de way he comes, and dat black trash don't dare stop him—not yit, leastways. (*He stops for a moment in the doorway, listening to the fur-*

off but insistent beat of the tom-tom.) Listen to dat roll-call, will you? Must be mighty big drum carry dat far. (*Then with a laugh*) Well, if dey ain't no whole brass band to see me off, I sho' got de drum part of it. So long, white man. (*He puts his hands in his pockets and with studied carelessness, whistling a tune, he saunters out of the doorway and off to the left.*)

SMITHERS (*looks after him with a puzzled admiration*). 'E's got 'is bloomin' nerve with 'im, s'elp me! (*Then angrily*) Ho—the bleedin' nigger—puttin' on 'is bloody airs! I 'opes they nabs 'im an' gives 'im what's what!

CURTAIN

SCENE TWO

The end of the plain where the Great Forest begins. The foreground is sandy, level ground dotted by a few stones and clumps of stunted bushes cowering close against the earth to escape the buffeting of the trade wind. In the rear the forest is a wall of darkness dividing the world. Only when the eye becomes accustomed to the gloom can the outlines of separate trunks of the nearest trees be made out, enormous pillars of deeper blackness. A somber monotone of wind lost in the leaves moans in the air. Yet this sound serves but to intensify the impression of the forest's relentless immobility, to form a background throwing into relief its brooding, implacable silence.

(JONES *enters from the left, walking rapidly. He stops as he nears the edge of the forest, looks around him quickly, peering into the dark as if searching for some familiar landmark. Then, apparently satisfied that he is where he ought to be, he throws himself on the ground, dog-tired.*)

Well, heah I is. In de nick o' time, too! Little mo' an' it'd be blacker'n de ace of spades heahabouts. (*He pulls a bandana handkerchief from his hip pocket and mops off his perspiring face.*) Sho'! Gimme air! I'se tuckered out sho' 'nuff. Dat soft Emperor job ain't no trainin' fo' a long hike ovah dat plain in de brilin' sun. (*Then with a chuckle*) Cheer up, nigger, de worst is yet to come. (*He lifts his head and stares at the forest. His chuckle peters out abruptly. In a tone of awe*) My goodness, look at dem woods, will you? Dat no-count Smithers said dey'd be black an' he sho' called de turn. (*Turning away from them quickly and looking down at his feet, he snatches at a chance to change the subject —solicitously*) Feet, you is holdin' up yo' end fine an' I sutinly hopes you ain't blisterin' none. It's time you git a rest. (*He takes off his shoes, his eyes studiously avoiding the forest. He feels of the soles of his feet gingerly.*) You is still in de pink—on'y a little mite feverish. Cool yo'selfs. Remember you done got a long journey yit befo' you. (*He sits in a weary attitude, listening to the rhythmic beating of the tom-tom. He grumbles in a loud tone to cover up a growing uneasiness.*) Bush niggers! Wonder dey wouldn't git sick o' beatin' dat drum. Sound louder, seem like. I wonder if dey's startin' after me? (*He scrambles to his feet, looking back across the plain.*) Couldn't see dem now, nohow, if dey was hundred feet away. (*Then shaking himself like a wet dog to get rid of these depressing thoughts*) Sho', dey's miles an' miles behind. What you gittin' figdety about? (*But he sits down and begins to lace up his shoes in great haste, all the time muttering reassuringly*) You know what? Yo' belly is empty, dat's what's de matter wid you. Come time to eat! Wid nothin' but wind on yo' stomach, o' course you feels jiggedy. Well, we eats right heah an' now soon's I gits dese pesky shoes laced up. (*He finishes lacing up his shoes.*) Dere! Now le's see! (*Gets on his hands and knees and searches the ground around him with his eyes.*) White stone, white stone, where is you? (*He sees the first white stone and crawls to it—with satisfaction.*) Heah you is! I knowed dis was de right place. Box of grub, come to me. (*He turns over the stone and feels in under it—in a tone of dismay*) Ain't heah! Gorry, is I in de right place or isn't I? Dere's 'nother stone. Guess dat's it. (*He scrambles to the next stone and turns it over.*) Ain't heah, neither! Grub, whar is you? Ain't heah. Gorry, has I got to go hungry into dem woods—all de night? (*While he is talking he scrambles from one stone to another, turning them over in frantic haste. Finally, he jumps to his feet excitedly.*) Is I lost de place? Must have! But how dat happen when I was followin' de trail across de plain in broad daylight? (*Almost plaintively*) I'se hungry, I is! I gotta git my feed. Whar's my strength gonna come from if I doesn't? Gorry, I gotta find dat grub high an' low somehow! Why it come dark so quick like dat? Can't see nothin'. (*He scratches a match on his trousers and peers about him. The rate of the beat of the far-off tom-tom increases perceptibly as he does so. He mutters in a bewildered voice*) How come all dese white stones come heah when I only remembers one? (*Suddenly, with a frightened gasp, he flings the match on the ground and stamps on it.*) Nigger, is you gone crazy mad? Is you lightin' matches to show dem whar you is? Fo' Lawd's sake, use yo' haid. Gorry, I'se got to be careful! (*He stares at the plain behind him apprehensively, his hand on his revolver.*) But how come all dese white stones? And whar's dat tin box o' grub I hid all wrapped up in oilcloth?

(*While his back is turned, the* LITTLE FORMLESS FEARS *creep out from the deeper blackness of the forest. They are black, shapeless, only their glittering little eyes can be seen. If they have any describable form at all it is that of a grubworm about the size of a creeping child. They move noiselessly, but with deliberate, painful effort, striving to raise themselves on end, failing and sinking prone again.* JONES *turns about to face the forest. He stares up at the tops of the trees, seeking vainly to discover his whereabouts by their conformation*).

Can't tell nothin' from dem trees! Gorry nothin' 'round heah looks like I evah seed it befo'. I'se done lost de place sho' 'nuff! (*With mournful foreboding*) It's mighty queer! It's mighty queer! (*With sodden forced defiance—in an angry tone*) Woods, is you tryin' to put somethin' ovah on me?

(*From the formless creatures on the ground in front of him comes a tiny gale of low mocking laughter like a rustling of leaves. They squirm upward toward him in twisted attitudes.* JONES *looks down, leaps backward with a yell of terror, yanking out his revolver as he does so—in a quavering voice*) What's dat? Who's dar? What is you? Git away from me befo' I shoots you up! You don't?—

(*He fires. There is a flash, a loud report, then silence broken only by the far-off, quickened throb of the tom-tom. The formless creatures have scurried back into the forest.* JONES *remains fixed in his position, listening intently. The sound of the shot, the reassuring feel of the revolver in his hand, have somewhat restored his shaken nerve. He addresses himself with renewed confidence.*)

Dey're gone. Dat shot fix 'em. Dey was only little animals—little wild pigs, I reckon. Dey've maybe rooted out yo' grub an eat it. Sho', you fool nigger, what you think dey is—ha'nts? (*Excitedly*) Gorry, you give de game away when you fire dat shot. Dem niggers heah dat fo' su'tin! Time you beat it in de woods widout no long waits. (*He starts for the forest—hesitates before the plunge—then urging himself in with manful resolution*) Git in, nigger! What you skeered at? Ain't nothin' dere but de trees! Git in! (*He plunges boldly into the forest.*)

SCENE THREE

In the forest. The moon has just risen. Its beams, drifting through the canopy of leaves, make a barely perceptible, suffused, eerie glow. A dense low wall of underbrush and creepers is in the nearer foreground, fencing in a small triangular clearing. Beyond this is the massed blackness of the forest like an encompassing barrier. A path is dimly discerned leading down to the clearing from left, rear, and winding away from it again toward the right. As the scene opens nothing can be distinctly made out. Except for the beating of the tom-tom, which is a trifle louder and quicker than at the close of the previous scene, there is silence, broken every few seconds by a queer, clicking sound. Then gradually the figure of the negro, JEFF, *can be discerned crouching on his haunches at the rear of the triangle. He is middle-aged, thin, brown in color, is dressed in a Pullman porter's uniform and cap. He is throwing a pair of dice on the ground before him, picking them up, shaking them, casting them out with the regular, rigid, mechanical movements of an automaton. The heavy, plodding footsteps of someone approach-*

ing along the trail from the left are heard and JONES' *voice, pitched on a slightly higher key and strained in a cheery effort to overcome its own tremors.*

De moon's rizen. Does you heah dat, nigger? You gits more light from dis out. No mo' buttin' yo' fool head agin' de trunks an' scratchin' de hide off yo' legs in de bushes. Now you sees whar yo'se gwine. So cheer up! From now on you has a snap. (*He steps just to the rear of the triangular clearing and mops off his face on his sleeve. He has lost his Panama hat. His face is scratched, his brilliant uniform shows several large rents.*) What time's it gittin' to be, I wonder? I dassent light no match to find out. Phoo'. It's wa'm an' dat's a fac'! (*Wearily*) How long I been makin tracks in dese woods? Must be hours an' hours. Seems like fo'-evah! Yit can't be, when de moon's jes riz. Dis am a long night fo' yo', yo' Majesty! (*With a mournful chuckle*) Majesty! Der ain't much majesty 'bout dis baby now. (*With attempted cheerfulness*) Never min'. It's all part o' de game. Dis night come to an end like everything else. And when you gits dar safe and has dat bankroll in yo' hands you laughs at all dis. (*He starts to whistle but checks himself abruptly.*) What yo' whistlin' for, you po' dope! Want all de worl' to heah you? (*He stops talking to listen.*) Heah dat ole drum! Sho' gits nearer from de sound. Dey's packin' it along wid 'em. Time fo' me to move. (*He takes a step forward, then stops—worriedly*) What's dat odder queer clickety sound I heah? Dere it is! Sound close! Sound like—sound like— Fo' God sake, sound like some nigger was shootin' crap! (*Frightenedly*) I better beat it quick when I gits dem notions. (*He walks quickly into the clear space—then stands transfixed as he sees* JEFF*—in a terrified gasp*) Who dar? Who dat? Is dat you, Jeff? (*Starting toward the other, forgetful for a moment of his surroundings and really believes it is a living man that he sees—in a tone of happy relief*) Jeff! I'se sho' mighty glad to see you! Dey tol' me you done died from dat razor cut I gives you. (*Stopping suddenly, bewilderedly*) But how you come to be heah, nigger? (*He stares fascinatedly at the other who continues his mechanical play with the dice.* JONES' *eyes begin to roll wildly. He stutters*) Ain't you gwine—look up—can't you speak to me? Is you—is you—a ha'nt? (*He jerks out his revolver in a frenzy of terrified rage.*) Nigger, I kills you dead once. Has I got to kill you ag'in? You take it den. (*He fires. When the smoke clears away* JEFF *has disappeared.* JONES *stands trembling—then with a certain reassurance*) He's gone, anyway. Ha'nt or not ha'nt, dat shot fix him. (*The beat of the far-off tom-tom is perceptibly louder and more rapid.* JONES *becomes conscious of it—with a start, looking back over his shoulder.*) Dey's gittin' near! Dey's comin' fast! And heah I is shootin' shots to let 'em know jes' whar I is! Oh, Gorry, I'se got to run. (*Forgetting the path he plunges wildly into the underbrush in the rear and disappears in the shadow.*)

SCENE FOUR

In the forest. A wide dirt road runs diagonally from right, front, to left, rear. Rising sheer on both sides the forest walls it in. The moon is now up. Under its light the road glimmers ghastly and unreal. It is as if the forest had stood aside momentarily to let the road pass through and accomplish its veiled purpose. This done, the forest will fold in upon itself again and the road will be no more. JONES *stumbles in from the forest on the right. His uniform is ragged and torn. He looks about him with numbed surprise when he sees the road, his eyes blinking in the bright moonlight. He flops down exhaustedly and pants heavily for a while. Then with sudden anger.*

I'm meltin' wid heat! Runnin' an' runnin' an' runnin'! Damn dis heah coat! Like a straitjacket! (*He tears off his coat and flings it away from him, revealing himself stripped to the waist.*) Dere! Dat's better! Now I kin breathe! (*Looking down at his feet, the spurs catch his eye.*) And to hell wid dese high-fangled spurs. Dey're what's been a-trippin' me up an' breakin' my neck. (*He unstraps them and flings them away disgustedly.*) Dere! I gits rid o' dem frippety Emperor trappin's an' I travel lighter. Lawd! I'se tired! (*After a pause, listening to the insistent beat of the tom-tom in the distance*) I must 'a' put some distance between myself an' dem—runnin' like dat—and yit—dat damn drum sounds jes' de same—nearer, even. Well, I guess I a'most holds my lead anyhow. Dey won't never catch up. (*With a sigh*) If on'y my fool legs stands up. Oh, I'se sorry I evah went in for dis. Dat Emperor job is sho' hard to shake. (*He looks around him suspiciously.*) How'd dis road evah git heah? Good level road, too. I never remembers seein' it befo'. (*Shaking his head apprehensively*) Dese woods is sho' full o' de queerest things at night. (*With a sudden terror*) Lawd God, don't let me see no more o' dem ha'nts! Dey gits my goat! (*Then trying to talk himself into confidence*) Ha'nts! You fool nigger, dey ain't no such things! Don't de Baptist parson tell you dat many time? Is you civilized, or is you like dese ign'rent black niggers heah? Sho! Dat was all in yo' own head. Wasn't nothin' dere. Wasn't no Jeff! Know what? You jus' get seein' dem things 'cause yo' belly's empty and you's sick wid hunger inside. Hunger 'fects yo' head and yo' eyes. Any fool know dat. (*Then pleading fervently*) But bless God, I don't come across no more o' dem, whatever dey is! (*Then cautiously*) Rest! Don't talk! Rest! You needs it. Den you gits on yo' way again. (*Looking at the moon*) Night's half gone a'most. You hits de coast in de mawning! Den you's all safe. (*From the right forward a small gang of negroes enter. They are dressed in striped convict suits, their heads are shaven, one leg

drags limpingly, shackled to a heavy ball and chain. Some carry picks, the others shovels. They are followed by a white man dressed in the uniform of a prison guard. A Winchester rifle is slung across his shoulders and he carries a heavy whip. At a signal from the GUARD *they stop on the road opposite where* JONES *is sitting.* JONES, *who has been staring up at the sky, unmindful of their noiseless approach, suddenly looks down and sees them. His eyes pop out, he tries to get to his feet and fly, but sinks back, too numbed by fright to move. His voice catches in a choking prayer.*)
Lawd Jesus!
(*The* PRISON GUARD *cracks his whip —noiselessly—and at that signal all the convicts start to work on the road. They swing their picks, they shovel, but not a sound comes from their labor. Their movements, like those of* JEFF *in the preceding scene, are those of automatons,— rigid, slow, and mechanical. The* PRISON GUARD *points sternly at* JONES *with his whip, motions him to take his place among the other shovelers.* JONES *gets to his feet in a hypnotized stupor. He mumbles subserviently.*)
Yes, suh! Yes, suh! I'se comin'.
(*As he shuffles, dragging one foot, over to his place, he curses under his breath with rage and hatred.*)
God damn yo' soul, I gits even wid you yit, sometime.
(*As if there were a shovel in his hands he goes through weary, mechanical gestures of digging up dirt, and throwing it to the roadside. Suddenly the* GUARD *approaches him angrily, threateningly. He raises his whip and lashes* JONES *viciously across the shoulders with it.* JONES *winces with pain and cowers abjectly. The* GUARD *turns his back on him and walks away contemptuously. Instantly* JONES *straightens up. With arms upraised as if his shovel were a club in his hands he springs murderously at the unsuspecting* GUARD. *In the act of crashing down his shovel on the white man's skull,* JONES *suddenly becomes aware that his hands are empty. He cries despairingly.*)
Whar's my shovel? Gimme my shovel 'til I splits his damn head! (*Appealing to his fellow convicts*) Gimme a shovel, one o' you, fo' God's sake!
(*They stand fixed in motionless attitudes, their eyes on the ground. The* GUARD *seems to wait expectantly, his back turned to the attacker.* JONES *bellows with baffled, terrified rage, tugging frantically at his revolver.*)
I kills you, you white debil, if it's de last thing I evah does! Ghost or debil, I kill you agin!
(*He frees the revolver and fires point blank at the* GUARD'S *back. Instantly the walls of the forest close in from both sides, the road and the figures of the convict gang are blotted out in an enshrouding darkness. The only sounds are a crashing in the underbrush as* JONES *leaps away in mad flight and the throbbing of the tom-tom, still far distant, but increased in volume of sound and rapidity of beat.*)

SCENE FIVE

A large circular clearing, enclosed by the serried ranks of gigantic trunks of tall trees whose tops are lost to view. In the center is a big dead stump worn by time into a curious resemblance to an auction block. The moon floods the clearing with a clear light. JONES *forces his way in through the forest on the left. He looks wildly about the clearing with hunted, fearful glances. His pants are in tatters, his shoes cut and misshapen, flapping about his feet. He slinks cautiously to the stump in the center and sits down in a tense position, ready for instant flight. Then he holds his head in his hands and rocks back and forth, moaning to himself miserably.*

Oh, Lawd, Lawd! Oh, Lawd, Lawd! (*Suddenly he throws himself on his knees and raises his clasped hands to the sky—in a voice of agonized pleading*) Lawd Jesus, heah my prayer! I'se a po' sinner, a po' sinner! I knows I done wrong, I knows it! When I cotches Jeff cheatin' wid loaded dice my anger overcomes me and I kills him dead! Lawd, I done wrong! When dat guard hits me wid de whip, my anger overcomes me, and I kills him dead. Lawd, I done wrong! And down heah whar dese fool bush niggers raises me up to the seat o' de mighty, I steals all I could grab. Lawd, I done wrong! I knows it! I'se sorry! Forgive me, Lawd! Forgive dis po' sinner! (*Then beseeching terrifiedly*) And keep dem away, Lawd! Keep dem away from me! And stop dat drum soundin' in my ears! Dat begin to sound ha'nted, too. (*He gets to his feet, evidently slightly reassured by his prayer—with attempted confidence*) De Lawd'll preserve me from dem ha'nts after dis. (*Sits down on the stump again.*) I ain't skeered 'f real men. Let dem come. But dem odders— (*He shudders—then looks down at his feet, working his toes inside the shoes—with a groan*) Oh, my po' feet! Dem shoes ain't no use no more 'ceptin' to hurt. I'se better off widout dem. (*He unlaces them and pulls them off—holds the wrecks of the shoes in his hands and regards them mournfully.*) You was real, A-one patin' leather, too. Look at you now. Emperor, you'se gittin' mighty low!

(*He sighs dejectedly and remains with bowed shoulders, staring down at the shoes in his hands as if reluctant to throw them away. While his attention is thus occupied, a crowd of figures silently enters the clearing from all sides. All are dressed in Southern costumes of the period of the fifties of the last century. There are middle-aged men who are evidently well-to-do planters. There is one spruce, authoritative individual—the* AUCTIONEER. *There is a crowd of curious spectators, chiefly young belles and dandies who have come to the slave-market for diversion. All exchange courtly greetings in dumb show and chat silently together. There is something stiff, rigid, unreal, marionettish about their movements. They group themselves about the stump. Finally a batch of slaves is led in from the left by an attendant—three men of different ages, two women, one with a baby in her arms, nursing. They are placed to the left of the stump, beside* JONES.

The white planters look them over appraisingly as if they were cattle, and exchange judgments on each. The dandies point with their fingers and make witty remarks. The belles titter bewitchingly. All this in silence save for the ominous throb of the tom-tom. The AUCTIONEER *holds up his hand, taking his place at the stump. The groups strain forward attentively. He touches* JONES *on the shoulder peremptorily, motioning for him to stand on the stump—the auction block.*

JONES *looks up, sees the figures on all sides, looks wildly for some opening to escape, sees none, screams and leaps madly to the top of the stump to get as far away from them as possible. He stands there, cowering, paralyzed with horror. The* AUCTIONEER *begins his silent spiel. He points to* JONES, *appeals to the planters to see for themselves. Here is a good field hand, sound in wind and limb as they can see. Very strong still in spite of his being middle-aged. Look at that back. Look at those shoulders. Look at the muscles in his arms and his sturdy legs. Capable of any amount of hard labor. Moreover, of a good disposition, intelligent and tractable. Will any gentleman start the bidding? The* PLANTERS *raise their fingers, make their bids. They are apparently all eager to possess* JONES. *The bidding is lively, the crowd interested. While this has been going on,* JONES *has been seized by the courage of desperation. He dares to look down and around him. Over his face abject terror gives way to mystification, to gradual realization—stutteringly)*

What you all doin', white folks? What's all dis? What you all lookin' at me fo'? What you doin' wid me, anyhow? (*Suddenly convulsed with raging hatred and fear.*) Is dis a auction? Is you sellin' me like dey uster befo' de war? (*Jerking out his revolver just as the* AUCTIONEER *knocks him down to one of the planters—glaring from him to the purchaser.*) And *you* sells me? And *you* buys me? I shows you I'se a free nigger, damn yo' souls! (*He fires at the* AUCTIONEER *and at the* PLANTER *with such rapidity that the two shots are almost simultaneous. As if this were a signal the walls of the forest fold in. Only blackness remains and silence broken by* JONES *as he rushes off, crying with fear—and by the quickened, ever louder beat of the tom-tom.*)

SCENE SIX

A cleared space in the forest. The limbs of the trees meet over it forming a low ceiling about five feet from the ground. The interlocked ropes of creepers reaching upward to entwine the tree trunks give an arched appearance to the sides. The space thus enclosed is like the dark, noisome hold of some ancient vessel. The moonlight is almost completely shut out and only a vague wan light filters through. There is the noise of someone approaching from the left, stumbling and crawling through the undergrowth. JONES' *voice is heard between chattering moans.*

Oh, Lawd, what I gwine do now? Ain't got no bullet left on'y de silver one. If mo' o' dem ha'nts come after me, how I gwine skeer dem away? Oh, Lawd, on'y de silver one left—an' I gotta save dat fo' luck. If I shoots dat one I'm a goner sho'! Lawd, it's black heah! Whar's de moon? Oh, Lawd, don't dis night eveh come to an end! (*By the sounds, he is feeling his way cautiously forward.*) Dere! Dis feels like a clear space. I gotta lie down an' rest. I don't care if dem niggers does cotch me. I gotta rest.

(*He is well forward now where his figure can be dimly made out. His pants have been so torn away that what is left of them is no better than a breech cloth. He flings himself full length, face downward on the ground, panting with exhaustion. Gradually it seems to grow lighter in the enclosed space and two rows of seated figures can be seen behind* JONES. *They are sitting in crumpled, despairing attitudes, hunched, facing one another with their backs touching the forest walls as if they were shackled to them. All are negroes, naked save for loin cloths. At first they are silent and motionless. Then they begin to sway slowly forward toward each and back again in unison, as if they were laxly letting themselves follow the long roll of a ship at sea. At the same time, a low, melancholy murmur rises among them, increasing gradually by rhythmic degrees which seem to be directed and controlled by the throb of the tom-tom in the distance, to a long, tremulous wail of despair that reaches a certain pitch, unbearably acute, then falls by slow gradations of tone into silence and is taken up again.* JONES *starts, looks up, sees the figures, and throws himself down again to shut out the sight. A shudder of terror shakes his whole body as the wail rises up about him again. But the next time, his voice, as if under some uncanny compulsion, starts with the others. As their chorus lifts he rises to a sitting posture similar to the others, swaying back and forth. His voice reaches the highest pitch of sorrow, of desolation. The light fades out, the other voices cease, and only darkness is left.* JONES *can be heard scrambling to his feet and running off, his voice sinking down the scale and receding as he moves farther and farther away in the forest. The tom-tom beats louder, quicker, with a more insistent, triumphant pulsation.)*

SCENE SEVEN

The foot of a gigantic tree by the edge of a great river. A rough structure of boulders, like an altar, is by the tree. The raised river bank is in the nearer background. Beyond this the surface of the river spreads out, brilliant and unruffled in the moonlight, blotted out and merged into a veil of bluish mist in the distance. JONES' *voice is heard from the left rising and falling in the long, despairing wail of the chained slaves, to the rhythmic beat of the tom-tom. As his voice sinks into silence, he enters the open space. The expression of his face is fixed and stony, his eyes have an obsessed glare, he moves with a strange deliberation like a sleep-walker or one in a trance. He looks around at the tree, the rough stone altar, the moonlit surface of the river beyond, and passes his hand over his head with a vague gesture of puzzled bewilderment. Then, as if in obedience to some obscure impulse, he sinks into a kneeling, devotional posture before the altar. Then he seems to come to himself partly, to have an uncertain realization of what he is doing, for he straightens up and stares about him horrifiedly—in an incoherent mumble.*

What—what is I doin'? What is—dis place? Seems like I know dat tree—an' dem stones—an' de river. I remember—seems like I been heah befo'. (*Tremblingly*) Oh, Gorry, I'se skeered in dis place! I'se skeered. Oh, Lawd, pertect dis sinner!

(*Crawling away from the altar, he cowers close to the ground, his face hidden, his shoulders heaving with sobs of hysterical fright. From behind the trunk of the tree, as if he had sprung out of it, the figure of the* CONGO WITCH-DOCTOR *appears. He is wizened and old, naked except for the fur of some small animal tied about his waist, its bushy tail hanging down in front. His body is stained all over a bright red. Antelope horns are on each side of his head, branching upward. In one hand he carries a bone rattle, in the other a charm stick with a bunch of white cockatoo feathers tied to the end. A great number of glass beads and bone ornaments are about his neck, ears, wrists, and ankles. He struts noiselessly with a queer prancing step to a position in the clear ground between* JONES *and the altar. Then with a preliminary, summoning stamp of his foot on the earth, he begins to dance and to chant. As if in response to his summons the beating of the tom-tom grows to a fierce, exultant boom whose throbs seem to fill the air with vibrating rhythm.* JONES *looks up, starts to spring to his feet, reaches a half-kneeling, half-squatting position and remains rigidly fixed there, paralyzed with awed fascination by this new apparition. The* WITCH-DOCTOR *sways, stamping with his foot, his bone rattle clicking the time. His voice rises and falls in a wierd, monotonous croon, without articulate word divisions. Gradually his dance becomes clearly one of a narrative in pantomime, his croon is an incantation, a charm to allay the fierceness of some implacable deity demanding sacrifice. He flees, he is pursued by devils, he hides, he flees again. Ever wilder and wilder becomes his flight, nearer and nearer draws the pursuing evil, more and more the spirit of terror gains possession of him. His croon, rising to intensity, is punctuated by shrill cries.* JONES *has become completely hypnotized. His voice joins in the incantation, in the cries, he beats time with his hands and sways his body to and fro from the waist. The whole spirit and meaning of the dance has entered into him, has become his spirit. Finally the theme of the pantomime halts on a howl of despair, and is taken up again in a note of savage hope. There is a salvation. The forces of evil demand sacrifice. They must be appeased. The* WITCH-DOCTOR *points with his wand to the sacred tree, to the river beyond, to the altar, and finally to* JONES *with a ferocious command.* JONES *seems to sense the meaning of this. It is he who must offer himself for sacrifice. He beats his forehead abjectly to the ground, moaning hysterically.*)

Mercy, Oh, Lawd! Mercy! Mercy on dis po' sinner.

(*The* WITCH-DOCTOR *springs to the river bank. He stretches out his arms and calls to some God within its depths. Then he starts backward slowly, his arms remaining out. A huge head of a crocodile appears over the bank and its eyes, glittering greenly, fasten upon* JONES. *He stares into them fascinatedly. The* WITCH-DOCTOR *prances up to him, touches him with his wand, motions with hideous command toward the waiting monster.* JONES *squirms on his belly nearer and nearer, moaning continually.*)

Mercy, Lawd! Mercy!

(*The crocodile heaves more of his enormous hulk onto the land.* JONES *squirms toward him. The* WITCH-DOCTOR'S *voice shrills out in furious exultation, the tom-tom beats madly.* JONES *cries out in a fierce, exhausted spasm of anguished pleading.*)

Lawd, save me! Lawd Jesus, heah my prayer!

(*Immediately, in answer to his prayer, comes the thought of the one bullet left him. He snatches at his hip, shouting defiantly.*)

De silver bullet! You don't git me yit!

(*He fires at the green eyes in front of him. The head of the crocodile sinks back behind the river bank, the* WITCH-DOCTOR *springs behind the sacred tree and disappears.* JONES *lies with his face to the ground, his arms outstretched, whimpering with fear as the throb of the tom-tom fills the silence about him with a somber pulsation, a baffled but revengeful power.*)

SCENE EIGHT

Dawn. Same as Scene Two, the dividing line of forest and plain. The nearest tree trunks are dimly revealed but the forest behind them is still a mass of glooming shadow. The tom-tom seems on the very spot, so loud and continuously vibrating are its beats. LEM *enters from the left, followed by a small squad of his soldiers, and by the Cockney trader,* SMITHERS. LEM *is a heavy-set, ape-faced old savage of the extreme African type, dressed only in a loin cloth. A revolver and cartridge belt are about his waist. His soldiers are in different degrees of rag-concealed nakedness. All wear broad palm-leaf hats. Each one carries a rifle.* SMITHERS *is the same as in Scene One. One of the soldiers, evidently a tracker, is peering about keenly on the ground. He points to the spot where* JONES *entered the forest.* LEM *and* SMITHERS *come to look.*

SMITHERS (*after a glance, turns away in disgust*). That's where 'e went in right enough. Much good it'll do yer. 'E's miles orf by this an' safe to the Coast, damn 's 'ide! I tole yer yer'd lose 'im, didn't I?—wastin' the 'ole bloomin' night beatin' yer bloody drum and castin' yer silly spells! Gawd blimey, wot a pack!

LEM (*gutturally*). We cotch him. (*He makes a motion to his soldiers who squat down on their haunches in a semi-circle.*)

SMITHERS (*exasperatedly*). Well, ain't yer goin' in an' 'unt 'im in the woods? What the 'ell's the good of waitin'?

LEM (*imperturbably — squatting down himself*). We cotch him.

SMITHERS (*turning away from him contemptuously*). Aw! Garn! 'E's a better man than the lot o' you put together. I 'ates the sight o' 'im but I'll say that for 'im. (*A sound comes from the forest. The soldiers jump to their feet, cocking their rifles alertly.* LEM *remains sitting with an imperturbable expression, but listening intently. He makes a quick signal with his hand. His followers creep quickly into the forest, scattering so that each enters at a different spot.*)

SMITHERS. You ain't thinkin' that would be 'im, I 'ope?

LEM (*calmly*). We cotch him.

SMITHERS. Blarsted fat 'eads! (*Then after a second's thought—wonderingly*) Still an' all, it might 'appen. If 'e lost 'is bloody way in these stinkin' woods 'e'd likely turn in a circle without 'is knowin' it.

LEM (*peremptorily*). Sssh! (*The reports of several rifles sound from the forest, followed a second later by savage, exultant yells. The beating of the tom-tom abruptly ceases.* LEM *looks up at the white man with a grin of satisfaction.*) We cotch him. Him dead.

SMITHERS (*with a snarl*). 'Ow d'yer know it's 'im an' 'ow d'yer know 'e's dead?

LEM. My mens dey got um silver bullets. Lead bullet no kill him. He got um strong charm. I cook um money, make um silver bullet, make um strong charm, too.

SMITHERS (*astonished*). So that's wot you was up to all night, wot? You was scared to put after 'im till you'd moulded silver bullets, eh?

LEM (*simply stating a fact*). Yes. Him got strong charm. Lead no good.

SMITHERS (*slapping his thigh and guffawing*). Haw-haw! If yer don't beat all 'ell! (*Then recovering himself-scornfully*) I'll bet yer it ain't 'im they shot at all, yer bleedin' looney!

LEM (*calmly*). Dey come bring him now. (*The soldiers come out of the forest, carrying* JONES' *limp body. He is dead. They carry him to* LEM, *who examines his body with great satisfaction.* SMITHERS *leans over his shoulder—in a tone of frightened awe*) Well, they did for yer right enough, Jonesey, me lad! Dead as a 'erring! (*Mockingly*) Where's yer 'igh an' mighty airs now, yer bloomin' Majesty? (*Then with a grin*) Silver bullets! Gawd blimey, but yer died in the 'eighth o' style, any'ow!

CURTAIN

The Plough and the Stars

BY SEAN O'CASEY

TO THE GAY LAUGH OF MY MOTHER
AT THE GATE OF THE GRAVE

CHARACTERS

JACK CLITHEROE (*a bricklayer*), *Commandant in The Irish Citizen Army.*	*Residents in the Tenement*
NORA CLITHEROE, *his wife.*	
PETER FLYNN (*a labourer*), *Nora's uncle.*	
THE YOUNG COVEY (*a fitter*), *Clitheroe's cousin.*	
BESSIE BURGESS (*a street fruit-vendor*).	
MRS. GOGAN (*a charwoman*).	
MOLLSER, *her consumptive child.*	
FLUTHER GOOD (*a carpenter*).	

LIEUT. LANGON (*a Civil Servant*), *of the Irish Volunteers.*
CAPT. BRENNAN (*a chicken butcher*), *of the Irish Citizen Army.*
CORPORAL STODDART, *of the Wiltshires.*
SERGEANT TINLEY, *of the Wiltshires.*
ROSIE REDMOND (*a daughter of "the Digs"*).
A BARMAN.
A WOMAN.
THE FIGURE IN THE WINDOW.

ACT I.—A living-room of the CLITHEROE flat in a Dublin tenement.
ACT II.—A public-house, outside of which a meeting is being held.
ACT III.—The street outside the CLITHEROE tenement.
ACT IV.—The room of BESSIE BURGESS.

TIME. Acts I. and II., November, 1915; Acts III. and IV., Easter Week, 1916. A few days elapse between Acts III. and IV.

The Plough and the Stars

ACT ONE

SCENE: *The home of the* CLITHEROES. *It consists of the front and back drawing-rooms in a fine old Georgian house, struggling for its life against the assaults of time, and the more savage assaults of the tenants. The room shown is the back drawing-room, wide, spacious and lofty. At back is the entrance to the front drawing-room. The space, originally occupied by folding doors, is now draped with casement cloth of a dark purple, decorated with a design in reddish-purple and cream. One of the curtains is pulled aside, giving a glimpse of front drawing-room, at the end of which can be seen the wide, lofty windows looking out into the street. The room directly in front of the audience is furnished in a way that suggests an attempt towards a finer expression of domestic life. The large fireplace on right is of wood, painted to look like marble (the original has been taken away by the landlord). On the mantelshelf are two candlesticks of dark carved wood. Between them is a small clock. Over the clock is hanging a calendar which displays a picture of "The Sleeping Venus." In the centre of the breast of the chimney hangs a picture of Robert Emmett. On the right of the entrance to the front drawing-room is a copy of "The Gleaners," on the opposite side a copy of "The Angelus." Underneath "The Gleaners" is a chest of drawers on which stands a green bowl filled with scarlet dahlias and white chrysanthemums. Near to the fireplace is a settee which at night forms a double bed for* CLITHEROE *and* NORA. *Underneath "The Angelus" are a number of shelves containing saucepans and a frying-pan. Under these is a table on which are various articles of delf ware. Near the end of the room opposite to the fireplace is a gate-legged table, covered with a cloth. On top of the table a huge cavalry sword is lying. To the right is a door which leads to a lobby from which the staircase leads to the hall. The floor is covered with a dark green linoleum. The room is dim except where it is illuminated from the glow of the fire. Through the window of the room at back can be seen the flaring of the flame of a gasolene lamp giving light to workmen repairing the street. Occasionally can be heard the clang of crowbars striking the sets.* FLUTHER GOOD *is repairing the lock of door, Right. A claw hammer is on a chair beside him, and he has a screw-driver in his hand. He is a man of forty years of age, rarely surrendering to thoughts of anxiety, fond of his "oil" but determined to conquer the habit before he dies. He is square-jawed and harshly featured; under the left eye is a scar, and his nose is bent from a smashing blow received in a fistic battle long ago. He is bald, save for a few peeping tufts of reddish hair around his ears; and his upper lip is hidden by a scrubby red moustache, embroidered here and there with a grey hair. He is dressed in a seedy black suit, cotton shirt with a soft collar, and wears a very respectable little black bow. On his head is a faded jerry hat, which, when he is excited, he has a habit of knocking farther back on his head, in a series of taps. In an argument he usually fills with sound and fury generally signifying a row. He is in his shirt sleeves at present, and wears a soiled white apron, from a pocket in which sticks a carpenter's two-foot rule. He has just finished the job of putting on a new lock, and, filled with satisfaction, he is opening and shutting the door, enjoying the completion of a work well done. Sitting at the fire, airing a white shirt, is* PETER FLYNN. *He is a little, thin bit of a man, with a face shaped like a lozenge; on his cheeks and under his chin is a straggling wiry beard of dirty-white and lemon hue. His face invariably wears a look of animated anguish, mixed with irritated defiance, as if everybody was at war with him, and he at war with everybody. He is cocking his head in such a way that suggests resentment at the presence of* FLUTHER, *who pays no attention to him, apparently, but is really furtively watching him.* PETER *is clad in a singlet, white whipcord knee-breeches, and is in his stocking feet.*

A voice is heard speaking outside of door, Left (it is that of MRS. GOGAN).

MRS. GOGAN (*outside*). Who are you lookin' for, sir? Who? Mrs. Clitheroe? . . . Oh, excuse me. Oh ay, up this way. She's out, I think: I seen her goin'. Oh, you've somethin' for her; oh, excuse me. You're from Arnott's. . . . I see. You've a parcel for her. . . . Righto. . . . I'll take it. . . . I'll give it to her the minute she comes in. . . . It'll be quite safe. . . . Oh, sign that. . . . Excuse me. . . . Where? . . . Here? . . . No, there; righto. Am I to put Maggie or Mrs.? What is it? You dunno? Oh, excuse me.

(MRS. GOGAN *opens the door and comes in. She is a doleful looking little woman of forty, insinuating manner and sallow complexion. She is fidgety and nervous, terribly talkative, has a habit of taking up things that may be near her and fiddling with them while she is speaking. Her heart is aflame with curiosity, and a fly could not come into nor go out of the house without her knowing. She has a draper's parcel in her hand, the knot of the twine tying it is untied.* PETER, *more resentful of this intrusion than of* FLUTHER'S *presence, gets up from the chair, and without looking around, his head carried at an angry cock, marches into the room at back.*)

MRS. GOGAN (*removing the paper and opening the cardboard box it contains*). I wondher what's this now? A hat! (*She takes out a hat, black, with decorations in red and gold.*) God, she's goin' to th' divil lately for style! That hat, now, cost more than a penny. Such notions of upperosity she's gettin'. (*Putting the hat on her head*) Oh, swank, what! (*She replaces it in parcel.*)

FLUTHER. She's a pretty little Judy, all the same.

MRS. GOGAN. Ah, she is, an' she isn't. There's prettiness an' prettiness in it. I'm always sayin' that her skirts are a little too short for a married woman. An' to see her, sometimes of an evenin', in her glad-neck gown would make a body's blood run cold. I do be ashamed of me life before her husband. An' th' way she thries to be polite, with "Good mornin', Mrs. Gogan," when she's goin' down, an' her "Good evenin', Mrs. Gogan," when she's comin' up. But there's politeness an' politeness in it.

FLUTHER. They seem to get on well together, all the same.

MRS. GOGAN. Ah, they do, an' they don't. The pair of them used to be like two turtle doves always billin' an' cooin'. You couldn't come into th' room but you'd feel, instinctively like, that they'd just been afther kissin' an' cuddlin' each other. . . . It often made me shiver, for, afther all, there's kissin' an' cuddlin' in it. But I'm thinkin' he's beginning to take things more quietly; the mysthery of havin' a woman's a mysthery no longer. . . . She dhresses herself to keep him with her, but it's no use—afther a month or two, th' wondher of a woman wears off.

FLUTHER. I dunno, I dunno. Not wishin' to say anything derogatory, I think it's all a question of location: when a man finds th' wondher of one woman beginnin' to die, it's usually beginnin' to live in another.

MRS. GOGAN. She's always grumblin' about havin' to live in a tenement house. "I wouldn't like to spend me last hour in one, let alone live me life in a tenement," says she. "Vaults," says she, "that are hidin' th' dead, instead of homes that are sheltherin' th' livin'." "Many a good one," says I, "was reared in a tenement house." Oh, you know, she's a well-up little lassie, too; able to make a shillin' go where another would have to spend a pound. She's wipin' the eyes of th' Covey an' poor oul' Pether—everybody knows that—screwin' every penny she can out o' them, in ordher to turn th' place into a babby-house. An' she has th' life frightened out o' them; washin' their face, combin' their hair, wipin' their feet, brushin' their clothes, thrimmin' their nails, cleanin' their teeth—God Almighty, you'd think th' poor men were undhergoin' penal servitude.

FLUTHER (*with an exclamation of disgust*). A-a-ah, that's goin' beyond th' beyonds in a tenement house. That's a little bit too derogatory.

(PETER *enters from room, Back, head elevated and resentful fire in his eyes; he is still in his singlet and trousers, but is now wearing a pair of unlaced boots—possibly to be decent in the presence of* MRS. GOGAN. *He places the white shirt, which he has carried in on his arm, on the back of a chair near the fire, and, going over to the chest of drawers, he opens drawer after drawer, looking for something; as he fails to find it he closes each drawer with a snap; he pulls out pieces of linen neatly folded, and bundles them back again any way.*)

PETER (*in accents of anguish*). Well, God Almighty, give me patience! (*He returns to room, Back, giving the shirt a vicious turn as he passes.*)

MRS. GOGAN. I wondher what is he foostherin' for now?

FLUTHER. He's adornin' himself for th' meeting to-night. (*Pulling a handbill from his pocket and reading*) "Great Demonstration an' torchlight procession around places in th' city sacred to th' memory of Irish Patriots to be concluded be a meetin', at which will be taken an oath of fealty to th' Irish Republic. Formation in Parnell Square at eight o'clock." Well, they can hold it for Fluther. I'm up th' pole; no more dhrink for Fluther. It's three days now since I touched a dhrop, an' I feel a new man already.

MRS. GOGAN. Isn't oul' Peter a funny lookin' little man? . . . Like somethin' you'd pick off a Christmas Tree. . . . When he's dhressed up in his canonicals, you'd wondher where he'd been got. God forgive me, when I see him in them, I always think he must ha' had a Mormon for a father! He an' th' Covey can't abide each other; th' pair o' them is always at it, thryin' to best each other. There'll be blood dhrawn one o' these days.

FLUTHER. How is it that Clitheroe himself, now, doesn't have anythin' to do with th' Citizen Army? A couple o' months ago, an' you'd hardly ever see him without his gun, an' th' Red Hand o' Liberty Hall in his hat.

MRS. GOGAN. Just because he wasn't made a Captain of. He wasn't goin' to be in anything where he couldn't be conspishuous. He was so cocksure o' being made one that he bought a Sam Browne belt, an' was always puttin' it on an' standin' at the door showin' it off, till th' man came an' put out th' street lamps on him. God, I think he used to bring it to bed with him! But I'm tellin' you herself was delighted that that cock didn't crow, for she's like a clockin' hen if he leaves her sight for a minute.
(*While she is talking she takes up book after book from the table, looks into each of them in a near-sighted way, and then leaves them back. She now lifts up the sword, and proceeds to examine it.*)

MRS. GOGAN. Be th' look of it, this must ha' been a general's sword. . . . All th' gold lace an' th' fine figaries on it. . . . Sure it's twiced too big for him.

FLUTHER. A-ah; it's a baby's rattle he ought to have, an' he as he is with thoughts tossin' in his head of what may happen to him on th' day o' judgment.
(PETER *has entered, and seeing* MRS. GOGAN *with the sword, goes over to her, pulls it resentfully out of her hands, and marches into the room, Back, without speaking.*)

MRS. GOGAN (*as* PETER *whips the*

sword). Oh excuse me! . . . (*To* FLUTHER) Isn't he th' surly oul' rascal.

FLUTHER. Take no notice of him. . . . You'd think he was dumb, but when you get his goat, or he has a few jars up, he's vice versa. (*He coughs.*)

MRS. GOGAN (*she has now sidled over as far as the shirt hanging on the chair*). Oh, you've got a cold on you, Fluther.

FLUTHER (*carelessly*). Ah, it's only a little one.

MRS. GOGAN. You'd want to be careful, all th' same. I knew a woman, a big lump of a woman, red-faced an' round-bodied, a little awkard on her feet; you'd think, to look at her, she could put out her two arms an' lift a two-storied house on th' top of her head; got a ticklin' in her throat, an' a little cough, an' th' next mornin' she had a little catchin' in her chest, an' they had just time to wet her lips with a little rum, an' off she went. (*She begins to look at and handle the shirt.*)

FLUTHER (*a little nervously*). It's only a little cold I have; there's nothing derogatory wrong with me.

MRS. GOGAN. I dunno; there's many a man this minute lowerin' a pint, thinkin' of a woman, or pickin' out a winner, or doin' work as you're doin', while th' hearse dhrawn be th' horses with the black plumes is dhriven up to his own hall door, an' a voice that he doesn't hear is muttherin' in his ear, "Earth to earth, an' ashes t' ashes, an' dust to dust."

FLUTHER (*faintly*). A man in th pink o' health should have a holy horror of allowin' thoughts o' death to be festherin' in his mind, for (*with a frightened cough*) be God, I think I'm afther gettin' a little catch in me chest that time—it's a creepy thing to be thinkin' about.

MRS. GOGAN. It is, an' it isn't; it's both bad an' good. . . . It always gives meself a kind o' thresspassin' joy to feel meself movin' along in a mournin' coach, an' me thinkin' that, maybe, th' next funeral'll be me own, an' glad, in a quiet way, that this is somebody else's.

FLUTHER. An' a curious kind of a gaspin' fer breath—I hope there's nothin' derogatory wrong with me.

MRS. GOGAN (*examining the shirt*). Frills on it, like a woman's petticoat.

FLUTHER. Suddenly gettin' hot, an' then, just as suddenly, gettin' cold.

MRS. GOGAN (*holding out the shirt towards* FLUTHER). How would you like to be wearin' this Lord Mayor's nightdhress, Fluther?

FLUTHER (*vehemently*). Blast you an' your nightshirt! Is a man fermentin' with fear to stick th' showin' off to him of a thing that looks like a shinin' shroud?

MRS. GOGAN. Oh, excuse me!
(PETER *has again entered, and he pulls the shirt from the hands of* MRS. GOGAN, *replacing it on the chair. He returns to the room.*)

PETER (*as he goes out*). Well, God Almighty, give me patience!

MRS. GOGAN (*to* PETER). Oh, excuse me!
(*There is heard a cheer from the men working outside on the street, followed by the clang of tools being thrown down, then silence. The glare of the gasolene light diminishes and finally goes out.*)

MRS. GOGAN (*running into the back room to look out of the window*). What's the men repairin' th' streets cheerin' for?

FLUTHER (*sitting down weakly on a chair*). You can't sneeze but that oul' one wants to know th' why an' th' wherefore. . . . I feel as dizzy as bedamned! I hope I didn't give up th' beer too suddenly.
(THE COVEY *comes in by door, Right. He is about twenty-five, tall, thin, with lines on his face that form a perpetual protest against life as he conceives it to be. Heavy seams fall from each side of nose, down around his lips, as if they were suspenders keeping his mouth from falling. He speaks in a slow, wailing drawl; more rapidly when he is excited. He is dressed in dungarees, and is wearing a vivdly red tie. He flings his cap with a gesture of disgust on the table, and begins to take off his overalls.*)

MRS. GOGAN (*to* THE COVEY, *as she runs back into the room*). What's after happenin', Covey?

THE COVEY (*with contempt*). Th' job's stopped. They've been mobilized to march in th' demonstration to-night undher th' Plough an' the Stars. Didn't you hear them cheerin', th' mugs. They have to renew their political baptismal vows to be faithful in seculo seculorum.

FLUTHER (*forgetting his fear in his indignation*). There's no reason to bring religion into it. I think we ought to have as great a regard for religion as we can, so as to keep it out of as many things as possible.

THE COVEY (*pausing in the taking off of his dungarees*). Oh, you're one o' the boys that climb into religion as high as a short Mass on Sunday mornin's? I suppose you'll be singin' songs o' Sion an' songs o' Tara at the meetin', too.

FLUTHER. We're all Irishmen, anyhow, aren't we?

THE COVEY (*with hand outstretched, and in a professional tone*). Look here, comrade, there's no such thing as an Irishman, or an Englishman, or a German or a Turk; we're all only human bein's. Scientifically speakin', it's all a question of the accidental gatherin' together of mollycewels an' atoms.
(PETER *comes in with a collar in his hand. He goes over to mirror, Left, and proceeds to try to put it on.*)

FLUTHER. Mollycewels an' atoms! D'ye think I'm goin' to listen to you thryin' to juggle Fluther's mind with complicated cunundhrums of mollycewels an' atoms?

THE COVEY (*rather loudly*). There's nothin' complicated in it. There's no fear o' th' Church tellin' you that mollycewels is a stickin' together of millions of atoms o' sodium, carbon, potassium o' iodide, etcetera, that, accordin' to th' way they're mixed, make a flower, a fish, a star that you see shinin' in th' sky, or a man with a big brain like me, or a man with a little brain like you!

FLUTHER (*more loudly still*). There's no necessity to be raisin' your voice; shoutin's no manifestin' forth of a growin' mind.

PETER (*struggling with his collar*). God, give me patience with this thing. . . . She makes these collars as stiff with starch as a shinin' band o' solid steel! She does it purposely to thry an' twart me. If I can't get it on th' singlet, how, in th' Name o' God, am I goin' to get it on th' shirt?

THE COVEY (*loudly*). There's no use o' arguin' with you; it's education you want, comrade.

FLUTHER. The Covey an' God made th' world, I suppose, wha'?

THE COVEY. When I hear some men talkin' I'm inclined to disbelieve that th' world's eight-hundhred million years old, for it's not long since th' fathers o' some o' them crawled out o' th' sheltherin' slime o' the sea.

MRS. GOGAN (*from room at back*). There, they're afther formin' fours, an' now they're goin' to march away.

FLUTHER (*scornfully*). Mollycewels! (*He begins to untie his apron*) What about Adam an' Eve?

THE COVEY. Well, what about them?

FLUTHER (*fiercely*). What about them, you?

THE COVEY. Adam an' Eve! Is that as far as you've got? Are you still thinkin' there was nobody in the world before Adam an' Eve? (*Loudly*) Did you ever hear, man, of th' skeleton of th' man o' Java?

PETER (*casting the collar from him*). Blast it, blast it, blast it!

FLUTHER (*viciously folding his apron*). Ah, you're not goin' to be let tap your rubbidge o' thoughts into th' mind o' Fluther.

THE COVEY. You're afraid to listen to th' thruth!

FLUTHER. Who's afraid?

THE COVEY. You are.

FLUTHER. G'way, you wurum!

THE COVEY. Who's a worum?

FLUTHER. You are, or you wouldn't talk th' way you're talkin'.

THE COVEY. Th' oul', ignorant savage leppin' up in you, when science shows you that th' head of your god is an empty one. Well, I hope you're enjoyin' th' blessin' o' havin' to live be th' sweat of your brow.

FLUTHER. You'll be kickin' an' yellin' for th' priest yet, me boyo. I'm not goin' to stand silent an' simple listenin' to a thick like you makin' a maddenin' mockery o' God Almighty. It 'ud be a nice derogatory thing on me conscience, an' me dyin', to look back in rememberin' shame of talkin' to a word-weavin' little ignorant yahoo of a red flag Socialist!

MRS. GOGAN (*she has returned to the front room, and has wandered around looking at things in general, and is now in front of the fireplace looking at the picture hanging over it*). For God's sake, Fluther, dhrop it; there's always th' makin's of a row in th' mention of religion. . . . (*Looking at picture*) God bless us, it's a naked woman!

FLUTHER (*coming over to look at it*). What's undher it? (*Reading*) "Georgina: The Sleepin' Vennis." Oh, that's a terrible picture; oh, that's a shocking picture! Oh, th' one that got that taken, she must have been a prime lassie!

PETER (*who also has come over to look, laughing, with his body bent at the waist, and his head slightly tilted back*). Hee, hee, hee, hee, hee!

FLUTHER (*indignantly, to* PETER). What are you hee, hee-in' for? That's a nice thing to be hee, hee-in' at. Where's your morality, man?

MRS. GOGAN. God forgive us, it's not right to be lookin' at it.

FLUTHER. It's nearly a derogatory thing to be in th' room where it is.

MRS. GOGAN (*giggling hysterically*). I couldn't stop any longer in th' same room with three men, afther lookin' at it! (*She goes out.*)
(THE COVEY, *who has divested himself of his dungarees, throws them with a contemptuous motion on top of* PETER'S *white shirt.*)

PETER (*plaintively*). Where are you throwin' them? Are you thryin' to twart an' torment me again?

THE COVEY. Who's thryin' to twart you?

PETER (*flinging the dungarees violently on the floor*). You're not goin' to make me lose me temper, me young Covey.

THE COVEY (*flinging the white shirt on the floor*). If you're Nora's pet, aself, you're not goin' to get your way in everything.

PETER (*plaintively, with his eyes looking up at the ceiling*). I'll say nothin'. . . . I'll leave you to th' day when th' all-pitiful, all-merciful, all-lovin' God'll be handin' you to the angels to be rievin' an' roastin' you, tearin' an' tormentin' you, burnin' an' blastin' you!

THE COVEY. Aren't you th' little malignant oul' bastard, you lemon-whiskered oul swine!
(PETER *runs to the sword, draws*

it, and makes for THE COVEY, *who dodges him around the table;* PETER *has no intention of striking, but* THE COVEY *wants to take no chances.*)

THE COVEY (*dodging*). Fluther, hold him, there. It's a nice thing to have a lunatic like this lashin' around with a lethal weapon!

(THE COVEY *darts out of room, Right, slamming the door in the face of* PETER.)

PETER (*battering and pulling at the door*). Lemme out, lemme out; isn't it a poor thing for a man who wouldn't say a word against his greatest enemy to have to listen to that Covey's twartin' animosities, shovin' poor, patient people into a lashin' out of curses that darken his soul with th' shadow of th' wrath of th' last day!

FLUTHER. Why d'ye take notice of him? If he seen you didn't, he'd say nothin' derogatory.

PETER. I'll make him stop his laughin' an' leerin', jibin' an' jeerin' an' scarifyin' people with his corner-boy insinuations! . . . He's always thryin' to rouse me: if it's not a song, it's a whistle; if it isn't a whistle, it's a cough. But you can taunt an' taunt—'m laughin' at you; he, hee, hee, hee, hee, heee!

THE COVEY (*singing through the keyhole*):

> Dear harp o' me counthry, in
> darkness I found thee,
> The cold chain of silence had
> hung o'er thee long—

PETER (*frantically*). Jasus, d'ye hear that? D'ye hear him soundin' forth his divil-souled song o' provocation?

THE COVEY (*singing as before*):

> When proudly, me own island
> harp, I unbound thee,
> An' gave all thy chords to light,
> freedom an' song!

PETER (*battering at door*). When I get out I'll do for you, I'll do for you, I'll do for you!

THE COVEY (*through the keyhole*). Cuckoo-oo!

(NORA *enters by door, Right. She is a young woman of twenty-two, alert, swift, full of nervous energy, and a little anxious to get on in the world. The firm lines of her face are considerably opposed by a soft, amorous mouth, and gentle eyes. When her firmness fails her, she persuades with her feminine charm. She is dressed in a tailor-made costume, and wears around her neck a silver fox fur.*)

NORA (*running in and pushing* PETER *away from the door*). Oh, can I not turn me back but th' two o' yous are at it like a pair of fightin' cocks! Uncle Peter . . . Uncle Peter . . . UNCLE PETER!

PETER (*vociferously*). Oh, Uncle Peter, Uncle Peter be damned! D'ye think I'm goin' to give a free pass to th' young Covey to turn me whole life into a Holy Manual o' penances an' martyrdoms?

THE COVEY (*angrily rushing into the room*). If you won't exercise some sort o' conthrol over that Uncle Peter o' yours, there'll be a funeral, an' it won't be me that'll be in th' hearse!

NORA (*between* PETER *and* THE COVEY, *to* THE COVEY). Are yous always goin' to be tearin' down th' little bit of respectability that a body's thryin' to build up? Am I always goin' to be havin' to nurse yous into th' hardy habit o' thryin' to keep up a little bit of appearance?

THE COVEY. Why weren't you here to see th' way he run at me with th' sword?

PETER. What did you call me a lemon-whiskered oul' swine for?

NORA. If th' two o' yous don't thry to make a generous altheration in your goin's on, an' keep on thryin' t' inaugurate th' customs o' th' rest o' th' house into this place, yous can flit into other lodgin's where your bowsey battlin' 'ill meet, maybe, with an encore.

PETER (*to* NORA). Would you like to be called a lemon-whiskered oul' swine?

NORA. If you attempt to wag that sword of yours at anybody again, it'll have to be taken off you an' put in a safe place away from babies that don't know th' danger o' them things.

PETER (*at entrance to room, Back*). Well, I'm not goin' to let anybody call me a lemon-whiskered oul' swine. (*He goes in.*)

FLUTHER (*trying the door*). Openin' an' shuttin' now with a well-mannered motion, like a door of a select bar in a high-class pub.

NORA (*to* THE COVEY, *as she lays table for tea*). An', once for all, Willie, you'll have to thry to deliver yourself from th' desire to practice o' provokin' oul' Peter into a wild forgetfulness of what's proper an' allowable in a respectable home.

THE COVEY. Well, let him mind his own business, then. Yestherday, I caught him hee-hee-in' out of him an' he readin' bits out of Jenersky's *Thesis on th' Origin, Development an' Consolidation of th' Evolutionary Idea of th' Proletariat.*

NORA. Now, let it end at that, for God's sake; Jack'll be in any minute, an' I'm not goin' to have th' quiet of his evenin' tossed about in an everlastin' uproar between you an' Uncle Pether. (*To* FLUTHER) Well, did you manage to settle th' lock, yet, Mr. Good?

FLUTHER (*opening and shutting door*). It's betther than a new one, now, Miss Clitheroe; it's almost ready to open and shut of its own accord.

NORA (*giving him a coin*). You're a whole man. How many pints will that get you?

FLUTHER (*seriously*). Ne'er a one at all, Mrs. Clitheroe, for Fluther's on th' wather wagon now. You could stan' where you're stannin' chantin', "Have a glass o' malt, Fluther; Fluther, have a glass o' malt," till th' bells would be ringin' th' ould year out an' th' New Year in, an' you'd have as much chance o' movin' Fluther as a tune on a tin whistle would move a deaf man an' he dead.

(*As* NORA *is opening and shutting door,* MRS. BESSIE BURGESS *appears at it. She is a woman of forty, vigorously built. Her face is a dogged one, hardened by toil, and a little coarsened by drink. She looks scornfully and viciously at* NORA *for a few moments before she speaks.*)

BESSIE. Puttin' a new lock on her door . . . afraid her poor neighbours ud break through an' steal. . . . (*In a loud tone*) Maybe, now, they're a damned sight more honest than your ladyship . . . checkin' th' children playin' on th' stairs . . . gettin' on th' nerves of your ladyship. . . . Complainin' about Bessie Burgess singin' her hymns at night, when she has a few up. . . . (*She comes in half-way on the threshold and screams*) Bessie Burgess 'll sing whenever she damn well likes!

(NORA *tries to shut door, but* BESSIE *violently shoves it in, and, gripping* NORA *by the shoulders, shakes her.*)

BESSIE. You little over-dhressed throllope, you, for one pin, I'd paste th' white face o' you!

NORA (*frightened*). Fluther, Fluther!

FLUTHER (*running over and breaking the hold of* BESSIE *from* NORA). Now, now, Bessie, Bessie, leave poor Mrs. Clitheroe alone; she'd do no one any harm, an' minds no one's business but her own.

BESSIE. Why is she always thryin' to speak proud things, an' lookin' like a mighty one in th' congregation o' th' people!

(NORA *sinks frightened on to the couch as* JACK CLITHEROE *enters. He is a tall, well-made fellow of twenty-five. His face has none of the strength of* NORA's. *It is a face in which is the desire for authority, without the power to attain it.*)

CLITHEROE (*excitedly*). What's up? what's afther happenin'?

FLUTHER. Nothin', Jack. Nothin'. It's all over now. Come on, Bessie, come on.

CLITHEROE (*to* NORA). What's wrong, Nora? Did she say anything to you?

NORA. She was bargin' out of her, an' I only told her to g'up ower o' that to her own place; an' before I knew where I was, she flew at me like a tiger, an' thried to guzzle me!

CLITHEROE (*going to door and speaking to* BESSIE). Get up to your own place, Mrs. Burgess, and don't you be interferin' with my wife, or it'll be th' worse for you. . . . Go on, go on!

BESSIE (*as* CLITHEROE *is pushing her out*). Mind who you're pushin', now. . . . I attend me place o' worship, anyhow . . . not like some o' them that go to neither church, chapel nor meetin' house. . . . If

me son was home from th' threnches he'd see me righted.
(BESSIE *and* FLUTHER *depart, and* CLITHEROE *closes the door.*)

CLITHEROE (*going over to* NORA, *and putting his arm round her*). There, don't mind that old bitch, Nora, darling; I'll soon put a stop to her interferin'.

NORA. Some day or another, when I'm here be meself, she'll come in an' do somethin' desperate.

CLITHEROE (*kissing her*). Oh, sorra fear of her doin' anythin' desperate. I'll talk to her to-morrow when she's sober. A taste o' me mind that'll shock her into the sensibility of behavin' herself!
(NORA *gets up and settles the table. She sees the dungarees on the floor and stands looking at them, then she turns to* THE COVEY, *who is reading Jenersky's "Thesis" at the fire.*)

NORA. Willie, is that th' place for your dungarees?

THE COVEY (*getting up and lifting them from the floor*). Ah, they won't do th' floor any harm, will they? (*He carries them into room, Back.*)

NORA (*calling*). Uncle Peter, now Uncle Peter; tea's ready.
(PETER *and* THE COVEY *come in from room, Back, they all sit down to tea.* PETER *is in full dress of the Foresters: green coat, gold braided; white breeches, top boots, frilled shirt. He carries the slouch hat, with the white ostrich plume, and the sword in his hands. They eat for a few moments in silence,* THE COVEY *furtively looking at* PETER *with scorn in his eyes.* PETER *knows it and is fidgety.*)

THE COVEY (*provokingly*). Another cut o' bread, Uncle Peter?
(PETER *maintains a dignified silence.*)

CLITHEROE. It's sure to be a great meetin' to-night. We ought to go, Nora.

NORA (*decisively*). I won't go, Jack; you can go if you wish.
(*A pause.*)

THE COVEY. D'ye want th' sugar, Uncle Peter?

PETER (*explosively*). Now, are you goin' to start your thryin' an' your twartin' again?

NORA. Now, Uncle Peter, you mustn't be so touchy; Willie has only assed you if you wanted th' sugar.

PETER. He doesn't care a damn whether I want th' sugar or no. He's only thryin to twart me!

NORA (*angrily, to* THE COVEY). Can't you let him alone, Willie? If he wants the sugar, let him stretch his hand out an' get it himself!

THE COVEY (*to* PETER). Now, if you want the sugar you can stretch out your hand and get it yourself!

CLITHEROE. To-night is th' first chance that Brennan has got of showing himself off since they made a Captain of him—why, God only knows. It'll be a treat to see him swankin' it at th' head of the Citizen Army carryin' th' flag of the Plough an' th' Stars. . . . (*Looking roguishly at* NORA) He was sweet on you, once, NORA?

NORA. He may have been. . . . I never liked him. I always thought he was a bit of a thick.

THE COVEY. They're bringin' nice disgrace on that banner now.

CLITHEROE (*remonstratively*). How are they bringin' disgrace on it?

THE COVEY (*snappily*). Because it's a Labour flag, an' was never meant for politics. . . . What does th' design of th' field plough, bearin' on it th' stars of th' heavenly plough, mean, if it's not Communism? It's a flag that should only be used when we're buildin' th' barricades to fight for a Workers' Republic!

PETER (*with a puff of derision*). P-phuh.

THE COVEY (*angrily*). What are phuhin' out o' you for? Your mind is th' mind of a mummy. (*Rising*) I betther go an' get a good place to have a look at Ireland's warriors passin' by. (*He goes into room, Left, and returns with his cap.*)

NORA (*to* THE COVEY). Oh, Willie, brush your clothes before you go.

THE COVEY. Oh, they'll do well enough.

NORA. Go an' brush them; th' brush is in th' drawer there.

(THE COVEY *goes to the drawer, muttering, gets the brush, and starts to brush his clothes.*)

THE COVEY (*singing at* PETER, *as he does so*):

Oh, where's th' slave so lowly,
Condemn'd to chains unholy,
Who, could he burst his bonds at first,
Would pine beneath them slowly?

We tread th' land that . . . bore us,
Th' green flag glitters . . . o'er us,
Th' friends we've tried are by our side,
An' th' foe we hate . . . before us!

PETER (*leaping to his feet in a whirl of rage*). Now, I'm tellin' you, me young Covey, once for all, that I'll not stick any longer these tittherin' taunts of yours, rovin' around to sing your slights an' slandhers, reddenin' th' mind of a man to th' thinkin' an' sayin' of things that sicken his soul with sin! (*Hysterically; lifting up a cup to fling at* THE COVEY) Be God, I'll——

CLITHEROE (*catching his arm*). Now then, none o' that, none o' that!

NORA. Uncle Pether, Uncle Pether, UNCLE PETHER!

THE COVEY (*at the door about to go out*). Isn't that th' malignant oul' varmint! Lookin' like th' illegitimate son of an illegitimate child of a corporal in th' Mexican army! (*He goes out.*)

PETER (*plaintively*). He's afther leavin' me now in such a state of agitation that I won't be able to do meself justice when I'm marchin' to th' meetin'.

NORA (*jumping up*). Oh, for God's sake, here, buckle your sword on, and go to your meetin' so that we'll have at least one hour of peace! (*She proceeds to belt on the sword.*)

CLITHEROE (*irritably*). For God's sake hurry him up ou' o' this, Nora.

PETER. Are yous all goin' to thry to start to twart me now?

NORA (*putting on his plumed hat*). S-s-sh. Now, your hat's on, your house is thatched; off you pop! (*She gently pushes him from her.*)

PETER (*going and turning as he reaches the door*). Now, if that young Covey—

NORA. Go on, go on.
(*He goes.*)
(CLITHEROE *sits down in the lounge, lights a cigarette, and looks thoughtfully into the fire.* NORA *takes the things from the table, placing them on the chest of drawers. There is a pause, then she swiftly comes over to him and sits beside him.*)

NORA (*softly*). A penny for them, Jack!

CLITHEROE. Me? Oh, I was thinkin' of nothing.

NORA. You were thinkin' of th' . . . meetin' . . . Jack. When we were courtin' an' I wanted to you to go, you'd say, "Oh, to hell with meetin's," an' that you felt lonely in cheerin' crowds when I was absent. An' we weren't a month married when you began that you couldn't keep away from them.

CLITHEROE. Oh, that's enough about th' meetin'. It looks as if you wanted me to go th' way you're talkin'. You were always at me to give up th' Citizen Army, an' I gave it up; surely that ought to satisfy you.

NORA. Ay, you gave it up—because you got th' sulks when they didn't make a Captain of you. It wasn't for my sake, Jack.

CLITHEROE. For your sake or no, you're benefitin' by it, aren't you? I didn't forget this was your birthday, did I? (*He puts his arm around her.*) And you liked your new hat; didn't you, didn't you? (*He kisses her rapidly several times.*)

NORA (*panting*). Jack, Jack; please, Jack! I thought you were tired of that sort of thing long ago.

CLITHEROE. Well, you're finding out now that I amn't tired of it yet, anyhow. Mrs. Clitheroe doesn't want to be kissed, sure she doesn't? (*He kisses her again.*) Little, little red-lipped Nora!

NORA (*coquettishly removing his arm from around her*). Oh, yes, your little, little red-lipped Nora's a sweet little girl when th' fit seizes you; but your little, little red-lipped Nora has to clean your boots every mornin', all the same.

CLITHEROE (*with a movement of irritation*). Oh, well, if we're goin' to be snotty!
(*A pause.*)

NORA. It's lookin' like as if it was you that was goin' to be . . . snotty! Bridlin' up with bittherness, th' minute a body attempts t'open her mouth.

CLITHEROE. It is any wondher, turnin' a tendher sayin' into a meanin' o' malice an' spite!

NORA. It's hard for a body to be always keepin' her mind bent on makin' thoughts that'll be no longer than th' length of your own satisfaction.
(*A pause.*)

NORA (*standing up*). If we're goin' to dhribble th' time away sittin' here like a pair o' cranky mummies, I'd be as well sewin' or doin' something about th' place.
(*She looks appealingly at him for a few moments; he doesn't speak. She swiftly sits down beside him, and puts her arm around his neck.*)

NORA (*imploringly*). Ah, Jack, don't be so cross!

CLITHEROE (*doggedly*). Cross? I'm not cross; I'm not a bit cross. It was yourself started it.

NORA (*coaxingly*). I didn't mean to say anything out o' th' way. You take a body up too quickly, Jack. (*In an ordinary tone as if nothing of an angry nature had been said*) You didn't offer me me evenin' allowance yet.
(CLITHEROE *silently takes out a cigarette for her and himself and lights both.*)

NORA (*trying to make conversation*). How quiet th' house is now; they must be all out.

CLITHEROE (*rather shortly*). I suppose so.

NORA (*rising from the seat*). I'm longin' to show you me new hat, to see what you think of it. Would you like to see it?

CLITHEROE. Ah, I don't mind.
(NORA *suppresses a sharp reply, hesitates for a moment, then gets the hat, puts it on and stands before* CLITHEROE.)

NORA. Well, how does Mr. Clitheroe like me new hat?

CLITHEROE. It suits you, Nora, it does right enough.
(*He stands up, puts his hand beneath her chin, and tilts her head up. She looks at him roguishly. He bends down and kisses her.*)

NORA. Here, sit down, an' don't let me hear another cross word out of

you for th' rest o' the night.
(*They sit down.*)

CLITHEROE (*with his arms around her*). Little, little, red-lipped Nora!

NORA (*with a coaxing movement of her body towards him*). Jack!

CLITHEROE (*tightening his arms around her*). Well?

NORA. You haven't sung me a song since our honeymoon. Sing me one now, do . . . please, Jack!

CLITHEROE. What song? "Since Maggie Went Away"?

NORA. Ah, no, Jack, not that; it's too sad. "When You Said You Loved Me."
(*Clearing his throat* CLITHEROE *thinks for a moment, and then begins to sing.* NORA, *putting an arm around him nestles her head on his breast and listens delightedly.*)

CLITHEROE (*singing verses following to the air of "When You and I Were Young, Maggie"*):

Th' violets were scenting th' woods, Nora,
Displaying their charm to th' bee,
When I first said I lov'd only you, Nora,
An' you said you lov'd only me!

Th' chestnut blooms gleam'd through th' glade, Nora,
A robin sang loud from a tree,
When I first said I lov'd only you, Nora,
An' you said you lov'd only me!

Th' golden-rob'd daffodils shone, Nora,
An' danc'd in th' breeze on th' lea;
When I first said I lov'd only you, Nora,
An' you said you lov'd only me!

Th' trees, birds an' bees sang a song, Nora,
Of happier transports to be,
When I first said I lov'd only you, Nora,
An' you said you lov'd only me!

(NORA *kisses him.*)
(*A knock is heard at the door, Right; a pause as they listen.* NORA *clings closely to* CLITHEROE. *Another knock, more imperative than the first.*)

CLITHEROE. I wonder who can that be, now?

NORA (*a little nervous*). Take no notice of it, Jack; they'll go away in a minute.
(*Another knock, followed by a voice.*)

VOICE. Commandant Clitheroe, Commandant Clitheroe, are you there? A messenger from General Jim Connolly.

CLITHEROE. Damn it, it's Captain Brennan.

NORA (*anxiously*). Don't mind him, don't mind, Jack. Don't break our happiness. . . . Pretend we're not in. . . . Let us forget everything to-night but our two selves!

CLITHEROE (*reassuringly*). Don't be alarmed darling; I'll just see what he wants, an' send him about his business.

NORA (*tremulously*). No, no. Please, Jack; don't open it. Please, for your own little Nora's sake!

CLITHEROE (*rising to open the door*). Now don't be silly, Nora. (CLITHEROE *opens door, and admits a young man in the full uniform of the Irish Citizen Army—green suit; slouch green hat caught up at one side by a small Red Hand badge; Sam Browne belt, with a revolver in the holster. He carries a letter in his hand. When he comes in he smartly salutes* CLITHEROE. *The young man is* CAPTAIN BRENNAN.)

CAPT. BRENNAN (*giving the letter to* CLITHEROE). A dispatch from General Connolly.

CLITHEROE (*reading. While he is doing so,* BRENNAN'S *eyes are fixed on* NORA, *who droops as she sits on the lounge*). "Commandant Clitheroe is to take command of the eighth battalion of the I.C.A. which will assemble to proceed to the meeting at nine o'clock. He is to see that all units are provided with full equipment: two days' rations and fifty pounds of ammunition. At two o'clock A.M. the army will leave Liberty Hall for a reconnaissance attack on Dublin Castle. —Com.-Gen. Connolly."

CLITHEROE. I don't understand this. Why does General Connolly call me Commandant?

CAPT. BRENNAN. Th' Staff appointed you Commandant, and th' General agreed with their selection.

CLITHEROE. When did this happen?

CAPT. BRENNAN. A fortnight ago.

CLITHEROE. How is it word was never sent to me?

CAPT. BRENNAN. Word was sent to you. . . . I meself brought it.

CLITHEROE. Who did you give it to, then?

CAPT. BRENNAN (*after a pause*). I think I gave it to Mrs. Clitheroe, there.

CLITHEROE. Nora, d'ye hear that? (NORA *makes no answer.*)

CLITHEROE (*there is a note of hardness in his voice*). Nora . . . Captain Brennan says he brought a letter to me from General Connolly, and that he gave it to you. . . . Where is it? What did you do with it?

NORA (*running over to him, and pleadingly putting her arms around him*). Jack, please Jack, don't go out to-night an' I'll tell you; I'll explain everything. . . . Send him away, an' stay with your own little red-lipp'd Nora.

CLITHEROE (*removing her arms from around him*). None o' this nonsense, now; I want to know what you did with th' letter?
(NORA *goes slowly to the lounge and sits down.*)

CLITHEROE (*angrily*). Why didn't you give me th' letter? What did you do with it? . . . (*He shakes her by the shoulder.*) What did you do with th' letter?

NORA (*flaming up*). I burned it, I burned it! That's what I did with it! Is General Connolly an' th' Citizen Army goin' to be your only care? Is your home goin' to be only a place to rest in? Am I goin' to be only somethin' to provide merry-makin' at night for you? Your vanity'll be th' ruin of you an' me yet. . . . That's what's movin' you: because they've made an officer of you, you'll make a glorious cause of what you're doin', while your little red-lipp'd Nora can do on sittin' here, makin' a companion of th' loneliness of th' night!

CLITHEROE (*fiercely*). You burned it, did you? (*He grips her arm.*) Well, me good lady—

NORA. Let go—you're hurtin' me!

CLITHEROE. You deserve to be hurt. . . . Any letther that comes to me for th' future, take care that I get it. . . . D'ye hear—take care that I get it!
(*He goes to the chest of drawers and takes out a Sam Browne belt, which he puts on, and then puts a revolver in the holster. He puts on his hat, and looks towards* NORA.)

CLITHEROE (*at door, about to go out*). You needn't wait up for me; if I'm in at all, it won't be before six in th' morning.

NORA (*bitterly*). I don't care if you never came back!

CLITHEROE (*to* CAPT. BRENNAN). Come along, Ned.
(*They go out; there is a pause.* NORA *pulls the new hat from her head and with a bitter movement flings it to the other end of the room. There is a gentle knock at door, Right, which opens, and* MOLLSER *comes into the room. She is about fifteen, but looks to be only about ten, for the ravages of consumption have shrivelled her up. She is pitifully worn, walks feebly, and frequently coughs. She goes over to* NORA.)

MOLLSER (*to* NORA). Mother's gone to th' meetin', and' I was feelin' terribly lonely, so I come down to see if you'd let me sit with you, thinkin' you mightn't be goin' yourself. . . . I do be terrible afraid I'll die sometime when I'm be meself. . . . I often envy you, Mrs. Clitheroe, seein' th' health you have, an' th' lovely place you have here, an' wondherin' if I'll ever be sthrong enough to be keepin' a home together for a man. Oh, this must be some more o' the Dublin Fusiliers flyin' off to the front.
(*Just before* MOLLSER *ceases to speak, there is heard in the distance the music of a brass band playing a regiment to the boat on the way to the front. The tune that is being played is "It's a Long Way to Tipperary"; as the band comes*

to the chorus, the regiment is swinging into the street by NORA'S *house, and the voices of the soldiers can be heard lustily singing the chorus of the song.*)

It's a long way to Tipperary; it's a long way to go,
It's a long way to Tipperary; to the sweetest girl I know!
Goodbye Piccadilly, farewell Leicester Square.
It's a long way to Tipperary, but my heart's right there!

(NORA *and* MOLLSER *remain silently listening. As the chorus ends, and the music is faint in the distance again,* BESSIE BURGESS *appears at door, Right, which* MOLLSER *has left open.*)

BESSIE (*speaking in towards the room*). There's th' men marchin' out into th' dhread dimness o' danger, while th' lice is crawlin' about feedin' on th' fatness o' the land! But yous'll not escape from th' arrow that flieth be night, or th' sickness that wasteth be day. . . . An' ladyship an' all, as some o' them may be, they'll be scatthered abroad, like the dust in the darkness!

(BESSIE *goes away;* NORA *steals over and quietly shuts the door. She comes back to the lounge and wearily throws herself on it beside* MOLLSER.)

MOLLSER (*after a pause and a cough*). Is there anybody goin', Mrs. Clitheroe, with a titther o' sense?

CURTAIN

ACT TWO

SCENE: *A commodious public-house at the corner of the street in which the meeting is being addressed from Platform No. 1. It is the south corner of the public-house that is visible to the audience. The counter, beginning at Back about one-fourth of the width of the space shown, comes across two-thirds of the length of the stage, and, taking a circular sweep, passes out of sight to Left. On the counter are beer-pulls, glasses and a carafe. The other three-fourths of the Back is occupied by a tall, wide, two-paned window. Beside this window at the Right is a small, box-like, panelled snug. Next to the snug is a double swing door, the entrance to that particular end of the house. Farther on is a shelf on which customers may rest their drinks. Underneath the window is a cushioned seat. Behind the counter at Back can be seen the shelves running the whole length of the counter. On these shelves can be seen the end (or the beginning) of rows of bottles. The* BARMAN *is seen wiping the part of the counter which is in view.* ROSIE *is standing at the counter toying with what remains of a half of whisky in a wine-glass. She is a sturdy, well-shaped girl of twenty; pretty and pert in manner. She is wearing a cream blouse, with an obviously suggestive glad neck; a grey tweed dress, brown stockings and shoes.*

The blouse and most of the dress are hidden by a black shawl. She has no hat, and in her hair is jauntily set a cheap, glittering, jewelled ornament. It is an hour later.

BARMAN (*wiping counter*). Nothin' much doin' in your line to-night, Rosie?

ROSIE. Curse 'o God on th' haporth, hardly, Tom. There isn't much notice taken of a pretty petticoat of a night like this. . . . They're all in a holy mood. Th' solemn-lookin' dials on th' whole o' them an' they marchin' to th' meetin'. You'd think they were th' glorious company of th' saints an' th' noble army of martyrs thrampin' through th' sthreets of paradise. They're all thinkin' of higher things than a girl's garthers. . . . It's a tremendous meetin'; four platforms they have—there's one o' them just outside opposite th' window.

BARMAN. Oh, ay; sure when th' speaker comes (*motioning with his hand*) to th' near end, here, you can see him plain, an' hear nearly everythin' he's spoutin' out of him.

ROSIE. It's no joke thryin' to make up fifty-five shillin's a week for your keep an' laundhry, an' then taxin' you a quid for your own room if you bring home a friend for th' night. . . . If I could only put by a couple of quid for a swankier outfit, everythin' in the garden ud look lovely—

BARMAN. Whisht, till we hear what he's sayin'.

(*Through the window is silhouetted the figure of a tall man who is speaking to the crowd. The* BARMAN *and* ROSIE *look out of the window and listen.*)

THE VOICE OF THE MAN. It is a glorious thing to see arms in the hands of Irishmen. We must accustom ourselves to the thought of arms, we must accustom ourselves to the sight of arms, we must accustom ourselves to the use of arms. . . . Bloodshed is a cleansing and sanctifying thing, and the nation that regards it as the final horror has lost its manhood. . . . There are many things more horrible than bloodshed, and slavery is one of them!

(*The figure moves away towards the Right, and is lost to sight and hearing.*)

ROSIE. It's th' sacred thruth, mind you, what that man's afther sayin'.

BARMAN If I was only a little younger, I'd be plungin' mad into th' middle of it!

ROSIE (*who is still looking out of the window*). Oh, here's th' two gems runnin' over again for their oil!

(PETER *and* FLUTHER *enter tumultuously. They are hot, and full and hasty with the things they have seen and heard. Emotion is bubbling up in them, so that when they drink, and when they speak, they drink and speak with the fullness of emotional passion.* PETER *leads the way to the counter.*)

PETER (*splutteringly to* BARMAN). Two halves . . . (*To* FLUTHER). A meetin' like this always makes me feel as if I could dhrink Loch Erinn dhry!

FLUTHER. You couldn't feel anyway else at a time like this when th' spirit of a man is pulsin' to be out fightin' for th' thruth with his feet thremblin' on th' way, maybe to th' gallows, an' his ears thinglin' with th' faint, far-away sound of burstin' rifle-shots that'll maybe whip th' last little shock o' life out of him that's left lingerin' in his body!

PETER. I felt a burnin' lump in me throat when I heard th' band playin' "The Soldiers' Song," rememberin' last hearin' it marchin' in military formation, with th' people starin' on both sides at us, carryin' with us th' pride an' resolution o' Dublin to th' grave of Wolfe Tone.

FLUTHER. Get th' Dublin men goin' an' they'll go on full force for anything that's thryin' to bar them away from what they're wantin', where th' slim thinkin' counthry boyo ud limp away from th' first faintest touch of compromization!

PETER (*hurriedly to the* BARMAN). Two more, Tom! . . . (*To* FLUTHER) Th' memory of all th' things that was done, an' all th' things that was suffering be th' people, was boomin' in me brain. . . . Every nerve in me body was quiverin' to do somethin' desperate!

FLUTHER. Jammed as I was in th' crowd, I listened to th' speeches pattherin' on th' people's head, like rain fallin' on th' corn; every derogatory thought went out o' me mind, an' I said to meself, "You can die now, Fluther, for you've seen th' shadow-dhreams of th' past leppin' to life in th' bodies of livin' men that show, if we were without a titther o' courage for centuries, we're vice versa now!" Looka here. (*He stretches out his arm under* PETER's *face and rolls up his sleeve.*) The blood was BOILIN' in me veins!

(*The silhouette of the tall figure again moves into the frame of the window speaking to the people.*)

PETER (*unaware, in his enthusiasm, of the speaker's appearance, to* FLUTHER). I was burnin' to dhraw me sword, an' wave it over me—

FLUTHER (*overwhelming* PETER). Will you stop your blatherin' for a minute, man, an' let us hear what he's sayin'!

VOICE OF THE MAN. Comrade soldiers of the Irish Volunteers and of the Citizen Army, we rejoice in this terrible war. The old heart of the earth needed to be warmed with the red wine of the battlefields. . . . Such august homage was never offered to God as this: the homage of millions of lives given gladly for love of country. And we must be ready to pour out the same red wine in the same glorious sacrifice, for without shedding of blood there is no redemption!

(*The figure moves out of sight and hearing.*)

FLUTHER (*gulping down the drink that remains in his glass, and rushing out*). Come on, man; this is too good to be missed!
(PETER *finishes his drink less rapidly, and as he is going out wiping his mouth with the back of his hand he runs into* THE COVEY *coming in. He immediately erects his body like a young cock, and with his chin thrust forward, and a look of venomous dignity on his face, he marches out.*)

THE COVEY (*at counter*). Give us a glass o' malt, for God's sake, till I stimulate meself from th' shock o' seeing th' sight that's afther goin' out!

ROSIE (*all business, coming over to the counter, and standing near* THE COVEY). Another one for me, Tommy; (*to the* BARMAN) th' young gentleman's ordherin' it in th' corner of his eye.
(*The* BARMAN *brings the drink for* THE COVEY, *and leaves it on the counter.* ROSIE *whips it up.*)

BARMAN. Ay, houl' on there, houl' on there, Rosie!

ROSIE (*to the* BARMAN). What are you houldin' on out o' you for? Didn't you hear th' young gentleman say that he couldn't refuse anything to a nice little bird. (*To* THE COVEY) Isn't that right, Jiggs? (THE COVEY *says nothing.*) Didn't I know, Tommy, it would be all right. It takes Rosie to size a young man up, an' tell th' thoughts that are thremblin' in his mind. Isn't that right, Jiggs?
(THE COVEY *stirs uneasily, moves a little farther away, and pulls his cap over his eyes.*)

ROSIE (*moving after him*). Great meetin' that's gettin' held outside. Well, it's up to us all, anyway, to fight for our freedom.

THE COVEY (*to* BARMAN). Two more, please. (*To* ROSIE) Freedom! What's th' use o' freedom, if it's not economic freedom?

ROSIE (*emphasizing with extended arm and moving finger*). I used them very words just before you come in. "A lot o' thricksters," says I, "that wouldn't know what freedom was if they got it from their mother." . . . (*To* BARMAN) Didn't I, Tommy?

BARMAN. I disremember.

ROSIE. No, you don't disremember. Remember you said, yourself, it was all "only a flash in th' pan." Well, "flash in th' pan, or no flash in th' pan," says I, "they're not goin' to get Rosie Redmond," says I, "to fight for freedom that wouldn't be worth winnin' in a raffle!"

THE COVEY. There's only one freedom for th' workin' man: conthrol o' th' means o' production, rates of exchange an' th' means of disthribution. (*Tapping* ROSIE *on the shoulder*) Look here, comrade, I'll leave here to-morrow night for you a copy of Jenersky's *Thesis on the Origin, Development an' Consolidation of the Evolutionary Idea of th' Proletariat.*

ROSIE (*throwing off her shawl on to the counter, and showing an exemplified glad neck, which reveals*

a good deal of white bosom). If y'ass Rosie, it's heartbreakin' to see a young fella thinkin' of anything, or admirin' anything, but silk thransparent stockin's showin' off the shape of a little lassie's legs!
(THE COVEY, *frightened, moves a little away.*)

ROSIE (*following him*). Out in th' park in th' shade of a warm summery evenin', with your little darlin' bridie to be, kissin' and' cuddlin' (*she tries to put her arm around his neck*), kissin' an' cuddlin', ay?

THE COVEY (*frightened*). Ay, what are you doin'? None o' that, now; none o' that. I've something else to do besides shinannickin' afhter Judies!
(*He turns away, but* ROSIE *follows, keeping face to face with him.*)

ROSIE. Oh, little duckey, oh, shy little duckey! Never held a mot's hand, an' wouldn't know how to tittle a little Judy! (*She clips him under the chin.*) Tittle him undher th' chin, tittle him undher th' chin!

THE COVEY (*breaking away and running out*). Ay, go on, now; I don't want to have any meddlin' with a lassie like you!

ROSIE (*enraged*). Jasus, it's in a monasthery some of us ought to be, spendin' our holidays kneelin' on our adorers, tellin' our beads an' knockin' hell out of our buzzums!

THE COVEY (*outside*). Cuckoo-oo!
(PETER *and* FLUTHER *come in again, followed by* MRS. GOGAN, *carrying a baby in her arms. They go over to the counter.*)

PETER (*with plaintive anger*). It's terrible that young Covey can't let me pass without proddin' at me! Did you hear him murmurin' "cuckoo" when he was passin'?

FLUTHER (*irritably*). I wouldn't be everlastin' cockin' me ear to hear every little whisper that was floatin' around about me! It's my rule never to lose me temper till it would be dethrimental to keep it. There's nothin' derogatory in th' use o' th' word "cuckoo," is there?

PETER (*tearfully*). It's not th' word; it's th' way he says it: he never says it straight out, but murmurs it with curious quiverin' ripples, like variations on a flute!

FLUTHER. Ah, what odds if he gave it with variations on a thrombone! (*To* MRS. GOGAN) What's yours goin' to be, maam?

MRS. GOGAN. Ah, a half o' malt, Fluther.

FLUTHER (*to* BARMAN). Three halves, Tommy.
(*The* BARMAN *brings the drinks.*)

MRS. GOGAN (*drinking*). The Foresthers' is a gorgeous dhress! I don't think I've seen nicer, mind you, in a pantomime. . . . Th' loveliest part of th' dhress, I think, is th' osthrichess plume. . . . When yous are goin' along, an' I see them wavin' an' noddin' an' waggin', I seem to be lookin' at each of yous hangin' at th' end of a rope, your eyes bulgin' an' your legs twistin' an' jerkin', gaspin' an' gaspin' for breath while yous are thryin' to die for Ireland!

FLUTHER. If any o' them is hangin' at the end of a rope, it won't be for Ireland!

PETER. Are you goin' to start th' young Covey's game o' proddin' an' twartin' a man? There's not many that's talkin' can say that for twenty-five years he never missed a pilgrimage to Bodenstown!

FLUTHER. You're always blowin' about goin' to Bodenstown. D'ye think no one but yourself ever went to Bodenstown?

PETER (*plaintively*). I'm not blowin' about it; but there's not a year that I go there but I pluck a leaf off Tone's grave, an' this very day me prayer-book is nearly full of them.

FLUTHER (*scornfully*). Then Fluther has a vice versa opinion of them that put ivy leaves into their prayer-books, scabbin' it on th' clergy, an' thryin' to out-do th' halos o' th' saints be lookin' as if he was wearin' around his head a glittherin' aroree boree allis! (*Fiercely*) Sure, I don't care a damn if you slep' in Bodenstown! You can take your breakfast, dinner an' tea on th' grave, if you like, for Fluther!

MRS. GOGAN. Oh, don't start a fight, boys, for God's sake; I was only sayin' what a nice costume it is—nicer than th' kilts, for, God forgive me, I always think th' kilts is hardly decent.

FLUTHER. Ah, sure, when you'd look at him, you'd wondher whether th' man was makin' fun o' th' costume, or th' costume was makin' fun o' th' man!

BARMAN. Now, then, thry to speak asy, will yous? We don't want no shoutin' here.

(THE COVEY *followed by* BESSIE BURGESS *comes in. They go over to the opposite end of the counter, and direct their gaze on the other group.*)

THE COVEY (*to* BARMAN). Two glasses o' malt.

PETER. There he is, now; I knew he wouldn't be long till he followed me in.

BESSIE (*speaking to* THE COVEY, *but really at the other party*). I can't for th' life o' me undherstand how they can call themselves Catholics, when they won't lift a finger to help poor little Catholic Belgium.

MRS. GOGAN (*raising her voice*). What about poor little Catholic Ireland?

BESSIE (*over to* MRS. GOGAN). You mind your own business, maam, an' stupify your foolishness be gettin' dhrunk.

PETER (*anxiously*). Take no notice of her; pay no attention to her. She's just tormentin' herself towards havin' a row with somebody.

BESSIE. There's a storm of anger

tossin' in me heart, thinkin' of all th' poor Tommies, an' with them me own son, dhrenched in water an' soaked in blood, gropin' their way to a shattherin' death, in a shower o' shells! Young men with th' sunny lust o' life beamin' in them, layin' down their white bodies, shredded into torn an' bloody pieces, on th' althar that God Himself has built for th' sacrifice of heroes!

MRS. GOGAN. Isn't it a nice thing to have to be listenin' to a lassie an' hangin' our heads in a dead silence, knowin' that some persons think more of a ball of malt than they do of th' blessed saints.

FLUTHER. Whisht; she's always dangerous an' derogatory when she's well oiled. Th' safest way to hindher her from havin' any enjoyment out of her spite, is to dip our thoughts into the fact of her bein' a female person that has moved out of th' sight of ordinary sensible people.

BESSIE. To look at some o' th' women that's knockin' about, now, is a thing to make a body sigh. . . . A woman on her own, dhrinkin' with a bevy o' men is hardly an example to her sex. . . . A woman dhrinkin' with a woman is one thing, an' a woman dhrinkin' with herself is still a woman—flappers may be put in another category altogether—but a middle-aged married woman makin' herself th' centre of a circle of men is as a woman that is loud an' stubborn, whose feet abideth not in her own house.

THE COVEY (*to* BESSIE). When I think of all th' problems in front o' th' workers, it makes me sick to be lookin' at oul' codgers goin' about dhressed up like green-accoutered figures gone asthray out of a toyshop!

PETER. Gracious God, give me patience to be listenin' to that blasted young Covey proddin' at me from over at th' other end of th' shop!

MRS. GOGAN (*dipping her fingers in the whisky, and moistening with it the lips of her baby*). Cissie Gogan's a woman livin' for nigh on twenty-five years in her own room, an' beyond biddin' th' time o' day to her neighbours, never yet as much as nodded her head in th' direction of other people's business, while she knows some as are never content unless they're standin' senthry over other people's doin's!

(BESSIE *is about to reply, when the tall dark figure is again silhouetted against the window, and the voice of the speaker is heard speaking passionately.*)

VOICE OF SPEAKER. The last sixteen months have been the most glorious in the history of Europe. Heroism has come back to the earth. War is a terrible thing, but war is not an evil thing. People in Ireland dread war because they do not know it. Ireland has not known the exhilaration of war for over a hundred years. When war comes to Ireland she must welcome it as she would welcome the Angel of God!

(*The figure passes out of sight and hearing.*)

THE COVEY (*towards all present*). Dope, dope. There's only one war worth havin': th' war for th' economic emancipation of th' proletariat.

BESSIE. They may crow away out o' them; but it ud be fitther for some o' them to mend their ways, an' cease from havin' scouts out watchin' for th' comin' of th' Saint Vincent de Paul men, for fear they'd be nailed lowerin' a pint of beer, mockin' th' man with an angel face, shinin' with th' glamour of deceit an' lies!

MRS. GOGAN. An' a certain lassie standin' stiff behind her own door with her ears cocked listenin' to what's being said, stuffed till she's sthrained with envy of a neighbour thryin' for a few little things that may be got be hard sthrivin' to keep up to th' letther an' th' law, an' th' practices of th' Church.

PETER (*to* MRS. GOGAN). If I was you, Mrs. Gogan, I'd parry her jabbin' remarks be a powerful silence that'll keep her tantalizin' words from penethratin' into your feelin's. It's always betther to leave these people to th' vengeance o' God!

BESSIE. Bessie Burgess doesn't put up to know much, never havin' a swaggerin' mind, thanks be to God, but goin' on packin' up knowledge accordin' to her conscience: precept upon precept, line upon line; here a little, an' there a little. But (*with a passionate swing of her shawl*), thanks be to Christ, she knows when she was got, where she was got, an' how she was got; while there's some she knows, decoratin' their finger with a well-polished weddin' ring, would be hard put to if they were assed to show their weddin' lines!

MRS. GOGAN (*plunging out into the centre of the floor in a wild tempest of hysterical rage*). Y' oul' rip of a blasted liar, me weddin' ring's been well earned be twenty years be th' side o' me husband, now takin' his rest in heaven, married to me be Father Dempsey, in th' Chapel o' Saint Jude's, in th' Christmas Week of eighteen hundhred an' ninety-five; an' any kid, livin' or dead, that Jinnie Gogan's had since, was got between th' bordhers of th' Ten Commandments! . . . An' that's more than some o' you can say that are kep' from th' dhread o' desthruction be a few drowsy virtues, that th' first whisper of temptation lulls into a sleep that'll know one sin from another only on th' day of their last anointin', and' that use th' innocent light o' th' shinin' stars to dip into th' sins of a night's diversion!

BESSIE (*jumping out to face* MRS. GOGAN, *and bringing the palms of her hands together in sharp clasp to emphasize her remarks*). Liar to you, too, maam, y' oul' hardened thresspasser on other people's good nature, wizenin' up your soul in th' arts o' dodgeries, till every dhrop of respectability in a female is dhried up in her, lookin' at your ready-made manœuverin' with th' menkind!

BARMAN. Here, there; here, there; speak asy there. No rowin' here, no rowin' here, now.

FLUTHER (*trying to calm* MRS. GOGAN). Now, Jinnie, Jinnie, it's a derogatory thing to be smirchin' a night like this with a row; it's rompin' with th' feelin's of hope we ought to be, instead o' bein' vice versa!

PETER (*trying to quiet* BESSIE). I'm terrible dawny, Mrs. Burgess, an' a fight leaves me weak for a long time aftherwards. . . . Please, Mrs. Burgess, before there's damage done, thry to have a little respect for yourself.

BESSIE (*with a push of her hand that sends* PETER *tottering to the end of the shop*). G'way, you little sermonizing, little yella-faced, little consequential, little pudgy, little bum, you!

MRS. GOGAN (*screaming*). Fluther, leggo! I'm not goin' to keep an unresistin' silence, an' her scattherin' her festherin' words in me face, stirrin' up every dhrop of decency in a respectable female, with her restless rally o' lies that would make a saint say his prayer backwards!

BESSIE (*shouting*). Ah, everybody knows well that th' best charity that can be shown to you is to hide th' thruth as much as our thrue worship of God Almighty will allow us!

MRS. GOGAN (*frantically*). Here, houl' th' kid, one o' yous; houl' th' kid for a minute! There's nothin' for it but to show this lassie a lesson or two. . . . (*To* PETER) Here, houl' th' kid, you.
(*Before* PETER *is aware of it, she places the infant in his arms.*)

MRS. GOGAN (*to* BESSIE, *standing before her in a fighting attitude*). Come on, now, me loyal lassie, dyin' with grief for little Catholic Belgium! When Jinnie Gogan's done with you, you'll have a little leisure lyin' down to think an' pray for your king an' counthry!

BARMAN (*coming from behind the counter, getting between the women, and proceeding to push them towards the door*). Here, now, since yous can't have a little friendly argument quietly, yous get out o' this place in quick time. Go on, an' settle your differences somewhere else—I don't want to have another endorsement on me licence.

PETER (*anxiously, over to* MRS. GOGAN). Here take your kid back, ower this. How nicely I was picked, now, for it to be plumped into me arms!

THE COVEY. She knew who she was givin' it to, maybe.

PETER (*hotly to* THE COVEY). Now, I'm givin' you fair warnin', me young Covey, to quit firin' your jibes an' jeers at me. . . . For one o' these days, I'll run out in front of God Almighty an' take your sacred life!

BARMAN (*pushing* BESSIE *out after* MRS. GOGAN). Go on, now; out you go.

BESSIE (*as she goes out*). If you think, me lassie, that Bessie Burgess has an untidy conscience, she'll soon show you to th' differ!

PETER (*leaving the baby down on the floor*). Ay, be Jasus, wait there, till I give her back her youngster! (*He runs to the door.*) Ay, there, ay! (*He comes back.*) There, she's afther goin' without her kid. What are we goin' to do with it, now?

THE COVEY. What are we goin' to do with it? Bring it outside an' show everybody what you're afther findin'!

PETER (*in a panic to* FLUTHER). Pick it up, you, Fluther, an' run afther her with it, will you?

FLUTHER. What d'ye take Fluther for? You must think Fluther's a right gom. D'ye think Fluther's like yourself, destitute of a titther of undherstandin'?

BARMAN (*imperatively to* PETER). Take it up, man, an' run out afther her with it, before she's gone too far. You're not goin' to leave th' bloody thing here, are you?

PETER (*plaintively, as he lifts up the baby*). Well, God Almighty, give me patience with all th' scorners, tormenters, an' twarters that are always an' ever thryin' to goad me into prayin' for their blindin' an' blastin' an' burnin' in th' world to come! (*He goes out.*)

FLUTHER. God, it's a relief to get rid o' that crowd. Women is terrible when they start to fight. There's no holdin' them back. (*To* THE COVEY) Are you goin' to have anything?

THE COVEY. Ah, I don't mind if I have another half.

FLUTHER (*to* BARMAN). Two more, Tommy, me son.

(THE BARMAN *gets the drinks.*)

FLUTHER. You know, there's no conthrollin' a woman when she loses her head.

(ROSIE *enters and goes over to the counter on the side nearest to* FLUTHER.)

ROSIE (*to* BARMAN). Divil a use o' havin' a thrim little leg on a night like this; things was never worse. . . . Give us a half till to-morrow, Tom, duckey.

BARMAN (*coldly*). No more to-night, Rosie; you owe me for three already.

ROSIE (*combatively*). You'll be paid, won't you?

BARMAN. I hope so.

ROSIE. You hope so! Is that th' way with you, now?

FLUTHER (*to* BARMAN). Give her one; it'll be all right.

ROSIE (*clapping* FLUTHER *on the back*). Oul' sport!

FLUTHER. Th' meeting should be soon over, now.

THE COVEY. Th' sooner th' betther. It's all a lot o' blasted nonsense, comrade.

FLUTHER. Oh, I wouldn't say it was all nonsense. Afther all, Fluther can remember th' time, an' him only a dawny chiselur, bein' taught at his mother's knee to be faithful to th' Shan Vok Vok!

THE COVEY. That's all dope, comrade; th' sort o' thing that workers are fed on be th' Boorzwawzee.

FLUTHER (*a little sharply*). What's all dope? Though I'm sayin' it that shouldn't: (*catching his cheek with his hand, and pulling down the flesh from the eye*) d'ye see that mark there, undher me eye. . . . A sabre slice from a dragoon in O'Connell Street! (*Thrusting his head forward towards* ROSIE.) Feel that dint in th' middle o' me nut!

ROSIE (*rubbing* FLUTHER'S *head, and winking at* THE COVEY). My God, there's a holla!

FLUTHER (*putting on his hat with quiet pride*). A skelp from a bobby's baton at a Labour meetin' in th' Phœnix Park!

THE COVEY. He must ha' hitten you in mistake. I don't know what you ever done for th' Labour movement.

FLUTHER (*loudly*). D'ye not? Maybe, then, I done as much, an' know as much about th' Labour movement as th' chancers that are blowin' about it!

BARMAN. Speak easy, Fluther, thry to speak easy.

THE COVEY. There's no necessity to get excited about it, comrade.

FLUTHER (*more loudly*). Excited? Who's gettin' excited? There's no one gettin' excited! It would take something more than a thing like you to flutther a feather o' Fluther. Blatherin', an', when all is said, you know as much as th' rest in th' wind up!

THE COVEY. Well, let us put it to th' test, then, an' see what you know about th' Labour movement: what's the mechanism of exchange?

FLUTHER (*roaring, because he feels he is beaten*). How th' hell do I know what it is? There's nothin' about that in th' rules of our Thrades Union!

BARMAN. For God's sake, thry to speak easy, Fluther.

THE COVEY. What does Karl Marx say about th' Relation of Value to th' Cost o' Production?

FLUTHER (*angrily*). What th' hell do I care what he says? I'm Irishman enough not to lose me head be follyin' foreigners!

BARMAN. Speak easy, Fluther.

THE COVEY. It's only waste o' time talkin' to you, comrade.

FLUTHER. Don't be comradin' me, mate. I'd be on me last legs if I wanted you for a comrade.

ROSIE (*to* THE COVEY). It seems a highly rediculous thing to hear a thing that's only an inch or two away from a kid, swingin' heavy words about he doesn't know th' meanin' of, an' uppishly thryin' to down a man like Misther Fluther here, that's well flavoured in th' knowledge of th' world he's livin' in.

THE COVEY (*savagely to* ROSIE). Nobody's askin' you to be buttin' in with your prate. . . . I have you well taped, me lassie. . . . Just you keep your opinions for your own place. . . . It'll be a long time before th' Covey takes any insthructions or reprimandin' from a prostitute!

ROSIE (*wild with humiliation*). You louse, you louse, you! . . . You're no man. . . . You're no man. . . . I'm a woman, anyhow, an' if I'm a prostitute aself, I have me feelin's. . . . Thryin' to put his arm around me a minute ago, an' givin' me th' glad eye, th' little wrigglin' lump o' desolation turns on me now, because he saw there was nothin' doin'. . . . You louse, you; If I was a man, or you were a woman, I'd bate th' puss o' you!

BARMAN. Ay, Rosie, ay! You'll have to shut your mouth altogether, if you can't learn to speak easy!

FLUTHER (*to* ROSIE). Houl' on there, Rosie; houl' on there. There's no necessity to flutther yourself when you're with Fluther. . . . Any lady that's in th' company of Fluther is goin' to get a fair hunt. . . . This is outside your province. . . . I'm not goin' to let you demean yourself be talkin' to a tittherin' chancer. . . . Leave this to Fluther—this is a man's job. (*To* THE COVEY) Now, if you've anything to say, say it to Fluther, an', let me tell you, you're not goin' to be pass-remarkable to any lady in my company.

THE COVEY. Sure I don't care if you were runnin' all night afther your Mary o' th' Curlin' Hair, but, when you start tellin' luscious lies about what you done for th' Labour movement, it's nearly time to show y'up!

FLUTHER (*fiercely*). Is it you show Fluther up? G'way, man, I'd beat two o' you before me breakfast!

THE COVEY (*contemptuously*). Tell us where you bury your dead, will you?

FLUTHER (*with his face stuck into the face of* THE COVEY). Sing a little less on th' high note, or, when I'm done with you, you'll put a Christianable consthruction on things, I'm tellin' you!

THE COVEY. You're a big fella, you are.

FLUTHER (*tapping* THE COVEY *threateningly on the shoulder*). Now, you're temptin' Providence when you're temptin' Fluther!

THE COVEY (*losing his temper, and bawling*). Easy with them hands, there, easy with them hands! You're startin' to take a little risk when you commence to paw the Covey!

(FLUTHER *suddenly springs into the middle of the shop, flings his hat into the corner, whips off his coat, and begins to paw the air.*)

FLUTHER (*roaring at the top of his

voice). Come on, come on, you lowser; put your mits up now, if there's a man's blood in you! Be God, in a few minutes you'll see some snots flyin' around, I'm tellin' you. . . . When Fluther's done with you, you'll have a vice versa opinion of him! Come on, now, come on!

BARMAN (*running from behind the counter and catching hold of* THE COVEY). Here, out you go, me little bowsey. Because you got a couple o' halves you think you can act as you like. (*He pushes* THE COVEY *to the door.*) Fluther's a friend o' mine, an' I'll not have him insulted.

THE COVEY (*struggling with the* BARMAN). Ay, leggo, leggo there; fair hunt, give a man a fair hunt! One minute with him is all I ask; one minute alone with him, while you're runnin' for th' priest an' th' doctor!

FLUTHER (*to the* BARMAN). Let him go, let him go, Tom: let him open th' door to sudden death if he wants to!

BARMAN (*to* THE COVEY). Go on, out you go an' do th' bowsey somewhere else.
(*He pushes* THE COVEY *out and comes back.*)

ROSIE (*getting* FLUTHER's *hat as he is putting on his coat*). Be God, you put th' fear o' God in his heart that time! I thought you'd have to be dug out of him. . . . Th' way you lepped out without any of your fancy side-steppin'! "Men like Fluther," say I to meself, "is gettin' scarce nowadays."

FLUTHER (*with proud ccmplacency*). I wasn't goin' to let meself be malignified by a chancer. . . . He got a little bit too derogatory for Fluther. . . . Be God, to think of a cur like that comin' to talk to a man like me!

ROSIE (*fixing on his hat*). Did j'ever!

FLUTHER. He's lucky he got off safe. I hit a man last week, Rosie, an' he's fallin' yet!

ROSIE. Sure, you'd ha' broken him in two if you'd ha' hitten him one clatther!

FLUTHER (*amorously, putting his arm around* ROSIE). Come on into th' snug, me little darlin', an' we'll have a few dhrinks before I see you home.

ROSIE. Oh, Fluther, I'm afraid you're a terrible man for th' women.
(*They go into the snug as* CLITHEROE, CAPTAIN BRENNAN *and* LIEUT. LANGON *of the Irish Volunteers enter hurriedly.* CAPTAIN BRENNAN *carries the banner of The Plough and the Stars, and* LIEUT. LANGON *a green, white and orange Tricolour. They are in a state of emotional excitement. Their faces are flushed and their eyes sparkle; they speak rapidly, as if unaware of the meaning of what they said. They have been mesmerized by the fervency of the speeches.*)

CLITHEROE (*almost pantingly*). Three glasses o' port!
(*The* BARMAN *brings the drinks.*)

CAPT. BRENNAN. We won't have long to wait now.

LIEUT. LANGON. Th' time is rotten ripe for revolution.

CLITHEROE. You have a mother, Langon.

LIEUT. LANGON. Ireland is greater than a mother.

CAPT. BRENNAN. You have a wife, Clitheroe.

CLITHEROE. Ireland is greater than a wife.

LIEUT. LANGON. Th' time for Ireland's battle is now—th' place for Ireland's battle is here.
(*The tall, dark figure again is silhouetted against the window. The three men pause and listen.*)

VOICE OF THE MAN. Our foes are strong, but strong as they are, they cannot undo the miracles of God, who ripens in the heart of young men the seeds sown by the young men of a former generation. They think they have pacified Ireland; think they have foreseen everything; think they have provided against everything; but the fools, the fools, the fools!—they have left us our Fenian dead, and, while Ireland holds these graves, Ireland, unfree, shall never be at peace!

CAPT. BRENNAN (*catching up The Plough and the Stars*). Imprisonment for th' Independence of Ireland!

LIEUT. LANGON (*catching up the Tri-colour*). Wounds for th' Independence of Ireland!

CLITHEROE. Death for th' Independence of Ireland!

THE THREE (*together*). So help us God!
(*They drink. A bugle blows the Assembly. They hurry out. A pause.* FLUTHER *and* ROSIE *come out of the snug;* ROSIE *is linking* FLUTHER, *who is a little drunk. Both are in a merry mood.*)

ROSIE. Come on home, ower o' that, man. Are you afraid or what? Are you goin' to come home, or are you not?

FLUTHER. Of course I'm goin' home. What ud ail me that I wouldn't go?

ROSIE (*lovingly*). Come on, then, oul' sport.

OFFICER'S VOICE (*giving command outside*). Irish Volunteers, by th' right, quick march!

ROSIE (*putting her arm round* FLUTHER *and singing*):

I once had a lover, a tailor, but he could do nothin' for me,
An' then I fell in with a sailor as strong an' as wild as th' sea.
We cuddled an' kissed with devotion, till th' night from th' mornin' had fled;
An' there, to our joy, a bright bouncing' boy

Was dancin' a jig in th' bed!

Dancin' a jig in th' bed, an' bawlin' for butther an' bread.
An' there, to our joy, a bright bouncin' boy
Was dancin' a jig in th' bed!

(*They go out with their arms round each other.*)

CLITHEROE'S VOICE (*in command outside*). Dublin Battalion of the Irish Citizen Army, by th' right, quick march!

CURTAIN

ACT THREE

The corner house in a street of tenements: it is the home of the CLITHEROES. *The house is a long, gaunt, five-story tenement; its brick front is chipped and scarred with age and neglect. The wide and heavy hall door, flanked by two pillars, has a look of having been charred by a fire in the distant past. The door lurches a little to one side, disjointed by the continual and reckless banging when it is being closed by most of the residents. The diamond-paned fan-light is destitute of a single pane, the frame-work alone remaining. The windows, except the two looking into the front parlour (*CLITHEROE'S *room), are grimy, and are draped with fluttering and soiled fragments of lace curtains. The front parlour windows are hung with rich, comparatively, casement cloth. Five stone steps lead from the door to the path on the street. Branching on each side are railings to prevent people from falling into the area. At the left corner of the house runs a narrow lane, bisecting the street and connecting it with another of the same kind. At the corner of the lane is a street lamp.*

As the house is revealed, MRS. GOGAN *is seen helping* MOLLSER *to a chair, which stands on the path beside the railings, at the left side of the steps. She then wraps a shawl around* MOLLSER'S *shoulders. It is some months later.*

MRS. GOGAN (*arranging shawl around* MOLLSER). Th' sun'll do you all th' good in th' world. A few more weeks o' this weather, an' there's no knowin' how well you'll be. . . . Are you comfy now?

MOLLSER (*weakly and wearily*). Yis, ma; I'm all right.

MRS. GOGAN. How are you feelin'?

MOLLSER. Betther, ma, betther. If th' horrible sinkin' feelin' ud go, I'd be all right.

MRS. GOGAN. Ah, I wouldn't put much pass on that. Your stomach, maybe's out of ordher. . . . Is th' poor breathin' any betther, d'ye think?

MOLLSER. Yis, yis, ma; a lot betther.

MRS. GOGAN. Well, that's somethin' anyhow. . . . with th' help o' God, you'll be on th' mend from this out. . . . D'your legs feel any sthronger undher you, d'ye think?

MOLLSER (*irritably*). I can't tell, ma. I think so. . . . A little.

MRS. GOGAN. Well, a little aself is somethin'. . . . I thought I heard you coughin' a little more than usual last night. . . . D'ye think you were?

MOLLSER. I wasn't, ma, I wasn't.

MRS. GOGAN. I thought I heard you, for I was kep' awake all night with th' shootin'. An' thinkin' o' that madman, Fluther, runnin' about through th' night lookin' for Nora Clitheroe to bring her back when he heard she'd gone to folly her husband, an' in dhread any minute he might come staggerin' in covered with bandages, splashed all over with th' red of his own blood, an' givin' us barely time to bring th' priest to hear th' last whisper of his final confession, as his soul was passin' through th' dark doorway o' death into th' way o' th' wondherin' dead. . . . You don't feel cold, do you?

MOLLSER. No ma; I'm all right.

MRS. GOGAN. Keep your chest well covered, for that's th' delicate spot in you. . . . if there's any danger, I'll whip you in again. . . . (*Looking up the street*) Oh, here's th' Covey an' oul' Pether hurryin' along. God Almighty, sthrange things is happenin' when them two is pullin' together.

(THE COVEY *and* PETER *come in, breathless and excited.*)

MRS. GOGAN (*to the two men*). Were yous far up th' town? Did yous see any sign o' Fluther or Nora? How is things lookin'? I hear they're blazin' away out o' th' G.P.O. That th' Tommies is sthretched in heaps around Nelson's Pillar an' th' Parnell Statue, an' that th' pavin' sets in O'Connell Street is nearly covered be pools o' blood.

PETER. We seen no sign o' Nora or Fluther anywhere.

MRS. GOGAN. We should ha' held her back be main force from goin' to look for her husband. . . . God knows what's happened to her—I'm always seein' her sthretched on her back in some hospital, moanin' with th' pain of a bullet in her vitals, an' nuns thryin' to get her to take a last look at th' crucifix!

THE COVEY. We can do nothin'. You can't stick your nose into O'Connell Street, an' Tyler's is on fire.

PETER. An' we seen th' Lancers——

THE COVEY (*interrupting*). Throttin' along, heads in th' air; spurs an' sabres jinglin' an' lances quiverin', an' lookin' as if they were assin' themselves, "Where's these blighters, till we get a prod at them," when there was a volley from th' Post Office that stretched half o' them, an' sent th' rest gallopin' away wondherin' how far they'd have to go before they'd feel safe.

PETER (*rubbing his hands*). "Damn it," says I to meself, "this looks like business!"

THE COVEY. An' then out comes General Pearse an' his staff, an', standin' in th' middle o' th' street, he reads th' Proclamation.

MRS. GOGAN. What proclamation?

PETER. Declarin' an Irish Republic.

MRS. GOGAN. Go to God.

PETER. The gunboat *Helga's* shellin' Liberty Hall, an' I hear that people livin' on th' quays had to crawl on their bellies to Mass with th' bullets that were flyin' around from Boland's Mills.

MRS. GOGAN. God bless us, what's goin' to be th' end of it all!

BESSIE (*looking out of the top window*). Maybe yous are satisfied now; maybe yous are satisfied now! Go on an' get guns if yous are men —Johnny get your gun, get your gun, get your gun! Yous are all nicely shanghaied now; th' boyo hasn't a sword on his thigh, now! Oh, yous are all nicely shanghaied now!

MRS. GOGAN (*warningly to* PETER *and* THE COVEY). S-s-sh, don't answer her. She's th' right oul' Orange bitch! She's been chantin' "Rule, Britannia" all th' mornin'.

PETER. I hope Fluther hasn't met with any accident, he's such a wild card.

THE COVEY. Fluther's well able to take care of himself.

MRS. GOGAN. God grant it; but last night I dreamt I seen gettin' carried into th' house a sthretcher with a figure lyin' on it, stiff an' still, dhressed in th' habit of Saint Francis. An' then, I heard th' murmurs of a crowd no one could see sayin' th' litany for th' dead; an' then it got so dark that nothin' was seen but th' white face of th' corpse, gleamin' like a white wather lily floatin' on th' top of a dark lake. Then a tiny whisper thrickled into me ear, saying', "Isn't the face very like th' face o' Fluther," an' then, with a thremblin' flutther, th' dead lips opened, an', although I couldn't hear, I knew they were sayin', "Poor oul' Fluther, afther havin' handin' in his gun at last, his shakin' soul moored in th' place where th' wicked are at rest an' th' weary cease from throublin'."

PETER (*who has put on a pair of spectacles, and has been looking down the street*). Here they are, be God, here they are; just afther turnin' th' corner—Nora an' Fluther!

THE COVEY. She must be wounded or something—he seems to be carryin' her.

(FLUTHER *and* NORA *enter.* FLUTHER *has his arm around her and is half leading, half carrying her in. Her eyes are dim and hollow, her face pale and strained looking; her hair is tossed, and her clothes are dusty.*)

MRS. GOGAN (*running over to them*). God bless us, is it wounded y'are Mrs. Clitheroe, or what?

FLUTHER. Ah, she's all right, Mrs. Gogan; only worn out from thravellin' an' want o' sleep. A night's rest, now, an' she'll be as fit as a fiddle. Bring her in, an' make her lie down.

MRS. GOGAN (*to* NORA). Did you hear e'er a whisper o' Mr. Clitheroe?

NORA (*wearily*). I could find him nowhere, Mrs. Gogan. None o' them would tell me where he was. They told me I shamed my husband an' th' women of Ireland be carryin' on as I was. . . . They said th' women must learn to be brave an' cease to be cowardly. . . . Me who risked more for love than they would risk for hate. . . . (*Raising her voice in hysterical protest*) My Jack will be killed, my Jack will be killed! . . . He is to be butchered as a sacrifice to th' dead!

BESSIE (*from upper window*). You are all nicely shanghied now! Sorra mend th' lasses that have been kissin' and cuddlin' their boys into th' sheddin' of blood! . . . Fillin' their minds with fairy tales that had no beginnin', but, please God, 'll have a bloody quick endin'! . . . Turnin' bitther into sweet, an' sweet into bitther. . . . Stabbin' in th' back th' men that are dyin' in th' threnches for them! It's a bad thing for any one that thrys to jilt th' Ten Commandments, for judgements are prepared for scorners an' sthripes for th' back o' fools! (*Going away from window as she sings*):

Rule, Britannia, Britannia rules th' waves,
Britons never, never, never shall be slaves!

FLUTHER (*with a roar up at the window*). Y'ignorant oul' throllope, you!

MRS. GOGAN (*to* NORA). He'll come home safe enough to you, you'll find, Mrs. Clitheroe; afther all, there's a power o' women that's handed over sons an' husbands to take a runnin'-risk in th' fight they're wagin'.

NORA. I can't help thinkin' every shot fired 'll be fired at Jack, an' every shot fired at Jack 'll be fired at me. What do I care for th' others? I can think only of me own self. . . . And there's no woman gives a son or a husband to be killed— if they say it, they're lyin', lyin', against God, Nature, an' against themselves! . . . One blasted hussy at a barricade told me to go home an' not be thryin' to dishearten th' men. . . . That I wasn't worthy to bear a son to a man that was out fightin' for freedom. . . . I clawed at her, an' smashed her in th' face till we were separated. . . . I was pushed down th' street, an' I cursed them—cursed the rebel ruffians an' Volunteers that had dhragged me ravin' mad into th' streets to seek me husband!

PETER. You'll have to have patience, Nora. We all have to put up with twarthers an' tormenters in this world.

THE COVEY. If they were fightin' for anything worth while, I wouldn't mind.

FLUTHER (*to* NORA). Nothin' derogatory 'll happen to Mr. Clitheroe. You'll find, now, in th' finish up, it'll be vice versa.

NORA. Oh, I know that wherever he is, he's thinkin' of wantin' to be with me. I know he's longin' to be passin' his hand through me hair, to be caressin' me neck, to fondle me hand an' to feel me kisses clingin' to his mouth. . . . An' he stands wherever he is because he's brave? (*Vehemently*) No, but because he's a coward, a coward, a coward!

MRS. GOGAN. Oh, they're not cowards anyway.

NORA (*with denunciatory anger*). I tell you they're afraid to say they're afraid! . . . Oh, I saw it, I saw it, Mrs. Gogan. . . . At th' barricade in North King Street I saw fear glowin' in all their eyes. . . . An' in th' middle o' th' sthreet was somethin' huddled up in a horrible tangled heap. . . . His face was jammed again th' stones, an' his arm was twisted around his back. . . . An' every twist of his body was a cry against th' terrible thing that had happened to him. . . . An' I saw they were afraid to look at it. . . . An' some o' them laughed at me, but th' laugh was a frightened one. . . . An' some o' them shouted at me, but th' shout had in it th' shiver o' fear. . . . I tell you they were afraid, afraid, afraid!

MRS. GOGAN (*leading her towards the house*). Come on in, dear. If you'd been a little longer together, th' wrench asunder wouldn't have been so sharp.

NORA. Th' agony I'm in since he left me has thrust away every rough thing he done, an' every unkind word he spoke; only th' blossoms that grew out of our lives are before me now; shakin' their colours before me face, an breathin' their sweet scent on every thought springin' up in me mind, till, sometimes, Mrs. Gogan, sometimes I think I'm going mad!

MRS. GOGAN. You'll be a lot better when you have a little lie down.

NORA (*turning towards* FLUTHER *as she is going in*). I don't know what I'd have done, only for Fluther. I'd have been lyin' in th' streets, only for him. . . . (*As she goes in*) They have dhriven away th' little happiness life had to spare for me. He has gone from me for ever, for ever. . . . Oh, Jack, Jack, Jack!

(*She is led in by* MRS. GOGAN *as* BESSIE *comes out with a shawl around her shoulders. She passes by them with her head in the air. When they have gone in, she gives a mug of milk to* MOLLSER, *silently.*)

FLUTHER. Which of yous has th' tossers?

THE COVEY. I have.

BESSIE (*as she is passing them to go down the street*). You an' your Leadhers an' their sham-battle soldiers has landed a body in a nice way, havin' to go an' ferret out a bit o' bread God knows where. . . . Why aren't yous in th' G.P.O. if yous are men? It's paler an' paler yous are gettin'. . . . A lot of vipers, that's what th' Irish people is! (*She goes out.*)

FLUTHER. Never mind her. . . . (*To* THE COVEY) Make a start an' keep us from th' sin o' idleness. (*To* MOLLSER) Well, how are you to-day, Mollser, oul' son? What are you dhrinkin', milk?

MOLLSER. Grand, Fluther, grand, thanks. Yis, milk.

FLUTHER. You couldn't get a better thing down you. . . . This turn-up has done one good thing, anyhow; you can't get dhrink anywhere, an' if it lasts a week, I'll be so used to it that I won't think of a pint.

THE COVEY (*who has taken from his pocket two worn coins and a thin strip of wood about four inches long*). What's th' bettin'?

PETER. Heads, a juice.

FLUTHER. Harps, a tanner.
(THE COVEY *places the coin on the strip of wood, and flips them up into the air. As they jingle on the ground the distant boom of a big gun is heard. They stand for a moment listening.*)

FLUTHER. What th' hell's that?

THE COVEY. It's like th' boom of a big gun!

FLUTHER. Surely to God they're not goin' to use artillery on us?

THE COVEY (*scornfully*). Not goin'! (*Vehemently*) Wouldn't they use anythin' on us, man?

FLUTHER. Aw, holy Christ, that's not playin' th' game.

PETER (*plaintively*). What would happen if a shell landed here now?

THE COVEY (*ironically*). You'd be off to heaven in a fiery chariot.

PETER. In spite of all th' warnin's that's ringin' around us, are you goin' to start your pickin' at me again?

FLUTHER. Go on, toss them again, toss them again. . . . Harps, a tanner.

PETER. Heads, a juice.
(THE COVEY *tosses the coins.*)

FLUTHER (*as the coins fall*). Let them roll, let them roll. Heads, be God!
(BESSIE *runs in excitedly. She has a new hat on her head, a fox fur around her neck, over her shawl, three umbrellas under her right arm, and a box of biscuits under her left. She speaks rapidly and breathlessly.*)

BESSIE. They're breakin' into th' shops, they're breakin' into th' shops! Smashin' th' windows, batherin' in th' doors an' whippin' away everything! An' th' Volunteers is firin' on them. I seen two men an' a lassie pushin' a piano down th' sthreet, an' th' sweat rollin' off them thryin' to get it up on th' pavement; an' an oul' wan that must ha' been seventy lookin' as if she'd dhrop every minute with th' dint o' heart beatin', thryin' to pull a big double bed out of a broken shop window! I was goin' to wait till I dhressed meself from th' skin out.

MOLLSER (*to* BESSIE, *as she is going in*). Help me in, Bessie; I'm feelin' curious.
(BESSIE *leaves the looted things in the house, and, rapidly returning, helps* MOLLSER *in.*)

THE COVEY. Th' selfishness of that one—she waited till she got all she could carry before she'd come to tell any one!

FLUTHER (*running over to the door of the house and shouting in to* BESSIE). Ay, Bessie, did you hear of e'er a pub gettin' a shake up?

BESSIE (*inside*). I didn't hear o' none.

FLUTHER (*in a burst of enthusiasm*). Well, you're goin' to hear of one soon!

THE COVEY. Come on, man, an' don't be wastin' time.

PETER (*to them as they are about to run off*). Ay, ay, are yous goin' to leave me here?

FLUTHER. Are you goin' to leave yourself here?

PETER (*anxiously*). Didn't yous hear her sayin' they were firin' on them?

THE COVEY *and* FLUTHER (*together*). Well?

PETER. Supposin' I happened to be potted?

FLUTHER. We'd give you a Christian burial, anyhow.

THE COVEY (*ironically*). Dhressed up in your regimentals.

PETER (*to the* THE COVEY, *passionately*). May th' all-lovin' God give you a hot knock one o' these day, me young Covey, tuthorin' Fluther up now to be tiltin' at me, and crossin' me with his mockeries an' jibin'!
(*A fashionably dressed, middle-aged, stout woman comes hurriedly in, and makes for the group. She is almost fainting with fear.*)

THE WOMAN. For Gawd sake, will one of you kind men show any safe way for me to get to Wrathmines? . . . I was foolish enough to visit a friend, thinking the howl thing was a joke, and now I cawn't get a car or a tram to take me home—isn't it awful?

FLUTHER. I'm afraid, maam, one way is as safe as another.

WOMAN. And what am I gowing to do? Oh, isn't this awful? . . . I'm so different from others. . . . The mowment I hear a shot, my legs give way under me—I cawn't stir, I'm paralysed—isn't it awful?

FLUTHER (*moving away*). It's a derogatory way to be, right enough, maam.

WOMAN (*catching* FLUTHER'S *coat*). Creeping along the street there, with my head down and my eyes half shut, a bullet whizzed past within an inch of my nowse. . . . I had to lean against the wall for a long time, gasping for breath—I nearly passed away—it was awful! . . . I wonder, would you kind men come some of the way and see me safe?

FLUTHER. I have to go away, maam, to thry an' save a few things from th' burnin' buildin's.

THE COVEY. Come on, then, or there won't be anything left to save.
(THE COVEY *and* FLUTHER *hurry away.*)

WOMAN (*to* PETER). Wasn't it an awful thing for me to leave my friend's house? Wasn't it an idiotic thing to do? . . . I haven't the slightest idea where I am. . . . You have a kind face, sir. Could you possibly come and pilot me in the direction of Wrathmines?

PETER (*indignantly*). D'ye think I'm goin' to risk me life throttin' in front of you? An' maybe get a bullet that would gimme a game leg or something that would leave me a jibe an' a jeer to Fluther an' th' young Covey for th' rest o' me days!
(*With an indignant toss of his head he walks into the house.*)

THE WOMAN (*going out*). I know I'll fall down in a dead faint if I heard another shot go off anyway near me—isn't it awful?
(MRS. GOGAN *comes out of the house pushing a pram before her. As she enters the street,* BESSIE *rushes out, follows* MRS. GOGAN, *and catches hold of the pram, stopping* MRS. GOGAN'S *progress.*)

BESSIE. Here, where are you goin' with that? How quick you were, me lady, to clap your eyes on th' pram. . . . Maybe you don't know that Mrs. Sullivan, before she went to spend Easther with her people in Dunboyne, gave me sthrict injunctions to give an occasional look to see if it was still standin' where it was left in th' corner of th' lobby.

MRS. GOGAN. That remark of yours, Mrs. Bessie Burgess, requires a little considheration, seein' that th' pram was left on our lobby, an' not on yours; a foot or two a little to th' left of th' jamb of me own room door; nor is it needful to mention th' name of th' person that gave a squint to see if it was there th' first thing in th' mornin', an' th' last thing in th' stillness o' th' night; never failin' to realize that her eyes couldn't be goin' wrong, be sthretchin' out her arm an' runnin' her hand over th' pram, to make sure that th' sight was no deception! Moreover, somethin's tellin' me that th' runnin' hurry of

an inthrest you're takin' in it now is a sudden ambition to use th' pram for a purpose that a loyal woman of law an' ordher would stagger away from!
(*She gives the pram a sudden push that pulls* BESSIE *forward.*)

BESSIE (*still holding the pram*). There's not as much as one body in th' house that doesn't know that it wasn't Bessie Burgess that was always shakin' her voice complainin' about people leavin' bassinettes in th' way of them that, week in an' week out, had to pay their rent, an' always had to find a regular accommodation for her own furniture in her own room. . . . An' as for law an' ordher, puttin' aside th' harp an' shamrock, Bessie Burgess 'll have as much respect as she wants for th' lion an' unicorn!

PETER (*appearing at the door*). I think I'll go with th' pair of yous an' see th' fun. A fella might as well chance it, anyhow.

MRS. GOGAN (*taking no notice of* PETER, *and pushing the pram on another step*). Take your rovin' lumps o' hands from pattin' th' bassinette, if you please, maam, an', steppin' from th' threshold of good manners, let me tell you, Mrs. Burgess, that's it's a fat wondher to Jennie Gogan that a lady-like singer o' hymns like yourself would lower her thoughts from sky-thinkin' to sthretch out her arm in a sly-seekin' way to pinch anything dhriven asthray in th' confusion of th' battle our boys is makin' for th' freedom of their counthry!

PETER (*laughing and rubbing his hands together*). Hee, hee, hee, hee, hee! I'll go with th' pair of yous and give yous a hand.

MRS. GOGAN (*with a rapid turn of her head as she shoves the pram forward*). Get up in th' prambulator an' we'll wheel you down.

BESSIE (*to* MRS. GOGAN). Poverty an' hardship has sent Bessie Burgess to abide with sthrange company, but she always knew them she had to live with from backside to breakfast time; an' she can tell them, always havin' had a Christian kinch on her conscience, that a passion for thievin' an' pinchin' would find her soul a foreign place to live in, an' that her present intention is quite th' lofty-hearted one of pickin' up anything shaken up an' scatthered about in th' loose confusion of a general plundher!
(*By this time they have disappeared from view.* PETER *is following when the boom of a big gun in the distance brings him to a quick halt.*)

PETER. God Almighty, that's th' big gun again! God forbid any harm would happen to them, but sorra mind I'd mind if they met with a dhrop in their mad endeyvours to plundher an' desthroy.
(*He looks down the street for a moment, then runs to the hall door of the house, which is open, and shuts it with a vicious pull; he then goes to the chair in which* MOLLSER *had sat, sits down, takes out his pipe, lights it and begins to smoke with his head carried at a*

haughty angle. THE COVEY *comes staggering in with a ten-stone sack of flour on his back. On the top of the sack is a ham. He goes over to the door, pushes it with his head, and finds he can't open it; he turns slightly in the direction of* PETER.)

THE COVEY (*to* PETER). Who shut the door? . . . (*He kicks at it.*) Here, come on an' open it, will you? This isn't a mot's hand-bag I've got on me back.

PETER. Now, me young Covey, d'ye think I'm goin' to be your lackey?

THE COVEY (*angrily*). Will you open th' door y'oul—

PETER (*shouting*). Don't be assin' me to open any door, don't be assin' me to open any door for you. . . . Makin' a shame an' sin o' th' cause that good men are fightin' for. . . . Oh, God forgive th' people that, instead o' burnishin' th' work th' boys is doin' to-day, with quiet honesty an' patience, is revilin' their sacrifices with a riot of lootin' an' roguery!

THE COVEY. Isn't your own eyes leppin' out o' your head with envy that you haven't th' guts to ketch a few o' th' things that God is givin' to His chosen people? . . . Y'oul hypocrite, if every one was blind you'd steal a cross off an ass's back!

PETER (*very calmly*). You're not goin' to make me lose me temper; you can go on with your proddin' as long as you like; goad an' goad an goad away; hee hee, heee! I'll not lose me temper.
(*Somebody opens door and* THE COVEY *goes in.*)

THE COVEY (*inside, mockingly.*) Cuckoo-oo!

PETER (*running to the door and shouting in a blaze of passion as he follows* THE COVEY *in*). You lean, long, lanky, lath of a lowsey bastard. . . . (*Following him in.*) Lowsey bastard, lowsey bastard!
(BESSIE *and* MRS. GOGAN *enter, the pride of a great joy illuminating their faces.* BESSIE *is pushing the pram, which is filled with clothes and boots; on the top of the boots and clothes is a fancy table, which* MRS. GOGAN *is holding on with her left hand, while with her right hand she holds a chair on the top of her head. They are heard talking to each other before they enter.*)

MRS. GOGAN (*outside*). I don't remember ever havin' seen such lovely pairs as them, (*they appear*) with th' pointed toes an' th' cuban heels.

BESSIE. They'll go grand with th' dhresses we're afther liftin', when we've stitched a sthray bit o' silk to lift th' bodices up a little bit higher, so as to shake th' shame out o' them, an' make them fit for women that hasn't lost themselves in th' nakedness o' th' times.
(*They fussily carry in the chair, the table and some of the other*

goods. They return to bring in the est.)

PETER (*at door, sourly to* MRS. GOGAN). Ay, you. Mollser looks as if she was goin' to faint, an' your youngster is roarin' in convulsions in her lap.

MRS. GOGAN (*snappily*). She's never any other way but faintin'! (*She goes to go in with some things in her arms, when a shot from a rifle rings out. She and* BESSIE *make a bolt for the door, which* PETER, *in a panic, tries to shut before they have got inside.*)

MRS. GOGAN. Ay, ay, ay, you cowardly oul' fool, what are you thryin' to shut th' door on us for?
(*They retreat tumultuously inside. A pause; then* CAPTAIN BRENNAN *comes in supporting* LIEUTENANT LANGON, *whose arm is around* BRENNAN'S *neck.* LANGON'S *face, which is ghastly white, is momentarily convulsed with spasms of agony. He is in a state of collapse, and* BRENNAN is almost carrying *him. After a few moments* CLITHEROE, *pale, and in a state of calm nervousness, follows, looking back in the direction from which he came, a rifle, held at the ready, in his hands.*)

CAPT. BRENNAN (*savagely to* CLITHEROE). Why did you fire over their heads? Why didn't you fire to kill?

CLITHEROE. No, no, Bill; bad as they are they're Irishmen an' women.

CAPT. BRENNAN (*savagely*). Irish be damned! Attackin' an' mobbin' th' men that are riskin' their lives for them. If these slum lice gather at our heels again, plug one o' them, or I'll soon shock them with a shot or two meself!

LIEUT. LANGON (*moaningly*). My God, is there ne'er an ambulance knockin' around anywhere? . . . Th' stomach is ripped out o' me; I feel it—o-o-oh, Christ!

CAPT. BRENNAN. Keep th' heart up, Jim; we'll soon get help, now.
(NORA *rushes wildly out of the house and flings her arms round the neck of* CLITHEROE *with a fierce and joyous insistence. Her hair is down, her face is haggard, but her eyes are agleam with the light of happy relief.*)

NORA. Jack, Jack, Jack; oh, God be thanked . . . be thanked. . . . He has been kind and merciful to His poor handmaiden. . . . My Jack, my own Jack, that I thought was lost is found, Oh, God be praised for ever, evermore! . . . My poor Jack. . . . Kiss me, kiss me, Jack, kiss your own Nora!

CLITHEROE (*kissing her, and speaking brokenly*). My Nora; my little, beautiful Nora, I wish to God I'd never left you.

NORA. It doesn't matter—not now, not now, Jack. It will make us dearer than ever to each other. . . . Kiss me, kiss me again.

CLITHEROE. Now, for God's sake, Nora, don't make a scene.

NORA. I won't, I won't; I promise, I promise, Jack; honest to God. I'll be silent an' brave to bear th' joy of feelin' you safe in my arms again. . . . It's hard to force away th' tears of happiness at th' end of an awful agony.

BESSIE (*from the upper window*). Th' Minsthrel Boys aren't feelin' very comfortable now. Th' big guns has knocked all th' harps out of their hands. General Clitheroe'd rather be unlacin' his wife's bodice than standin' at a barricade. . . . An' th' professor of chicken-butcherin' there, finds he's up against somethin' a little tougher even than his own chickens, an' that's sayin' a lot!

CAPT. BRENNAN (*up to* BESSIE). Shut up, y'oul' hag!

BESSIE (*down to* BRENNAN). Choke th' chicken, choke th' chicken, choke th' chicken!

LIEUT. LANGON. For God's sake, Bill, bring me some place where me wound 'll be looked afther. . . . Am I to die before anything is done to save me?

CAPT. BRENNAN (*to* CLITHEROE). Come on, Jack. We've got to get help for Jim, here—have you no thought for his pain an' danger?

BESSIE. Choke th' chicken, choke th' chicken, choke th' chicken!

CLITHEROE (*to* NORA). Loosen me, darling, let me go.

NORA (*clinging to him*). No, no, no, I'll not let you go! Come on, come up to our home, Jack, my sweetheart, my lover, my husband, an' we'll forget th' last few terrible days! . . . I look tired now, but a few hours of happy rest in your arms will bring back th' bloom of freshness again, an' you will be glad, you will be glad, glad . . . glad!

LIEUT. LANGON. Oh, if I'd kep' down only a little longer, I mightn't ha' been hit! Every one else escapin', an' me gettin' me belly ripped asundher! . . . I couldn't scream, couldn't even scream. . . . D'ye think I'm really badly wounded, Bill? Me clothes seem to be all soakin' wet. . . . It's blood. . . . My God, it must be me own blood!

CAPT. BRENNAN (*to* CLITHEROE). Go on, Jack, bid her good-bye with another kiss, an' be done with it! D'ye want Langon to die in me arms while you're dallyin' with your Nora?

CLITHEROE (*to* NORA). I must go, I must go, Nora. I'm sorry we met at all. . . . It couldn't be helped—all other ways were blocked be th' British. . . . Let me go, can't you, Nora? D'ye want me to be unthrue to me comrades?

NORA. No, I won't let you go. . . . I want you to be thrue to me, Jack. . . . I'm your dearest comrade; I'm your thruest comrade. . . . They only want th' comfort of havin' you in the same danger as themselves. . . . Oh, Jack, I can't let you go!

CLITHEROE. You must, Nora, you must.

NORA. All last night at th' barricades I sought you, Jack. . . . I didn't think of th' danger—I could only think of you. . . . I asked for you everywhere. . . . Some o' them laughed. . . . I was pushed away, but I shoved back. . . . Some o' them even sthruck me. . . . an' I screamed an' screamed your name!

CLITHEROE (*in fear her action would give him future shame*). What possessed you to make a show of yourself, like that? . . . What way d'ye think I'll feel when I'm told my wife was bawlin' for me at th' barricades? What are you more than any other woman?

NORA. No more, maybe; but you are more to me than any other man, Jack. . . . I didn't mean any harm, honestly, Jack. . . . I couldn't help it. . . . I shouldn't have told you. . . . My love for you made me mad with terror.

CLITHEROE (*angrily*). They'll say now that I sent you out th' way I'd have an excuse to bring you home. . . . Are you goin' to turn all th' risks I'm takin' into a laugh?

LIEUT. LANGON. Let me lie down, let me lie down, Bill; th' pain would be easier, maybe, lyin' down. . . . Oh, God, have mercy on me!

CAPT. BRENNAN (*to* LANGON). A few steps more, Jim, a few steps more; thry to stick it for a few steps more.

LIEUT. LANGON. Oh, I can't, I can't, I can't!

CAPT. BRENNAN (*to* CLITHEROE). Are you comin', man, or are you goin' to make an arrangement for another honeymoon. . . . If you want to act th' renegade, say so, an' we'll be off!

BESSIE (*from above*). Runnin' from th' Tommies—choke th' chicken. Runnin' from th' Tommies—choke th' chicken!

CLITHEROE (*savagely to* BRENNAN). Damn you, man, who wants to act th' renegade? (*To* NORA) Here, let go your hold; let go, I say!

NORA (*clinging to* CLITHEROE, *and indicating* BRENNAN). Look, Jack, look at th' anger in his face; look at th' fear glintin' in his eyes. . . . He, himself's afraid, afraid, afraid! . . . He wants you to go th' way he'll have th' chance of death sthrikin' you an' missin' him! . . . Turn round an' look at him, Jack, look at him, look at him! . . . His very soul is cold . . . shiverin' with th' thought of what may happen to him. . . . It is his fear that is thryin' to frighten you from recognisin' th' same fear that is in your own heart!

CLITHEROE (*struggling to release himself from* NORA). Damn you, woman, will you let me go!

CAPT. BRENNAN (*fiercely, to* CLITH-

EROE). Why are you beggin' her to let you go? Are you afraid of her, or what? Break her hold on you, man, or go up, an' sit on her lap!
(CLITHEROE *trying roughly to break her hold.*)

NORA (*imploringly*). Oh, Jack . . . Jack . . . Jack!

LIEUT. LANGON (*agonizingly*). Brennan, a priest; I'm dyin', I think, I'm dyin'!

CLITHEROE (*to* NORA). If you won't do it quietly, I'll have to make you! (*To* BRENNAN) Here, hold this gun, you, for a minute. (*He hands the gun to* BRENNAN.)

NORA (*pitifully*). Please, Jack. . . . You're hurting me, Jack. . . . Honestly. . . . Oh, you're hurting . . . me! . . . I won't, I won't, I won't! . . . Oh, Jack, I gave you everything you asked of me. . . . Don't fling me from you, now!
(*He roughly loosens her grip, and pushes her away from him.* NORA *sinks to the ground and lies there.*)

NORA (*weakly*). Ah, Jack. . . . Jack. . . . Jack!

CLITHEROE (*taking the gun back from* BRENNAN). Come on, come on.
(*They go out.* BESSIE *looks at* NORA *lying on the street, for a few moments, then, leaving the window, she comes out, runs over to* NORA, *lifts her up in her arms, and carries her swiftly into the house. A short pause, then down the street is heard a wild, drunken yell; it comes nearer, and* FLUTHER *enters, frenzied, wild-eyed, mad, roaring drunk. In his arms is an earthen half-gallon jar of whisky; streaming from one of the pockets of his coat is the arm of a new tunic shirt; on his head is a woman's vivid blue hat with gold lacing, all of which he has looted.*)

FLUTHER (*singing in a frenzy*):

Fluther's a jolly good fella! . . .
Fluther's a jolly good fella!
Up th' rebels! . . . That nobody can deny!

(*He beats on the door.*)
Get us a mug or a jug, or somethin', some o' yous, one o' yous, will yous, before I lay one o' yous out! . . . (*Looking down the street*) Bang an' fire away for all Fluther cares. . . . (*Banging at door*) Come down an' open th' door, some of yous, one o' yous, will yous, before I lay some o' yous out! . . . Th' whole city can topple home to hell, for Fluther!
(*Inside the house is heard a scream from* NORA *followed by a moan.*)

FLUTHER (*singing furiously*):

That nobody can deny, that nobody can deny,
For Fluther's a jolly good fella,
Fluther's a jolly good fella,
Fluther's a jolly good fella . . .
Up th' rebels! That nobody can deny!

(*His frantic movements cause him to spill some of the whisky out of the jar.*)

Blast you, Fluther, don't be spillin' th' precious liquor! (*He kicks at the door.*) Ay, give us a mug or a jug, or somethin', one o' yous, some o' yous, will yous, before I lay one o' yous out!
(*The door suddenly opens, and* BESSIE, *coming out, grips him by the collar.*)

BESSIE (*indignantly*). You bowsey, come in ower o' that. . . . I'll thrim your thricks o' dhrunken dancin' for you, an' none of us knowin' how soon we'll bump into a world we were never in before!

FLUTHER (*as she is pulling him in*). Ay, th' jar, th' jar, th' jar!
(*A short pause, then again is heard a scream of pain from* NORA. *The door opens and* MRS. GOGAN *and* BESSIE *are seen standing at it.*)

BESSIE. Fluther would go, only he's too dhrunk, . . . Oh, God, isn't it a pity he's so dhrunk! We'll have to thry to get a docthor somewhere.

MRS. GOGAN. I'd be afraid to go. . . . Besides, Mollser's terribly bad. I don't think you'll get a docthor to come. It's hardly any use goin'.

BESSIE (*determinedly*). I'll risk it. Give her a little of Fluther's whisky. . . . It's th' fright that's brought it on her so soon. . . . Go on back to her, you.
(MRS. GOGAN *goes in, and* BESSIE *softly closes the door. She is moving forward, when the sound of some rifle shots, and the tok, tok, tok of a distant machine-gun bring her to a sudden halt. She hesitates for a moment, then she tightens her shawl round her, as if it were a shield, then she firmly and swiftly goes out.*)

BESSIE (*as she goes out*). Oh, God, be Thou my help in time o' throuble. An' shelter me safely in th' shadow of Thy wings!

CURTAIN

ACT FOUR

The living-room of BESSIE BURGESS. *It is one of two small attic rooms (the other, used as a bedroom, is to the Left), the ceiling slopes up towards the back, giving to the apartment a look of compressed confinement. In the centre of the ceiling is a small skylight. There is an unmistakable air of poverty bordering on destitution. The paper on the walls is torn and soiled, particularly near the fire where the cooking is done, and near the washstand, where the washing is done. The fireplace is to the Left. A small armchair near fire. Two small windows at Back. A pane of one of these windows is starred by the entrance of a bullet. Under the window to the Right is an oak coffin standing on two kitchen chairs. Near the coffin is a home-manufactured stool, on which are two lighted candles. Between the two windows is a worn-out dresser on which is a small quantity of delf. Tattered remains of cheap lace curtains drape the windows. Standing near the window on Left is a brass standing-lamp with a fancy shade; hanging on the wall near the same window is a vividly crimson silk dress, both of which have been looted. A door on Left leading to the bedroom. Another opposite giving a way to the rest of the house. To the Left of this door a common washstand. A tin kettle, very black, and an old saucepan inside the fender. There is no light in the room but that given from the two candles and the fire. The dusk has well fallen, and the glare of the burning buildings in the town can be seen through the windows in the distant sky.* THE COVEY *and* FLUTHER *have been playing cards, sitting on the floor by the light of the candles on the stool near the coffin. When the curtain rises* THE COVEY *is shuffling the cards,* PETER *is sitting in a stiff, dignified way beside him, and* FLUTHER *is kneeling beside the window Left, cautiously looking out. It is a few days later.*

FLUTHER (*furtively peeping out of the window*). Give them a good shuffling. . . . Th' sky's gettin' reddher an' reddher. . . . You'd think it was afire. . . . Half o' th' city must be burnin.'

THE COVEY. If I was you, Fluther, I'd keep away from that window. . . . It's dangerous, an', besides, if they see you, you'll only bring a nose on th' house.

PETER. Yes; an' he knows we nad to leave our own place th' way they were riddlin' it with machine-gun fire. . . . He'll keep on pimpin' an' pimpin' there, till we have to fly out o' this place too.

FLUTHER (*ironically*). If they make any attack here, we'll send you out in your green an' glory uniform, shakin' your sword over your head, an' they'll fly before you as th' Danes flew before Brian Boru!

THE COVEY (*placing the cards on the floor, after shuffling them*). Come on, an' cut.
(FLUTHER *comes over, sits on floor, and cuts the cards.*)

THE COVEY (*having dealt the cards*). Spuds up again.
(NORA *moans feebly in room on Left.*)

FLUTHER. There, she's at it again. She's been quiet for a good long time, all th' same.

THE COVEY. She was quiet before, sure, an' she broke out again worse than ever. . . . What was led that time?

PETER. Thray o' Hearts, Thray o' Hearts, Thray o' Hearts.

FLUTHER. It's damned hard lines to think of her dead-born kiddie lyin there in th' arms o' poor little Mollser. Mollser snuffed it, sudden too, afther all.

THE COVEY. Sure she never got any care. How could she get it, an' th' mother out day an' night lookin' for work, an' her consumptive husband leavin' her with a baby to be born before he died.

VOICES IN A LILTING CHANT TO THE LEFT IN A DISTANT STREET. Red Cr . . . oss, Red Cr . . . oss!

. . . Ambu . . . lance, Ambu . . . lance!

THE COVEY (*to* FLUTHER). Your deal, Fluther.

FLUTHER (*shuffling and dealing the cards*). It'll take a lot out o' Nora—if she'll ever be th' same.

THE COVEY. Th' docthor thinks she'll never be th' same; thinks she'll be a little touched here. (*He touches his forehead.*) She's ramblin' a lot; thinkin' she's out in th' counthry with Jack; or, gettin' his dinner ready for him before he comes home; or, yellin' for her kiddie. All that, though, might be th' chloroform she got. . . . I don't know what we'd have done only for oul' Bessie: up with her for th' past three nights, hand runnin'.

FLUTHER. I always knew there was never anything really derogatory wrong with poor, oul' Bessie. (*To* PETER *who is taking a trick*) Ay, houl' on, there, don't be so damned quick—that's my thrick.

PETER. What's your trick? It's my thrick, man.

FLUTHER (*loudly*). How is it your thrick?

PETER (*answering as loudly*). Didn't I lead th' deuce!

FLUTHER. You must be gettin' blind, man; don't you see th' ace?

BESSIE (*appearing at door of room, Left; in a tense whisper*). D'ye want to waken her again on me, when's she's just gone asleep? If she wakes will yous come an' mind her? If I hear a whisper out o' one o' yous again, I'll . . . gut yous!

THE COVEY (*in a whisper*). S-s-s-h. She can hear anything above a whisper.

PETER (*looking up at the ceiling*). Th' gentle an' merciful God 'll give th' pair o' yous a scawldin' an' a scarifyin' one of these days!

(FLUTHER *takes a bottle of whisky from his pocket, and takes a drink.*)

THE COVEY (*to* FLUTHER). Why don't you spread that out, man, an' thry to keep a sup for to-morrow?

FLUTHER. Spread it out? Keep a sup for to-morrow? How th' hell does a fella know there'll be any to-morrow? If I'm goin' to be whipped away, let me be whipped away when it's empty, an' not when it's half full! (*To* BESSIE *who has seated herself in an armchair at the fire*) How is she, now, Bessie?

BESSIE. I left her sleeping quietly. When I'm listenin' to her babblin', I think she'll never be much betther than she is. Her eyes have a hauntin' way of lookin' in instead of lookin' out, as if her mind had been lost alive in madly mindlin' memories of th' past. . . . (*Sleepily*) Crushin' her thoughts . . . together . . . in a fierce . . . an' fanciful . . . (*she nods her head and starts wakefully*) idea that dead things are livin', an' livin' things are dead. . . . (*With a start*) Was that a scream I heard her give? (*Reassured*) Blessed God, I think I hear her screamin' every minute! An' it's only there with me that I'm able to keep awake.

THE COVEY. She'll sleep, maybe, for a long time, now. Ten there.

FLUTHER. Ten here. If she gets a long sleep, she might be all right. Peter's th' lone five.

THE COVEY. Whist! I think I hear somebody movin' below. Whoever it is, he's comin' up.

(*A pause. Then the door opens and* CAPTAIN BRENNAN *comes into the room. He has changed his uniform for a suit of civies. His eyes droop with the heaviness of exhaustion; his face is pallid and drawn. His clothes are dusty and stained here and there with mud. He leans heavily on the back of a chair as he stands.*)

CAPT. BRENNAN. Mrs. Clitheroe; where's Mrs. Clitheroe? I was told I'd find her here.

BESSIE. What d'ye want with Mrs. Clitheroe?

CAPT. BRENNAN. I've a message, a last message for her from her husband.

BESSIE. Killed! He's not killed, is he!

CAPT. BRENNAN (*sinking stiffly and painfully on to a chair*). In th' Imperial Hotel; we fought till th' place was in flames. He was shot through th' arm, an' then through th' lung. . . . I could do nothin' for him—only watch his breath comin' an' goin' in quick, jerky gasps, an' a tiny sthream o' blood thricklin' out of his mouth, down over his lower lip. . . . I said a prayer for th' dyin', an' twined his Rosary beads around his fingers. . . . Then I had to leave him to save meself. . . . (*He shows some holes in his coat.*) Look at th' way a machine-gun tore at me coat, as I belted out o' th' buildin' an' darted across th' sthreet for shelter. . . . An' then, I seen The Plough an' th' Stars fallin' like a shot as th' roof crashed in, an' where I'd left poor Jack was nothin' but a leppin' spout o' flame!

BESSIE (*with partly repressed vehemence*). Ay, you left him! You twined his Rosary beads round his fingers, an' then, you run like a hare to get out o' danger!

CAPT. BRENNAN. I took me chance as well as him. . . . He took it like a man. His last whisper was to "Tell Nora to be brave; that I'm ready to meet my God, an' that I'm proud to die for Ireland." An' when our General heard it he said that "Commandant Clitheroe's end was a gleam of glory." Mrs. Clitheroe's grief will be a joy when she realises that she has had a hero for a husband.

BESSIE. If you only seen her, you'd know to th' differ.

(NORA *appears at door, Left. She is clad only in her nightdress; her hair, uncared for some days, is hanging in disorder over her shoulders. Her pale face looks paler still because of a vivid red spot on the tip of each cheek. Her eyes are glimmering with the light of incipient insanity; her hands are nervously fiddling with her nightgown. She halts at the door for a moment, looks vacantly around the room, and then comes slowly in. The rest do not notice her till she speaks.*)

NORA (*in a quiet and monotonous tone*). No . . . Not there, Jack. . . . I can feel comfortably only in our own familiar place beneath th' bramble tree. . . . We must be walking for a long time! I feel very, very tired. . . . Have we to go farther, or have we passed it by? (*Passing her hand across her eyes*) Curious mist on my eyes. . . . Why don't you hold my hand, Jack. . . . (*Excitedly*) No, no, Jack, it's not. Can't you see it's a goldfinch. Look at th' black-satiny wings with th' gold bars, an' th' splash of crimson on its head. . . . (*Wearily*) Something ails me, something ails me. . . . Don't kiss me like that; you take my breath away, Jack. . . . Why do you frown at me? . . . You're going away, and (*frightened*) I can't follow you! Something's keeping me from moving. . . . (*Crying out*) Jack, Jack, Jack!

BESSIE (*who has gone over and caught* NORA's *arm*). Now, Mrs. Clitheroe, you're a terrible woman to get out of bed. . . . You'll get cold if you stay here in them clothes.

NORA. Cold? I'm feelin' very cold; it's chilly out here in th' counthry. . . . (*Looking around, frightened*) What place is this? Where am I?

BESSIE (*coaxingly*). You're all right, Nora; you're with friends, an' in a safe place. Don't you know your uncle an' your cousin, an' poor oul' Fluther?

PETER (*about to go over to* NORA). Nora, darlin', now——

FLUTHER (*pulling him back*). Now, leave her to Bessie, man. A crowd 'll only make her worse.

NORA (*thoughtfully*). There is something I want to remember, an' I can't. (*With agony*) I can't, I can't, I can't! My head, my head! (*Suddenly breaking from* BESSIE, *and running over to the men, and gripping* FLUTHER *by the shoulders*) Where is it? Where's my baby? Tell me where you've put it, where've you hidden it? My baby, my baby; I want my baby. My head, my poor head. . . . Oh, I can't tell what is wrong with me. (*Screaming*) Give him to me, give me my husband!

BESSIE. Blessin' o' God on us, isn't this pitiful!

NORA (*struggling with* BESSIE). I won't go away for you; I won't. Not till you give me back my husband. (*Screaming*) Murderers, that's what yous are; murderers, murderers!

BESSIE. S-s-sh. We'll bring Mr. Clitheroe back to you, if you'll only lie down an' stop quiet. . . . (*Trying to lead her in*) Come on, Nora, an' I'll sing something to you.

NORA. I feel as if my life was thryin' to force its way out of my body. . . . I can hardly breathe. . . . I'm frightened, I'm frightened, I'm frightened! For God's sake, don't leave me, Bessie. Hold my hand, put your arms around me!

FLUTHER (*to* BRENNAN). Now you can see th' way she is, man.

PETER. An' what way would she be if she heard Jack had gone west?

THE COVEY (*to* PETER). Shut up, you, man!

BESSIE (*to* NORA). We'll have to be brave, an' let patience clip away th' heaviness of th' slow-movin' hours, rememberin' that sorrow may endure for th' night, but joy cometh in th' mornin'. . . . Come on in, an' I'll sing to you, an' you'll rest quietly.

NORA (*stopping suddenly on her way to the room*). Jack an' me are going out somewhere this evenin'. Where I can't tell. Isn't it curious I can't remember. . . . Maura, Maura, Jack, if th' baby's a girl; any name you like; if th' baby's a boy! . . . He's there. (*Screaming*) He's there an' they won't give him back to me!

BESSIE. S-ss-s-h, darlin', s-ssh. I won't sing to you, if you're not quiet.

NORA (*nervously holding* BESSIE). Hold my hand, hold my hand, an' sing to me, sing to me!

BESSIE. Come in an' lie down, an' I'll sing to you.

NORA (*vehemently*). Sing to me, sing to me; sing, sing!

BESSIE (*singing as she leads* NORA *into room*):

Lead, kindly light, amid th' encircling gloom,
Lead Thou me on.
Th' night is dark an' I am far from home,
Lead Thou me on.
Keep Thou my feet, I do not ask to see
Th' distant scene—one step enough for me.

So long that Thou hast blessed me, sure Thou still
Will lead me on;

(*They go in.*)

BESSIE (*singing in room*):

O'er moor an' fen, o'er crag an' torrent, till
Th' night is gone.
An' in th' morn those angel faces smile,
That I have lov'd long since, an' lost awhile!

THE COVEY (*to* BRENNAN). Now that you've seen how bad she is, an' that we daren't tell her what has happened till she's betther, you'd best be slippin' back to where you come from.

CAPT. BRENNAN. There's no chance o' slippin' back now, for th' military are everywhere: a fly couldn't get through. I'd never have got here, only I managed to change me uniform for what I'm wearin'. . . . I'll have to take me chance, an' thry to lie low here for a while.

THE COVEY (*frightened*). There's no place here to lie low. Th' Tommies 'll be hoppin' in here, any minute!

PETER (*aghast*). An' then we'd all be shanghaied!

THE COVEY. Be God, there's enough afther happenin' to us!

FLUTHER (*warningly, as he listens*). Whisht, whisht, th' whole o' yous. I think I hear th' clang of a rifle butt on th' floor of th' hall below. (*All alertness*) Here, come on with th' cards again. I'll deal. (*He shuffles and deals the cards to all.*)

FLUTHER. Clubs up. (*To* BRENNAN.) Thry to keep your hands from shakin', man. You lead, Peter. (*As* PETER *throws out a card*) Four o' Hearts led.
(*The door opens and* CORPORAL STODDART *of the Wiltshires enters in full war kit; steel helmet, rifle and bayonet and trench tools. He looks round the room. A pause and a palpable silence.*)

FLUTHER (*breaking the silence*). Two tens an' a five.

CORPORAL STODDART. 'ello. (*Indicating the coffin.*) This the stiff?

THE COVEY. Yis.

CORPORAL STODDART. Who's gowing with it? Ownly one allowed to gow with it, you knaow.

THE COVEY. I dunno.

CORPORAL STODDART. You dunnow?

THE COVEY. I dunno.

BESSIE (*coming into the room*). She's afther slippin' off to sleep again, thanks be to God. I'm hardly able to keep me own eyes open. (*To the soldier*) Oh, are yous goin' to take away poor little Mollser?

CORPORAL STODDART. Ay; 'oo's agowing with 'er?

BESSIE. Oh, th' poor mother, o' course. God help her, it's a terrible blow to her!

FLUTHER. A terrible blow? Sure, she's in her element now, woman, mixin' earth to earth, an' ashes t'ashes an' dust to dust, an' revellin' in plumes an' hearses, last days an' judgments!

BESSIE (*falling into chair by the fire*). God bless us! I'm jaded!

CORPORAL STODDART. Was she plugged?

THE COVEY. Ah, no; died o' consumption.

CORPORAL STODDART. How, is that hall? Thought she moight 'ave been plugged.

THE COVEY. Is that all? Isn't it enough. D'ye know, comrade, that more die o' consumption than are killed in th' wars? An' it's all because of th' system we're livin' undher?

CORPORAL STODDART. Ow, Oi knoaw. Oi'm a Sowcialist moiself, but Oi 'as to do moi dooty.

THE COVEY (*ironically*). Dooty! Th' only dooty of a Socialist is th' emancipation of th' workers.

CORPORAL STODDART. Ow, a man's a man, an 'e 'as to foight for 'is country, 'asn't 'e?

FLUTHER (*aggressively*). You're not fightin' for your counthry here, are you?

PETER (*anxiously, to* FLUTHER). Ay, ay, Fluther, none o' that, none o' that!

THE COVEY. Fight for your counthry! Did y'ever read, comrade, Jenersky's *Thesis on the Origin, Development an' Consolidation of th' Evolutionary Idea of the Proletariat?*

CORPORAL STODDART. Ow, cheese it, Paddy, cheese it!

BESSIE (*sleepily*). How is things in th' town, Tommy?

CORPORAL STODDART. Ow, Hoi fink hit's nearly howver. We've got 'em surrounded, hand we're clowsing hin hon the bloighters. Ow, hit was honly a little bit hof ha dawg foight.
(*The sharp ping of the sniper's rifle is heard, followed by a squeal of pain.*)

VOICES TO THE LEFT IN A CHANT. Red Cr . . . oss, Red Cr . . . oss! Ambu . . . lance, Ambu . . . lance!

CORPORAL STODDART (*excitedly*). Chroist, that's hanother hof hour men 'it by that blawsted snoiper! 'e's knocking abaht 'ere, somewheres. Gawd, when we gets th' bloighter, we'll give 'im the cold steel, we will. We'll jab the belly haht hof 'im, we will!
(MRS. GOGAN *comes in tearfully, and a little proud of the importance of being directly connected with death.*)

MRS. GOGAN (*to* FLUTHER). I'll never forget what you done for me, Fluther, goin' around at th' risk of your life settlin' everything with th' undhertaker an' th' cemetery people. When all me own were afraid to put their noses out, you plunged like a good one through hummin' bullets, an' they knockin' fire out o' th' road, tinklin' through th' frightened windows, an' splashin' themselves to pieces on th' walls! An' you'll find, that Mollser in th' happy place she's gone to, won't forget to whisper, now an' again, th' name o' Fluther.

CORPORAL STODDART. Get it aht, mother, git it aht.

BESSIE (*from the chair*). It's excusin' me you'll be, Mrs. Gogan, for not stannin' up, seein' I'm shaky on me feet for want of a little sleep, an' not desirin' to show any disrespect to poor little Mollser.

FLUTHER. Sure, we all know, Bessie, that it's vice versa with you.

MRS. GOGAN (*to* BESSIE). Indeed, it's meself that has well chronicled, Mrs. Burgess, all your gentle hurryin's to me little Mollser, when she was alive, bringin' her somethin' to dhrink, or somethin' t'eat, an' never passin' her without liftin' up her heart with a delicate word o' kindness.

CORPORAL STODDART (*impatiently but kindly*). Git it aht, git it aht, mother.
(THE COVEY, FLUTHER, BRENNAN *and* PETER *carry out the coffin, followed by* MRS. GOGAN.)

CORPORAL STODDART (*to* BESSIE, *who is almost asleep*). 'Ow many men is in this 'ere 'ouse? (*No answer. Loudly*) 'Ow many men is in this 'ere 'ouse?

BESSIE (*waking with a start*). God, I was nearly asleep! . . . How many men? Didn't you see them?

CORPORAL STODDART. Are they hall that are hin the 'ouse?

BESSIE. Oh, there's none higher up, but there may be more lower down. Why?

CORPORAL STODDART. All men in the district 'as to be rounded up. Somebody's giving 'elp to the snoipers, hand we 'as to take precautions. If Oi 'ad my woy, Oi'd make 'em all join hup, hand do their bit! But Oi suppowse they hand you are all Shinners.

BESSIE (*who has been sinking into sleep, waking up to a sleepy vehemence*). Bessie Burgess is no Shinner, an' never had no thruck with anything spotted be th' fingers o' th' Fenians. But always made it her business to harness herself for Church whenever she knew that God Save The King was goin' to be sung at t'end of th' service; whose only son went to th' front in th' first contingent of the Dublin Fusiliers, an' that's on his way home carryin' a shatthered arm that he got fightin' for his King an' counthry.
(*Her head sinks slowly forward again.* PETER *comes in to the room; his body is stiffened and his face is wearing a comically indignant look. He walks to and fro at the back of the room, evidently repressing a violent desire to speak angrily. He is followed in by* FLUTHER, THE COVEY *and* BRENNAN, *who slinks into an obscure corner of the room, nervous of notice.*)

FLUTHER (*after an embarrassing pause*). Th' air in th' sthreet outside's shakin' with the firin' o' rifles, an' machine-guns. It must be a hot shop in th' middle o' th' scrap.

CORPORAL STODDART. We're pumping lead in on 'em from every side, now; they'll soon be shoving up th' white flag.

PETER (*with a shout*). I'm tellin' you either o' yous two lowsers 'ud make a betther hearseman than Peter! proddin' an' pokin' at me an' I helpin' to carry out a corpse!

FLUTHER. It wasn't a very derogatory thing for th' Covey to say that you'd make a fancy hearseman, was it?

PETER (*furiously*). A pair o' redjesthered bowseys pondherin' from mornin' till night on how they'll get a chance to break a gap through th' quiet nature of a man that's always endeavourin' to chase out of him any sthray thought of venom against his fella-man!

THE COVEY. Oh, shut it; shut it, shut it!

PETER. As long as I'm a livin' man, responsible for me thoughts, words an' deeds to th' Man above, I'll feel meself instituted to fight again' th' sliddherin' ways of a pair o' picaroons, whisperin', concurrin', concoctin', an' conspirin' together to rendher me unconscious of th' life I'm thryin' to live!

CORPORAL STODDART (*dumbfounded*). What's wrong, Daddy; wot 'ave they done to you?

PETER (*savagely to the Corporal*). You mind your own business! What's it got to do with you, what's wrong with me?

BESSIE (*in a sleepy murmur*). Will yous thry to conthrol yourselves into quietness? Yous'll waken her . . . up . . . on . . . me . . . again. (*She sleeps.*)

FLUTHER. Come on, boys, to th' cards again, an' never mind him.

CORPORAL STODDART. Now use of you gowing to start cawds; you'll be gowing out hof 'ere, soon as Sergeant comes.

FLUTHER. Goin' out o' here? An' why'r we goin' out o' here?

CORPORAL STODDART. All men hin district to be rounded up, and 'eld hin till the scrap his hover.

FLUTHER. An' where'r *we* goin' to be held in?

CORPORAL STODDART. They're putting 'em in ha church.

THE COVEY. A church?

FLUTHER. What sort of a church? Is it a Protestan' Church?

CORPORAL STODDART. I dunnow; I suppowse so.

FLUTHER (*dismayed*). Be God, it'll be a nice thing to be stuck all night in a Protestan' Church!

CORPORAL STODDART. Bring the cawds; you moight get a chance of ha goime.

FLUTHER. Ah, no, that wouldn't do. . . . I wondther? (*After a moment's thought*) Ah, I don't think we'd be doin' anything derogatory be playin' cards in a Protestan' Church.

CORPORAL STODDART. If Oi was you Oi'd bring a little snack with me; you moight be glad of hit before the mawning. (*Sings*):

Oi do loike a snoice mince poy,
Oi do loike a snoice mince poy!

(*The snap of the sniper's rifle rings out again, followed simultaneously by a scream of pain.* CORPORAL STODDART *goes pale, and brings his rifle to the ready, listening.*)

VOICES CHANTING TO THE RIGHT. Red Cro . . . ss, Red Cro . . . ss! Ambu . . . lance, Ambu . . . lance! (SERGEANT TINLEY *comes rapidly in, pale, agitated, and fiercely angry.*)

CORPORAL STODDART (*to sergeant*). One of hour men 'it, Sergeant?

SERGEANT TINLEY. Private Taylor; got 'it roight through the chest, 'e did; han 'owl in front hof 'im has 'ow you could put your fist through, hand arf 'e's back blown awoy! Dum dum bullets they're using. Gang hof Hassassins potting at hus from behind roofs. That's not ploying the goime; why down't they come hinto the howpen hand foight fair!

FLUTHER (*unable to stand the slight*). Fight fair! A few hundhred scrawls o' chaps with a couple o' guns an' Rosary beads, again' a hundhred thousand thrained men with horse, fut an' artillery . . . an' he wants us to fight fair! (*To* SERGEANT) D'ye want us to come out in our skins an' throw stones?

SERGEANT TINLEY (*to* CORPORAL). Are these four all that are 'ere?

CORPORAL STODDART. Four; that's hall, Sergeant.

SERGEANT TINLEY (*vindictively*). Come on, then; get the bloighters aht. (*To the men*) 'Ere, 'op hit aht! Aht hinto the streets with you, and if a snoiper sends hanother of hour men west, you gow with 'im! (*He catches* FLUTHER *by the shoulder.*) Gow hon, git aht!

FLUTHER. Eh, who are you chuckin', eh?

SERGEANT TINLEY (*roughly*). Gow hon, git aht, you bloighter.

FLUTHER. Who are you callin' a bloighter to, eh? I'm a Dublin man, born an' bred in th' city, see?

SERGEANT TINLEY. Oi down't care if you were Broin Buroo; git aht, git aht.

FLUTHER (*halting as he is going out*). Jasus, you an' your guns! Leave them down, an' I'd beat th' two o' yous without sweatin'!

(PETER, BRENNAN, THE COVEY *and* FLUTHER, *followed by the soldiers, go out.* BESSIE *is sleeping heavily on the chair by the fire. After a pause,* NORA *appears at door, Left, in her night-dress. Remaining at door for a few moments she looks vaguely around the room. She then comes in quietly, goes over to the fire, pokes it and puts the kettle on. She thinks for a few moments, pressing her hand to her forehead. She looks questioningly at the fire, and then at the press at back. She goes to the press, opens it, takes out a soiled cloth and spreads it on the table. She then places things for tea on the table.*)

NORA. I imagine th' room looks very odd, somehow. . . . I was nearly forgetting Jack's tea. . . . Ah, I think I'll have everything done before he gets in . . . (*She lilts gently, as she arranges the table.*)

Th' violels were scenting th' woods, Nora,
Displaying their charms to th' bee,
When I first said I lov'd only you, Nora,
An' you said you lov'd only me.

Th' chestnut blooms gleam'd through th' glade, Nora,
A robin sang loud from a tree,

When I first said I lov'd only you, Nora,
An' you said you lov'd only me.

(*She pauses suddenly, and glances round the room.*)

NORA (*doubtfully*). I can't help feelin' this room very strange. . . . What is it? . . . What is it? . . . I must think. . . . I must thry to remember. . . .

VOICES CHANTING IN A DISTANT STREET. Ambu . . . lance, Ambu . . . lance! Red Cro . . . ss, Red Cro . . . ss!

NORA (*startled and listening for a moment, then resuming the arrangement of the table.*)

Trees, birds an' bees sang a song, Nora,
Of happier transports to be,
When I first said I lov'd only you, Nora,
An' you said you lov'd only me.

(*A burst of rifle fire is heard in a street near by, followed by the rapid rok, tok, tok, of a machine-gun.*)

NORA (*staring in front of her and screaming*). Jack, Jack, Jack! My baby, my baby, my baby!

BESSIE (*waking with a start*). You divil, are you afther getting' out o' bed again!

(*She rises and runs towards* NORA, *who rushes to the window, which she frantically opens.*)

NORA (*at window, screaming*). Jack, Jack, for God's sake, come to me!

SOLDIERS (*outside, shouting*). Git awoy, git awoy from that window, there!

BESSIE (*seizing hold of* NORA). Come away, come away, woman, from that window!

NORA (*struggling with* BESSIE). Where is it; where have you hidden it? Oh, Jack, Jack, where are you!

BESSIE (*imploringly*). Mrs. Clitheroe, for God's sake, come away!

NORA (*fiercely*). I won't; he's below. Let . . . me . . . go! You're thryin' to keep me from me husband. I'll follow him. Jack, Jack, come to your Nora!

BESSIE Hus-s-sh, Nora, Nora! He'll be here in a minute. I'll bring him to you, if you'll only be quiet—honest to God, I will.

(*With a great effort* BESSIE *pushes* NORA *away from the window, the force used causing her to stagger against it herself. Two rifle shots ring out in quick succession.* BESSIE *jerks her body convulsively; stands stiffly upright for a moment, a look of agonized astonishment on her face, then she staggers forward, leaning heavily on the table with her hands.*)

BESSIE (*with an arrested scream of fear and pain*). Merciful God, I'm shot, I'm shot, I'm shot! . . . Th' life's pourin' out o' me! (*To* NORA) I've got this through . . . through you . . . through you, you bitch, you! . . . O God, have mercy on me! . . . (*To* NORA) You wouldn't stop quiet, no you wouldn't, you wouldn't, blast you! Look at what I'm afther gettin', look at what I'm afther gettin' . . . I'm bleedin' to death, an' no one's here to stop th' flowing blood! (*Calling*) Mrs. Gogan, Mrs. Gogan! Fluther, Fluther, for God's sake, somebody, a doctor, a doctor!

(*She staggers frightened towards the door, to seek for aid, but, weakening half way across the room, she sinks to her knees, and bending forward, supports herself with her hands resting on the floor.* NORA *is standing rigidly with her back to the wall opposite, her trembling hands held out a little from the sides of her body, her lips quivering, her breast heaving, staring wildly at the figure of* BESSIE.)

NORA (*in a breathless whisper*). Jack, I'm frightened. . . . I'm frightened, Jack. . . . Oh, Jack, where are you!

BESSIE (*moaningly*). This is what's afther comin' on me for nursin' you day and night. . . . I was a fool, a fool, a fool! Get me a dhrink o' wather, you jade, will you? There's a fire burnin' in me blood! (*Pleadingly*) Nora, Nora, dear, for God's sake, run out and get Mrs. Gogan, or Fluther, or somebody bring a doctor, quick, quick, quick! (*As* NORA *does not stir*) Blast you, stir yourself, before I'm gone!

NORA. Oh, Jack, Jack, where are you!

BESSIE (*in a whispered moan*). Jesus Christ, me sight's goin'! It's all dark, dark! Nora, hold me hand! (BESSIE'*s body lists over and she sinks into a prostrate position on the floor.*)

BESSIE. I'm dyin', I'm dyin' . . . I feel it . . . Oh God, oh God! (*She feebly sings.*)

I do believe, I will believe
That Jesus died for me;
That on th' cross He shed His blood,
From sin to set me free. . . .

I do believe . . . I will believe
. . . Jesus died . . . me;
. . . th' cross He shed . . . blood,
From sin . . . free.

(*She ceases singing, and lies stretched out, still and very rigid. A pause. Then* MRS. GOGAN *runs hastily in.*)

MRS. GOGAN (*quivering with fright*). Blessed be God, what's afther happenin'? (*To* NORA) What's wrong, child, what's wrong? (*She sees* BESSIE, *runs to her and bends over the body.*) Bessie, Bessie! (*She shakes the body.*) Mrs. Burgess, Mrs. Burgess! (*She feels* BESSIE'*s forehead.*) My God, she's as cold as death. They're afther murdherin' th' poor inoffensive woman!

(SERGEANT TINLEY *and* CORPORAL STODDART *enter agitatedly, their rifles at the ready.*)

SERGEANT TINLEY (*excitedly*). This is the 'ouse. That's the window!

NORA (*pressing back against the

wall). Hide it, hide it; cover it up, cover it up!

SERGEANT TINLEY (*going over to the body*). 'Ere, what's this? Who's this? (*Looking at* BESSIE) Ow Gawd, we've plugged one of the women of the 'ouse.

CORPORAL STODDART. Whoy the 'ell did she gow to the window! Is she dead?

SERGEANT TINLEY. Ow, dead as bedamned. Well, we couldn't afford to toike any chawnces.

NORA (*screaming*). Hide it, hide it; don't let me see it! Take me away, take me away, Mrs. Gogan!
(MRS. GOGAN *runs into room, Left, and runs out again with a sheet which she spreads over the body of* BESSIE.)

MRS. GOGAN (*as she spreads the sheet*). Oh, God help her, th' poor woman, she's stiffenin' out as hard as she can! Her face has written on it th' shock o' sudden agony, an' her hands is whitenin' into th' smooth shininess of wax.

NORA (*whimperingly*). Take me away, take me away; don't leave me here to be lookin' an' lookin' at it!

MRS. GOGAN (*going over to* NORA *and putting her arm around her*). Come on with me, dear, an' you can doss in poor Mollser's bed, till we gather some neighbours to come an' give th' last friendly touches to Bessie in th' lonely layin' of her out.
(MRS. GOGAN *and* NORA *go slowly out.*)

CORPORAL STODDART (*who has been looking around, to* SERGEANT TINLEY). Tea there, Sergeant. Wot abaht a cup of scald?

SERGEANT TINLEY. Pour it hout, Stoddart, pour it hout. Oi could scoff hanything just naow.
(CORPORAL STODDART *pours out two cups of tea, and the two soldiers begin to drink. In the distance is heard a bitter burst of rifle and machine-gun fire, interspersed with the boom, boom of artillery. The glare in the sky seen through the window flares into a fuller and deeper red.*)

SERGEANT TINLEY. There gows the general attack on the Powst Office.

VOICES IN A DISTANT STREET. Ambu . . . lance, Ambu . . . lance! Red Cro . . . ss, Red Cro . . . ss!
(*The voices of soldiers at a barricade outside the house are heard singing.*)

They were summoned from the 'illside,
They were called in from the glen,
And the country found 'em ready
At the stirring call for men.
Let not tears add to their 'ardship,
As the soldiers pass along,
And although our 'eart is breaking,
Make it sing this cheery song.

SERGEANT TINLEY *and* CORPORAL STODDART (*joining in the chorus, as they sip tea*).

Keep the 'owme fires burning.
While your 'earts are yearning;
Though your lads are far away
They dream of 'owme;
There's a silver loining
Through the dark cloud shoin-
ing,
Turn the dark cloud inside out,
Till the boys come 'owme!

CURTAIN